D1558789

BERNANOS

HANS URS VON BALTHASAR

BERNANOS:
AN ECCLESIAL
EXISTENCE

Translated from
the German and the French
by Erasmo Leiva-Merikakis

A COMMUNIO BOOK
IGNATIUS PRESS   SAN FRANCISCO

Title of the German original:
Gelebte Kirche: Bernanos
third edition
© 1988 Johannes-Verlag, Einsiedeln, Trier

Cover by Roxanne Mei Lum

© 1996 Ignatius Press, San Francisco
All rights reserved
ISBN 0-89870-576-2
Library of Congress catalogue number 95-79888
Printed in the United States of America ∞

TO LOSE ONE'S LIFE FOR ONE'S HONOR,
TO LOSE ONE'S HONOR FOR ONE'S SOUL.

Motto on an old Spanish noble house

CONTENTS

PART ONE

A CHRISTIAN AND A WRITER

CONTENTS

PART TWO

THE CHURCH: A PLACE FOR LIVING

PART THREE

CONTEMPORARY MAN

TRANSLATOR'S NOTE

One aspect of the genius of Hans Urs von Balthasar is his knack for making the subject of his study come alive before the reader. The sterling theologian never hesitates to make himself the servant of his chosen theme, all the more so when his focus is on someone with the spiritual depth and creative stature of Georges Bernanos, surely the greatest Catholic creative writer of the twentieth century. The impression we receive as we follow von Balthasar's patient unfolding of the thoughts, images, and characters that populate Bernanos' universe is not so much of an analyst probing his inert material as of a sorcerer conjuring up intact the overpowering presence of a great-souled human being. Let the qualifier "intact"—referring to the comprehensiveness of treatment, the thoroughness of the exposition, and the absence of all interpretive violence—suffice for the moment in explaining the considerable length and occasional complexity of the pages that follow. Von Balthasar has here accomplished for Georges Bernanos what in another book he achieved for Karl Barth, author of the multivolume *Church Dogmatics*, and what he likewise did, in the smaller format of the monograph in the second and third volumes of *The Glory of the Lord*, for a significant number of great Christian poets and thinkers: the miracle of distilling without denaturing, of compressing without reducing, of interpreting without distorting.

The secret of von Balthasar's "miracle" is in itself quite simple: judicious quoting of the primary source and careful juxtaposing of texts and commentary, in such a way that the selected passages are not so much "proof-texts" for theological theories as a tranquil forum from which Bernanos can speak to the reader with unhampered freedom. But the actual realization of such a simple formula also requires the intuitive brilliance unique to von Balthasar. And that is the essence of von Balthasar's service to Bernanos: to have provided him with a space of contemplative leisure and a context within the total ecclesial Mystery of Christ out of which he can speak his mind in such a way that he can be clearly heard and genuinely understood. The Swiss theologian quotes the French novelist and cultural critic well and at length, so that not the least feature of the present volume lies in its being a thematic "anthology" of many of the best texts in Bernanos.

The English translator thus owes a great debt of gratitude to Maurice de Gandillac, whose French version of the present work—*Le Chrétien Bernanos* (Paris: Éditions du Seuil, 1956)—proved an indispensable companion. It offered me on a "silver platter", as it were, all of the passages from Bernanos in the French original. Given the very great space occupied in this book by Bernanos' texts (I estimate a good 20 to 25 percent), it is highly doubtful whether a translation into English (or, indeed, any other language) could have been prepared from von Balthasar's text alone, since here Bernanos of course appears in German translation. De Gandillac has already accomplished for all future translators the huge labor of compiling within the covers of one book the original of all texts quoted by von Balthasar.

In addition, de Gandillac has put many quotations and references in context by detailing situations, persons, and cultural movements. As well, he has identified the correspondence by date and recipient where von Balthasar has a mere bibliographical symbol, and he has at times given a fuller form of some quotations that von Balthasar gives more skeletally. Finally, I have followed de Gandillac's lead in breaking up the massive paragraphs of the German text into more digestible portions.

I am thankful to David Schindler and David Spesia, of *Communio Catholic International Review*, for having insisted that I undertake a project that bolstered my personal life in surprising ways by putting me for nine months in the daily company of two extraordinary hearts and minds. Stanley Nel, Dean of the College of Arts and Sciences of the University of San Francisco, made this translation and other projects possible by granting me a year's leave of absence from my teaching post.

As always I am humbly grateful to my wife, Mireya Letayf, for her warm interest and day-to-day encouragement in seeing this translation through to the end. Two friends, Michael Torre and Patrick Carey, provided a crucial stimulus by often requesting sample passages of my work as I produced it. In many ways, then, the book belongs to these three.

E. L.-M.
Chihuahua, México
11 June 1995
Solemnity of the Holy Trinity

BIBLIOGRAPHICAL REFERENCES
IN THE FOOTNOTES

We here give the date of first publication, followed by the publisher and date of the edition referenced. Square brackets enclose the abbreviated title of the work.

Finally, we give the literal English translation of the works' titles as used in the present volume.

I. WORKS OF FICTION
AND HAGIOGRAPHY

Madame Dargent (1922). Plon, 1955.   [*Madame Dargent*]
   —*Madame Dargent*

Sous le soleil de Satan (1926). Plon, 1926.   [*Soleil*]
   —*Under Satan's Sun*

Saint Dominique (1926). Gallimard, 1939.   [*Dominique*]
   —*Saint Dominic*

L'Imposture (1927). Plon, 1929.   [*Imposture*]
   —*The Imposture*

La Joie (1928). Plon, 1929.   [*Joie*]
   —*Joy*

Une Nuit (1928). Plon, 1955.   [*Nuit*]
   —*A Night*

Dialogue d'ombres (1928). Plon, 1955.   [*Dialogue d'ombres*]

—*Conversation among Shadows*

Jeanne relapse et sainte (1929). Plon, 1934.   [*Jeanne*]

—*Joan, Heretic and Saint*

Un Crime (1935). Plon, 1935.   [*Crime*]

—*A Crime*

Journal d'un curé de campagne (1936). Plon, 1936.   [*Curé*]

—*Diary of a Country Priest*

Nouvelle Histoire de Mouchette (1937). Plon, 1937.   [*Mouchette*]

—*Mouchette's New Story*

Nouvelles (containing *Dialogues d'ombres, Madame Dargent, Une Nuit*). (1955). Plon, 1955.   [*Nouvelles*]

Monsieur Ouine (1943). Plon, 1946.   [*Ouine*]

—*Monsieur Ouine*

Dialogues des Carmélites (1949). Le Seuil, 1949.   [*Carmélites*]

—*Dialogues of the Carmelites*

Un Mauvais rêve (1959). Plon, 1950.   [*Rêve*]

—*An Evil Dream*

II. CRITICAL WORKS AND LECTURES

Lettre à Frédéric Lefèvre. Plon, 1926.

—*Letter to Frédéric Lefèvre*

Une Vision catholique du réel. Revue générale belge, 1927.

 —*A Catholic Vision of Reality*

La Grande peur des bien-pensants (1931). Palatine, 1947. [*Peur*]

 —*The Great Fear of the Right-Thinking*

Noël à la maison de France. Cité des Livres, 1931.

 —*Christmas at French House*

Les Grands cimetières sous la lune (1938). Plon, 1938. [*Cimetières*]

 —*The Great Cemeteries under the Moon*

Scandale de la vérité (1939). Gallimard, 1939. [*Vérité*]

 —*The Scandal of Truth*

Nous autres Français (1939). Gallimard, 1939. [*Français*]

 —*We, the French*

Lettre aux Anglais (1942). Gallimard, 1946. [*Anglais*]

 —*Letter to the English*

Le Chemin de la Croix-des-Ames (1942–1945). Gallimard,
1948. [*Croix*]

 —*The Way of the Cross-of-Souls*

La France contre les robots (1944). Laffont, 1947. [*Robots*]

 —*France against the Robots*

Les Enfants humiliés (1949). Gallimard, 1949. [*Enfants*]

 —*The Humiliated Children*

La Liberté, pourquoi faire? (1953). Gallimard, 1953. [*Liberté*]

 —*What for, Freedom?*

Le Crépuscule des vieux (1956). Gallimard, 1956.   [*Crépuscule*]

— *Twilight of the Bawds*[1]

III. OTHER REFERENCES

Cahiers du Rhône. Seuil, 1949: *Georges Bernanos: Essais
    et témoignages.*   [*C. du R.*]

Bernanos par lui-même. Seuil, 1954. Ed. by Albert Béguin.
    Col. "Ecrivains de toujours".   [*Bernanos*]

Bulletin trimestriel de la Société des Amis de Georges Bernanos.
    Starting in December 1949.   [*Bul.*]

Georges Bernanos. *Das sanfte Erbarmen: Briefe des Dichters.*
    Intro. by A. Béguin; selected and trans. by Hans Urs
    von Balthasar. Einsiedeln: Johannes Verlag, 1951.   [*Erbarmen*]

Georges Bernanos. *Die Geduld der Armen: Neue Briefe.*
    Intro., selected, and trans. by Hans Urs von Balthasar.
    Einsiedeln: Johannes Verlag, 1954.   [*Geduld*]

Georges Bernanos, *Lettres à Jorge de Lima.* Privately printed.
    Rio de Janeiro, 1953.

---

[1] In order to echo something of the significant rhyming pun in Bernanos' title (he replaces *vieux*, "old men", as counterpart for *dieux*, "gods", in the title of Nietzsche's famous work *The Twilight of the Gods*), I have ventured to use "bawds" instead of "old men" in English. Bernanos' contempt for the senile pandering of conventional ideas is conveyed equally well, I think, by this word. — TRANS.

FOREWORD

The flourishing of Catholic literature, which blossomed so splendidly with Bloy, Péguy, Claudel, and Bernanos during the first half of the twentieth century, seems to have left no heirs. We often regret this fact. But we have done very little to make our own what we have already been so richly given.[1] Some also hold it against theological authors that nowadays they are too concerned with writers of literary works instead of plying their own trade. But I would not have written this book if someone else had done it; and, at the same time, it could just be that in the great Catholic literary figures we find more originality and vibrancy of thought—an intellectual life thriving superbly in a free and open landscape—than we do in the somewhat broken-winded theology of our time, which is satisfied with quite slender fare.

Let me explain myself. It is by no means the intent of this book to make Bernanos into any kind of "Church Father" or saint, or even into a "lay theologian": he would be the first to respond to such an idea with a loud laugh. But no one can keep him from being a thinking Christian—a *courageously* thinking Christian—of our time. No one can keep him from having derived his faith, not from textbooks, but from the catechism and a stormy prayer life, from the reception of the sacraments and the daily wounds inflicted by the sin and blindness of the world: his faith was to him the living truth, which must suffice in mastering the most terrible questions of existence. Whoever puts on God's weapons in order to resist the devil's tricks on the evil day and be able to stand firm and unshakable; whoever stands there girt with truth, clothed with the armor of justice, shod with the readiness to proclaim the gospel of peace; whoever takes up the

---

[1] I have here excluded the following passage, which would be somewhat out of place within the body of an English version of this book: "There exists no comprehensive book in German, for instance, on any of the writers named. This may be due to the fact that, while the French go to great lengths to learn German, few in Germany possess a good command of modern French, which is presently undergoing massive change. Despite its nationalism, the nineteenth century created a truly universal literature through the power of its language, while this creative power has been debilitated, ironically, in the present age of Europe's emerging unity."—TRANS.

helmet of salvation, the sword of the Spirit, which is the Word of
God, covers himself with the shield of faith so as to extinguish all
the flaming arrows of the demon and continually prays in the Spirit
with a storm of insistent pleas (cf. Eph 6:11–18): will such a one
—by the sheer feel and friction of so many weapons imposing their
shape on his body—not experience in the end something of God's
power over our life? And is this not something that someone who
has merely read many books will never experience?

There is no use trying to dissect the natural and supernatural components in Bernanos, no use asking what in him was innate intuition
and what the charism of prophecy, what mere sensitivity and what
discernment of spirits, what fine writing and what the gift of tongues,
what in his anguish had natural causes and what was imposed on him
by faith. It belonged to his particular mission as layman that both
things were inseparable: that his nature, with all its volcanic force,
was from the outset compelled by the gentle predominance of grace,
because this rough man in his depths housed a loving child who stood
defenseless and disconcerted before every real love, above all the love
of God in Christ. Because he loved, he had a feel for the truth, including the truth of the times; and, because he felt, he had reactions
that were interiorly more delicate and exteriorly harsher and fiercer
than our own. While the rest of us sleep, he has long since risen and
set out to listen to the night. He fulfilled Christ's injunction to consider "the fig tree and all the other trees": "When their buds burst
open, you see for yourselves and know that summer is now near"
(Lk 21:29). There are Christian truths that cry out with full throat
from the events of the times, and they thus manifest that they are
timely, that their time has come; but one must have the courage to
hear them cry out. The courage, which is perfected by the trembling
of his anguish, was one of the fundamental qualities of Bernanos the
Christian. He demonstrated such courage above all to his Mother, the
Church, whom he loved tenderly and painfully, the same Church into
whose face he also cried shame when in his opinion she had failed.
Granted that he too hastily threw together into the same pot shrewd
political diplomacy and cowardly slyness: in his impatience, he could
barely stomach the humiliations inflicted on the earthly Church, her
need to coexist with the powers that be, the limitations and slowness
imposed by her hierarchical structure. But not only did he time and
again take back overly gruff statements and, through thick and thin,

bare his heart to protest his childlike fidelity and devotion to the Church. Beyond this, he possessed in his depths an almost unerring sense of equilibrium in all that pertains to Christian existence; and, whenever this seemed to him to be disturbed—not in the Church, but in Christianity at large, at the level of lived faith—then he threw his whole life with all its weight into the scales, as when in a storm at sea a man leans out over the waves in order to make the capsizing sailboat regain its balance.

We would be saying too little if we called Bernanos a "practicing Catholic". What makes him a creator of Christian literature is not the fact that he daily went to Mass, or, if he couldn't, that he prayed the texts of the Mass at home,[2] that he went to confession every week,[3] prayed his Rosary daily "like any pious old lady", and "never went to bed without having prayed his Compline".[4] What made him a Christian writer was that he did these things with a conviction that welled up from the deepest parts of his being and that very evidently constituted the culture-medium, as it were, for all his creative activity as a writer. Anyone who is familiar with what is at stake and has the eyes to see knows that everything he created is *ecclesial existence that has been given form*: existence derived not merely from an abstract, individual faith but from the specific faith that cannot be had elsewhere, that is, the faith of the Church, which is the communion of saints and whose wellsprings of grace—the sacraments—nourish the life of faith. "Whoever does not eat my flesh or drink my blood. . . ." For this reason it is perhaps not after all a waste of time for a cleric like myself to concern himself with this living testimony of a great Christian and break through the somewhat embarrassed proscription of silence with which the clergy has until now largely surrounded the creative writer.

The goal of the book is, therefore, quite modest: simply to convey what Bernanos wanted to say as the Christian he was. Thus, at the center of our study stands the Church, and indeed the Church as source of joy, which is what she was for Bernanos: as communion of saints, which is to say, as love become reality and as treasure house of the sacraments, which were for him the very origin and form

---

[2] *To Amoroso Lima*, March 13, 1940 (*Esprit* 8 [1930]: 203).

[3] *Hochland*, 1949, 524.

[4] *To Amoroso Lima*, March 13, 1940.

of Christian life. Compared with these aspects, the written Word of God took second place. Bernanos was no great reader of the Bible; the Old Testament in particular was wholly foreign to him. His book was Christ's commandment of love and its contemplation in human life.

Our presentation strives to be objective. Whoever is seeking for paradoxes and rare sensations will be disappointed. Nor is it at all my purpose to utter through someone else's mouth things that I myself "simply cannot say", although Bernanos himself occasionally proceeded in just such a manner. It is really so unimportant to say things about the weaknesses of our Church, which anyone can find out should he be interested. But it is infinitely important to allow her marvelous mysteries, which nearly no one knows or cares to know, to shine forth resplendently from the work of a great writer. What is at stake here is precisely this light, and not the work of a man, even if we are about to contemplate the Church, not theoretically, but through the work of this particular man.

I am not a simple Bernanos enthusiast; but I know what his rank is. To speak about him always makes one ask the question concerning rank. Happily, he cannot be systematized or reduced to theses. But we should be able to detect the irreducible point out of which such living creations can spring forth. This book, then, remains a scaffolding that can be removed once the building is standing: once, that is, the writer's spirit has passed into the hearts he wanted to enkindle.

The first part will start us off with personal and biographical considerations and continue with methodological problems; our thought will thus proceed from the life to the form. The second part will then develop this form. The third part, which we had to shorten perhaps excessively, will show how the form impresses its shape on the life within time and the present moment.

All quotations are translated directly from the French exclusively for the present book, since not all existing translations offer the exactness required for our purposes. I am quite conscious of not having reached the blithe elegance of the original diction.[5] It has not

---

[5] The present translator has rendered quotations directly from French into English, just as the author translated them from French into German; and von Balthasar's sentiment must be echoed here, exponentially! Whenever there exists any ambiguity of interpretation, I have naturally followed von Balthasar's lead.—TRANS.

been possible to give summaries of the contents of Bernanos' works. Such summaries could never, in any event, substitute for reading the works themselves. Although having read Bernanos is not an absolute prerequisite for reading the present volume, such reading should at least follow it.

I owe particular thanks to my friend Albert Béguin, who made available to me unpublished letters and papers that helped to enhance my perception of Bernanos' character. However, I have tried to work as little as possible with texts that as yet remain unavailable. Bernanos' life, so full of interior tension and drama, could be surveyed only in broad outline. Especially in this area we will have to await the publication of the French edition of the letters, which will reveal many individual episodes for the first time and place others in their proper light.[6] An exhaustive biography will not be possible for decades to come, until material that is too personal and too close to us will have entered the cool objectivity of history. But the work itself, which has already been published in all its parts, can already now be considered and judged in its full form. And it is with the work that this study concerns itself.

---

[6] Von Balthasar was writing before the publication of a large portion of Bernanos' letters, edited by Albert Béguin: *Correspondance* (Paris: Plon, 1971).—TRANS.

PART ONE

A Christian and a Writer

I. THE SPIRIT

1. The Measure of Man

Bernanos fought for man. He rose up against everything in the modern world and Church that openly or secretly threatens the full appointed measure of man. The lower lip begins to quiver, the vein in his temple swells, and the whole man rises slowly from his chair, with uncanny composure. The first lightning rends the darkness, and soon, with a clap of thunder worthy of God himself, the torrential downpour begins rattling the windows. But the storm passes, and the same man who a moment ago contained within himself the whole orchestra of the Gorge of the Wolves and of the Flying Dutchman is now smiling at us with all the childlikeness of a spring morning, trickling drops of water after the night's storm. He engages everything human in himself in his fight for man. One step deeper into his being, and he would have been a great actor: he bears his heart, his soul, his innermost thoughts on his lips; with him, the most secret reality becomes a gesture; in the long run, he is unable to confine anything to silence. Throughout his life he remained a big child who could not be angry for longer than an hour, and for this reason no one could hold a grudge against him.

In all of his activity and writing, it is he himself who emerges: the man Georges Bernanos. Everything, even the last sentence he wrote, bears the specific weight of this human being. He vouches for what he says, he guarantees it with his own person. Whoever doesn't believe him has his work cut out for him. He is honorable to the foundations: like Nathanael, he is "a man without guile". He is immediately prepared to commit himself totally to any honorable undertaking. But he does not sit "comfortably" with people. Whoever runs against his grain does not escape unscathed. Whatever in the world is simply not right is so unbearable to him that his life becomes a burden for him as a consequence. Sin, in his view, disfigures the human countenance, so dear to him. A sense of honor then stirs within him, and he cannot let sin go unavenged.

His first heroine, Mouchette, was a grand conception. She wants

to break out of her musty bourgeois existence into the frantic freedom of youth. Almost without realizing it, she falls into the captivity
of the devil, and the novelist dispatches a spiritual Perseus to liberate the fettered Andromeda who has fallen prey to the sea monster.
But, if Donissan fights his battle in the highest supernatural sphere,
the writer does not presume to claim for himself the experience of
mystical nights. He knows that he needs still other earthly supplies;
and so he arms himself with a knight's spear. Anger arouses him: it is
the strongest thing about him, and also the most dangerous for him.
He strives to submit his anger to the discipleship of the Christ who
brandished a whip; and, in all reality, we can affirm that Bernanos
hurled his bolts of lightning only in order to liberate the truth. The
target, which he strikes without exception, has first been eyed by
his incorruptible glance: he has reached a judgment that is cool and
without prejudice. When the red stream rises into his eyes, this is
not a blurring of his vision but the final sign that he is about to
shoot.

But how immensely difficult does this then make the counterbalance: patience! *Patientia pauperum*, "the patience of the poor": he made
this phrase something of a personal motto. Such patience did not come
easy to him; he had to struggle for it in the endless passing of time,
inch by inch, day by day, hour by hour: he had to learn how the unbearable had nonetheless to be borne. He was acquainted with danger, and he strove to go out and meet it. In contrast to Péguy, who
could accumulate whole storehouses of ancient hatreds and drag out
deep-seated rancors through the whole of very long books, Bernanos'
outbursts of anger remain short and episodic. And, in contrast to Bloy,
such outbursts never degenerate into sessions of grumbling and vili-
fication: not only is the thundercloud soon swept away by his good
humor; it even receives a kind of interior light. His humor sparkles
even in his gloomiest letters, much as these convey his disgust and
weariness with life. Aware as he is of the dangers of a temperament
like his, he also knows that at a deeper level he possesses an innate
spiritual faculty to regain equilibrium, and this organ never deserts
him. It gives him the measure of man at the center of his being. This
is the Latin *mensura*, which a Frenchman of ancient heritage has in
his blood and against which so many of this nation have sinned, in
the certainty that they will always land upright on their own feet.
Like Péguy and Claudel, Bernanos took his stand in the old France

of King Louis and Joinville, of Joan of Arc and Corneille, of Rabelais and Francis de Sales.[1]

Bernanos, then, speaks from the perspective of such a measure of man into an age that has lost all measure. He speaks from the perspective of an incarnate Christianity into a spiritualized Church and a materialized world; and if he then wants to bring them both together again by means of violent strokes, he aims for them to meet at the center of the measure. With the support of the living tradition he can then commission the Christian to go out wholly exposed and vulnerable, to undertake long journeys, and this in two directions: inwardly, to undertake the adventure of heaven and hell, properly the adventure of the mystic and of the most daring kind of spiritual missions (audacious, yes, but ventured by God himself and sustained and underwritten by the Church); and outwardly, to undertake the Christian responsibility for the world that belongs to the individual layman: in a de-Christianized spiritual milieu the layman must be bold enough to engage the Church's sense for the discernment of spirits. This almost violent expansion of horizons in both directions was continually undertaken by Bernanos after he had solidly taken his stand upon an unquestionable Christian and ecclesial center that he took for granted.

Had this not been so, then the farther he advanced in his labors, the more inevitably would Bernanos have lost his balance and necessarily been thrown off his track. The early novels, especially *Under Satan's Sun*,[2] have to be interpreted with latitude in light of the later ones if they are not to appear distorted and exaggerated. The later works, in which sheer creative genius and immediacy are perhaps no longer so striking, nevertheless have undergone a steady process of clarifying the writer's basic intent and have thus attained the balance

---

[1] For this reason, Bernanos must always be considered within the French context: he cannot be exported in isolation, especially not into a Germany that, with Péguy, he terms a "failed Christianity" and that occasionally would like to take possession of him in order to put him to æsthetic uses much less balanced than his own. We must have an ear for the volume at which a word of his is uttered and hear his invectives within the totality of the French orchestra. A Frenchman can absorb spiritual material in greater quantities and more quickly than his German counterpart, and a Frenchman can also produce spiritual material more easily, while the German takes it more seriously "into his blood".

[2] We will normally give literal translations of the French titles of Bernanos' works and refer in a note to the actual title given in published English translations. *Sous le soleil de Satan* was published in English as *The Star of Satan*.—TRANS.

for which he strove from the beginning. This masterful balance is most resplendently persuasive in *The Diary of a Country Priest* and in *Dialogues of the Carmelites*.

The Catholic balance, in the final analysis, is anchored in the supernatural mystery of Christ, which is to say, neither in natural qualities of character (how could Peter then ever have become a "rock"?) nor in a systematic formula that can be analyzed rationally and comprehended. In the same way in which we cannot get to the bottom of the relationship between humanity and divinity in Christ, neither can we fathom the relationship, in the Church and thus in ecclesial existence, between institutional "closure" and mystical "openness". Ecclesial balance does not mean taking refuge in the Church as visible institution and thriving there quietly in a human sense. The saints have shown this sufficiently. But neither does it mean being so burned up and consumed by the divine truth—God in oneself, loss of world, experience of the Cross—that the result is the dissolution of the right form and healthy tranquillity necessary to human and ecclesial existence. The "spirituals" who opt for such imbalance will then construe the concrete life of the Church as something to be forever hounded, denounced, and pilloried as a degenerate form of true pneumatic existence that must tirelessly be exposed as such. The Catholic Church has always condemned such allegedly "pneumatic" (or purely spiritual) raging, and indeed not at all for merely practical reasons having to do with civil order, but because it is not in keeping with the spirit of a God who became man and because it profoundly contradicts the Christian imperative to love. We are to recognize the sphere of Christ's disciples, not as the place where whitened sepulchers are being torn open within and without the Church, but as the place where love is gently at work covering a multitude of sins. And the balance that only the Holy Spirit can produce in a man allows the blast of the pneumatic's gale—which indeed is sent, among other things, to demolish what is rotten—to spend itself and to return to the hidden stillness and humility of human love.

There does, of course, also exist a higher balance *among* the individual missions in the Church: the lack of measure or excessive measure of a saint or any other prophetic voice, viewed in isolation, could have its counterpart and justification in the deficient measure of a specific community or of Christendom and the Church herself within a given period or situation. In this case the individual mis-

sion ought not to be interpreted outside its own context; it belongs
to Christian love to do that much justice to an individual mission,
all the more so as the sent person in question was not following his
own inclinations but exercising strict obedience toward God when
he entered upon his way, which served as a sign and warning to all
others. Nothing is more serious and urgent to the Church's total life
of love than for those who thus expose themselves at such risk to be
sheltered within the common economy of love and truth. This is only
possible, however, if such vocational paths are considered and read,
not in a psychological and biographical manner, but rather ecclesially,
with a sense for mission. In other words, unusual vocations should
become occasions, not for sensationalism, curiosity, or advertising for
non-Catholic consumption (as if to show that we Catholics, too, still
have a couple of prophetic types!), but rather for pondering and taking to heart what God is here intending to send us as a grace to be
welcomed.

Bernanos belongs to the "poor in spirit" whom the Spirit has
stripped down as representatives of all men, those who are "naked"
in spirit and "whose teeth chatter":[3] he has a claim to the mantle of
the Church's love.

His concern is man. The loveliest projects proposed by the Church
will not change the world if they are not realized by man. And if these
projects intend to create a certain kind of man, at the same time they
cannot help presupposing man: "To be sure, the Church's doctrine is
also mine. But here I am speaking of men and of the way they apply
that doctrine. This is the only thing that interests me today."[4] "It's
undeniable that one cannot reasonably hope to confront last-model
tanks and airplanes with outdated machines. Why then should I not
have the right to examine with the same criterion the kind of man
with which the democracies intend to win the war? The average citizen of these democracies appears to me in many regards to be as
outmoded as would be the case if a Newport or a Spad of 1917 were
to face today's Spitfires and Hurricanes."[5] "It's all very nice to put

---

[3] *Enfants*, 224.
[4] *Anglais*, 148.
[5] *Croix*, August 1942, 237–38.

social projects on paper. But what we must know is the kind of men you intend to populate them with."[6]

It is not the ideologies of the age that trouble Bernanos, but the fact that, "if we compare the man of 1939 with that of 1914, and these two men to their common ancestor of 1789, it would seem that our national human material—to use a word in fashion—has been greatly impoverished",[7] so much so that we cannot totally reject the hypothesis that there has occurred "a profound crisis, a deviation, and a perversion of human energy".[8] In earlier centuries, "moral, social, and political transformations took place very slowly", in keeping with man's right measure: "With each new crisis he could find those appropriate reflexes of self-defense or adaptation that in almost identical instances had served his forebears well." Nowadays the very possibility of adaptation is questioned:

> The tragedy of our new Europe is precisely the lack of adaptation between man and a rhythm of life that no longer follows the beat of his own heart but rather the dizzying rotation of turbines, a rhythm under continual acceleration. . . . I'll go farther and say that such adaptation appears to me less and less possible. . . . A machine can do good or evil, indifferently. A more perfect machine—that is, one that is more efficient —should correspond to a more reasonable, a more human humanity. But has the civilization of machines improved man? Have they made man more human? I could abstain from answering, but I think it more convenient to make my thought more explicit. In all probability, machines have changed nothing in man's basic wickedness—up until now, in any event; but they have exercised this wickedness, making it grow strong, and they have revealed to man the power of his wickedness, the fact that the exercise of this power in a certain sense has no boundaries.[9]

"We are not witnessing the natural end of a great human civilization but the birth of an inhuman civilization that can take root only by virtue of a vast, immense, and universal sterilization of the highest values of life."[10] The substitution of these highest values by realities of a quantitative order (money and numbers)[11] and the technicaliza-

---

[6] *Français*, 241.
[7] *Robots*, 119.
[8] Ibid., 150.
[9] Ibid., 153–56.
[10] Ibid., 174.
[11] Ibid., 182f.

tion of the spirit by psychology[12] are events that attack the power of judgment and the conscience of a free man at the deepest level and that tear apart what makes man superior to animals: his free, serene, and sublime ability to be responsible. "Obedience and irresponsibility: these are the two Magic Words that tomorrow will open up the Paradise of the Civilization of Machines."[13]

We would do well to be extremely careful in the conclusions we draw in the face of the humanitarian protestations made by the modern conscience of man and of humanity: it is entirely possible that only neuro-pathological phenomena are involved.[14] "Let us distrust the kind of compassion that God has not blessed and that is nothing but a movement of the viscera. Man's nerves have their contradictions, their weaknesses, but the logic of evil is as strict as hell."[15] Our novelist remains just as distrustful with regard to all the psychological and religious evasions of spiritual spheres of calm and contemplation that the machine age has to offer. In the final analysis, the only role that a contemplative person could still play in a machine age consistent with itself is that of a brake. "The only kind of interior life the Technician could just barely allow would be that necessary for modest introspection, under the surveillance of a doctor, with the goal of developing an optimism that would result from eliminating, to the very roots, all desires that cannot be realized in this world."[16] For, "if man's salvation is to be found here below in the increasingly more efficient manipulation of all the planet's resources, then, the moment you make the idea of salvation come down to earth from heaven, the contemplative life will be seen as an escape or a refusal."[17] It is evident that this writer does not expect the power to transform life from any other religion but the Christian, and it follows that he can expect only Christians to assume responsibility for the true measure and proportions of man in this world. But at the same time we can see what an excessive demand is made here of the Christian: in an age that, according to Bernanos, is necessarily and increasingly los-

---

[12] Ibid., 195f., 207f.

[13] Ibid., 219.

[14] Nietzsche, too, quite correctly suspected as much; but, from an identical insight, Bernanos does not draw Nietzsche's philosophical conclusions.

[15] *Robots*, 156–57.

[16] Ibid., 209–10.

[17] Ibid., 209.

ing this measure, he would have the Christian take the measure of man upon himself, which is to say, to take under his charge nothing less than freedom of spirit and the faculty to be a free, responsible, decision-making agent. Anxiously we ask ourselves what the writer intends to give the Christian he is so overtaxing before he sends him on his way. At this point it is time to examine the shape of his work.

The work falls into two almost equal halves: cultural criticism and narrative work. The writings dedicated to a critique of culture offer analyses of the epochal figure defined by contemporary humanity both inside and outside the Church, of the relationship between the Church and the world, and of the historical origins and future prospects of the present situation. The narrative work in appearance takes its departure from a very different place: from the innermost realm of the Church's heart, where the mystery of life contained within Christian doctrine takes the purest existential form possible among men. In other words, the narrative work begins with the figure of the *saint*, and indeed also with the mystery of evil, which is intimately connected with the saint and can be recognized as such only from his watchtower.

This second half of the work derives its image of man from the highest Christian reality: namely, from the following of Christ—a reality rooted in grace that always both elevates and overtaxes "nature" (otherwise grace would not be grace!). In the concrete, this means that Bernanos the novelist derives his image of man from the saints of the Church, who are constellations looming high over the life of Christians and all men and pointing out the way but who are also human beings like ourselves. It is here that Bernanos would have us find the essence and the measure of man. "*Experience has shown me too late that human beings can be explained, not by their vices, but, on the contrary, by whatever they have kept that is intact, pure, by that which remains in them of their childhood, regardless of how deeply we may have to look for it.*"[18] Here human nature appears like the calyx of a flower in bloom, open to grace, determined and directed by grace, summoned by grace and launched on extraordinary adventures with God, that surpass all human comprehension in their magnificence. These adventures are literally incomparable, which is to say, as *unique and unrepeatable* as God's graces always are. By contrast, even the greatest

---

[18] *Anglais*, 92.

human passion always remains "typical": think of Tristan, Don Juan, Faust! The "adventures" we speak of can be categorized solely by means of those forms of socialization assumed by God's grace in the world: namely, God's Word and sacraments in the Church. It is from such a wellspring that we will have to draw the truth informing the lives of Bernanos' saints.

But what is the behavior, in our contemporary world, of the Christian who has taken such a stance and whose sole "norm" is grace? This is the question posed by the other series of writings. And here, if we don't want to misunderstand Bernanos at a fundamental level, we will have to grasp that everything depends on this: God's revelation in Christ, in his Church, and in his saints—in the whole of Christian life—*cannot and will not provide ready-made recipes* for overcoming the problems of this world, of history, of the development of culture, the State, technology, and so on. If this were so, man would be robbed of his deepest responsibility and freedom, and precisely the Christian, as compared to the non-Christian, would find himself at a frightful disadvantage that could never be compensated by the number of privileges. The *one and only thing* God's revelation does provide us with are *archetypes* or *models* that, necessarily and in keeping with their very essence stand *above* the level of worldly questions and, like stars, shed their light down upon them. If Christ himself wasted hardly a word concerning the State or culture, and no word at all concerning art or science, it was so as not to commit the blunder of meddling in the Father's work of creation, and also in order not to rob man, the laboring king of creation, of the earnestness of his accomplishments by applying some magical formula. It would therefore be foolish to expect more from this writer than he can give as a Christian. It would be wholly misguided to juxtapose the works of cultural criticism, with the mountain of questions they evoke, and the novels, in such a way that one hoped to find all the ready-made answers in the latter.

The saint, behind whom Christ always stands, does surely reveal the measure of man, but not in such a way that his unique and extraordinary destiny can be imitated as such. The saint is no recipe but rather an archetype or model who gives orientation, a figure who coaches and supports. And the question of how the Christian in the world conducts himself as someone filled with the spirit of the saints, and also of how the visible Church, the bearer of Christ's mission consisting of clergy, religious, and laymen, can discharge this mission in the contemporary world: this second question is a different one that every time must be asked anew, albeit never without looking at the models. "Have you also sufficiently preached about the exceptional character of heroic vocations? Because, to tell the truth, my country is not populated with exceptions but with ordinary citizens."[19]

If we were to put both realms on the same level (like a question with its adequate answer), then we would not escape the danger of making the saints *supermen* instead of ordinary men steered by grace: we would make them into titans who, much to the astonishment of all smaller contemporaries, confronted the superhuman demands of the world and showed themselves equal to them, although not without suffering and death. We cannot overlook the fact that here precisely lay the danger for the young Bernanos, something we can see especially in *Under Satan's Sun*: Donissan is the saint as hero, dragon slayer, and conqueror of the abyss. But the same tendency is still active in the next two novels: Cénabre is a "hero" confronting evil, and even Chantal, like some fetching animal tamer, is victorious over the wild beasts that besiege her, even though it costs her her life. The last shimmer of this ambiguity had wholly disappeared by the time he wrote *The Diary of a Country Priest*; but it was already no longer detectable in the dark novels of the early 1930s. The youthful gesture that wanted to master existence and rout all its evils, armed with the mysteries of the Cross and brandishing them like sword and whip, had now yielded to the spirit of the Beatitudes, to the hunger and thirst for justice, to the patience of the poor. Now even the adventures of the saints are absorbed into the veiled ordinariness of Christian existence; and yet, in the case of the country priest and of little Blanche, those adventures do not for all that cease to be their own quite special and unique paths.

Both halves of Bernanos' work mirror one another. The cultural criticism shows that the novels are, and intend to be, much more than mere narratives: they are an interpretation of existence and of revelation in view of the present situation. For their part, the novels demonstrate that the critical works are nourished from much deeper sources than may at first appear. Precisely in their incongruity with one another, precisely in the open manner in which they reject one another, these two halves prove why they genuinely belong together

---

[19] *Français*, 243−44.

and why together they display the truly Christian image of man;[20] they thus also exhibit Bernanos' sense of measure. In this way, along-side the country priest, his friend Olivier, the foreign legionnaire, can appear as an exponent of the whole culture-critical aspect, and both can extend their hand to one another in a deep and indispensable pact of friendship: in this handshake they are creating the Catholic balance.

The quality and greatness of a man today can most correctly be read in the imperturbable way in which he can look at phenomena just as they are. Such a person can see without "pre-judice", that is, without judging in advance; he will judge only on the basis of what he has really seen for himself. All of Goethe's excellence is to be found pre-cisely in this. Bernanos possesses a similar power of vision. The vital-ity of his style can conceal for us the long look he takes at things; the heat of his temper can distract us from the coolness of his intellect; the impatience of his demands can make us miss the deep, Christian patience with which he suffers existence; the fact that his equilibrium could variously be considered either troubled or threatened at the psy-chological level can hide the solidity and stability that were his in the deeper domain of the person: despite all his being tossed to and fro by the events of life, by the scandal he encountered, by the rising and falling waves of anger and depression, such stability gave this man an extraordinary sense of security. He did not at all worry for himself, for his own salvation, and not in the least concerning his catholicity: "I have never been a restless soul. . . . I feel at home in the Church. I am not afraid of losing in one instant all the fruits of the effort made to enter into the Church, because that is where I was born."[21] "There is no honor in just being a Frenchman, . . . nor is there any honor in just being a Christian. We did not make the choice. 'I am a Christian, revere me!' This is what the Princes of the High Priests, the Scribes and the Pharisees love to proclaim. What we should rather say, and humbly, is: 'I am a Christian, pray for me!' We did not make the choice. . . . We find ourselves in this great adventure because God

---

[20] This is the only image of man Bernanos gives. Whether he likes it or not, "man" as such is always measured by Bernanos against the norm of "Christian man". But, precisely for this reason, "Christian man" could never, in Bernanos' view, be one-sidedly supranaturalistic.

[21] *To Amoroso Lima*, January 1940, *Esprit*, 192.

put us there."[22] "I am not a convert, and I am almost ashamed to admit it because for about twenty years now it's been fashionable to be a convert, perhaps because converts speak a great deal, speak enormously about their conversion. . . . Must I add that clerics have a fine palate for this sort of people?"[23] "For me, the Catholic faith is an element out of which I could not live any more than a fish out of water": but he can say this only because the Catholic reality produces for him a tight and indissoluble solidarity with all men, particularly those outside the Church.[24] As with the elder son in the parable who "was always with me" (Lk 15:31), his seniority in the Church gives him the right to speak an open word or two about conditions in the house, while converts either rave enthusiastically about everything or else take deep offense at all the well-known scandals.

It is true that Léon Bloy[25] and, occasionally, also Ernest Hello[26] are mentioned with praise. But at the decisive moment Bernanos cannot be mistaken for either of these: he is not one of these "self-assured good old fellows, a guy of Bloy's ilk, or even a braggart".[27] To his best friends he complained bitterly that they had fashioned an image of him as "rebel and anarchist":[28] coming from the Action Française, he insisted that he had left it the moment he understood that the principles of order the Action was developing were not rooted deeply enough in the divine order. Who, in fact, could be less a rebel than Bernanos, who daily, with a schoolboy's diligence, affirmed and assumed his own lot as well as that of mankind and of his age?[29]

It is surely possible that, when those he terms *les imbéciles*—and among whom he numbered above all the half-educated, the *littérateurs*,

---

[22] *Français*, 26–27.

[23] *Liberté*, 267–68.

[24] Ibid., 267–69.

[25] *Peur*, 107, 138, 177, 189; *To Dom Besse*, July 1918, *Bull.* 11, 3; *Croix*, September 1940, 47, and February 1942, 195; *Erbarmen*, 59.

[26] *To Lagrange*, May 31, 1905, *C. du R.*, 21; *To a Young Man from the Berry* [*Charreyre*], December 1945, *Bul.* 2–3, 21.

[27] *To Amoroso Lima*, February 2, 1940 (*Esprit*, 197).

[28] *To a Friend*, July 2, 1934 (*Bul.* 2–3, 21). (In a text von Balthasar will quote much later, however [p. 583; *To Luc Estang*, May 31, 1947; *Bul.* 1, 7], Bernanos will define himself as an "anarchist," but not without first having specified [*Croix*, May 1943, 341] that by anarchy he does not understand revolt but rather a "spontaneous disorder" that is less dangerous than a "perverted order".—Note by the French translator, Maurice de Gandillac, *Le Chrétien Bernanos*, 29.)

[29] *Français*, 32f.

and dishonest Christians—busy themselves with his thought, they abuse it by applying it in all kinds of nonsensical ways both inside and outside the Church. What Bernanos wanted to produce from his soul was good bread to nourish all the household;[30] and is it his fault if from it others instead brew a poison? And granted that he may not always have been wholly innocent in this regard: Would it not then be our task to protect him against himself? We would then have to protect his real depth against what is superficial about him, protect the pure child that he so ardently wanted to be against all false maturity and the danger of histrionics; in a word, protect the measure of man so dear to his heart against all the excessive ways in which he himself, with irate love, wanted to protect it.

2. Christian Boldness

Bernanos was a bold Christian, and he was conscious of the fact. That he lived so submerged in anguish is evidence neither for nor against this fact. The boldness in question has nothing to do with innate vitality or even with character; it derives, rather, from the seriousness with which Bernanos appropriated his faith. Precisely because Bernanos had no possibility of separating himself from his faith, of distancing himself from it or entertaining any doubts concerning it,[31] neither could he bargain with it. "One must open oneself up to the truth from top to bottom."[32]

But, as he himself insists time and again, the creative writer is no theologian; and so, for him, faith can never assume the serene form of a more or less coherent system of thought. Bernanos vehemently rejects such a notion:

I have no system, because the systematic spirit is a form of madness. Systems are good only for madmen. Common sense teaches us that, by pretending to simplify, systems complicate everything, while life itself,

---

[30] *Enfants*, 206–7: "My sufferings are those of any ordinary man, but most ordinary men pass alongside them without seeing them for what they are. If I run after him, what I hold out to him is a measure of flour, a flour he knows well. 'I have some at home', he says. With this flour I can only teach him how to make his own bread. And it is with just this bread that I would like to nourish him."

[31] *Cimetières*, 240.

[32] *To Dom Besse*, September 3, 1918; *Bul.* 11, 11.

while seeming to complicate, in fact simplifies everything. Nor do I have any "principles", for the simple reason that I feel no need whatsoever to impose a kind of constitution upon my conscience, to live with my conscience under a constitutional regime. . . . I have no need of principles, because I am a Christian. I have no principles, but I have a faith, and this faith, which compels me to love my neighbor, invites me to understand him, which is the surest and most loyal means of loving him. . . . I have always made an effort to write what I thought—inflexibly—and when you write inflexibly what you think, it's difficult not to teach yourself something day by day, and this takes away your desire to teach things to other people.[33]

What this means is that Bernanos followed no plan and that he did not infer what he said from anywhere in particular. He attempted to live face to face with truth, to see it simply, just as it was, to speak it as precisely as he could, and to assume its consequences for him. "You don't play with the truth any more than with fire, and, whatever precautions you take with it, the honor of him who serves the truth consists in feeling its bite sooner or later."[34] "At certain moments just seeing is in itself such a harsh trial that you wish God would shatter the mirror."[35] This sets him apart from the "intellectual" that he did not want to be, and as which, even if he had been, he would not have wanted to speak to his fellow human beings.[36] Intellectuals remained for him one of the most suspicious phenomena of modern civilization: "Consciously or not, they dream of a world governed by pawns, because they themselves are pawns."[37] They are full of theories they have come up with out of the blue, and they insist on looking at reality exclusively through these.

Nor did Bernanos seek to undergird his work with *history*. Whenever he did consider history, as in *The Great Fear of the Right-Thinking*, he looked at it exactly as he would a slice of the present: he considered it in view of the present moment in order better to understand his own time. "The *imbéciles* think that I spend my time mourning for a lost past. I honor the past, because it has made us what we are, and I do not consider myself capable of ever denying those from whom

[33] *Anglais*, 76–77.
[34] *Liberté*, 297.
[35] *Soleil*, 283.
[36] *Croix*, April 1942, 213.
[37] Ibid., September 1942, 246.

I have come. I honor the past but think only of the future, while all the little Communist or Fascist intellectuals think only of the present, which is to say, of themselves."[38] "It is true that I deeply love the past, but only because it allows me to understand the present, to understand it better, which is to say, to love it better, to love it more usefully, to love it despite its contradictions and follies, which, seen with the eyes of History, almost always have a moving meaning that disarms one's wrath or contempt."[39] The simple vision of what is, unbiased by any theories or by history itself, has made some characterize Bernanos as possessing a prophetic gift (we will deal with this expressly later on); but he himself always dismissed all appeals to the supernatural and the extraordinary in this connection, claiming for himself solely the merit of using his reason correctly. What he sees and foresees could be seen or at least surmised and intimated by all others, provided they had the courage to expose themselves to the truth.

And, in truth: this writer lives, thinks, and works by virtue of his courage. "I have always striven to awaken those who sleep and to keep the others from falling asleep. This is a labor that does not bring in great profits or great honors but instead closes off many possibilities of employment. No matter!"[40] Walking such a path, you do not endear yourself to others, and you acquire the reputation of a malcontent and an agitator: from the perspective of those who have chosen a tranquil middle course, you are one who "walks on the edge". But does not the Christian have a right to freedom of speech and the duty to avail himself of this right? "The Son of Man was betrayed by all of us. But at least I hope I did not sell him. I have never refused anyone the portion of truth available to me. I have always replied face to face to whoever asked me for it. I have always replied with a manly tongue, and not with shameful phrases that, with detestable unction, fuse together what is just and what is unjust, the rich and the poor, the victim and the torturer. God willing, the liars will never have me; they have never yet had me."[41] "I am ashamed to say I am one of the very few Catholics who ever dares to speak this way in

---

[38] Ibid., 245–46.
[39] *Robots*, 135.
[40] *Liberté*, 299.
[41] *Vérité*, 71.

public."[42] "I am not a prudent man. Thinking is not for me a task or a pleasure: it is a risk."[43] "When risk comes to you, the most important thing is to face it, because it would be even more dangerous to turn your back to it. Prudence would then only be the alibi of cowards."[44]

The bold venture of speaking openly concerns everything that must urgently be said in Church and State in order to restore the public atmosphere to health, as an aid for the wavering in spirit and for those who have been terrorized, disgusted, and desiccated by the silencing and repressing of the truth. In a word, it concerns everything no one dares to say in the way it must be said. "The way it must be said" is here the sober way, without pathos or bitterness, without the will to wound or to take a secret revenge, without servile grumbling or supercilious gloating. Rather, it must be that specifically Christian way of speaking that is close to sacramental confession in its gravity and to a physician's advice in its objectivity and that finds its clean tone in the at once modest and proud competence of the baptized person who makes his home in the Church and there enjoys the full rights of citizenship. The courage so to speak rests above all on the fact that the truth can be trusted to have its effects, in contrast to all those anxious efforts to be helpful through political arrangements, diplomatic ruses, and little doses of wisdom *ad usum delphini*, as if a "truth" that appeared masked, dressed up, decorated, and hung with the garlands of human beautification in this manner could still make an impression on persons with a deep moral sense.

But who could today escape the influence of such artifices, which have appropriated the most enormous means of propaganda and practically possess a monopoly on the means whereby the truth is disseminated among men? Bernanos gives us a clear answer: Only the person who has preserved his freedom even in the sphere of his social and political life. "You young people who are reading this book: consider it with lively curiosity. For this book is the testimony of a free man."[45] Soon no more such men will be found: "I belong to a race

---

[42] *Liberté*, 136.
[43] Ibid., 302.
[44] Ibid., 308.
[45] *Cimetières*, 344.

of ordinary people which is daily becoming rarer: I am an ordinary person who has remained free, someone whom propoganda has not yet trained to jump through all the hoops held in front of him."[46]

> As you know, I am a novelist who has stopped writing novels, that is, stopped doing what he loved to do above all, in order to try to say what others would probably have said better in his place if they had had the courage to say it. But they prefer to become ministers of the government, or members of the French Academy, or, who knows, even archbishops. From that moment on, they become optimists. I have absolutely no interest in becoming either a minister or a member of the Academy. Perhaps some of you won't be surprised to hear that I have already refused membership in the Academy. But you'll surely be much more surprised to learn that they have tried to make me a minister, because I really don't have the right face for that. . . . And as far as archbishop goes, I can't say, because I've never been asked.[47]

Why speak so freely?

> Well now, it isn't only because I have the right to do so, it's because I also have the power. I have lost my country—so be it! It's even probable I will never see it again, or that at least I will not be laid to rest there, because transportation is very expensive and no one extends credit to the dead. No matter! I have at my disposal all the freedom that can be dreamed of by a writer without wealth who is also the father of six children. This portion of freedom is not great, but I possess it wholly. In a country [such as Brazil] where the best land costs two hundred francs a hectare, or, if you go far enough from the cities, only one *louis*, a family like mine is assured never to die of hunger. God willing, I'll never be condemned to write serial articles or to give erotic advice in fashionable newspapers or to give autograph sessions at booksellers' or to be the slave of contending parties. I will not play Giono's game or that of some country literary aristocrat or that of the pseudoinnocents who dance their attendance upon the Academy as they would upon an aged wealthy aunt (not so, Monsieur de Pesquidoux? not so, my dear La Varende?). I am free to have my own opinion concerning General Franco without thereby entering the ranks of Monsieur Francisque Gay. I can have great respect for Monsieur Maritain and yet also regret his womanish daydreaming about the Jews and democracy, for which he receives an ovation from the public at the Ambassadeurs. I can read *Tête*

---

[46] *Liberté*, 151f.
[47] *Liberté*, 298.

d'Or with admiration and nevertheless state publicly that Monsieur Paul Claudel smells of sulphur when he writes about the Sacred Scriptures in the *Nouvelle Revue Française* and that he has left in Brazil the reputation of a most cunning businessman, someone who is far more closely related to Turelure than to the virginal Violaine. What else do you want to hear? That the democrats of *Temps présent* act unjustly when, after promising their readers authentic Mass wine, they set before them instead the stale dregs from their cruets. Yes, yes indeed: this is what I think, my dear Fumet.[48]

I have the right to find clerical circles very little to my liking, and there are thousands of priests and monks who, without saying it, share my opinion on this point. But it would be unjust to make these circles responsible for a kind of deformation [in the Church] that is due to very different causes. After two thousand years of Christianity, a Christian should be able to live in the open air. Christians should be able to live the Christian life. However, for two or three centuries now, your very vocabulary has been that proper to a besieged place, to an island battered by the sea. It's a vocabulary of conservation, of self-defense, of mutual aid, of coöperation: you prefer everything except a conqueror's vocabulary. But the Christian people is a conquering people. . . . The Church has abandoned nothing of her dogmas; she has developed her doctrine supernaturally and made it more specific. The Church, moreover, is not only a congregation of the faithful: she is a human society, and she suffers from not having been able to carry out completely the immense enterprise of her temporal fulfillment. While remaining irreproachable from the standpoint of his faith, at the social and human levels the modern Christian offers only a prodigiously weakened reflection of what Christian Man was at one time.[49]

But when, impressed by the writer's words, Christians rush to effect their "temporal realization" and begin to build the earthly city in the spirit of the City of God, they again encounter Bernanos' hand raised in warning. And his new veto, even more than his previous exhortations, must be heard under the sign of Christian boldness:

Christians without a brain and poor priests without a conscience, scared at the idea that they will be treated like reactionaries, invite you to Christianize a world that, along with all its resources, is being deliberately and openly organized in such a way that it can do without Christ, that it can

---

[48] *Français*, 67–68.
[49] Ibid., 211–12.

assure a justice without Christ, a justice without love, the same justice in whose name Love himself was scourged with rods and put on the Cross. Young people who listen to me: I think there are many among you who are really Christians, who live their faith. The people I speak of are appealed to in the name of justice; this is the way in which today a real blackmail is practiced on the consciences of the unfortunates I have just mentioned, and it makes them tremble. It isn't that they lack virtue or zeal, but they lack character, and, without exactly realizing it, they show signs of the same blindness and commit the same error as the clergy in the nineteenth century: in the name of order, this clergy ended up attributing a kind of divine right to the bourgeoisie. Since power has now changed hands, those I speak of have developed the idea of another divine right, that of the proletariat.—*You will know the tree by its fruits*: this is what Scripture teaches you. A certain kind of justice is known by its fruits, even when it adorns itself with the name *social*. . . . That justice that is not according to Christ, in other words, justice without love, quickly becomes a rabid beast.[50]

This passage was quoted to show that Bernanos does not hesitate to grapple with all parties when it seems to him that the truth requires it. To him all parties and programs are suspect simply by their very existence, especially in our time. He never allows his truth to walk the streets alone, bereft of the person answerable for it and of the courage that lets itself be killed for it and that, in today's world, is the only thing that guarantees it the weight of a serious truth:

At the present moment I know of no system or party to which one could entrust a true idea with the least hope of finding it intact or even recognizable on the following day. I possess a small number of true ideas. They are dear to me, and I will not send them to the Public Welfare Office—not to say to the public house—because the prostitution of ideas has become a State institution the whole world over. All the ideas one sends out into the world by themselves, with their little pigtails on their back and a little basket in their hands like Little Red Riding Hood, are raped at the next corner by some slogan in uniform."[51]

The more progress is made by the technical organization of the modern world, the more infallibly truth itself enters the realm of organization and its means and methods, and the more normal an attitude of conformism becomes for all—Christians and non-Christians

[50] *Liberté*, 165–67.
[51] Ibid., 208.

alike; the more quickly, too, those free spirits will die out who, until two centuries ago, constituted the normal manifestation of the Christian personality: in the last century, they were already reduced to those "solitaries" of Kierkegaard and Nietzsche, who swam so laboriously against the stream, and today they survive only in very rare examples like Bernanos. And, because very few people still possess the sensorium with which to perceive the difference between free and conformist speech, the very voice has to be raised a little louder than previously.

"The individual has at his disposal only a small number of means —and this number is shrinking by the day—with which to resist the pressure of the mass, like a submarine resisting the water's pressure."[52] But the pressure of the modern State is incomparably stronger and infinitely more efficacious than that of any system in the whole course of history: "Modern civilization . . . is perfectly capable of getting the ordinary citizen little by little to barter away his higher freedoms in exchange for the simple guarantee of the lower freedoms: for instance, he will give up his right to freedom of thought—now become useless, since it seems ridiculous not to think like everyone else—in exchange for the right to listen to the radio and watch movies every day."[53]

Bernanos speaks as long as there is still time: "It seems to me that only a limited time has been given us."[54] "This is not perhaps the time or the place to say these things; but I will say them. I hasten to say them because our time to say them is limited."[55] He says them vehemently, because "I violently detest all violence, and in the first place that which is most hateful of all, the kind of violence inflicted today on people's spirits under the name of 'propaganda', which is the code name for the universal organization of mendacity."[56] But he himself wants to be neither vehement nor violent, for "violence always dissipates and squanders one's energies. . . . We escape into wrath and disdain to exempt ourselves from having to act and judge."[57] However, it belongs to the mission of the individual, of the solitary, that

---

[52] *Croix*, January 13, 1945, 474.
[53] Ibid., 475.
[54] *Liberté*, 81.
[55] Ibid., 246.
[56] Ibid., 12.
[57] *Croix*, September 1943, 375.

his condition and the word whereby he expresses himself should be different from that of the crowd: "In order for a room to be adequately warm, the fireplace itself must be red-hot. Even if the heat there is excessive, it doesn't matter, because you can always open the windows. But if the fireplace is only just warm, the room temperature quickly falls below zero."[58]

We should never isolate Bernanos from a "communion of saints", which for him always takes very concrete form. As solitary as he always lived, and as much as he may have fled from all bonds that strove to incorporate him into the official literary mills of the big cities, it was nevertheless impossible for him in the long run to live without friends and conversation. His spiritual need for expansion revealed the feminine side of his heart:[59] this was manifested in the endless outbursts in monologue form that he allowed himself when in the company of friends. He would then dazzle with his wit and his irony, his seething wrath and his humor. Even the monologues in his books (for instance, in the *Grands cimetières*, full of long, formal speeches in the classical style) are at least addressed to an imaginary public, that is, to a "thou"—whether friend or enemy—without which this Christian could not have lived for a moment, in the same way that all his books were written in public places in order not to lose his essential communication with other men.

> I write in cafés and bars, risking being taken for a drunkard, something I would perhaps in fact be if our powerful Republics did not slap pitiless taxes on the alcohol that comforts us. Instead of which, year in and year out, I down these overly sweet *café-crème*, with a fly inside. I write on café tables because I could not for long do without the human face and the human voice, which I think I have managed to speak about in a noble way. . . . I write in the open spaces of cafés as not long ago I used to write in railroad carriages, *so as not to be fooled by imaginary creatures, so as to rediscover the right measure of joy or of sorrow by casting a glance at an unknown passerby.*[60]

---

[58] *Letter*, June 30, 1943; *Bul.* 5, 9.

[59] See the *Souvenirs* of Vallery-Radot, published in the first two *Bulletins* of the Bernanos Society. The most telling text is found in *Bul.* 2–3, 28: "He harbored within himself a feminine nature—nervous, irritable, coquettish—which the male in him dominated but which now and then showed through."

[60] *Cimetières*, ii–iii.

No, Bernanos knows nothing of the pathos of the solitary, like
Kierkegaard and Nietzsche. Like every deep person, he is alone; but,
like Péguy, he remains an ordinary "Christian in a parish". And he
musters up his courage, not before an imaginary public in a lecture
room, but eye to eye with his neighbors, whom he forces to listen to
him. While the two Nordics gathered a whole arsenal of masks with
which to camouflage their seven hapless solitudes, Bernanos never
wears a mask. Each of his words reveals his heart and therefore goes
straight to the heart. For this reason it is impossible to think ill of
even his harshest words. They swim on a current of glowing love
that would like to communicate its heat to everything it touches.

3. Gentle Compassion

This writer's courage is not exhausted in the battle for the measure of
man and the value of the person against all forms of anticivilization. It
makes itself felt also in his portrayal of Christian man as the only true
measure and the only salvation of man as such. Now the Christian
lives on grace.

Like no other Christian writer of modern times, Bernanos is the
minstrel of grace. He is so far from being such in a Jansenistic or Protestant sense that, at the same time and without any contradiction whatever, he is also the extoller of man's original freedom, given him
by God at creation. We will not find any other explanation for this
unity than that given by his own interior religious experience. The
little we know about Bernanos' early period reveals a stormy and most
animated and dramatic wrestling with God. Seasons of deep darkness
and despair alternate with lightning-like certitudes and encounters.
We are entitled to term "mystical" neither the first nor the second;
they are simply states of soul experienced by a man of prayer who believed and struggled with great vehemence. None of the writers who
enthused him in his youth could have been accountable for this: not
Balzac, and Drumont even less; surely not Maurras or Léon Daudet,
and not even Barbey d'Aurevilly. Bloy's influence can first be detected
in 1917, when everything essential seems to have been long decided
in Bernanos' inner life. Hello and Dostoyevsky, too, seem to have
been more a reënforcement than an inspiration. Bernanos time and
again insisted that his heroes and heroines sprang almost complete

from the depths of the world of his childhood; and the same could be said about the quality of religious experience that permeates all his works.

How could we describe this experience? At the very beginning there doubtless stands God's action of grasping for his soul. "At the moment of my First Communion the light began to shine on me", and the boy interprets this light as pointing "to death". The fundamental insight, which will be his to the end, is as follows: "To live and die" for God, "to hasten the coming of his Kingdom", for "glory and fame are empty things . . . when God is not at the center of them, always and absolutely."[61]

At the same time, however, fear awakens in the boy, fear in the face of death; but, at a deeper level, the anguish of sensing the abyss gaping wide behind the appearances of the ephemeral and the intimation of the enormous power of eternity to destroy existence as if by suction. To such nakedness and vulnerability is then added Bernanos' extraordinarily acute faculty for sensing the reality of sin, that lower abyss that opens precisely in the face of the divine abyss. And then here, together with the painful experiences of maturing (when the paradise of his childhood seemed to vanish definitively and, along with it, his naïve understanding with God), he begins to make attempts to "overcome" his self-abandonment to God, to do away with the stripped-down existence imposed upon him. Then there are his long years of service in the ranks of the Action Française. Bernanos did feel a deep kinship with those valid viewpoints and traditions that the Action nonetheless took into its custody and administered in a most invalid manner. Beyond this, however, his involvement with the Action was also a flight into an exaggerated form of order, measure, and constraint, all of which the young man Bernanos intensified to the point of pretentiousness and even dandyism, by means of which he endeavored to create a counterweight to the claim the Absolute was making upon him.

The resulting despair awakening secretly in his heart, the experience of his own resistance, of the "pride that is habitual to me",[62] of the "full and continual anguish"[63] that accompanied him then, the

---

[61] *To Lagrange*, March 1905, *C. du R.*, 19.
[62] *To His Fiancée*, 1919 (unpublished letter).
[63] *To J. M. Maître*, September 17, 1918; *C. du R.*, 33.

experience of an existence exposed to the elements, as it were,[64] the no-exit dialectic of the heart that feeds on itself and becomes increasingly more tangled—a dialectic that knows about self-surrender and yet also feels called to give shape, to create[65]—the deep voices from the abyss "that assail me with a tone so noble and so bent on justice that I don't know how to defend myself against them when they begin raising in me their wild uproar":[66] all these things rush forward to converge in the form that the experience of the absolute will assume in *Under Satan's Sun*. There is a haunting phrase, borrowed from Léon Bloy, that like a stroke of lightning illumines for an instant Bernanos' personal situation at this time: "I find myself between the Angel of light and the Angel of darkness. I look at one and then at the other with the same ravenous hunger for the Absolute."[67]

His deepest Christian insights were gained as a result of much suffering:

> I know it well: it is not the trial that tears you apart but the resistance you offer to it. I let God snatch away from me anything he wants me to give him. At the first movement of submission, everything becomes serene. Pain thus finds its balance within itself: it is as if it had established itself immovably within the majesty of order. . . . I know, I know—but what does it matter that I know? . . . I am surely not unaware that God wants all of me, and I always have something I want to keep from him: I make a ridiculous effort to outwit him. It's as if I were trying to evade his glance, which he has so firmly settled upon me, forever.[68]

Out of these experiences, however, the writer derives not only his praise for the grace that overcomes them but also the demonic grandeur of those who resist God, of those who yield to the abyss and its seductive magic: "By an effort of the pride habitual to me, I construct out of my sufferings grand characters that are so attractive, so impressive, and afflicted with such noble despair that they could make a tiger weep."[69]

---

[64] "Until daybreak, until the rising of the frightful sun, sheltered under hope's highest peak, circled with darkness, what is it that we can then still hold out over the abyss in our torn hands?" (*To J. M. Maître*, August 26, 1919; *C. du R.*, 36–37).

[65] To give shape to and create what, if not this self-surrender itself, this plunge into the unfathomable? And is not such a feat already something demonic?

[66] *To Dom Besse*, 1917; *Bul.* II, 2.

[67] *To Vallery-Radot*, January 17, 1926; *Bul.* I, 3.

[68] *To Dom Besse*, August 1918; *Bul.* II, 4.

[69] *To His Fiancée*, 1917 (unpublished letter).

And for a time he succumbs to the danger of losing the measure of man to the unmeasurableness of the abyss, the danger of abandoning the hiddenness of faith's middle course in order to peer almost greedily into the extremes. Christ in the night of his Passion, the Christian mystic and charismatic, indeed the priest who, endowed with sacramental power by virtue of his function, searches for Christ's tracks in the abyss: Would this not be the Archimedean point standing on which one could see hell as it truly is and lift it from its foundations? According to Bernanos' own interior experience, a man afflicted with original sin cannot undertake this descent without God compelling him and without a certain holy violence on the part of God and of grace. This being so, must there not also be something demonic in such a survey of the unfathomable—something related to demonic possession, to being abandoned to the laws of hell (even in the absence of sin!) and to the rigors of its struggle with God? But it is the final and most daring thesis of *Under Satan's Sun* that, in this being delivered over to the demon—an event that is necessary in Christianity—the demon is always overcome and subjected into God's service by Christ's superior power.

The dimension of revolt and refusal, however, the experiences of genuine despair, of radical hopelessness and abandonment by God, all of which can be undergone only in hell: these provide the formal preconditions for that deed of love whereby Christ and, in his wake, the holy heroes who descend with him can become the conquerors of eternity. The unfortunate thing here is the fact that the saint appears under the emblem of the hero, or, more broadly stated: that love appears under the emblem of power.

How penetrating a diagnosis Bernanos made in this connection in 1918, eight years before the novel's publication: "I dreamed of concentration, of unity. Instead of being reformed exteriorly, progressively, following the discipline of Saint Ignatius, I was attempting to reform myself interiorly. Since the idea of God, little by little, is crowding out in me all others—so I thought—let's put it squarely in the center of my moral life with one clean blow. . . . To have but *one* source of energy and activity, only one angle of vision. . . . To believe in order to understand, to understand in order the better to believe." But, at the same time, dialectical to this desire, Bernanos clearly sees that this unity cannot be constructed piecemeal: it can only be created: "Another possesses the secret of the word that creates. . . . Only, he doesn't speak. . . . Will I forever, forever, remain a useless servant? This *fiat* is more difficult to utter than all the others."[70]

It is very important that Bernanos was not satisfied with his attempt, in *Under Satan's Sun*, to master the abyss. The creation that did emerge from his efforts was not the final form of what he had intimated and dreamed of: "*This book does such little justice to my great dream!*", he inscribed in his parents' copy,[71] and to Vallery-Radot he writes: "Yes, I have finished my book. Reading it through greatly disheartened me. *No, I did not produce my fury of a dream! One can see its face passing back and forth behind the bars, or its huge shadow on the insurmountable wall.*"[72]

And yet, how much had been gained by his tremendous first production! How much wrongheadedness had simply been demolished, never to rise again! If Bernanos continued to pray and struggle, how much easier it would now be for him to set things straight for himself, building on what he had already attained! For, to tell the truth, man is indeed the being who walks between two abysses, and he is delivered from hell through Christ's abandonment by God, and God's grace has assumed this frightful, hard-as-steel, graceless form, and God has really given his Church and her sacraments and his chosen saints a participation in his battle with hell. None of these things should be forgotten or made to lose its bite.

We could for a moment compare Bernanos' way with Karl Barth's, the path he followed from his *Commentary on the Letter to the Romans* to his *Church Dogmatics*. The former, with its demonic exaggerations, would be surpassed by the balanced serenity of the later works, but at the price of a certain loss of genius. The points of departure are similar in both authors, despite the distance between them; and in both of them it is the formal exaggeration of the early works that produces the intensity of the desired shock of their vision.

Continual humiliations that succeed one another blow by blow are necessary in both the exterior and interior destiny of the proud writer if he is going to be increasingly dissuaded from forcing the ways of grace with man into a system—even if this were the "system" of the Cross and the descent into hell—dissuaded also from collapsing sanc-

---

[70] *To Dom Besse*, September 3, 1918, *Bul.* 11, 5.

[71] *Pour une iconographie*, *Bul.* 2–3, 2.

[72] *To Vallery-Radot*, February 25, 1925; *Bernanos*, 154.

tity and heroism into a paradoxical unity disconcerting to Christians and non-Christians alike. Day-to-day difficulties, illness, personal, family, and political disappointments without number and almost without measure: all of these rained down on Bernanos' life and persistently disassembled everything in him that smacked of acquired Stoic *grandezza*,[73] until at last, beneath it all, what reëmerges was his naked child's heart, which laughed and wept in the sun and the rain of grace; at times, indeed, he even laughed with one eye and wept with the other. He became a man whose small childlike maneuvers to impress the adults could be overlooked with a smile, because these masquerades could almost be said to intensify his childlike openness.

Already in 1918 he wrote: "There is a verse in my *Imitation of Christ* that is enough to make me cry for help: *I shall not tire of praying, I shall not ever tire, until your grace returns to me and you speak to me interiorly.* It is both my humiliation and my hope to feel so utterly poor and weak when this voice becomes silent in my heart. I can no longer do without God for a single instant, *and he knows it.* . . . The only thing between paradise and myself is the divine wing that covers me. *Sub pennis ejus sperabis* [thou shalt hope under the shelter of his wings]."[74] His life became one great act of standing at attention before God, of waiting for God's commands, of making himself available to God. "If God calls me, he'll put everything in order. I leave everything up to him."[75] Only in God can we live and breathe.[76] This visceral feeling is but the flip side of the "dangerous gift that was bestowed on me: a very concrete feel for Grace".[77] Such "feeling", however, is no dry organ for cognition but rather a sensing through love, a scenting of every fragrance that wafts from the beloved, something so tender that it can only be expressed through the *gift of tears*. Bernanos can speak about God's grace, about the *"douce pitié de Dieu"*,[78] only with eyes overflowing.

It is, in fact, striking that he endows all his heroes, whether men

[73] See *Sur la sottise du stoïcisme*; *C. du R.*, 39.

[74] *To Dom Besse*, September 1918; *Bul.* 10, 17.

[75] *To Dom Besse*, July 1918; *Bul.* 10, 2.

[76] "Starting with our first cry, the air we breathe is not pure. No, indeed, it is not pure" (*To Vallery-Radot*, March 20, 1925, 112).—"Alas, my friend, we live and die enclosed by denseness" (*Letter*, October 9, 1925; *C. du R.*, 39).

[77] *To Vallery-Radot*, March 20, 1925; *Bernanos*, 112.

[78] "God's tender mercy."

or women, with this same quality.[79] But what is involved is something quite different from sentimentalism; rather, it is what Surin demanded throughout his life: a heart denuded before the all-consuming sweetness of God's love. Everything harsh and seemingly cruel that Bernanos put into his stories always, by contrast to Claudel, serves the one purpose of making the moment of conquest by grace emerge with all the purity and precision possible. This is most striking in the *Country Priest* and in the *Dialogues of the Carmelites*. The full craft of Bernanos' art as a writer is here concentrated on the one end of extinguishing all human prejudices and objections against the truth of divine love and making all situations transparent to their very foundations, that God's glance and call may penetrate them. The dying words of the country priest provide the very simple leading theme of all Bernanos' works: "Qu'est-ce que cela fait? Tout est grâce" [What does it matter? Everything is grace!][80]

This truth is so absolute that there cannot exist any problematic tension or dialectic between "merit" and "grace" because, even though grace does indeed "strike" man from the outside,[81] it also makes a claim upon him and appropriates him from within. The word "merit" has no other meaning for Bernanos than the manner whereby the whole man makes himself radically present and available to the action of grace. For Bernanos, "merit" as such should nowhere be given separate consideration. "I believe in the efficacy of works within the strict limits that the Church commands me to believe in it—no more, no less."[82] "I am not responsible for what I have created. . . . *Virtus de illo exibat.* . . ."[83] I am responsible for what I have not been."[84] It is precisely because he has not merited them that he can demand from God "such great things as the resurrection of the dead and life everlasting".[85] "No one is as shamelessly greedy for grace, and as foolishly wasteful with it, as I. In every respect, a thankless beggar."[86]

[79] See *Soleil*, 278; *Imposture*, 21; *Joie*, 122; *Ouine*, 77; *Curé*, 299; *Liberté*, 276.
[80] *Curé*, 324. (This, the last sentence of the book, is very poorly translated in the only existing English version by Pamela Morris [Macmillan Co., 1937; Image Books, 1954, 1974] as "Grace is everywhere"—an entirely different statement.—TRANS.)
[81] *Joie*, 238, 303; *Français*, 285.
[82] To Amoroso Lima, February 2, 1940 (*Esprit*, 196).
[83] "A power went out from him."
[84] Words reported by Pezeril in *Bernanos et sa mort*; *C. du R.*, 343.
[85] Inscription on a copy of *La joie* (1933); *Bul.* 2–3, 15.
[86] To Dom Besse, August 1919; *Bul.* 11, 10.

As far as he is concerned, once he has received grace, his tears are full of bitterness, an experience already familiar to Saint Augustine: "If only I at least had the bitter consolation of saying to myself that the good Lord has been particularly severe in my case! But no! Not at all. What I have received is more like the ratio of a hundred thousand francs to one *écu*.[87] But his graces trickle like water between my fingers."[88] And all his portrayal of sin and distance from God (often throughout whole books, from the first to the last page) serves the writer only to awaken the feeling of unsurpassable bitterness lodged in a lost heart, because there is no other way to prepare to receive God's sweet grace. The writer hopes to touch a last residue of honor abiding even in hardened hearts, so as to awaken it to life. "We would be branded with ignominy for all eternity if we still pretended to pit our feeble forces against the pitiless thunder of grace as it multiplies its blows."[89] His whole life long Bernanos had to drink such bitter dregs, without ever turning them into a perverse means of feeling the sweetness of grace more deeply or of gaining deeper insights into its workings. There is a phrase of Bérulle's that he liked to repeat toward the end of his life: "*S'offrir par des humiliations aux inspirations* [through humiliations we offer ourselves to inspirations]", and this phrase has a much more naïve and truly Christian meaning, summing up as it does the fundamental bittersweet experience of his long life as literary artist.

The world, with all its hatred and all its blindness, will recognize that it is lost *within God's immense mercy like a small pebble in the sea*[90] only when it becomes aware of the abyss of its loss in the presence of the splendor of grace. "With very few exceptions, it is the common lot of man to die with the feeling that you have not accomplished your task. At the hour of death's agony, each of us will have to experience this greatest of all tearings, just before crossing the threshold and awakening to find ourselves immersed in God's sweet mercy as in the cool depths of the dawn."[91] The whole of existence thus becomes one long yearning to cross the boundaries. With the exception of New-

---

[87] An obsolete French coin formerly worth three francs.—TRANS.
[88] *To Vallery-Radot*, September 1933 (unpublished letter).
[89] *To Maître*, September 17, 1918; *C. du R.*, 33.
[90] *Croix*, February 1942, 195.
[91] Ibid., January 13, 1945, 471.

man, we will hardly find any other Christian of modern times who
had his glance set on eternity with such existential longing, awaiting
the rising of the colossal sun of God's grace at his own death and at
the world's end.

Already in 1933 he was writing these magnificent words: "The
hunt has taken us far away, much farther than we thought of going
before evening came, and now we must confront the darkness and
the beasts of the gloom. We must pitch camp, we must hold out until
morning. O the sweetness of this death, O only morning!"[92] "Five
minutes of paradise will make everything well."[93] "In any event, it's
lovely to say to oneself that, *lost in this abyss of universal joy, human
suffering continues to speak with the good Lord with its gentle voice*—gentle
human Suffering, so pensive, so patient, and always so meticulous in
fulfilling its task to the very end, until it has reached its goal, until
the moment of the innocent arrival of glory, until the first Morning
dawns."[94] "May you be present there, to pluck something of my first
glance without any sadness, of my first glance only just barely opening
on what I have so much yearned for!"[95] "Will we ever have longed
for it ardently enough—the end of the world?"[96]

The letters abound with such passages; and especially those letters
that will inevitably result in the breakup of a deep human relationship are written in the context of eschatological expectation as the
sole horizon before which Christians can argue with, and part company from, one another: "*A Dieu, Maurras! A la douce pitié de Dieu!*
until we are united one day in God's sweet mercy as in an everlasting
morning."[97] And we read something similar at the end of the most
important letter Bernanos wrote to Amoroso Lima, in which there
likewise takes place a sort of solemn parting.[98]

By his words and by his attitude, Bernanos became the steady *witness*
for grace. The permanent fear of death he had to bear was but the salt

---

[92] *To Vallery-Radot*, 1933; *Bul.* 1, 3–4.

[93] *To a Woman Friend*, November 24, 1934; *Bul.* 2–3, 22.

[94] *To Amoroso Lima*, March 1, 1940; *Esprit* 8 (1950): 200.

[95] Inscription to a friend on a copy of *La Joie*, 1933; *Bul.* 2–3, 15.

[96] *To Vallery-Radot*, September 1933; *Bernanos*, 117.

[97] *C. du R.*, 142.

[98] Georges Bernanos, *Das sanfte Erbarmen: Briefe*, intro. by A. Béguin, selected and trans.
by H. U. von Balthasar (Einsiedeln: Johannes Verlag, 1951), 87.

that kept his hope fresh and uncorrupted and that lent the eternity he so much hoped for the quality of being present to him at all times. "If we do not bear witness to the revealed truths, what's the good of calling ourselves Christians?"[99] People could always sense that Bernanos bore witness with his life. He himself knew that, through his profession, he served God just as much as a priest through his ministry.[100] What he wrote to a young writer applies equally to himself: "If the good Lord really wants you to bear witness, you must expect to work a lot, to suffer a lot, to have ceaseless doubts about yourself, whether in success or in failure. Because, seen in this way, the writer's profession is no longer a profession: it's an adventure, and above all a spiritual adventure. And all spiritual adventures are Calvaries."[101]

Like few Christians, perhaps even (when you consider the enormous effect of writers) like few priests in our time, the Christian creative writer Georges Bernanos became a minstrel, an interpreter, and a mediator of divine grace. Already in the trenches of the First World War we see him acting as an apostle,[102] and, through his assiduous correspondence, we see him increasingly become a kind of lay father confessor to countless seekers. The letter of August 1947 shows how intelligently and frankly he could help even priests.[103] We finally see his willingness to receive the many visitors who took up so much of his time: "I never have time to write; but I have made it my duty to receive anyone who shows up at my house, and it happens all too often that I have to lose a whole hour in the company of an idiot. . . ."[104] On his deathbed he handed over to a priest the care of those entrusted to him.[105]

The grace of God shines forth from this life, a life that great and merciless trials "drove home to the foot of the Cross"[106] but that in the process lost none of its fullness of freedom and grandeur. Grace does not subject nature to itself in the same way that one trains wild animals and turns them into domesticated house pets. As Bernanos'

---

[99] *To Charreyre*, August 1946; *Bul.* 4, 6.
[100] *To Dom Besse*, Ascension 1919; *Bul.* 11, 24.
[101] *To Charreyre*, December 1945; *Bul.* 2–3, 24.
[102] *To Dom Besse*, September 3, 1918; *Bul.* 11, 4–6.
[103] *C. du R.*, 58.
[104] *To Benoît*, early 1948; *Bul.* 4, 10.
[105] Pézeril, "Bernanos et sa mort": *C. du R.*, 458.
[106] *To Maître*, September 17, 1918; *C. du R.*, 33.

example shows, grace does it by freeing nature from the false constraints that, in its helplessness or its defiance, nature has fashioned for
itself. In our age, when human nature has been rendered innocuous,
there are only very few persons who are still willing to give grace
the opportunity for its gentle compassion also to show an inexorable
face that exacts merciless demands. Groaning under his enormously
burdened life, Bernanos nevertheless did nothing but offer thanks to
grace. This is what makes him a perfect model in an age when the
greater spirits seek their mainstay in revolt and the lesser spirits derive
from this a right to bleat a little against the order of the world. Despite all the blunt curses he hurled at the "dog's life" that was his lot,
Bernanos did not for a single instant—even in one little corner of his
soul—allow himself to be tempted by the thought of pointing an accusing finger at God's sweet mercy or asking it to give an account of
itself. He knew very well that man's "why?" always misses the point,
because such a question is addressed to a God of justice, while this
writer's flaming heart stands before the wounded and pierced Heart
of God, which has given the last drop of its blood. "What if one of
our blows should stray and strike the bloodied Face?"[107]

---

[107] *To Massis*, October 1926; *Bul.* 17–20, 10.

II. THE LIFE

1. Youth

Georges Bernanos was born in Paris on February 20, 1888, at 26, rue Joubert, in a house that has since been destroyed. His paternal ancestors came from Lorraine, and his maternal forebears from the Berry. Alleged Spanish origins on the father's side have proven incorrect and, with them, the descent of the family from a branch of the same name that settled in Santo Domingo. Bernanos' father was an interior decorator, a kindhearted petty bourgeois who had worked his way up to prosperity by his work in the most flamboyant and sumptuous Makart style. He had, for example, decorated and furnished the Turkish embassy in Paris. In 1898 Monsieur Bernanos bought a spacious country house in Fressin (Pas-de-Calais), where Georges would spend the happiest years of his youth. Before this, the family had spent their vacations in their modest house in Pellevoisin (Berry). To his mother Hermance, née Moreau, a pious and meditative woman, Georges owed the greatest influence on his character. The boy grew up together with his older sister, Marie-Thérèse, on these plains close to the sea, with their endless roads that lead nowhere. To hike on these to the point of exhaustion became emblematic for the basic feeling for existence that would characterize the grown man. "The inordinate temptation to jump secretly over the hedge and simply to dash out into the night"[1] is the temptation of all children in the writer's stories, and it was also his own.

> I have never loved anything except roads. The road knows where it is going. Not tomorrow, but today! Already today! Beautiful and dear road, you are a friend that makes me dizzy with your enormous promises! The man who built the road inch by inch . . . now no longer recognizes it; but he believes in it: for it is his great possibility, a breakthrough as experienced in fairytales, the endlessly unfurling miracle of solitude and flight, the sublime arc that soars up into the blue. . . . The most desolate of men derives patience and hope from the sight of a road, dreaming

---

[1] *Mouchette*, 9.

57

that perhaps another way exists for his soul besides death. Whoever has never seen a road in the first rays of the dawn, between its two rows of trees, wonderfully fresh and alive, does not know what hope is.[2]

"Ah, to flee! To hear your soles crunch on the firm, glistening, softly undulating ground, like a path leading you to an unimaginable freedom! In his hips he felt the quiver of his gait, a movement without goal, without end, without limits."[3] In his most difficult years, around 1933, Bernanos thought of the roads of his youth as a last possible consolation; they became for him the symbol of the life he still hoped for: "The road ahead of us can yet perhaps be very beautiful, perhaps we'll yet see resplendent mornings rise upon it. . . . In any case, the road is there come what may, and in the end it will glide into the sweetness of eternity."[4] The latter can already be heard in the distance: "If you press your ear to the ground and hold your breath, you will eventually perceive a kind of dull rumble, wholly unlike all the other sounds of the plain. It echoes in the hollow of your chest and constricts your heart: it is the great surge of the springtime over in Roulers and Briville."[5]

The Bernanos family cultivated friendly relations with all the clergy of the vicinity. In his passion for photography, the father loved to capture the faces of his visitors in countless pictures, some of which still exist. In these the young Georges can now and then be seen, his face with its sharp features peering maliciously as he sits between two priests playing chess. Or we can see him dressed in clerical garb himself—probably at the instigation of his mother, who had dreams of consecrating him to God—playing the reverend father as he strikes half-genuine, half-pompous poses. Some photographs show the beaming face of a child with huge, wide-open, enraptured eyes that seem to be looking at nothing but wonders instead of earthly realities. These eyes must have seen those deep and simple things the writer would feed on throughout his life, the things to which he would continually have recourse as the only wellspring that could nourish his writing.[6]

---

[2] *Ouine*, 71.

[3] *Rêve*, 164.

[4] Georges Bernanos, *Die Geduld der Armen: Neue Briefe*, intro., selected, and trans. by Hans Urs von Balthasar (Einsiedeln, Johannes Verlag, 1954), 42.

[5] *Ouine*, 47.

[6] See the section "Childhood and Hope" in Part 2, Chapter 3 below.

But these same eyes could make sharp observations; realities entered them before the elaboration of concepts: the face of this priest reveals humility, holiness, a hidden life in God, while that other face communicates only mediocrity and stupidity. Bernanos' eyes knew how to close before God in prayer, for the boy, raised in the normal practice of the Church's life, was never a purely formal Catholic: in this respect he never needed to "convert". His eyes, likewise, learned how to fly over paper: lying on his stomach, the boy spent whole afternoons on the carpet of his father's well-stocked library and consumed all of Balzac, Barbey d'Aurevilly, and Drumont, the anti-Semite who would become the unexpected hero of his first critical book.

"At what moment and by what miracle did the faultlessly turning line explode? When did he, half-unconsciously, leave his childhood? . . . The tomorrow that until now had been only a pale image of yesterday, quietly awaiting him under the horizon ahead, the tomorrow that every morning was again encountered without any surprise: it is no more! O wonder! Life had suddenly detached itself from him like a stone from the slingshot!"[7] For Bernanos, as for Péguy, this transition remained *the* tragic moment of existence: the haunting image, never to be overcome, of man's fall out of his paradise. Everything that followed would be at once the primordial remembrance of what had vanished and the presentiment of what would be recovered in eternity.

The years spent in the lower grades at Notre-Dame des Champs, and to a lesser degree the years when he was with the Jesuits at one of those horrible French boarding schools (dark, dirty, heartless, and tasteless), remained in his bones for the rest of his life as the very embodiment of dread. Indeed, throughout his life Bernanos retained an aversion for the Society of Jesus. As a man he would remember "the black winters, the stinking classrooms, the dining rooms with their greasy breath, the endless and crushing High Masses during which the only thing that an overtired little soul could share with God was its boredom".[8] His First Communion took place during this period, on May 11, 1899, and the event became decisive for his interior development. This was when death and the fear of death first emerged in him, from then on to remain ever present. The boy consecrated

---

[7] *Ouine*, 14–15.

[8] *Cimetières*, 79.

his life to God. If he considered a vocation as priest or missionary, it was clearly due to the impression of how brief life was and how exacting God's presence.

Soon his choice of vocations became clarified as the deeper intentions of Providence were manifested: "The surrender of his own life and death" to God was to occur within the lay state, "because a layman must do battle in many fields where the cleric cannot do much."[9] The writer's profession appeared to him then as "the sole means given me to express myself—which is to say, to live". For him, writing was no mere "freeing up of the inner man", but rather "the condition of my moral existence. . . . If you were to bury my calling, you would be burying me along with it, as well as the thoughts that give me life. Then I would be nothing more than an automaton in the world. This sacrifice is not demanded of me."[10]

At boarding school Georges was a shy and withdrawn young man who, out of defiance and to set himself apart from the others, deliberately went unkempt. At this time, too, the "sensitivity" that later on gave him so many problems and so much matter for reflection, gained the upper hand. From 1901 to 1903, he was at the minor seminary of Notre-Dame des Champs, and then until 1904 at the minor seminary of Bourges, where he felt better and entertained a good relationship with two young priests who were family friends. One of these, Msgr. Lagrange, who later would be the vicar general of Bourges, has preserved a number of very telling letters written by Bernanos at age seventeen.[11] These letters reveal his defenseless sensitivity, his states of anguish, and an arrogance induced by the need to compensate. They were written at the Collège Sainte-Marie in Aire-sur-le-Lys, where the young man was a boarder for the last time. His diploma as *bachelier*, dated July 2, 1906, bears the signature of "Aristide Briand, Minister of Public Education". In 1907 short stories began to appear in royalist newspapers.

While studying law in Paris, in December 1908, he gave his name to the Action Française Party, and he became an ardent and noisy champion of the monarchical idea, often involved in quarrels, scuffles, and street battles. In 1909 an article of his ("The Effects of the

---

[9] *Erbarmen*, 22.
[10] *Geduld*, 19.
[11] *C. du R.*, 13–27.

Democratic Prejudice in the World of Letters")[12] appeared in a small newspaper of the Latin Quarter (*Soyons Libres*). The piece was written from prison, where Bernanos was doing time as punishment for his participation in the Thalamas riot. It is composed in the insolent, grandiloquent, and artificially measured style that belonged to good tone in his circles and is a strident polemic against decadent literature. Instead, Bernanos proposes an ideal consisting of interior concentration and discipline.

In the same year he wrote a brief essay on Léon Daudet, whose solitary experience of the storm raging between the abyss of faith and that of despair Bernanos admired.[13] The adventures undertaken by him during his vacations are recounted by a friend of his youth, Henri Tilliette.[14] And the young student also wrote poems that have not been preserved, which he read to his friends as they strolled up and down in the Luxembourg Gardens.

From October 5, 1913, to August 1, 1914, he accepted Daudet's invitation to take over as editor of the small newspaper *L'Avant-Garde de Normandie*, in Rouen, for twenty-four francs per month.[15] In each number he wrote the lead political article, and here he published his first three short stories, already exhibiting his characteristic terseness.[16] He becomes engaged with the president of the Ladies of the Action Française in Rouen, Jeanne Talbert d'Arc, who descended in direct line from the family of Joan of Arc. Bernanos was a loyal and devoted husband and father to his wife and children; he was a kind of patriarch for numerous relatives and friends who attached themselves to his family, and with this little tribe he moved from place to place and, finally, across the ocean. Nevertheless, no one will ever be able to estimate the measure of restlessness, worry, and suffering imposed on him by this existence in the family circle. This was not so much due to the ceaseless hunt for daily bread that, considering the number of mouths to feed, was hardly ever enough, nor to the frequent changes in places of residence, something that resulted from his interior unrest and, at times, from his feelings of guilt: no sooner had the household settled down than it would be disrupted anew, and with

---

[12] *Bul.* 14, 3-6.

[13] Ibid., 7-9.

[14] Ibid., 13f.

[15] *Bul.* 17, 44.

[16] One of these, "The Mute Woman", may be read in *Bul.* 2-3, 9f.

each move valuable manuscripts would once again be lost. Bernanos'
trials in this connection, rather, derived from the frequent clashes between the writer's temperament and the reprehensible behavior of his
children, some of whom caused him sorrows beyond words, which
he mostly bore in silence. Thus, his marriage became for him a road
of atonement deeply assented to, which he trod humbly in the thicket
of our existence as sinners. He kept to this road unwaveringly, but he
never glorified it. As in the case of other great Christian writers, what
this road represented for him above all was the Cross. He wanted all
the "saints and heroes" whom he saw high above himself to be virginal.

He experienced the First World War from beginning to end as a
volunteer in the Sixth Dragon Regiment, in which he was promoted
to brigadier. Brave in battle but sluggish when confined to the base,
he dumbfounded his comrades by his continual scribbling in students'
notebooks, but he immediately crossed out what he had just written.
Nothing is more astonishing than the slowness and effort with which
this prolific mind arrived at the definitive form of a composition.
Later on, not only the books but even "the least newspaper article
and the drafts for his casual conferences would go through not only
three or four but even ten or twelve quite different versions", some of
which have been preserved.[17] "I decided to proceed with my work,
onward from day to day, from line to line, with uninterrupted com-
pulsion. I will show you my manuscript. You will see how much I
have crossed out and how much new material I have added. I have
learned to endure a whole day in despair before a blank sheet of paper,
just in order not to lose one true thought."[18]

We do not know how many things Bernanos drafted and rejected
until at last, at thirty-eight years of age, he published his first novel.
To Massis he confessed: "I realize I needed twenty years in order
to create in my head an imaginary world of rare proportions." The
war years did not dissipate him. His amazing letters to Dom Besse, a
Benedictine monk of Ligugé and the chaplain of the Action Française,
show that in the midst of the War's upheaval he maintained an iron
will that disciplined him in both the intellectual and the religious do-
mains. Uncompromisingly, he held on to his practices of prayer: the

---

[17] According to Béguin in *Bul.* 2–3, 7.
[18] *Geduld,* 35.

Rosary, the Angelus, Compline—all of which he observed to the end of his life, "but I don't on that account consider I've paid back what I owe."[19] In the trenches he tried to recollect himself and to pray the Little Office.[20] He wrestled with God for the meaning of his life, but also for the spiritual meaning of his age and of the war, which appeared to him to be "the sensory translation of the great things God is presently bringing to pass in the world of souls, the invisible storm that may be detected even at the edge of the material world".[21]

This last quotation makes us feel that Léon Bloy has been through here. Bernanos discovered Bloy "in 1917, while convalescing in Vernon", and at reading him he "rolled in the grass on the banks of the Seine, literally crying with anger".[22] To be sure, the war letters to his confessor, to his fiancée, and to his friends all bear the mark of that forced unity of *Sturm und Drang* and arrogantly aristocratic form that at times had to act provisionally as the crude vessel into which the volcanic contents were poured. The cry to God was authentic; but the spiritual hunger and thirst were howling so loudly in his soul that they did not allow the quiet of contemplation, in which alone God's whispered answer becomes audible, to expand and take hold. Bernanos remained distrustful—to the point of self-defeat—of everything he could attain in his literary endeavors, even after the thousandth attempt at fashioning the precisely desired form. "The only advantage of my present confusion is that I cling to nothing."[23] He would nurture a lifelong insecurity concerning his own creative powers. The great fame to which he was not personally closed and at which he was not loathe to hint would never cloud over his sense of self-criticism or diminish his distrust concerning the final judgments of his own literary conscience.

The end of the war, gray and sobering, the retreat from a heroic existence to the rank of ordinary citizen, the way the forces engaged at the front were then consumed and wasted by the mendacious powers back home: all of this would remain for Bernanos a symbolic and

---

[19] *Erbarmen*, 96.
[20] *Geduld*, 9f.
[21] Ibid., 10.
[22] *Erbarmen*, 59.
[23] *Geduld*, 14.

unforgettable situation. In *The Humiliated Children*, written on the occasion of the Second World War, he would once again ponder the whole problematic of 1918. His attitude toward war as such, however, would become more and more conflictual. On the one hand, he was aware of the power of war to purify, to sanctify even, by putting people squarely before the Last Things.[24] War can be an occasion for God's judgment to become crystal clear,[25] and for people to learn how to die well.[26] But he was equally aware of the dirtiness of war,[27] especially when its endeavors are not guided by the people's convictions but when the strings are being pulled by the cold calculations of diplomacy and finance.[28] Bernanos took a long look at the conditions in which a war must be fought in the twentieth century: advanced weapons technology falsified and made impossible a genuine human involvement in war; the ability to kill was now exercised without any sense of personal responsibility; millions of men were now herded like cattle to the slaughterhouses of the front;[29] and the traditionally honorable soldier's profession was now transformed into a mere trade put at the disposal of any tyrant giving orders.[30] The more he considered these things, the greater Bernanos' distrust of the way Christians can embellish the horrors of war with a philosophical appeal to the natural law,[31] the greater his distrust in particular of the way church people can neatly stake out territories labeled "right" and "wrong".[32] Here, Bernanos took a decisive step beyond Péguy, who did indeed stress the opposition between a duel as "war for the sake of honor" and a tactical battle but who never applied this distinction to the present age.

Nevertheless, we could not describe Bernanos as a pacifist, for never —in order to arrive at an allegedly higher, "purely Christian" conception—did he skip over the dimension where the nation's earthly power and honor are legitimate. Nothing was more abhorrent to him

[24] *Croix*, 96, 203f., 358.
[25] *Erbarmen*, 32; *Geduld*, 10.
[26] *Croix*, 218f.
[27] *Geduld*, 9; *Enfants*, 99.
[28] *Enfants*, 27f., 67f.; *Vérité*, 30; *Cimetières*, 239; *Robots*, 111f.; *Bul.* 16, 4f.
[29] *Curé*, 162, 269; *Cimetières*, 11, 173f., 331; *Robots*, 65f., 70f.
[30] *Robots*, 161, 168f., 215.
[31] *Cimetières*, 93; *Enfants*, 133f.
[32] *Cimetières*, 187f.

than the short-circuit mode of thought that seeks to substitute super-natural virtues (such as humility, repentance, love of enemies, and so on) for nonexisting civil virtues or that endeavors at least to gain an ascendancy over these.[33] Similarly, he was willing to live with the paradox in which the Church finds herself when she, proclaiming the gospel of the powerlessness of heavenly love on earth, does so using in part earthly means of power.[34] And just as war, honorably waged, imposes the highest ethical demands on both the people and the individual, the same holds as well, and even more so, for peace, which for Bernanos was a hazardous enterprise demanding the greatest efforts, not a pillow on which to collapse.[35] What happens during a war must remain alive and ineffaceable in the memory of the nation[36] so that the peace that follows will not turn to rot but rather take hold and grow.

For Bernanos the end of the war posed the question concerning the path he should now take. His quickly growing family had to be supported: it could not live on articles alone. After three years of uncertainty in which he experienced growing states of anxiety, he finally decided toward the end of 1922 to accept a position as an insurance salesman. This was his first bitter humiliation.

2. Maturity

Here we stand before an extraordinary paradox: Bernanos, the foe of every form of middle-class security and the proponent of every bold venture, someone besides who throughout his life could not handle money and was incapable of effecting the simplest accounting operation in the household budget without making a mistake, now, starting in 1924, began traveling across France from his home in Bar-le-Duc in order to convince people to buy life-insurance policies, an occupation aided by his talent as an actor. Tortured as he was by this contradiction, he could tolerate his existence only because he now also

---

[33] See *Croix*, 296f., 460; *Français*, 42; *Cimetières*, 157f.

[34] *Français*, 118; and see 322f.

[35] *Croix*, 332–335, 384, 427f.; *Enfants*, 132.

[36] *Croix*, 441.

set to work with more determination than ever on the task of giving shape to his dreams. "The energy expended for nothing, for less than nothing: for idle trash" left him "every evening completely wiped out, with pounding brain and constricted heart".[37] Still he wrote, in railroad carriages, in waiting rooms, and at night in hotel rooms. He wrote a play that has been lost, and then the short novel *Madame Dargent*, which appeared in 1922 in the *Revue Hebdomadaire*. In a very limited space, this work examines the theme of the demonic aspect of a writer's existence, which would later be developed at greater length in *An Evil Dream*. This was a symbolic beginning, exposing the writer's critical self-judgment with much the same words he would later have God the Father speak to Luther.[38]

At this time he entered a friendship that would endure a lifetime: that with Robert Vallery-Radot. In letters full of impatient prompting and touching concern for the other, Bernanos gives us a first demonstration of his ministry with souls as he tried to convince Vallery-Radot of his mission as writer.[39] We have the following account by Vallery-Radot:

At that time he began to search for himself in dark, abrupt, elliptical novels that exude the atmosphere of a nightmare. He showed them to me, anxiously awaiting my judgment, . . . always full of doubt about his own talent and yet with the feeling of an inner world pressing to be born—something heavy, dark, threatening, and secret, like the silent pressure of a storm. . . . He liked to say he had read nothing, which was a great exaggeration. His masters were Balzac, Bloy, Barbey d'Aurevilly, Dostoyevsky, and Conrad (especially his *Heart of Darkness*). Few contemporaries, except Péguy. He had just discovered Pirandello as well as Proust. He was greatly interested in Léon Daudet, the physician and analyst of states of soul, the author of *Hérédo* and *The World of Images*, and he was fascinated by Freud's psychoanalysis. He was obsessed by a truth into whose face very few dare to look: that we dream our life instead of living it, perhaps because our present life is but the dream of a future one we will come to know only on the other side of death. . . . He made the discovery that in human love each one takes from the other only what nourishes his own passion: that we aren't really looking for a true exchange but for a poison, a drug with which to narcotize

[37] *Geduld*, 24.
[38] *Esprit*, October 1951, 443.
[39] *Geduld*, 23f.

our interior boredom and disgust with existence and thus flee from the horrible truth. These investigations coincided in him with states of nervous anxiety that shook him awake at night and gave him the sensation he was experiencing death's agony in advance. . . . He loved firearms, swords, horses, the hunt, good food, above all venison and French wines of good years—all natural joys. No one was ever less a *littérateur* than he, and in this sense he was right when he said he had read nothing: he never read for the sake of reading, but only in order to rediscover the dream that lived within him. This is why he had such a taste for murder mysteries, especially Simenon's: in these he saw parables of our spiritual life, signs of other worlds. This is also the reason why he often went to the movies: films were for him the darkroom of dreams.[40]

Bernanos brought his friend Vallery-Radot his first big manuscript, now the third part of *Under Satan's Sun*. Despite all its weaknesses, it remains the boldest of his works and the key to all the rest.

He had read the life of the Curé d'Ars and had been profoundly moved by this saint and the shape of his destiny: he was almost denied priestly ordination because of his lack of intellectual talent, and yet he was able to shake his age awake. He drew the whole world to his confessional, foretold the future, healed the sick, read the real state of souls, and wrestled face to face with the devil, who in his rage set the priest's mattress on fire. This saint straightaway transported Bernanos by the pure simplicity of his childlike heart, which loved only God and sinners' souls. He now wanted to portray a country priest in the midst of the twentieth century who, without being a slavish copy of Vianney, would nevertheless reflect his chief characteristics by embodying an adversary of religious conformism and godless science; and he also wished to have his hero undergo his own anxieties and fears.[41]

Vallery-Radot counseled the uncertain and hypersensitive young author, who later too—usually to his subsequent regret—would listen rather too much than too little to others' judgments: he would excise whole parts of chapters and almost mutilate characters in his novels when some reader in a publishing house demanded it.[42] *Under Satan's Sun* was published by Plon in the "Le Roseau d'Or" series, edited by Maritain, Fumet, and Lefèvre. Prefaced by Vallery-Radot and highly

---

[40] *Bul.* 1, 9-10.

[41] *Bul.* 2-3, 25.

[42] See the samples of restored texts of the novel *Joy*, in: *Bul.* 12-13, 1f.; *Esprit*, December 1952, 945f.

praised by Léon Daudet in two articles, it instantly attained enormous success.[43]

Somewhat overwhelmed, Bernanos left the insurance company, exclaiming: "I have no more interest in insuring the life of my contemporaries, which in any event is for the most part hardly worth it."[44] Three years before he had suffered a serious illness that brought him to the very edge of the "dark threshold",[45] and the difficult period of convalescence had turned his continuous travels into a torture. He now hoped to live from his royalties. In August 1926, he moved with his family to Bagnères-de-Bigorre, where his father soon died. The cancer of the liver that consumed him became for the son a palpable image of evil, "a likeness of its monstrous fruitfulness in souls. I continue to work in the midst of this quintessential anguish that reaches down to the foundations. I am living in advance the experience of my own death agony",[46] which in fact was also caused by liver disease.

He was asked to interpret his novel, so dark and difficult to understand. He gave his explanation in a letter to Frédéric Lefèvre, in a conference he gave at Brussels ("A Catholic Vision of Reality"), and in a conference entitled "Satan and Us".[47] But the book did not satisfy him. At once he began work on a second book, which would eventually become the double novel *The Imposture* (*L'Imposture*, 1927, originally entitled *The Darkness*) and *Joy* (*La Joie*, 1928). The progress he made here is evident. The barely tolerable theological ambiguity of his first work, which we will later discuss, has been overcome. In the context of his new breakthroughs, that ambiguity can now be seen as an exaggerated version of a profoundly Christian view of existence, which now emerges more clearly and serenely. The remaining dross would have to be washed away by life itself: years later, the interior purification undergone would enable him to write *The Diary of a Country Priest.*

In these years two new humiliations awaited him, even more bitter than the first. He had devoted the best portion of his youthful fire to

---

[43] Texts cut by Maritain from this first edition of *Sous le soleil de Satan* have recently been restored in a critical edition by William Bush.—TRANS.

[44] *Erbarmen*, 24.

[45] *Geduld*, 23.

[46] Ibid., 34.

[47] A surviving fragment of this conference may be read in *Bul.* 12–13, 22f.

the royalist movement, but already early on he had distanced himself interiorly from the intellectual leader of the Party, Charles Maurras. Bernanos never denied the power of admiration that attracted him to Maurras; but he was put off by Maurras' un-Christian ways, by the hardness of his soul, and by his tendency to make an organized party out of an open movement. In 1913 Bernanos had written: "Maurras defends our entire tradition: the lucid images of our writers, the method of our thinkers, the politics of our kings, the religion that formed our conscience."[48] But in 1919 Bernanos began to draw back from the Action Française: "I have neither the taste nor the ability to be a civil servant."[49]

In 1926, when Maurras and his movement were condemned by the Vatican and membership in the Action was punished with heavy sanctions, Bernanos became profoundly agitated. In his letters to Massis he revealed the deep dichotomy in his soul: "The line between subjection and evasion is devilishly uncertain: it is the difference between the heroic and the cowardly solution."[50]

> My intention had been to use my laughable means in order to provoke a scandal, just as in certain illnesses the doctor raises the fever. I'd have given anything to shake Catholics out of their unbearable silence. The Pope has spoken, and Maurras should have disappeared into the background. Better put: now it is only us they should have listened to. Our outraged and painful cries would surely have produced the necessary clarifications. . . . The majority of Catholics in the Action Française would in this way have become conscious of themselves as an independent power, and so Maritain's entire theoretical project would have become a living reality.[51]

Although this dream of rendering genuinely Catholic an Action taken away from Maurras' hands was a manifest fantasy, again in 1928–1929 Bernanos made himself available to the Action as a spokesman. This he was until 1932, when a difference of opinion concerning an election dispute, something secondary in itself, degenerated into a fierce duel with articles, engaged in by both sides with wounding vehemence.

---

[48] *Bul.* 17–20, 2. This issue of the *Bulletin trimestriel* gives all the documents dealing with Bernanos' break with the Action Française as well as references to the pertinent passages in his books.

[49] *Geduld*, 19.

[50] *Bul.* 17, 11.

[51] Ibid., 13.

The result of the affair was that in the end, and much too late, what was plain for all to see was the total irreconcilability of the positions on both sides. Maurras, Daudet, and Pujo now showered upon Bernanos a whole battery of reproaches, whose mean-spiritedness was plain as day and which spared the "traitor" no public humiliation, even of the most personal sort. Against these, Bernanos defended himself as best he could, all the while exhibiting marks of painful respect for the once-loved Maurras. As always when an opponent wanted to lure him into giving free rein to contempt, he clung to an image of childhood, the original ideal that had to continue breathing under all the rubble and that he in no way wanted to wound.[52]

The most difficult thing about this public thrashing was that it occurred at the same moment Bernanos was heading for a crisis that proved most threatening to his interior balance and self-confidence. After the double novel, in 1931 he produced his first critical work, *The Great Fear of the Right-Thinking* (*La Grande peur des bien-pensants*, originally entitled *France Capitulates*). It contains a critical intellectual and spiritual history of France since the Franco-German War, with particular reference to the French political Catholicism of the time, whose defeatist retreat, conditioned by fear, was exposed by Bernanos with uncompromising fury. Unfortunately, it was the figure of the anti-Semitic traditionalist Drumont who provided him with all the hooks on which to hang the analysis of the events. One cannot shake the feeling that the work, while offering so many genial particulars and an overall vision that is so profoundly correct, nevertheless employs a thoroughly mistaken tone whose youthful arrogance was hardly tolerable now in the author's maturity. What was taking place was the interior liquidation of Maurras and his program, soon to be followed by the exterior one as well. But Bernanos here seems to have arrived at a barrier. He still produced a few small works: *Saint Dominic* (*Saint Dominique*, published in a review in 1926), *Joan of Arc* (*Jeanne d'Arc*, 1929), two short novels: *A Night* (*Une Nuit*) and *Conversation among Shadows* (*Dialogue d'ombres*), both in 1928. Then, silence.

For a few months, together with his friend Vallery-Radot, he was literary editor for *Le Figaro*. But he soon left Paris for the provinces, and, afflicted with both interior and exterior instability, he moved with his family from place to place: Clermont-de-l'Oise, Toulon, La

---

[52] Ibid., 54.

Bayorre (near Hyères). His success with the reading public was diminishing, and he experienced financial difficulties and even real distress.
Already in 1926 we hear him speak of his "wild desire to drop everything and dash off to America".[53] His words of repulsion and disgust at the state of Europe, France, and the Church now invaded his
whole discourse, and his formulations attained an unheard-of sharpness: "With all my forces I have striven for greatness, the greatness
God himself desires we should seek—I mean, out of the dark abyss
of my nakedness, to the point of being disgusted with myself. . . .
I have truly become a humiliated being. And so, if greatness should
ever really touch me, I have no right to count on anything except
being incinerated on the spot."[54] His publisher was pressuring him to
produce other best-sellers. Bernanos put up a half-hearted resistance
that often turned to anger. He protested that he did not write for
the wide public, that he was being taken for someone else, that he
needed time to rebuild his interior front, that he was in the midst of
searching and groping, "pushing himself to the maximum" and therefore "terribly sensitive".[55]

But his measure was not yet full. While ranting so strongly against
modern technology, Bernanos was a motorcycle enthusiast: he used
it as an instrument to help him work out his impatient and highly
concentrated energies and to vent his need for speed. One day, near
Montbéliard, he had to swerve around a car that was backing out onto
the road. To avoid hitting a child standing on the other side of the
road, he crashed against a wall and fractured both his legs. From that
moment on, the proud man became a cripple who had to be content
with walking laboriously using two canes.

Vallery-Radot describes for us his external appearance: "At age
thirty Bernanos was resplendently handsome. His light blue eyes—
blue as the sky—under his high and straight forehead were continually sparkling with a childlike smile, and they attracted your glance
as soon as you saw the pale, manly face. His regular features were
not yet swollen. He did not yet have the stoutness that weighed him
down later on. Rather, he had the elegance of a chivalry officer in
civil clothes, with brisk movements and the hint of a challenge."[56]

---

[53] *Bul.* 17–20, 14.
[54] *Erbarmen*, 54–55.
[55] Ibid., 68.
[56] *Bul.* 1, 9.

And Fumet says the following: "He was tall and bore his head high, looking at you with that improbable glance given only by violet eyes. He had a conquering nose and his moustache, turned up at the tips, sat over fleshy lips ready to break into laughter."[57] And again Vallery-Radot:

> For hours on end he loved to produce grandiose monologues sparkling with wit, during which he would develop loaded character sketches of known personalities, masterpieces of truthfulness and vivacity in which, unbeknownst to himself, Bernanos conjured up the spirit of Ezekiel, Æschylus, Aristophanes, and Rabelais. All the while he would give forth gargantuan belly-laughs, speaking through his nose with puckered lips and pacing incessantly back and forth, tearing at his lion's mane with both fists and relighting a hundred times the pipe that had gone out a hundred times. We thus witnessed firsthand the interior work of this imagination, which was uninterruptedly haunted by prophetic visions, or better: we were transported by Bernanos' imagination far out of this mediocre world, as if we were in Elijah's chariot in the midst of galloping multitudes of angels on Judgment Day.[58]

The bad months spent at La Bayorre brought back the old states of anguish in an intensified form.[59] It is time to say a few words about these states. *Anguish* was for our author a kind of medium for poetic knowledge, the prerequisite for his descents into the underground of souls, that utter interior nakedness and exposure by virtue of which he could capture the softest vibrations of a concealed and precious truth that remained hidden from others. Thus, his works had for him the value of something he had paid for with his heart's blood: "It appears unbearable to me that one could derive profit from what I have created in one uninterrupted state of anguish and enduring so many agonies."[60] This anguish had inhabited him ever since his childhood; it was very likely the cause that, once when he was alone at home in Fressin, made him shoot with a rifle at the numerous fancy mirrors in his father's house. His anguish is difficult to classify, since it can be called neither mystical in the strong sense of the word nor

---

[57] *Bul.* 2–3, 4.
[58] Ibid., 29.
[59] *Geduld*, 45.
[60] Ibid., 47.

pathological. It was apparently something, rather, that was to serve his particular task as Christian writer. He would never have to compel himself artificially to suffer the tortures of hell experienced by his characters Cénabre and Ouine in order to portray their full reality. Knowledge of these tortures was communicated to Bernanos, in the first place, by his own very vital faith and, in the second place, by the states of anguish he was subjected to. The Benedictine Paulus Gordan has written very perceptively concerning Bernanos' experience of anguish:

> The eruptions of his colossal temperament and the explosive power of his spirit were easier to bear than the heavy and leaden torment of the mysterious states of anguish that often enough haunted Bernanos, otherwise sparkling with so much life. Such was surely the high purchase price, carefully weighing sorrow for sorrow, that Bernanos paid for the prophetic visions he received, in order then to condense them into a novel or fashion them into lightning-bolts for an essay. In these experiences he would look at himself as something of an observer, and the extreme alertness of his consciousness, which was constantly registering and comparing states of soul, would only heighten his suffering. Nothing and no one was in a position to make things easier for him. . . . He himself would then, with full clarity, recount similar afflictions he had suffered earlier on, for instance the long period of anguish that preceded the birth of his first work, *Under Satan's Sun.* . . . This state of anguish had all the signs of a death agony and was accompanied by the frightening physical manifestations of a quickly advancing serious disease. His doctors assured him that his organism was in good order: among my papers I still have a medical document I was to give him in order to calm him down. And yet, with the clairvoyance so particular to him both in the bodily and the spiritual realms, . . . he seemed to know and see through to his problems better than his doctors. . . . Thus, I believe I was a witness to his prophetic agony, in which he accepted death as life's highest accomplishment.[61]

It is interesting in this connection that Bernanos from early on thought highly of *physicians* and sought out their company. When he still came frequently to Paris, he would stay with a doctor friend of his, Dr. Lafitte. "He greatly loved medicine and liked to be with doctors. He developed a serious interest in this science, which he

[61] Paulus Gordan, "Erinnerungen an Georges Bernanos", in: *Hochland*, 1949, 522–23.

considered indispensable for the psychologist."[62] His works abound with medical images and metaphors of startling precision, which often involve the portrayal of diseases, the description of medical procedures, or the examination—with cool medical objectivity—of sexual processes.[63] In no novel is a doctor absent as counterpart to the perceptive priest. Despite the fact that the doctor often represents in Bernanos the unbelieving and, therefore, dangerous alternative to the priest as one endowed with true, sacramental power and who therefore has knowledge of the supernatural harm that can come to souls, nevertheless most of these physician figures are portrayed in a very noble light. They would have doubtless taken an even more positive form if Bernanos had not had to wait until his sojourn in Brazil to meet the great Catholic poet and physician Jorge de Lima, who became an intimate friend and spiritual advisor.

In the meantime—we are in 1934—the negative elements in his life continued to have their effect. He was harried by former friends, endured physical misfortunes, faced serious financial worries continually, experienced an interior uncertainty about the direction in which his literary work should proceed, suffered ongoing states of anguish that again intensified and, last but not least, felt a profound disgust at political developments in France and Europe. All of these things converged for Bernanos to such an unbearable degree that, without giving anyone notice, he suddenly left the country, leaving behind his furniture, his father's library, and a great number of his own manuscripts and drafts. He settled in Mallorca, where he hoped to begin a new existence. A contract with his publisher, cosigned by the Société des Gens de Lettres, allowed him a very modest income provided he regularly submitted a certain number of manuscript pages. Under this external pressure and the discipline he had painfully acquired, he produced in the course of the next two years, first, the trilogy of novels that belongs to the author's gloomiest works (*A Crime, An Evil Dream, Monsieur Ouine*), and then, immediately following these, *The Diary of a Country Priest.*

---

[62] *Bul.* 2–3, 29.

[63] Here are a few examples of Bernanos' frequent medical allusions: *Peur*, 149; *Cimetières*, 183, 346; *Curé*, 168, 186; *Ouine*, 137; *Rêve*, 244; *Français*, 203; *Enfants*, 219, 221, 236f., 245; *Anglais*, 11, 85, 92, 142f., 164, 168; *Robots*, 91, 93, 155, 172, 185, 191f.; *Croix*, ix, 19, 37, 102, 109, 205f., 219, 228, 267, 305, 314, 337, 338; *Liberté*, 20, 59, 106, 107, 119, 123, 127, 142, 161, 196, 201, 221, 235; *Erbarmen*, 121; and so on.

On first conceiving this last work, he experienced a feeling of liberation: "It seems to me I can now again write with clarity, because I am really without anger. . . . I think that, after my friend's adventures, I will also write the memories of his youth. . . . And, after these two books, I will have fulfilled my destiny. Souls will have eaten my bread."[64]

> I don't like to talk about this book, because it is very dear to me. While writing it, more than once I thought of keeping it for myself. . . . I wanted to put it in a drawer, and it would have been published only after my death. This would have made my friends rejoice. I mean, we would have rejoiced together: they in this world, I in the other, and my little priest between us, at the borderline between the visible and the invisible—O you who are the cherished confidant of my joy! What a shame that we control the fate of our books about as much as we control our existence! . . . I love this book as if it hadn't come from me. My other books I have not loved. *Under Satan's Sun* is a fireworks display, ignited on a stormy evening in the midst of gales and showers. *Joy* is only a whisper, and the song of praise we expect never breaks through. *The Imposture* is a stone face that nevertheless weeps real tears. If it should be presented to me on Judgment Day, I wouldn't dare to confront this work and say to its face: "I don't know you", because I indeed know that it contains a part of my secret."[65]

A Crime (1935), out of which the companion story *An Evil Dream* (published only in 1950) developed by a very complicated process,[66] represents the fusion of the murder-mystery motif with a metaphysical concern. As such, it is a preliminary study for what is perhaps Bernanos' most profound, and surely his most dense and challenging, narrative creation. We speak of *Monsieur Ouine*. The novel was begun already in 1931, to be finished in Brazil in 1940 and published in Rio de Janeiro in 1943. With characteristic hesitation, Bernanos describes it both as a "dismal pissing wall" and "Job's dunghill" *and* as "my best work" and doubtless "the greatest effort of my life as a writer".[67] In what concerns *A Crime*, its author remained inwardly

---

[64] *Erbarmen*, 50–51.
[65] *Le Cahier*, November 1936; quoted from *Bernanos*, 173.
[66] Albert Béguin has patiently unraveled this process in his critical edition of *Un mauvais rêve*.
[67] *Bernanos*, 165–68.

unsure: "The murder mystery soars to a higher plane", he says;[68] and he asks: "Seriously, now: do you not think I have disgraced myself with this *Crime?*"[69] In *An Evil Dream* he attempted to produce a focused analysis of the younger generation's feeling for existence. "I could have named this novel 'At Rope's End' [*Au bout du rouleau*]", he wrote. "My characters aren't wrecks like [Julien] Green's sad figures. They are beings who have lost their sense of life and can do nothing but make extravagant gestures within the nothingness of their despairing souls, until they perish. They are the rubble of ancient families, or the failed products of recent ones, but this can be seen only if one possesses a gift for observation. In any event, this book is harsher than *The Imposture.*"[70]

In *Monsieur Ouine*, in turn, this tendency to perform an analysis of the *Zeitgeist* is surpassed in favor of a thoroughly metaphysical concern. Nowhere else did Bernanos go so far beyond the limits of what may be said and portrayed. Compared with *Ouine*, the *Country Priest* gives the impression of being simplistic and popular in its appeal. *Ouine* is the orthodox "purification" of that exploration of the depths of existence which in *Under Satan's Sun* was expressed in a perhaps more titanic form but also one that in many ways was grossly distorted. *Monsieur Ouine* concludes the fictional portion of Bernanos' works. The writer's imagination could still have easily produced a great number of living figures, as he had assured his publisher in connection with *Mouchette's New Story*; but the events of the times called him to another manner of engagement.

The deepest crisis had been overcome with the move to Mallorca, just before which, in 1933, he had written: "I have lost faith in myself, in the same way that people lose faith as such."[71] But when the Spanish Civil War now broke out, a new blow awaited him there in Mallorca. After his disillusionment with the parties of the right in France, he now experienced a far greater chagrin at the spectacle of Catholic Fascism in Spain. *The Great Cemeteries under the Moon* (1938) is a mighty cry of indignation from a Christian conscience in the face of the hypocrisy of a supposedly Catholic movement and its

---

[68] Ibid., 170.
[69] *Geduld*, 52.
[70] *Bernanos*, 172.
[71] *Erbarmen*, 44.

crimes committed in the name of religion. Despite the fact that it is grounded in a very particular happening, this book is sure to remain influential for a long time to come. What we must call the "hidden priestly quality" in Bernanos—that compassion which is ready to descend into any hell so as to save a soul—erupts in an elemental way in the context of the war's horrors. The following important account by our author casts a penetrating light on his existence as a writer:

> I began to write *Mouchette's New Story* as I saw poor wretches ride by in trucks, sitting between armed men, their hands on their knees, their faces covered with dust, but very erect, wonderfully erect, with their heads raised high, with the dignity characteristic of Spaniards even in the most awful moments of misery. Early the next day they would be shot: that was the only thing that was clear to them. They could understand none of the rest. Even if they had been interrogated, they would have been unable to defend themselves. Against what? They would first have had to be told. Now then: what impressed me was the impossibility for these poor people to understand the horrendous game in which their life was trapped. . . . I did not, of course, make a conscious decision to use this experience as the basis for a novel. . . . What remains true, however, is that, if I hadn't seen these things, *Mouchette's New Story* would never have been written.[72]

In 1938 our author returned to Toulon for a short time, but then, disgusted with the capitulation in Munich and awaiting the arrival of Hitler as he had prophesied in *The Great Cemeteries*, he carried through with his intention of emigrating to South America.

3. From Primal Forest to Desert

In July, 1938, along with his family, now enlarged by the addition of several relatives and friends, Bernanos undertook the journey to Paraguay, which had always appeared to him as the land of his childhood dreams.[73] After failing to settle there, he next turned to Brazil, where he remained until the summer of 1945 and where he had many places of residence. All in all, these were happy years, due mostly to the generosity and helpfulness of a great number of influential

[72] *Candide*, June 17, 1937; quoted from *Bernanos*, 178.
[73] See the letter in *Erbarmen*, 55f.

friends and admirers who often covered Bernanos' expenses without
his knowing it and who continually found new houses for him when
some experiment had failed. The places where he lived were Itipaiva,
Juiz de Fora, Vassuras, Pirapora, Barbacena, and Rio. The longest sojourn was near Barbacena, in a small place called Cruz das Almas
(Cross of souls), which was to give its name to the title of a large
collection of essays, *Le Chemin de la Croix-des-Âmes*, literally "The
Way of the Cross-of-Souls". He passionately followed the course of
world events and commented on it in weekly articles in the press.
He was soon broadcasting ardent exhortations to the French and to
the Allies over the radio, and in this way he became one of the most
important spiritual pillars of the Resistance back in France.

Around 1938 the figure of Péguy, whom he already knew well,
came even more strongly into the foreground. *The Scandal of Truth*
(1939) and *We, the French* (1939) show the great extent to which
Bernanos recognized in this older brother all of his own deepest concerns and how influenced he was by his language. Bernanos' here
severed his last bonds with the circles of the right, just as Péguy had
had to part ways with leftist politics. Both met in a common and
higher middle-ground that from then on had to provide the spiritual
and intellectual foundation for the France of the future. Alone on his
fazenda, he now developed a predilection for expressing himself in
the form of Bloy's diaries. The book that is perhaps his most beautiful, *The Humiliated Children*, published posthumously in 1949, is an
in-depth reflection on his leading themes. The *Letter to the English*
(1942), the four volumes of collected meditations on the times, entitled *The Way of the Cross-of-Souls* (1942–1945), and *France against the
Robots* (1944) all show the world the same face: the splendid gesture,
the uncompromising glance, the wounded heart offered to all and—
behind it all—the unseen, laborious detail work that fashioned effective form.

Bernanos loved the people of Brazil, which, in its best representatives, welcomed and honored him with true greatness of soul. He
confided his deepest concerns and trials to people like the genial
Jorge de Lima, the government minister Fernandes and his wife, the
politician Virgilio de Mello Franco, and many others. With others,
like Amoroso Lima, he had hefty disagreements,[74] and he was inti-

---

[74] See Bernanos' letters to him in *Erbarmen*, 78–103.

mate friends with many religious, such as Father Paulus Gordan, who
had so many profound things to say about Bernanos. Less than ever
was he spared painful and dramatic experiences in his own home,
and these contributed to keeping alive the tragic undertones of his
life. He commented: "It seems that the Bernanos home is an unsolvable problem."[75] The strongest crises of anguish occur during these
years.

In 1945 the author returned with his family to his country. He was
enthusiastically received in Paris, but he immediately withdrew to
the country: he spent time in Sisteron, Bandol, and La Chapelle-
Vendômoise. From these places he hurled articles in the style of
prophetic irritation at the press of the liberation period, with the
intention of bringing some clarity into the confusion then reigning
in people's consciences and of forcing them to make clear distinctions and take firm positions. Many young people wrote him, and he
answered each one with the same conscientiousness. He gave conferences in Belgium, at the "International Meetings" in Geneva, at
the Sorbonne, and in various cities in Switzerland, and these took
the form of ardent exhortations for the honor and dignity of the free
man, warnings against modern technocracy and the totalitarian mind-
set. His words affected people so deeply that his hearers felt with
trepidation that standing before them was indeed someone who had
looked into the face of Medusa. The part of hope that was still left
him did not derive from this world, as may be seen in the collection
of his conferences, entitled *What for, Freedom?* (1953). He now began
to feel hostility from different quarters, and his financial difficulties
were renewed. But it was above all the disgust of his spirit and his
thoroughgoing disillusionment with his country, which had learned
nothing of spiritual value from the trials of war and the Occupation,
that determined his decision to leave for Tunisia. One last time he
here undertook the attempt to give some shape to his life, to recollect himself in order to write what was to be his supreme work, a
life of Jesus he had been planning. Shortly before his death, in fact,
he made a vow to dedicate himself exclusively to this project. He
now received a request to write the dialogues for the film scenario by
Father R. L. Bruckberger, O.P., based on Gertrud von le Fort's *Song*

---

[75] *Geduld*, 84.

at the Scaffold (Die Letzte am Schafott). This would be the occasion for Bernanos' last and purest work, on which he worked with total dedication and which he completed shortly before his death. Albert Béguin was to adapt it to the stage. Despite its deep, spiritual interiority, *Dialogues of the Carmelites* became one of the greatest theatrical successes of the time. As he worked, Bernanos had before him only the film scenario and not the original novella, and so he created anew the beautiful story of the German poetess from his own interior intuition, enriching it with wonderful episodes. No material could have been more apt for him than this apotheosis of mystical anguish and love, than this nobility of soul elevated and shaped by the ecclesial form of Carmel. It is as if he were able to store away in this ark what was most precious in his own existence, which he had continually offered up in sacrifice and which had been taken out of his hands from the outset. The magical qualities of this work as vessel of the spirit—a work that is perfect also in its formal aspects—proves one last time how correct Bernanos' poetics is. According to this poetics, great form is but a sign for the presence of an even greater life, that of the truthful, uncompromising, free personality that knows how to bow in obedience before God and the Church.

A serious disease of the liver required his immediate transfer to Paris, where he died on July 5, 1948, at the American Hospital in Neuilly after undergoing an unsuccessful operation. He was buried in the family vault in Pellevoisin. Down to his last days and hours, for which we have the precious testimony of the Abbé Daniel Pézeril, who accompanied him to the end,[76] Bernanos maintained the incomparable spontaneity and immediacy of a heart that has remained childlike and never hardened. On receiving the anointing of the sick, he exclaimed: "How moving! How wonderful!" While being taken to the operating room on a stretcher, he sang the Marseillaise. And on the eve of his death he said to his wife: "Now I am entering the Holy Agony." Finally, already engaged in the struggle with death, he whispered a mysterious phrase that could have been uttered by his character, the Abbé Donissan: "*A nous deux!*", which could be roughly rendered as: "Now it's only the two of us!"

---

[76] See *C. du R.*, 341–58; abridged in *Erbarmen*, 126–29.

III. THE DIMENSIONS OF REASON

1. Reason That Transcends

Why should we be concerned with the blank spots on the map, which are daily becoming smaller? Still, and forever, the true unknown is our soul. Our soul and nothing else is the landscape of all surprises and adventures. . . . You say to me: *I leave adventures to the restless and the bums. I myself hate the unforeseen. I run my little life like a double-entry account. Mystery is the pastime of those who have the time for it; but I don't have the time.* But, come now: try as hard as you may, there will always be an adventure you have to undergo despite yourself, one you'll perhaps be experiencing already tomorrow. Better get your feet wet a little now, just to begin getting used to it. . . . The most sedentary of people will have to experience it, and it is a greater and more marvelous adventure than any of those you read about in books. . . . Yes, of course: I mean death, your death, yours, your very own unique one. A deathbed is only a bed like any other, as long as the dying person retains his last connection with the living—I mean that tireless heart that puts up a fight to the very end. But as soon as the poor exhausted chest becomes filled with a solemn silence, the most vulgar bed then appears to me to be a miraculous little boat that suddenly lifts anchor and departs. . . . This is how the great adventure begins.

Don't say too many bad things about bums, then, since all of you—even the most meditative and settled—will, at least at a certain moment, become people who take to the road without knowing where they will sleep that night, adventurers out to discover a new world. And what a world! You will suddenly recognize—without ever having seen it—the invisible universe to which your body had no access and away from which you carefully turned your interior glance. . . . It was here, however, that, almost unbeknownst to you, your soul had long been cultivating its habits, its history, its life, here that it moved secretly, silently, like those fish in the ocean depths that at times are hauled up to the daylight by the lead of a plumbline. Here is where the great passions breathe, passions unknown to the majority of men except for their final, almost imperceptible tremor at the surface of their poor lives. Here is where mysterious forms may be surprised and caught."[1]

---

[1] "Satan et nous"; *Bul.* 12–13, 24.

All of Bernanos is in this passage, which is a provocation aimed at getting the bourgeois to come out of his hollow immanence and enter the place through which he will have to walk at his death, the place through which he has therefore long since been walking during his life. For it is only out of that place, as locus of a person's true depth, that one can live in reality. It is interesting to note that the conference from which the passage is taken, entitled "Satan and Ourselves", was given in the same year that Heidegger's *Being and Time* was published and ten years after the publication of Freud's *Introduction to Psychoanalysis*. But for Bernanos, *the transcendence* afforded by death is not only the means for acquiring knowledge of life but the true locus within which we move and exist. And this place of the soul is not for him, as it is for Freud, the depth of our subconscious but the abyss of life in God. But Bernanos conceives this in such an enormously real manner that we would not be able to understand anything about the events that occur within time, regardless of how dramatic a form they may take, except out of that depth in which we live our truth before God. Far from emptying immanence of its proper weight and tension, looking at immanence from God's perspective is what really confers upon it the superabundant fullness of meaning that is forever tearing open the net of temporality. Hence the seemingly exaggerated role played by the *death agony* in Bernanos, as the locus and hour from which the truth erupts over every single instant of life and as the unveiling of the depths of one's being that had always participated in even the most superficial of our deeds. In our superficiality and sinfulness, we are making a continual effort to close up the access to this abyss of truth: "No one suspects the price of the immense effort the frivolous must make to come to the end of their destiny, while the drama lurks behind each of their pleasures: several times a day they must pass, smiling, right by its gaping gullet, certain in any event that sooner or later they will fall into it. For you can count those who stick to their wager to the last, those who evade the tender majesty of death's agony and who succeed in making their own death something impure."[2]

The writer in some sense "superintends" the truth of life; and so he has the duty to keep awake people's sense for the tremendous adventure: this adventure consists in the truth that, beyond all pleasure

---

[2] *Rêve*, 52–53.

or dread, beyond all terror or bliss, the depth of eternal life may be experienced at each moment of our ephemeral existence. *And this locus of transcendence is made manifest at the two extremes: at the entrance into and at the exit from life, at birth and at death,* in the poverty of childhood and in the denudation of the dying, in the double slopes of the stream of existence—opposed to one another and yet identical: that leading to the child and that leading to the old man. "All day long", writes the country priest, "I've had nothing but childhood images in my head. I think of myself as someone dead." And: "It seems I've gone backward the whole way traveled since God drew me out of nothingness. At first I was nothing but this spark, this incandescent grain of dust created by divine charity. And once again I am nothing but this within the unfathomable Night. But the grain of dust hardly glows anymore; it is going out."[3] "Death demands only one thing: that we keep the promise made on the first morning of our days. For all its earnestness, the smile of death is not less sweet and gentle than the other."[4]

The passion informing Bernanos' life can be called eschatological because it is forever revealing the bare and eternal depths of existence. "The only thing between paradise and myself is the divine wing that covers me."[5] The outdoors is a constant lure to take flight: "What does a flying being need to conquer the third dimension? Wings! Wings, and one initial impulse that dares to soar. . . . This pierces my heart. Is one single gesture of faith rewarded with a whole new world? Shall we stop at the limits of the darkness? Shall we die a wretched little death having ventured nothing, when the wind that comes from another universe is already striking us in the face?"[6] This wind is the call of eternity, the glance of God under which our existence must be lived: "The divine glance has settled upon us, so firm and yet so tender. And this has awakened something in our nature's sheath, full as it is of instincts and habits, whether acquired or inherited. Something has stirred only one time, but it cannot be undone. It's finished. Now we can no longer deceive ourselves. We must either break our bonds or die."[7]

---

[3] *Curé*, 122.

[4] Ibid., 67.

[5] *To Dom Besse*, September 1918; *Bul.* 11, 7.

[6] *To Maître*, 1919; *C. du R.*, 35.

[7] *To Maître*, August 26, 1919; *C. du R.*, 37.

But, in what concerns this lucid realization that our being is ordered to death in the sense that, in its depths, it is always gaping open toward eternity: Of how many men could we say that they truly live, that they are truly alive? The country priest feels the edge of sorrow as he considers this: "How many men will never have the least idea of supernatural heroism, without which there cannot be any interior life? And yet it is precisely on this life they will be judged! All you have to do is think about it a little and the thing appears certain and self-evident. And then, what? Then, once death has stripped them of all the artificial limbs with which society equips the people of their ilk, they will see themselves just as they are, just as they have been without knowing it: frightful undeveloped monsters, mere human stumps." The priest then remembers, however, that all of us have our origin in eternity and that at least the child possesses a kind of dark memory of truth: "It is rare for a child not to have had some kind of interior life, in the Christian sense of the term, at least in embryonic form. On some day or other the impulse of his young life gained the upper hand, and the spirit of heroism stirred in the depths of his innocent heart. Not much, perhaps, but still enough for his small being to have vaguely sensed—and perhaps darkly accepted—the immense risk of salvation, which is the whole substance of the divine element in human existence."[8]

Such is the very heart of Bernanos' experience of existence: our existence on earth is darkened by the fact that we originate in the Light and must return to the Light. Because we are redeemed beings in an eschatological sense—that is, already in the midst of time—for that very reason is it so unbearable for creation and God's children to have to sigh at possessing their redemption only in hope. But this unbearable sighing itself, which is continually bursting us open, is the pledge and guarantee of the Spirit. In the end, no one has expressed this feeling with regard to the world better than Bernanos himself, in a dazzling dedication he inscribed in a copy of his novel *Joy*:

> Blessings on the thunder! And, in addition, I demand the resurrection of the dead and life everlasting for tomorrow. No, not for tomorrow: for today, for this very day!
> "But you don't deserve so much", says God.

---

[8] *Curé*, 124.

"Listen, my God. That's just it! Tomorrow you'd perhaps refuse it to me. Give it to me right away!"

Having said this, you'll know by reading this book (and the others) that, even though I'm a specialist in Joy, I'm also a very good hand at death agonies. May I not fail at mine! . . .

May you be present there when I arrive, in order to receive something of my first glance without any sadness, of my first glance just barely opening on what I have so long yearned for.[9]

Bernanos' *manner of perceiving time* derives from this foundation of eternity within time; this never leads him, however, to try to capture a stagnant "eternal moment" as the rightful possession of man but is a reality that manifests itself continually in an unstoppable current that flows toward birth and death. Bernanos' perception of time is not merely a formal æsthetic problem involving his work; rather, it is something that determines the theological, or, better still, the Christian, atmosphere of his narratives. This has been best understood by Pierre Emmanuel, who, as poet, possesses a particular empathy in the matter:

A novel of Bernanos' [he has written] pursues two different directions at once: first, it moves toward its resolution; but then it also moves toward the deepening of its characters, who are in quest of a time that is never lost, a past that is always present and, in some of them, a kind of childhood state that subsists in them and whose mysterious imprints show through their acts. Regardless of how inexorable the fate may be that leads Simone Alfieri [the heroine of *An Evil Dream*] to her final crime, we know at every moment that this woman remains free, but free in a region of herself of which she knows nothing and for which she possesses something like a furious nostalgia. Time, in Bernanos, is never a one-way road leading to death. . . . Bernanos never condemns anyone, because he knows that a person's interior time never runs out, that the weightiest decisions are never definitive. He knows that there is always a possibility open for changing the past at its very root. This is perhaps the reason for the care he takes never to enclose his characters within too strict a story, the reason for allowing the drama to burst open, since all the circumstances and many of the motivations remain

---

[9] *Bul.* 2–3 (1933), 15.

understated. For, beyond all apparent causes, the deepest cause of every human action can only be intimated obscurely.[10]

But precisely this allusive character of the narrative is necessary in order to involve the reader, who himself thus participates in the drama's events. The tension of Bernanos' novels, then, always resides simultaneously in the two directions we have noted: the movement toward the conclusion of the story and the movement into the depths of the persons involved. This is so true that Bernanos can at the same time create a murder-mystery novel and a metaphysical drama, an art he shares with Dostoyevsky and Poe, although each of them possesses his own conception of time. And the tension at the murder-mystery level can in the end become such a formal epiphany of the metaphysical content (we think here of *Monsieur Ouine* and *An Evil Dream*) that the crime must necessarily remain unsolved—something unheard of in murder-mystery literature—since all the tension is absorbed into the metaphysical depths. Even though other elements do indeed come into play in these novels, above all the social character of guilt, nevertheless the chief concern always remains the adventure of the soul, its being cast on the shores of the eternal, the absolute, the divine, which is ceaselessly manifesting itself at the borders of finite life. To be sure, knowledge of the full and fully revealed dimensions of the transcendent would kill anyone unprepared for such a revelation. In order to withstand it, one would have to be God himself in human form, or someone abiding close to him, which is to say, a saint. And just as grace conceals heaven from mortals, so too does it conceal hell: "If God were to open our senses to the invisible world, which of us would not fall dead—yes, dead—at the sight, at the mere sight, of all the hideous, all the abominable proliferations of evil?"[11] But sin has dulled our sense of sin; we are "protected by this turtle-shell".[12]

The writer's role, however, is to expose the truth. Therefore, he cannot achieve his goal without the saint, whom he must employ as a visible figure, or at least as an invisible standard, and the task of *divination*, which is his very element as a writer, cannot at base be distinguished in the writer from the work of *prophecy*.

---

[10] *La Nef*, March 1951; reprinted in *Bul.* 6, 11.
[11] *Ouine*, 164.
[12] *Agenda*, January 26, 1948; *Bernanos*, 147.

If at this juncture Bernanos did not become an Expressionist without any stable form, he owes this to his sense for the Catholic reality, the measure for which was communicated to him in his youth by Charles Maurras. Mistaken as his involvement with Maurras may have been, still Bernanos never fully succumbed to the enticement: even at the time of faithful membership in the Action Française, Bernanos retained his personal freedom and kept his deeper ideals intact, in much the same way Péguy had done at the time of his Socialist sympathies. We must realize, moreover, that Bernanos' association with the Action was to him a protective shield against his lethal inner visions: it was for him the "marble track" in which "he rolled, without detour and unyielding, toward his goal."[13] Even more: the Action Française afforded him a training in that very intimate feeling for form that, in his mature work, would never allow him to give shape to the decisive and exemplary transcendental reality except within the framework of rigorous spiritual discipline. Indeed, in Bernanos such discipline always leads to the preëstablished ecclesial "track", which is there precisely to direct toward God those paths that are most mortally dangerous because in themselves they lead nowhere and are dead ends.

Hence, Bernanos' *ambivalent judgment of the Action Française* and its leader. In the face of both the liberal and the clerical bourgeois reaction, Bernanos launched a proud and furious defense of the culprit Maurras. The moment the Church condemned him, Bernanos declared himself openly for him, although he had already parted ways interiorly with Maurras. And the moment certain political constellations made Maurras' return to the bosom of the Church desirable, Bernanos distanced himself more vigorously than ever from him, as if each time he were defending the best the Action had to offer against the Action itself. And this second position became the definitive one. The Bernanos who had been a snobbish *camelot du roi* in his youth[14] would be humiliated by Providence and thrown out of his "marble track" and every saddle he was to sit upon. But he would retain, intact to the end, the spirit he had brought with him to the Action Française—the spirit he falsely believed the Action would safeguard and which he brought back out untouched when he left it: we speak

---

[13] *To Maître*, 1919; *C. du R.*, 35.

[14] The *camelots du roi* (pages of the king) were a royalist organization of young Frenchmen. —TRANS.

of the spirit of Catholic and French *form*, which here in Bernanos more than elsewhere becomes the soaring form of a soul that allows itself to be hurled without resistance across the abyss. Bernanos accomplished this while expressly rejecting the way Maurras demonized this abyss[15] and, as we will later show, by basing himself ever more consciously on the supernatural archetypes of existence Christ has given the Church: the sacraments. In the sacraments the saint is time and again catapulted through regions lacking all natural paths, and this results in the truth of existence being laid bare. *This reality, which shatters every natural standard of measurement, is the very content of the sacraments; but the sacrament also impresses its form on life, on everyday existence, on the community. It is liturgy and adoration, measure and appeasement.* What for Bernanos became the intrinsic form of his life necessarily also became the intrinsic form of his work, of his literary creation.

2. *Prophetic Reason*

Bernanos was conscious of the fact that the true measures of existence, which surpass the grasp of reason, did reveal themselves to his experience as a thinker by way of intuition. Half-seriously and half-smilingly, he rejected the role of prophet: "People who regard me much too highly treat me like a prophet."[16] "Friends of mine, blinded by an excess of good will, at times attribute to me prophetic views. Alas, I have never foretold anything! I announce misfortunes many others are expecting like me, but they pretend not to be expecting them because they are responsible for them."[17] "I regret having to speak, almost despite myself, a language that is a little too impassioned, something that every time gives my very modest forecasts the false appearance of prophecy. I prophesy nothing. Most of the events I seem to be announcing are already under your noses, but the public refuses to see them, refuses above all to consider their magnitude."[18]

But Bernanos did not deny the fact that he possessed a free voice that, against the flood of servitudes of our present age, inevitably gave the impression of being prophetic:

---

[15] *Français*, 287–90.
[16] *Liberté*, 13.
[17] *Croix*, February 1941, 95.
[18] Ibid., September 1944, 248–49.

A prophet isn't really a prophet until after his death, and until then he isn't a man people want to be seen with. I am not a prophet, but it so happens that I see what others see as I do, but they don't want to see it. The modern world today is stuffed with businessmen and policemen, but it needs to hear a few liberating voices. A free voice, regardless of how sullen, is always a freeing voice. Voices that make free are not tranquilizing, reassuring voices. They aren't content with inviting us to wait for the future as one waits for a train. The future is something that must be overcome. We don't endure the future: we make it.[19]

All of this amounts to the following: *reason*, if it is to be worthy of the name, must be prophetic not only by way of exception; *reason is prophetic in its very essence*, because existence is itself the creative act of transcendence. Bernanos was very far from having developed any kind of "theory" on the prophetic character of reason: he repeatedly stressed the fact that he was no philosopher ("I am so unphilosophical", he wrote to Lima)[20] and no theologian.[21] But everywhere in his writings there dart forth short reflections on what reason can and should be when it functions correctly, hints as to what reason intends to accomplish in the mind and the work of this particular writer. "Shall we die a wretched little death having ventured nothing, when the wind that comes from another universe is already striking us in the face?" This question is answered a little later in the same letter, when Bernanos affirms: "I lie down on the bed of the waves and of the wind—I get my direction. Once we bring order into our thought, it overflows even in the heart [*Il faut mettre seulement de l'ordre dans sa pensée, pour qu'il déborde jusqu'au cœur*]."[22] For, when it orders itself, thought transcends its own order, in the direction of the "heart" in Pascal's sense, the heart as reason's "freest power". Cartesian *ratio* is not denied, but it has not been given a depth it must decide to embrace. "There is nothing comparable to the eminent dignity of thought. But shall its freest power forever be nailed down? There is no abstraction in the world. When you try to explore it through analysis, all the little precision instruments explode in your hands. . . . We must proceed to the great face-to-face encounter! If only we could make contact with things through the tip of the sublime, the tip that

[19] *Liberté*, 11.
[20] *To Amoroso Lima*, June 16, 1942; *Esprit*, 208.
[21] *Cimetières*, 213.
[22] *To Maître*, 1919; *C. du R.*, 35.

pierces our own heart!''[23] All of this is not for a moment meant in a philosophical sense but, as the next letter shows, only in a Christian sense. That there is no abstraction in the world derives from the fact that God is no concept and Christ no generic being, that the Cross is no random suffering and Christian anguish and hope no universal human feelings. Grounded in a God who became man, all of this converges at the fine tip of a uniqueness that by the same token is absolute freedom.

We could therefore equally say that reason's ability to transcend itself along with existence constitutes Christian faith. For Bernanos, *faith* is not a mere affirmation of propositions held to be true but a decision undertaken with one's whole existence in response to Christ, on the basis of the fact that he has already transferred us out of the darkness and into the light. Insofar as faith is such a decision, it is freedom itself and hence the motor-force of reason. "A man who reasons before believing, admiring, or loving, instead of reasoning only afterward, as if reason were what created faith, admiration, and love, while in reality it is made only to supervise them": such a person is not "capable of foreseeing how, again this time, mankind is to be saved".[24] For his reason is not *creative*, as it is at the culmination of the decision of faith; at most it may be said to "register", an activity that dispenses with interior decision making and commitment and hence with the highest and most efficacious truth. We here encounter for the first time the *diagnosis of obedience* that is so important in Bernanos, obedience being that noble Christian virtue that nowadays is so easily looked upon as the lowest of vices. Whether addressing civil or ecclesiastical authorities, Bernanos cannot impress upon them enough the fact that "sabotaging this high and indispensable faculty of the soul called 'judgment' can only lead to great disasters. . . . People trained to obey blindly are the very ones who will suddenly disobey blindly. To obey without discussion does not at all mean the same thing as to obey without understanding, and total docility is not as far as we think from total revolt. Christian obedience, by its very nature, has a heroic character."[25] People who nowadays are the victims of propa-

---

[23] *To Maître*, August 10, 1919; *C. du R.*, 36.
[24] *Croix*, 392.
[25] Ibid., 465.

ganda are at the same time its secret accomplices: "They believe in everything for the same reason they believe in nothing. If you went to the bottom of their apparent credulousness, you would find that it is only a form of the refusal to judge and that these people are suffering from a paralysis of their conscience."[26]

The particular form of a believing reason, which is this writer's organ to attain to knowledge, is therefore characterized by two things: first, it is a wholesale casting of oneself into God ("the bed of the waves and the winds") accomplished by transcending all barriers; second, with regard to the world, it is a personal and solitary decisiveness and commitment. And the freedom of reason consists in the unity of these, its two aspects. Thinking is self-surrendering trust. Thinking is solitary decisiveness. Thinking is freedom. And it is this we must now examine.

There is hardly a passage of Scripture Bernanos quotes more frequently than the fourth verse of Psalm 90 (91): "He will cover you with his pinions, and under his wings you will find refuge." "This is the word of one who rocks us in his arms—us, his poor wretched children. Who could touch us resting on that breast from which all light issued forth?"[27] This *condition of being nestled in God* is the source of all fruitful living. "We can be worth anything only if we sacrifice ourselves and forget ourselves completely, for the sake of God and his cause." This is why "God will in due course desire that *everything* let go of us, so that we will be able to find support only in him", and Bernanos adds significantly: "that is to say, in our awareness of Good and Evil, of what is just and unjust, which he has put in us".[28] Already in his youth he had written: "If God is calling me, he will arrange everything. I leave it up to him."[29] And the painful experiences of alienation and repeated submission become for Bernanos archetypal experiences of the cognitive spirit, which can see clearly only when God's clear eyes are resting upon it.

> I know it well: it is not trial that tears you apart but the resistance you offer to it. I let God snatch away from me anything he wants me to give

[26] Ibid., 478.
[27] *To His Wife*, June 1918; *Erbarmen*, 29.
[28] *To Amoroso Lima*, June 1940; *Esprit*, 204.
[29] *To Dom Besse*, July 1918; *Bul.* 11, 2.

him. At the first movement of submission, everything becomes serene.
Pain thus finds its balance within itself: it is as if it had established itself
immovably within the majesty of order. . . . I know, I know—but what
does it matter that I know? . . . I am surely not unaware that God wants
all of me, and I always have something I want to keep from him. I make
a ridiculous effort to outwit him. It's as if I were trying to evade his
glance, which he has firmly settled upon me, forever.[30]

And again one year later: "The divine glance has settled upon us,
so firm and yet so tender. . . . What do we care that we will never
know rest—never!?"[31] Indeed, Bernanos would know no rest in himself, and no rest either in mere art, the art of this world, or in its
earthly organ, "sensitivity". "The war has brought sensitivity to its
knees. From now on it's impossible to put it to any good use. What
we need is a rehabilitation of the will, which alone, I feel, can take
us a long way. All or nothing: this is our password. . . ."[32] And so,
he can reassure his friends: "With God's grace, I will at least give
everything I can give: I'll keep nothing back. . . . In this at least I
will never disappoint you."[33]

Self-surrender is the ground of reason because it allows itself to
be hurled by God into the depths God wants the creative writer to
plumb, depths that cannot be reconnoitered from a safe retreat but
only by abandoning oneself to them. What Bernanos is allowed to
taste in return is faith experiences that start from faith and proceed to
experience, located somewhere between the two—between the non-
vision of faith and the vision of the mystic. It is not for nothing that
mysticism plays so prominent a role in Bernanos, and yet not as a
piece of curiosity or sensationalism upon which he focuses a hagiographic spotlight. His priests' ability suddenly to know souls from the
inside and to see into them is something bestowed only on them as
saints; but, once we posit the miracle of grace and faith, this is almost
the natural unfolding and explicitation of the cognitive possibilities
contained in the act of self-surrender. However, we must continually
repeat the fact that all of this has its proper locus only within the
Church. What is involved here is not at all some kind of ruthless ex-

---

[30] Ibid., August 1918; *Bul.* 11, 4.

[31] *To Maitre*, August 26, 1919; *C. du R.*, 37.

[32] *To Dom Besse*, August 1918; *Bul.* 11, 4. (There may be something of a pun in the use
here of the word "password", in French *mot d'ordre*.—TRANS.)

[33] *To Pury*, May 21, 1931; *Erbarmen*, 49.

ploitation of religious potencies for the sake of obtaining cold knowledge, an enhancement of the realm of knowledge, if you will, as in
the projects of a Swedenborg or a Jacobi. What is involved, rather, is a
sober Christian existence in the Church, for the sake of serving one's
neighbor and one's age. Within this context, Bernanos is willing to
allow reason a "divinatory character", an interior certitude that rests
as much on the activity of *ratio* itself as it does on its self-surrender
in faith and on its decisiveness and freedom, exercised through this
act whereby reason ventures all.

To a young worker Bernanos writes:

> You see, it is very difficult to proceed as you request, by a series of ques-
> tions and answers, as the Church herself does when she defines error
> by approving or condemning certain propositions. . . . *Anathema sit!* . . .
> You say to me: *We feel you are right.*[34] Yes, indeed, that's exactly it: the
> operation of the mind we call judgment. We must either get to the point
> where we *feel we are right* or we must resign ourselves to having eternal
> discussions with ourselves, as the poor damned souls in hell must have
> with the greatest logician of them all, whose name is the devil. *Every
> comprehensive judgment is a risk, a wager. But the superstition, or rather the
> idolatry called Technology, closes our eyes to the divinatory character of Reason,
> which must either make a choice at the right moment or resign itself to a perpetual
> condition of doing without.*[35]

The reference to the *kairos*—the right historical moment for acting
and the knowledge it presupposes—is particularly significant in connection with such supernaturally clairvoyant reason. "In momentous
public-affairs transactions, nothing can take the place of what we're
tempted to call (doing some violence to our vocabulary) 'innate experience', that sixth sense that cannot be communicated to another
and is impossible to capture in a formula."[36] But, if it is to be a living truth, the momentous thinking of Church authorities and theologians, too, must possess something of this daring character of a reason
exercised within a *kairos*. In this respect it is not different from reason
as used by statesmen.

---

[34] Throughout this passage, there is a pun on the French expression *avoir raison*, which
means "to be right" but which literally translated would be "to have reason".—TRANS.

[35] *To Charreyre*, April 1946; *Bul.* 4, 5. (The last sentence is italicized by von Balthasar,
while Bernanos underlines only the word *choice*.—Note of the French trans.)

[36] *Croix*, August 1942, 242–43.

Our thought is judged to be too revolutionary—as if all thought were not
revolutionary by definition, as if the thought of Saint Thomas Aquinas
had not been revolutionary in comparison to the Scholasticism of the
eleventh and twelfth centuries, to the point of being condemned by the
bishop of Paris and the archbishop of Canterbury. In no way do I excuse
the Jacobins of 1793 for having brought in solemn procession into the
sanctuary of Notre-Dame in Paris a woman of ill repute, transformed
by them into the goddess Reason just for the occasion. But, after all,
human reason, too, has been redeemed by Christ, and, as such, it has
its place within the Church of God: it is not an intruder there. And a
blind conservatism, for its part, under the pretext of preserving social and
religious institutions from the excesses of the critical spirit, has favored
the advent of an order that does not have the characteristics of even a
human order; in this manner, such conservatism has opened the way to
the divinization, not of reason, but of race and instinct.[37]

Reason thus conceived, moreover, is and remains a redeemed reason, which is to say, a reason that listens, a reason that has surrendered to God and his moment-to-moment interventions. At this pin-
nacle, reason—even creative reason—is receptive, and nothing can be
snatched from it by force. As the young Bernanos considered how to
build his life, he had to struggle with despair, and he wrote: "I can see
only too clearly that, here, what must be done is not to build but to
create, and Another possesses the secret of the word that creates. . . .
Only, he doesn't speak. . . . Will I forever, forever, remain a useless
servant? This *fiat* is more difficult to utter than all the others."[38] Indeed, when he considers the forms reason assumes in Christians of
our age, the sheer horror of it again reassures him concerning his own
convictions. Some lose their dignity through their *perfidie caressante*,
by betraying their faith in their eagerness to flatter the Modern Spirit:
with frightening suppleness they adapt their sensibilities artificially to
the spirit of the times, and they confuse this attitude with the Christian act of discerning the signs of the times. Others make their own
all the excesses of the critical method in order to apply these within
the Church and thus court the favor of the "scientifically minded".
Bernanos bypasses both kinds of Christians and returns to the foundation: "Not one of them gives himself wholly, and yet this is what

---

[37] Ibid., February 1942, 190–91.
[38] *To Dom Besse*, September 3, 1918; *Bul.* 11, 5.

is required. We must open up to the Truth from top to bottom."[39]
Only in this way does one come to be "naked in the face of scandal",
becoming a thermometer by which the temperature of the age may be
read: "Precisely because I'm only a poor devil I feel the blows coming
from farther off. I'm used to being struck, and no one worries too
much about me. Nothing protects me from scandal; I have no honors
to keep me warm. . . . I am naked in the face of scandal, as naked
as you yourself will be along with me before the just Judge, naked
as a worm. It is therefore easy for me to detect before you do that
the wind is turning northward. So, when my teeth begin chattering,
watch out. It probably means that it will snow tomorrow."[40]

With regard to his use of reason, the Christian has this in common
with the prophet: precisely because his spirit is so malleable and defenseless with respect to God can it be so hard and unyielding with
respect to the world: *ponam faciem tuam durissimam* [I will make your
face hard as flint]. Self-surrender to God contains within itself the
commitment to the truth at all costs: "I can do without everything, except the veneration [*culte*] of sincerity and truth."[41] "Nothing in my
life as an artist rests on deceit."[42] Bernanos is ready both to endure
and to provoke every possible "scandal for the sake of truth [*scandale de la vérité*]". He sees himself as belonging to the "generation of
confrontation",[43] which does not shy away from conflict and even
looks for it when necessary. Thinking authentically is a virtue that
requires courage;[44] it is one and the same thing as the feat of daring
that results in a great deed. "The thought of a great people is its
historical vocation."[45] At this point, Bernanos can still not be concerned with the scandal provoked in the weak: "How can you expect
me to avoid scandalizing certain small sissyish souls? This belongs to
the very nature of things. The blood of the Cross scares them."[46]
It should be stressed, however, that scandal is not at all in itself for

[39] Ibid., Ascension, 1919; *Bul.* 11, 11.
[40] *Enfants*, 225.
[41] *To Jorge de Lima*, April 1939; *Lettres inédites* (Rio de Janeiro, 1953), 12.
[42] *To Belperron*, November 1934, in *Erbarmen*, 63; and see *Rêve*, crit. ed., 323.
[43] *Anglais*, 26.
[44] *Liberté*, 15.
[45] Ibid., 16.
[46] *To Massis*, February 12, 1926; *C. du R.*, 40.

Bernanos a standard for the truth, nor does he think that it ought to be fostered at all costs.[47] But there are certain truths that possess an inner quality that alone renders them lovable: the courage with which they intervene. "For, much to the embarrassment of the imbeciles, it is only bold, conquering thoughts that sprout wings and command a following."[48]

However, we must not in this connection forget the warning of Madame Lidoine in the *Dialogues of the Carmelites*, to the effect that such courage is not a virtue acquired once and for all that may be activated at will: "Come what may, we must never count on anything except the sort of courage God bestows day by day, penny by penny, as it were",[49] and this courage is usually accompanied by the sting of anguish and fear. The courage to confront what we must derives from an interior decision and invites others to follow in this decision. But such a decision creates persons who are essentially solitary. Only these can be the building stones of a true community, to withstand the quicksand of modern, atomized society. "I think it is not too high a price if I must pay with a little *solitude* for certain modest privileges that no one would dream of denying me—even if this amounted only to the right to speak, as I do, frankly and calmly, the right to speak in my name and in my name only."[50]

Bernanos knew well that, abiding in this solitude, a person will be attacked from every front. And so he writes in July 1943:

> There was only a handful of us between the press of the right—paid by the enemy, drafted by the people of the Academy, and blessed by the archbishops—and the press of the left, which incidentally was infinitely less rich and powerful, being financed marginally from the budget of the Komintern. The hypocrites of the right could not forgive us for speaking the truth, and the hypocrites of the left bitterly reproached us for speaking the whole of it. Alas, at that time we could speak freely without being silenced or censured. But we could see newspapers and magazines closing their doors to us, because their terrorized editors, fearing boycotts, were very hesitant to publish us.[51]

---

[47] *To Bourdel*, February 1935, in *Erbarmen*, 67; and see *Rêve*, critical ed., 332f.
[48] *To Dom Besse*, Ascension, 1919; *Bul.* 11, 11.
[49] *Carmélites*, 135.
[50] *Liberté*, 83.
[51] *Croix*, July 1943, 354.

Bernanos believed that in our age a serious writer could exercise his craft only by struggling against the pressure of that superpower, money, and against the political configurations created by the power of money; but this is not to say that such an obstacle—which, seen from the outside, is reason enough for despair—does nothing but exhaust a writer's energies: in fact, it can also increase them. "I am a man like you, exactly like any one of you. But I feel what you do not feel, what you endure without feeling it: the immense pressure brought to bear upon all of us, at every hour of the day and night, by a universal and anonymous conformism that has at its disposal inexhaustible resources as well as ingenious and implacable methods aimed at nothing but the deformation of our minds and spirits."[52]

This explains Bernanos' ever more irreconcilable aversion for Claudel, who, according to Bernanos, yielded to the pressure of money and thus lost the clear voice of a witness for the truth.[53] This explains, too, his disdain for all congresses, prizes, academies, for all intellectual associations that, at least in our day, cannot dispense with money and politics. To Jorge de Lima he writes: "The opinion I have of the Academy doesn't only concern the Brazilian Academy but every Academy in the world. They have a contagious spirit of imposture about them that perverts even the most immune persons who enter these societies, which are more ridiculous than Freemasonry because they are silly and accomplish nothing."[54] In Bernanos' view, such associations function on the principle that the compromises and complicities of society and the "socialization" of truth itself in the end free the individual from the solitary task of deciding his own future. "They prefer to believe that everything will be taken care of thanks to a certain number of international commissions of a juridical, economic, or financial stamp, and thanks to a generous encyclical from the Sovereign Pontiff, which Catholics will applaud, taking great pains moreover not to follow its prescriptions if these interfere with the way they run their business affairs."[55]

For the same reason, Bernanos also had great distrust of all those organizations within the Church that rely on impressive numbers—

---

[52] Ibid., 473.

[53] *Cimetières*, 10, 103, 158, 188, 247f., 308; *Enfants*, 71, 96f., 117, 145, 208f., 256; *Français*, 68; *Curé*, 223f; *Croix*, 145.

[54] *To Jorge de Lima*, January 5, 1945; *Lettres inédites*, 58.

[55] *Croix*, September 1942, 250.

whether of members or of projects—to keep alive the illusion that they are contributing to the dissemination of the power of truth in the world. "I also think I understand very well the *atmosphere* of all these associations, groups, committees, and so on. . . . Here, what always wins the day are compromise solutions. Unfortunately, compromise solutions are generally mediocre solutions. This amounts to saying that, even if in the beginning worthy causes were involved, inspired by intelligent and energetic persons, sooner or later these associations, groups, and committees are destined to reflect the compromise opinion of all-too-average, mediocre people."[56] But the truth knows nothing of averages and compromises; its very essence as truth is to proceed to its appointed end and to reveal itself as truth precisely by following this straight course. "At one time it was said—alas, it is still said!—that the truth is to be found at a precise middle point. We might as well proclaim openly then that the natural place of truth is between two lies, like a slice of ham between the two slices of bread in a sandwich. As far as I'm concerned, the best means of reaching the truth is to proceed unswervingly to the very end of what's true, whatever the risks involved."[57]

For Bernanos, his *freedom* rested on his *poverty*, no less *within the Church* than elsewhere, and his freedom allowed him both to see and to speak the truth. Truth in the Church lies not only in the structures and their guardians but in the sense of faith and Christian existence of all. And whenever there is some indication that this equilibrium is affected, the free individual has the right to raise his voice, even in the Church. "I don't boast of being a philosopher, an economist, or even less a theologian. I'm only a simple observer, and I say what I see. I say it as I want and when I want. When a writer has a few friends scattered throughout the world, and when poverty doesn't frighten him—that is, when he's willing to do without a car and a refrigerator—then he'll always find a way of printing his books. You can silence him only by killing him."[58] And if the strength of the cleric consists in the fact that he speaks by virtue of his ecclesial office and not in his

---

[56] *Lettres brésiliennes*, June 30, 1943; *Bul.* 5, 9.
[57] *Croix*, March 1944, 409.
[58] Ibid., August 1943, 366.

own name, the strength of the layman consists in his speaking in no name but his own.[59]

At the moment we are not yet discussing whether Bernanos was objectively justified in his daring remonstrances; what we are considering is his intense awareness of the freedom of the Christian, and this is something that exudes tremendous grandeur and pride: "If I don't keep silent it's because it strikes me as villainous to sacrifice the honor of the whole Christian people to certain private interests, respectable as these may be. I must speak because no one wants to speak in my place."[60] "Granted, I write truths that are dangerous. I write them without pleasure. I write them because thousands of priests and simple believers around the world think like me on these matters. The priests can't say them, and the laymen don't dare to say them. As for me, I both can and dare to. I prefer to deflect toward my person all manner of misunderstanding, rancor, and hatred that could hurt others but cannot really do very much to me, since I don't expect anything from anyone."[61]

At times, however, Bernanos could raise his tone to the level of a certain *hybris*: "Thousands of priests and monks think as I do, but they are perfectly right in keeping silent, just as I am right in speaking. I speak so that they can keep silent without remorse."[62] You always find people who "don't at all like the fact that an honest Communist worker can say to his comrades: 'What do you know! There are after all some good fellows among the Catholics! They're not afraid of saying the truth, even to the bishops. That's not the way it is among us, where the guy who grumbles is immediately excluded by being labeled a Trotskyite'."[63] And this is why Bernanos the individual had emphatically to raise his voice: "There always exists a Catholic brand of Fascism. There exists a powerful Catholic Fascist opinion. When we say this, we're immediately accused of compromising the Church. What has compromised the Church is the fact that the Fascists have for too long been almost the only ones to speak within it, and using the tone of masters. We, in turn, have firmly resolved to raise our

---

[59] See ibid., February 1943, 313–14.
[60] Ibid., September 1943, 372.
[61] Ibid., September 1940, 51.
[62] *Français*, 141.
[63] *Croix*, February 6, 1945, 487.

voice, not to outshout theirs, but in order to be heard everywhere, even in Rome."[64]

It was not Bernanos' intention to combat against and banish the side of diplomacy and compromise in the Church, for diplomacy and compromise are inseparable, and he knew that these are a part of the form of the Church while she sojourns in this world. But, within this same Church, he had to create—with a certain violence when necessary—a space where the counterbalance might act with vigor: and this counterbalance was the individual, the layman for whose benefit the diplomatic apparatus exists and is justified if it keeps to its place. Now, the voice of the individual resounds in a most undiplomatic manner, and so we turn to hear a sampling of some of its blunter accents:

> Just a few months more and, in the face of the tremendous trial the world is about to undergo,[65] one of these astute little diplomatic monsignori, for instance, with fat fingers and a sly smile, will perhaps appear as incongruous in the Church as he would have at the time of Saint Peter. . . . "But these monsignori belong to the Church!", someone will object. No doubt, I reply. And we poor devils, both believers and unbelievers, we make up precisely that world with which the eternal Church has sent them to negotiate. And this is why we have the perfect right to express our opinion about these negotiators who have been created for us, for our use. Here goes, then: We don't like them one little bit! And they persuade us even less than we like them. What's the good of them, then? None whatsoever! They belong to an order of things that has become obsolete, as outmoded at their level as the Noble Guards and the Swiss Guards at the Vatican. . . . I'm not too concerned about causing scandal by these words. For my part, I'm done with laughing. Like a great number of honest people across the world, I'm done with laughing.[66]

I know the clerical party. I know the extent to which it lacks both heart and honor. I have never confused it with the Church of God. The Church is charged with protecting the poor, but the clerical party is always the cunning go-between of the evil rich, the more or less conscious but indispensable agent of every kind of simony. Once more, those people are going to ask: "What is this Catholic writer then asking for? He must be lacking something, since he's evidently so unhappy. Let's try

---

[64] Ibid., March 1944, 412.
[65] Bernanos is writing in 1939.
[66] *Vérité*, 60–64.

to give it to him so he'll leave us in peace!" It would never occur to them, of course, that I'm ashamed of them. . . . They would certainly never ask themselves the question that is so familiar to every Christian, provided he's neither a coward nor an imbecile: "What opinion of Christ and his doctrine is a person of good will going to form as he observes me, knowing I am a Christian?" I'm ashamed of them, I'm ashamed of myself, I'm ashamed of our impotency, of the shameful helplessness of Christians in the face of the dangers threatening the world. *What? We're supposed to be the Church of Christ?*[67]

These last words are important: they show that Bernanos never broke his solidarity with the Church, even in the midst of his harshest and most reviling criticism. He always included himself in the common guilt of all Christians, and he judged himself along with the others: "When I speak of the Catholic masses, *I judge myself along with them*, since I am only one unit within the whole." And he immediately claimed his portion of responsibility in this community of guilt: "When I denounce our scandalous impotency, I should receive the approval of those who have the heavy charge of guiding us, those who in the future will bear a responsibility it would be more just to let fall on us."[68] We repeat: What concerns us here for the moment is not the content of the criticism, but Bernanos' tone and his will (which for him corresponds to a necessity) to bear witness with his whole existence, a witness that could become effective only through the risk he took with his life: "If we don't bear witness to the revealed truths, why call ourselves Christians? And surely, the events of the time themselves would in the end infallibly demonstrate that revelation is right. But our risk and our honor consist precisely in our sacrificing our reputations and our lives in order that the experiences of evil may not be pushed too far. For the good Lord has not sent us out to the nations only in order to declare to them, once the catastrophe has taken place: I told you so!"[69]

At the conclusion of every critical tirade stands the individual, the man Bernanos, with tears in his eyes, exhausted from the intolerableness of the scandal:

---

[67] Ibid., 68–70. (The italics are von Balthasar's.—TRANS.)

[68] *Croix*, December 1940, 69–70. (The italics are von Balthasar's.—TRANS.)

[69] *To Charreyre*, April 1946; *Bul.* 4, 6.

I say it, I repeat it, and I'll never tire of proclaiming it: The present state of the world is a disgrace for Christians. Was the sacrament of baptism bestowed on them simply to allow them to judge from on high, and with contempt, those unhappy unbelievers who, for lack of something better, pursue an absurd undertaking, uselessly striving to establish by their own means a kingdom of justice without Justice, a Christianity without Christ? We continually repeat, with tears of helplessness, laziness, and pride, that the world is becoming de-Christianized. But it isn't the world that has received Christ—*non pro mundo rogo*[70]—but rather we who have received Christ for the world. It's from our Christian hearts that God is withdrawing, it's we who are becoming de-Christianized, wretches that we are![71]

The prophetic element in Bernanos we witness here is nothing but the freedom common to all Christian persons, only raised to the level of a specific mission and thematic content within the communion of saints. We understand freedom here as the bold risk taken by thought, as the commitment of the person to the truth it has discerned, as that total personal stance that is the result of a certain worldview and makes reason clear-sighted. The structures of the Church are eternal and supratemporal; her official representatives are formed primarily on the basis of this supratemporality. It is the business of the layman, by contrast, to detect and to suffer the consequences of the ever-present, ever-pressing relevance of God's revelation by bringing it to bear within the sphere of the life of the world at the present hour. Total trust in God, which makes the soul transparent to the spirit, is paid for in the world with the solitary commitment to God's unabridged truth. This constitutes freedom, the third characteristic of reason.

3. Reason as Freedom

The pathos of freedom that smolders all through Bernanos' work has nothing to do with liberalism. No one is more deeply convinced than he concerning the "communion of saints", that commonality of destinies and responsibilities that reaches into the most intimate regions of a person. This is, simply, a Christian pathos, the pathos of Paul and Augustine and, if he had remained Catholic, of Luther too. But,

---

[70] "I do not pray for the world."

[71] *Français*, 36.

since what is involved here is the most communal of all Christian
possessions, we should look upon it, not as a particular possession
of the baptized, but rather as the essence and very face of man as
such, called as he is to the vision of God. At this point nature and
supernature can no longer be distinguished, for it is only by engaging
in the risk of grace that man becomes truly free as a person.

> If someone defends freedom of thought only for himself, he is by the
> same token already disposed to betray it. It's not a question of knowing
> if this freedom makes people happy, or if it even makes them moral.
> It's not a question of knowing if freedom favors evil more than good,
> because God is the master of both evil and good. It's enough for me if
> freedom makes man more man, *more worthy of his awesome vocation as man,*
> *of his vocation according to nature but also of his supernatural vocation, because*
> *the one whom the Liturgy of the Mass invites to participate in the Divinity itself*
> —divinitatis consortes[72]—*could not possibly renounce any part of his sublime*
> *risk.*[73]

"*The freedom of man, the indivisible solidarity existing between his rational-*
ity and his freedom, gives the human person its sacred character."[74]

Freedom and reason are one, just as freedom and truth are one:
"Whoever opens himself up indifferently to both what is true and
what is false is already ripe for every sort of tyranny. The passion for
truth goes hand in hand with the passion for freedom."[75] For this
reason, it is not enough to see in freedom the guarantee of merely
earthly well-being, as conceived "by those American democrats for
whom Freedom has not ceased being a terrific business deal for the
last hundred and fifty years."[76] Freedom is not in the first place a
right but a duty, a burden, an honor,[77] exactly the same as reason.
Ignoring this truth is the reason why authentic freedom has been lost
to mankind: "A continually growing number of human beings refuse
to embrace the heroic part of freedom, they refuse to wager with Pascal on eternal values."[78] "Capitalists, Fascists, Marxists—all of these
people are similar. Some of them deny freedom, and some of them

---

[72] "Partakers of the Godhead."

[73] *Robots*, 44–45. (The italics are von Balthasar's.—TRANS.)

[74] *Liberté*, 39. (The italics are von Balthasar's.—TRANS.)

[75] *Liberté*, 143.

[76] *Croix*, May 1943, 339.

[77] *Anglais*, 249.

[78] Ibid., 222.

pretend to believe in it, but believing or not in freedom is no longer a matter of much importance because in any event no one knows what to do with it any more."[79]

The horrendous possibility of an entropy of freedom, which was Péguy's nightmare, now arose for Bernanos too. Addressing his contemporaries, he says: "How different you already are from all those who went before you in the course of the ages! How less precious a thing freedom already is in your estimation! How easily you put up with things, how deft you are at enduring! And, alas, your children will be capable of putting up with even more, of enduring even more. For you have already lost the most precious of your freedoms, or what you've kept of it is but a small portion that every day is growing smaller."[80] "What your forebears once called 'freedoms' you're already calling 'disorders' and 'illusions'."[81] "You're being told: *Freedom cannot die.* But it can die, it can die in men's hearts. Just recall for a moment: thousands upon thousands, no, millions of young men who were just like you suddenly lost their taste for freedom, as you lose your sleep or your appetite. . . . These young men were not savages. They were the sons of the very ancient and illustrious German Christendom, your very neighbors."[82] "The day is perhaps not far off when leaving our key in the lock of our front door so that the police can enter our house night and day will seem to us as natural as opening our briefcase for searching at every request."[83] In the 1920s, "millions and millions of people no longer believed in freedom, that is, they no longer loved it, they no longer felt its necessity. They were only accustomed to it in some way, and it was enough for them if they spoke its language. For a long time the State had been deriving strength from everything its citizens abandoned with full consent."[84] For, "free man has only one enemy: the pagan State."[85] And when man no longer loves freedom, he no longer loves love either, for "only the free man can love."[86]

[79] *Robots*, 47.
[80] *Liberté*, 141.
[81] *Robots*, 50.
[82] *Liberté*, 178–79.
[83] *Robots*, 54.
[84] Ibid., 91.
[85] *Anglais*, 242.
[86] Ibid., 239.

But how could this most intimate of realities ever be taught in the manner of a technique or a speculative proposition? For we have here the very core of man, that apex that enables him to pierce through the cloud of temporality and advance into the eternal. "A harsh, cruel, and atrocious experience will prove to them[87] that freedom cannot be taught to anyone, cannot even be given to anyone, that freedom is an interior force and a power of the soul. A free people is one that has a certain proportion of proud men, and if this proportion is not reached, then one must still try to agree on the meaning of basic words [like freedom]."[88] But precisely the word *freedom* is slowly being devalued and falling into obsolescence.

All we hear about these days is order, obedience, discipline, instructions —not only for the present but also for the future—as if these were the only positive realities on which everyone were agreed, as if the myth of Freedom should play in the imagination of the world's peoples the same episodic role that the illusion of love plays in the experience of a young realistic person of the bourgeoisie. . . . The risks of freedom are immense, and the Democracies contain millions of people who are inclined to think that freedom is not worth these risks, because the goods we expect from it for the most part belong to the category of invisible goods, while tyranny offers us very tangible ones.[89]

And so Bernanos takes up "that terrible formula of Lenin's" and puts it in the mouth of the amazed man-in-the-street: "Freedom? What for?"[90]

God, however, "refuses to save man without his coöperation".[91] Without boldly engaging the whole of his person, man cannot reach his goal. The furious battle for freedom that Bernanos fought had nothing to do with traditionalism or nostalgia for the good old bourgeois world or, even, for an alleged "golden era" of Christendom. Bernanos' battle was the simple and fundamental defense of man as such. Indeed, we may ask whether anyone except Christians can still fight this battle today. It is Christians, and not the bourgeois world,

---

[87] Bernanos refers here to the "generation of free men" that will emerge tomorrow "from the ruins of the dictatorships", free men who will not "give lessons in how to be free" but who will live like free men.—Note of the French trans.

[88] *Anglais*, 211.

[89] *Croix*, May 1943, 338.

[90] *Anglais*, 214; *Liberté*, passim; *Robots*, 86.

[91] *Croix*, January 13, 1945, 471.

who are in a position to understand that freedom is not a privilege but
a task and that "only a free man is capable of serving", that "service,
by its very nature, is a voluntary act, the gift that a free man makes
of his freedom to whomever he pleases, to whatever he judges to be
above him, to whatever he loves", that "Satan's *non serviam*[92] is not
a refusal to serve but a refusal to love."[93] In our day, only Christians
can still be the saviors of freedom and, hence, of mankind; consequently, it is they who are responsible before God for the world's
destiny. "Unbelievable as this may sound, it hits the nail on the head
to say that we Christians hold ourselves to be solely responsible for
human freedom, because we are responsible for it before God."[94] But,
while making such an affirmation, Bernanos well knew and did not
hide the fact that the advance guard of Christianity, which is fighting
and dying for freedom, can be found in enemy territory, far from the
gates of the visible Church:

> O you free men, dying without friend or priest, your poor eyes still full
> of the sweetness of home. . . . You, free men dying with defiance in
> your mouths; and you too who are weeping as you die—and you, above
> all you who ask yourselves bitterly if you are not dying in vain! The sigh
> that escapes your breasts shattered by bullets is heard by no one, but
> that feeble breath is the breath of the Spirit. I'm not here speaking the
> language of pulpit oratory or of some neo-Catholic poet. I'm affirming
> an unshakable truth, as simple as two plus two make four. You, free men:
> a great number of you would be very surprised to learn that you are
> marching as the advance guard of Christianity. . . . For the men chosen
> by God to preserve his word are not always the same as those he chooses
> to carry it out.[95]

Such an affirmation, however, is far from releasing the Church from
responsibility. On the contrary: "We expect from the Church the
same thing that God expects from her: that she should form truly
free men, a race of free men who will be particularly effective because for them freedom is not only a right but a mandate, a duty
for which they will render an account to God."[96] On reading the
minutes of a symposium held by the Center of Protestant Studies,

---

[92] "I will not serve."
[93] *Robots*, 87.
[94] *Anglais*, 250.
[95] Ibid., 244–45.
[96] Ibid., 249.

Bernanos found himself in full agreement with Jacques Ellul, who stated that "the Church of Christ remains alone in the defense of man—of man's power to invent, to suffer, to demand, in a word, man's freedom."[97] And, by following this idea, we see Bernanos set off in an unexpected direction: "The Church has a tremendous role to play. She will play it sooner or later: she will be forced to play it. For the Catholic Church already condemned the modern world, at a time when it was difficult to understand the reasons for a condemnation that the facts now justify every single day. The famous Syllabus [of Errors], for example, which today's democratic Christians are too cowardly ever to dare to speak about, was looked upon in its day as a kind of purely reactionary manifesto. Today it appears prophetic."[98]

The fundamental principle of Bernanos' "theory" of reason is: "Whoever judges commits himself [*Qui juge, s'engage*]",[99] for it is not possible to live without making decisions: "To live is to choose [*Vivre c'est choisir*]".[100] And here he seems to be applying this principle to the Church herself. The solidarity between reason and commitment, truth and freedom, has been amply demonstrated in the experience of the modern world: because the world is becoming unfree, it is also becoming dumb. This same solidarity must be deeply felt by the Church: for the Church cannot be an accomplice to the growing indifference to truth and falsehood or an accomplice to the sham truths disseminated by irresponsible modern propaganda. For this very reason, whether she likes it or not, the Church must take upon herself the responsibility for freedom and also, inseparable from it, the responsibility for reason.

4. Catholic Reason

That the Catholic Church is the true Church was not a "problem" for Bernanos; but precisely for that reason, it was not an advantage either that merely needed to be tapped. In the same breath that Bernanos acknowledged the Church's truth, he had to proclaim her obligations. If she is the true Church, then she has to give truth, to create truth,

---

[97] *Liberté*, 108.
[98] Ibid., 145–46.
[99] Ibid., 143.
[100] *Soleil*, 85.

and within herself in the first place. Only this will enable her to beam
forth the truth that is *lived* within her, for a truth that is not lived
cannot help the world. If the Catholic Church is the true Church,
then we must obey her unquestioningly, for all haggling concerning
ecclesial obedience would be a sign of lack of faith and at the same
time of foolishness. But this obedience can only be an obedience born
of freedom and leading to freedom, for truth and freedom are one.

In a questionnaire he once filled out for his publisher, Plon, Bernanos entered: "Catholic since baptism, not even a convert!"[101] Bernanos
did not think roughly "along the lines" of the Church: Bernanos'
thought grew directly out of the Church. He laughed in the face of
anyone who wanted to see in him a problematic Catholic, perhaps
even a secret heretic. The famous letter to Amoroso Lima says it all:
"I have never been a restless soul. Contrary to what some pitiable
priests think, with all the coarseness of my nature I feel coarsely at
home with obedience and discipline. In no way do these bring me the
elation (or the appeasement) of a difficulty that has been overcome
or a humiliation to which one has acquiesced. This is probably why I
seem to make so little fuss about it. I feel at home in the Church. I'm
not afraid of losing in one instant all the fruits of the efforts made to
enter into the Church, because that is where I was born."[102] But Lima
insists, suspecting him of being secretly tempted to heresy. Bernanos
replies with a tone of bitter reproach: "It's really funny that, after having read my books, you could imagine me discussing with theologians
some point in the doctrine of the Fathers or in conciliar decisions."[103]
"How could I have spoken in such a bantering tone of the abyss I had
slid by if that abyss had been heresy?"[104] On his deathbed he would
declare: "As for me, I aspire only to obey. If the pope should speak, I
would be the first to follow."[105] And there are numerous other texts
in this vein: "If they drove me out of the Church, I couldn't live five
minutes outside of her. I'd immediately find my way back in, in bare
feet, wearing a hairshirt, with a rope around my neck: in a word,
meeting all the conditions you would care to impose, and gladly!"[106]

---

[101] January 11, 1925; *Bul.* 1, 3.
[102] *To Amoroso Lima*, January 1940; in *Esprit*, 192.
[103] Ibid., March 1, 1940; *Esprit*, 200.
[104] Ibid., *Esprit*, 199.
[105] Pézeril, *C. du R.*, 351.
[106] *Français*, 144.

"Bernanos used to say that, without faith, he could not live one single minute, formulate one single thought, move one little finger".[107]

Although Bernanos' love for the Church did have its painful aspects, this in no way speaks against this love: "The truth is I love the Church painfully. I love her as I love life itself with all its pains. I accept the Church as she is, I strive to accept her as she is, and it seems to me—at least if I ever were worthy of it—that at the end of this acceptance I should receive my humble part in the immense effort of the Church's ascent."[108] But such an unconditional and affirmative acceptance can be given only to a truly *Catholic* Church. This is the reason for Bernanos' zealous vigilance that no one should transform the Church into a "heresy" in the original sense, in modern parlance into a "party": "When I believe that the Church is always right, I don't understand this in the same sense as the Fascists who write on walls that the Duce is always right." What makes for the difference is precisely the openness reigning in the very bosom of the Church: "No party man would dare to write the things I write."[109] The bishops themselves against whom Bernanos carried on his polemics "know very well that under no pretext" would he "write one word against the Church"; and he adds: "I quite agree that my opinions aren't to everyone's liking, but who could speak without risk of scandal? The very fact that a thought is expressed by means of words is a permanent scandal in the world. So what could we then say of the written word?"[110]

Without yet touching on the mysteries that lie at the heart of the Church, we must at least make preliminary mention here of the irreducible dialectic peculiar to the Church's existence and resting on her twofold reality: for the Church is both eternal and temporal, infallible and fallible, immaculate in herself and yet sinful in her members. In her first aspect, the Church requires the most childlike obedience and an open love for the truth entrusted to her, a truth she freely dispenses and simply *is*—in her deepest identity as Bride and Body of Christ, as communion of saints, and as "love". In her second aspect, the Church

---

[107] Gordan, *Bernanos au Brésil*; in *Bul.* 6, 4.
[108] *Français*, 225.
[109] Ibid., 227.
[110] *Cimetières*, 216.

requires open judgment, criticism, and even humiliation, things the
Christian cannot spare the Church provided he lays claim to his part
in the burden of guilt. We must realize, however, that the relationship
between both these aspects can never be defined with clean precision
for two reasons: first, because the visibility of the Church belongs to
the mystery of Christ's Incarnation and, second, because Christ's truth
can never be subject to exhaustive judgment by the believer. Nevertheless, it would be just as wrong to allow the second aspect (that
the Church must be examined, understood, and judged just as she is
at a given moment in time) simply to be absorbed into the deeper
attitude of faith. Every apologetical approach that seeks to argue away
the Church's aspect of being sinful in her members in fact harms the
Church more than it helps her. This is precisely what completes the
structure of human reason: its faculty of judging boldly, both by its
internal processes and in the public forum. We would be wounding
the very heart of reason if, at the last moment, we were to refuse
to exercise the duty imposed by a bold freedom, under the pretext
of obeying the Church and preserving an ecclesial disposition: "The
truth concerning Ethiopia! The truth concerning Spain! The truth
concerning the Reds, the Blacks, the Whites, the Blues, the Greens,
and the Purples, the truth concerning the Rainbow! But, you say,
'there are dangerous truths'? Well, then: spell them all out, and they
will correct one another. You're systematic in your support of every
manner of prestige. Why, it's every manner of truth that we should
be defending! Every kind of prestige has been created for the truth,
and not the truth for the prestige."[111] "Since you're not willing to
go in your lying all the way to mortal sin, let lies be and stop teasing
them. Don't rile up lies for nothing!"[112]

It is in this context that we should examine Bernanos' continuous
polemic against a certain official "church style" of expression, which
got on his nerves not only because of its pampered traditionalism
and verbose pomposity but because it could not help but scandalize
the undiscriminating outsider: "You are the only ones in the whole
world—absolutely the only ones!—to find this unctuous style touching, elegant, admirable. It is so unnatural that we must at times ask
ourselves with trepidation whether it is still capable of conveying one

---

[111] *Français*, 130.
[112] Ibid., 133.

sincere thought or feeling."[113] Remarks of this sort and other equally harsh turns of phrase[114] so give evidence of deep wounds inflicted on a soul starving for truth that we may not simply dismiss them as hot-tempered exaggerations. Bernanos knew the priestly soul. It was easy for him to penetrate this so-called "clerical" style from the inside and sustain it for pages, to the point that he seemed in earnest and yet gave himself away with all his veiled allusions. A good example of this procedure is the bishop's letter to Canon Gerbier at the end of the first part of *Under Satan's Sun*.[115] Perhaps no task of Bernanos' was more clearly defined than his duty to cleanse the Church's atmosphere of all the kitsch and other forms of untruth clinging to ecclesial institutions and traditions in our day. The laity of the Middle Ages would have blown away such layers of dust with much less hesitation than its counterpart in the modern world. Bernanos was irritated, not by the imperfection and sinfulness of churchmen, but by the view that these failings must be argued away at all costs with pious pretexts. How more wonderful by far to see all of it as it is and to love the Church nonetheless! "It's enough for me to know that, if things are this way (at least judging by human appearances and logic), God must have wanted it this way; that he knows what he does; and that he does not expect us to pluck out our eyes so as not to see any more than he expects us to castrate ourselves so as not to sin against the sixth commandment."[116]

We must only listen carefully to Bernanos to learn how love and indignation, obedience and the critical spirit, can interpenetrate fruitfully in a Christian heart, without detriment to either:

Whenever I point an accusing finger at the Church, it is never with the ridiculous intention of contributing to her reform. I do not believe that the Church can be reformed in her human aspect, at least not in the way in which Luther and Lamennais understood it. I do not long for a perfect Church: after all, she is a living reality! Like the most humble and most destitute of her children, she goes hobbling along from this world to the next. She commits faults and atones for them, and whoever for one moment looks away from all her pomp will hear her praying and sobbing along with us in the darkness. If this is so, why point an

---

[113] *Vérité*, 57–58.
[114] See, for instance: *Croix*, 75; *Cimetières*, 231; *Français*, 169f., 213.
[115] *Soleil*, 245f.
[116] *To Amoroso Lima*; in *Esprit*, 192.

accusing finger, you will ask. Why, because it's in her very nature to be
the accused, in the line of fire! Everything that I have, I have from her,
and nothing can reach me except through her. The scandal that comes
to me from her has wounded me directly in my soul, at the very root of
hope. It may be that no other scandal exists except the one the Church
gives the world. I defend myself from this scandal with the only means
at my disposal: the effort to understand. You advise me to turn my back
to the problem? It's possible I could do that. But I'm not speaking in the
name of the saints; I'm speaking in the name of all the honest people who
resemble me like brothers. Have sinners been entrusted to you? Well,
then: the world is full of miserable people whom you have disappointed.
*No one would dream of throwing such a truth in your face if you consented to
acknowledge it humbly.* They don't reproach you for your faults. They're
not shattered by your faults but by your pride. Doubtless you'll answer
that, whether proud or not, you are the keepers of the sacraments that
are the gates to eternal life and that you don't refuse them to anyone
who is in the proper state to receive them; that all the rest is only God's
business. . . . "What more can you want?", you ask. *Dear God, we'd like
to be able to love!*[117]

We should add here what Bernanos says, echoing Mounier whom
he quotes, concerning bad taste and kitsch in religious art, in his opinion an openly discredited currency and a symptom of deep-seated untruths and impurities: this ranges from the occasional dilution even
of liturgical language all the way to the "arid, hasty, and hopeless
stylizations" of so-called modern art, especially in France but elsewhere as well, and everything that nowadays is called "sour kitsch"
and has succeeded to the "sweet kitsch" of the Saint-Sulpice style.[118]
We should also deal already here with Bernanos' battle against the
remains of the "Christian humanism" of the Baroque schools, tatters
that have been handed down to our age and that hardly command
credibility any more. Of this humanism Jacques Maritain has said that
"it has been rehearsed to the point of nausea, divine nausea, for it's
the World produced by this sort of humanism that God himself is in
the process of vomiting."[119]

As he searched for a genuine form and expression of divine truth
that would be unassailable even in purely human terms, he hit upon

---

[117] *Cimetières*, 114–15. (The italics are von Balthasar's.—TRANS.)

[118] *Français*, 137.

[119] Ibid.

the last encyclical of Pius XI, written practically on his deathbed. "An old exhausted pope sees the swastika fluttering over his city and, driven to the edge by this outrage, he emits a cry of pain and wrath, a full-throated human cry, and the whole universe replies with a sort of deep bellowing that makes the Masters of the nations shake in their boots. The cry of a man: this is something that in the near future will be priceless, when night and day, on the high places of the Spirit, all we'll be able to hear will be the clitter-clatter of type-writers, striving to cover over the noise of machine-guns."[120] On his own deathbed Bernanos was still desperately straining to hear again this voice he so yearned for: "Why doesn't the pope speak?" he asked. "You have only to put people on their own two feet and they walk!"[121]

Thus we see that everything converges for Bernanos on the question of how the existential truth becomes realized within the Church. The universal truth that Christ is may be participated in within his Church on one condition: that the people who make up the Church know that Christ is divine life and a divine Person. This is why everything in the Church that is supporting structure and scaffolding can never represent the *whole* truth of the Church—and under "structure and scaffolding" we may list the official priestly functions, the hierarchy and its special infallibility, and the various aspects of the clergy's life that derive from these structures. Official structures and functions are channels that insure that the divine graces and truths arrive intact at the place they are intended to reach, namely, the hearts of the faithful, which is the ultimate field where God's grace is realized and bears fruit. Everything just listed under "structures" is the means; grace in the hearts of the faithful is the goal. The structures of the Church do possess a divine guarantee that they will remain in their essence un-touched by sin and that the gates of hell will not overpower them, and this reassurance is an inestimable privilege for all. But for the "field of realization", which has not received such guarantees, the same state of affairs would in fact be a hindrance: for, did not the gates of the underworld close over the Son of Man? Did not his death become the very condition for his own and every other resurrection? Must not

[120] Ibid., 136–37.
[121] Pézeril, *C. du R.*, 351.

the Christian and, with him, the whole Church of all living Christians daily die to the old man in order daily to rise again and be born anew? *This* is true discipleship and imitation of Christ, and not the death-free state of invulnerability such as can be enjoyed only by the forms and structures and the graces of the Risen Christ contained within them. In this "field of realization" the priest does not stand higher than the layman, or the layman higher than the priest; only one person could ever make a claim to superiority here, the very person who would never do so: the saint. The saint is the one who lives the truth of the Church and therefore the full form of Catholic reason, which as such is the full form of all reason and reveals reason's prophetic character, in the original sense of the word: an utterance from God representing God.

The Christian writer of fiction, as layman and as representative and defender of the laity, can do nothing other than portray the figure of the saint (cleansed, to be sure, of all the untruths that often have turned it into a figure of kitsch) and strive with all his faculties to realize in his life and work the existential side of ecclesial truth. Bernanos continually defended himself against being mistaken for a theologian; he would not even enter into dialogue with them, so little did he feel called to change, renew, or suggest even the smallest thing at the level of theoretical ecclesial truth. "I am by no means an expert in theology. Here I am speaking as I always do, following the letter and the spirit of the penny catechism, the only one I'm sure of knowing."[122] But what transformation when the dry truths of the catechism are submerged like Japan flowers in the water of life! How they now blossom with the "fullness of Christ", a fullness of life, but not only of life but also a fullness of truth. For the Spirit of God is the Spirit who here and now directs the course of Christian existence, a reality that few have expressed more beautifully than Thomas Aquinas; and this Spirit is the Spirit of truth, of counsel, of knowledge, wisdom, and science, the Spirit who reveals in the midst of time and history the abyss of the riches of Father and Son. Bernanos enriched the Church in marvelous ways in the whole sphere of existential truth. He strengthened and corrected the center of gravity, and in this way he helped restore the balance between theory and life, a balance that every new generation of Christians must strive to attain.

---

[122] *Cimetières*, 213.

With original impact, he made all of us again aware of the specific weight and "water-displacement capacity" of Christian life and sanctity. And if all theoretical formulations of Christian truths must in the end be said to have been abstracted from salvation history and, most centrally, from the concrete life of the God-Man, then it should not surprise us that nothing can more benefit and stimulate theology than the existence of lived holiness in the Church. This, at least, is what the ordinary state of affairs could and ought to be.

Consequently, Bernanos always portrayed *the Christian person in the act of commitment* and in the vulnerability endemic to Christian judgment and action—something that often enough takes the form of suffering what is inflicted. In keeping with his heart's vision, he portrayed the *priest*, not in the performance of his "holy functions", but in dialogue with sinners, in the inevitability of difficult situations, humanly exposed and yet venturing forward into all the individual cases for which general theories no longer sufficed and in which the crucial thing was the ability to make correct and on-the-spot Christian decisions on the basis of the insight given by the Holy Spirit. Bernanos showed the priest at prayer. This prayer, however, was by no means a secure refuge from the dangers of action but rather the act of becoming even more exposed before God.

Thus, the person in the *religious state* was initially the object of bitter criticism by Bernanos for having apparently withdrawn to a more protected place and situation; but in the end Bernanos justified the consecrated religious life by virtue of its risking a greater nakedness and defenselessness before God and before all the powers of both the upper and the nether abyss. Such denudation is the lived truth of contemplation.

Finally, often taking himself as example, Bernanos portrayed the *layman* as the person who must bear the naked brunt of responsibility for the world. To the layman God has not given the help of sacramental power and ecclesial office, so he will not be able to entrench himself behind these as tactical cover; nor has God given the layman the yoke of ecclesial obedience: such obedience would dispense the layman of his specific responsibility in having to make judgments and take bold steps in the world, and freedom from ecclesial obedience in fact enables the layman to be a Christian in the world who dares all and is exposed to all.

In all states of life within the Church, the "place" where existential

ecclesial truth becomes a reality is the precise point where the supernatural ecclesial structures (to which the priestly office also belongs)
and the world, or "nature", intersect; and, as far as such realization of
truth is concerned, this point of intersection is the very center of the
Church. Bernanos in no way fell victim to the imbalance of "laicism":
his heroes are just as much priests and nuns as they are laymen. This
crossroads is the privileged place of the layman in the Church for the
sole reason that *here* no other state of life takes precedence over the
lay state, and any exemplary fulfillment of the Christian vocation by
a priest or a religious occurs here only for the sake of the Church
consisting of all God's people.

By contrast to theoretical and dogmatic truths, it belongs to the intrinsic coherence of *existential* truth that a person can successfully demonstrate it to the world only by risking a personal commitment and by
casting one's own existence into the balance. As with Péguy and Bloy
and, later on, Mauriac as well, this is what every reader of Bernanos
continually senses, and this is what lends real weight to their utterances. Bernanos never ceases to put all of himself into the figures he
creates and the thoughts he formulates: he is the unwieldy creature
made of clay into which God wafts his breath, the big clumsy fellow who wins others with his sense of humor, his good-naturedness,
his wit, his heartfelt loyalty, his childlike readiness to laugh and to
cry; in a word, he wins others by virtue of a soul receptive to all
that is human, a soul the reader can almost take by the hand and
which, like a deft potter, seems to have to apply only the pressure
of a thumb to the ever-malleable material in order for the images
and forms to appear that Bernanos wants to present to the reader.
But, out of this complex personality that both laughs and cries, there
continually shimmers forth something greater, acquired in the experience of total dependency on God: something at once terrible and
demanding, a prophetic wisdom that, proffered in such a vessel, will
from this point on never let go of the reader. This peculiar "something", however, which is the presence of Bernanos' soul in his work,
could not for a moment be mistaken for his saints and heroes; and
yet he knows that both he and they are made out of the same stuff
—the Lord's grace; both he and they bear witness to their origins
as best they can—the saints in a magnificent way by following their
unswerving path, he himself limping along clumsily and often falling:

and precisely for this reason they both belong together within the all-embracing truth of the one Lord.

The presence of the man Bernanos in everything he dares to say, in everything he—as he so well formulates—"advances", confers on his every word, by virtue of an inexplicable paradox, both the greatest gravity and a humanizing gentleness often bordering on humor. And this is how it should be when a layman preaches. The priest in the pulpit is too completely identified with his official function to allow himself such "musical accompaniment", and for the most part the same holds true for the saint who has been chosen and sent. The layman who steps forth with Christ's truth must put his own life at times in the foreground and at times in the background. He is both self-affirming and self-effacing. He points to his own life because Another is living in him. Humor is the tool he uses to shatter the shell and expose the serious contents of the hidden core. He receives unconditional competence by the very fact that he acknowledges his incompetence. Bernanos has communicated something of this basic quality of the layman to all his figures, even his priests and saints, and this quality about them brings them so close to us that, even in their most exorbitant experiences, we feel they are people just like us.

~

In 1944 Bernanos was requested by his friend Fernando Carneiro to write a brief autobiographical sketch to be used by Carneiro in a conference. Instead of this, Bernanos handed his friend a sort of interior portrait of his ideals in which the features and stages of reason we have been examining here are summarized in a luminous way. The occasion of this statement guarantees that what Bernanos is revealing here are highly personal convictions. He takes his bearings from the *honnête homme*, the exalted human ideal of the *Grand Siècle*—the seventeenth century—and in so doing he turns a confessional utterance into an objective criterion. The main part of this unpublished document reads as follows:

> 1. I turn to the kind of man that the seventeenth century called the *honnête homme*:[123] the frank, fair, cultivated man; the gentleman.

---

[123] The typically French expression may be generally rendered as the "frank, fair, and culti-

The *honnête homme* is the man who, while fulfilling the duties of his profession, mission in life, and rank, searches throughout his life—through all possible circumstances and experiences of life—not for the solution of particular problems, but for the clearest possible idea of the general problems that confront a free mind, and he does this in order to organize these problems reasonably, by the order of their import and urgency, and thus to grasp the total net of relationships that binds these problems among themselves. The *honnête homme* is quite willing to be mistaken concerning many of the details in this picture; he is satisfied if its proportions are correct.

2. The *honnête homme* knows how to run the risk of judging, for judging is always a risk. Judging is an aristocratic, indeed, seignorial act. This gift is possessed from birth, although it can be reënforced by the education of the mind, just as that other gift called good taste is possessed from birth—I mean, from nature—and can also be developed by practice and experience.

In a country of savages, the superior man, the divine man, would obviously be the technician, the specialist, even if all he could do were to pull teeth. What would be the good here of a man with general ideas? A great civilization is the one with the greatest number of men capable of judging, that is, capable of formulating comprehensive views, because such men form opinion, clarify it, render it healthy, and open it up to the great currents of thought. Next to such people, technicians and experts are but manual laborers and subordinates. A civilization of technicians is a pretentious civilization of underlings.

3. The direst lack of our age is an aristocracy of the spirit.

4. Modern man adores systems because these dispense him from the daily risk of judging. The system judges for him.

5. The *honnête homme* fears nothing so much as being taken in, especially being taken in by himself. He well knows that he cannot avoid all prejudices, but he strives to recognize his own and be fully aware of what they are. And he has a tremendous distrust of every truth capable of reënforcing prejudice, so that he acknowledges such truth reluctantly.

Whatever the particular system may be, *one is always taken in by it.*

6. The role of the *honnête homme*, of the aristocracy of the spirit, is precisely to sustain in the greatest possible number of people a certain freedom of spirit, which makes a civilization naturally rebellious to system, for systems invade only civilizations in a state of decadence.

7. When the insolence and fanaticism of the expert and the technician

---

vated person" or "gentleman". In the course of the document, Bernanos will make his own understanding of the term clear.—TRANS.

are no longer contained within their bounds by the irony of the *honnête homme*, then. . . .

8. When I speak of an aristocracy of the spirit, one would be mistaken in imagining that I'm thinking of a very small, disdainful, and overly refined élite. *Nothing could be more false*. There are many people in the world who fit the classical definition of the *honnête homme*, and they come from all classes and even every level of education. For what makes them to be what they are is their capacity to judge and not merely an acquired knowledge: they all share the same free and disinterested attitude of spirit. Lack of education perhaps makes them fall more often than others into certain errors of detail; but as soon as a dialogue begins, they recognize these errors at once, and we easily come to agreement on our overall views.

9. N.B. The one who is least worthy of the name of *honnête homme* is surely the little professional intellectual, the intellectual parasite. The role of this intellectual vermin is precisely to keep the *honnêtes gens*—the honest people—from coming to an understanding among themselves, from seeing clearly what is before them, and from finding bold solutions.

10. Léon Bloy clearly saw that the mediocre priest is, spiritually speaking, a monster; but, from the perspective that concerns us here, such a priest also belongs to the lowest and most nefarious species of the intellectual parasite. Nothing is farther removed from the aristocracy of the spirit than the mediocre priest.

—I think, my dear Carneiro, that you should make some room at the beginning of your conference for this definition of the *honnête homme*. It will perhaps suffice to help you avoid all further discussion with the imbeciles who refuse me the right of saying that modern society is ill constructed; they refuse me this right, that is, if I do not first prove to them that I am capable of construing another kind of society.

This spontaneous document unites all the main elements of Bernanos' "method": it provides the deepest insight into what "spirit" is (the free and bold commitment to the total truth, the aristocratic elevation above the slavery of individual facts) and, hence, also the most serious possible foundation for the superiority of the older culture over today's civilization of systems. The ascendancy of the system in all realms, including theology, against which Bernanos fought with the same weapons as did Péguy—for instance, in his splendid pamphlet, *L'Esprit de système* [The system-building spirit][124]—is the sign that the

---

[124] Gallimard, 1953.

prophetic and Catholic character of reason is well on its way to vanishing. If the priest is supposed to represent the apex of reason, he could not do so merely by mastering a theological system; rather, in keeping with Peter's call to the Cross (Jn 21:18), he would have to do it by the radical commitment of his existence. The holy priest who embodies the fulfillment of the highest truth is the greatest and best proof for the fact that truth becomes creative when it is realized by a person's bold commitment. Therefore, all those priests who, instead of representing the truth and their commitment to it, represent only themselves and are committed only to their own interests more than deserve and invite a "critique of clerical reason", despite the fact that they may at the same time be irreproachable in their obedient fidelity in the realms of ecclesial doctrine and discipline.

The only question that remains here—and we will save it for the conclusion of the book—is whether the tone and atmosphere that are the medium for Bernanos' critique are always the most adequate for his purposes. We are hardly inclined to answer in the affirmative. Anger and indignation at times render his voice less clear, by contrast to the measured tones of the voice of the *Grand Siècle*, which Bernanos himself presents as model. We would have to defend Bernanos and protect him against himself on the basis of his purest inflections; we would have to interpret him—and, at times, correct him—on the basis of the sublime heights he states are his goal when he defines himself and his purpose. Bernanos quite readily accepted such a judgment, all the more so as he made no claim to sanctity (the meeting point of truth and life) for himself; what he called his own, rather, was the humor of the discrepancy between truth and life in his person, and the trembling emotion sparked by the grace that was nonetheless given him.

It is thus that the circle is closed: to the openness of existence, to its adventure beyond death and the abyss, ending in life eternal, corresponds the prophetic character of reason, which has as both prerequisite and result the attributes of commitment, audacity, and freedom. The Church, moreover, is the place where reason attains its denudation, completeness, and catholicity. Not least important, this occurs within the dialectic of obedience in faith and ecclesial self-criticism, which together make up the painful earthly form of eternal love, through which the *zelus Dei*—God's wounded zeal for man— is manifested here below.

IV. THE DREAM OF THE IMAGINATION

The word *dream* is present everywhere in Bernanos. It appears both in the novels and in the critical writings. It covers such an enormous range of experience that it is almost too much for a single concept to encompass. If we seek in Bernanos for an *existential*, it is in the dream that it becomes tangible. Everything in Bernanos—both the best and the worst—is to be found under the sign of the dream. For this reason we may at first be inclined to dismiss as meaningless, or at least as illimitable, a concept that can mean so many things. This would be unjust. For even though in this case, as elsewhere in Bernanos, no philosophical theory may be elaborated on the relationship between existence and the power of the imagination, nevertheless the lines traced by his treatment of the dream, as they cross one another time and again, yield a clear pattern that constitutes the background before which the whole drama of this life and work is played out. As usual, what we must first do here is listen carefully to what Bernanos says and means, all the while trying to detect one first level of coherence by identifying various groups of motifs and different layers of signification. Nothing here must be forced; everything must be kept loose and interpreted as living signs: that is, we must not attempt to separate Bernanos' "abstract thought" from the concrete reality of his characters' and his own lived experience.

1. The Dream of Existence and Eternity

The basic and comprehensive meaning of "dream" in Bernanos may be construed from the prophetic form of reason, and therefore of existence, which we have discussed. To be human means to undergo the adventure of eternity, which has its decisive and central turning point in death. To be human, therefore, means both things at once: to understand oneself in one's uniqueness as a being oriented through death *toward* eternity (as a being who is *becoming* eternal) *and* to see and understand oneself nevertheless within temporality *from* the perspective of eternity (as a being who already, and continually, is becoming

eternal). Consequently, our every situation, our every decision, and
even our every real thought possesses a gleaming quality that reveals
man's relatedness to the eternal or, even more, the very foundation
of eternity. This confers on existence a perspectivism identical with
the fact that man is spirit, and this perspectivism can always and necessarily be experienced and interpreted in two ways that run counter
to each other. When man is conscious of himself as living within
temporality, then the manner in which eternity dawns through all his
acts must appear like the opening up of the depths of a dream, of a
space of consciousness that looms into man's temporal reality with all
the intensity of the memory of a physically experienced dream, or
like the sensation of a dream image that is present but that the sleeper
cannot draw up into the sphere of waking consciousness. "The average man", wrote Bernanos, "is by no means proud of his soul. The
only thing he wants to do is deny it. He denies it with immense
relief, as one wakes from a terrible dream."[1] Conversely, the sense
of eternity's depth can acquire such preponderance as the source of
everything most real and significant in a person, it can so become
the very basis of meaning and the locus of ideation, that, considered
from this perspective, all the phenomena of temporality begin to be
experienced as steeped in an unreality peculiar to themselves: as mere
images in a dream.

We might at first be tempted to trace these motifs in Bernanos
to some aspect of the Romantic and Idealist traditions, such as Albert Béguin has described in his book *L'Âme romantique et le rêve*.[2]
But, despite a surface similarity, the core of the dream experience in
Bernanos is something quite different, something more primal and
without apparent derivation. We can already see this from the fact
that there is nothing "Romantic" about Bernanos in the ordinary
sense of the word, no trace of reverie or vague nostalgia. Everything
about him has a manly clarity, hardness, and resolve. We would be
more on track if for an instant we thought of some connection with
Freud, not Freud the interpreter of dreams, but Freud the researcher
into the depths of the soul. Bernanos is familiar with, and closely
follows, this method of depth analysis; but he does not stop there.
This, too, is for him the path to the expression of something deeper:

[1] *Liberté*, 232.
[2] "The Romantic Soul and the Experience of Dreams", 1939.

the self-transcendence of the whole of existence into an eternity for or against God; and this depth of resolve, which reaches down to the very source of the underground waters of eternity, is what is present in a man's every act and state of consciousness.

The expression of such depths may be detected in the normal pattern of Bernanos' narrative technique: it is as if the most important decisions have already been made in advance; and the temporal course of events, which in fact results *from* a decision already made in eternity (although seeming to develop *toward* that decision), appears by comparison to be but the delayed rumble of a thunder whose lightning has rent the sky elsewhere. In *Under Satan's Sun* we read: "The marquis' glance hesitated for a second, surveyed him from head to foot, then suddenly hardened. The pale blue of his pupils turned green. At this moment Germaine could have read her destiny in them."[3] "Her disappointment was so strong, her disdain so immediate and decisive, that in reality the events that are to follow were, so to speak, already inscribed in her."[4] "Through her noisy despair she felt a vast silent joy emerging like a presentiment. . . . From that moment on, her impending destiny could be read in the depths of her insolent eyes."[5] "But the fatal sign was already written on the wall."[6]

Similar passages may be found in *Mouchette's New Story*: "The revolt beginning to snarl in her is a blind and mute demon. But does it deserve the name of revolt? Rather, it may be called the sudden feeling, shattering like a lightning bolt, that she is turning her back on the past, that she is venturing her first step, the decisive step toward her destiny."[7] The interior dimension becomes even more manifest in the episode of Mouchette's suicide: "The gesture of suicide really frightens only those who are never tempted in that direction, those who will surely never be tempted, because that black abyss welcomes only the predestined. The person who already possesses the will to murder ignores this for the time being and will realize it only at the last moment. The last glimmer of consciousness in a suicide, if he is not a madman, must consist of stupor—a frantic amazement."[8]

---

[3] *Soleil*, 13.
[4] Ibid., 37.
[5] Ibid., 41.
[6] Ibid., 74.
[7] *Mouchette*, 142–43.
[8] Ibid., 220–21.

We must note that the term "predestined" does not here have its conventional theological meaning; rather, it denotes the condition of a soul that has long lived on and been nourished by a reality that is fully unveiled to the soul only at the very end. And yet, because this veiled mystery belongs to eternity, it cannot remain totally hidden from temporal consciousness, which apprehends it by means of a "presentiment" everywhere at work in Bernanos. Mouchette's father had, "for the first time, the presentiment of a near and inexplicable danger".[9] The Abbé Menou-Segrais is agitated by "the foreboding of a strange and inevitable event".[10] The country priest remarks: "A serene man would smile at my anguish. But, can one control a presentiment?"[11] Mainville feels he is "discerning . . . something like the shadow and presentiment of a misfortune",[12] and later he is again "seized by a kind of dark foreboding".[13] The motif recurs everywhere: "You can tell a mediocre person by this feature: generally, he is quite insensitive to the announcement of impending catastrophes, while the presentiment of a misfortune is for a strong soul a thousand times more anguishing than the misfortune itself. To have a presentiment is not the action of a mediocre man. . . . A certain degree of optimism is what, in imbeciles, provides the exact measure of their cowardice."[14]

At this crossroads we recognize the convergence of many of the main tracks of Bernanos' thought. Dying, for instance, means for him "going to the bottom" of things; dying constitutes the decisive act of self-recognition and of cognition as such. Then, too, there is the truth that one cannot be one's own spectator while living one's life but ought to be just that at the moment of dying. On the other hand, however, Bernanos insists that the anticipation of the death agony during life can be a man's—and certainly a writer's—highest organ of cognition. Finally, we see that, for Bernanos, the remembrance of youth is an inexhaustible source of dreams for existence, something that enables our fluid existence to remember its eternal origins.

---

[9] *Soleil*, 33.
[10] Ibid., 100.
[11] *Curé*, 163.
[12] *Rêve*, 41–42.
[13] Ibid., 124.
[14] *Croix*, February 1943, 183.

But let us return to the subject of dreams.

We are now in a position to understand why, referring to a shallow philosophy of progress, Bernanos can say that it "risks slowly drying up in souls, along with the religious sense, the faculty of dreaming, which is the very source of hope".[15] And, concerning his hero Drumont, he comments: "How could he say everything? There is in him this power of dreaming that burdens the life of a man and overwhelms him with its immense weight, making the transition to the humblest and most ordinary act (like writing a letter, paying a visit, settling accounts) something extremely painful, cutting."[16] The ability to dream is here one and the same thing as the fundamental act of thinking, which is why thinking can precisely be described as a *machine à rêves*, a "dreaming machine".[17] The dreaming faculty is also one with the power of the imagination to create the horizons in which the individual images and concepts then find their place. As so often, it is in a letter to Jorge de Lima that Bernanos makes the most decisive statements concerning this subject:

> I write you today to thank you for your fine article on *Monsieur Ouine*. You put it in a marvelous category: that of oniric, or dream, literature. I would be so pleased if the first random critic didn't term it "surrealist". Nothing is more real or more objective than dreams. But there are many narrow-minded people who admit only Zola's brand of reality. How dumb the world is, so dumb it makes you cry, but you never forget it can be saved by infinite Mercy. Why can't they understand how logical things can become oniric, and logically, for instance in hypnosis and in novels? This is because nothing is as lucid as a dream. And is there anything more conscious than the intoxication of art? Ah, my dear Jorge! Life is full of imagination, and from it come the good images, like those of a luminous intelligence such as yours. From here I send you the warm greetings of an awakened sleeper.[18]

In the novel *A Crime*, the problem of the oniric imagination arises in the character of the genial little judge. This man sees the lines of convergence of fragmentary clues beginning to glimmer in his spirit's depths—his "subconscious"—focusing on an imaginary center that

---

[15] *Peur*, 194.
[16] Ibid., 126.
[17] *Rêve*, 89.
[18] *To Jorge de Lima*, November 15, 1943; *Lettres inédites*, 57.

he cannot perceive consciously. In fact, this depth is the true depth of reality, of his authentic life:

> "Here, I have a question for you", he asks the inspector. "Do you dream?" "You ask if I dream?" "I mean: Do you now and then have dreams?—Not the kind of dream that is only a chaos of images, the kind that the sleeper himself can hardly believe in. I mean real dreams, the kind of dream that is so logical and believable that it seems to last beyond the time of sleeping. These are the dreams that have a place in our memory and belong to our past. . . . Yes, my dear fellow: . . . sometimes it happens that I doubt the reality of certain very recent facts simply because they match my . . . my dreams too well, which are nothing but plain dreams. I couldn't call them by any other name."[19]

But did this man not continue "in full light of day, with a creature of flesh and blood, the conversation he had begun the previous night with an imaginary character, a ghost—nothing"?[20] " 'For three days now I haven't been able to recognize myself', the little judge admitted sadly. 'I dream awake: that's the word! It's a rather unusual state. . . . Suppose, my dear fellow, that an idea comes to me in a dream. All right, it happens to everyone. If I open my eyes, swish! . . . , the idea flies off. But then it clings there, somewhere, in some nook in my brain, like a bat clinging to the beams of the ceiling.' "[21]

By dreaming and giving free rein to his imagination, the judge comes within reaching distance of the unlikely solution that could never have been found through mere analysis. His work here resembles that of the writer, which we will later discuss expressly. Both judge and writer are for Bernanos exponents of a reason that is functioning correctly. The waking dreamer is aware of the fact that his whole temporal existence by no means corresponds to ultimate wakefulness; but he has neither the power nor the motive to perceive the oniric aspect of existence as an intolerable barrier, a glass house whose walls he must shatter at all costs. It is not at all the case that he is about to smother imprisoned in this dream world. His situation, rather, is that of a person who knows the way out and already possesses it in advance in his intimate depths: for such a person, as a result, both time and eternity reciprocally take on the character of a dream. (The

---

[19] *Crime*, 177–79.
[20] Ibid., 188.
[21] Ibid., 191–92.

same basic experience, parenthetically, may be found in Sartre's *Les Jeux sont faits*, only here the this-worldly and the other-worldly characterize one another and grind each other down dialectically, while in Bernanos the two distinct realities open up to the religious depths of existence.)

In the face of eternity, nothing earthly can claim to possess ultimate reality. To his friend Paulus Gordan, Bernanos writes: "The only precaution I recommend is not to take either me or my books too seriously, or my trials either: these may be great, but Providence allows me to see them as such only when they are past."[22] The course of life resembles the wavy line traced by dolphins in the sea. Their bodies half-emerge out of the water, only to dive back down at once. Our life proceeds from dream to dream: dream at the surface, dream in the depths, this-worldly dream and other-worldly dream. Dreams are the blossoming projection of the imagination, the experience that confers splendor and depth on the thinness of our existence. Thus, one of his characters finds "what is banal and inferior wrapped in the magic of a dream—of the one and only dream of a poor life that had never experienced anything of consequence except this one matter of conscience that was its undoing, this one and only doubt, this one and only magic spell!"[23] But, conversely, the miserliness of existence, which keeps it from developing into fullness, also belongs to the realm of dreams: "These mud-stained folk . . . go and come as in a dream, eking out the little that remains to them in their store of memories. . . . What a short step from this diminished life to death itself!"[24]

Within this twin-sighted expanse, the dream is at one with the consciousness of a living being. The more spirit a being possesses, the more it dreams. When viewed in Monsieur Ouine's distorting mirror, this truth can lead to the following reflections:

> "What do you expect, Madame Marchal?", said Philippe. "An imbecile shouldn't dream of becoming a musician or a poet. Monsieur Ouine says that death is always caused by a dream." . . .
>
> "Die of a dream? What are you babbling about there, Monsieur Philippe? You're only repeating words without understanding them."

---

[22] *To Paulus Gordan*, in *Bul.* 5, 6.

[23] *Soleil*, 274.

[24] *To His Wife*, 1917 or 1918; *Erbarmen*, 30.

Philippe shrugged his shoulders and said: "If people didn't dream, . . .
I suppose they'd live to be old, much older than usual. Maybe they'd
live forever."

"What about animals, Monsieur Philippe? Don't they also die?"

"Animals dream in their own way. If we could read in their brain, we
would surely see that they too desire what they don't have, and they
don't exactly know what. This is what dreaming is."

"So then Monsieur Ouine doesn't dream?"

"Yes", said the child. "But he didn't allow himself to for a long time.
I don't want anything, he used to say, nothing good and nothing bad.
Nowadays he claims that he's opened up to dreams like an old rotten
boat is open to the sea."[25]

This experience remains profoundly ambiguous and hence, in the
end, indifferent, not in the sense of Idealist and æsthetic indifference,
but in the sense that it is the matter of the decisive choice that will
orient this final indeterminateness of existence either toward God or
toward the world of pure dreams as ultimate goal. In the latter case,
we would arrive at the essence of evil, the "evil dream". The heroine
of *A Crime* gives us a precise indication of when the threshold has
been crossed: "Who could carry us farther away and more reliably
than our dreams? . . . dreams into which none but ourselves ever enters. . . . But only few people know how to dream. To dream is to
lie to oneself, and in order to lie to oneself one must first learn how
to lie to everyone."[26] And she addresses these final deceitful words to
the boy she has already deceived: "The world is full of people who
don't conceal anything because they have nothing to hide. They are
nothing. . . . But you kept silent. And yet silence itself would not for
long have been for you an effective protection. The moment would
have come when you'd have had to wear a mask, or, rather, masks,
an infinity of masks, one mask for every day of your life."[27]

When we interpret existence, thought, and the spirit itself on the
basis of the imagination, then we risk the very strong and almost
unavoidable temptation of seeing life as a lie, of embracing life by
embracing it as a lie that one seeks and loves for its own sake. As
we shall see, Bernanos interpreted the essence of evil in this sense;
but by no means did he view existence itself as a necessary lie simply

---

[25] *Ouine*, 221–22.

[26] *Crime*, 225.

[27] Ibid., 224.

because it rests on the imagination: on the contrary, Bernanos vigorously opposed any attempt at a demonic systematization of existence.
At its root, the imagination remains indifferent; it can be elevated to
the highest level of art and religion, or it can be put to the worst and
lowest uses. There exists a "fatal hour when the imagination, which
is at once powerful and childlike, accelerates its rhythm and begins
to poison thought instead of making it fruitful".[28]

For the moment, let us leave the phenomenon of the imagination
with these considerations of its lack of differentiation, which also connotes its limitlessness. In the next chapters we will see how certain
realities emerge with ever more dominance to impose bounds and
limits *from the outside* on the oniric nature of the present life. For, in
and of itself, life does not feel any such limitations. For now let us
just say that the definitive *interior* limit of life's character as dream is
death, which Bernanos describes magnificently as the "liberation of
the truth caught within it": "And if I could die for the truth, then
I would be freeing myself along with it, and I could escape with
the truth into *the Light without dreams*."[29] And, while God is being
described with this phrase, we must not forget the complementary
truth: that hell is the end of the "evil dream" whose internal logic
is progressive self-destruction leading, precisely, to hell as natural ex-
tremity. The final description of Mouchette is that she is "defeated,
hurled out of her dream, . . . stripped of everything, even of her
dream";[30] and Ouine portrays in sinister fashion the self-destruction
of the evil dream: "What could you possibly need my secrets for? . . .
Their complexity now appears to me as vacuous as the complexity
of dreams. Is it even secrets we're still dealing with here? I would
like to be able to hate them, but I neither hate them nor love them.
Without my knowing it, their malice has slowly given out. They are
like those wines that are too old, without taste, of a pale pink, which
before dying have eaten through the cork of the stopper and even
gnawed at the bottle's glass sides."[31]

---

[28] *Joie*, 173.
[29] *Enfants*, 257. (The italics are von Balthasar's.—TRANS.)
[30] *Soleil*, 197.
[31] *Ouine*, 236.

2. *The Poet's Dream and Reality*

Bernanos always viewed his poetic vision under the image of the dream. It is in the image of the dream that the poet[32] himself may find the characteristics of a reality that emerges creatively out of nothingness, with all the proximity and concreteness of what has been experienced: only in the dream is there access to such a reality. And, if the writer succeeds in casting such an experience in adequate form, then the access to it is extended to all those who are gifted with the same capacity to dream. Proper to the work of art is an interior space of immediate and tremendous truth, a sphere that has no continuity with the flatness of everyday truth; but the poet must pay for the existence of this truth with his very substance. Thus, Bernanos says in connection with Drumont: "He grew old too late and too abruptly, all of a sudden, following the example of so many heroes, or, to speak his own language, of so many *vocati*, those 'called' souls and *sacrificial beings, born and matured in their dream, who draw a vision of the world out of themselves, out of themselves alone, from their own interior life*. It may be that this vision is mistaken in more than one point; but it has such astounding verisimilitude that it confounds the analysts and the prudent, making them for a moment lose all trust in their numbers and statistics."[33]

For Bernanos, the event of literary creation is something inextricably bound up with the total history of the writer's existence. His work is the *anamnesis* and the creative provocation (in the literal sense of "calling forth") of what in him is closest to eternity, to God, of what in him is most intimately nestled in the kingdom of purity: in a word, his work is the memory of his *childhood*. The child knows everything. For the forgetfulness and sense of loss of the later years—beginning with all that is buried under and overshadowed in our maturity—the child remains the inexhaustible dream source: it is the child in the poet who produces all the true and real figures that are born from the poet's soul and that vie in reality with any living person.

---

[32] "Poet" and "poetic", here translating the German *Dichter* and *dichterisch*, are used in a general sense to refer to the creative writer. These words do not in this context refer to the writer of poetry as opposed to the writer of prose. In this sense, Bernanos is a "poet", which says a great deal more about him than the simple term "writer".—TRANS.

[33] *Peur*, 257. (The italics are von Balthasar's.—TRANS.)

What Bernanos says in this connection is unfalteringly precise, both as theory and as personal confession. Let us listen to him: "As for my books, what's good about them comes from far off, from my youth, from my childhood, from the deep wellsprings of my childhood."[34] "Childhood is always magical."[35] When the lady of a manor near Fressins believed she recognized in the figure of the count in *The Diary of a Country Priest* the very image of her father and wrote her objections to Bernanos, he replied with a confession that lays open the sources of his creative activity:

> I began *The Diary* one evening last winter, having absolutely no idea where I was going with it. How many novels have I begun in this way, which never got past page twenty because they weren't taking me anywhere! No matter! As soon as I take pen in hand, what at once begins emerging before me is my childhood, a very ordinary childhood like all the others; and yet, it is from it that I draw everything I write as from an *inexhaustible fountain of dreams*: the faces and landscapes of my childhood, all mixed up, confused, shuffled helter-skelter by this peculiar unconscious memory that makes me what I am—a novelist and, God willing, also a poet. You can understand this, can't you? . . . This is what happened with your father. . . . You're not wrong in assuming that, when I wrote down the name of Torcy, the memory of your father was present to me; but this memory is everywhere, often unbeknownst to me, in the first part of my book. . . . How can I help it? From a certain moment on, I'm not inventing anything: I simply retell what I am *seeing*. People I have loved pass before me on the screen, and I recognize them only a long time afterward when they have already stopped acting and speaking. Or it happens that I don't recognize them at all, because they've been transformed little by little, forming, in conjunction with others, part of an imaginary creation more real to me than any living person.[36]

And these real creations, all of them born from the poet's maternal soul, now inhabit the souls of thousands and thousands of others, and here too they are more real and more active than most so-called real living persons, for they are children of an authentic fruitfulness of the spirit. These real figures, moreover, are in solidarity with both

---

[34] *To Paulus Gordan*, in *Bul.* 5, 6.

[35] *To Assia Lassaigne*, November 3, 1945; *Bul.* 6, 11. In Bernanos, the word "magical" has a very pure resonance, connoting "full of enchantment".

[36] *To Madame de La Noue*, 1935; *Bul.* 1, 5. (The italics are von Balthasar's.—TRANS.)

the eternal weal and the woe of the poet who created them, for better or for worse. Michelangelo cannot reach his eternal bliss without his Adam and his Lorenzo de' Medici, any more than Bernanos without his children, who are the imperishable reality he succeeded in creating, because they arose from that source of eternity in him that was a childhood intimately bound to God:

> Unknown companions, dear old brothers: one day we'll arrive together at the gates of the Kingdom of God. You are indeed a weary band, a harassed band. You are white with the dust of the roads. Dear hardened face, I've not been able to wipe off your sweat! Your eyes have seen both good and evil; they have fulfilled their task, they have braved both life and death: they have never surrendered their vision! When we meet again, old brothers, I will find you just so: just as I dreamed of you in my childhood. For it was to meet you that I had set out—I was running toward you. At the first turn in the road I would have seen the glowing red flames of your eternal watchfires. My childhood belonged only to you. And on one certain day, a day known to me, I was perhaps worthy to become the head of your unyielding band. May God not will that I should ever again see the roads where I lost trace of you, at the hour when adolescence lengthens its shadows, when the juices of death come to flow into the heart's blood and course all through our veins! Roads of the Artois country, at the very end of autumn; roads wild and pungent like beasts, roads rotting in the November rain, clouds galloping like horses, rumblings in the heavens, dead waters. . . . I would arrive home, push the iron gate, and bring my boots reddened by the storm close to the fire. Dawn came well before my fictional characters—still barely formed, memberless embryos—returned to their haunts deep in the silence of my soul: Mouchette and Donissan, Cénabre, Chantal, and you, the only one of my creations whose face at times I thought I clearly saw, you, to whom I did not dare to give a name—beloved curé of an imaginary Ambricourt. Were you then my masters? Could you possibly be such even today? Ah, I know well how vain such a return to the past is. My life is indeed already full of the dead. But the deadest of the dead is the little boy I once was. Still, when the hour comes, it is he who once again will take his place at the head of my life; it is he who will gather up the years of my poor life, down to the last one. And, like a young commander rallying his disorderly troop of veterans, it is he who will be the first to enter the House of the Father.[37]

---

[37] *Cimetières*, iv–v.

We know with what incredible effort and slowness Bernanos worked, with how alert a reason, how unflagging a devotion: the best image would be that of a sweating peasant. And, one more thing, he worked in continual despair: "Do whatever I may, I shall never, never turn my wretched person to better advantage or bring in a greater harvest. Such a thing, alas, is easy only in dreams."[38] This great appeal to childhood as a source of dreams by no means implies a feeling of distance from the earth but rather an almost superhuman obligation. Thus it is with total seriousness that, while expressing his heartfelt gratitude to a critic he admires, Claude E. Magny, Bernanos says of himself: "I am a novelist, that is, a man who lives his dreams, or relives them without knowing it. Therefore, I may be said to have no 'intentions', in the sense normally given this word. But you make me better understand this world in which at one time I pushed forward, from page to page, in the darkness, guided by an instinct similar in kind, perhaps, to the sense of orientation birds have."[39] Vallery-Radot is right when he states: "Bernanos did not create literature. What he did as he wrote was truly to give his soul, his flesh, and his blood, because all of his heroes—both the worst and the best—are his very own ghosts that he bears within him."[40] It would here, then, be appropriate to see a distant analogy to the Eucharist within the human realm: for it is not in vain that the image of the pelican may be applied both to Christ and to the writer. Julien Green's assertion that the writer's attitude toward his characters is like God the Father's toward his creatures once again casts light on the impenetrable mystery of Christian literature: for the soul of the poet must be pure indeed in order to give birth to unclean creatures and follow them intimately on their dark paths without itself becoming impure but rather helping to redeem the foulness of the prodigal son by its own purity.

This is where we see the barrier emerge that flings the writer back from the dream of God-likeness (so fondly dreamed by Claudel: the poet as vicar of the Logos!) and into the ambiguities of the æsthetic dream. For the poet does more than simply deplete his own life by pouring it into the phantoms in his books. (And, parenthetically, will

---

[38] *To Vallery-Radot*, September 1933; *Bul.* 9, 2.
[39] *To Claude E. Magny*, August 18, 1946; *Bul.* 4, 7.
[40] *Souvenirs*, in *Bul.* 2–3, 28.

he truly be able to make his marionettes intercede for him when his turn comes to render an account before the one who is the only real Creator?) No: he will have to ask himself seriously, perhaps with fear and trembling, whether he has not denied his fellowmen the real substance of his Christian love by the sheer force of bestowing it upon his dreams. Indeed, he will have to ascertain whether, in his conspiracy with the sinners and criminals he has invented, he has not already trespassed the allowable limits and, in a manner more pregnant with consequences than he realizes, scattered in the world an evil seed whose rank growth he can no longer contain. On this matter we must be clear that what is involved is not the Romantic problematic of the golem or the demonic visions of an E. T. A. Hoffmann: our concern, rather, is with the sober Christian realization that the creation of literature is an activity within the realm of existence for which an account must be given.

In this connection we reflect on the figure of the old Ganse in *An Evil Dream*, a writer in the mold of Balzac or Zola, prolific as a nature goddess, who with unscrupulous sensuality has squandered his life by pouring it into his work. Now in his old age his imagination is running dry, and he is at a loss as to where to turn. His dreams continue to proliferate uncontrollably like a sputtering motor running on empty; but his interior life is devastated, since he has allowed all of his human substance to pass over into the universe he has created. He would perhaps be willing to grant himself some peace in order to buy time

> if it weren't that, by an atrocious irony, his overheated imagination could not stop multiplying to the point of absurdity, as in a nightmare, these unfinished creatures mingled with tatters of stories. The swarming of these creatures in his brain gave the wretched man the illusion, ceaselessly reborn, of the creative power he had lost. Thus it is that he began ten different novels, hell-bent on finding his way—his way out. . . . But, as he felt this interior solitude expanding about him—the solitude that is the damnation of the depleted artist—he clung with all his strength, like a shipwrecked man, to the collaborator he had long grown used to. Her mere presence evoked at once his real life and his dreamed-of life.[41]

---

[41] *Rêve*, 101–2.

Precisely this "collaborator", however, Simone Alfieri, about whom Ganse has begun a new book that is to fuse reality and dream definitively, happens to be the heroine of *An Evil Dream*, the double murderess who commits her crimes simply by following the internal logic of evil. She is the imagination of the old Ganse become reality; she is his golem, "his likeness", and "his mirror",[42] the living proof that the writer's dreams have an enormously dangerous resonance in the realm of reality.

Years before, Bernanos had already wrestled with this theme in the eerie novella *Madame Dargent*. It is significant enough that with his very first opus, produced in 1922, the novelist is already treading the terrain of great literature. The wife of a famous writer is on her deathbed, but she cannot die because in her death the whole of her life is becoming present, visible to her like an exact reflection in the water. She had loved her husband. As for him, however, after loving her for a brief while, he had again turned to the characters in his novels, nourishing their intensity by all kinds of flirtatious and parallel affairs. What could the poor woman do to enter into the locked dream-world of the man she loved? She transformed herself into his characters. "I am yourself, do you hear me?—*yourself!* . . . What you have dreamed of, I have lived. . . . My portion in life, what I have been, is all those women you have dreamed up, dearer to you than the living! Madame Guebla, Monique, Mademoiselle de Sergy, old Gambier's granddaughter, the heroines of your plays and novels. . . . I had indeed read your books! How I pursued all these women in your books! With what famished curiosity! Despite all your talent, you had only given them a dubious existence, a slight, intangible form. But I gave them something better: a body, real muscles, a will, an arm." In her delirious dream she slowly begins revealing what all of this means: she has killed the boy whom her husband had ostensibly adopted but who in fact was the child of a mistress; and she has also killed this woman. When, in his unbelief, the novelist demands proof of her deeds, she hurls at his feet the pearl necklace he had seen his mistress wearing a hundred times. In death the horrible truth is revealed, the truth of an illustrious writer's existence: "Take your share of my burden!", the dying woman cries out. "A secret, *this secret*, is what's

---

[42] Ibid., 62.

holding me back in life! I must tell it, must confess it, must scream
it out. I must expel it from me, must void myself of it!" He then
strangles her, to reduce to silence something too terrible. But the last
sentence of the novella gives us only a tentative sum-up: "But who
knows? More than one murderous image that the writer has rid himself of still stirs in a book ten centuries afterwards."[43] Here the act of
literary creation stands in close proximity to adultery: the woman is
merely giving external fulfillment to the internal consequences of her
husband's deeds. And such proximity borders on the demonic region
of the æsthetic, as defined by Kierkegaard.

The novella *Madame Dargent* is the best commentary on *An Evil
Dream*. Aside from the oniric character of sin, to be examined later,
we may say that the latter book centers at once on the psychological situation of detachment already mentioned by Bernanos: that is,
the way a writer's figures acquire a living autonomy by becoming
detached from the soul of their creator. There are certain "turning
points in a book" where the author "no longer feels he is master of
the characters he has slowly seen forming under his eyes. He remains
simply a spectator of a drama whose meaning has just suddenly escaped him."[44] And yet he remains responsible for this meaning: after
all, it is he who has started the characters off on the way they now
must follow to the end with total consistency, without bothering to
consult him. Ganse's collaborator is full of his creatures; she is "choking on them": "Yes, I am really smothering. If I take much longer in
becoming myself again, I'll never be able to do it. After all, imperfect
as these creatures may be, they belong to you, they are something
that came from you. Don't deny it: they give you a little comfort
in spite of everything. . . . They live in me: they just move in, they
multiply in me without difficulty—go ahead, laugh! And I don't have
any hope, not the least hope—what am I saying? not the tiniest bit of
hope!—of drawing them out of myself to take my turn in unloading
them into a novel."[45]

Involved here is a nonphysical, perverted act of procreation that
renders the real act of love impossible ("you have killed my taste for
love", Simone says at one point to Ganse)[46] but that nonetheless pro-

---

[43] *Nouvelles*, 279–88.
[44] *Rêve*, 233–34.
[45] Ibid., 83.
[46] Ibid., 84.

duces a real birth in the world: "I will soon bring you the solution [*dénouement*] you've been searching for for six months", Simone reassures Ganse.[47] What is meant is the murder she is pondering: "This scares you a little, doesn't it? Come on, admit it! I look like I've come out of one of your machines! Here you are suddenly having a conversation with one of your characters, and you have no way of making her get back into your outline for the book. There she is, walking off by herself!"[48] No one but Ganse leads her to commit the murder.[49]

It is true, to be sure, that both the novel and the novella operate within a world from which faith is absent. And it could be that the step into reality, taken by a believing writer who has truly surrendered to God, would lead in the exactly opposite direction. Was it not, after all, for the sake of the saints that Bernanos lived and wrote? And did these saints not emerge with radiant freshness from his imagination? While writing *Joy* he confesses: "I am living with two delightful saints [Chantal de Clergerie and the Abbé Chevance], two real saints I invent as I go along. Everything is so luminous that I can think of nothing else, and my heart is enthralled."[50] And he can extricate these true dreams from the tangle of illusions and mirages of false dreams:

> As far back in my past as I can go, I can't remember having had many illusions. An illusion is a cheap dream, a rag-doll dream, the kind of dream that too often is grafted onto a precocious experience, the dream of the future accountants of this world. Yes, I too have had my dreams; but I more than knew they were dreams. An illusion is a stillborn dream, a midget dream, to scale with a child's size. But I would have nothing but wildly unbounded dreams—otherwise, what's the good of dreaming? And this is precisely why they didn't disappoint me. If I were to live again, I'd try my best to have even bigger ones, because life is infinitely greater and more beautiful than I had imagined, even in dreams, and I am smaller. I have dreamed of saints and heroes, skipping all the intervening forms of our species, and now I realize that these intervening forms barely exist and that only the saints and the heroes count. The intervening forms are like bland porridge, a real potpourri: take a

---

[47] Ibid., 88.
[48] Ibid., 91.
[49] See ibid., 104.
[50] *To Massis*, August 15, 1927; *C. du R.*, 44.

sampling from anywhere at random and you'll know what all of it tastes like. And such a gelatinous mass wouldn't even deserve a name if the saints and the heroes didn't give it one, didn't give it their own name, which is Man. In short, it's by virtue of the saints and the heroes that I am: it's they who from my earliest days sated me with dreams and kept me from illusions. . . . Everyone pressured me to become a practical young man, otherwise I would starve to death. But in actuality it's my dreams that nourish me. Bigots, military men, and grownups in general have been absolutely useless to me. I've had to find other patron saints, like Donissan, Menou-Segrais, Chantal, Chevance. It's from the hand of these, my heroes, that I eat my daily bread.[51]

Who could question this proud and childlike confession on Bernanos' part or doubt that he did indeed nourish his dream figures with his heart's blood? Once again, only he himself is here entitled to draw the boundaries, to set up the marker pointing to the danger that can lurk in the dream of sanctity, the danger Bernanos held before himself as a warning in the unmistakable form of his frightful Abbé *Cénabre*, the unbelieving and, indeed, possessed priest who was an analyst of mystical states. Writing about saints is his vocation and his passion. But one sentence of *The Imposture* reveals his whole evil secret all at once: "This author's art, or, rather, his happy formula, when plumbed to the bottom, may be defined as follows: to write about sanctity as if charity did not exist."[52] In this case, everything becomes counterfeit, because "the only sure means of knowing is to love."[53] We must listen to the devastating analysis that Bernanos makes of Cénabre's literary activity. Here, he is obviously pillorying the methods of that mystic *cum littérateur*, Henri Bremond; but it is also certain that, in so doing, he is far from forgetting himself:

It's not possible to read him without a feeling of discomfort; but only one of these very saints he has mutilated could wrest his secret from him. . . . No matter how simple and soothing, how enveloping and insistent his art always was, they always refused themselves to its wiles. Just the preface of his last book is fifty pages long, and these are full of prudent silences, reservations, and veiled hints, as if the poor man, in his fear, were backing away as much as possible, to avoid the inevitable confrontation. For, as soon as the rebellious witness appears, the careful balance is broken. . . . The pages multiply, and the book drags on inter-

---

[51] *Enfants*, 199–200.
[52] *Imposture*, 29.
[53] *Croix*, August 1940, 39.

minably, like a cruel dream punctuated with starts. And all of a sudden the author . . . wakes up, abruptly losing his composure, and plunges again into the dispute with a kind of rage. This makes the reader feel uneasiness mingled with astonishment. From where this sudden anger? What happens is that, when violence is inflicted on the truth, a frightful irony rises through the lying words much as the stench gives away the presence of a corpse. For all others, this irony is imperceptible; but the arrogance of the Abbé Cénabre cannot fail to know its bite. Anxious to flee from himself, and in addition smitten with his imaginary characters, whom he substitutes almost unconsciously for the real ones and whom he strains to regard as the real ones, Cénabre finds himself, alas, always only himself, at the end of his crooked road. What his saints lack is precisely what has justly been refused to him. His every effort to conceal this only reveals his own deficiencies a little better. What can we say. . . ? In order to give some consistency to his ghosts he has stripped himself of his treasure: the precious lies that would have camouflaged him as they have camouflaged so many others to the end. . . . He sees himself naked.[54]

Precisely this realization that his heroes and saints have torn off all his soul's clothing is what provides the transition to Cénabre's discovery of the fact that he no longer believes and to his act of opening up to the evil spirit.

The writer's great danger, from which his profession always separates him only by a hair's breadth, is *the* vice of vices, the essence of original sin, which is also the cause for the downfall of Cénabre, Ganse, and Ouine—the sin of Eve in paradise and of all her guilty children: *curiosity*, or, expressed in a more theological way, knowledge without love, the kind of knowledge that is not paid and vouched for with one's existence and suffering, the forced anticipation of the vision God wants to bestow through grace but into which impatient man bites as he bit into the forbidden apple. We know that everything in Bernanos is oriented toward vision: the vision of God's hidden mysteries, the vision of concealed sanctity, the vision of souls as they are before God, and also the vision of evil and hell exactly as they are in the eyes of the Redeemer. For this very reason the sin against such vision can be portrayed by Bernanos only in all its immeasurable

---

[54] *Imposture*, 30–31.

enormity. But how close this sin of curiosity is to the literary creative act! We read the following concerning Cénabre:

> The only truly fertile joys he ever derived from belief were precisely those of a curiosity wholly focused on the problem of this supernatural life, whose reality he would never dream of denying today any more than in the past. Indeed, at present [in the last years of his possession], no less than in the past, he was exasperated by the crudeness and inherent poverty of the theses of rationalism, of the ridiculous and pretentious daydreaming of psycho-physiology, or, still worse, of the school of psychiatry in fashion. The only problem that interested him, then, had already been stated and would always remain so.[55]

Thus, although he had in the meantime become an unbeliever, he continued to lead "this secret, impenetrable life, in which his strange genius had spent itself animating the characters born of his dream—his holy men and women."[56]

The same occurs with Ganse and his collaborator, who lives the evil dream to the end, a dream out of which curiosity precipitates like a quintessence: "She could barely remember the chain of circumstances—interconnected among themselves by the delirious logic of a dream—that had brought her to that point or for what purpose she had come there. The only sensation that subsisted in the midst of this terrible swooning of her soul was the kind of professional curiosity she had learned in the school of old Ganse",[57] "that pinch of curiosity, of impatience, which she knew so well and which she had felt every time at decisive moments".[58]

Monsieur Ouine, finally, is the work in which the theme of the *identity of curiosity and damnation* is developed to its conclusion. And if the figure of André Gide stands at the source of the character of Ouine, it is precisely because, for Bernanos, Gide represents the archetype of the curious man: "The only virtue of this great man is a curiosity that is so greedy, so cruel even, that it seems to be a form of lust."[59] Ouine calls curiosity "the most powerful instrument of dissolution",

---

[55] *Joie*, 297.
[56] Ibid., 304.
[57] *Rêve*, 233.
[58] Ibid., 246.
[59] *Croix*, February 1, 1945, 483.

and he carries it "to the point of hatred".[60] The greedy curiosity of Ouine and Cénabre (and both are here but mouthpieces of Bernanos) extended only to the hidden world of the spiritual. The dying Ouine says: "Curiosity is eating me up. It digs up and gnaws away at the little left me. Such is my hunger. Why wasn't I curious about *things*? My hunger has been only for souls. But why am I saying 'hunger'? I've lusted after them with another desire that doesn't deserve the name of hunger. . . . With what jubilation I've entered these modest consciences, so little different from one another in appearance, so common, like little brick houses without luster, blackened by habit, by prejudice, by stupidity. . . . They would all of a sudden surrender their secret to me, but I didn't hurry to take it."[61]

Curiosity is the great danger Bernanos always keeps in front of his eyes so as not to succumb to it: "Thanks to God, I think I have never really felt that low form of congeniality called curiosity. The great calamity—among many others—of those unfortunates who received from Providence a critical spirit like a bunch of thorns in the heart is their condition of being curious by necessity, or, if I may be so bold, by vocation."[62] Bernanos, then, knew exactly what he was doing when he distinguished between dream and illusion. Without having explicitly named it, he was evidently aware of the fact that *the dream is delimited* by a higher reality, and this fact keeps us from concluding that saints and heroes are nothing but protuberances of the writer's dreaming soul, intensified versions of his own self, mirror images of himself, whose truth lies only in the psychological substance of dreams. A disdainful guffaw was his consistent reaction to such "ridiculous and pretentious daydreaming on the part of psychophysiology and psychiatry", burdened as they are with the "thorns of the critical spirit". Nothing is more real than *the saint* who, in his quality as saint, breaks out beyond literature's dream sphere: he is the "rebellious witness" against Cénabre's attempt at æstheticizing spirituality, so real that he strips the æsthete mercilessly of all his dreamy tinsel and leaves him standing there "naked".[63]

---

[60] *Ouine*, 146.

[61] Ibid., 241 (corrected text).

[62] *Sur la poésie: Préface pour les poèmes de Jorge de Lima* (Rio de Janeiro, 1939); in *Bul.* 15–16, 11–12.

[63] *Imposture*, 30–31.

Even if every other vision of the world were based on the imagination, and in that sense had its origin in dreams, still there would exist *one* vision that would absolutely transcend this description and operate in a region above it: that is the vision or intuition the saint has into souls, the supernatural *charism of cardiognosis* (or "ability to read in men's hearts") normally possessed by both Bernanos' priests and his other saints. This is the unexpected and yet *logically derived absolute point that informs all of Bernanos' vision, even on the literary plane.* What is involved is, not æsthetic intuition as defined by Schelling (the identity of the ideal and the real), but the participation—conferred by grace and realized within the ecclesial community and for its benefit —in the truly real vision of invisible spiritual reality as God himself sees it. The nebulous dream zone, which is to say, the whole zone of man's relative faculty to think and imagine, is transcended, so that the saint soars beyond it to become immersed in the resplendent blue skies of visionary certainty. In the end, literary creation aspires only to be a humble and prayerful participation, paid for with suffering, in the saint's charism of reading into men's hearts. Bernanos knows what he is doing when he dares to grasp the moment when this inner eye opens in the spirit of a saint:

> Like the radiance of a hidden glimmer, like an inexhaustible source of brightness flowing through him, an unknown sensation, infinitely subtle and pure, without any admixture, was moving through him, little by little, toward the principle of life and as it went was transforming him in his very flesh. Just as a man dying of thirst opens up totally to the water's keen coolness, he did not know whether what had in some sense pierced him from side to side was pleasure or pain. Did he at that instant know the price of the gift that was being given him, or this gift itself? Through so many tragic struggles, in which his will seemed at times to waver, he still retained this power of sovereign lucidness throughout his life, and yet he was never clearly aware, no doubt, of the power he had. The reason is that nothing resembled less the human experience of slow investigation, going from observed fact to observed fact, with continual hesitations and almost always stopping midway—when human experience, that is, is not hoodwinked regarding the extent of its own cleverness. The Abbé Donissan's interior vision preceded every hypothesis and imposed itself by its own weight. But, once this sudden evidence had overwhelmed the spirit, the understanding already acquired could discover the reason for its certainty only very slowly, by way of a detour. The same is the case with a man who awakens before an unknown landscape he discovers

suddenly in the dazzling noon light: even though his eyes have already taken in the whole horizon, he himself emerges only gradually from the depths of his dream.[64]

This text, of an admirable philosophical density and clarity, provides us with an unambiguous criterion: *Truth lies in the saint's way of seeing.* "Sanctity" here is to be understood, not only in a moral sense, but as an existentially lived ecclesial ministry that communicates the competence of judging together with Christ and also consequently, as a prerequisite to such judgment, the faculty of seeing souls just as they are. Nor are we speaking here of an exceptional and purely subjective privilege in which the community does not participate and in which it therefore has no interest; we are speaking, rather, of a function for the benefit of all. This becomes intelligible provided (as we will later show) we do not dichotomize between the institutional offices of the Church and the sanctity of the Church but rather see them as the two poles, in tension with one another, of one and the same archetypal sphere. The individual Christian existence of the average Catholic is subjected to the criterion of this vision of sanctity in a twofold manner. First, he is confronted with the criterion of sanctity in the sacramental and objective form that the Word of God also has in the Church: seen and judged by God's Word, a Catholic's existence is laid bare to its very foundation (cf. Heb 4:12–13). And, second, he is also confronted with the criterion of sanctity in the existential, subjective form of the holy person. This person, the saint, can walk through an average Catholic existence and polarize it—like a confused jumble of steel splinters—in the direction of the truth, a truth that such a Catholic could not otherwise have found. Such radical reorientation can become a terrible judgment, humanly speaking, and a seemingly excessive challenge for the Christian paralyzed with banality. These two poles of sanctity were brought close together by Bernanos already in *Under Satan's Sun* in order to emphasize the fact that they belong together: Donissan suffers in his official function as confessor, which puts him in a position of exercising his gift of clairvoyance in this office, as if the objective power of vision that every priest possesses by virtue of his office had only coincidentally become subjective as well in Donissan's case. From this perspective, sanctity is a reflection

---

[64] *Soleil*, 193.

of the Church's infallibility becoming manifest within the sphere of experience.

Let us consider the passage in which the intensity of Donissan's interior vision is most powerful, the passage where we see Mouchette, the sinner, judged and consumed by Donissan's words during confession. He tells *her* her sins and describes exactly what he sees in her:

> What she was hearing was not a judge's verdict or anything that surpassed her understanding—that of a dark and wild little animal. No: what she was hearing (and told with a terrible sweetness) was her own story, the story of Mouchette, not at all dramatized by some theatrical director and enriched with strange and peculiar touches, but quite the contrary: her own story in summary, reduced to nothing, seen from the inside. That particular sin that is eating us up: how little substance it leaves our life with! What she saw being consumed in the fire of his words was . . . herself, and she could conceal nothing from the pointed and sharp flame that penetrated into the last nook, into the last fiber of her flesh. In rhythm with the rising and falling of that formidable voice that resounded in the bowels of her being, she felt the heat of her own life increase or decrease. The voice was at first distinct, using everyday words, and her terror welcomed it like a friendly face in a frightening dream. Then the voice became more and more commingled with the interior testimony—the wrenching whisper of a conscience polluted at its own deep source—to such an extent that the two voices blended to form but a single lament, like a solitary gushing of crimson blood.[65]

The words spoken in sacramental confession are mightier than any conscience. They awaken to a salutary remorse the slumbering conscience entangled in its own lies, and they take it up into something greater than itself: the truth, which, in order to make free, must first capture with sovereign authority a conscience kicking and screaming with animal savagery: "The way I have seen you makes it impossible for you to escape me, despite all your cunning. . . . Out of yourself you have drawn only empty dreams, which always met with disappointment. . . . You think you're free? *That* you could only have been in God."[66] Mouchette will henceforth be unable to escape imprisonment by the Word. In the end it is a matter of indifference whether,

---

[65] Ibid., 203–4.
[66] Ibid., 207.

in a paroxysm of fear, she attempts to commit all possible crimes and thus deliver herself to Satan's power, or she finally capitulates and accepts the Word of grace as one conquered by it. She is the creature marked by the Word, the woman who has had the Word's brand burned into her like a head of cattle: she has now become a possession of her Master. And this introduces the second aspect: the event of her being judged because a saint, in passing, has touched her life. For this, too, we have a text of unsurpassable lucidity:

> Certain simple men, who are born for some quiet work, are suddenly thrust by an extraordinary encounter into the heart of things, as by one single stroke of lightning that is quickly extinguished. They must then make a supreme effort: we see them apply themselves—to the last minute of their incomprehensible life—as they strive to recall and recapture the thing that never recurs, the thing that fulminated their back that one instant. This spectacle is so tragic and so profoundly bitter that the only comparable thing is the death of a little child. Vainly do they retrace their past step by step, memory by memory; vainly do they spell out their life, letter by letter. The reckoning is there before them, and yet the story no longer makes sense. They have become strangers, as it were, to their own adventure: they can no longer recognize themselves within it. The tragic element has pierced them from side to side, so as to kill someone else standing beside them. How could they remain insensitive to this injustice perpetrated by fate, to the evil-doing and stupidity of chance? Their greatest efforts will make no more progress than the shiver shaking an innocent and unarmed animal: *when they die they undergo a fate beyond their powers.* For, regardless of how far an average spirit may reach —even if we allow that through symbols and appearances he may now and then have touched the real—still it cannot be that he has usurped the lot of the strong, which is not so much the knowledge of the real as it is the feeling of our incapacity to seize it and keep it whole: the ferocious irony of the true.[67]

We are here made privy to the lethal character of redemptive truth and to the reason why God seldom bestows it other than within the fire-proof containment of the sacraments: otherwise, men would perish in their dream world under the cataract of this light. Nevertheless, the imaginative Christian writer humbly ventures to make himself malleable to this truth and attempts to see souls with the eyes of the saint. He looks at the first Mouchette through the eyes of Donis-

---

[67] Ibid., 275–76. (The italics are von Balthasar's.—Trans.)

san; and, on his own responsibility, he dares to look at the second Mouchette through these same eyes, although he no longer names them expressly. And, at bottom, it is the writer's humility that keeps him from assuming her visible redemption himself.

3. The Evil Dream and Sanctity

We have just seen, in the example of this episode involving Mouchette, how Bernanos can consider simultaneously, under the category of the dream, the most positive and the most negative reality: most positive is the act of literary creation, and most negative is the world of evil. According to Bernanos (and here we are tempted to think of Schopenhauer), the dream is all at once the exponent and the existential instance of this-worldliness as judged (that is, as exactly measured and adjusted) by real truth: the dream is the revelation of the world in all its character as mere appearance, a character of which man at times becomes conscious by way of a presentiment without, nevertheless, his being able to tear away the veil. The authentic poet dreams in the direction of the truth; but the Evil One, on the contrary, loves appearances for their own sake, and he weaves himself into the dream of evil as into a cocoon: he dreams in the direction of nothingness. Here the particular form of "dream logic" itself becomes symbolic: for here we can observe how the sinner yearns—secretly or openly— to abolish all the ontological laws dictated by a waking logic, as well as the dreamer's will to ensconce himself in the dream and displace the threshold of awakening. This is an essentially solitary world, since in the dream there can take place no authentic communication, and this too is pregnant with meaning: the sinner has fallen in love narcissistically with his own closed-off microcosm, or, better, his "microchaos"; and so, he populates the theater of the world solely with the chimeras of his own fantasy.

"Out of yourself you have drawn only empty dreams, which always met with disappointment."[68] This statement of Donissan to Mouchette should be writ large over Bernanos' trilogy of evil: *A Crime*, *An Evil Dream*, and *Monsieur Ouine*, for it defines precisely what the three books have in common.

---

[68] Ibid., 207.

In *A Crime* we witness the web spun by mendacity, loved and sought after for its own sake and accepted despite its inevitable end: "Yes, I have loved lies. I don't mean useful lies, that abject form of lying that is only a means of self-defense like any other, employed with regret and shame. . . . I have loved lying as such, and it has rewarded me handsomely. It has given me the only freedom I could enjoy without constraints, because, if the truth sets us free, still it places on our deliverance conditions that are too hard for my pride to accept, and lying imposes no conditions at all. There is one thing: in the end it kills you. It is killing me now."[69]

In *An Evil Dream*, Madame Alfieri, quite different from the Evangéline of *A Crime*,[70] has an even more conscious experience of the "delirious logic of dreaming"[71] and the "inexorable unfolding of nightmares":[72] these involve at once a painfully and obsessively exact process of calculating and a nonchalance and carelessness that define the enjoyment of the devious and the illogical for their own sake. Simone Alfieri finds her "satisfaction" in dreams, and Olivier, who tears this net of dreams, then becomes entangled in the web that sin continues to spin as Simone invites him to share her dreaming solitude.[73] For her, lying is "a marvelous evasion, a relaxation that always works, a rest, a forgetting", for "she was one of those—more numerous than we think—who love lying for its own sake, who employ lies with profound cleverness and insight, those also who truly value lying only when true and false mingle in it so intimately that they become one thing and come to have a life of their own, creating another life within ordinary life."[74] Along this path, however, Simone becomes the prey of the dreams that consume her, and, since this is precisely what she wants and strives for, in the end self-hatred is revealed as the source of all her motivations:

---

[69] *Crime*, 231.

[70] In *A Crime*, the heroine was bound by an accursed love to Evangéline Souricet, grand-niece by marriage of the heroine's victim. It was to assure Evangéline her inheritance that the heroine killed. This heroine then became Simone Alfieri in *An Evil Dream*, and here she found another Evangéline, but in the form of a character in a novel. It is this woman, poorly imagined by Ganse, who becomes embodied in Simone and gives free rein to Simone's will to murder.—Note of the French trans.

[71] *Rêve*, 233.

[72] Ibid., 237.

[73] Ibid., 160.

[74] Ibid., 193.

The only hatred she had ever truly known, lived, and drunk to the dregs was hatred of herself. How clear it all was now! Why was she realizing it so late? She had hated herself since childhood, at first without knowing it, then with a sly and hypocritical ambition, the kind of frightful solicitude with which a poisoner surrounds the victim she one day intends to slay. . . . She had never forgiven herself, and would never forgive herself, for having failed where many other women succeeded who were worth much less than herself: but these others had known how to act, while she had only had dreams, without ever succeeding in controlling them. Her dreams had invaded her life, smothered her soul and will. Ever since the first awakening of adolescence, they were sucking up her energies, depleting her life's sap.[75]

This condition, of course, was a marvelous windfall for Lipotte, the psychoanalyst: "[We are dealing]", he says, "with a bad[76] dream of childhood long since forgotten, forgotten for twenty, thirty, forty years, a dream that has made you suffer all along under twenty different names, and not one of these names is its true one."[77] And Simone admits: "Yes, by a hair's breadth I would have gone on in calm and blissful ignorance of my true self. . . . So many girls . . . are quite satisfied with little vices, with bad dreams that are chalked up to nerves—the same dreams that did the job at age thirteen and will continue to do the job until we die."[78] But then came her first marriage, her first murder, and, with it, the great lie. *An Evil Dream*, however, wants to go farther: it wants to capture, within the category of the dream, the feeling for life of a whole generation of modern youth, of all those young people who at base no longer love anything, least of all themselves, and who, with an uncanny indifference to both life and death, renounce existence willingly in the same way they had only just enjoyed it, with dissipation and boredom as starting points.[79]

In *Monsieur Ouine* both themes are carried to their conclusion: the analysis of sin and that of the *Zeitgeist* under the sign of unreality, and this both for the individual personalities (at whose center Ouine

---

[75] Ibid., 243.

[76] The text plays on the ambiguity of the French word *mauvais*, which in normal usage means "bad", but "evil" in the more precise moral and theological sense.—TRANS.

[77] *Rêve*, 108.

[78] Ibid., 81.

[79] See ibid., 132; and "Notes et Variantes" of the critical edition, 283.

stands, but all others find their place in his constellation) and for the collective. In a manuscript passage omitted from the printed version of the book, we witness a burial service and requiem Mass at which the "dead parish"[80] unwillingly assists. It is a text in which this second aspect of the unreality of the collective receives particularly striking expression: "As the priest . . . took off his black chasuble and seemed to head for the pulpit (actually he went only as far as the communion rail), a muffled grumbling rose from the depths of the church. It was not so much a murmur of impatience as the kind of groan that escapes a sleeper buried in his dream."[81] Ouine gives the explanation for it, he who, in his "half-sleep, rich in dreams",[82] himself appears to be a material out of which all possible dream images may be formed: "The amazing thing is that you can imagine him in any situation whatsoever, true or false, ordinary or unusual, tragic, comic, or absurd: he lends himself to everything, he is matter for all possible dreams."[83] This is the same Ouine who, at the end of his dream adventure with souls, will have to call everything into question: "Have I really done what I have just said? . . . Or have I only desired it? Have I dreamed it?"[84] Even the extraordinary Jambe-de-Laine is a dreamer at bottom ("Does she dream?"),[85] and particularly Steeny, who is brother to the young men in *An Evil Dream*, entered with full consciousness into the world of sin as into a dreamable world obedient to the laws of dreams: "The world of laziness and dreams that had once submerged his weak forebear—the fabulous horizon, the lakes of oblivion, the magnificent voices—abruptly opened up for him, too, and he felt himself strong enough to live there among so many ghosts, glared at by their thousands of eyes, until he had to take the ultimate misstep: with us here, there is no chance of winning; the only thing you can do is fall. Monsieur Ouine himself will fall."[86]

---

[80] *Monsieur Ouine* was published in German under the title *Die tote Gemeinde*. *La Paroisse morte* (The dead parish) is apparently a title Bernanos himself also considered for this novel. —TRANS.

[81] *Bul.* 11, 13.

[82] *Ouine*, 18.

[83] Ibid., 43.

[84] Ibid., 242.

[85] Ibid., 79.

[86] Ibid., 21–22.

The eloquent symbol for the dream character of the whole trilogy is homosexuality, a theme with an oblique, shadowy presence in all three novels: homosexuality as the perversion of love into self-love or lack of love, which amounts to the same thing, for a love-partner of the same sex is but a duplication and a mirror of the self. For Bernanos, sexual inversion is the efficacious sign or "sacrament" of sin and therefore the best means for making it visible. Moreover, the spiritual reality behind this sign is nothing other than unreality, nothingness itself: the attempt to displace the one and only reality instituted by God and usurp its place. Thus, the dream stands here, no longer for the projection of an idea by the soul, but rather for the evacuation of all meaning, the dilution of being, a vacuum, a distorting mirror, and the dissolution not only of a person's substance but, more comprehensively, even of the form in which this substance can express itself. There exists a (philosophical) idealism of godlessness that is the adequate expression for the loss of being through sin.

Bernanos underwent a certain evolution in his manner of portraying this "nothingness". He was convinced that evil cannot be portrayed from the outside, from a bystander's perspective, and that a certain internal experience is required for this that is not at all, in itself, necessarily evil: such an experience, in the last analysis, is based on Christ's own descent into temptation and hell. Bernanos, consequently, was always careful not to describe evil simplistically from the standpoint of the world of light and love, or hell from the standpoint of heaven. Thus, in his first attempt, Bernanos tried his hand at understanding the unreality of evil as a function of the underlying reality of Satan, and he interpreted all lies by reference to the ultimate "truth" of Satan, the "Father of Lies", whom he endeavored to bring into full evidence by making him emerge naked out of all his phantoms and disguises. By this procedure Bernanos accomplished one thing: by flying in the face of a shallow rationalism, he compelled the reader to acknowledge the reality of hell and its particular form of existence. In the soul of Mouchette, Satan was at first nothing but a "dream, . . . barely distinguishable from other dreams"; but he soon becomes an indisputable certainty, "real and living, companion and executioner, now lamenting and languishing—a fountain of tears; now insistent, brutal, eager to coerce; then again, at the decisive instant, cruel, devouring, all of him present in a painful and bitter burst of laughter, at first a servant but now the master."[87]

For Donissan himself, Satan becomes the reality to which all dreams have referred: "Alas, everything is no more than a dream, and the shadow of a dream!", the Evil One whispers to Donissan. "Everything was only a dream, except for your slow ascent toward the real world, your birth, your growing expansion. Raise yourself up toward my mouth, and listen to the word that contains all knowledge!"[88] We again see something similar in *The Imposture*, in which the image of the demon, present from the outset, emerges ever more clearly through the fog: Cénabre "already knew that this humiliating laughter [of his] was only the external manifestation of a certain and abundant reality, a concrete life, to which he had always wanted to remain a stranger. In his inability to deny the evidence, he was reduced to delaying its sudden, inevitable outburst."[89]

But already here, and increasingly so with every new novel, Bernanos became ever more conscious that he was portraying evil with means that were ultimately in contradiction to it: these means derived from an abundant life of the spirit, whereas what should have been shown was the death of the spirit, and from the harmonious coherence of the spirit, whereas what should have been conveyed was the dissolution of all logic. Is not the demonic, precisely, the breaking-off of all communication? The projection of the reality of the divine world of grace (which now lies behind, having become invisible) forward into the world of perdition and hell creates a univocal view of reality that is too naïve because purely imaginative, and as such it can no longer withstand the deeper logic of evil. Contrary to Bernanos' deeper intention, the appearance of Manichaeism in the early works necessarily emerged at the point where he wanted to portray *simultaneously* both the character of Satan's kingdom as dream (that is, its character as absolute, intrinsic appearance) *and* its univocal truth and reality as standing in ontological communion with the kingdom of grace. One of these terms had to cancel out the other; and, in fact, it was the second element—uncritical and purely imaginative—that questioned and finally displaced the first category, which is specula-

---

[87] *Soleil*, 201.
[88] Ibid., 271.
[89] *Imposture*, 75.

tive and in itself by far the more important. This is why the first element henceforth disappears more and more behind the second element; but this does not occur as a retraction of the absoluteness and definitiveness of damnation but as a way of surpassing the first manner of portraying evil by driving it to its ultimate consequences. Only in the "trilogy" does evil become fully incarnate by being considered from within, and hell is no longer merely the buttress of "dreams" but the consummation of the spirit's disintegration.

But there then arises the *question about the reality from whose perspective dream can be judged as dream and, hence, confined to its unreality*. In *The Imposture* and in *Joy*, it is doubtless the saint who, in the midst of the phantasmal masquerade of the Evil One, constitutes the counterpole of reality. (This is dramatized in the central portion of *The Imposture* by the satyr-play on bourgeois Catholicism and in *Joy* by the devil's five marionettes.) What happens, however, when the saint himself disappears, either by being utterly reduced as a character (like the Curé de Fenouille) or by disappearing altogether (as in *An Evil Dream*, *A Crime*, and *Mouchette's New Story*)? Where can we then find a distancing standard of judgment? In this case, it can no longer be manifested directly; the world of perdition is indeed shut off from heaven; it acknowledges no criterion that can judge it; if such a thing were attempted, the demonic viewpoint would only laugh at it as a childish endeavor. There is no priest to reach into the night of the second Mouchette or into the suicidal world of Philippe and Olivier, and, even when Ouine does converse with his parish priest, not the slightest communion in the truth results. *At this point the writer himself assumes the role of the priest. As he walks with his shadowy heroes through Hades, he, Orpheus, is still very much alive.* And the steps he takes toward nothingness do measure out a real distance from it. When a Christian turns his back on heaven in order to walk with his brothers, he yet has a relationship with God even by way of his back! Donissan is the man who looks away from heaven in order to look toward hell: "As for me", he says, "ever since my childhood I have lived less hoping for the glory we will one day possess than sorrowing for the glory we have lost."[90] He has heavenly bliss behind him—like the Christ Child as he comes down from heaven and must turn his glance toward the Cross and hell, and like the Crucified himself, who creates the

---

[90] *Soleil*, 238.

most expressive and (on earth) unsurpassable form of his relationship to his Father precisely out of his abandonment by God. In the final analysis, the reality by which the dream of evil must be measured is the Cross. The Crucified renounced heaven in order to be annihilated along with sinners; and, precisely for this reason, the Cross is the reality that measures and judges both nothingness and hell. No one can experience a deeper and more comprehensive abandonment by God than the eternal Son of the Father. The ever-deeper reality that shatters the dream of sin is not the imagined figure of Satan but the Cross, which has been fashioned in such a way that it reaches the very bottom of the abyss. Donissan himself knew this,[91] and Bernanos too, with the passing of time, had nothing else left to him. Sin has no depth—this he would come to see clearly at the end of his life— because it "makes us live at the surface of ourselves. We will again go back into ourselves only to die, and there is where he awaits us."[92]

---

[91] Ibid., 284–85.
[92] *Agenda*, January 24, 1948; in *Bernanos*, 147.

V. THE WRITER'S MISSION

1. Calling

An enormous question still awaits an answer: How can the literary work, which is a work of dream and fantasy, possibly be created without incurring guilt? Out of the fog of existence's appearances there do indeed emerge certain blocks of solid rock: evil, which tugs the writer downward, and, even more emphatically, holiness, which delivers and buoys him upward. But how can the poet himself secure his creative craft, housed as it is within the realm of the imagination, with regard to these fundamental realities, which surpass purely human capabilities? The only way of achieving this is if the poet is empowered by reality itself to undertake his literary activity, if, that is, he is authorized to accomplish his æsthetic work by virtue of an authentically Christian call of grace. In this manner, the results of his work will partake in the privileges of grace.

The *call* to be an artist in the Church and the *inspiration* attendant upon such a call are more than a distant analogy: by no means are we dealing here with the secularization of a sacred concept. God "called" Bezalel and his companions "by name" and "filled them with a divine spirit of skill and understanding and knowledge in every craft" (Ex 31:2–3), not in order for them to produce things in keeping with their own imagination, but, under a bond of obedience to Moses, for them to execute on earth the dwelling of God that Moses had seen on the holy mountain. Moses himself had to acknowledge the direct nature of this call from God and abide by it (Ex 35:30f.).

The young Bernanos grew up surrounded by priests, and, indeed, his mother did all she could to steer him in the direction of the priesthood. Although he sensed in himself an unmistakable call from God, he could not decide for the priesthood. At his First Communion he had the insight that the whole of life must be "read" from the standpoint of death: "I thought of becoming a missionary, and in my thanksgiving after Mass . . . I asked this of the Father as sole gift." And six years later he racked himself with the question: "Did I lose my vocation through my own fault? Is this hypersensitivity the

only thing I've ever possessed? I don't know; but it still seems to me
that my path is not in that direction." But God's plan for him was
already becoming clearer. The same young man who did not believe
he was called to be a priest, when looking back at his First Communion, could not for a moment entertain any doubts regarding his
having been especially chosen. For him there was no other possibility
of living except by keeping his glance steadily fixed on God. He knew
"that, in order to be happy, a person must live and die for him, working for the advent of his Kingdom, according to one's age, position
in life, available means, wealth, and personal inclinations." There is a
way of following Christ that is not that of interiority and flight from
the world, the way of public life in society: Jesus, Bernanos notes,
"was an unknown carpenter but also a preacher".[1] And only now
could he see what had lain as a seed within his wish to become a
missionary: "If I don't have the intention of becoming a priest it's,
first of all, because I don't think I have the vocation for it, but then
too because a layman can fight on many levels where the cleric cannot
accomplish much."[2]

Through all the vicissitudes of his existence, Bernanos would always
remain one thing, unchangeably: a herald of his faith and a keeper of
his neighbor's soul. From the wartime letters to his confessor we can
see the extent to which such an apostolate was second nature to him.
From all of his letters—from the enthusiastically youthful ones to
his skeptical and pleasure-seeking friends in the army all the way to
the kindly and wise ones of his late years—what we hear above all
else is Bernanos' direct, unabashed, but also effortless concern for his
brother's eternal salvation. For the laymen and isolated priests who
found their way to him, he became a guide pointing the path a person
must follow to discover the meaning and manner of being a Christian
in our time. Increasingly, he lived the selfless life of a missionary in
the lay state: "I never have time to write; but I have made it my
duty to receive anyone who shows up at my house, and it happens
all too often that I have to lose a whole hour in the company of an
idiot."[3] Once he established contact with someone, he assumed the
person into his very soul and from then on carried him forward. On

---

[1] All these passages from a letter *To Lagrange*, March 1905; *C. du R.*, 19.
[2] *To Lagrange*, March 1905; *C. du R.*, 22.
[3] *To Benoît*, early 1948; *Bul.* 4, 10.

his deathbed he had to turn over the care of these souls to the priest who was caring for his own: "To this one you'll have to say this. . . . And, please, look after this other one. . . . As for this one, right now you can't do anything for him, because . . . ; but I have great hope: pray for him. Love this other one for me—he's suffered so much!"[4] In Bernanos we can see the perfection of what the priesthood of the laity can be.

Nevertheless, his care for souls remained a function of his particular vocation as steward of the Word. He once summed up this decisive insight in a clear though reserved formula: "The writer's vocation is often—or, rather, is at times—the other aspect of a priestly vocation." To the young poet to whom he addressed these words, Bernanos was in fact lending features that were precisely his own; in so doing, he was describing his own career as one sent. Because he was called from above, he would have to draw everything out of himself, and his first attempts at writing would exhibit "the kind of awkwardness that is precisely the mark of a deep sincerity". He would not succeed in using any of the literary tricks that are the earmarks of his contemporaries, the devices whereby "a professor, for instance, can conjure up a momentary illusion." He was "like a man who wants to solve certain mathematical problems without knowing the Pythagorean rule of three. He first has to find it all by himself, rediscover it as the boy Pascal had to reinvent geometry." In other words, "you shall be an original writer or nothing at all. If the good Lord really wants you to bear witness, you must expect to work a lot, to suffer a lot, to have ceaseless doubts about yourself, whether in success or in failure. Because, seen in this way, the writer's profession is no longer a profession: it's an adventure, and above all a spiritual adventure. And all spiritual adventures are Calvaries."[5]

The word "vocation" ceaselessly flowed from his pen, and to underscore its importance he put it into solemn Latin: "No, I am not a born writer. If I were, I would not have waited until I was in my forties to publish my first book. . . . And I do not reject this name of 'writer' only out of some kind of inverted snobbery. . . . Every vocation is a calling—*vocatus*—and every call wants to be transmitted. Those I am calling are obviously not numerous. They will change

---

[4] Pézeril, *C. du R.*, 348.
[5] *To a Young Man from the Berry* [*Charreyre*], December 1945; *Bul.* 2–3, 24.

nothing in the way this world is run. But it's for them, yes, for them that I was born."[6] "Whatever great thing we do is first done within us, almost without our knowing it, by that interior power that seems to answer to a mysterious call. Such is the meaning—both for whole nations and for individuals—of the word 'vocation', from *vocatus*— 'called'. Being called does not depend on us, but not answering the call does depend on us."[7] "The older I get, the better I understand that my modest vocation is truly a vocation—*vocatus*. The good Lord must call me every time he needs me (and this occurs often, and with a threatening tone!). At such times I get up sulking and, as soon as I've finished my task, I go back to my very ordinary life."[8] Most intellectuals are the kind of people whose own inflated spirit gets in the way of their hearing the voice from above: "But I am not speaking, of course, of the scientist, artist, or writer, whose vocation is to create and for whom the intelligence is not a profession but a vocation."[9] And now we can understand better this other statement Bernanos made on his deathbed: "I am not responsible for what I have created. . . . *Virtus de illo exibat*. . . .[10] I am responsible for what I have not been."[11]

The man who has been sent out no longer lives his own life; he subjects himself to the conditions of the mission, which become his own measure and form. Bernanos spoke about this mission with emphatic gravity; when he spoke in this connection, he shed all histrionics and stood naked before us in the full body of his mission:

> I too, my friend, am playing for my vocation and my life. You'll tell me that these, for me, are really big words; but truly great words are like truly great nobility: they are never out of place. Our vocations are what they are. *They are*, and that's all: they have been given to us. I don't think we could be dispensed from them any more easily than a religious from his vows. . . . I did not make myself a writer. I became one only very late, and not very willingly. . . . In short, it seems to me I've respected my vocation. It hasn't been for me a source of honors or gain. I have not treated it like a mistress but like a revered companion. . . . We must both

---

[6] *Cimetières*, iii.

[7] *Anglais*, 16.

[8] *To Gordan*; in *Bul.* 5, 6.

[9] *Robots*, 181.

[10] "A power went out from him."

[11] Pézeril, *C. du R.*, 343.

be saved together, not by omission or by abstention, but by fulfilling each other to the end. Can you understand me? . . . My vocation, my work, and my life must come to be one thing, all of which I must then raise up to him."[12]

Understood in its Christian sense, however, mission always means vicarious representation: standing willingly in the place of another, being called in the place of those not called. And if this holds for the man ordained to the priestly office, it also holds no less for the layman. Called out of the relative anonymity of the laity, the individual layman takes up the Word in his own place at God's bidding. Time and again, Bernanos justified his strokes of boldness by appeal to this representative, ecclesial function.[13] He sought the theological locus appropriate for him in the Church in this connection. He was a herald, a preacher, a missionary, but not from the ranks of the hierarchy. As such, he could only be a kind of God-appointed spokesman for the people and for the ecclesial *sensus communis*:

> It is true that, in the last few years, a great effort has been made to try to ridicule the mission of the writer. I believe in this mission as naïvely as Hugo and Michelet. I do not claim that this mission could not be better accomplished than by ourselves. But, to keep to only this one example, there is no longer anything in Europe that resembles those preachers of the Middle Ages who, both in France and in Italy, were the very voice of the people. The Church limits herself at present to her essential, indispensable duties. She teaches morality and theology, administers the sacraments, negotiates treaties and concordats. She gets as little involved as possible with poor sinners, and she avoids like the plague being troublesome to governments. It is true that she defines oppression admirably; but these impeccable definitions, which delight the philosophers, are not a very great help to the oppressed, because the Church almost always avoids designating the oppressors by name. Under these conditions, what writer worthy of the name would refuse to speak for those who can only keep silent any more?[14]

---

[12] *To Amoroso Lima*, March 13, 1940; *Esprit*, 202.
[13] *Français*, 141.
[14] *Croix*, February 1942, 196.

The mission from above, as innermost truth of a life and a vocation, drives both to give all they can and demands from both that they forsake their thrones and submit entirely to the sovereign law of grace. Neither one's art nor one's self has the right to protest against the mission. The self is poor straw that flares up in the conflagration of the command received. Already as a boy Bernanos could write that "we can come to be worth something only through total self-sacrifice and self-forgetting, for the sake of God and his cause", through "the offering-up of both one's life and one's death".[15]

This is the source of Bernanos' disinclination to engage in self-questioning and self-interpretation. For him, looking at oneself, the γνῶθι σεαυτόν (*gnothi sauton*),[16] is always a vain and fruitless endeavor, since the essential does not lie in the self but in the task entrusted to one: "I really don't know whether or not I am worthy of such trust, and I've resigned myself to not knowing it, because I have long since renounced knowing myself, at least in the sense this is understood by the Wise of this world. . . . How can you take inventory of a warehouse if you don't have the keys to it and if Providence stores there whatever it pleases? . . . *I am not this.* . . . *I am not that.* What is the point of knowing what you are not? . . . Why tell about yourself when you can give yourself?"[17] "My books and I are one, and you *never* speak about yourself usefully. Speaking about yourself is almost always a trap of the devil."[18] And we must quote the magnificent lines Bernanos wrote to a young woman he had befriended. Here he gives the ultimate justification for refusing to set out on a quest for self-knowledge: silent respect before the interior mystery that dwells within the soul as a tender guest and which, within our spirit, is more than the spirit itself:

> By what right . . . would you so insist on knowing what you are? This has no importance whatever. Do I, for one, know what I am? There are duties to be fulfilled, sorrows to be suffered, injustices to embrace. Above all, there are illusions to be lost. . . . A desire for self-knowledge, I swear to you, is the itch of imbeciles. Your sweet genius consists in being what you are without knowing it and without thinking about it,

---

[15] *To Lagrange*, May 31, 1905; *C. du R.*, 21.
[16] The "Know thyself" of the Delphic oracle.—TRANS.
[17] *To Amoroso Lima*, late 1938; *Esprit*, 189.
[18] *To Amoroso Lima*, March 5, 1939; *Esprit*, 190.

with that exquisite naturalness I so love and which is a grace of God. Yes, God's sweet mercy is within you. Don't ask her to explain herself, to justify herself. Don't bore her with endless chatter and discussions. Close the window, close the door, don't let anyone in. Allow his mercy to smile and pray within you. And when she weeps, say nothing.[19]

What we here see penetrating deeply and expressly into the mission and condition of the writer is the ultimate mystery contained in Christianity: that the Christian must "unbecome"[20] his own self in order to find—in the space cleared by this "unbecoming"—his Lord and Guest and, along with him, the sole valid eternal idea of his self and of the task assigned it within time. At first, in the face of the divinely commissioned task, the self appeared as nothing—mere, indifferent, interchangeable material that then becomes suffused with something precious, unique, irreplaceable. And now an astounding thing happens: by virtue of this receptivity, this same self, as a bearer of the divine mandate, itself becomes something necessary, indispensable, and precious. The idea of the literary work as being a Christian commission is a living idea in God, which means a lived idea. This divine idea, therefore, claims for itself the life of the writer whom it indwells and consumes like a flame in the brushwood, and from the outset it deprives the burning substance of any say in the matter. *The material that the writer himself is, is not available to him for his work, since it would never suffice for that purpose or be of any use. It burns for God, and God alone gives him both his life and his work as a gift.*

"I write as I suffer and as I hope, and if I am not necessarily a good judge of my writings, at least I have good knowledge of my hope and my suffering: the material these are made of is sturdy and ordinary; you can find it anywhere. . . . It's possible that my coarse sincerity acts . . . as a stimulant, and certain delicate stomachs can in the end digest only ordinary household bread."[21]

---

[19] *To a Woman Friend*, March 23, 1933; *Bul.* 2–3, 16.

[20] Von Balthasar here uses the unusual word *entwerden* to refer to the process whereby the Christian is emptied of his natural self in order to be filled with Christ. Even though the literal rendering "to unbecome" is clumsy in English, by contrast to the elegant precision and nuance of *entwerden* in German, its very unusualness should call attention to the uniqueness and radicalness of the spiritual event it describes.—TRANS.

[21] *Enfants*, 193.

I am a writer—can I help it? The instrument I use is contemptible when I am unskillful with it. . . . No matter! It's my instrument, the only one available to me, and I did not deserve that the good Lord should assign me another. . . . I wouldn't want to be taken, myself, for that instrument. Normally, the people of my profession complain that, pen in hand, they can communicate only a ridiculously small portion of the interior world whose secret they hold. I could never call myself a good judge of an interior world where I am perhaps fooled by a simple trick of perspective. The fact is I have never observed it from the outside, and I've never established myself there in the strict sense. After these many years, I have hardly built anything there. I live there like a shipwrecked man on an island or like a child in a garden. But this garden is like all other gardens, except that the light there is doubtless a bit harsher than elsewhere. I had never realized this peculiarity, and if I see it today it's because age and weariness have in the end made me realize that I have always not so much enjoyed this light as I have confronted it, overcome it, stared it in the face. Far from thinking I have expressed only a small number of the feelings that animate me—that give me a soul—I am amazed that, by some incomprehensible gift, by some miracle, they have in fact provided material for a lifetime of work. What I would like to share is this gift, it's the only alms I'm capable of giving; and it is precisely this gift that is the incomparable, the incommunicable thing. My sufferings are those of any ordinary man, but most ordinary men pass alongside them without seeing them for what they are. If I run after him, what I hold out to him is a measure of flour, a flour he knows well. "I have some at home", he says. With this flour I can only teach him how to make his own bread.[22]

If Bernanos then adds the comment: "And it is with just this bread that I would like to nourish him", this in no way contradicts his recognition that his own naked self could never satisfy his brother but only the gift in the writer that is God and that the writer can be a steward of only if he has first lavished himself upon that gift.

At the conclusion of *The Humiliated Children*, the following immortal sentences burst forth out of his struggle for the meaning of his existence as a writer:

More and more I have come to understand that I will add nothing to the truth whose depository I am: I could never pretend otherwise. It is

---

[22] Ibid., 205–7.

I myself who should rise to this truth's stature, for she[23] is smothering within me. I am her prison and not her altar. The smile I owe her is that of my own person. I will set her free only at my death; and if I died for her, I would be setting myself free along with her. I could then flee in her company into the light without dreams. In the meantime, and until my task is accomplished, we will be face to face, she and I. The real drama will be played out between us. My literary *œuvre*—if that is what it is—will add nothing to this.[24]

His calling to be a writer was identical for Bernanos with his standing before God, his moral existence. Soon after the end of World War I, the young veteran writes: "The literary profession has no attraction for me: it is being imposed on me. It is the sole means given me to express myself—which is to say, to live. For everyone else, writing is an emancipation, a freeing up of the inner man. But for me it is something else besides: the condition of my moral life. . . . This is why the affliction has no cure. If you were to bury my calling, you would be burying me along with it, as well as the thoughts that give me life. Then I would be nothing more than an automaton in the world. This sacrifice is not demanded of me."[25]

2. Pathos

The flame that burns in the writer and prepares the bronze of his work for casting is more than just a mystical fire burning up toward God. It is the fire God brought to ignite the earth, the flame of God's suffering at the hands of his world, "the red brand of love and shame", of the scandal that grace must endure in the kingdom of sin. Most precisely, it is *the flame of the "zeal for God"* that consumed the prophets and the apostles, the zeal of man for God and of God for man. This flame is stoked by sin: the fact that sin—such great and such frightful sin—exists only makes the *zelus Dei* flame up all the more infallibly.

---

[23] Bernanos has so vivid and intimate a conception of *the truth* entrusted to him by God that he is compelled to personify it in highly dramatic form. Only the use of the feminine pronoun, for *la vérité*, can here convey something of the impact of the original.—TRANS.

[24] *Enfants*, 257–58.

[25] *To Dom Besse*, 1919; *Bul.* 11, 8–9.

Sin is the occasion and the condition for the blazing of this divine zeal; but, the deeper love penetrates into the realm of darkness, the greater the danger that the zeal will contract the internal taste of sin, as a source, not of pleasure, but of bitterness, not as an allurement and a careless sliding into sin, but in the form of a bitter *contempt* for a human race that has turned its back from the mystery of crucified love.

When Bernanos selected the anti-Semite Drumont as the hero of his private French intellectual history, he was close to succumbing to such a temptation to harbor contempt. " 'If our youth is what you say, how could you hold up to it as teacher one of the most embittered . . . of our French writers . . . ?' I shall answer: I do this in order to help our youth in perhaps recovering what the scion of a great family can never altogether allow to die: a certain heroic feeling for justice and injustice; and if the exhaustion is hopeless and the death agony near, then at least there's bile and absinthe, the voluptuousness of contempt."[26]

Even after the time of his first book, Bernanos continued to drink out of these poisoned wells. But the taste that this left in his mouth made him recognize the danger (the very personal danger!) such views posed to him. At the beginning of *The Great Cemeteries* he writes: "At one time I believed in contempt";[27] but "contempt is worthless to me; in me it is always the sign of a momentary depression. And, besides, I have noticed that indignation only had on the people of whom I am speaking the effect of inflating their arrogance beyond all measure."[28] And in conclusion: "When you've gotten to this point and you've had this experience of life and men, then contempt becomes an impossible intoxication, a wine that no longer has the time to go to your head because it's spewn out the moment it's drunk."[29] These are statements we should read alongside these lines to Jorge de Lima: "Above all, you must not believe . . . that I distance myself from people through contempt. If I held them in contempt, they would be coming to me in throngs, because men are mad over whatever disdains them. They only really began to distrust me the day I

---

[26] *Peur*, 302.
[27] *Cimetières*, 1.
[28] *Anglais*, 152.
[29] *Enfants*, 198.

resolved to understand them and love them."[30] Toward the end of his life he recollected himself to take a global glance at both the dangers before him in this connection and what could save him from them: "I am going to try to live here as far as possible from those things I would be too tempted to hate and above all to hold in contempt. At a distance you are in a better position to rediscover something of the secrets of that sweet mercy of God, outside of which you cannot really come to know anything about human beings or their miseries."[31] And these words to a young poet sound like a last will and testament: "You should above all be afraid of turning sour as you undergo trials that are inevitable. A sour artist is no longer an artist, just as a sour spinster is no longer a woman.... For God's sake, don't become sour. Remain available and free."[32]

This is why Bernanos always, and ever more forcefully, rejected the label of *révolté* ("rebel" or "agitator", Camus' "man in revolt"), which certain admiring zealots would have liked to pin on him as a title of honor.[33] "[Certain words I have spoken,] misunderstood, have often made me seem to be a rebel. In fact, there is nothing of the rebel about me.... In the spirit of revolt there is a principle of hatred or of contempt for mankind. I'm afraid that the rebel will never be capable of bearing as much love for those he loves as he bears hatred for those he hates."[34] For Bernanos, the only authentic "spirit of revolt" was that contained in the fire of Christianity, of the Cross, and of martyrdom, and it would be a grievous error to try to render it innocuous: "We have never claimed that the first Christians were rebels or agitators in the eyes of the theologian; but we would like to be allowed to note that that is exactly what they were taken for in the eyes of the Empire, in the judgment of all the Empire's traditionalists. How can it be helped? No matter how decided you are not to fall from one excess into its opposite, it is still very unpleasant to hear nice, plump cathedral canons talking about the Sermon on the Mount as if it were a conservative manifesto."[35]

---

[30] April 7, 1940; *Lettres à Jorge de Lima*, 26.
[31] To Benoît, May 11, 1947; *Bul.* 4, 9.
[32] To a Young Man from the Berry [*Charreyre*], December 1945; *Bul.* 2–3, 24.
[33] To a Woman Friend, July 2, 1934; *Bul.* 2–3, 21.
[34] *Français*, 32–34.
[35] *Anglais*, 247.

Yes, granted: zeal for God would always burn in Bernanos to such an extent that the *bien-pensants* ("the right-thinking", that is, "those who think with conventional correctness") would always be able to sniff in him the scent of an agitator. And, indeed, he knew enough about an attitude that to him appeared to be even more dangerous than revolt, and that was *disenchantment*. In the disenchanted person the only voice has been silenced that could still have kept the heart lively and alert as the person grew old: the voice of the child I once was, whose angel ceaselessly contemplates the face of God: "I want to teach [this child] how to suffer. I don't want to turn him away from his suffering. I prefer to see him in revolt than in disenchantment, because most of the time revolt is only a transition, while disenchantment no longer belongs to this world. It is as full and dense as hell itself."[36] In this icy place, all fire from above has been extinguished. The only person who can be disenchanted is the one who has not grasped that the world is a dark marvel. Disenchantment is a sign of stupidity.

"Life brings no disillusionment. Life speaks only one word, and it keeps it. Too bad for all those who say the opposite. They are impostors and cowards. People disappoint, that is true enough, but only people. Again, too bad for all those who are poisoned by such disappointment. This is due to a malfunction in their soul: their soul does not eliminate toxins. As for me, people have not disappointed me, nor have I disappointed myself either. I expected something worse, and that's all. The first thing I see in man is his misery. The misery of man is the wonder of the universe."[37] Elsewhere Bernanos writes with more vehemence and less pity:

> I am not disappointed; nothing has disappointed me, in the precise meaning of the word. The least disappointment would have reduced me to silence, I swear it. The only thing that can truly disappoint you is something you love, and I could never have the strength to endure being disappointed by something I love. Neither life nor people have disappointed me or shall ever disappoint me. Whoever has deceived me has deceived me only in appearance: it is I who deceived myself. I wanted to appear to suffer beyond my capacity, against the very promise of the good Lord, and so I invented consolations for myself. Did I then disappoint myself?

---

[36] *Enfants*, 195.
[37] *Cimetières*, 280.

The very notion now seems to me too flattering. I lacked courage, and that's all.[38]

But, in his flight from cold disappointment, Bernanos found himself thrown back into the oven of fiery *indignation*, especially when *malheur*, "misery", bore down with all its weight as the debt of sin and the zeal for God refused to enter into any compromise with it. Is not God himself indignant over sinners? And is not indignation practically a part of love?

> Indignation is not at all, like contempt, a refusal of the soul; indignation is not an attitude of the miserly heart. The contemptuous person has first begun by holding himself in contempt and, by that very token, has disqualified himself. Contempt is exercised only from a low level, whereas you couldn't become indignant unless you had already reached a certain elevation that you have to maintain at all costs if you don't want to blush with shame. The person capable of indignation cannot escape the torturing necessity of examining his own conscience. The conclusion of this examen will always be unfavorable to him, because indignation is nothing if it isn't the cry of a conscience outraged by scandal; but this indignant conscience at the same time doesn't feel it has the strength to carry such outrage to its perfection, in the manner of our saints and heroes, by making it lead to prayer and action. If the Lord had not become indignant against the Pharisees, I would gladly write that indignation is a sign of weakness. But what am I saying? We know too well that what cries out in us could not have held back its cry. We wish that this painful part of our being would keep silent out of virtue, but we don't wish for it to remain inert and passive under the goad of lies. God grant that some day we'll look at injustice through and through, with eyes that are so lucid, so pure that we'll be able to live with it without having to partake of it.[39]

Let us not think that this groping for the ideal position between indignation and acceptance, equidistant from revolt and resignation, is an idle psychological game. What is involved here is the pathos that alone makes the art of Christian literature possible, the fundamental attitude presupposed by everything else. We speak of the attitude that can neither be described nor lived except in terms of Christian theology, and this, consequently, makes this attitude to be itself a mystery

---

[38] *Enfants*, 193–94.
[39] Ibid., 215–16.

of faith: this is the possibility, extended to the Christian and adequate to him, of participating in the unfathomable identity of love and wrath in God, that is, in the gesture whereby God both chooses out of grace and spews out of his mouth in condemnation. Abstract thought will never be able to approximate or grasp this identity; at most, it will attain to an equally abstract dialectic of judgment consisting of two opposed and mutually exclusive gestures. But God becomes concrete for us in Christ, and it is to Christ as Redeemer that the whole authority to judge is entrusted. In a most radical way, we can affirm that there is no access to the attitude that makes the creation of Christian literature possible other than the attitude of Christ himself. This attitude is also bestowed on the Christian by grace in a most mysterious manner. Such a Christlike stance makes the Christian strong and pure enough to descend into the realm of scandal and have contact with the dark mystery there without himself becoming tainted with it. On the other hand, he is also made so rich in love and self-surrender that, as he participates with Christ in this mystery of evil, he does not set himself apart from all the rest, like the "pure" of the Old Testament and the Pharisees of the New, in such a way that genuine communion with all becomes impossible. This necessary condition for the creation of Christian literature cannot be had at a lower price: it is one and the same as the necessary condition for Christian existence as such.

Here is where the *problem of the imbecile emerges*, which is to say, the problem of the brother whose invincible weakness of spirit bars him from an in-depth understanding of things, the brother who is easily scandalized, who always opts for penultimate rather than fundamental principles, and with whom communication must nonetheless be established. For the believer, such communication can only be a cause of suffering; but, as Bernanos intuits with supernatural clairvoyance, this suffering at once adapts the believer to his task and keeps him unsullied: for, if both these effects did not coincide, how could we speak of suffering? "No, I lay no claim to any kind of supernatural vocation. I don't quite think that the good Lord brought me to this world only to have me suffer along with the imbeciles. I would then harbor too great a regret for failing to become a saint, for missing the sublime opportunity of some day becoming the patron saint of imbeciles. But I know there is a part of my soul mysteri-

ously attuned to theirs and miraculously preserved. By what miracle?
By being a Christian: that's the miracle! If I weren't a Christian, it's
obvious I'd be an imbecile, although I'm not sure what variety of
imbecile."[40]

The writer must doubtless experience a "contact" between his personal life and the object he shapes. Much has been made of this contact, and it has led the "imbeciles" astray into believing that the writer
must possess a de facto existential experience of the things he is mold-
ing into literature. Now, under "imbeciles" we must in this case include even the greatest non-Christian writers and most literary critics
and historians. From our perspective, however, we must affirm that
this "contact" between the writer and his subject matter cannot occur
without sin and without offense to God's love and compassion other
than through the mystery of Christ, who "became sin for us" (2 Cor
5:21) although he had not committed one single sin (Heb 4:15).

Thus, the writer has the twofold and yet single function of burning
in the same *fire of scandal* that burns the imbecile, without nevertheless
simply burning along with the imbecile but rather as a Christian who,
because he is involved as a sufferer, can also be a helper and, because
he is a helper, can also be a creator: " 'Never, never', I once wrote
a long time ago, 'never will we grow tired of scandalizing the imbeciles.' I now understand that I could only hurl this naïve challenge at
myself. Either the statement is meaningless or the only thing it could
mean is: 'I will never grow tired of being scandalized, of sharing the
scandal of the imbeciles.' For this is really the scandal I share, it's the
one I'm in tune with."[41]

However, while the imbecile's reaction to being scandalized by the
Church is to flee into conformism, pietism, and clericalism, such flight
is denied the writer; and, since he is scarcely in a position to "escape
into sanctity", the writer must remain in the fire as one defending himself "against being overwhelmed, which is to say, against despair."[42]
His particular suffering, which is greater than that of his brothers
who take scandal, is not a direct and personal suffering: "No scandal
could wound me, as a Christian, directly, even if it came from the
Sovereign Pontiff. I say this because I know myself, I know what lies in

---

[40] Ibid., 194–95.
[41] Ibid., 213.
[42] Ibid., 215.

man.''[43] The Christian writer's suffering is indirect, altruistic, social; to be precise, it is a "cosuffering" ("com-passion," "sym-pathy"),[44] which opens up to the writer the depths of Christian understanding and love: "I do not disdain others. Far from disdaining them, I would like to understand them better, because to understand is already to love. What separates human beings one from another, what makes them into enemies, probably has no profound basis in reality. The differences our experience and our judgment eagerly feed on are, in fact, insubstantial. They would vanish like dreams if we could manage to look at them with truly liberated eyes, because the worst of our misfortunes is not being able to give to another anything except such an impoverished image of ourselves."[45] But the only person who can reach such depths of authentic fellowship is the one who admits into his being the pliancy of divine grace, which flows from nowhere but the Cross. *Truth is to be found only in forgiving along with grace, only in looking at the creature along with God's very glance:* this is a truth that is twofold because it is both a creation of grace and the result of the life of man, and this twofoldness makes it just as much a mystery, strictly speaking, as the twofold unity of love and wrath we have previously seen.

Many religious writers have striven to look at the creature with the eyes of God, in order to grasp the truth about it on the basis of this "primal ground". But Bernanos is the only one among them who has in full earnest seen the real fusion and, indeed, the *ultimate identity that exists between the truth of literary creation and the truth of salvation.* And not only did Bernanos see this identity: it was on the basis of it that he both wrote his works and lived his life. The truth of salvation is the absolutely unique event whereby the lost creature, which of itself is nothing but lies and decay, attains through grace to its truth in God, and this truth is not something merely imputed to the creature but something internally belonging to it and really present within it. This transformation occurs by virtue of an event that simultaneously involves an act by God's unfathomable and creative mercy *and*, within it, the possibility of a lie surrendering itself to the truth, which is to say, an act of confession. And, if the writer has any function in this

---

[43] *Anglais*, 98.
[44] *To Benoît*, May 11, 1947; *Bul.* 4, 9.
[45] *Cimetières*, 78.

process of transformation (and he does), then it is the function of a ministry within the Church that intends to serve by helping others attain to the truth. We speak here of the unusual role of being a sort of "lay confessor" in the Church, which is revived in Bernanos, similar to the way he previously described himself as a "lay preacher" —God's voice emerging from the people: "a priest, unfinished but not for that the less admirable", in the words of his friend Vallery-Radot.[46] Here we are at the opposite pole of a Kierkegaard, with his separation of the æsthetic from the ethical, or of a Claudel, with the breach he interposes between the muse and grace. We are standing, in fact, within the sanctuary of the Christian artist's responsibility for the work and the figures he creates.

Let us examine the matter more closely. If the writer is to find his way in the gloom, his outlook on the dark path of creatures must always come from eyes that are simultaneously fixed on God. God, however, keeps silent for the most part. Although he is the God of grace, he is veiled in incomprehensible harshness. Even when he is a near God in eager pursuit of man, he remains a God of the heights, so that his eternal love must react ironically to the capers of human destiny. It is to this God that the writer looks for the standard of truth. Never, not even when he must yield to indignation, can the writer swim against God's current. "I am too old and I have been through too much for me to wrangle with the Creator over his works and give him lectures on literature, especially on stylistics."[47] There is only one thing that helps against both anger and resignation: *prayer*. "Saints do not become 'resigned' to anything, at least not as the world understands it. If they suffer in silence the injustices that agitate the mediocre, it's only the better to turn against Injustice—against the brazen face of Injustice—all of the powers of their great soul. Outbursts of anger, those daughters of despair, rant and rave, twisting like worms. In the end, prayer is the only revolt that remains standing erect."[48]

The most decisive statements in this connection are found in the *Country Priest*. Here we see the demonstration of the fact that only prayer is or could ever be the sole medium and atmosphere of ab-

---

[46] *Souvenirs*; in *Bul.* 2–3, 28.
[47] *To a Woman Friend*, March 23, 1933; *Bul.* 2–3, 15.
[48] *Cimetières*, 14.

solute truth. By contrast to prayer, solitary reflection is an activity that shuts itself off: "For a person with the habit of prayer, mere reflection is too frequently but an alibi, a sly way of confirming ourselves in a predecided design. The reasoning process easily leaves in the shadows what we desire to keep hidden there. The man of the world reflects in order to calculate his chances: let him. But how much weight can 'our chances' have for us, who have once and for all accepted the terrible presence of the divine in every instant of our poor lives?" Unless he loses his faith, the person consecrated to God cannot "have a vision of his own interests that is as clear, as direct—we'd almost say as ingenuous and naïve—as that of the children of the world."[49]

And so the young priest seeks a way of extending his prayer into every aspect of his everyday life, a way of turning each and every thing into a "conversation between the good Lord and me".[50] The world of prayer becomes for him *the* criterion for the truth of any given thought. His priest friend from Torcy strengthens him in this respect: "When it happens that some idea comes to me (one of those ideas, I mean, that could be useful to souls—why bother with the other kind . . . ?), I strive to bring it before the good Lord. I immediately make it come into my prayer. It's amazing how it changes appearances at once. At times you can't even recognize it."[51] This holds above all for evil, which the Christian must come to see and recognize. But he must not do so with his own eyes but must attempt to come to see evil with the eyes of God, which is to say, in prayer. Speaking about injustice, the Curé de Torcy says to his younger colleague: "Above all, don't imagine you'll make it back off by staring into its eyes like a lion tamer! You wouldn't escape its fascination, the vertigo it instills. Don't look at it any more than you strictly have to, and never look at it without praying."[52]

Later on the Curé d'Ambricourt begins to grasp the connection between prayer and an understanding of his fellowmen. He asks himself how it can be that it is precisely the monks who live separated from the world and appear to be "daydreamers" who seem to "en-

[49] *Curé*, 13–14.
[50] Ibid., 33.
[51] Ibid., 59.
[52] Ibid., 73.

ter daily more deeply into an understanding of other people's misfortunes. What a strange dream and a unique opiate this, which, far from making the individual withdraw within himself and become isolated from his neighbors, rather brings him into solidarity with all, in a spirit of universal charity!"[53] Those mystics in Bernanos who dispose of the gift of *cardiognosis*—the ability to see into the soul of another —have not come by it anywhere but in prayer. The connection is noted by the simple priest who reads into the soul of the countess' daughter in this supernatural fashion. In his diary he enters: *"I ask myself whether this kind of vision is not bound up with my prayer, whether it isn't perhaps my prayer itself."*[54] Such reading into souls, moreover, is for Bernanos the very model and ideal of the artistic vision, but it is unattainable because given as pure charism. Prayer is the only way for an average man to partake authentically of God's interior world and manner of seeing things. If the Christian possesses purity of soul and makes a radical effort at practicing the high "art" of prayer (as opposed to the dilettante who "at times strikes the keys of the piano at random, with the tip of his fingers"),[55] then he is capable of feeling at home in the vision of God. Perhaps Bernanos was not a contemplative in the sense of the monks of former ages, who had a great deal of time in which to allow themselves to be "borne" into eternity: for this he was too impatient. But he was a systematic and persevering man of prayer. Above all he was an open, unarmed, dialogical soul who allowed himself time and again to be brought back from anger, indignation, and what we could call "combative prayer" to a mode of converse with God abounding in the tears of self-surrender and, increasingly with the years, attaining even to *indifference*—something he achieved at tremendous cost. Once again it is the Curé d'Ambricourt who, in his final interior state, gives us what is doubtless a reflection of something Bernanos himself had experienced: "Some day you will understand that prayer is precisely this way of weeping, the only tears that are not cowardly."[56] "It's obvious that I'm praying better now. Before, my prayer was like a stubborn pleading. And even when, for instance, the reading of the breviary held my attention, I felt a con-

---

[53] Ibid., 119–20.
[54] Ibid., 151. (The italics are von Balthasar's.—TRANS.)
[55] Ibid., 120.
[56] Ibid., 250.

versation with God unfolding within me—now imploring, now insisting, at times even domineering. Yes, I wanted to wrest his graces from him, to do violence to his tenderness. At present it's difficult for me to come to desire anything at all. . . . Is this good? Is this bad? I don't know."[57]

Now the eyes of heaven open up for the writer, too. These are eyes whose love is infinitely more tender than what we had imagined grace could be, and for this reason it is also less perceivable for men; also infinitely more patient than anything we can imagine, and for this reason they take long in intervening, precisely when we have come to the end of our patience and are hoping for some moral solution. And they are seemingly much more brazen in the eternal light with which they shine, and more inexorable in their mysterious foresight, than anything we could imagine under the name of love. Bernanos knows exactly what he is about when he speaks of the "reproach full of kindness" that is the "reply of Providence" to his "jeremiads": "I have often noted, or thought I sensed, this barely perceptible irony (unfortunately I can't find another word for it). We'd say it was an attentive mother shrugging her shoulders at the awkward steps taken by her little child. Ah, if we only knew how to pray!"[58] The irony of heaven is not that of distant majesty but of loving compassion: "I am always struck by the idea that the mercy of the Lord of lords always has something unique and decisive about it. I'd be so bold to say it has the character of a free and magnificent irony."[59]

We will perhaps nowhere come to know the interior being of Bernanos better than in the light of his saints, for instance in the outlook of the Curé d'Ambricourt, an unusually austere, wholly unsentimental and realistic character who precisely because of these qualities can forgive others and lead them to conversion.[60] The priest can achieve these things only by virtue of a paradox accessible only to love: namely, that he, though a person more sensitive than others to the injustices committed against him, can nonetheless experience them as one who forgives them almost before they are committed. He actually experiences the quality of injustice not at all in himself

---

[57] Ibid., 252.
[58] Ibid., 91.
[59] *To Dom Besse*, August 1919; *Bul.* 11, 10.
[60] See *Curé*, 90.

but rather in God, since it is against that that the injustice is in all truth committed. Let us recall the following statement by the country priest at the moment of dying:

> It's also very comforting to say to myself that no one ever incurred the guilt of having been too harsh with me; much less could I here pronounce that big word, "injustice". Indeed, I'm quick to give credit to those souls who are capable of finding a source of strength and hope in their own vivid sense of the wrong of which they are the victims. But, for myself, I simply can't help it: I will always be loath to declare myself even the innocent cause or the mere occasion for someone else's failures. Even on the Cross, as he brought his holy humanity to its perfection through his death agony, our Lord did not declare himself the victim of injustice: "They know not what they do."[61]

Bernanos often stressed the objectivity of his outlook,[62] his repugnance for all sensationalism and prurience. Chronic curiosity, the essential characteristic of Monsieur Ouine, is wholly inadequate for the perception of the truths of the soul. From the very outset of his career as novelist, Bernanos already understood that evil can never be recognized and understood through evil, that the "magic of sin", to which the superficial sinner succumbs so often and so gladly, is in fact a false magic: "What son of woman, having experienced pleasure, is not aware of its bitter deceit? And if he says to himself that he is *fooled* every time, then I'll have to call him a very pleasant airhead . . . who's left nothing for the devil to do because the devil does not write in the sand."[63]

The writer's charity, which together with God's charity accompanies his characters through the experience of sin and utter night, is not so much a love accosted by temptation as one that must suffer under the bitterness of temptation to the point of being driven beside itself. Thus emerges in Bernanos, as a concrete image of God's grace, the figure of the one exclusively human person who cannot be tempted and who, precisely for this reason, is the one who most suffers along with all others: *Mary*. With reference to her, Bernanos always exhibited a well-advised and tender discretion: he did not pronounce her name needlessly. But, at the end of his little priest's pilgrimage, he

---

[61] Ibid., 316.
[62] *Cimetières*, 89.
[63] *To Vallery-Radot*, January 17, 1926; *Bul.* 1, 3.

could no longer refrain: at this point she must come forth as the being who follows the paths of sinners with eye and foot, walking along with them with unspeakable sadness. For, can we think of a single Marian apparition where the Virgin was not seen to weep?

"I was afraid that, on opening my eyes, I would see the face before which every knee must bend. And I did see it. . . . It was also the face of a child, or of a very young girl, without any radiance. It was the very face of sadness, but a sadness I did not know and in which I could have no part. It was so close to my heart, my wretched human heart, and yet I could not reach it. There is no human sadness exempt from bitterness, but that sadness was all gentleness; and no human sadness exempt from revolt, but that sadness was all acceptance. It made me think of some vast night—wonderfully soft and boundless." In the presence of this innocence that suffers, the little priest comes to understand that, "by some marvel, God at that time had to cast a veil over this virginal sadness. Blind and hard-hearted as men may be, they would otherwise have recognized their own precious daughter by this sign, the last-born child of their ancient race, the heavenly hostage around whom all the demons were now roaring. And they would all have stood up together to form a bulwark around her with their mortal bodies."[64]

The Romantic pathos of the final image should not make us overlook the fact that what is involved here for Bernanos is a fundamental criterion: namely, that *the sadness of the Virgin Mother is the refutation that renders impossible every attitude of revolt against the dark mystery of Providence*. Mary is more radical than Ivan Karamazov but also than all existentialists—both the philosophers and the poets—who set out to interpret existence by the criterion of the nonacceptability of a situation of guilt. *In order to arrive at the truth, the outlook of the writer on creatures must always keep before itself the outlook of Mary.* "The gaze of the Virgin is the only truly childlike gaze, the only truthful child's gaze ever to dwell on our shame and our misfortune. Yes, my boy. In order to pray well to her you must first feel on yourself the gaze of these eyes that are looking . . . not exactly with indulgence—because indulgence is inseparable from some bitter experience. They are looking, rather, with tender compassion, with painful surprise, with still other sentiments that remain inconceivable and unnamable to us, sen-

---

[64] *Curé*, 237.

timents that make her younger than sin, younger than the whole race from which she is descended."[65] For Christian literature, Mary's existence is not only an object or a content: it is a fundamental *form*, that is, the concrete norm that must mold both the Christian writer's vision of the world and his work.

However, it is not idle if, besides Mary, Bernanos calls upon the other inhabitants of heaven, too, to lend him their eyes. While the country priest is meditating on the revolt of sinners and ponders the dark mysteries of demonic possession and cruelty, this nostalgic sigh escapes him: "Ah, if we could only look upon these poor, mutilated creatures with the *eyes of the Angel!*"[66] And his friend, the Curé de Torcy, expressly encourages him to "pray to the Angels": "We don't pray enough to the Angels. They frighten theologians a little bit, on account of those ancient heresies of the Eastern churches. . . . The world is full of Angels."[67] Not far from the angels, who are simply creatures in their purest state, stands the child—the child who each of us was and who throughout our lives judges us, "adults" who have tragically outgrown our purity and thus become falsely so-called "grownups". Bernanos takes this child as the fundamental criterion for his literary creation, trying as best he can to hold his ground before him: "We shouldn't speak 'in the name' of childhood: what we should do is *speak its own language.* From book to book it is this forgotten language I seek, poor imbecile that I am, as if such a language could be written down or had ever been written down. No matter! Now and then I can actually reclaim some of its inflections."[68] "What does my life matter? The only thing I want is for it to remain faithful to the end to the child I once was, . . .—the child I was and who at present is like an ancestor to me."[69] "I write in order to justify myself. In whose eyes? I've already told you, but I'll face the ridicule of telling you again: in the eyes of the child I was. It doesn't matter whether he has stopped talking to me or not. I'll never resign myself to his silence. I will always answer him."[70] When Bernanos, the grown man, undertakes some difficult work and is overwhelmed at the prospect,

---

[65] Ibid., 232.
[66] Ibid., 111. (The italics are von Balthasar's.—TRANS.)
[67] Ibid., 229.
[68] *Cimetières*, v. (The italics are von Balthasar's.—TRANS.)
[69] Ibid., 79.
[70] *Enfants*, 195.

it is to that child he turns: "Dear God, how I wish I could express these very simple truths in the language of childhood!"[71]

But, although Mary and the saints and also the angels and the child have to stand there for Bernanos as witnesses of the truth, in the end they are all only images and transparencies of the *gaze of God* himself, of the God moreover who assumed human form and, though without sin, descended into the abyss of sin in order to be the fullness of all in all. Bernanos wants to create literary works in the Word of God, who became a human word but wholly without lies. Bernanos does not seek refuge from the attacks of hell in the WORD in his condition of majesty, of unassailable and sublime eternity, the Word who already in advance has defeated evil and all its revolt. No: the Word to whom he flees is the Word who came into the midst of our abyss, there to become man, child, suppliant, and sufferer, the Word who can contain and embrace man's whole way from childhood to death because he became weaker than a child and more despoiled than a dying man. It is thus that the incarnate Word became the very measure of human existence and was established as Judge over all flesh:

In the words of the Curé de Torcy:

> Don't you see that any imbecile picked at random could not help but be moved by the sweetness, the tenderness of the Word as conveyed to us by the Holy Gospels? That's the way our Lord wanted it. In the first place, it's the way it should be. Only weaklings and ponderous "thinkers" believe themselves obliged to roll their eyes and show us the white part before they even open their mouth. And then, it's the way of nature itself. For the little child resting in his crib and taking possession of the world with freshly opened eyes, isn't life all gentleness and caress? And yet, how hard life is! But, if you look at things as you ought, you'll notice that this first welcome life gives us isn't as deceiving as it might seem, because the only thing death asks of us is that we keep the promise made on that first morning of our days. The smile of death, although graver than the other, is not for all that any less gentle and caressing. In short, with the tiny the Word becomes tiny.[72]

---

[71] *Cimetières*, 241.

[72] *Curé*, 66–67.

And when the dying Curé d'Ambricourt says: "There was never an old man in me. . . . For the first time in years, or perhaps for the first time ever, it seems to me that I am face to face with my youth, looking at it without distrust",[73] what is occurring is a Christian encounter in God's Word, an encounter the more important half of which the philosopher of "existence unto death" has discarded. "For, what first emerges out of the depths of every death agony is the sweetness of our childhood."[74]

Two secrets envelop the awareness of a living being, reminding us of the twofold mystery of Mary's gaze: astonished surprise and anguish. "This double secret remains buried within the memory of our earliest childhood, the time of childhood more surfeited with milk than a sick man with bromide or morphine, the time of childhood that is wordless and almost sightless, ignored by all and inviolable—because the crib is not less deep than the grave."[75] Awe and anguish envelop existence and underlie every glance that both reason and sensuality direct in this world at man and his destiny. And this awe and this anguish find their ultimate expressive form in the Christ Child's capacity for wonderment and in the death agony of the God-Child on the Cross. The unity of these stances remains the horizon in the light of which Bernanos understood his life and creative activity and toward which he would always steer them. The world of the child (but of the holy, Christian child), steeped in the mysteries of baptism and confirmation, and the world of death (but of a holy, Christian death), steeped in the mysteries of anointing and the Eucharist and culminating in the handing over of the person from earth to heaven, and both of these worlds reflected one in the other: no, beyond this Bernanos had nothing to say. The clash between them gave birth to the Beatitudes of the Sermon on the Mount: "Blessed are the poor" and the "pure"—those who have been laid bare on the Cross and in death; "the meek and the patient", from whom the power of existence here below has been taken away; "those who hunger and thirst" just as the Word of God died of thirst on the Cross. For every hope of mankind derives from this encounter.

---

[73] Ibid., 316.
[74] *Ouine*, 94.
[75] Ibid., 233 (corrected text).

"The patience of the poor will not perish for all eternity", says the Psalmist. And a little farther on he cries out: "You will not put me to shame forever". This cry, this sublime challenge, is the whole substance of our heritage. We live *within* this extraordinary word. The human race, all its variety, each of us in the attitude proper to him—as in a bronze casting, everything has here been seized at its most vital and been set for all centuries to come. . . . Know that, from the Garden of Olives to Calvary, our Lord has in advance experienced and expressed all agonies —even the most humble, even the most desolate, and therefore yours too. . . . Many theologians believe that, in Jesus Christ at the moment of his Passion, human nature was abandoned to the experience of every feeling a man is capable of.[76]

"The truth" for us is everything Christ was from his childhood to his death, and the eternal and infinite dimension of this truth was revealed in the Resurrection. "Even the most humble of truths was redeemed by Christ, . . . just like anyone at random from among us Christians. The humblest truth, I say, has a share in the divinity of him who deigned to put on our nature—thus making us *consortes ejus divinitatis* [partakers of his divinity]."[77]

We continually forget, however, that this event whereby our nature and history are lifted up and transformed into the nature and history of Christ, and whereby we thus attain to our truth before God, is not an action that occurs necessarily, as by a law of nature. This event is realized by God in a deed of the most extraordinary freedom, and by virtue of his absolutely creative love, which makes an unfathomable choice and election coincide with God's wisdom. "How little we know what a human life is in reality! Our own life, for instance. To judge ourselves by what we call our 'acts' is probably as useless as judging ourselves by our dreams. Christ[78] chooses, according to his justice, from among this jumble of dark things, and

---

[76] *To Maître*, August 26, 1919; *Bul.* 1, 3.

[77] *Vérité*, 57.

[78] This passage presents us with a textual problem, theologically speaking. Both the original French and von Balthasar's German translation have "God" instead of "Christ" here. But how could "God" be said to raise anything "up toward the Father"? This mediating role would appear to be Christ's. Still, it is difficult to imagine that both Bernanos and von Balthasar could have overlooked the problem. God can raise others up to himself but not "to the Father": this would be a purely Gnostic proposition, positing "the Father" as a higher divine being above "God".—TRANS.

whatever he raises up toward the Father in a gesture of presentation suddenly bursts with splendor and begins to shine like a small sun."[79] The writer is transported ecstatically by this gesture of transformation, though he knows very well he cannot imitate it. But it is enough for him if his creative activity may, by sheer force of humility and prayer, become a sign pointing toward the only *poiesis* that can hold its own in the face of eternity. It is enough for him if, in the shadow of the marvel of redemption, he is allowed to attempt to cast upon the "dark things" of this world the glance of the grace of the Cross, the glance of that first and, alas, bloody transformation.

The writer remains fully conscious of the separating distance; it is significant that he is continually warning the reader against taking his words and works too seriously, full of pathos as they are: "The only precaution I recommend is not to take either me or my books too seriously, or my trials either: these may be great, but Providence allows me to see them as such only when they are past."[80] Bernanos loved to laugh, and his great guffaws more than qualify him for a role as "Catholic rascal", the buffoon who knows that in all human actions there is a residue of playacting and who consequently loves to jingle the bells hanging over his own head. He rejected as boring and false the earnest, pathetic image of him that his friends tended to fashion.[81] Where his person was concerned, Bernanos time and again let out a sudden *"qu'importe!"* (what does it matter?) in order to change the subject, and this exclamation was only the obverse of the supernatural burden bearing down upon his life and work with all the weight of the criteria for the truth that invade our poor temporal world out of God's absoluteness. Bernanos said "No matter!" only to restore the Catholic equilibrium in his life. Where Léon Bloy remained a humorless zealot bent on overturning everything around him but seldom bringing gladness, in Bernanos' case the wide swings of the pendulum always gravitated around the Catholic center. He owed the love with which he was so richly endowed, not to his zeal, but to the gleam in his childlike eyes.

---

[79] *Curé*, 103.
[80] *To Paulus Gordan*, in *Bul.* 5, 6.
[81] *To a Woman Friend*, July 2, 1934; *Bul.* 2–3, 20.

Because the criteria of Bernanos' literary task derived from God's world of eternity, he could not rely on them as one would on temporal, human *security*. For the manner in which God's truth appeared and was freely given to us follows the path leading from the passing awe of the Child in the crib to the passing anguish of the dying Jesus on the Cross. Faith, the form of God's truth for us, bears the imprint of this story's trajectory, even when it must speak without any doubt or hindrance as the mouthpiece of the truth. In this way, faith can confront the uncertainty of unbelief, fitting it precisely as a top fits its box. But faith cannot fit the smug self-certainty of bourgeois writers and Christians.

> All those Christians listening to me will kindly have to forgive me. If there were only one stranger to our faith among them, it is to him alone I would be speaking at this moment. I would have to blush too much if such a person imagined I was addressing him out of the depths, or better, out of the vacuum of my security as a believer as out of a safe and warm lair: in a word, if he imagined I remained a stranger to his own situation of risk. It is not true, no, it is not true at all that faith is a security, at least not in the human sense of the word. . . . Faith has nothing in common with the kind of evidence of which the truism *two and two make four* is the most frequent example.[82]

The evidence, rather, lies in God's gaze and choice, in his free judgment, and it is from this evidence that Bernanos' peace and security came: "God sees and judges. This certainty I have that he sees and judges has sustained me all my life. This is why I have always been able to look squarely at the doctors of the Law, the scribes and the Pharisees, without disdain or anger, but also without illusion, in the way in which Christ himself invites me to do it."[83]

This form of certainty does not so much connote a person ruling over anything but rather a person himself being ruled, and this significantly affected Bernanos' whole conception of literary work: "If he finds a suitable subject, any professional writer whatever will be quick to adapt it to his own scale and needs, which is to say, to the scale and needs of his public. God forbid that I should become the total master of the subject I have chosen. The subject is rather what shows

---

[82] *Liberté*, 270.
[83] *Croix*, June 1941, 132.

me the way."[84] The country priest, when he once attended a conference with his fellow priests and heard a lecture by a historian on the causes of the Reformation, is "flabbergasted" by the smug feeling of "security" of the audience, and he asks himself whether this is "the sign of a great faith" or rather "of great unconscious arrogance". He continues: "Not one of these men could ever believe the Church to be in danger, for any reason whatsoever. I don't think my trust is less than theirs, but it's of another kind." And, in order at least to hint at this difference, he adds: "After all, the Church is not an ideal to be realized. She already exists, and they are inside."[85] The object of the whole novel was to transcend the easier and more reasonable moral solution and ascend to the mystery of redemption, to transcend, too, the look of human compassion that "forgives all because it understands all" and enter into the abyss of the suffering God. In the same way, in this scene of the priests' conference, the moralized faith of these clerics has to be transcended so that the deeper mystery of ecclesial existence can emerge in all its splendor, for only in the context of the Church's life can there take place anything like participation in the act whereby the incarnate God hurls himself into the abyss.

3. The Object

The descent of God into the flesh—all the way to the Cross and hell itself—was the total, superabundant object of Bernanos' task as writer. This was the goal toward which his whole work strove; everything else—the portrayal of both the divine and the hellish in the world— remained a prolegomenon, but of a very special sort: given the impossibility of plumbing the main and ultimate theme to its depths, the preparatory stages also have a definitive, permanent quality about them, and they cannot be left behind. On his deathbed (and what great decisions did Bernanos not make on his deathbed?) he made the for him superhuman decision of never again writing anything other than a *Life of Jesus*. "It seems to me that the Lord is asking of me this total self-stripping. Do you agree?" And the Abbé Pézeril, who was with

---

[84] *Satan et nous*, July 1927; *Bul.* 12, 23.
[85] *Curé*, 42.

him to the end, agreed with this decision, because in it he saw the opportunity for one final purification before Bernanos made his passage to eternity. To this, the writer replied: "Now I have a reason to live. . . . It's hard, it's terribly hard. . . . But I've made my decision: from now on I'll speak only about Jesus Christ. . . . And don't think that I want to write any novels! . . ."[86] What particularly concerned him in this endeavor is clear from the many questions the mortally ill writer asked of an exegete who visited him regarding the temptations of Christ. It must have belonged in the very center of Christ's plans that he, the All-Pure One, should descend into the abyss of temptation. The *Life of Jesus* by Bérulle, which someone gave him to read, impressed him as unbearably contrived and artificial: "This man has to pinch himself in the spirit in order to have any ideas. . . . No, this isn't at all what I would like to do. Actually, it's exactly the opposite. I would like to speak about Jesus Christ in a very simple manner to people who no longer know him. I would like to speak about him at a church entrance or from behind a pillar, since I am no less poor than the rest of them." And about the apostles he would have liked to show that, until the Resurrection, they understood little or nothing, that they were "human beings . . . like ourselves".[87] Above all else, however, Bernanos would have wanted to portray the Child of God in his suffering on the Mount of Olives, to portray this, not as the chance destiny of Jesus alone, but as *the* all-embracing reality of all human existence, both of the holy and the unholy, both of those who surrender their lives to God and of those who refuse to do so. The agenda of 1948, the last year of his life, has preserved for us in this connection what must be the deepest statements Bernanos ever wrote. They shed much light on the hidden foundations of his own vision of things, which are also those of the Christian vision as such.

Bernanos' endeavor was to show that Christ's suffering is the a priori of all possible human suffering, because it infinitely surpasses and undergirds the suffering of any and all sinners. "He suffered a kind of suffering about which we cannot have the faintest idea, a kind of suffering we have never experienced. . . . We have become hardened to Pain as we have to Evil. We are protected by this shell, to which

---

[86] Pézeril, *C. du R.*, 352.
[87] Ibid., 345–46.

every generation adds a new layer. As for him . . ."[88] This distance
in suffering is that between the absolute and the merely inchoative,
and it gave Bernanos the right to draw a conclusion that is clinched
by his boundless feeling for the solidarity uniting all men in their
single human nature. The Church Fathers themselves could not have
expressed it in a more profound and simple fashion than Bernanos,
who in so doing avoided the temptation of sliding into the facile terms
of an Origenistic theory of universal redemption:

> We really and truly want what he wants. Without knowing it, we really
> want our sorrows, our sufferings, our solitude, and we only imagine that
> what we want is our pleasures. We imagine that we fear our death and
> want to flee from it, whereas we really desire this death as he desired
> his. Just as he sacrifices himself on every altar where Mass is celebrated,
> so too does he undertake to die again in every man entering his death
> agony. We want everything he wants, but we don't know that we want
> it. We don't know ourselves; sin makes us live at the surface of ourselves.
> We will again go back into ourselves only to die, and it's there he awaits
> us.[89]

On the basis of these statements, whose adamant character has no
need of a commentator, Bernanos then dared to take a final step and
ground in Christ all of human existence and the world as such. Surely without
realizing it, Bernanos in so doing coincided with the christocentrism
of the newer theology, not for theoretical reasons, but by virtue of his
direct and prayerful contemplation of the being of Jesus: "The point
is not to conform our will to his, because his will is in fact already
ours. When we rebel against his will, it's only at the cost of tearing
apart our own interior being, at the cost of a monstrous scattering of
ourselves. Our will has been united to his since the beginning of the
world. He created the world together with ourselves. How soothing
to think that, even when we offend him, we can never quite stop
desiring what he desires in the innermost sanctuary of our soul!"[90]
We can then see that this thoroughgoing grounding of the whole of
human nature in Christ—even of that nature's freedom and its whole
realm of choosing—leaves intact all the Lord's freedom to judge over

---

[88] *Agenda*, January 26, 1948; *Bernanos*, 147.
[89] Ibid., January 24, 1948; *Bernanos*, 147.
[90] Ibid., January 23, 1948; *Bernanos*, 146–47.

good and evil precisely *because* it subjects the realm of human freedom to Christ's. In this way, human freedom is not explained in a merely philosophical way by deriving it from the God of abstract theology; rather, it is grounded by reference to the concrete foundation of creation: namely, the Logos who became man and suffered. Here we should say after Saint Augustine: "*Christus interior intimo meo* [Christ is more at the center of my being than I am myself]." And this Christ is not solely the Lord of Glory: so long as men continue to sin and to suffer, Christ is present among them in the form of one dispossessed, Christ the Stranger, indeed, Christ the Refugee, that most holy "Suppliant" about whom Péguy had already written immortal lines in his work *Les Suppliants parallèles* and who now also appears in Bernanos: "He did not come as a conqueror but as a suppliant. He took refuge in me, under my care, and I must answer for him before his Father."[91]

The saints in Bernanos' novels stand in a very subtle relationship with the most important figures of saints in recent history. Certain features from the life of the Curé d'Ars were consciously and openly used in developing the hero of *Under Satan's Sun*, and this modern saint can easily be recognized as well in the Abbé Chevance and in the Curé d'Ambricourt. The figure of Chantal de Clergerie, the heroine of *Joy*, was influenced by two of Bernanos' favorite women saints: first of all, Thérèse of Lisieux; then, as the heroine enters in earnest into the mystical battle with the hell that surrounds her, the presence of Joan of Arc becomes apparent, to the terrible end of whose life Bernanos devoted a separate little work. The borrowings are so evident that Bernanos repeatedly referred to Donissan as a "second Curé d'Ars" and often alluded to these saints in the novels themselves.[92] Nevertheless, what is involved here is not a copy or replica in the naturalistic or idealistic sense but something far deeper that might well be unique to Bernanos in all of Christian literature. Behind it stands an image of Christian sanctity that the writer never formulated theoretically. He envisioned the saint as someone who had been prepared by God to become an image of divine truth and revelation for a specific moment

[91] Ibid., January 19, 1948; *Bernanos*, 146.
[92] *Soleil*, 270; *Joy*, 34, 38; and so on.

in the history of the world. The saint is thus a person commissioned to represent a particular divine task, and this mission asserts itself in his life in such a way that the saint becomes its servant without knowing it and even though he may refuse to obey. Through it all, he is empowered by grace, and in the end he has served God as best he could. In his service, or better, in his mission, people are able to "read" God's Word, the answer God gives to a particular time and its questions. The saints are not merely—or even mainly—persons who go to God and who, as they disappear in the direction of God, manage to make a little rip in heaven, as it were, through which a few rays of eternity escape. First and foremost, the saints are messengers who come from God to the world in the company of Christ with a message in words for men—although such "words" may be proclaimed through their silence, their lives, their sufferings, and their death. Jean-Marie Vianney and Thérèse Martin were two such "words of God" whom it was impossible not to hear, words spoken by the Holy Spirit in whom the Spirit concretizes anew something of Christ the eternal Logos ("the Spirit will take from what is mine. . . ."). Eager for the most valid instances of sanctity, Bernanos turned precisely to these "words" with a sort of divinatory certainty. He "distilled" them, so to speak, out of their limited historical situation and, through literary creativity, lent them a new corporality, not arbitrarily or by slavishly compulsive imitation, but empowered to do it by the freedom of the Christian man, who is entitled to do precisely this: to extricate a subject from its letter in order to lend the spiritual a new presence in the spirit.

Bernanos' literary activity shows that he was conscious of what a fortunate occurrence it is when the charism of sanctity meets the charism of the creative word. In such a case, what the saint has lived —even though he himself has not perhaps received from God the gift of expressing it in words—may be put into the hands of a craftsman of language who is rooted within the same ecclesial sphere as the saint, which is where God appoints his messengers. Such was certainly the case of Jean-Marie Vianney and largely also that of Thérèse of Lisieux. This convergence of vocations, moreover, does not at all abolish the distance between saint and writer. Bernanos himself was "nothing but a writer" and had no other tool at his disposal: "I did not deserve for God to assign any other to me. I know very well that a saint, for instance, would smile at this very poor means of touching hearts.''[93] And yet, Bernanos the writer was enabled by God to lend his voice to things Jean-Marie Vianney would have wanted to say in his shabby sermons and which he was so incapable of saying that, as has been shown, he had to copy out of a sorry though unctuous manual for preachers. Bernanos likewise took up things that Thérèse of Lisieux expressed in the *bien-pensant* style of her century, and which she thus more hid behind garlands of roses than gave clear form to (the very things, parenthetically, that Péguy had already formulated in a very different key in his *Mystery of the Holy Innocents*). And, finally, Bernanos spoke for Joan of Arc herself, uttering statements she longed to hurl at her judges but had instead to leave unsaid. What succeeded in Bernanos was something that had never succeeded before: he lent the saint such a truthful voice that, through it, sanctity as grace and mission became absolutely credible for the listener, while at the same time, for the speaker himself, it remained not merely an insignificant, everyday voice but a painfully humbled voice whose failure was always imminent.

What hagiography has ever found the precise tone in which the two poles unite to become one and the same thing? In Bernanos' figures of saints, the most sublime grace combines with the most ordinary banality, the most dazzling insight into the world and sin with the most innocent lack of vision in what concerns the saint's own election. Total sincerity combines with equally total humility, but a humility that is not an acquired virtue but rather the manifest inexperience, inaptitude, and uselessness of a young priest still wet behind the ears and of a young girl facing life and not knowing how to handle the situation. In Bernanos' saintly characters we witness the simultaneity of deep, inexplicable anguish—a sense of abandonment—and an equally deep sobriety and steadiness, the simultaneity of the ridiculous and the majestic, of light humor and unsurpassable earnestness. And all of it occurs, not as an abstract "coincidence of opposites", but as a believable, unique, clearly contoured reality immersing the saint in the thick of life. The shape of such an existence is not so much viewed by Bernanos from the outside (which would necessarily lead to its being evaluated and judged from a perspective alien to it) as it is developed from the inside: it is the saint himself who has his experiences, ponders, takes notes, reflects again on the basis of these,

---

[93] *Enfants*, 205.

and this process unfolds through the (literarily speaking) very unusual technique of the inextricable interweaving of the voice of the character with the voice of the author, whose interventions in his work are often unmistakable.

What makes such a technique possible is solely the fact that Bernanosian discourse occurs, not at the level of psychology or historiography, but at the level of the ecclesial missions, which, without detriment to their individual personal uniqueness, can be made by grace to interpenetrate in an almost trinitarian manner. We have only to think of cases like that of Dominic and his prior, of Francis de Sales and Jane Frances de Chantal, of Jean-Marie Vianney and his little Roman martyr. The price the writer must pay in order to enter with the saint into such a symbiosis of mission is, of course, nothing less than his life: the price of sanctity itself, in other words, understood, not as a moral or canonical quality, but as the result of having been uniquely and irreversibly called by God to sacrifice oneself for the sake of his own purposes—sanctity as the process whereby one becomes dispossessed of one's own will and the management of one's life through the supernatural task imposed by God. Bernanos therefore saw himself entitled to speak about his spiritual mission with the same absolute seriousness "with which a religious [speaks] about his vows".[94] And a friend said of him: "Yes, there was in Bernanos a priest, unfinished but not for that the less admirable, a 'priest' for whom sanctity retains its original meaning of *separation* from the world, consecration to God alone."[95]

If Bernanos was capable of making his saints credible, then, it was because he engaged his own substance and not just his literary talent. If he had borne them only within his imagination, Bernanos would not have been able to bring them to reality beyond the world of dreams. But, since he was continually bestowing his own life upon them, he was able to introduce his imagination into the interior reality of the saint, without nevertheless trespassing where he should not or incurring any profanation. Bernanos was so aware of this that the satanic counterpart to his little Chantal could not be anything other than a writer who writes about sanctity without even dreaming of giving away his own life: such is "the Abbé Cénabre, the fa-

---

[94] *To Amoroso Lima*, March 13, 1940; *Esprit*, 202.
[95] Vallery-Radot, *Souvenirs*; in *Bul.* 2–3, 28.

mous author of a book on *Florentine Mystics*," whose peculiarity it
is "to write about sanctity as if charity did not exist".[96] In the first
pages of *The Imposture*, from which these words are taken, we can still
clearly detect Bernanos' violent aversion for hagiographic journalism
in the style of Henri Bremond. His anger, however, was directed not
only against this unfortunate and hollow writer but against the usual
manner of writing about saints' lives: "True heroes do not think of
themselves as heroes any more than true saints think of themselves as
saints. While awaiting the Church's decision—often late in coming
—and even long thereafter, the saints must entrust the care of their
renown to learned canons, who naturally refashion them into their
own image and likeness."[97] Out of the concrete lives of the saints
these pious prelates then not only concoct a distillate of highly refined moral virtues, but also, what is worse, they create well-behaved
embodiments of the conventional *bien-pensant* mentality or paragons
of an infantilism that has been substituted for the divine childlikeness
of the New Covenant. The saint, whoever he may be, is a "child",
not in the natural, but in the supernatural sense: in Novalis' language,
a "synthetic" child. His innocence and "ignorance" are what they are
only if they can hold their ground all the while knowing the reality of the abyss, indeed, in the very midst of their experience of the
abyss. This is why little Chantal must be dragged so roughly out of
the unawareness that envelops her, to be handed over for profanation
to the demons lurking about her. For the saint to be revealed and
exposed, hell itself must be exposed and revealed along with him,
and this disclosure is a task Bernanos does not spare us. Of himself
he says: "I find the right voice, *la voix juste*, only when I speak as
a Christian",[98] and by this he meant his manner of speaking about
evil, which neither underestimates nor exaggerates the mysteries of
the abyss. This countertheme, too, should not take its norm from
man, for man cannot measure the depths of the abyss. Man, rather,
has the double tendency either to veil these depths from himself or,
on the contrary, to stare at them with morbid curiosity, while the
Apocalypse at one and the same time shows them to us and forbids
us "to investigate the depths of Satan" (Rev 2:24).

---

[96] *Imposture*, 29.
[97] *Cimetières*, 190.
[98] *To Paulus Gordan*; in *Bul.* 5, 6.

The measure of the abyss is known only to the One who holds
the keys of death and hell in his hand (Rev 1:18), the One who,
being the incarnate fullness of divinity, is himself the measure of all
human sanctity. Thus, in Bernanos, the saints are transparencies of
Christ. Their personal destiny is unimportant in itself, but it reveals
something of the one thing necessary: Christ's suffering love. Unbeknownst to her, it is little Chantal's vocation to help carry the guilt
of the world, and she utters words the implications of which she cannot possibly understand. The old and mad grandmother, whose guilt
for murder Chantal is helping to bear in atonement, is literally carried back into the house on her granddaughter's shoulders as Chantal
whispers in her ear:

> "Don't be afraid. Now I am strong enough to carry you. I wish you
> were heavy, much heavier, as heavy as all the sins in the world. You
> see, Mama, I've just discovered something I've known for a long time:
> it can't be helped, but we just can't escape from one another any more
> than we can escape from God! The only thing we have in common is
> sin." She brought her mouth close to the dripping forehead and suddenly
> impressed her lips upon it. The docile head rolled over limply, letting
> go, eyes shut. . . . "Mama", she whispered, catching her breath, "I seem
> to be carrying you, but it's you who are carrying me. . . . Don't ever
> let go of me!" Her glance, drunk with exhaustion and light, was full of
> calm defiance.[99]

In the *Country Priest* there are situations that, almost unintention-
ally and in any case with most tactful restraint, evoke a christological
analogy to the Lord's Passion: the nocturnal fall into the mud, the
vomiting of wine and blood, the smeared face and the cloth of little
Séraphita, the priest's death scene in the attic room in the presence of
the mortally ill friend who, after a fashion, may be said to be "crucified along with him" as absurd fellow sufferer. . . . In this connection
André Bazin says with great insight:

> The æsthetic value [of these Christlike scenes] derives from their theo-
> logical value, and both resist direct explication. . . . None of the situ-
> ations that obviously refer to a Gospel passage is there simply because
> of that resemblance. Each of them possesses its own meaning, which is
> biographical and contingent: it depends upon the rest of the story and
> elucidates it. . . . The christological resemblance is only secondary. . . .

---

[99] *Joie*, 138–39.

The life of the Curé d'Ambricourt in no way "imitates" that of his
Model: it does not imitate it; it *repeats* it. Each man must bear his own
cross, and every cross is different. But all crosses are the one Cross of
the Passion. On this priest's forehead the sweat caused by his fever is a
sweat of blood.[100]

Human suffering receives its proper reality by being brought into relation with the suffering of God. Man knows that he cannot suffer
God's suffering; but this suffering communicates something of its divine reality to man, and grace is nothing other than this communication. For God's suffering, too, occurs within a human nature like
ours, and so, at the conclusion of *Joy*, the window is opened wide on
the Lord's Passion and Eucharist. Chantal's love can now no longer be
spoken of without also naming the source of the rays that are beaming
so powerfully from her: "Humanly, like a man, he loved man's humble inheritance—his shabby hearth, his table, his bread and wine—
the gray country roads, made golden by a recent shower, the villages
with their smoking chimneys, the little houses behind thorny hedges,
the peace that settles with the descending evening, the children playing at a doorstep. Humanly did he love all of this, in the manner of
a man, but as no man had ever loved it or would ever love it. With
such purity, in so tight an embrace, with the heart he had made for
just that with his own hands."[101] So runs the tear-spotted introduction
to the narrative of the institution of the Eucharist in the presence of
the traitor. For the deepest aspect of Christianity is God's love for the
earth. Other religions also know that God is rich in his heaven. What
remained unheard of, unimaginable, until the coming of Jesus is that
God should have wanted to be poor along with his creatures, that in
his heaven he should have wanted to suffer because of his world and
did in fact make that suffering a reality, that through his Incarnation
he put himself in a position of demonstrating to his creatures this his
suffering out of love. And, if the suffering of man points only to that
of the Son of Man behind him, then the Son through his suffering
points to *the wounded Heart of the Father*. This is the final goal aimed
at through all of Bernanos' work.

   In a copy of *The Diary of a Country Priest* the author inscribed the

[100] From an article in *Cahiers du cinéma* on Bresson's film based on Bernanos' novel; quoted
in *Bul.* 7–8, 29–30.
[101] *Joie*, 251.

following dedication in 1936: "When I am dead, please tell the sweet kingdom of this Earth that I loved it more than I ever dared to say."[102] He found in his own heart the impulse for a love he had previously attributed only to Christ. Even if some of his best friends have done so, it is false to think of Bernanos as having primarily an Old Testament image of God. To be sure, his God is a zealous, a jealous God: "The most inhuman of man's passions has in him its ineffable image. As the Jews of old intuited without understanding it, he is a jealous God. Yes, God is jealous. In him there is this pensive and severe desire, this keenness and eagerness for his creatures."[103] And in the light of suffering, also of the Christian suffering of the soul's dark night, the Old Testament, not exactly beloved by Bernanos,[104] suddenly begins to beam forth the eternal riches it contains: "A certain passage, often read and reread, a certain verse in the Book of Job, the terrible cry wrenched from the tough Jewish heart by universal malice, the despairing irony of the Psalms—this testimony coming from the depth of the ages and smelling of the grave, which a sanctimonious old gal sleepily recites to the purring of a rickety harmonium: all of it suddenly took on its eternal meaning."[105] What Bernanos desires, however, is not the bare-bones exposure of this gesture of jealousy on the part of God the Father. He wants for it to become incarnate in the heart of the Son of Man: "The danger", he writes for himself in his agenda, "of imagining the love of God as a love of condescendence. God yearns for his creature with a desire the least representation of which would reduce us to dust. This is why he hid this desire in the deepest recesses of the gentle, suffering heart of Jesus Christ."[106] And here it becomes evident that from all eternity the content of God's jealous zeal was his *pathos*—his passionate love—for his creatures. This and this alone is what the crib and the Cross reveal. This alone is what constitutes the scandal and the folly of Christianity, "the masterful absurdity, and the sublime challenge of this small number of thinking animals whose contribution, when all is said and done, is to have brought to the world the good news of Pain divinized."[107] For

---

[102] *Bernanos*, 52–53.
[103] *Joie*, 42–43.
[104] *Bul.* 2–3, 25.
[105] *Joie*, 121.
[106] *Agenda*, January 18, 1948; *Bernanos*, 146.
[107] *Joie*, 121.

this very reason, we repeat, resignation is not possible within Christianity. To the Abbé Chevance, Chantal declares: "I am not resigned to anything. Resignation is a sad affair. How could you resign yourself to the will of God? Do you 'resign' yourself to being loved?" And Bernanos adds: "She could see this clearly, all too clearly. It was just that the will of God doubtless contains a part that poor human love cannot quite manage to dissolve so as to incorporate it fully into its own substance. Man's great thirst, man's eternal Thirst, has turned away from the springs of living waters and has preferred gall and vinegar, has desired only bitterness."[108]

From this perspective we cannot say that Schopenhauer was completely wrong when, for very different reasons, he praised compassion (*Mitleid*, "suffering-with") as being the highest virtue. The suffering creature is not redeemed *from* suffering but *within* suffering and *through* suffering. Redemption does not release it *toward* a God who is beyond all suffering: rather, it is redeemed *by a God who suffers along with it*, not to say even more correctly that *the* Sufferer is simply God himself (on the Cross), while the creature is only a cosufferer. Little Chantal's suffering is as such the locus where "joy"—which is also the title of the work—bursts forth: "The idea, the certainty of her impotency had now become the dazzling center of her joy, the very core of the flaming star. This helplessness itself is what made her feel united to the Master she still could not see. It was this humbled part of her soul that plunged into the abyss of all sweetness." But the welling-up of joy spends itself, and out of the receding waters again emerges the black reef of pain: "At this sign, Mademoiselle de Clergerie knew that the last stage of her journey had been completed, that her humble sacrifice had been accepted, and that all the anguish and doubts of the last few hours—even her remorse—had just now disappeared into the abyss of God's stupendous compassion."[109]

We have seen that, for Bernanos, Christ is the very foundation of man's psychic life, the "ground" to which should be traced those paradoxes in the life of man's soul that in themselves must remain inexplicable. In other words, Bernanos' psychology refers us first and last to his Christology. In the present context this fact acquires an even deeper meaning, for even Christology now becomes an expres-

---

[108] Ibid., 110.
[109] Ibid., 247.

sion and an extrapolation, within the world, of theology properly so called, that is, of the truth about God himself. *La douce pitié de Dieu*: this phrase of ardent intimacy, which we can literally though somewhat clumsily translate as "the sweet mercy of God", is incessantly used by Bernanos and constitutes one of the cornerstones of his thought. The phrase may, in fact, be said to communicate the reality that bears all else within it, because it implies, not merely that God exercises mercy upon the perishing out of his safe retreat in the fortress of eternity, but that he exercises compassion as genuine "compassion", which is to say, that God suffers right along with those suffering. The dark stream of all human questioning in the end arrives at this revealed truth, which, being genuinely and purely Christian, could not have been derived solely from the Old Testament: "This world . . . appears to our mortal eyes to be the permanent exhibition of every possible form of ignorance and hatred. But one day we will know with certainty that it is lost within God's immense mercy like a little pebble in the sea."[110]

4. The Idea of Literature

Only after friends pressured him to provide some sort of interpretation regarding his mysterious first novel did Bernanos begin—after the event and as a secondary activity—to reflect on the meaning and intention of his literary work. The essential is contained in his *Letter to Frédéric Lefèvre*[111] and in the essay *A Catholic Vision of Reality*.[112] The eruptive formulas that here express his point of view as an author manage to bring very exactly under one heading the various aspects we have been examining at greater length: the prophetic character of reason, the writer's *pathos*, and, finally, its object—the divine *pathos* or the tragic depth of creaturely existence.

In the *Letter*, Bernanos declares that what drove him at the most elemental level to write was the double platitude consisting, on the one hand, of a rationalism without faith and, on the other, of a moral-

---

[110] *Croix*, February 1942, 195. (Lines written in connection with the death of Stefan Zweig. —Note of the French trans.)

[111] In the series "Chroniques du Roseau d'Or", no. 2 (Plon, 1926) 383–95.

[112] In the *Revue Générale Belge*, April 15, 1927.

ism within the Church: "This disgust, which in our case was quite lucid, was also felt in darker, less conscious ways by a great number of others. The very palpable trial of the war had awakened in many souls what I shall call *the tragic sense of life*, the need to relate our immense human misfortune to the great laws of the spiritual universe, the need to incorporate this misfortune into a spiritual order. The problem of Life is the problem of Pain. . . . The wail wrenched from a humiliated heart is prayer being born, the spring shooting up from a saturated soil."[113] If it emerges from so deep a level, it is because sin is so unfathomable, so much deeper than merely moral guilt. Bernanos defines sin from the perspective of faith: it is nothing less than "a deicide", the murder of God! Only this can explain why sin wreaks such catastrophes in the cosmos, and why the Cross is so much more than just the restoration of justice: beyond this, it is the answer a suffering love gives to the murder the sinner intends for it:

> Where, then, will the union of Creator and creature, victim and executioner, take place? In the suffering that is common to both. We are at the center of this stupendous drama, we are at the very heart of the Most Holy Trinity. What am I saying? That this sort of inconceivable hurricane can occur within God himself? . . . And we live at ease and unaware in the midst of this horrific whirlwind of love! If, by an impossibility, it were to change the course of its unwavering spiral by one inch, it would proceed to uproot whole worlds. . . . *Suffering* is the bread God shares with man, the *temporal image of the divine possession to which we are called.* . . . From his privileged friends God asks what he himself gave: lavish suffering. . . . *The drama is no longer played out in hell; from now on it is played in the heart of the God-Man, where mankind has its root*—this heart pierced with a lance where our race, itself wounded open, mingles with his its own blood, squandered without measure. . . . Haven't I said it? Haven't I written it? *This particular man, though himself in despair, can lavish hope with full hands.*[114]

Art can be nothing other than a breakthrough that shatters all the closures of morality, philosophy, and, yes, æsthetics itself, so as to enter into this sphere where the unity of all truth reigns supreme: "We cannot live outside of the real. And the real, the truly positive

---

[113] "Chroniques", 384. (The italics are von Balthasar's.—TRANS.)

[114] Ibid., 391–94. (The italics of the last sentence are Bernanos'; all the rest are von Balthasar's.—TRANS.)

dimension of life, surely cannot consist in a few moments of sensual or intellectual exaltation, or even of vague religiosity. The real is that subterranean sheet of suffering that suddenly bursts to the surface like the waters of an underground river."[115] *Either art is more than art or it is nothing:*

> In its highest and most perfect expression, art is still a search. Even shaped by a genius, the work of art retains the gesture and the form of an impulse despite the sublime immobility it may enjoy. Indeed, the kind of sacred joy that fills us with its marvelous presence [when we come into contact with a great work of art] contains as well the goad of an expectation, and the most wonderful sort of hope is born of our sated desire. . . . We can't deny it: art has an end other than itself. Its perpetual search for a manner of expression is only the feeble image or symbol of its perpetual search for Being as such. Would *Racine*, for example, have reached his point of perfection if he hadn't one day, with one sublime stroke, surpassed moral man and rediscovered man the sinner? No cause other than this could explain his continual bitterness, the indefinable shiver of sorrow perceivable everywhere, or the silence into which he suddenly lapsed, or his death. This happy rival of Corneille learned of the exhausting struggle undergone by his magnanimous older colleague. And we can doubtless believe that then, impatient as he already was to achieve great fame, Racine passionately desired to please a public that the author of the *Cid* had sated with sublimeness and that was looking for a different entertainment. But it was not with Greek or Roman sublimeness that this young man had dreamed of filling his eager heart. . . . Already in the triumphant cry with which the conquering, loved, and famous adolescent welcomes life we can detect the barely perceivable crack, the sighing of a joy mingled with anguish, the intense search for a more urgent and more profound truth. Who will follow him all along his arid path? Until he sees her, Phædra, suddenly emerge, born of his art, pale with a lust that has been squeezed to the point of torture, her little secret hand resting on the shoulder of her insignificant friend; yes, and in his Phædra's dying eyes Racine recognizes the face of a sister and his own remorse.[116]

A Catholic Vision of Reality (1927) does not attain the weightiness of these utterances. Bernanos' main intention in this conference was to impress upon his readers the fact that, without the depth of evil,

---

[115] Ibid., 395.
[116] Ibid., 385–88.

reality must remain an unknown and that all efforts of modern literature to come to know evil through evil must necessarily fail. Proust, Gide, and all those who have tried to plumb the abyss of evil in man by means of psychology or by a process of uninhibited "stripping-down" have experienced the shipwreck of absolute boredom, of the void with nothing to say. To reconnoiter hell by means of "analysis" results in the kind of disintegration that in the end leads precisely to hell. Such "analysis" will never produce the desired "synthesis" of hell, which can be achieved only from the standpoint of its opposite, namely, God. Thus, the imaginative writer cannot perform his task without the aid of *theology*, because "art . . . needs one thing above all else: namely, truth." But this truth, which no one can any longer discover for himself, is nevertheless not foreign to man: what God is saying to him lies buried at the very bottom of his memory of Being: "It may well be that our wretched and suffering species retains, in the deepest recess of its hereditary memory, the recollection of that evening of all evenings when the first human couple saw, for the last time, that Truth which they had just insulted, saw it descending slowly below the horizon like an immense star, while the accursed earth was being overtaken, at a frightful speed, by the shades of the first of all nights."

In his *Eve*, Péguy had ventured the same monumental act of anamnesis: in the face of the Cross—center of the world's history of suffering—Péguy undertook to recollect the truth of man's condition in his first origins, the fullness of his innocence, and at the same time he projected forward to the end of time a firm hope in the restoration of *paradise*. Eden—Cross—grace—and rebirth: this remains the line of the horizon against which alone the catastrophe of evil may be measured. Only the person with a sense for the fullness of truth can know what parts of it have been lost. Literature, according to Bernanos, does not deserve its name if it does not break through all the appearances of the foreground of existence in order to penetrate into the widest possible sphere of the world's redemption. This very breakthrough is the essential movement animating literature. This is to say that Bernanos' conception of literature and the act of literary creation constitutes the opposite pole of every sort of Old Testament or Puritanical and Jansenistic legalism. If we listen to his pronouncements on this subject, we are initially astonished to find such expansiveness of outlook and such cosmic optimism in the man to whom so many like to attribute a dark and harsh intransigence. We would more naturally have sought for such openness in Claudel, on whom Bernanos did not look with favor, but more for personal than objective reasons. Claudel's grand gesture of embracing the whole world and reaching out to all of redeemed creation is found in Bernanos as well, only Bernanos transports us to the foot of the Cross, to the center of the freely given redemptive event; and Claudel's wide-open joy, already possessed in the fullness of its results, remains in Bernanos compressed within its cause as a wellspring within its narrow source, but his joy is not for all that any weaker in its explosive power. Bernanos' "violence" is but the tempestuous force of his affirmation of redeemed creation.

We must listen to him as he speaks about lyric poetry:

> To be always impassioned is the natural condition of the poet. Poetry takes hold of us with its waves—eternal, torrential, generous. All the world's great poets have been like this. Only in our time has poetry become fragmented into little compositions and cold wordiness: at best it produces sporadic episodes. To cite one representative of the Americas, the poetry of Whitman is a poetry of massive, gigantic passion; it is never poetic fragment. The modern world has mutilated and deformed art, confining it to little details, little cubes, little ironic poems, little lyrical sweets—if indeed we can give the name of "lyricism" to this nonchalance, this platitudinousness, and this discomfort that are tending to corrupt modern poetry. What modern poetry is lacking is incarnation: it desperately needs to be rooted both in heaven and in the earth, as well as in the hell to which it must descend. Today's poetry lives outside of the world. Like everything else, today's poetry has become deformed. . . . There are painters who complain that the Church no longer supports them in our time with her patronage, that she has abandoned and forgotten them. What these artists forget is the incompatibility that exists between unity and fragmentation, particularity and catholicity, fashion and eternity, exhibitionism and modesty. . . . This particular world has lost its vocation to truth and passion, and it has delivered itself exclusively to the cold calculation of destruction. As with the devil, it is lacking in passion, in holy folly. It is pure lie. What has happened is that it has become neurotic and impotent in a petty way, without the grandeur of folly, without the agitated majesty of passion. It lacks interiorization; thus, in our world, the language of the interior man appears to us forced, repressed, and all too abstemious: what happens is that men have lost the vision of the immense interior distances traveled

by the saints, who appear to be so calm and airtight. If we were to look well into it, we would, quite on the contrary, see in the interior man's expression an oceanlike agitation and an anguish for perfection that are a road without end—the road of a creation oriented toward eternity. And this road . . . is a road of messages proclaimed, of universal communion, of participation in truth and beauty of all kinds, of a generous anxiety regarding perfection. And all of this can be transmitted "apostolically", as it were, immensely multiplied, poured out, lavished with full hands on all those who thirst for poetry. There is . . . a great need for poetry to be also communion, wholesome universality, and not a calculated artifice without any heroism or humanity. All the interior man does is scream in order to make the world shudder with his cries; but this world shudders only at wars, bombs, cataclysms. Our corpselike world needs the scandal of poetry, just as it needs the scandal of truth, because scandal does not consist in telling the truth but in not telling it entire, without introducing little gaps and little shifts that disfigure it, both as poetry and as truth. There's no question about it: a world that bombs its own monuments has forever lost the need for the monumental.[117]

This spirited diatribe from the year 1942 structures Bernanos' poetics around passion as its center, not, to be sure, sensual passion, but a cosmic *pathos* that is as big as the world. This is what the young Bernanos meant in 1915 when he spoke of "playing on my great organ", which he contrasted to the superficial and sentimental dilettantism of those who merely "stroke the piano's keyboard". If we go even farther back to the sources, what we doubtless discover at base is Bernanos' *sensibilité*, the "sensitivity" the boy and the young man continually mentioned and which he both fostered and feared, a personal characteristic that made him a hypersensitive instrument of every sort of impression and state of soul and predestined him to be a writer. By age twenty he had managed to contain this predisposition through a will to service and self-surrender. After four years of war, the then thirty-year-old Bernanos had finally bridled his hypersensitivity, or rather made it permeable to his religious experience and placed it at its service. In 1918 he writes: "After four years of solitude my sensitivity cannot hold out. It must fall to its knees. My anguish is full and continual. Some days are horrendous. We would

---

[117] *To Jorge de Lima*, January 1942; *Lettres inédites*, 45–48.

be branded with ignominy for all eternity if we still pretended to pit our feeble forces against the pitiless thunder of grace as it multiplies its blows."[118] Again, in the same month, he writes to his confessor: "After four years of solitude, of endless pondering, of useless interior debates . . . don't you see? You can't even take refuge in being mediocre. The war has forced sensitivity to its knees. It's no longer useful for anything. What we need is a restoration of the will. . . . All or nothing—that's the password."[119] And a year later he writes the following to defend himself against the suspicion of arrogance and religious presumption: "I am the weakest of all, the most unstable, the most cowardly—*a slave*—and, if anyone, it's *I* who shall have to crawl along the long, the very long road, with my sensitivity flayed alive, until I reach Him!"[120] Already ten years previously, in his article "The Effects of the Democratic Prejudice in the World of Letters" (1909), the young Bernanos had devoted a whole section to "making sensitivity useful". This is a significant text, which shows to what extent his present improvisation on the "great organ of passion" had its roots in the distant years. For Bernanos, the only way of overcoming sensitivity decisively was through *la grande passion*, which concentrates a person's subjectivity by focusing it interiorly:

> It's from the ashes of these Muses, on whose chin time eventually grew a beard,[121] that was born this horde of scribblers who are eternally occupied with themselves and for whom art is only one means among others (albeit the most direct and delicate) of adding some salt to their pleasures and prolonging their exquisite thrills. War must be declared on this spineless race! These voluptuaries don't really know how to *feel*. True feeling is not the endless multiplication of successive sensations, of as diverse or contradictory a nature as possible. True feeling results from binding sensations forcefully around one central passion and thus exalting the powers of our sensitivity. Sorry is the person who has never known the rough pleasure of hearing at the bottom of his being the blow of an insult and then all his nerves silently entering the rhythmic harmony of one undivided hatred! Though agitated by pleasures as de-

---

[118] *To Maître*, September 17, 1918; *C. du R.*, 33.

[119] *To Dom Besse*, August 1918; *Bul.* 11, 4.

[120] *To Maître*, August 26, 1919; *C. du R.*, 37.

[121] Bernanos is speaking of the "women of 1830—Estelle, Hermance, or Mélanie—who experienced a veritable death through the reading of verses just before going to dine at the tax collector's."—Note of the French trans.

licious as they are fugitive, let them never tire of rallying these simple
and strong convictions, because it is to these that we owe it if at times
we can see our interior unity emerge before us like a clap of thunder.[122]

The article on Léon Daudet, which appeared around this same time,
applies this ideal of a free and blazing subjectivity ("freedom of will
as foundation of human consciousness, with redeeming faith going
before it and, behind it, despair and nothingness!")[123] to define a poetics in a nutshell.

The central core, the fundamental event of such a poetics, is precisely this *concentrated and dramatic I*, which is always giving birth to
itself anew from the ashes of its sensitivity but which can then express
itself freely by means of this sensitivity since it has now overcome its
tyranny:

> The most beautiful . . . drama . . . [is] the effort of the lyrical genius
> to attain the most purely denuded moral truth through the world of
> images. Thus it is that Dante and Shakespeare assail sensitivity with fire
> and sword, not in order to draw from it haphazardly a few sublime cries,
> but to discover there the cry of nature herself, surprised at her elemental
> labor. These great visionaries call out to one another from heaven to
> heaven. Their work, stripped of all sentimentality, remains from age to
> age as changing and throbbing as life itself and appears to evolve along
> with life. Within their work, every man can bound and breathe freely.[124]

It is clear that this ideal, inspired by the Action Française, of a tragic
discipline in which the self as charioteer reined in the feelings as a
team of horses could not hold its ground for long. The ever-deeper
humiliations inflicted by Bernanos' existence robbed his ego's idol of
its crown, in order to place it on the head of grace alone. Nevertheless, although the Christian alchemy active in this life did recombine
the elements of his make-up in a different manner, it did so without
destroying them or substituting others for them. Dante and Shakespeare—to whom Balzac must be joined, from Bernanos' youth, and,
later on, Dostoyevsky—are not idle names Bernanos drops at random. They point ahead to Bernanos' own cosmic poetics, to his intimate relationship with nature (both external and internal, higher and

---

[122] *Bul.* 14, 6.
[123] Ibid., 9.
[124] Ibid., 7.

lower nature), to his ferocious rejection of everything that smacked of Jansenism or legalistic Christianity or also of a conception of the Church that would cut her off from the world. We hardly need stress this last point. Bernanos speaks witheringly about "these edifying priests whose bloodless zeal gushes inexhaustibly through endless unreadable books"[125] and who were legion in the nineteenth century, particularly in France but everywhere else in the Church as well. *The Great Fear* was one sustained invective against the "spirit of the sacristy" and the odor of shut-in Catholicism. More important to us here is the other side of the coin: the great breakthrough into the true and real world: "A poet, like a king, is at home everywhere", says Bernanos in 1927 in a conference he gave at Rouen to introduce his friend Robert Vallery-Radot. "The young artist who trembled so and looked so delicate among so many others you would have believed stronger than he but who in fact were overtaken and left behind by the event—this same young artist, with one fell blow, took his stance precisely where Gœthe wanted to see the poet: at the heart of things."[126]

This passion for the whole, for the world, for things, places Bernanos in the company of the Whitman he just mentioned; and it also makes him look at traditional classicism[127] in an ambiguous light. In the context of the modernists' abstractness, which has let go of the real world, Bernanos is an admirer of classicism: "I adore the clarity of Racine, and I detest the verses of Monsieur Cocteau in the same way that I detest a certain kind of pious, episcopal poetry, for instance, which is falsely called Catholic and is produced for exclusively clerical uses." But he goes on to say: "I love the poetry of mystery, which is a very different thing from the incomprehensible poetry of many poets of our time, who have confined themselves to pure 'logomachy'—nothing but verbal heroics."[128] This affirmation provides the background for the following admission by Vallery-Radot concerning his vain efforts to get Bernanos to appreciate Racine: "I never could make him understand Racine. One evening when I was

---

[125] *Imposture*, 70.

[126] *Bul.* 12–13, 28.

[127] In the context of French literary history, "classicism" and "the classics" normally refer to the literature of the "siècle classique," which is to say, the seventeenth century, and not to the classics of the ancient world or classics in general.—TRANS.

[128] *To Jorge de Lima*, April 1939; *Lettres inédites*, 12.

reading *Andromaque* to him, he burst into a vicious diatribe against the classics, whose only reason for existing, he insisted, was to fill the professors' breadbasket."[129] What is odious to Bernanos, however, was not the extremely formal quality of classical works: he was, after all, no destroyer of form. Detestable to him, rather, was the mummification of the classics, their forcible hibernation within the laboratories of the "science" of literature. True classicism, as shown by the first strong passage concerning Racine, is quite capable of being open to the true and the real. Hence, everything always leads back to the one alternative: the choice between a Catholic literature that is open and deeply bound to the world, or a sectarian and Jansenistic pseudoliterature that is shut off in a vacuum and has lost the world —and it is a matter of indifference whether the latter bears a clerical or a surrealistic-abstractionist stamp: "There is literature and there is literature. There is the literature of the *littérateurs*, which—like certain experiments in the chemistry lab—is constructed and deconstructed in glass jars that may be transparent but also airtight. But there is also the kind of literature that, like the perfumes of Baudelaire's *Flowers of Evil*, pierces through the glass wall of testtubes and jars and diffuses among the mass of men, there to trigger reactions that its author had never expected. This phenomenon is no longer a literary phenomenon."[130] This is where a literary work becomes Christian, and also prophetic and charismatic in the sense we have discussed: it is henceforth endowed with the power of bearing witness.

We have been continually stressing the unity of literary creation and Christian mission. But we must also remain conscious of the dangers of such an assertion, which led Kierkegaard to make a sharp dichotomy between the two. The proximity of literary inspiration and prayer can also become banalized in an intolerable manner, as is demonstrated by *Prayer and Poetry*, a key work by Bernanos' archenemy, Henri Bremond. The one thing we cannot expect from Bernanos is that he reduce to conceptual form the dialectic without which no progress can be made here. Bernanos knew this dialectic, knew it to satiety, but as something experienced by a poor man

---

[129] *Souvenirs*; in *Bul.* 1, 11.
[130] *Croix*, December 1943, 386.

who, to his distress, viewed the writer's task imposed on him as a
"dog's life". His *Humiliated Children* perhaps sheds more light on this
experience than the most accomplished formulas of dialectical theology. In this work Bernanos' meditation on the writer's task reached
its unsettling conclusion. Despite all his enthusiasm for the splendor
of the world, Bernanos remained *the* Christian writer who devoted
himself with a holy sobriety to examining the right measure of man,
something that cannot be abstracted for a single moment from the
two poles of sin and grace. What Bernanos understood by *nature*,
therefore, is never the same thing as what natural religion (and this
includes Gœthe and German idealism) has understood by it since the
time of the Renaissance:

> We do not deny the existence of mystery, but we would like to make a
> distinction between mystery and the mysterious, between true mystery
> and the unknowable and indeterminate. We think it a great misfortune
> to try to approach God, not out of a desire for the light, but out of a taste
> for the darkness, because Night is always more or less an accomplice of
> the shameful part in ourselves. . . . The fool who constructs theories
> and makes judgments may still move the Angels to pity. He is practicing
> his unreason within the space of God's mercy, as a baby relieves itself in
> its diapers. By contrast, when a cynical brute whips his fury into ecstasy
> and is panting from his exertion to enter into the great All, then heaven
> and earth are dismayed. For we French still believe that life has been
> made for man and not man for life.[131]

From this perspective we can understand Bernanos' passionate rejection of a poetry such as that of the Comtesse de Noailles, who
here naturally stands for many poets of her kind, such as Rilke, Gide,
and Valéry. Nor did Bernanos hesitate in telling her this to her face,
shortly after the publication of *Under Satan's Sun*:

> Your all too generous and all too gracious friendliness is . . . cruel with-
> out knowing it. I do not deserve it. I can no longer as much as open one
> of your books without blushing for not having let you know that, for a
> long time now, they have been my familiar enemies. With all my strength
> I thrust away all this commotion you make with your distant oceans and
> your rustling leaves. One of the goals of my life is to renounce you to-
> tally. When I say that no voice except yours brings me with more danger

---

[131] *Français*, 13–14.

the whispering of these confused noises out there—noises to which I would like to remain a stranger—I am not speaking for a public and not even for you. I am only bearing to myself a witness that in any event only I can hear. . . . When, in this or that café or literary salon, one of those despicable simpletons I know so well speaks about Nature, he is lying. *Whoever has not resisted Nature, whoever has not wrestled with it for his soul, knows absolutely nothing about what Nature is.* Our continual concern is to protect against Nature what it is its very essence to annihilate: the free human will. This has been the unimaginable paradox ever since Adam! And this tells us a great deal about what the rest of creation has become in relation to man, who is now an incomprehensible scandal in the midst of universal determinism.[132]

Even when creating literature, the Christian is not called to experience intoxication of any kind: he is called to act out of a stronger love. Everything that contributes to the person's dissolution into an anonymity within nature can only contradict the truth of existence. The greater passion Bernanos demanded in his letter to Jorge de Lima was a spiritual and not a fleshly or cosmic passion: it is the fire of the Holy Spirit, which "groans" and "smolders" not only within the children of God but in all of creation, urging on the birth of the definitive shape of the kingdom of redemption. Hence, the artist's efforts become an activity of keen renunciation, but guided by the compass that points the way to the earliest possible realization of love:

> When the moment arrives for me to sit down to work, the time of desire is past, love is dead—at least in appearance: for at times it seems to me that it has only withdrawn to the deepest part of my being, to the farthest recess of my consciousness. I no longer love my book once I have begun writing it, but I *want* it with an invincible will. And, if I may use without ridicule an expression such as this concerning works as modest as mine, I would have to say I want my book *with a tragic will*, a naked will that has been reduced to the essential, like a landscape devoured by the sun. Yes, indeed: once I begin writing a book I have already become detached from it long before, *but I write it precisely in order to recover its lost source at all costs, the movement of soul that gave it birth.*[133]

---

[132] *La Table Ronde*, April 1954, 183.

[133] *Luther*, in *Esprit*, October 1951, 435. (The italics of the final sentence are von Balthasar's; the others are the translator's.—TRANS.)

5. *The Impossible Vocation*

The young Bernanos labored under the burden of blatant self-assurance and pretension: "I write this book for me and for you—yes, for you who are reading me: for you and no one else. I swore to move you, either with friendship or with fury—what, after all, is the difference? I here give you a book bristling with life."[134] Such is the opening of *The Great Fear*, whose author wants to *émouvoir*, that is, to "touch", to "move", to "make shudder", to "put a person beside himself", and he trusts that his pen can do this. And yet, from the outset, this proud tone is but the exterior mask of an interior insecurity and even despair. Precisely what he is so proud of—his literary talent—makes him a wavering Christian: "I am very afraid of again incurring the sin of literature and of speaking too well about myself", he writes to his spiritual director. And again a few days later: "All I have at my disposal is a very poor language that is frightfully literary, a language that hangs ridiculous garlands all about the simplest and sincerest of thoughts. *Bombinantes in vacuo*, [as Saint Paul would say]: 'they make an empty noise. . . .' Nevertheless, this is the best I can offer, and there I stand babbling in the presence of the good Lord."[135] This despair, too, is perhaps nothing but vanity, and how well it fits his desire to move! Ever-deeper humiliations were required to make Bernanos expressly renounce this initial tone and attitude. At the beginning of *The Great Cemeteries* he again refers to that word *émouvoir*: "That's the way I was speaking at the time of *The Great Fear*, seven years ago. At present I'm no longer very concerned with making people 'shudder', at least not with fury."[136]

We can surely ask ourselves whether the *Cemeteries* are not in fact much more moving in their actual effect than the story of the betrayal by France. But, in his solitary exile in South America, his disorientation regarding his public led him even more deeply into the thicket of questions regarding meaning: "If I really knew for whom I am speaking in this way, I would no longer dare to do so. But I am beginning to know less and less for whom it was I spoke before, and for whom I am speaking at present. I speak like a man feeling

---

[134] *Peur*, 13.
[135] *To Dom Besse; Bul.* 11, 5.
[136] *Cimetières*, 3.

his way, and from now on no scornful smile will throw me off. And
besides, I no longer have any desire to 'move' people."[137] Bitter experiences had in the meantime taught Bernanos what it meant to be
a writer, not only in a material but also in a spiritual sense, a writer
and *nothing but* a writer, and a Christian writer to boot, a writer of
books about saints and heroes: what it meant, in other words, to be a
person who must *dream his way* to the highest reality, a person whose
only ratification within reality is his own dream. Whatever attitude
he adopted would be false. Should he join his own life to his work
as its demonstration and guarantee? But, in this case, what could be
the value of his poor life compared to that of the saints and heroes
he brought forth? Or should he keep his life for himself and separate
it completely from his work? But what could possibly be the value
of his dreams if he failed to pay for them with his own life?

The questionableness of his literary activity, however, moved to a
new depth when he inquired concerning his reader. Throughout his
life Bernanos struggled with the question of what possible readership
was ripe for him. The year 1934 found him thrashing about for a
sense of direction. He had by now reached a deadend: enthusiasm
over his first great success had waned, and his second success (the
Country Priest and the book on the Spanish Civil War) was still not
in sight. Everyone was advising him to continue along the road he
had taken and produce *de la littérature alimentaire*, "books that keep you
well-fed".[138] Was he not a writer? Should he not submit to the laws
of his profession? Was he not writing for his readers? And, beyond
this, did he not have to provide for his wife and six children? But the
price to pay was "the prostitution of our poor talents", and Bernanos
refused to pay it. Speaking about the literary profession, he writes to
his editor: "In a word, there's no success in store for us",[139] and he
tries to explain his situation to him:

> The reason for many misunderstandings is that those who love my work
> and understand it love me too, but without understanding me. People
> ascribe too much merit to what I do. Whether they are right or wrong
> in this matter, it is ridiculous to imagine me using schemes and formulas
> that are adequate at best for specialists who know how to fill orders

---

[137] *Enfants*, 258.
[138] *To a Woman Friend*, May 17, 1934; *Bul.* 2–3, 17.
[139] *To Bourdel*, October 15, 1934; *Rêve* (crit. ed.), 320.

they've been given. And I might add that such methods have nothing dishonest about them. It's just that they're beyond my reach, that's all! I come along with a Number 12 Express shotgun full of cartridges, and they want me to knock off little thrushes, arguing that these are always better than nothing. . . . It would really be too silly to have waited forty years to write *Under Satan's Sun* and then end up in the skin of a worthy gentleman *with ever so many engagements*.[140]

Half a year later, at the beginning of 1935, Bernanos wrote his publisher a whole treatise on different kinds of readerships. He distinguished between authors who write for a well-defined, preëxistent, and invariable circle of the half-educated[141] and adapt themselves to their readers' very moderate needs (as examples he mentioned at random Colette and Bordeaux, Maurois and Mauriac) and, at the opposite end, those other, rarer authors who must create their own reading public: "To be sure, this doesn't happen without difficulties. Even supposing an initial success due to the shock of surprise, the most difficult things still remain ahead, and after the honeymoon come the partial failures, the misunderstandings, the quarrels, and the reconciliations. But, through it all, the household finds its balance, and if the writer does not become discouraged, if he perseveres in the search for himself and strives to renew himself ceaselessly, then the union becomes perfect—or nearly so." Some reproached him for having "lost contact with [his] public". He replied by saying that he had to break a bone that would have set wrong; that he could not bring himself to fashion a marketable literary trick out of the genuine scandal his first three novels had provoked; and that he was restructuring his front and expected his readership to understand this as a sign of honesty.[142]

After all the acclaim surrounding the success of *The Diary of a Country Priest* had spent itself, there again set in, around 1940, the same sense of alienation from his readers. Again Bernanos became aware, with more clarity than ever, that this relationship was governed by a sort of law: "Catholic circles", he writes, "have given me what they

---

[140] *To Bourdel*, June 26, 1934; *Bul.* 2–3, 19–20.

[141] Bernanos' actual wording, which von Balthasar here paraphrases, is: "an indeterminate sort of public, educated and yet without very specific preferences."—Note of the French trans.

[142] *To Bourdel*, February 1935; *Rêve* (crit. ed.), 333–34.

can give to whoever does not flatter them: exactly nothing. Apparently they have nothing to say to a writer who, after both *Under Satan's Sun* and *The Diary of a Country Priest*, twice sacrificed the potential material profits of a great success to what he believed was his duty, a writer who twice lost—and by his own choice!—an immense public from which he could have drawn honor and fortune if he had only made a few concessions."[143] He let go of a great "public" in order to keep the small company of his friends. But did even these understand him? In many a letter he had to do battle like a Don Quixote against the illusory image of himself that they (even the best of them: Robert Vallery-Radot and Amoroso Lima) had constructed in their heads. Were these men of letters, who so delighted in reading his magnificent style, really the readers for whom he was writing? What had they to do with the small child he was, the small child whose wordless language he gropingly sought and whom he had set up as judge over all his pen-pushing? And yet, "precisely this is what makes you prick up your ears, my fellow wayfarers scattered throughout the world, you who one day opened my books haphazardly or out of boredom. What a peculiar idea, to write for those who have a disdain for all writing! What a bitter irony, to aim at persuading and convincing when my deepest certainty is that the portion of the world still capable of being redeemed belongs only to the children, the heroes, and the martyrs!"[144]

But this is not all. Bernanos was a Catholic writer; but the readers he was envisioning were not Catholics, those who were living in the light of the truth, but the others, those outside of this light:

Although a Catholic writer, I often speak to those whom Catholic writers never address. . . . These mostly speak to the well-known type of unbeliever who feels *drawn by the Church* and is continually repeating: *How lucky you are to believe! How I envy you!*, as if faith were an inexhaustible source of consolations that makes us immune to the misfortunes of this life. . . . My inclination, rather, is to write for the ill-disposed and mischievous minds. Who are these "mischievous minds" in the judgment of many Catholics? They are people whom the devil pushes to slight or misunderstand us, the believers, to deny our talents and our virtues. But, as a matter of fact, it is highly probable that a great number of

---

[143] *To Amoroso Lima*, January 1940; *Esprit*, 195.
[144] *Cimetières*, v.

these mischievous minds have nothing to do with the devil. Perhaps
it's the good Lord himself who has made them particularly sensitive to
our defects, our ridiculous stances, the often scandalous contradiction
between our principles and our lives, and to many other things besides,
in order to humble in us the pharisaical pride that has made survive
among us the synagogal spirit even after the synagogue itself has been
destroyed.[145]

We must admit, however, that, apart from its resplendent sincerity, the method Bernanos employed to address these estranged spirits
was often very paradoxical. He did not lead the recalcitrant step by
step closer to the truth: that was the clever recipe of the well-behaved
apologetics he so despised. Bernanos, rather, hurled the unbeliever directly into the—for him incomprehensible—center of things, hurled
him into what must for him have been the darkest core of the mystery
that alone casts light on all that surrounds it. Using such a method,
how could Bernanos put his hope in anything other than grace, which
can affect one hidden individual imperceptibly but could never transform an empirically tangible "community of readers"? And, if he
should happen to address the Catholics among them expressly, then
his tendency was to do it from the opposite standpoint, from the
perspective of unbelief and the world's outlook, as in that martial
"Sermon of an Unbeliever to the Catholics on the Feast of Little
Thérèse"[146] which Bernanos placed in the mouth of an "honest ag-
nostic of average intelligence" and for which he could expect little
enthusiasm from the conventional wisdom of the *bien-pensants*.

Driven into such straits from so many different sides, the work of a
writer such as Bernanos must inevitably take place under the sign of
an apparent futility with no exit in sight. What he was striving after
was surely something impossible: to build a lasting structure with the
most perishable of stones, to produce something holy and supernatural through an occupation subject to vanity like no other, and this
using a vain and unholy material: the life and substance of the writer
himself.

---

[145] *Croix*, October 1944, 447–48.
[146] *Cimetières*, 250–75.

On the one hand, Bernanos was impelled by the need to sacrifice his life totally to his literary vocation: "My books and I are one."[147] "It seems to me I've respected my vocation. . . . We must both be saved together . . . by fulfilling each other to the end."[148] "This morning I was reading *Joy* again. . . . If I really knew how to read my own books well, I would probably find prefigured in them everything that is happening or will happen to me."[149] And the life he devoted to his literary mission did indeed have to remain a genuine human life, free from the poison of literature: "I am the last person in the world to look at himself through literature. No one has a keener horror than I do of committing such a hideous equivocation."[150] And he advised his friends to take the same attitude toward him: "People take me to be a paradoxical individual, and all I am is a man with common sense."[151] And, just as real life should not become fanciful under the influence of literature, so too the literary work should not be the duplication or poor imitation of life but rather its mysterious transformation: "In my opinion, the work of the artist never is the sum total of his disillusionments, sufferings, doubts, and of all the good and evil of his life. Rather, it is his life itself, only transfigured, illuminated, reconciled."[152]

But this is precisely where the questionableness of such a prospect begins: for such a transformation can be neither understood nor experienced by the writer, nor can he expressly strive after it: "I well know that we can never taste the new wine of this reconciliation of ourselves with ourselves except after the grapes have been gathered in, just as my physical pain can last long after its cause has stopped. Having attained it at the cost of an immense effort, we continue to yearn for it even after it's been achieved. This is because our interior joy doesn't belong to us any more than the work it gives life to. We must therefore give our joy away a bit at a time, so as to die empty, so as to die like newborns."[153] Here again we confront the mystery of mortal agony and rebirth, death and childhood, as the true locus

---

[147] *To Amoroso Lima,* March 5, 1939; *Esprit,* 190.
[148] Ibid., March 13, 1940; *Esprit,* 202.
[149] July 8, 1934; *Bernanos,* 162.
[150] *To Vallery-Radot,* January 17, 1926; *Bul.* 1, 3.
[151] *To Bourdel,* February 1935; *Rêve* (crit. ed.), 335.
[152] *To Michaelis; C. du R.,* 49.
[153] Ibid., 49.

beyond all other experiences, for the sake of which our life must be surrendered; and this sacrifice, which empties out our life, at the same time fills up the mission, which in the case of the artist is one and the same as his work. However, the Christian mystery of death and resurrection (which, according to Paul, occurs on a daily basis) cannot be resolved on this earth, because, when a person is doing the dying, he cannot feel that he is at the same time rising from death, and the person who has risen with Christ cannot feel that he no longer dies, although, even as he dies, he lives in the faith of the Resurrection. For this same reason, for the artist the relationship between his life and his work remains rationally irresolvable: "I do not pretend to justify my books with my life, or my life with my books."[154] What Bernanos was, therefore, was not a saint, not an extraordinary man, but only a writer! And when he gave himself, what was it he was giving? What are we being enriched with?

> Every writer, at one time or another, must have felt what I feel: the prick of an unrightable blunder. But he has felt it only to dismiss it at once. "At bottom", they will say, "you are complaining because Mouchette will never read the *Story of Mouchette*. Stop the farce! Did you really write it for her? . . ." I don't know what to answer. My misfortune is precisely not being able to answer. I chose to walk down a street with no exit, but I didn't know it had no exit. But I won't tire of trying to find one. The others have long since accepted the situation. "We'll never come out of it? All right, then. Let us make ourselves at home. Only, let's get organized!" I'm quite ready to accept not being heard by anyone on the other side of the wall, but I don't accept people thinking that I'm comfortably settled in my solitude.

There then follows an invective against Claudel, who had created a very comfortable artist's existence for himself as a successful author holding government posts as a diplomat and directorships of literary societies:

> "What do you mean, then?", they will again object. "What you want is for Monsieur Paul Claudel to be the man of his books? Are you the man of yours? Are you the country priest, or Donissan, or Chantal?" I am not the man of my books, but at least I don't lie to my books. My life does not lie to my books: my life says nothing, my life keeps silent. . . .

---

[154] *Enfants*, 205.

My life does not disturb my books. She[155] sits in her corner, knitting by the fire. Now and then she pushes back into the fireplace with her foot the log that rolls off. She watches over the family's pot of soup and tries not to cry until the day's done and everybody is in bed.[156]

The "old man who daily dies" experiences every possible manner of humiliation; but he must not renounce this daily suffering unto death under the pretext that what is here dying is in any event no longer worth anything.

And the person who is humiliated in this way in his life will also be so in his work. With what ambitions the young Bernanos had made his debut as writer! What pride quivers throughout his first articles and even in his first fictional masterpieces! The mature man, by contrast, saw before him the fragmentary pile of what he had done: half of it novels, half of it critical works. Where was the totality, the integrated whole?

Take into account, you my dear old companions, that the good Lord gave me only this one means of moving (*émouvoir*) you to sympathize with the things I love. The only instrument I deserved was this street organ[157] I'm playing underneath your windows. When I was still young, I did now and then turn the handle with my fingertips, bending down my head a bit too dramatically toward my poor little grind-mill. This is over now. . . . I can no longer take this object to be a masterpiece of instrument making. I've been carrying it around for too long. The strap is cutting into my shoulder. I'll continue to grind until the mill is empty, and that's all. I'll give it back to God empty, and I'll even try to polish it carefully one last time before I die, not in the hope of impressing the heavenly musicians, but for the honor of the profession. . . . The old boy has changed sidewalks; the old boy has changed sidewalks with the concierges and the cops. . . . I'll conclude my career as devoted street singer in a country without streets or roads—unless perhaps you think you can still hear me. For, you see, it isn't my song that's immortal but what I sing about.[158]

---

[155] The feminine personification comes more naturally in French, since "my life", *ma vie*, is a feminine noun.—TRANS.

[156] *Enfants*, 205-9.

[157] The French for "street organ", *orgue de Barbarie*, gives Bernanos the occasion for evoking, with gentle self-deprecation, what he considers to be the rough and primitive qualities of his work.—TRANS.

[158] *Enfants*, 189-90.

And then Bernanos holds before us the deeply moving final image of *The Humiliated Children*. The author contemplates his cottage in Brazil, and it becomes a symbol for the "open house" his life has been. Many strangers pass by and take a look inside:

> My house is surely not what they expect, but it belongs to them. It is open. I'm happy that I built my life so poorly that anyone can just walk in as you would into a windmill. And, if I may be allowed to continue the comparison, I would add that I don't regret having gone such a long way across the sea, because in this country I've found, if not the house of my dreams, at least the house that best fits my life, a house made for my life. Its doors have no locks, its windows no panes, its bedrooms no ceiling, and the lack of a ceiling makes it possible to discover in it everything that in other houses remains hidden: what the backside of the beams, girders, and rafters really looks like; the pink-spotted pale grayish gold of the smooth, worn tiles; the thick patches of shadow that the daylight can barely gnaw at and that seem to grow even blacker in the light of our lamps; the uneven ridge of the walls where phantom rats run, nowhere else to be seen and strangely respecting our corn and manioc; the extravagant bats and those enormous black May-bugs, armored with black steel and yet so fragile that the least drop of insecticide hurls them to the ground like bullets, stone dead. Of such a house I suppose one could say it is an open house! . . . We are in the hands of every passerby just as we are in the hands of God. And may we—my books and I—always, together, remain at the mercy of every passerby![159]

---

[159] Ibid., 209–11.

PART TWO

The Church:
a Place for Living

I. COSMOS AND SALVATION

1. Man

We have now surveyed the whole space defined by Georges Bernanos' existence. In every respect we have seen his life to be a permanent striving toward the ever-greater truth. To the same degree that he continuously cast his life and the full weight of his person into the balance, he also denied, ceaselessly and emphatically, that he could in any sense himself be the truth. What shimmers in his face is only the reflection of the fire itself. What man is cannot be told from "reading" him, unless we mean that a truth, although not his own, merely becomes illuminated through Bernanos. This truth is Christ: creation belongs to him as God-Man and Redeemer, and he has impressed the seal of his lordship deep into the innermost being of creatures. And on this earth the visible and symbolic realm of his lordship is the Church, which will be the central theme of this second part of our study.

Christ, however, is not only Lord of the Church. He is also Lord of the world and of man. All power has been given to him in heaven and on earth. Everything was made in him and for him, and by him was everything redeemed. His Kingdom is boundless, while Peter's kingdom comes up against painful boundaries. Because Christ is Lord of the wolves as much as of the sheep, he can send the sheep out into the midst of danger and death, and yet not "one hair on their head is touched" despite all torture and persecution. If the Christian dares to address boldly the darkness of a world that has turned its back on God, it is by the power of this universal dominion of Christ and not on the general basis of a conventional humanism. And, in so doing, the Christian directs the world not only to the Lord of Glory but also to the Son of Man. Having lost all communication with sinners, the Son of Man descended into the abyss, and there, on its impracticable and lost roads, he created paths through the most impassable terrain precisely through his own walking, slipping, and falling. He is himself the Way, and, as Truth, he is also the instruction on how this Way

217

is to be walked. The resistance that sin puts up against him can be resolved nowhere but in himself.

> For as long as the passing of the ages does not modify its characteristics, an animal species is born, lives, and dies according to its own laws, and the part assigned to it in the immense drama of creation consists of only one role, which is indefinitely repeated. Our own species too, to be sure, does not escape this monotonous law of gravitation. It revolves around its immutable destiny like a planet around the sun. And yet, also like this planet, our species is all the time being borne along with its sun toward an invisible star. It is not its destiny that makes it mysterious but its vocation. For this reason, the historians do not really know very much about its actual history. When confronting our race, historians are very much like a theater critic in the presence of an actor about whose private life he knows absolutely nothing. The same actress may play Rosine at an interval of twenty years, and it's still the real Rosine. But the adolescent actress has become a woman.[1]

Much to the comfort of those who fear relativism more than the deadly rigidity of concepts, the so-called (physical) "nature" of man can be considered immutable; but the concrete "essence" or "idea" that the living Creator entertains concerning his living creature, and which both Creator and creature together unfold within a living history—*this* may be understood only through the *kairos* of time:

> I believe this world will end one day. I believe that our species, as it moves toward its end, retains in the depths of its consciousness much to throw off the psychologists, the moralists, and other such ink-lapping brutes.[2] It would seem that what really rules our affective life is the foreboding of death. What, then, will happen to our affective life when death's foreboding will have been replaced by the presentiment of the catastrophe that is to swallow up our whole species? Clearly, our old vocabulary will come in handy. Don't we use the same word "love" to refer both to the desire that makes two young lovers join their trembling hands and to the black whirlpool into which Phædra falls with arms outstretched and howling like a she-wolf?[3]

---

[1] *Cimetières*, 85–86.

[2] Bernanos here has the nearly untranslatable "*et autres bêtes à encre*", a satirical phrase mocking the self-appointed scientific "experts of the soul" with all their theories and analyses.—TRANS.

[3] *Cimetières*, 86.

Bernanos feels his tentative way along human "nature" by groping with the modality of man today, affected as he is by a sense of
his destined end, a sense of a line of death leading directly to an approaching eternity, a sense of the immanence of dying in every moment of his life. Bernanos has no access to "human nature" other
than the sobering experience of man as he encounters him in the
present, man at a moment in his history when more than ever he is
called upon to decide absolutely for or against God. Twentieth-century
man, in Bernanos' view, has been deprived of the possibility of assuming a stance of philosophical neutrality by finding a center within
himself:

> Many a priest doesn't even dare pronounce the name of the devil. What
> have they made of the interior life? The dreary battlefield of the instincts.
> What have they made of morality? A hygiene of the senses. Grace is no
> longer anything but a way to reason fairly and appeal to the intellect.
> Temptation is a carnal appetite that tends to bribe the intellect. With such
> views they can barely account for even the most superficial episodes of
> the great battle being waged within us. Man is said to search only for the
> pleasant and the useful, with his conscience guiding his choices. This is
> good for the abstract man we find only in books, that "average man" who
> is in fact nowhere to be found in reality! Such childish notions actually
> explain nothing. In such a universe of sensible, reasoning animals, there
> is nothing left for the saint, except perhaps to convict him of madness.
> And, naturally, this too is already being done. But this doesn't solve the
> problem. Each of us—oh, if you could only remember these words of
> an old friend!—each of us is in some way or another, and in succession,
> a criminal and a saint. At one moment we are impelled toward the good,
> not by a careful examination of its advantages, but, clearly and strangely,
> by an impulse of our whole being, by an outpouring of love that makes
> suffering and renunciation the very object of our desire. The next mo-
> ment we are tormented by a mysterious taste for self-degradation, for
> delights that taste of ashes, for the vertigo of animality and an incom-
> prehensible nostalgia for it. Why, what possible difference can then be
> made by the experience of the moral life, accumulated over the centuries?
> What difference can then be made by recalling the example of so many
> wretched sinners and their distress? Yes, my child, remember this: evil,
> like goodness, is loved and served for its own sake.[4]

---

[4] *Soleil,* 232–33.

But when man has no center in himself, then the double abyss surrounding him above and below is in reality one and the same: man is the creature designed to designate God, the creature hurled in the direction of God,[5] and only his fear of so excessive a goal, only his will not to move in such a direction, opens up under him the other abyss: "It is this despair [of himself] that leads man to degrade and debase himself, as if to inflict vengeance on himself, inflict vengeance on his immortal soul."[6] The possibility of an internal contradiction in man first arises because man in reality is more and must be more than simply himself (his "nature"), and when man denies this his destiny, then he is actually trying to abolish himself:

> There is in man a secret, incomprehensible hatred, not only of his fellowmen, but of himself. We can give this mysterious feeling whatever origin or explanation we want, but we must give it one. As far as we Christians are concerned, we believe that this hatred reflects another hatred, a thousand times more profound and lucid: the hatred of the ineffable spirit who was the most resplendent of all the luminaries of the abyss and who will never forgive us his cataclysmic fall. Outside the hypothesis of an original sin, that is, of an intrinsic contradiction within our nature, the notion of man does become quite clear, only it is no longer the notion *of man*. When this occurs, man has gone straight through the definition of man, like a handful of sand running between his fingers.[7]

Bernanos has no thought of doing away with the "nature" of man in Jansenistic fashion. After all, who has exalted man's innate and natural freedom more than he? Nevertheless, he cannot tolerate our thinking about man for a single instant bereft of his supernatural and "superhuman" divine goal: "Paganism was not the enemy of nature, but only Christianity can enhance and exalt nature, only Christianity can raise nature to the true measure of man and of man's dream."[8] "We can even say that Christianity divinizes man. . . . Whoever claims to belong only to a human order will sooner or later fall under the unshakable law of the juggernaut State. Whoever awaits the arrival only

---

[5] Von Balthasar here has a play of words difficult to translate: "*Der Mensch ist der auf Gott hin Entworfene und Geworfene.*"—TRANS.

[6] *Robots*, 64.

[7] *Liberté*, 252–53.

[8] *Curé*, 29.

of the kingdom of man will find himself deprived of the Kingdom of God, which is to say, deprived of justice, because man's triumph in this world can be obtained only by means of a pitiless discipline."[9] The "natural vocation of man" cannot be separated from his "supernatural vocation".[10] Man remains a puzzle without solution if he is not seen and understood in God:

> Are they really so certain of what they have stretched out before them, there on their operating table? What if man were not what they believe? What if one day their definition of man turned out to be false or incomplete? . . . What if man were really created in the image of God? If there is indeed in man even a small measure of freedom, no matter how small we imagine it, what would be the result of their experiments other than the mutilation of an essential organ? What if there did exist in man this principle of self-destruction, this mysterious hatred of self we call original sin and which their technicians have not failed to note since it explains all the awful disappointments of history? It's true that they chalk this up, not to man, but to a bad organization of the world. But what if they were wrong? What if injustice resided within man himself and all external constraints did nothing but reinforce its evil-mindedness? *What if man could become fulfilled only in God?* What if the delicate operation of amputating his divine part—or at least of atrophying this part systematically until it falls off withered, like an organ in which the blood no longer circulates—what if this operation resulted in turning man into a ferocious beast? Or, even worse perhaps, into a permanently domesticated beast? Or even less: into an abnormal, deranged being?[11]

Bernanos is not content with considering this loss of the sense of man as theoretically possible; he goes about verifying it precisely in his time through personal experience. A "hardening", a "stiffening", a "sclerosis in men's consciences", the "drying up of the deep wellsprings of the soul": such is the "universal phenomenon" he cannot avoid acknowledging in his day "with a heartfelt and almost religious anguish, with a sacred awe". And he exclaims: "God is leaving, God is withdrawing from us. How empty and, at the same time, how heavy he leaves us!" There was a time when we "were lighter and freer", and this "even in the midst of error, sin, and injustice", because "this

---

[9] *Anglais*, 248.
[10] *Robots*, 44–45.
[11] *Liberté*, 154. (The italics are von Balthasar's.—TRANS.)

interior freedom was himself. We have lost it, and along with it we
have lost God, and to recover it we will have to do more than desire
it again, or whimper over its loss, or search in the pharisaism of social
justice for a type of alibi that can by no means fool God."[12]

The kingdom of enforced immanence, reigning in an amputated
nature, is for Bernanos identical with the harshness and inhumanity
of tyranny. This is why he is such a declared enemy of both brown
and red totalitarianism, as also of the democratic ideologies that prepared the way for them. Only where man understands himself by
reference to God are human dignity and culture possible: "A civilization disappears with the kind of man, the type of humanity, that has
issued from it."[13] Now, the mysterious peak whereby man surpasses
the world and nature, and which at once constitutes both his most
external and most internal reality, has three names in Bernanos, which
interpenetrate and point one to the other: *freedom, love, simplicity.*

Freedom and love are one and the same, "because there is no responsibility without freedom, and love is a free choice or it is nothing".[14] God himself is nothing but the abyss of an incomprehensible
and free choice of love. And, thus, the creation too is above all "an act
of love" and not of reason or justice; and whoever would approach
creation, with its "moaning of universal suffering that is not silent
by day or by night", on the basis of either reason or justice must
necessarily founder and become enraged against the injustice of the
Creator of the world: "You rebel against the cruelty of this world in
the name of reason and justice. And, indeed, a long experience has
shown that this path will lead you only to revolt, despair, or absolute
negation."[15] Only love can understand love; mere intellect, wanting
to proceed on the basis of mere logic, must necessarily result in re-
bellion against God, in negation of God. Bernanos knows whereof he
speaks, and in saying these things he does not want to be confused
with Protestants or Jansenists: If it is true that we are created in the
image of God,

---

[12] Ibid., 186–87.
[13] *Robots,* 57.
[14] *Liberté,* 274.
[15] Ibid., 276.

how could we possibly disdain [the intellect], one of man's highest faculties? You reply that, without expressly disdaining it, I have just declared it powerless. Not at all. [The intellect] is not powerless. It is not
powerless to draw certain advantages from creation, but it is incapable
of penetrating its deepest meaning, incapable of "com-prehending" or
embracing it in the literal sense of the word. If creation were the work
only of [divine] intelligence, then human intelligence could do nothing
better than discover a few of its laws. . . . Creation is a work of love. Reduced to its own forces, the intelligence thinks that all it finds in nature
is indifference and cruelty; but it's its own cruelty it's discovering there.
Properly speaking, it isn't suffering as such the intelligence is condemn-
ing but what appears to it to be an anomaly, a waste, a bad organization
of suffering. The intelligence is crueler than nature [left to its own laws
and devices, the intelligence will attempt to wipe out those who suffer
as miscarried examples of humanity]. In reality, the intelligence does not
grow indignant over suffering; rather, it rejects suffering just as it rejects
a badly constructed syllogism, which nevertheless the intelligence may
later on itself use according to its methods once it has corrected the
errors in the syllogism. Whoever speaks of Suffering as an intolerable
violation of the soul or, simply, as a fundamental absurdity is sure to
receive the approval of imbeciles. But, compared to the small number of
those who experience a sincere revolt, how many others are there who,
in their revolt against suffering, are only looking for a more or less sly
justification for their own indifference and selfishness in the face of those
who suffer? If this were not so, then by what miracle does it happen that
precisely those who accept the most humbly, and without understanding
it, the permanent scandal of suffering and misery are almost always the
very same ones who devote themselves the most tenderly to the care of
the suffering and the miserable, for instance, Saint Francis of Assisi and
Saint Vincent de Paul?[16]

No: "the scandal of the universe is not suffering but freedom",[17] and
freedom cannot be explained at the level of mere reason but only at
the level of love, and indeed not of a mental love but of a simply
loving love, or, what amounts to the same, at the level of sanctity.
This is the source of all miracles: "Everything truly beautiful in the
history of the world happens unbeknownst to us through the mysterious accord of man's humble and ardent patience with the sweet

---

[16] Ibid., 278–80.
[17] Ibid., 280.

mercy of God. . . . We must all 'overcome' life. But the only way of overcoming life is to love it."[18]

The encounter of these two things, however—of the gentle patience of the suffering man with the gentle mercy of God—is the encounter of the two individuals who can understand one another, whose adequacy for one another reaches over all else, and this in the abyss of the mystery of freedom and love, in whose darkening depths suffering makes its home. At this level, everything remains incomprehensible for the nonsuffering intellect; but it is precisely here that the day of ultimate reason begins to dawn:

> At this very moment somewhere in the world, in a corner of some lost church, or even in some ordinary house, or at the turning of some deserted road, there is a poor man joining his hands and, from the depths of his misery and not fully aware of what he is saying, or without saying anything, he is thanking the good Lord for having made him free, for having made him capable of loving. And somewhere else, I don't know where, there is a mother hiding her face for the last time in a little chest that will no longer throb with life, a mother by her dead child, offering up to God the moaning of her exhausted resignation; and it is as if the Voice that hurled the suns out into the vast stretches of space as a hand hurls out grain, as if the Voice that makes the worlds tremble, had just whispered gently in her ear: "Forgive me. One day you will know, you will understand, you will thank me. Right now the only thing I expect from you is your forgiveness. Forgive me." These two, the exhausted mother and the poor man, are located at the very heart of the mystery, at the heart of universal creation, enfolded in the very secret of God. What can I tell you about it? Language is at the service of the intellect. And what these two persons have understood, they have understood by a faculty superior to the intellect, although not at all in contradiction to it; or, rather, they have understood it by a deep and irresistible movement of the soul that engaged all its faculties at once, that engaged their whole nature at its very depths. . . . Yes: at the moment when this man and this woman accepted their destiny and accepted themselves, ever so humbly, the mystery of creation was being enacted in them. By thus running, without knowing it, the full risk of their human conduct, they were experiencing total fulfillment in the charity of Christ and themselves becoming "other Christs", according to Saint Paul's expression. In a word, they were saints.—To engage one's whole being: what a prospect! It's

---

[18] *Sur un album*; in *Bul.* 12–13, 4.

no secret that, in our life, most of us engage only a very slender part, a ridiculously small part of our being, like those fabulously wealthy misers who formerly were thought to spend only the profits generated by their income. A saint does not live on the profits generated by his income, or even on his income alone. He lives on his capital, he engages his soul totally. This is what makes the saint different from the merely wise man, who secretes his wisdom as a snail secretes its shell—only in order to find shelter within it. . . . We say to ourselves with horror that countless men are born, live, and die without having used their soul one single time, really *used* their soul, even if only to offend the good Lord. . . . Could Damnation perhaps consist in discovering too late—much too late, after death—that one has a soul that has lain absolutely unused, in discovering it still carefully folded into four, and ruined, like certain precious silks, through lack of use? Whoever uses his soul, regardless of how awkwardly, is by that very fact already participating in universal Life. He is entering into harmony with the tremendous rhythm of this Life, and by the same token he is entering straightaway into the communion of saints, which is that of all men of good will to whom Peace has been promised—the invisible Church about which we know that she includes pagans, heretics, schismatics, and unbelievers whose names God alone knows.[19]

Never has Bernanos been more inspired when speaking about the mystery of freedom as love. Never has he demonstrated with more mastery how little he has to do with Jansenism or Manichaeism and, although he forcefully rejected its diluted forms, how much he stands in the most sterling tradition of Christian humanism, which runs from the Fathers through Thomas Aquinas all the way to Corneille, Newman, and Péguy. In this tradition, there is no such thing as a genius who has no love. Man may continue to be called a "rational animal", but only on condition we acknowledge that the full idea of *ratio* can unfold only within the free venture of love and that this love is nothing other than sanctity! Then, and only then, can humanism come to be one with the flame of the gospel:

Those who have such difficulty understanding our faith are those who have formed only a very imperfect idea of man's eminent dignity within creation, those who do not put man in his place within creation, in the place to which God raised him in order to be able to come down to him

---

[19] *Liberté*, 280–83.

there. We have been created in the image and likeness of God because we are capable of loving. The saints have a genius for love. But do please note that this particular genius is not like that of the artist, for instance, which is the privilege of a very small number of people. It would be more precise to say that the saint is the man who knows how to find within himself—and make well up from within the depths of his being—the water of which Christ spoke to the Samaritan woman: *Those who drink of it shall never thirst again. . . .* It is there inside each one of us, this deep cistern open to the heavens. Its surface is indeed cluttered with refuse, broken branches, and dead leaves that give off the stench of death. On it beams the cold and harsh spotlight of the reasoning intellect. But, underneath this diseased layer, the water at once becomes ever so limpid and pure! Still a little deeper down, the soul finds itself in its native element, infinitely more pure than the purest of waters: the uncreated Light that bathes the whole of creation—in him was life, and this life was the light of men.[20]

Here, the purest characteristic of the spirit's essence is revealed: its singleness, or *simplicity*. Bernanos can never praise it enough. Without his quite knowing it, this conviction inserts him into a tradition that leads from the Gospel to the Neoplatonic Fathers with their concept of *heniaiôs*, to medieval mysticism and the spirituality of the seventeenth century, down to Bernanos himself, who quite simply returns to the Gospel. The true depth of the soul, which has become blocked by all sorts of clutter, is its unity, while sin in its essence is multiplicity and dispersion. "There is only one order: the order of charity."[21] Charity, divine love, in the end orders and unifies man, not with a view to his own unity but aiming at the unity of God himself. Such is the very mystery of holiness: "It is so difficult to be simple! But worldly people say *the simple* in the same way they say *the humble*, with the same condescending smile. What they should say is: *the kings.*"[22]

The secret of all Bernanos' saints lies in this seamless unity of supernatural and childlike singleness and simplicity: "You were simple then, and you've remained simple", Cénabre says to Chantal. "Few simple beings exist. We should say of simplicity what the Jews used to say of Yahweh: Whoever sees it face to face risks death!"[23] And

---

[20] Ibid., 287.
[21] *Curé,* 167.
[22] Ibid., 303.
[23] *Joie,* 271.

the country priest writes: "The holiness of God! The simplicity of God, the terrible simplicity of God, which damned the pride of the Angels! Yes, the demon must have attempted to see it face to face, and he, the magnificent flaming torch at the very peak of creation, plunged in one swoop into the night."[24] The holy man is all aglow with this blinding simplicity that no creature can look upon. Bernanos describes the young Chantal in terms of "the extreme supernatural simplicity of her life, the hiddenness of her devotion, her naïve horror of all confusion, disorder, and of everything that can disturb the clean sincerity of words, acts, and intentions."[25] "Chantal's only craft is . . . a devastating simplicity. The weak man and the impostor are always more complicated than the problem they want to solve, and, thinking they are surrounding their adversary, they gnaw interminably all around their own person. By contrast, the heroic will throws itself into the very heart of danger and makes good use of it, just as a good strategist turns around the enemy's abandoned artillery to strike the fleeing troops in the back."[26]

This is why the ideal is never self-knowledge, which in any event is not possible, but on the contrary an ultimate looking away from self. "No one but I", says Cénabre to Chantal, "can help you see clearly within yourself." But the girl replies at once: "I no longer need to see clearly within myself. It's too late for that. What does it matter to me what I am and what I am not? . . . The closer I get to the goal, the less I desire to know this."[27] And, if Cénabre's ultimate sin consisted in his wanting to investigate the mystery of the saints by means of a curiosity devoid of love (that is, devoid of the spirit of simplicity), then the ultimate grace of the saint is that curiosity can only ricochet off the shield of his simplicity and shatter into fragments: "All of a sudden, however, this curiosity tasted disappointment since it remained without an object. Chantal's slender and contracted little figure now only expressed a resignation that was so humble and mysterious that he began to feel a kind of terror. The word he was about to utter suddenly withered on his lips."[28]

[24] *Curé*, 230.
[25] *Joie*, 62–63.
[26] Ibid., 131–32.
[27] Ibid., 277.
[28] Ibid., 282–83.

The whole secret of *Joy*, moreover, is surely that Chantal—although immersed without knowing it in the abyss of God's simplicity—is wrenched from this holy shelter by the complicated sin she wishes to take upon herself, and she is dragged into an environment wholly alien to her in which she can only be a victim. But it is Chantal's secret that, even in an atmosphere of sin and of clever and cynical machinations, she can, by the power of her simplicity, remain the dominant character who knows how to defeat her enemies—apparently with their own weapons but in reality with a superior secret weapon. Or, as Bernanos wrote to a religious shortly before his own death: "It's true that the Gospel is written for *the simple*, and that only simplicity gains us access to it. But, if there do exist souls who have received the gift of simplicity, there are many others who have not received it. So, for the sake of these, it is perhaps good to make oneself complicated in order to lead them elsewhere little by little."[29] It belongs to the "economy" of simplicity (in the old theological sense of the term) that it can take on the form of sin and the form of the reflective intellect without losing itself.

Now, there exists another name for simplicity, for a divine quality communicated to us by grace that is defined by the singleness and seamlessness of the divine Being: this other name is *purity*. The Middle Ages spoke of the "pure" Being of God. But, in man, purity is a quality that can be conceived only as applying to the totality of man's being, consisting of both body and soul. In its specific form as chastity, purity is the precondition for the simplicity characteristic of the person who can and wants to know himself, not in himself, but in God. Impurity and unchasteness are not merely (as Thomas Aquinas usually describes them) an external obstacle to pure knowledge untroubled by the senses; they are, in fact, the internal destruction of the light that shines only in God. Unchasteness, according to the country priest's profound meditations, is secretly the same thing as unbelief, for faith is the evidence and knowledge of things in God, not in man himself, while unchasteness is one and the same as the curiosity to know oneself and all things only in oneself, a truth about which Freud has taught us a great deal. Unchasteness is also one with madness, because reason remains intact only when it transcends itself

---

[29] *To a Priest*, August, 1947; *C. du R.*, 57.

in the direction of God. The abuse of the sexual faculty for loveless
self-enjoyment presupposes, as a basic spiritual attitude, the abuse of
the rational faculty for loveless self-knowledge, and this can be nothing other than madness: "I have not lost my faith, because God has
deigned to preserve me from impurity. Such a comparison, alas, would
probably make the philosophers smile! And it's obvious that the most
disorderly of personal lives could not put a reasonable man so far off
course that he would, for example, begin to doubt the truth of certain axioms in geometry. But there is an exception: madness. After
all, what do we know about madness? What do we know about lust?
And what do we know about the secret dealings between these two
things?"[30] The Curé d'Ambricourt then reminisces about his youth
as a very poor boy, about all the abominations he witnessed: "What
would have been the use of *understanding* these things? I had seen them.
You don't understand lust; you *see* it. I had seen those wild faces, suddenly frozen into an indefinable smile. Dear God! Why don't we realize more often that the mask of pleasure, stripped of all hypocrisy,
is precisely the mask of anguish? . . . What if madness and lust were
really one and the same thing?"[31]

Sitting in his confessional, a priest can be overcome "as by a kind
of vertigo" by those eternally identical whisperings that are "like the
writhing of worms and the stench of the grave": "The image of a
perpetually open wound emerges, through which the substance of our
wretched species is flowing out. What accomplishments could man's
brain not have attained if the poisonous fly [of lust] hadn't laid its larva
within it!" Neither Bernanos nor his hero, however, can be accused
of prudery or, what amounts to the same thing, of sexual obsession.
No one has dealt with this theme more soberly than our author. This
gives him the right to call things by their name: "Whoever has any
experience of sin cannot ignore the fact . . . that lust is constantly
threatening to smother both virility and intelligence under its para-
sitic vegetation and hideous luxuriance. Since it can create nothing,
lust is reduced to staining—in its very seed—the frail promise of
humanity. Lust is probably at the origin, at the very source, of all
the blemishes of our race." And the young priest concludes with this
decisive insight:

---

[30] *Curé*, 140.
[31] Ibid., 140–41.

Purity is not something prescribed for us like a punishment. Experience shows that it is one of the mysterious but self-evident conditions for that supernatural knowledge of oneself—of oneself in God—which is called faith. Impurity does not destroy this knowledge; rather, it abolishes the need for it. You no longer believe because you no longer desire to believe. You no longer desire to know yourself truly. This profound truth —the truth about yourself—no longer interests you. And it is useless to say that the dogmas that only yesterday had your assent are still present in your mind, that only reason rejects them. What's the difference, if we can only really possess what we desire? This is so because for man there is no such thing as total and absolute possession of anything. You no longer desire. You no longer desire your joy. You could only love yourself in God, so now you no longer love yourself.[32]

Thus, only faith is truly an act involving the whole of man: it is not a transcendence of the spirit over the body; it is an act whereby both the body and the spirit, together, transcend toward God. We can, then, understand the following reflection, which the country priest interjects in the midst of his dark night of the soul, when he feels his faith is wholly hidden or even that it has been taken from him: "At times it seems to me that [my faith] has withdrawn, that it's subsisting in a place where I wouldn't have looked for it—in my flesh, in my wretched flesh, in my blood and in my flesh, my perishable but baptized flesh."[33]

All of this explains why Bernanos, as also Claudel, thunders so loudly against the alleged ideal of *self-knowledge*. The only true self-knowledge occurs in God, and there man does not see himself but, through faith, God. This vision of God is the truth of what man is. To look back upon himself is already untruth, impurity. This is a constant theme in the letters,[34] and it is precisely the idea Bernanos is portraying in the figure of little Chantal.[35]

Bernanos provides the check test of this truth by a ruthless analysis exposing the folly of the "cult of personality":

---

[32] Ibid., 142–43.
[33] Ibid., 138.
[34] See above, 161f.
[35] See *Joie*, 277.

Monsieur Massis is very excusable, and perhaps even deserves our esteem, for having entered a marriage with himself the moment he left his
childhood, under the species[36] of Pascal or at least of some other worthy
citizen of Port-Royal. Similarly, and around the same age, Monsieur de
Montherlant glued himself to some grandee bent on anarchy and misog-
yny, who had perhaps borrowed his face and bearing from his first Jesuit
confessor. It is I who am mad to think that these bizarre couples are,
in fact, but single beings, mad to denounce them as impostors, when in
actuality I am standing before two unfortunates: having been born more
or less devoid of all deep sincerity, these have worked on themselves for
twenty years to fashion a semblance of sincerity through the trickery
of an imaginary personality, from which they surely expect in return
the kind of security the slave receives from his master, and at the same
price.[37]

(It is significant in this connection that, in a letter that signals the
lowest point of his despair and self-reproach, our author expresses the
desire to dissolve the troubled marriage of Georges Bernanos with
"Bernanos Georges".)[38] "Personality development" as an ideal is not
only a lie; it is also an enslavement, for freedom is to be found in
God alone, in the Infinite One, who delivers us through love from
the chains and dungeons of our finitude and hence gives us the only
possibility of moving, not toward a permanent end, but toward a new
beginning. The anthropology Bernanos here sketches culminates in a
teaching concerning true and false time: on the one hand, theological
and christological time as open-endedness into the future and, on the
other hand, immanent and finite time that is wholly subject to an
inexorable end.

Toward the end of his own life, Bernanos considered his situation
as follows:

The time is past for me to go any farther. Where would I go? The only
thing that matters any more at my age is not to go backward. . . . The
idea of going backward inspires me with a feeling different from noble

---

[36] By using the technical theological word *species* here, Bernanos indicates that the stu-
diously self-created persona of a Massis and a de Montherlant amounts, at the spiritual level,
to an unholy and willful parody of the genuinely redeeming miracle of transubstantiation,
whereby Christ is truly present "under the species" (or appearances) of bread and wine, in
order to become the eternal nourishment of man.—TRANS.

[37] *Enfants*, 114–15.

[38] *To Vallery-Radot*, September 1933.

indignation. It frightens me. If I stride toward my end, like everyone else, it's with my face turned toward what is beginning, what doesn't cease beginning, what, once begun, never begins again. O victory! Every step backward brings me closer to death, or to what we are barely allowed to call by this name—the only thing that may be feared by a free man whose chains Christ has shattered: the fatalism of failed and lost lives, destiny, fate, all the world's determinisms together—those of blood, race, habits, and also those of our own errors and faults, the Fatalism that no one escapes except by casting himself forward. I know I'm not one who has cast himself forward more often than anyone else; but I've never believed I've arrived, and perhaps I'm actually farther away than I think.[39]

Here there yet again emerges the image of the young boy and the endless road on which he is walking. He has set out, will not turn back, and does not know whether the road has an end. This is the road on which all of them are walking—both the good and the evil characters, and Bernanos himself in their midst. Already in his first book, toward the very beginning, this is Bernanos' image of man:

It's from there it set out, and it went farther than the Indies. . . . Happily, for Christopher Columbus, the earth is round: no sooner had the legendary caravel lifted anchor than it was already on the return route. . . . But another route can always be attempted—straight, unveering, which always moves farther away and from which no one returns. If Germaine, or those who will follow her in the future, could speak, they would say: "What's the use of setting out once and for all on your good road, which leads nowhere? . . . What do you expect me to do with a universe that is round as a ball of thread?" Such and such a person seemed born for a quiet life, and yet a tragic destiny awaited him. We call this a surprising and unforeseeable development. . . . But "developments" are nothing: the tragic element lay in that person's heart.[40]

But this element, which is here called tragic because it shatters a person's peace, is always in Bernanos precisely the element that redeems and confers bliss. The truly evil person is in the end only a caricature of the saint whose "chains Christ shattered" so that, along his endless road, he might be able to find God, and his fellowman in God:

[39] *Enfants*, 107–8.
[40] *Soleil*, 18–19.

Indeed, all of you imagine that the only natural thing is the search for pleasure. But this, my dear fellow, is a childish point of view. I think a person should, on the contrary, go beyond himself and renounce himself. You did renounce yourself once and for all, even though I must admit it was painless! The fact still remains, however, that a truly superior man has a natural tendency toward self-sacrifice: he naturally tends to offer himself up for some object superior to himself, and he risks becoming what we call a hero or a saint. Such a thing succeeds only one time in a thousand. "Many are called and few are chosen", you quip? What remains is vice. . . . I'm not far from believing that Madame Alfieri is a kind of saint—a saint without miracles, to be sure! A sad saint. My very pious mother—God rest her soul!—used to say that sad saints make for poor saints. . . . Imagine someone whose sanctity had a flaw in it, a crack through which boredom slips in. . . . That sanctity would little by little be poisoned, rotted, liquefied by boredom.[41]

And, since man is in this way coerced to go beyond himself, it may be that Cénabre is right when he says that "we are always tempted beyond our powers."[42] Man is overtaxed—this is his very being; and so, he cannot by the power of his nature meet the demands made upon him, but only by the power of grace, in an act of freely responding love. And sin consists in the refusal to do so.

2. Nature

Man can be saved only in his totality: soul and body; this is why faith is not sufficient without the work of the body, that is, without purity. This, too, is why he cannot be saved without the nature of which he is a part, in which he lives and moves, and which is his most faithful companion on his adventure and the mirror of his interior truth. Bernanos wastes no time on the idea of a natural happiness independent of human beings and destiny. He sees nature only as the locus and companion of man, existing in open or secret dialogue with man. By no means is nature a place of refuge to shelter what in man remains imperiled: nature is just as exposed, as sternly overtaxed, and as inexorably sacrificed as man himself. Nature is, for Bernanos, the

---

[41] Rêve, 64–65.
[42] Joie, 279.

Eve-like companion who shares man's destiny with him,[43] the reality to whom man remains indebted because, next to God, man receives everything from nature. To despise nature like the Jansenists, or to turn one's back on her, would be the vilest of betrayals. Rather, man must embrace her with a tender, virile love.

It is significant that in Bernanos' life we encounter only two profound experiences connected with landscapes. It is odd that, even though for decades he had the most magnificent views of the French and Spanish Mediterranean coast before his eyes, he hardly wasted a word on them. Nor did he devote a single word to the beauties of the ocean he must have seen on his transatlantic voyage or to the magic of Rio de Janeiro. He did speak of the landscape of his youth: the endless, rain-sodden, forsaken, windswept lowland bordering on the gloomy North Sea, with its roads leading nowhere, its scattering of poor villages, its fields offering no shelter except by their very openness and breadth. And much later there was the landscape of Brazil: the untamed heart of the country, at the edge of the virgin forest, where once again he experienced, although in a very different way, an overwhelming feeling of unshelteredness. All the novels reflect the first experience; and the critical works—especially the most beautiful among them, *The Humiliated Children*—would be unthinkable without the Brazilian landscape: "The blue hill, and the vast plain toward the sea, with the sun on the dunes, . . . the hollow road still full of shadows, and the pastures all around with their hunchbacked apple trees, and the light fresh as the dew": this is the landscape Mouchette will never forget.[44] The dark drama of *Under Satan's Sun* begins in such scenery, and the same landscape will to the end be an indispensable and almost human player. When well beyond midnight the conversation between Mouchette and the count has reached an impasse and the unknown and inexplicable danger raises its head, the window "suddenly opened without a sound. A blast of the cold north wind, tasting of salt, burst in—coming from the high seas, but having picked up on its way all the stale vapors of the marshes. The sudden draft blew the papers scattered on a table up to the ceiling and drew from the glass of the lamp a long red flame that settled as soot. The

---

[43] Nature—a feminine noun in both German and French—is here personified as "*Schicksalsgefährtin*".—TRANS.

[44] *Soleil*, 15.

wind became even cooler. From one end of the park to the other, the awakened pines groaned as with a single voice."[45] And the young Abbé Donissan finds himself led around this same landscape as in the circles of the most tangled of labyrinths, only now the setting has become even more nocturnal and is steeped in a sinister silence.[46] After the horrific night spent struggling with Satan, it is again within this same landscape that the priest meets the murderess at the break of day: "The pale dawn rose gradually around them, and all they could see was its pathetic reflection on their faces. To the right, barely emerging from the fog, the hamlet nestled among the hills was a desolate sight to behold. Within the immense plain, at a seemingly infinite distance, the only thing alive was a slender thread of smoke above an invisible roof."[47]

Even more significant is the tone with which Bernanos opens Donissan's personal drama in the novel's second part, which was actually written first: "He opened the window. He was still awaiting he did not know what. Through the shadowy chasm drenched in rain, the church glistened feebly as if it were the only living thing about. . . . *Here I am*, he said, as if in a dream."[48] And one of the high points of the book is the thoroughly "theologized" landscape that serves as backdrop to the tragic conversation on God, the devil, and man between Donissan and the priest of the neighboring parish: "The more the harsh voice rose in the wind and the sun, the more the stalwart little garden resisted it with the full strength of its life. The May breeze rolled its gray clouds in the sky, and now and then it halted their vast herd above the horizon. It was then that a stream of dazzling light, grazing over the whole of the gloomy plain like the flashing of a saber, came to burst into flames in the magnificent hedge."[49]

In *Joy*, we find that destiny and nature are even more intimately interwoven. Nowhere will we find a landscape more permeated by grace. The first landscape is described in the following terms: "The joy of

[45] Ibid., 34.
[46] Ibid., 151–52.
[47] Ibid., 205.
[48] Ibid., 251.
[49] Ibid., 288.

the day, the day blossoming on an August morning with all its sap and dazzling brightness, . . . burst resplendently in every window'', implying that the theme of the title should first of all become manifest in nature. But the parenthetical remark indicated by the ellipsis above already points to the fact that the joyful splendor of the landscape is interiorly threatened: "but the treacherous scents of autumn were already in the too heavy air''. As the novel develops, both things are demonstrated: eternity contained in a single instant, the imperishability of joy . . . *and* the perishableness of this eternal instant and the transformation of joy into darkest suffering; and yet, this suffering always remains a disguise of eternal joy: "It was the joy of the day, and—by virtue of who knows what perishable brilliance —it was also the joy of a single day, of a unique, irretrievable day, so delicate and fragile in its implacable serenity. This was the day when, on the burning summit of the dog-days, the insidious haze appears for the first time, crawling for the moment above the horizon but descending some weeks later upon the exhausted earth, the ravaged meadows, the sleeping water, with the smell of withered leaves."[50]

It is into just this imperishable and yet already perishing landscape that, in the next sentence, the young woman enters. For the time being she can feel in herself only the first half of the truth—that reflecting imperishability: "She listened to her heart throb, and this was surely not from either terror or idle curiosity, since for weeks and weeks now, without her paying much attention to it, every hour of her life had been full and perfect. It seemed to her that all her powers together could not have added anything to this fullness, much less detracted from it."[51] Only the memory of the death of her father confessor, the Abbé Chevance, begins to reflect the other side of the reality:

> It had happened one evening toward winter's end. The wan day gleamed in the panes of his shabby room. . . . Suddenly, all the light of the dying day had burst in his glance, while he exclaimed with a strong, loud voice: "My daughter, I know what you need. And it will come at its own time, because souls have their own seasons. Yes, indeed: there are such seasons! I know every season because I'm an old peasant from the Meuse region. Frost will come, even in May. Does this keep our yellow-

---

[50] *Joie*, 32.
[51] Ibid., 33–34.

plum trees from blossoming? Does the good Lord control his springtime, measuring the extent of sun and showers? Let's let him throw all his goods out the window!"[52]

It is not in her encounter with sinners but in her encounter with nature that Chantal begins to experience her transformation, her sense of being wrenched out of her refuge in God. This is a sign for the extent to which the supernatural drama (that is, the imitation of the Lord's Passion on the Mount of Olives) is in the end an interior drama over and beyond all attacks of the Evil One: "What, then, was the power of lies for it to be able to alter to such a great extent the very face of the saints in the wretched sight of men? Suddenly the narrow familiar universe in which she had been born and had lived took on a new appearance, like those landscapes too full of light and vibrancy: at sunset they are suddenly engulfed, and they emerge again slowly, hardly recognizable, as if rising from the abyss of the night. It seemed that inanimate objects themselves had become alien to her."[53] Later on, as the net of the Evil One tightens around its victim, it is again the landscape that manifests the reason for her puzzling alienation. Now the landscape itself has become transformed into a monster ready to leap:

> She barely dared to open her eyes and fix her glance on the soft and hard lines of the hills: she was afraid she would suddenly see them closing about her. The hillsides crisscrossed by living hedges, the white road, the suspended shadow of the tiny valley cut by the Soulette, . . . this whole peaceful landscape appeared to her transfigured in the immobile light—enormous, expectant, like a giant animal lying in ambush for its prey. In the past, terror had induced the same alarm—repressed at once —before the heaping spectacle of the big city. But even this land before her now was no less powerful, no less greedy. It had taken the shape of man's desires; it had been kneaded over and over by sin. It was a land belonging to sin.[54]

Once Chantal has become accustomed to her new life of danger, however, and to the impending sense of an oblation that is steadily becoming more inescapable, the landscape again changes its appear-

---

[52] Ibid., 39–40.
[53] Ibid., 50.
[54] Ibid., 119–20.

ance. While at first it had seemed to be on the side of the attackers, now it unveils its own sacrificial countenance as victim.[55] But the landscape does not for this reason become a "consolation" for Chantal, or indeed a place where she may escape from her innermost destiny. Even in his suffering, man remains lord over nature, and she remains his servant and the mirror of his sorrow. However, nature does receive man, her suffering lord, into her arms the way a servant unfolds a soft linen sheet to wrap her martyred master: to our earthly eyes this covering appears infinitely greater than the poor suffering body, and in this respect it is a shelter. Human suffering, its incomparable quality notwithstanding, is reflected in nature as if resounding in an echo chamber with a thousand reverberations, in an endlessly changing pattern, and such empathy on the part of nature seems to justify and appease man's suffering. The following page is one of the most masterful Bernanos ever wrote:

> The day glided down from its zenith in broad diagonal waves that struck the tall, white stone walls and flowed down their sides, only to well up again in many-colored clusters at the four corners of the lawns—yellow and purple with the dahlias, pink and white with the carnations—until it died out in the darkening green of the wood's edge. But, in a manner of speaking, this was only the symphony's main theme, set within the orchestra's tightly constructed movement. The immense tidal wave of light had already shattered in the air against some translucent reef, and the invisible wind was playfully scattering its foam in the most inaccessible places—in the cleft of an embankment steeped in shadows, in the tiniest leaf of a lilac bush, or in the summit of a black pine tree. It was not so much the day's vast and universal final bursting as a cunningly lit conflagration in very dry brushwood: the instantaneous wave of flames leapt from one twig to another like a minuscule scarlet tongue. At certain moments of a summer that has been too oppressive, nature, instead of opening up and stretching out under the sun's dazzling caress, seems on the contrary to withdraw within herself—mute, crazed, immobile—with the stupid surrender of a prey that has felt the clamp of the victor's jaws on its side, at the vital spot. And, indeed, it was assiduous biting —millions upon millions of persistent little bites, a vast and unending nibbling—that was brought to mind by this stiff rain of rays falling from

---

[55] In German, *das Opfer* refers both to the act of "sacrifice" and to the person of the "victim". It seems that here both meanings are intended, and I thus translate using both English terms.—TRANS.

an unfeeling sky, this downpour of white-hot darts of light, this bound-less suction by the solar star.[56]

And the landscape must again be incorporated at the end of all the struggles—after the battles with the grandmother, with the irre-deemable father, with the cynical psychiatrist; after the possessed priest has accosted her with the inexorability of a sinner who demands re-demption but does not have a single drop of love to give; after the mystery of the night of the spirit and of betrayal has run its course and the night has been transformed by virtue of a sacrifice, and just before Chantal falls into unconsciousness from sheer exhaustion and overexertion. The landscape at this moment appears reduced to its most simple possible spiritual form; it offers nothing but a similitude of the spiritual events: "She slowly approached the window, opened it wide, and breathed in the burning air. She then returned toward him with the same slow gait, smiling: 'What a summer,' she said, 'don't you think? You end up regarding the light with resentment, as if it were an enemy. Its intensity will make the winter look all the blacker.' 'Precisely so', he replied with the same calm. 'We hate the night, and yet the day is not less hard to withstand.' "[57] And, while in the house Chantal's terrible destiny is being accomplished, Cénabre is wandering outside through the ink-black, stormy night. Everything is said and known the moment "a drop of rain fell on Cénabre's hand —hot, heavy, and scented like a drop of nard. It was the quintessence of the swooning day."[58]

This treatment of landscapes, however, appeared to Bernanos to be still much too symbolic, perhaps too pathetic as well, as in the wholly fantastic portrayal of nature in the early novella *A Night*, which is set in a South American virgin forest the writer had never seen. What a distance from this youthful Romanticism to Bernanos' experience of Brazil in the 1940s! But *Conversation among Shadows* is already quite close to *Joy* in many of its details: it is set on a rainy day under a tree, on the shores of the flooded Rance, and with the last sentence comes the extraordinary breakthrough of the sun through the shooting rain

---

[56] *Joie*, 193–94.
[57] Ibid., 284.
[58] Ibid., 300.

—a truly eschatological sight: "The pale blue sky appeared through a long tear to the west, and the disheveled sides of the clouds lit up all at once. The last throb of the wandering sun suddenly shone in the rain's thousand facets."[59] The later books handle landscape even more sparingly. As was the case with *The Imposture*, in which an urban, in-doors atmosphere of a very intense sort always remained connected with the actions of the characters, so too with the landscape in *A Crime*: landscape does not for one moment become a theme independent from the human action, which takes place in an imaginary mountain village supposedly near Grenoble; but all the place names have been borrowed from the northern region of Pas-de-Calais, Bernanos' native area. Only toward the end, when everything is straining toward the revelation and at the same time becoming unraveled, does landscape once again emerge, painted in broad strokes,[60] as a landscape of perdition, above all as abyss: deep below the cliff, the murderess and her young companion contemplated "the river's formidable current, the rolling of the stones on its bottom". Significantly, this river is the Bidassoa, a river defining a border. On its other shore we see the Spanish customs officer, and Bernanos describes it at its very mouth, where it hurls itself out into the sea. It is this river that will receive the corpse of the boy and again spew it out, while the murderess is strolling in a burned-out and calcinated pine forest, moving toward the final destiny she herself has chosen.[61]

Likewise, in *Monsieur Ouine*, we will find no landscape described for its own sake. The shreds of nature that do manage to peer through here and there are themselves tainted with the curse affecting the characters. These can expect no spark of assistance from the desolate land they inhabit, no more than the little Mouchette of 1936 received any sympathy from the hard, nocturnal, rain-drenched nature that surrounded her as mute witness to her suffering. There is something almost clinical in the precision with which Bernanos describes the escarpment and the pond in which Mouchette drowns. In these works of the middle period, only seldom do we encounter a gust of cosmic breath such as is blowing in the night through which the old Devandomme is walking in search of his son-in-law, a suspected

[59] *Dialogue d'ombres*; in *Nouvelles* (Plon ed.), 139.
[60] *Crime*, 222f.
[61] Ibid., 239.

murderer: "Now is the hour of the night that no man knows perfectly or has entirely possessed, the hour that holds all the senses at bay while the ever-denser gloom is filling the expanse of the heavens and the saturated earth seems to sweat an even blacker ink. The wind has hidden somewhere (but where?); it is roaming about in the depths of immense deserts, of majestic solitudes where the echoes of the wind's wild gallops have, one after the other, come to die. A breeze, a breath, a whisper, a swarm of invisible things is gliding thirty feet above the ground as if floating on the density of the night."[62]

Only in the *Country Priest* does nature again recover some consistency as a result of its connection with the book's winning hero. Everything remains quite understated, of course, in keeping with the work's chamber-music-like quality. We witness a conversation on the deserted town square, while a flock of doves flies back and forth at regular intervals. Overhead, the two persons can hear the "whoosh of their wings",[63] and gradually the birds' revolutions come to be expected unconsciously, like "the swish of an enormous sickle" swooping down apocalyptically from heaven.[64]

Or we see the young priest portrayed as one night he leans at a window looking out over an alien and unknown world: "I've just spent a whole hour at my window despite the cold. The moonlight creates in the valley a kind of luminous velvet cover, so light that the movement of the air unravels it in long strands that rise obliquely up to the sky and seem to glide there at vertiginous heights. And yet they are very close to us, so close that I can see some floating in tatters at the top of the poplars. What fantastic illusions! To tell the truth, we don't really know anything about this world of ours: we are not in the world."[65]

On another night, during the decisive conversation with the countess—the hardest battle the little priest will have to fight—the landscape again exudes a silent significance: "The logs were hissing in the fireplace. Through the open window and its fine linen curtains could be seen the huge lawn, lying under a taciturn sky and delimited

---

[62] *Ouine*, 101.
[63] *Curé*, 129.
[64] Ibid., 132.
[65] Ibid., 160.

by the black barrier of the pines, like a stagnant pond of putrescent water."[66]

Only three years later, when Bernanos found himself at the end of the world, transplanted to the edge of the virgin forest, where nature was gigantic and basically still untouched by human hand, the novelist's sense of landscape again came through with an elemental force. Time and again he returned to nature's landscapes whenever he wanted to portray his own spiritual situation. Bernanos' interior position was a very solitary one, and therefore it was linked almost necessarily to nature. But by no means did he have a sentimental dependency on nature: despite his keen sensitivity, his outlook on nature always remained most manly: "The small hill to the side of which our isolated house clings is called *Cruz das Almas*—the 'Cross of Souls'. It opens out on a vast horizon of bare and wild ridges that ride horseback on one another for hundreds of kilometers. To the south they fall headlong into the sea, and to the north they gradually disappear into the boundless *sertão*." [67]

This landscape served all Bernanos' purposes: it became the "great organ" on which the writer played.[68] In *The Humiliated Children* he gains momentum with a mighty prelude. He describes the courtyard where he works, and then the house behind him, which "habitually and continuously, my dear friends, resounds with shouts, quarrels, and reproaches hurled in three different languages. The grave reply comes from the eccentric macaws, those huge clowns all painted in yellow, blue, scarlet, and Veronese green."[69] He then describes himself at his work table, his mind on eternal things, resolutely committed to work despite everything, despite the war and the general collapse of civilization. France is on the horizon, and the war. Then he begins to consider the land around him:

> The dry and the wet divide up the year between themselves. In one season, the cattle wander about filling themselves; in the other, they empty themselves out and slowly cave in, buried up to their bellies in a poisonous grass turned into an indigestible substance, a kind of mineral

---

[66] Ibid., 166.
[67] *Croix*, preface (1941), 1.
[68] *To His Fiancée*, 1915 (unpublished letter).
[69] *Enfants*, 106.

poison, by the sun's chemical fury. I do not hate this country, nor could I say I love it. I would love it if it could love me, if it were capable of the exchange to which the lands of our Old World have accustomed us. But Europe's old soil has everything from us, and this land has received nothing from anyone. For centuries now it has been ruminating only its hunger and thirst.[70]

This is the solitary land of solitary men, with whom no conversation is any longer possible, men who have withdrawn from themselves and, with all the more reason, from all culture: "My own image has never weighed much or occupied much space, but at present it has shrunk in the extreme. It no longer bothers me. I do not in the slightest feel the need to conform my life to it or to sacrifice anything to it."[71] And then the book again takes up landscape in order to aid in the understanding of man. This time Bernanos does not turn to the bare, interminable plains to the south but to the land to the north, which grows denser until it reaches the virgin forest,

the dwarfed, shapeless forest whose gradual creeping has come to cover an enormous portion of the earth—the thick-set and irresistible woods with limbs contorted by thirst, squatting on their knock-kneed thighs, clinging with their millions of misshapen arms to cables that have very little of the vegetable left in them, giant lianas so dried out that they sound like a drum when struck with the finger. Only some weeks ago I thought this forest had reached the outer limit of decrepitude: it was ready to collapse into dust on a soil that had been baked and rebaked until it was harder than bricks. And just look at it now: it has risen from its decay and is once again green, swollen with water, bursting under its bark shell, thrusting forward its low forehead—covered with a new woolly fleece—thrusting forward this forehead of a bull. On all sides he is pressing in on our little chalk-and-clay house. He is scenting a path through the logs of our corral: he would indeed make short work of knocking down both house and corral if he were not about to begin being tortured by thirst until the next season. . . . I am not speaking here of mere brushwood. I'm speaking of a waterless forest, a martyred forest, the forest as Tantalus, dying of thirst during ten months out of the year within earshot of the distant grumbling of rivers and waterfalls.[72]

[70] Ibid., 109.
[71] Ibid., 111.
[72] Ibid., 183–84.

Even the rain no longer has anything human or civilized about it:

> In no way did it evoke the familiar image of a cloud that bursts, rather
> that of a river flowing majestically, or of an enormous liquid ark between
> heaven and earth: it was reconciliation, peace, forgiveness, universal re-
> mission of sins, a deeper and sweeter slumber, a second night within
> the night. And yet I clearly knew it would not bring salvation to this
> country, even less, rest and sleep. It would not in two months restore the
> twisted forest, nor would it set free knotted joints and limbs misshapen
> by contraction. It would only transform these hardened invalids into
> monsters more powerful than any of the athletes in our French forests.[73]

Here Bernanos had found the equivalent to the infinitely fruitless
landscapes of his youth: this was the theological landscape of his late
period, evoking Tantalus and the Minotaur. He had very little interest
now in the landscapes of the middle period, the Mediterranean vistas
so dear to Maurras but that now meant nothing to Bernanos and in
no way corresponded to his destiny. But the Brazilian landscape of
Cruz das Almas had become a permanent part of him: "I feel I have
the right to speak about it now, because my destiny is humbly united
to its destiny, my effort to its effort, my poverty to its poverty. I no
longer consider it from the outside: I am within."[74] After having left
behind him "the last train station and the last bridge", it is here at the
end of the world that Bernanos grinds away at his street-organ, and
he begins that unforgettable meditation on his vocation, on the meaning of his activity as a writer, for which the landscape just described
provided only a stimulus. The meditation ends with the very moving
image of the "open house" we have quoted above when dealing with
the writer's profession. There we saw how the house and the open
landscape interpenetrate, as do the material and the spiritual senses of
the image—bitter irony and fervent prayer.

In the end, "the black, black forest" becomes for him "like a place
of refuge", and he wonders "why the people native to this land fear it
so".[75] His "vertiginous solitude" slowly distances him from the cities
he had loved so much ("O my age-old cities, my human cities!") and,
indeed, from the whole world of culture and form so vitally impor-

---

[73] Ibid., 185.
[74] Ibid., 186–87.
[75] Ibid., 232.

tant to him—as if nature were applying a merciful yet inexorable loop around "culture and civilization" and compelling it to abandon itself to a greater reality. And Bernanos is not a man ever to have refused a gesture of self-surrender: "Within this sterile forest, where the snakes are more numerous than the birds, within such an immense lair, the word 'poverty' no longer has its ancient meaning, the lovely meaning we formerly gave it. Poverty here is nothing but an affliction that kills people in the depths of their solitude, much as they are killed by dysentery, fever, or typhus."[76]

It is precisely in such a form that nature cannot be excluded from Bernanos' vision of the world and history. Under the mask of the elegant man who knew his way around Parisian literary circles, Bernanos secretly remained the man who had come from the country and was returning to the country. Although he was doubtless a rather fanciful farmer and *fazenda* owner (he did not, in fact, know much about agriculture and plantations), he was nevertheless one who had to take his stance at the more vast and all-embracing level of reality. Thus, there was no remaining in France for Bernanos after he had returned home from Brazil. After a sojourn in a house in Sisteron (Basses Alpes) that had no electricity, running water, or window panes, and then in Bandol (Var) and La Chapelle-Vendômoise (Touraine), he felt driven to the edge of the African desert. Here he finally felt at ease, even though every inch of his daily existence was a struggle, and he would have to be carried away as a dying man. This was the same theological desert without which neither Rimbaud nor Claudel (in *The Satin Slipper*), neither Lyautey nor Psichari, neither Saint-Exupéry nor Charles de Foucauld, could live: the silent, expectant bed on which Paris can lay its head once its racket has given out.

3. The World

Once, after the war, Bernanos was invited to give a lecture in Porrentruy, at the western edge of the Swiss Jura mountains. As the train moved in the evening through the dark gorges, he had "the feeling of going toward a retreat of serenity, of tranquil security, a protected nook of the world". Speaking to his audience about this feeling, he

[76] Ibid., 248.

added at once: "I said to myself that I could probably do something better than come to disturb your peace. But, you know, there are no more 'protected nooks' in the world. This world no longer protects anyone or offers anyone security. It no longer defends anyone; rather, it is the world that needs defending, it is we who must save the world."[77]

Bernanos' first concern was the world and not the Church, because the Church is only a means for the redemption of the world. It is as if he were standing at the crossroads between the two Testaments: at the place where the chosen people had to expand into a universal people, where the Jews had to decide to allow the pagans "sitting in darkness and the shadow of death" (Lk 1:79) to enter into the possession of the ancient promise. Today the chosen people are the Christians, and all who turn their back on the Church and sit in darkness—whether before or after Christ—nevertheless, at base, still have a share in the promise and indeed in the redemption, no longer by virtue of Abraham, but now of Christ, even though this may occur unbeknownst to them and despite their waywardness, indifference, and even hatred. It is not the Church that is being redeemed but the world, and the Church is the light for the redemption of the world. Not only the Christian but man as such is called to salvation, for "God wills that all men be saved", and he expects the Church to pray for all (1 Tim 2:1–6). This world no longer belongs to itself; it belongs to the *Kyrios*, the Lord, who has branded its flesh like a slave's to mark it as his own inalienable property. But it is a very worldly world indeed, and by no means already "Church", and less than ever are its thoughts on conversion. Bernanos had no interest in theoretical theology. As a writer he faced the concrete world. He saw and felt its spirit; he experienced it all the deeper as he himself was Christian and sinner simultaneously. He was well acquainted with resistance and the overcoming of resistance, with self-surrender to both evil and grace, with the slavery of sin and Christ's lordship over the slave, with the will of the Evil One and the higher will of Christ. And Bernanos did not for a moment take the depths of sin and the perdition it involves any less seriously simply because of his conviction that redemption had been accomplished. Is not the first effect of redemption precisely that it has introduced into the world the means whereby to take the full

---

[77] *Liberté*, 298–99.

measure of sin? "If I had not come and spoken to them, they would have no sin; but as it is they have no excuse for their sin" (Jn 15:22). But neither can there be any question of the measure of darkness surpassing the measure of light: for a Christian, the real "world" can be envisioned only in a Johannine manner—namely, in the suffering but dramatic way in which the Cross confronts (and is adequate to overcome) hell. The existence of redemption (and its sign in the world: the Church) suffices to insert a thorn into the world's flesh. This "thorn" is the "spirit" in the Pauline sense; and if the "world" is the "flesh", also in Paul's sense, then both of these together do not indeed yield an image of man, or even less of the God-Man, since the flesh and the spirit are at war with one another. And yet, and yet: the spirit *intends* the flesh, Christianity *intends* the world, and when the flesh refuses to admit the spirit into itself, this is less bad (for this is the blindness native to the flesh) than when the spirit purposes to get through without the flesh. In the world's present age, the shaping of the flesh by the spirit necessarily takes on the form of struggle and suffering; and yet, from this lethal wrestling of love, result a unique character and fruitfulness that foreshadow the eschatological unity of spirit and flesh.

The country priest's reflections on Church and State lead him to the insight that the pre-Christian State was the fullest expression of the curse pronounced against Adam—this because of that State's practice of slavery as a legal institution, a form of publicly sanctioned injustice that reduced to "despair a race of sacrificed people, a people without name, without history, without possessions, without allies". Now,

> the institution [of slavery] is dead, and the Ancient World crumbled along with it. . . . It will not ever be reinstated. . . . Injustice will never again enjoy a legal status: that's over and done with. But, for that very reason, it now exists in a state of dispersion throughout the world. Not daring any longer to use injustice for the welfare of only a small number, society has thus condemned itself to pursuing the destruction of an evil it bears within itself, an evil that, banished from the laws, reappears almost immediately in people's accepted customs, there to begin again its tireless hellish circle, only in reverse. Whether it likes it or not, society must now share in man's condition; it must risk the same supernatural adventure as man. Formerly, society was indifferent to good and evil,

acknowledging only the law of its own power. But Christianity gave it a soul, a soul to lose or to save.[78]

The Curé d'Ambricourt shows these lines to his colleague, the Curé de Torcy, who agrees with him and adds: "Modern society can deny its master all it wants. The fact remains that it too has been redeemed. It can no longer be enough for it to administer the common heritage. Like all of us, whether it likes it or not, society itself has had to set out in search of the Kingdom of God. And this Kingdom is not of this world. Society, therefore, will never be able to halt in this search."[79] This is why, he continues, Paul was not in a hurry to abolish slavery: "He simply said to himself that Christianity had let loose in the world a truth that nothing could henceforth stop because this truth was already to be found in advance in the deepest part of men's consciences and because man immediately recognized himself mirrored in it." The world may indeed entertain nostalgic dreams of its past and again attempt to recast the ideal of slavery on a higher level. It is too late! "By wedding himself to poverty, our Lord so elevated the poor man's dignity that no one will ever be able to bring him down from his pedestal."[80] And, when the world attempts to replace slaves with machines, even then it will not be able to wipe out poverty in this way. The Soviet Russians were an ambiguous sign to us: an anti-Christian sign insofar as they wanted to achieve an *earthly* paradise, but at the same time a Christian sign insofar as they could not help searching for *paradise*:[81] "The peoples of the earth no longer go to Mass or to hear sermons, and they are ignorant of the catechism. But the vision they bear within themselves, in their very entrails and unbeknownst to them, is that of a society that in fact has never existed, a society the incredible arrival of which their ancestors have awaited from century to century: the harmonious *polis* or society, with brotherhood as emblem."[82]

Bernanos was convinced that this *cité harmonieuse*, a notion that significantly originated with Péguy, was an echo of the Kingdom of God and that as such it stood within the Church's purview as an as-

[78] *Curé*, 57–58.
[79] Ibid., 59.
[80] Ibid., 60.
[81] Ibid., 61f.
[82] *Anglais*, 146.

signed task for her administration: "An earthly paradise in the style of Rousseau . . . may still be a weak, stale, and almost unrecognizable image of the Kingdom of God. Such an image does not directly contradict the Kingdom, as does, for instance, capitalist society."[83] "Fascism, Hitlerism, and Communism will one day, in the light of history, be judged to be monstrous deformations of the ancient idea of Christendom",[84] and this idea is "at once spiritual and temporal": it envisions "a vast pilgrimage by Humanity toward the golden age of the Beatitudes found in the Gospel."[85]

This ideal should not be wrested away from the earth's peoples. The Americans and the Puritans would like to abolish it by reducing it to a pure moralism. On the contrary, we should come to see that the French Revolution arrived too late. Christians should actually have made it happen much earlier, "and the Church would have been its godmother".[86] For the leaven activating mankind's every major awakening to salvation is to be found within the Church, all the more so when the Spirit incites men from within to the very thing to which the Church is calling them from without: "Christian honor can be outraged in the unbeliever as well as in the believer, because it is this honor that has formed the conscience of one and of the other, having been communicated to both."[87] "The human race [in Europe] is Christian. Whether we regret the fact or not, it is Christian."[88] And Bernanos therefore exclaims: "Listen to me, both believers and unbelievers: every weakening of the Christian spirit is a catastrophe for both of you. We are in solidarity in the face of the peril threatening us. Whether we save ourselves or perish, it shall be together."[89]

Even in his blackest portrayals of the lost modern world, Bernanos' persistent intention was to show that these human shades we call men remain marked by the Christian reality precisely in their shadelike existence: "It's frightful to see the extent to which all these people exert themselves to disobey the commandments of God, a God in whom

---

[83] *Robots*, 82f.
[84] *Anglais*, 188.
[85] Ibid., 183.
[86] *Robots*, 83.
[87] *Anglais*, 207.
[88] Ibid., 146.
[89] Ibid., 155.

they no longer believe. For it is useless for them to go to such lengths
to be scoundrels with naturalness. . . . It would seem that vice exas-
perates rather than appeases their old Christian blood, which torments
them. The most cynical have an air of bad priests about them."[90] And
Olivier, who here acts as Bernanos' messenger, then addresses Simone
Alfieri and, through his mistress, all of sinful humanity: "Come on,
now! Christianity is in the very marrow of your bones! And do you
know what the result of your celebrated postwar 'demoralization' has
been? It has brought back the notion of sin—the notion of sin but
without grace, fools that you are!"[91] A little before this, the psychoanalyst Lipotte had declared: "Christianity may indeed continue to
dissolve little by little all on its own. Still, our Western world isn't
quite able to eliminate the most subtle and harmful of its poisons.
All these people appear to be rushing headlong on a mad search for
pleasure, but somewhere within themselves, in some secret corner of
their lives, they have an altar consecrated to suffering. And if they're
dashing after gold—which after all is nothing but the material sign
for pleasure—they do it with a residue of shame, because Poverty
—holy Poverty—is still an awesome presence to them."[92] For his
part, the Curé de Fenouille explains to the village doctor that, even if
mankind succeeded in ridding itself of the very instinct for purity and
impurity and imagined it had disinfected the world of all morality,
even then mankind would retain a nostalgia for purity and grace, like
"a poisonous thorn in the hearts of men", but this nostalgia could
express itself only in perverted and monstrous forms.[93]

But what dialogue could be possible between Christianity and a
world whose despair impelled it to put up a wild struggle and which
was digging its way ever more deeply into its refusal to believe? The
question is mortally dangerous for the Christian: it judges him, and
may even be said to be *the* judgment that he must undergo. The less he
can "do" about it, the more he should ascribe to himself the guilt for
the condition of today's world. The world's refusal is the world's disappointment with the Church. Who would dare affirm the contrary?
And so, the Church has as her first task the obligation to see and to
hear: "Pious persons doubtless have a lot of things to say to unbeliev-

---

[90] *Rêve*, 161.
[91] Ibid., 162.
[92] Ibid., 115.
[93] *Ouine*, 208.

ers, but often they could also have a lot of things to learn from these
unhappy brothers, and they risk never knowing what those things are
because they never stop talking."[94] Thus, Bernanos once imagined
that, on the feast of Thérèse of Lisieux, an unbeliever climbs the pulpit and preaches a sermon to the congregation—and, to be sure, it is
no fervorino, but rather one of the most beautiful in all of modern
homiletic literature, and in any event the most impressive and useful.
The unbeliever holds a mirror up to the pious congregation, in which
it can see how the world sees it from the outside and what the world
has with perfect right expected from it but which they have never delivered: "It is you, divine people, who since Christ's Ascension have
been his visible person on this earth. Admit that you're not always
recognizable as such at first glance."[95] And a few pages before, we
read: "It isn't enough to reply that God entrusted himself to your
hands. The hands to which Christ entrusted himself then were surely
not friendly hands, although they were consecrated hands. What does
it matter that you have succeeded to the synagogue, and that this succession is legitimate? For us, who expect only from you the sharing of
a gift you proclaim to be ineffably sublime, it doesn't matter whether
or not God entrusted himself to your hands. What matters to us is
what you're making of it."[96]

And now Bernanos himself climbs into his layman's pulpit:

> For years now we've been searching here, there, and everywhere for
> those responsible for the decay of Christianity, and all the while they've
> been on the inside. Those who cause the world's perdition are mediocre
> Christians, mediocre priests, blissful Christians who most frequently also
> happen to be the *beati possidentes*—the blissful affluent. . . . And their very
> mediocrity should not serve them as an excuse! We have much less to
> fear from cynical consciences than from perverted and false consciences.
> The most heinous acts in history have not been perpetrated by the most
> heinous people but by cowards and weaklings.[97]

For there is only one step from Pauline weakness in Christ to a weakling's betrayal of Christ—the step from hidden faith to hidden faith-
lessness. Bernanos hits the bull's-eye and brings forth good proofs:

---

[94] *Croix*, March 1941, 102.
[95] *Cimetières*, 262.
[96] Ibid., 256.
[97] *To Sister Marie de Loyola*, May 1941; *Croix*, 125.

I am therefore free, perfectly free to tell them to their face that they are committing a crime against Christianity by pretending to justify themselves through a new casuistry of law, justice, and honor. And it isn't out of ignorance that they're acting in this way. They know very well what Christian order is, since they have learned it in the Catholic schools almost all of them attended. But they have for so long felt themselves incapable of restoring that order—which means incapable of assenting to the sacrifices necessary for such a restoration—that they have consciously preferred defeat. . . , because such defeat released them from all responsibility, . . . just as a bankrupt man burns down his factory in order to dodge his creditors.[98]

With this we have arrived at the very heart of the problem: Christianity as a ready-made, self-contained and self-evident affair, which is therefore devoid of any mystery, existing "alongside" the world as a "perfect society" parallel to the other, imperfect one—in the end, Christianity as one idea among many other ideas, no longer the leaven and the grain of wheat, the active principle that, in order to have its effect, must enter the world, die there, and dissolve within it, so that, once it again bursts through to new birth like an ear of corn, it will be both things beyond distinction: the field of the world but transformed into the power of the Word. That pre-packaged and "perfect" Christianity would no longer be Christianity at all, and the world, having seen through it, would rightly treat it with indulgence, realizing it was merely one of its own ideological products.[99]

For Bernanos, the Church stands and falls with her ultimate solidarity with the world:

The Church, as a matter of fact, is a movement, a striding force, whereas so many pious men and women seem to believe, or pretend to believe, that she is only a shelter, a refuge, a sort of spiritual haven: through her windowpanes one may take pleasure in watching the passers-by— the people who belong outside, those who aren't paying boarders of the house—trudging through the mud. . . . But I myself can't help loving them. I feel in utter solidarity with these people who haven't yet found what I myself have received without deserving it, without even having asked for it, and I've enjoyed it from the cradle, so to speak, by a kind of privilege the gratuity of which frightens me. . . . How could I not feel

---

[98] Ibid., 125–26.
[99] *Enfants*, 149–53.

gravely and profoundly committed in the face of those who, in order to learn this language [of faith] must invest great pains in forgetting their own, the language they have always used?[100]

To be a Christian can be nothing other than to accept from grace, in union with Christ, the responsibility for the non-Christian world. Just as the world bears the brand of Christ, so too the Christian bears the brand of the world. The one and only requirement is that Christianity must for this very reason be kept clean of all forms of the worldly spirit and all politization of its convictions,[101] that its salt may not go stale, since it can only be called "salt" if it is the salt *of the world*. Such responsibility, moreover, can only be love. Bernanos loved the world; and, if the Church was his open and painful love, the world was his secret and tacit love: "When I am dead, please tell the sweet kingdom of this Earth that I loved it more than I ever dared to say."[102]

A good proof of this love is the way Bernanos totally renounces the usual methods of apologetics intended to convince the unbeliever of the truth of Christianity. At bottom, Bernanos builds no bridges; what he does is tear down all the sham linkages between the world and the Church in order to make these face one another, each as its clean self. This is, indeed, the Johannine way: to move from alleged dialogue—which becomes more and more fraught with impossibility and misunderstanding—back to pure confrontation of light and darkness. In this confrontation, the light must suffer, and the hour of darkness appears to win the day. But, once one has despaired of all possibility of mutual understanding on an earthly basis, grace breaks through with its final synthesis. Already the first novel strove to arrive at a situation in which "forehead knocked against forehead" (the literal meaning of "con-front-ation"), and all other novels followed suit. The encounter between Christ and Satan was the central confrontation, but it shed its light on every other: that between Donissan and the murderess, between Donissan and the dead child, Donissan and the rationalistic Curé de Luzarnes, Donissan and the French Academy.

We should take careful note of how, gradually, each of these encounters becomes a defeat for Donissan, most frightfully in the awful

---

[100] *Liberté*, 267–69.
[101] *Enfants*, 155–56; *Français*, 112.
[102] *Bernanos*, 53.

scene involving the failed miracle, when Donissan judges himself: "I am lost. . . . I was crazy. . . a dangerous madman. . . . I will execute myself."[103] After the narrative has reached this culminating point, the redemptive mysteries of the descent into the pit of hell are inexorably revealed, down to their ultimate, unbearable consequences. And then, in a kind of satyr-play by way of epilogue, Bernanos ventures to bring on the scene an old member of the French Academy who is identical to Anatole France. Flanked by two rationalists, one lay and the other clerical (the doctor and the Curé de Luzarnes, respectively), France goes to visit Donissan, a priest in the image of the Curé d'Ars. Here, Bernanos gives detailed descriptions of the pious emotions produced in the famous writer, known for his delicate skepticism, by the atmosphere of the bare rectory and the little room in which Donissan whips himself until he draws blood. At first, France is repulsed. But that evening, sitting alone in the little village church where he must wait for a long time under dingy kerosene lamps while people search the roads in vain for the disappeared Donissan, another mood takes hold of him, just as strong as the first: a gentle curiosity about religious phenomena. Finally, he begins to entertain a kind of Arcadian daydream: he, Anatole France, fondles the idea of converting in old age. Would this not cast a by no means uninteresting light retrospectively on his literary *œuvre*, adding a final dimension that would unify and reconcile the whole? This meditation in a country church affords Bernanos the opportunity to indulge in a pastiche of France's undulating style. The rhythm of the narrative, which has been breathless in the previous pages, suddenly becomes measured and expansive. For many pages it now loses itself in the calm meanderings of a pastoral psychological mood, until the moment when, out of casual curiosity, the old satyr draws back the curtain of the confessional and in the semi-darkness sees the saint sitting there: "Two big shoes . . . , the fold of a weirdly draped cassock . . . , one long skinny leg", then "a vague whiteness, and suddenly the awesome face, lit up by God's lightning." Simultaneously, Bernanos returns to his own style: "A teacher of irony finds his master and awakens in confusion from a slightly silly though tender dream. He opens wide the door, takes one step back, sizes his strange companion up with one

---

[103] *Soleil*, 309.

glance and, without yet daring to challenge him, takes his stand before him."[104]

Bernanos would never go any farther than this. In his early work there was still the occasional conversion. But toward the end we don't have even this, as if, in the context of such earnest confrontation, an explicit conversion would have an anticlimactic effect or merely distract us from the truly essential. In *Under Satan's Sun* what we do get at the very end is the supposed final prayer of the holy priest of Lumbres, the "supreme lament" and "loving reproach" he sends up to his Judge in heaven. However, he has "something different to say" to the famous writer who has come from so far away looking for him. "In the darkness, his black mouth looked like a wound torn open by the explosion of a final cry, and it did not emit any other sound." But "his whole body" was like a "dreadful provocation": "You wanted my peace?", the saint exclaimed. "Come and take it!"[105]

Essentially speaking, there was nothing else Bernanos could add to this in all the rest of his work. Cénabre and Chevance, Cénabre and Chantal, the country priest and the countess, the Curé de Fenouille and his "dead parish", the unknown priest who meets Madame Alfieri, the murderess, on the road: all of these characters are placed by Bernanos before one another and are made to confront one another, and the defiant challenge they pose to one another says more than any single spoken word or accomplished act could. Even though each of these encounters means a descent into hell, none of them could nevertheless be called tragic. None of Bernanos' "saints" is a tragic figure; they are all bearers of joy, and from the depths of their souls gleams the silver laughter of Sister Constance. Tragic is what the face of the world can be when it turns against the saints burning with rage:

What else can happen? What more could they do than Nero and Tiberius? Is not the Lord's shameful death the disguise of all disguises? They dressed the master of creation in the guise of a slave and nailed him to the wood like a slave. Earth and hell together could never go beyond such a monstrous and sacrilegious act of roguishness. Giving men to beasts as food and making them into torches: Doesn't this evoke the idea of some hor-

---

[104] Ibid., 359–60.
[105] Ibid., 363.

rible farce? Yes, of course: we will always be stunned by suffering and death. But what could these grotesque shenanigans mean in the sight of the Angels? They would doubtless make them laugh, if Angels could laugh.[106]

---

[106] *Carmélites*, 165.

II. THE CHURCH

1. The Priestly Office and Holiness

Just as man is always surpassing his present reality in order to move in the direction of God, so too the Church is engaged in outgrowing her present earthly form and assuming the form of God's eschatological Kingdom. This is why the Church is always open to the world envisaged by God's redemptive deed. Because from the outset the Church always surpasses her own reality, we cannot say that her visible aspect simply coincides with her invisible aspect, although the two do constitute one single reality. The situation is similar to that of man: the here-and-now reality of his body imparts to his soul, too, a here-and-now reality, even though this does not mean that the soul can be wholly reduced to the categories of sensory perception: "Indeed, nothing seems to be better regulated and more strictly ordered, hierarchized, and balanced than the exterior life of the Church. But her interior life overflows with the wondrous freedoms, we could almost say with the divine extravagances, of the Spirit—of the Spirit that blows where he will."[1] Bernanos then reminds us of the theologians' distinction between the "body" and "soul" of the Church. Whoever belongs to the body has a right to all the privileges of the "Catholic, Apostolic, and Roman order"; but millions of persons in the world partake of the Church's interior life "almost without knowing it", in the same way as, for example, millions can share interiorly in a culture such as the French without themselves being French.[2] The Church is present wherever there is genuine, selfless love, because love is community, ultimately community in the absolute, community effected in God and by God, and, therefore, in the end it can only be one community; or, what amounts to the same thing: the Church is present wherever there is holiness. With this we confront the duality that is decisive for Bernanos' whole conception of the Church and that also justifies it, even though all sorts of restrictions

---

[1] *Liberté*, 283.
[2] Ibid., 23.

will subsequently have to be made concerning this twofold character. The visible Church finds her fundamental expression in the priestly office and in the sacraments this office administers; "but the invisible Church is the Church of the saints."[3]

> *There can be no question whatsoever of opposing the visible Church and the invisible Church.* Just consider that the visible Church is not only the ecclesiastical hierarchy. She is you, she is me—which means the Church is not always a pleasant thing. At times it's even been a very unpleasant thing to have to look at the Church close up, in the fifteenth century, for instance, at the time of the Council of Basel. In such cases one is naturally tempted to regret the fact that *the* Church is not the invisible Church alone. Yes, one regrets that a cardinal can be recognized from far away by his beautiful scarlet cape while a saint, during his lifetime, cannot be told by any peculiarity of dress. . . . Alas, I am well aware of the fact that what here appears to be a jest is at times for many souls a torturing idea. We are wrong to think that the visible Church and the invisible Church are in reality two Churches. The visible Church is actually what we can see of the invisible Church, and this visible part of the invisible Church varies with each of us. For, the less worthy we are of knowing the Church's divine reality, the better we know what she has about her that is human. If this were not so, how could you explain the odd fact that those who are most entitled to be scandalized by the flaws, the distortions, and even the malformations of the visible Church —I mean the saints—are precisely the ones who never complain about them?[4]

The fact that the Church's visible and invisible aspects do *not* co-incide is the greatest boon God could have given his Church:

> Oh, yes, of course: if the world were the masterpiece of an architect bent on symmetry, or of a logic professor—in other words, of a deist God—then the Church would offer a spectacle of perfection and order. Holiness would be the first privilege of those in charge, and every step of the hierarchy would correspond to a higher degree of holiness, all the way up to the holiest of all, who of course would be our Holy Father the Pope. Come now! Is this the kind of Church you would want? Would you feel at home in such a place? Allow me to laugh! Instead of feeling at home, you would stop at the threshold of this congregation of supermen,

---

[3] Ibid.

[4] Ibid., 284–85. (The italics are von Balthasar's.—TRANS.)

turning your cap in your hands, like a poor beggar at the door of the Ritz or of Claridge's. The Church is a family home, a father's house, and there is always disorder in this kind of home. Often the chairs lack a leg, the tables are stained with ink, and the jars of jam empty out all by themselves in the cupboards. I know what I'm talking about, because I've experienced it.[5]

Since we live in a sinful order, this visible and invisible aspect of the Church cannot in the end help taking on the traits of the Pauline conceptual pair of "flesh" and "spirit", for Christ became not only a "body" but indeed "flesh", flesh without sin but with the weaknesses attendant upon sin:

No one can doubt the fact that the Church involves governance. But, as such, her action is extremely slow and awkward, and her inertia colossal. You would think that God half-paralyzes her members in order to develop her interior life all the more! The Church's body is massive, and we can well understand the illusion of this earth's demi-gods who, fooled by that body's gigantic proportions, think that the only source of fear for them is the Church's body. They approach it with great caution, barely graze it with their fingertips, and then little by little begin gaining courage until they think they've won the contest. "Pshaw! Is that all there was to it?", they muse. They have no way of knowing that the reactions of this huge body are absolutely different from anything in their experience. . . . The Body of the Church moves only when impelled by the interior Being dwelling with it. This Being is normally absorbed in contemplation and prayer but is also extraordinarily sensitive to certain mysterious warnings and signs that only it perceives. And, naturally, the Body always finds the Spirit's impulse to be initially painful. The Body of the Church is never more wretched than at the very moment when the Spirit is about to triumph.[6]

We could develop this last thesis one-sidedly until we produced a dialectic that would identify the ever-greater abasement and humiliation of the visible, official Church as coinciding with the ever-greater liberation of the interior Church of love. We cannot deny the fact that Bernanos did occasionally go a step too far in this direction. But the feeling for ecclesial authenticity, innate in him as a Frenchman and a Catholic living within a very ancient tradition, served him as an

[5] Ibid., 285.
[6] *Anglais*, 237.

organ for regaining equilibrium, and he did always in fact recover his balance. But Bernanos did not conceal his central concern. In a time when the Church's official and organizational aspect appeared continually to gain the upper hand, Bernanos—precisely for reasons of ecclesial balance—campaigned for the Church of the saints with all the energy and spontaneity native to him. But he did not for a moment forget that particular, exemplary holiness—and this alone concerned him—needs the official Church, her support, and her help in order to do its proper work more urgently than it needs bread. We could even say that, for Bernanos, the saint—which means the subjective following of Christ and the realization of his holiness within the sphere of the human person—is simply unthinkable without the objective holiness of the Church, of her official ministry, and of her sacraments. No other Catholic writer—not even Bloy, Péguy, or Claudel—has ever dealt with this side of holiness more convincingly. The connection between the saint and the priesthood and its sacraments, the transposition to the former of the divine holiness objectively contained in the latter, so that it becomes subjective, personal holiness: this is the exact point where Bernanos' saintly heroes begin to emerge. But precisely for this reason he was also entitled to stress this other aspect: that the whole of the hierarchical and sacramental order in the end is there for the saint, that is, for the subjective sanctification of Christians in general, for those who at base have already been made holy through baptism. The sacramental order exists for this fundamental sanctification of all and does not function only accidentally or marginally, as it were, for the subjective sanctification of the special elect who are termed "saints" in a qualified sense. By the same token, the "saint" in the narrow sense of the word becomes a person who has been appropriated by the Church and hence a person who, in his own way, exercises an "official" function within the Church: he appears as the exemplary goal and end of all hierarchical activity. The "canonization" of saints by the hierarchy is the latter's recognition that in heaven there obtains a different, invisible "hierarchy", which does not suspend the earthly one but grows straight across it and develops beyond it: "When we consider the strict discipline that keeps every member of this great ecclesiastical body almost ruthlessly in his assigned place —from the modest curate all the way to the Holy Father with his privileges, titles, and we'd almost say his peculiar vocabulary—does it not strike us as an extravagance when we witness these sudden, at times very sudden, promotions of obscure nuns, simple laymen, or even beggars who are abruptly made patron saints, protectors, and occasionally even doctors of the Universal Church?"[7]

From this perspective we can understand the explosive hymn of triumph to the Church of the saints with which Bernanos concludes his *Joan, Heretic and Saint.* We must listen to it in order for our ears to catch the leitmotifs of everything that will follow:

The hour of the saints is always coming. *Our Church is the Church of the saints.* If someone approaches her with distrust, he will think he is seeing only closed doors, barricades, and spyholes—a sort of spiritual police station. *But our Church is the Church of the saints.* If only he could become a saint, what bishop would not give up his ring, miter, and crozier? What cardinal would not give up his purple? What pope would not give up his white robe, his chamberlains, his Swiss guards, and all his temporal power? Who would not desire to have the strength to dare this admirable adventure? For sanctity is an adventure, we might even say the only adventure. Once you have understood this, you have reached the very heart of Catholic faith, you have felt the thrill in your mortal flesh of a terror different from that of death—the terror of a superhuman hope. *Our Church is the Church of the saints.* But who worries about the saints? We would like them to be venerable old men full of experience and politics, but in fact most of them are children. And children stand alone against all others. The clever shrug their shoulders and smile, saying: "What saint owed much to the churchmen?" Ha! Why bring in the churchmen? Why should this or that person, who is sure that the Kingdom of Heaven can be acquired like a seat in the French Academy —by cultivating connections with everybody—have access to the most heroic of men? God did not create the Church so that the saints would prosper but for the Church to transmit their memory, lest a whole torrent of honor and poetry should be lost along with the divine miracle. Let some other church show off its saints! *Ours is the Church of the saints.* Into whose care would you put this flock of angels? History would, all by itself, have shattered them with its summary method and its narrow and harsh realism. But our Catholic tradition bears them along, without wounding them, in its universal rhythm. Saint Benedict with his crow, Saint Francis with his lute and his Provençal verses, Joan with her sword, Vincent de Paul with his shabby cassock, and our last arrival—so odd, so secretive, at once tortured by entrepreneurs and simoniacs and yet always with her mysterious smile: Thérèse of the Child Jesus. Do we

[7] *Liberté*, 283–84.

really wish that all of these would have been placed, during their lifetime, in golden shrines and decked out with bombastic epithets, then to
be lauded with genuflections and incense? Such niceties are only good
for cathedral canons! The saints lived and suffered like us. They were
tempted like us. They carried their full load, and more than one of them,
without letting go of his burden, lay down under it to die there. . . . All
of the Church's tremendous superstructure—her wisdom, force, supple
discipline, magnificence, majesty—is nothing of itself unless charity an-
imates it. But human mediocrity can look in that grandeur for a solid
reassurance against the risks of the divine. No matter! The least little
child attending catechism classes knows that the blessing imparted by
all the churchmen in the world together will bring peace only to those
souls already prepared to receive it—that is, to men of good will. No
ceremony can dispense us from loving. . . . We have great respect for
administrative officers, the military police, surgeon-majors and cartogra-
phers, but our heart is with the men of the vanguard, our heart is with
those who get themselves killed.[8]

Bernanos loved this last thought so much that he again puts it on
the lips of his country priest: "A sentence I read I don't know where
has been haunting me for two days: My heart is with those in the
vanguard, my heart is with those who get themselves killed.—Those
who get themselves killed . . . Soldiers, missionaries . . ."[9]

Bernanos' whole trend of thought and all of his emphases should alone
have sufficed to separate him forever from the Action Française. How
could someone whose faith envisioned the Church in the manner we
have just seen ever have opted for *order* and against the freedom of the
Holy Spirit? No: in this connection, too, he was ever a follower of
Péguy. The chaplain's Good Friday sermon in the Carmelite church
of Compiègne, during the French Revolution, once again says everything and sums up Bernanos' whole stance in very mature form:

What can I say? In less somber times, the homage due his divine Majesty
easily takes on the character of a simple ceremonial, all too similar to
the one observed to honor the kings of this world. I am not saying
that God does not accept this kind of homage—although we must say
that the spirit that inspires them belongs more to the Old than to the

---

[8] *Jeanne*, 61–66.
[9] *Curé*, 272.

New Testament. But at times he grows weary of it, if you'll excuse the expression. The Lord always did live and still continues to live among us like a poor man, and the moment always arrives when he decides to make us poor like himself. He does this that he might be welcomed and honored by the poor, in the manner of the poor, and that he might thus again enjoy what he had experienced so frequently back then, on the roads of Galilee: the hospitality of the destitute, their simple welcome.[10]

The New Covenant finds its ultimate truth in discipleship; all official functions of the ecclesial institution remain at the service of the concrete following of Christ. The prioress is not overly distraught by the ongoing persecution of priests during the Revolution: "When priests are wanting," she says, "there is an overabundance of martyrs, and the balance of grace is thus restored."[11]

We can therefore affirm that, for Bernanos, *the ecclesial drama is played out between the priest and the saint*, as representatives of the two equally strong and equally important poles of objective holiness (ordination, authority, sacrament) and subjective holiness, the latter of which continually adheres to and depends on the first and cannot distance itself from it for a single instant. But this image of the two poles, true as it is, still does not wholly reveal what is ultimately crucial here: the movement the saint accomplishes when he makes the objective holiness of the Church become subjective holiness in his person. Always within the Church, and without in the slightest leaving her behind, the saint transcends the sphere of objectivity and official functions. This transcending is one and the same as Christian freedom: it always constitutes an enormous event, a feat of "daring unto God", a kind of explosion. Luther—for whom Bernanos had a great and painful interest and for whom he daily prayed—abandoned the sphere of the Church through his act of explosive transcendence. He acted wrongly: he should have exploded *within* both himself and the Church, and then he would probably have become a saint. Bernanos, however, did not want to show merely that the Church's official functions are indispensable to the saint as a sort of springboard from which to soar. In a way that made him more deeply Catholic than any of the other great Catholic writers, Bernanos would demonstrate how the Church's official functions and ministries are what makes the saint's leap to sanc-

[10] *Carmélites*, 145–46.
[11] Ibid., 150.

tity at all possible, and indeed not only by providing a mere elevation from which to jump but by tracing the precise line of flight that
sanctity must follow. Bernanos showed how the priestly office in this
way fulfills one of its highest ecclesial functions. The priestly office
and ministry "launch" the saint and "offer" him up sacrificially; and,
by the very fact that the priestly office "launches" him, the saint is
sustained by it.

"Saints don't pass through our midst without wreaking a lot of
havoc, but something's got to be sacrificed!"[12] Such, understandably,
is the attitude of the clergy with regard to the bothersome fellow in
the Church who later, after his death, will come up for canonization.
The saint "bursts open" an order that has become too narrow and
encrusted, and when is he to do this if not during his lifetime? The
dean who appears in the *Country Priest* is by no means conceived as
a caricature. He is voicing one very legitimate side of the Church's
life when he speaks of the burden God loads upon his Church when
he gives her a saint:

> God preserve us from reformers! . . . God preserve us also from saints!
> Hold your objections and allow me to be a little whimsical! Listen to me
> first. As you know, the Church raises to her altars—and this usually a
> long time after their death—only a very small number of the exception-
> ally just. Their teaching and heroic examples first have to undergo the
> test of a very rigorous inquest. Only then do they become the common
> treasure of all the faithful. But don't forget that these are not at all free
> to draw on this treasury without any supervision. With all due respect,
> we could say that in the end these admirable persons are like wines of
> inestimable value, but slow in the making, which cost the vintner so
> much effort and care and yet are destined to titillate the palate only of
> his grand-nephews. . . . I'm only kidding, of course. Nevertheless, you'll
> note that God seems to be wary of multiplying among us secular priests
> —his regular troops, so to speak—saints who are rich in prodigies and
> miracles, those supernatural adventurers who at times make the hierar-
> chy's officials tremble. Is not the Curé d'Ars an exception? Isn't there
> an insignificant proportion between the venerable host of irreproachable
> and zealous clerics who consecrate all their strength to the crushing tasks
> of the ministry and those who are canonized? And yet, who would dare
> claim that the practice of heroic virtues is the privilege of monks, or
> indeed of simple laymen?

---

[12] *Soleil*, 264.

Quite aside from the slightly disrespectful and paradoxical character of such a jest, do you now understand how I could in a certain sense be right when I say: "God preserve us from saints"? Too often they have been a trial for the Church, before becoming her glory. And I am not even speaking about those incomplete and failed saints who swarm all about the real ones and are like nickels and dimes to their solid greenbacks: like all huge coins, they are more of a nuisance than a help! What shepherd, what bishop would want to be in command of such troops? They do have the spirit of obedience, granted! But even so . . .[13]

This sigh from the clergy is justified; Bernanos was quite careful not to take too lightly this harangue of the good dean in defense of the "regular troops" who practice a hidden heroism that is rewarded with no decorations. But, even though Bernanos was not primarily concerned with miracles and other extraordinary charisms, his all-consuming interest nevertheless was sanctity. Decisive for him was the fact that nothing can take the place of sanctity in the Church and that the very genus "Christian" stands and falls with sanctity. Thus, when he spoke in his own name, he used rather different language:

> What most matters is to know what exactly a Christian person is. For there does exist a "type", or model, of the Christian person, and this type is determined by the Church herself: it is the saint. The saints are the army of the Church. Can we judge the strength of a people by the quality of its diplomats? Well, then: the Church's diplomats aren't really worth much; and, precisely because they are merely average, they don't yield their place very easily. They are like bumbling jugglers who have to start their trick twenty times over. But the Church in arms—this is what counts! . . . The Church in arms is the Church in deployment, with the saints in the first line of battle.[14]

The Church must bear the burden of sanctity because the Church is herself borne by the saints. In 1947 Bernanos gave a conference in Algeria to the Little Sisters of Charles de Foucauld on "*Our Friends the Saints*". Though brightened by humor, the delightful conference was meant in dead earnest. In it, he compared the Church to a "huge transportation company, transportation to paradise, that is", and the saints to those who organize the transportation. For two thousand years there have been innumerable catastrophes, derailments, and crashes,

---

[13] *Curé*, 80–81.
[14] *Anglais*, 245.

but thanks to the saints the enterprise is still functioning: "Without the saints, this I can tell you, Christianity would long since have become a gigantic heap of ruins, a pile of overturned locomotives, burned-out railway cars, twisted rails, and tangled scraps of iron—all of it rusting under the rain."[15] The stationmaster and the train conductor are men standing alone, while thousands sit in the cars. Either the safety or the undoing of this great multitude depends on the responsibility of these solitaries.

The saint is the person whom God himself has singled out. Even though often he is so unlike the others, still he is the "type" of the Christian. He is the "idea" from which one may deduce what it means to be a Christian. Insofar as this is possible to sinners and fallible human beings, the saints—in their following of Christ—embody with full purity what in the others remains admixed with all manner of earthly dross and cannot therefore be exhibited in all its brightness. We can easily understand here why a writer concerned with beauty and purity of form would have selected the saints as his heroes. There exists a theological and ecclesiological æsthetics that has nothing to do with æstheticism. The purity of human beauty here converges with supernatural beauty. Within this sphere, all the tragic antics that normally surround the garden-variety heroes produced by novelists suddenly lose all their weight and validity in order to make way for other laws, the specific laws of sanctity. Such a fact will astonish only literary critics, because the Christian, for his part, should long since have been accustomed by the Gospel to locate the common rule and "type" for all Christian life in the highest individual case: "I have dreamed of saints and heroes, skipping all the intervening forms of our species, and now I realize that these intervening forms barely exist and that only the saints and the heroes count. The intervening forms are like bland porridge, a real potpourri: take a sampling from anywhere at random, and you'll know what all of it tastes like. And such a gelatinous mass wouldn't even deserve a name if the saints and the heroes didn't give it one, didn't give it their own name, which is Man."[16]

---

[15] *Liberté*, 265–66.
[16] *Enfants*, 199–200.

2. Obedience

Holy is the person to whom a mysterious grace gives the force to pass beyond the boundaries of mediocrity (and, hence, beyond every mean and average) to enter a unique destiny that becomes the norm by which to measure mediocrity. This crossing of boundaries occurs by virtue of a call from God and thus is an act of obedience. At this level, the way leads into a wholly untrodden and pathless territory, all the more so as this way is, to the end, a following of the suffering Christ, whose abandonment by God and descent into the hour and place of darkness was a sheer treading in the pathless, or better, a *being trodden* and *being dragged* through the pathless. The more this way adheres to Christ, the more sightless it becomes.

Such transcending, however, cannot lead outside the Church but only deeper into her. Thus, obedience to God can only be an ever-deeper ecclesial obedience. It may indeed be that, when the average Christian obeys the Church, he does so in an average manner: that is, he adheres to her when she explicitly demands something of him, and for all the rest he lives his life and makes his decisions according to his own feelings and with a free responsibility all his own. Things stand very differently with the saint. His act of crossing over into "the sightless and pathless" largely robs him of this supposed average freedom in order to give him a different and higher freedom in God. The saint, then, by contrast to the average Christian, will cling to the injunctions and instructions of ecclesial authority, which for him becomes most concrete in his father confessor and his spiritual director. It belongs to the essence of this obedience that the one giving injunctions cannot himself accompany the one obeying on his way. It remains an absolutely solitary way shrouded in unseeing night.

Nevertheless, no one can really walk upon this way unless a representative of the Church starts him on it and orders him to do it, and unless this representative maintains deep contact with the one he has "launched", whatever shape this contact may assume and however it may be described. Nowadays we would be tempted to speak of a relationship of "remote control", provided this technological image could include the much greater freedom of both God and the one obeying, and provided we did not lose from sight the ever-present element of surprise for the Church's representative in charge; for the flight trajectory of the saint who has been thus "launched" infallibly

leads in a different direction from anything that could have been foreseen. The ecclesial representative in charge must, through an absolute
obedience to God, change his standpoint when necessary in order to
follow the developing curve and not arrive too late at the "landing",
for which he must be present. This ineffably subtle relationship, defined by a wholly indispensable accompaniment from a distance that
is really no distance at all, involves, in fact, a *community in solitude*
that in the last analysis is rooted in the christological and trinitarian
mystery, here transposed into the ecclesial realm: the Son on earth is
accompanied by the Father in the Holy Spirit, from the "distance" of
heaven, which is no distance at all.

This relationship between the saint and his ecclesial guide has interior dimensions that are as rich and varied as the number of cases
involved. Bernanos portrayed this relationship on four different occasions: in *Under Satan's Sun*, in the relationship between Donissan and
his advisor, Menou-Segrais; in *Joy*, in that between Chantal and her
confessor, the Abbé Chevance; in the *Country Priest*, in the relationship of the little priest with his friend, the Curé de Torcy, who guides
him in such a paternal way; and in the *Dialogues of the Carmelites*, in
that of little Blanche with both her prioresses. To round off the picture, we also have the short study on Joan of Arc, and, as almost
perfectly inverted mirror images and demonic caricatures, we have,
in *A Crime*, the relationship between the alleged priest and the young
altar boy and, in *Monsieur Ouine*, that between Ouine and Philippe,
which we will have to deal with later.

Those who obey can be priests or laymen, men or women; but
those in command can only be priests or (in the case of the prioresses) those who have received official authority in the name of
the Church. It is never a question of those in command acting as
private individuals who, even as Christians, ascribe to themselves the
authority to do what they must do. This would constitute the most
terrible *hybris* imaginable. But, by virtue of the office they hold, they
perform their task in keeping with the charge given them, and they do
so with the same sober certainty with which the one in their charge
obeys. In the priestly office, it is not more difficult to lead on the
way of sanctity one God has called than it is, also by virtue of the
priestly office, to absolve him of his sins or to anoint him unto eternal
life. The expropriation of all private and personal elements is equally
great on both sides; such expropriation or dispossession is the absolute

presupposition for that most mysterious of all acts of love, whereby the objective holiness of the Church (which is the holiness of Christ himself) enters into the subjective holiness of the one called (who as such can only enact and portray the holiness of the Church).

In this connection, the scenes between Donissan and Menou-Segrais are most fundamental. In their inexorable clarity and their hardness, which is but the hardness of true love, they are a precisely aimed punch in the face of modern personalism, both inside and outside the Church. Personalism can never attain the highest level of the person, since it remains tethered to the laws of the self. The heights are reached only by ecclesial obedience: "God and your bishop, my child, have given you a master, and that is me." Donissan then looks "with a curiosity full of fright at this old priest, normally so polite and now suddenly so stiff, so imperturbable, and with so hard a glance in his eyes".[17] This older priest, the dean of Campagne, is a humanist and a scholar, and in his advanced age he no longer engages much in spiritual direction. He is the precise opposite of Donissan with his wild zeal for souls. And Menou-Segrais expressly puts his finger on this difference: "You have just entrusted yourself into my hands. . . . But do you know what hands these are? I'll tell you: they are the hands of *a man you don't regard very highly*."[18] In actual fact, the dean possesses deep goodness and even tenderness, but he must conceal these for the sake of his function. Chevance will tell his penitent the reason for this: "Divine love is a thousand times harder and stricter than justice. For a long time God can still grant us the grace of loving us as we love little children. But the hour must arrive when we learn —at the price of what anguish!—that the most inhuman of all man's passions has in God its unutterable image and that he is . . . a jealous God."[19]

Menou-Segrais bids the young priest set out on his adventure by confirming his vocation in the name of the Church:

> We find ourselves at that hour of life (it strikes for everyone) when truth imposes itself all on its own with irresistible evidence, the hour when each of us has but to stretch out his arms in order to rise in one single stroke to the surface of the darkness and enter the light of God's sun.

---

[17] *Soleil*, 102.
[18] Ibid., 100.
[19] *Joie*, 42–43.

At such a time human prudence is tantamount to entrapment and folly. Sanctity . . . [is] a vocation, a call. You will have to rise to where God is awaiting you—rise or be lost. Expect no human aid. Fully aware of the responsibility I'm taking on, and having tested your obedience and simplicity one last time, I have thought it good to speak to you in this way. By entertaining doubts concerning not only your strength but also God's plans for you, you were heading for an impasse. Running my own risk and danger, I now return you to your road. I hereby turn you over to those awaiting you, to the souls whose prey you'll be. . . . May the Lord bless you, my little child![20]

In the midst of his temptations, Donissan knows exactly the portion allotted to him, even if his trials distort its image: "From the position of mediocrity where, to his despair, he felt he was languishing, the words of the Abbé Menou-Segrais transported him to a height that made the fall inevitable. Was not his former sense of abandonment preferable to this joy that would now leave him in the lurch?"[21] Then the solitary priest sets out on his road. Menou-Segrais follows him with his glance as he goes. He "no longer has any hope of reading in such a secretive heart".[22] He inquires among those of his confrères who may know more than he but learns nothing from them. With prayerful anxiety he accompanies, unseen, the one whom he has launched on the ways of sanctity. Indeed, later on, after the "miracle", when Donissan again comes to him for a manifestation of conscience and stutteringly hints at his dark secret, Menou-Segrais expressly dismisses him, leaving him alone with his secret: "'What fate awaits you then, my son?' The young priest lightly shrugged his shoulders. 'I will not ask you your secret. Once I would have been entitled to do so. But at present we are parting roads, you and I, and already you no longer belong to me.' 'Don't speak like that', the Abbé Donissan whispered, his eyes dark and staring. 'Wherever I may go, no matter how far down I sink, . . . I will remember your charity'."[23]

Menou-Segrais completed his work. After listening to his protégé without "any surprise", with "an attention that was calm, indifferent to the person, barely interested in the facts, with a hint of haughty

---

[20] *Soleil,* 110–11.
[21] Ibid., 139.
[22] Ibid., 141.
[23] Ibid., 237.

compassion",[24] he still gives Donissan a few last bits of advice, especially on what he should and should not say to his confessor. The manner in which Menou-Segrais releases Donissan "unto God" shows the degree to which the Church's guidance prepares for direction by God himself, and how little the former stands in competition with the latter. The theme is again taken up when Chantal finds herself forcibly abandoned at the death of her father confessor, who henceforth can accompany her only in "spirit" through his earlier instructions.

Donissan's obedience is perfect. He is so humble and childlike that "his spiritual director's barely displayed desire to be contradicted a bit"[25] remains unsatisfied. The young priest feels how hard submission is; but he knows precisely that his obedience to divine guidance is undergoing its "tensile test" by his being required to submit to the person of Menou-Segrais. He also grasps the fact that a certain nonunderstanding belongs to the exigencies of his way and that therefore another—the officially delegated priest—must take his place in understanding what he himself is not given to see. The darkening of his faith and hope—something exacted from him in the place and for the benefit of others, to the point that he seriously feels damned—would be impossible without his depositing all of his trust in obedience. Without knowing "the secret of this big child",[26] Menou-Segrais has "seen clearly [in Donissan] from the first day" and discerned in him the sign of his being chosen for the experience of the dark night of the soul.[27] For this very reason, he can also, when the moment comes, understand correctly the words of contradiction that escape Donissan.

Donissan believes that his mission must be interpreted in the sense that God is demanding of him that he should "pursue Satan into the very souls" of people, in such a way that he "cannot avoid endangering his own peace of soul, his priestly honor, and even his eternal salvation".[28] When the older priest protests sharply against such ideas, Donissan answers his director "calmly" that he is suffering from "a great illusion". Donissan "does not seem to realize how removed such words are from his usual tone of respect and humility. 'I can have no doubts about the will that is urging me on', he says, 'nor about the

[24] Ibid., 226.
[25] Ibid., 118.
[26] Ibid., 120.
[27] Ibid., 232.
[28] Ibid., 236.

fate that awaits me.' "²⁹ Then a certain intuition begins to dawn on
Menou-Segrais: he is on the track of Donissan's secret. With difficulty
he brings himself to admit that Donissan must have made "something
like a dangerous vow or a promise", or, if not a vow or a promise ("I
could never have emitted such without my confessor's permission"),
then "something similar to these": he has perhaps formulated the desire to offer his own eternal happiness to God as a forfeit to redeem
the souls of the lost.³⁰

At this point the "masterful surgeon of souls, always firm in his
prudence and his sovereign good sense", must intervene.³¹ He forbids the young priest to foster such thoughts any further. In them
he recognizes the effect of satanic temptation, not indeed temptation
as sin, but the way a "saint" can deliver himself over to Satan on
account of sin. It is not the business of man to bring this power of
the demon into play, even if it serves the work of redemption. To be
sure, the interior laws of the night of the soul sneer at all attempts
by psychology to comprehend them. Menou-Segrais knows this, and
he understands the unique form—comparable with none other—that
freedom assumes in the saint whom the Church has "launched": he
offers his plunge to God by giving him subsequently, as it were, what
God has already, preliminarily, taken from him—which is nothing less
than the light of his soul and his hope for salvation. From the outset
this man had uttered his Yes to God; what God now does in him
is to subject him to suffering, strip down his soul, impress spiritual
stigmata upon him. The one suffering such things ought not to think
that he must still offer himself to God in any active sense. The only
thing he must do is not to flee, in particular from the extraordinary
graces God imposes upon him. The responsibility for them falls back
on God but also on his Church. The Church's authorities can at no
moment feel that they are left as unparticipating bystanders without
responsibility for what goes on in a saint's life, not even in his most
extreme adventures and dark nights. It was through ecclesial obedience that the saints first entered upon their way. The Church, in
her place, and God, in his, were the ones who propelled them upon
the road of sanctity. The saints belong to the sacrificial matter of the

²⁹ Ibid.
³⁰ Ibid., 241.
³¹ Ibid., 242.

Holy Mass that the Church publicly and sacramentally offers up to God.

It is thus that Menou-Segrais, having shouldered his burden of responsibility, elevates his priestly hands:

> Unbelieving fools do not admit the existence of saints. Devout fools imagine they sprout all by themselves like the grass of the fields. Only few people know that the tree is all the more fragile as it is rare in kind. Your own destiny, to which so many other destinies are doubtless bound, stands at the mercy of some blunder, some abuse of grace—even involuntary—some hasty decision, some ambiguity, some misunderstanding. *And you have been entrusted to me! You belong to me! How my hands tremble as I offer you up to God! I am not allowed a single mistake. How brutal a thing it is for me not to be able to fall to my knees alongside you and join you in a profound thanksgiving!*[32]

But the case of Donissan is no longer a merely private case of conscience for which his spiritual director could assume responsibility. He has become a public case, and his director no longer has the right to make decisions on his own: "On all of this", he tells Donissan, "I must now consult our superiors. My own support won't take you very far! At the same time, you must not conceal anything. And then . . . , yes indeed, what then? Who knows when you'll be able to overcome the defiance of some, the pity of others, and the opposition of all! Will you *ever* overcome all of this?"[33] This means that the responsibility Menou-Segrais must now share with the bishop represents for him an intensified responsibility with regard to Donissan: he takes it upon himself to hurl him not only into the arms of God (and Satan) but also into the huge machinery of the Church's administration, between the wheels of which we can foresee that the young priest is about to be crushed: "From now on, and for an indefinite period of time, everybody will look on you as nothing but an insignificant little priest full of imagination and self-sufficiency, half-dreamer, half-liar, or perhaps a madman. You must therefore undergo the penance that will surely be imposed on you, the temporary silence and oblivion of some monastery. Accept it, not as an unjust punishment, but as something necessary and justified. . . . Have you understood me this

---

[32] Ibid., 243. (The italics are von Balthasar's.—TRANS.)
[33] Ibid., 244.

time?"[34] After doing penance for five years at La Trappe,[35] another part of his punishment will be his assignment to work under the Curé de Luzarnes. This priest is a small-time rationalist with nothing to prepare him for Donissan's interior adventure: he is a typical representative of a Church overstrained by the presence and life of her saints.[36] Consequently, Donissan allows responsibilities to be piled on him that he simply cannot bear, and all of this leads to the catastrophe of the failed miracle: " 'I take everything upon me', he concluded after a barely noticeable hesitation, punctuating his words with a cutting gesture full of conviction."[37] "Go and give the child's little corpse back to his mother!"[38]

The report on Donissan that the Curé de Luzarnes writes up is wholly conditioned by the situation: he can see only what he can perceive through the veil of clerical ideology, and the one he wears is dense indeed.[39] But it is characteristic of Bernanos that he wants to see, and actually can see, the truth even through the holes of such a mask as this. Characteristic too, at a deeper level, is the fact that even the severe limitations of the Curé de Luzarnes can no longer in any way touch the God-sustained truth of the miracle worker. The wheel track that Menou-Segrais had traced is too deep and too straight for anyone else to come along and deflect. And the mystery of suffering has now entered too far into its passive phase for anyone's misdirected active interventions (including Donissan's own by virtue of his despair) to affect it adversely.

The relationship of obedience again emerges between the Abbé Chevance and the young woman Chantal. Here, too, such a relationship is indispensable for Chantal to advance on her way, and this results in both her deliverance from some burdens and her assumption of others. But in this case the screw is turned a few times tighter than in *Under Satan's Sun*. The first increased difficulty is the death of Chevance. Although he has left the girl in a wonderful state

---

[34] Ibid., 231.
[35] Ibid., 248.
[36] Ibid., 275.
[37] Ibid., 282.
[38] Ibid., 296.
[39] Ibid., 272f., 289f.

of both natural and grace-given unawareness and has schooled her for her coming trials, Chevance dies at the very moment when these are about to begin. Consequently, nearly all of the help Chantal will receive from the hierarchical Church in the future will have to be drawn from her memory of the teachings and example of the dead Chevance. Then there is a second difficulty, and this is the manner of Chevance's death, which is something incomprehensible for both Chantal and all other onlookers. The dedicated, humble, and merry man dies the atrocious and smothering death of a sinner. This horror forever deprives her of a part of her ability to understand: it leaves her with her friend the priest to be deposited in God. She herself had offered this open flank to suffering. By unburdening her, Chevance had prepared her more effectively for her coming passion than by any lesson he could teach her: "The old priest had taken something with him, or at least a precious part of herself had drowned, as it were, in his silent and solemn death agony, incomprehensible to her. No, it was not her hope in God, which was the very source of her life. Nor was it her innocent sense of security, which was subtler and firmer than any calculation on the part of restless souls. It was simply that the severe master was no longer there, the one who steadily plucked from her her mysterious joy so that she would not feel the burden of its supernatural weight."[40]

While he was still alive, things were easy: "She had long striven not to keep anything for herself. She made an effort to pass on to others the alms that fell upon her day by day from heaven. And why should she have thought twice about it? Only one thing was required of her: to give the old priest an exact account of what she received. He, however, was made even more impenetrable by his incredible meekness, and he patiently waited for the measure to be full and for God to reveal himself to this heart that already overflowed with him, though without knowing it."[41] Everything in Chantal is so in its right place and she is so innocent that she cannot be hurled without transition into the realm of sinners. The terrible disenchantments she is about to experience in the dark kingdom in some sense have to be outdone in advance by one massive disenchantment within the kingdom of light, the Church—a disenchantment that will serve as foun-

---

[40] *Joie*, 37.
[41] Ibid., 37–38.

dation for all else. This comes with the alienation that the priest's horrible death inserts between her and Chevance, "the fundamental disenchantment that must sooner or later steel a heart predestined for God." And this alienation is the crucible and the mold within which the whole melting process of Chantal's passion can later on occur in the way intended by God and without peril to her.[42] Only now can the inevitable come to pass; God becomes for her "invisible and mute", and the dark cloud of a supernatural sadness overshadows her soul: "Very young children who have known only smiling human faces confront their first harsh glance without any fright, but with a kind of curiosity full of amazement. In the same way, the bitterness of Chevance's death had not weakened Chantal's trust, although the memory she retained of it abided like a shadow between her and the divine presence, which was the sole source of her life."[43] And we have only to think of Mary, the Mother of the Lord, to grasp the truth of the following statements, which Chantal makes to the psychiatrist La Pérouse while trying to explain why she is not afraid of him: "We often know more about evil than people who have only learned to offend God. I have seen a saint die, I who am speaking to you, and it isn't at all what people imagine, it isn't at all like what we read in books. You have to hold your footing before such a spectacle: you feel the very framework of the soul crack. I then understood what sin is."[44] She was overcome by "vertigo in the presence of old Chevance's prostrate corpse", and this she remembers at the end when she must confront the traitor priest; but the bed she recalls is empty: "Today, like yesterday, she could not expect any help or consoling word from the friend of her soul. . . . She knew it had been decreed from all eternity that she would arrive alone at the last bend of the road."[45] Nevertheless, in her solitude she still remains wholly intent on the absent priest, and she continues to obey him across death's wide expanse: "By a rare wonder, she accomplished a movement of soul as pure and innocent as any of those awkward gestures that ravish a mother's heart with love and pity: she vaguely feared having disobeyed him; and so she turned to her old master in

[42] Ibid., 42.
[43] Ibid., 50.
[44] Ibid., 230.
[45] Ibid., 242.

the way a newborn baby moans in her sleep. What would he have said? What would he have thought?"[46]

Chevance, however, had himself suffered his unfathomable death in atoning substitution for the apostate, and the old priest had prepared his spiritual daughter for the same fate. It is therefore not astonishing if in the end Cénabre and Chantal meet one another "in Chevance", in his spirit and work, which consisted precisely in bringing them together. Chevance had broken open[47] a breach in the bad priest's impenetrable armor, and through it Chantal can now enter to complete her sacrifice. Both the victim and the executioner are now made one by the fact that God is absent to them both. Cénabre is aware of this fellowship, and this is his defeat. "Neither Chevance nor you can give me back God," he says to Chantal, "and yet . . . he is more absent from you than from me."[48]

Just as it is love that impels Chevance to offer up the young woman as sacrificial atonement, so too the Curé de Torcy precipitates his young friend, the country priest, into an oblative action, and he does so with all the compassion of a higher, Catholic love: "Even though your shoulders aren't very broad, you have a lot of heart, and you deserve to serve in the infantry. But remember what I now say to you: Don't lose your spine. Once you go to the infirmary, you'll never get out. Your makeup doesn't suit you for a war of attrition. March bravely on and see to it that you meet your end quietly one day in a trench, without having even unhitched your backpack."[49] The little priest shows perfect docility to the Curé de Torcy and also to his actual superior, the dean of Blangermont:[50] "My superiors can disown me if they so wish, since they have the right to do so."[51]

The *Country Priest* has lost the harsh ruthlessness of the first novel, in which the chief goal was to demolish the temple of the Philistines; but under its softer, more "human" surface it contains a no less inexorable and absolute truth. The country priest's battle with himself

---

[46] Ibid., 249.
[47] Ibid., 280.
[48] Ibid., 281–82.
[49] *Curé*, 72.
[50] Ibid., 158f.
[51] Ibid., 168.

is much harder precisely because he is physically much weaker than Donissan: "If I yielded to the temptation of complaining to anyone at all, the last bond between God and me would be shattered, and it seems I would be passing over into the eternal silence."[52] Silence finally becomes a martyrdom for him; he feels obligated to keep the secret of the countess, and this finishes him off: "I must keep silent. . . . When I think that all it would surely have taken a moment ago for me to reveal this secret would have been a word, a pitiful glance, a simple question perhaps! . . . It was already on my lips, and it's God who held it back. Indeed, how well I know that another's compassion can be such a comfort for a moment, and I am far from disdaining it. But it doesn't quench your thirst. It flows through your soul as through a sieve."[53] The Curé de Torcy knows this, and that is why he is both jovial and harsh at once, despite all the tenderness of his soul.

At this point we can see the full significance of the *Mystery of Joan of Arc*. Already in Bloy, Péguy, and Claudel, Joan of Arc had been something wholly other than a "national saint": she was a luminous instance that cast a unique and dazzling light on certain hidden truths of the Christian life. This is true above all in Péguy's three or four books dedicated to her. For Bernanos she becomes the occasion of demonstrating the relationship obtaining in the Church between official ministry and personal sanctity. Donissan, Chevance, and the country priest had been priests who assumed the role of sacrificial "victims". Their relationship to the Church's representatives who offered up the oblation of their lives was a relationship of ecclesial obedience among members of the hierarchy. These "victims" were wonderful examples of the unity of official ministry and personal love in their discipleship of the Son: they embodied the unity of both the shepherd's care and the shepherd's death as it had been recommended, indeed, commanded to Peter by the Lord when Jesus bestowed his official ministry upon him (Jn 21:18f.). The "offerers"—Menou-Segrais and the Curé de Torcy, for instance—did not have less ecclesial love than did their "victims"; in this they were united to the Father of Jesus in his action of delivering over his Son. This trinitarian image was by rights much more intrinsic and deep to the situation than the

[52] Ibid., 144.
[53] Ibid., 283.

relationship of the "victim" to the occasion of his sacrifice, namely, the sinner as executioner. But what if sin lives in the Church herself, if sin anchors itself most securely precisely where the Church is most vulnerable—in her hierarchical structure? What if the horror occurs that the face of Satan should begin to glimmer in the very heart of that trinitarian image, which is the relationship of ecclesial obedience? And since holiness cannot cease being holy, in this case the man holding the office would become an inverted principle: he would become an offerer of sacrifice, not in his capacity as one who loves, but as sinner.

All of Bernanos' efforts in his *Joan, Heretic and Saint* go to showing that the tribunal that condemned Joan of Arc was "regular", and that, "wonder of wonders", it was "a tribunal made up of churchmen".[54] Péguy makes Joan's judges to be a choir of the damned. Claudel, for his part, degrades them into representatives of all bestial vices: they are nothing but a subspecies of man and empty masks. In Bernanos, however, they are indeed scoundrels, but they possess demonic greatness and are exercising their offices with legitimacy: "It would be useless, by means of overly subtle distinctions, to try to turn this regular and regularly constituted tribunal into an exceptional case, a kind of tragic Punch-and-Judy show. To reduce such shabby ruses to nothing, only one fact suffices: the holy Inquisition itself intervened in the trial. The seal of the apostolic delegate is to be seen alongside that of the bishop of Beauvais, at the bottom of the iniquitous sentence."[55] The sentence remains uncontested until the opening of the trial of rehabilitation. All the original judges end their lives in very high offices and positions of honor.[56]

This is the Church, even if represented by the most unworthy of men, and still the Church even if violated in her holiest sphere: the hierarchical Church, doing sinfully what she should have done out of love—namely, offering up what is holy to God. In the midst of the official Church, sanctity agonizes. Bernanos apostrophizes Joan as follows: "They saw your pale cheeks ravaged by fever. They saw the beads of sweat on your small stubborn forehead, and the quivering of your mouth, when, in the stuffy courtroom, you suddenly

[54] *Jeanne*, 15.
[55] Ibid., 17–18.
[56] Ibid., 25f.

refused to resist them any longer after so many days of harassment, and you surrendered your word and your oath, you, the finest flower of chivalry!"[57] Behind this picture of a prey that is being hunted down and driven in circles into an ever narrower impasse, of an animal that begins to tremble as it approaches the horror, do we not sense the presence of the "Second Mouchette" almost palpably? This Mouchette is a darker sister of Joan of Arc, but her destiny can be best understood when we consider her alongside Joan's experience. And, just as *Mouchette* is a work of compassion for the inescapable suffering of creatures, so too *Joan*: "As we approach the finale and we see the harassed saint begin to totter as she is forced from hour to hour to engage in her own naïve and fragile defense, an unexpected pity for her judges suddenly takes hold of you."[58] For the moment, however, it is the judges themselves who are absorbed in self-pity as they strain themselves through a show of compassion to preserve their victim from the fires of hell. Should she not recant, then she is excluded from the communion of saints and forever abandoned to her damnation: "They open out their arms to her, entreating her and calling out to her soul with tender words."[59] There then succeeds in happening what no human power could have brought about: the holy equilibrium of a soul belonging to God is disturbed at its very center, wounded and broken. The knife has bored its way into the person's deepest mystery and has imposed there a lethal opening:

> The words she has just heard in silence, with her precious little head bent humbly toward the ground, have cut her off from everything that lives, from the Holy Universal Church, from a forgiven universe. They have wounded her to the quick in her soul's very heart, at the source itself of her being, which was her tender, her pure hope. Or, rather, it's love, her innocent love, the sweet name of Jesus itself, which has just burst in her heart. You, the bishops of Thérouanne and Noyon, masters Beaupère, Midi, Erart, and Maurice, licentiate Venderès and licentiate Marguerie: she is yours, take away her prostrate body. . . . Whoever possessed the secret of this strange moment would have the key to all the rest; but the secret is well kept. . . . Like those insects that insert a worm in the heart of their living prey, they have made doubt enter her child's soul. And, once its sordid fruit has come full term, they no

---

[57] Ibid., 33.
[58] Ibid., 37.
[59] Ibid., 50.

longer recognize their victim. They search for her and beg her to give them what, through their fault, she is no longer capable of giving: a pure, untouched word that would bring them certitude or forgiveness. They have literally stolen her soul. Still for two days, and with growing impatience, they will vainly shake this corpse. And finally, weary of the ridiculous struggle, they will cast their broken toy into the fire.[60]

Indeed, in the midst of the Church sanctity does agonize. The human sacrifices of Vizlipuzli are repeated here at a much more subtle and cruel depth, a level Claudel never reaches: this agony is a spiritual, more, an ecclesial agony. As Péguy had intuited, it is when they rob Joan of her Christian hope that her torturers have perfected her sacrifice in the image of the sacrifice of the Cross. But Bernanos is here the first to show that this is a sacrifice effected by the Church. Time and again he evokes the distinction that Père Clérissac, O.P., makes between suffering *for* the Church and suffering *through* the Church, that is, *at the hands of* the Church. The "mystical blood",[61] which overflows from the heart of the Church and runs down in atonement over those armed with daggers, is a blood that flows in communion with him who, on the Cross, was the most solitary of all. It is the blood that pours into the chalice of the Church's Holy Sacrifice. The Chantal of *Joy* is, pure and simple, but the transposition of this drama into our own time. Bernanos remained fixated on this mystery: "Whoever possessed the secret of this strange moment would have the key to all the rest." Just as many mystics remain fixated before the Cross as they see the Redeemer's physical body being drained of blood in its forsakenness, so too Bernanos would not be made to budge from the contemplation of this same suffering in the Lord's Mystical Body: *"We must look at this agony face to face. Or, better, we must enter into it. How deep it is, and how cold! All the fire of the executioner's stake cannot succeed in warming it."*[62]

The saint is the person who, in the true sense of the word, has been *cast forth*. He is handed over, hurled out, by God himself: "God does not keep any of us like a precious bird in a cage. . . . He hands over his best friends. He gives them free of charge to the good, to the bad,

---

[60] Ibid., 57–60.
[61] *Dominique*, 38.
[62] *Jeanne*, 60. (The italics are von Balthasar's.—TRANS.)

to everybody, just as he himself was handed over by Pilate: 'See here! Take him! Here is the man!' " [63] And what God does, the Church, too, does after him; and she does it both through her good and her bad members. In paradoxical communion, it is both Cénabre and Chevance who hand Chantal over. But the saint hurls himself forward: "This stripping down of hope—this is the only thing that matters. All the rest is nothing. On the road you have chosen—no! on the road on which you have *cast* yourself!—you will be alone, most definitely alone." [64] "At the decisive moment he accepts the struggle, not out of pride, but driven by an irresistible *impulse*. . . . He was born for war; every bend on his road will be marked by a spurt of blood." [65] "The heroic will *hurls itself* into the heart of danger and makes good use of it." [66] But, when it is no longer possible to hurl oneself actively into suffering, then, in order to continue his movement forward, the saint needs another who will do the hurling for him and keep him on the right trajectory. And who would take this task upon him if not out of obedience to the Church and by virtue of an official ministry? It is this objective ministry that must strengthen the "hurler" so that he will possess the power necessary to lend a vicarious force to the weakness of the one being hurled. Thus, sanctity has a retroactive effect on the official ministry, something that Menou-Segrais is well aware of: "Ever since this blockhead entered my life, he draws everything to himself without realizing it. He leaves me no rest. His mere presence forces me to choose." [67] And, addressing Donissan directly, he says: "You've turned me inside out like a glove. . . . It is you who are forming me." [68]

3. Sacramentality

This whole mystery of the relationship between objective and subjective sanctity in the Church will now no longer be investigated in either a psychological or a more general anthropological manner. In order to

---

[63] *Joie*, 231.

[64] *Soleil*, 242. (The italics are von Balthasar's.—TRANS.)

[65] Ibid., 129. (The italics are von Balthasar's.—TRANS.)

[66] *Joie*, 121. (The italics are von Balthasar's.—TRANS.)

[67] *Soleil*, 92.

[68] Ibid., 109–10.

be lived, such a mystery presupposes a concept of the Church given only in Catholicism. This is why Bernanos—who stakes everything on this one card: the existential living of the mystery of the Church —was, eminently and exclusively, a Catholic writer. The sphere of mysticism, the boundaries of which Bernanos incessantly crossed, was for him the place not only where the naked divine essence may be experienced by man but also where the experiential encounter occurs with the God who became Man, in his suffering and Resurrection: the God who became ecclesial. The mystic is the Christian who is given to experience subjectively something of the mystery of that sphere by whose life and truth every believer objectively lives his Christian life. This means, therefore, that every believer has fundamentally and objectively died both to the world and to his self and that he is given to live by virtue of a superworldly grace into whose sphere he has been transferred: henceforth, he lives on the basis of a "mystery" (*mysterium, sacramentum*) whose essence transcends all his natural capabilities and limitations, a "mystery" into which he must lose himself in total trust. The mystic has only one privilege: somehow to "see" what the ordinary Christian can "only" believe. This "seeing" is a variously structured experiencing, touching, hearing, and tasting of the reality of God-become-man, and for Bernanos it became *the* central criterion insofar as he, as a writer, had to be intent on rendering truth—even supernatural truth—perceivable by the senses. It was neither curiosity nor a kind of churchly aristocratism that urged him to explore the mystical domain but rather the strictest requirements of a "Catholic æsthetics".

If it is true that "the just man lives by faith", then the believing Christian lives by virtue of the "sacrament", that is, by the total truth that is the truth of God in Christ and in the Church. This Church in her wholeness, as Mystical Body of Christ, is the "total sacrament". She is this at that depth where she is at once Body and Bride, the mystery of love of the one Flesh, Spouse without wrinkle or stain, Holy Church, or, as Bernanos liked to say: "the Church of the saints". But, at just as primary a level and in no way secondarily, this same Church is also the Church of hierarchical ministry and of the individual sacraments, and both these things—official ministry and sacraments—are for the Catholic a participation in the total sacrament of the "communion of saints". The ordained ministry and the sacraments are vessels of divine life; and, if these give the ordinary

Christian a share in a divine and ecclesial mystery whose content he cannot directly experience, the saint who does experience it is also present in the Church, and he becomes for all others a revealer of their own truth. In his contemplation the saint is given to see, not this or that heavenly "object", but indeed the very reality of Christian life. In the saint we see fully displayed, not only what becomes of a person who fully surrenders to the content of faith, but even more so what this content can bring about in such a person: his life becomes the demonstration of the content of the individual sacraments that, each in its own way, contain a participation in the life of Christ that makes discipleship possible. The saint's life becomes a manifestation of the essence of the official ministry, because through him we can see by whose power it is that the hierarchical minister acts and commands. Finally, the saint's life also exhibits the relationship existing between the official Church and sanctity, and between the sacraments and sanctity, because in the saint all of these relationships enter into the light of explicit vision and experience. It goes without saying that Bernanos nowhere intended to give us a theoretical ecclesiology. What we will seek to do here is to show the theological background presupposed by all of his literary activity, without which we cannot understand the first word concerning his characters' actions. As a writer, he dared to hope that his figures, both the good and the bad, would themselves manifest or allow the reader to guess at the mystery that animated them. This hope is a Christian hope: it is a hope that the proof of the truth of Christianity comes from the "spirit and power" of Christian existence, which can persuade unbelievers who would never be converted by apologetical discourses or theological treatises. And, precisely because Bernanos would have liked to show unbelievers the very essence of Christian existence, he took the way, not of "ethics", but of "mysticism", which means the mystery of God's Incarnation: the Church in her saints.

The use of the word "sacrament" in Bernanos is highly peculiar. Not infrequently he uses it to refer to human experiences that have nothing to do externally with the sacraments of the Church but that, rightly or wrongly, are received and celebrated like holy actions, states, and realities. This can sometimes occur as a parody of the real sacraments and at other times as a reference—over and beyond the individual sacraments—to the wholly sacramental character of ecclesial and human existence.

To the parodic genre belong expressions such as: "Opportunism has become a kind of sacrament";[69] "the sacrament of the police force";[70] "the government ministers [of France, with their official civil-servant souls], think they alone are capable of providing our country with well-schooled lackeys, . . . and they look on a steady supply of these as a kind of sacrament";[71] "France thought she had found herself in [Pétain], this nearly century-old Tartuffe: and she received from him, with ecstasies of reverence and love, the sacrament of shame";[72] "the hypocrites of Vichy invited us through wicked priests to bless the providential catastrophe that would permit us to atone for our sins without wiping them out and without effacing their harmfulness and scandal: this would presumably occur by the power of an eighth sacrament—the sacrament of dishonor. We replied that it was not Providence that had signed the armistice."[73] And, with great sarcasm, Bernanos writes: "By the grace of a new Sacrament—the Sacrament of Bikini—Man truly becomes Spirit, but in a quite different way from what he had imagined."[74]

The tone changes drastically, however, when Bernanos compares the events of war, and more particularly the life of the soldier in submission to wartime laws, with a kind of sacrament or Mass: "We were low-quality saints, a race of very inferior saints", he says of himself and his comrades-in-arms of the First World War.

> By its daily repetition, our sacrifice had little by little taken on the character of a rite that we performed in a state of culpable distraction, just as a worldly priest says his Mass in twenty minutes. . . . It would not have occurred to any of us to think of himself as a kind of priest, but anyone who could speak our language could perhaps have made us understand that from that moment on we were marked, marked forever, and that there could no longer be any question of any administrative power whatever restoring us just as we had been to the world we had left. . . . We had been members . . . of a slightly suspicious, nonrecog-

---

[69] *Peur*, 138.

[70] Ibid., 315.

[71] *Croix*, February 1944, 403.

[72] Ibid., January 1943, 294.

[73] Ibid., 375.

[74] *Liberté*, 213.

nized church. . . . And it is true that the Great Citizens liquidated our
church in six months, but they didn't manage to do away with us. The
Great Citizens could do nothing against the Sacrament. Because you're
a discharged soldier for only a few days, but you remain a defrocked
priest forever.[75]

Bernanos, furthermore, compares the trenches to "muddy cloisters",[76] and, concerning the "heroes" that had become such, "unbeknownst to them", he says that "their sanctity could not survive
the war."[77] About the postwar period that strove to wipe from its
memory all traces of the war, Bernanos writes that everyone rushed
to the "grills" in order to obtain there "a certificate of general absolution endowed with a plenary indulgence".[78] But, "once the rite
was performed and the sacrament dispensed", everyone realized that
the military men were only civilians after all and that the "priests",
therefore, had abandoned "their priestly anointment along with their
vestments"![79]

When Édouard Daladier attempted to give the Second World War
a pseudoreligious ideological character and spoke of a "Crusade",
Bernanos remarked that the word he would have expected was "Sacrament".[80] Very soon, he would call Pétain "the priest and celebrant"
of a new holy action, namely, the "Surrender of France", which is
written in capital letters because what is involved is truly a religious
act. And, if he didn't fear incurring "blasphemy by this application of
the words of the Holy Sacrifice of the Mass", Bernanos would dare to
write concerning Pétain that it was "in him, with him, and through
him that France capitulated".[81] Indeed, for him, Pétain's policies most
closely resembled a black Mass: "We wondered if, in the craze of her
hysterical despair, France were not looking in all of this for a kind
of horrible inebriation, just as the simultaneously satanic and devout
lover of Des Esseintes [in Huysmans' novel *Against the Grain*] slips a
consecrated host into her adulterous mouth."[82] Through this many-

---

[75] *Enfants*, 11–13.
[76] Ibid., 21f.
[77] *Robots*, 98.
[78] *Enfants*, 40.
[79] Ibid., 45–46.
[80] Ibid., 73.
[81] *Croix*, preface, 3.
[82] Ibid., preface, 4.

sided use of the vocabulary of "sacrament", Bernanos' fundamental concern becomes clear: war could be an honorable, ascetic, and purifying action, and the Church Fathers did once conceive it as such; when it is this, then it comes close to possessing a kind of sacramental efficacy. The abuse of war by the new modern states is, therefore, the abuse of something mysteriously connected with a certain kind of sanctity.[83]

We stand on very different ground, however, when Bernanos says the following concerning the hypocrites in the Church "who have neither heart nor brains": "You are the scandal of the Church. But it is necessary that this scandal exist: in it, Christ wants to hide from our reason, our judgment, our very conscience. Only the heart can look for him and find him there. *You are the sacramental species of the Sacrament of God's Permanent Humiliation!*"[84] And he bores more deeply still when he writes the following epigraph to a *Life of Jesus* begun in Brazil: "*One must oneself be destitute* [misérable] *to partake without blasphemy in the sacrament of destitution* [misère]."[85] In the same text, Bernanos speaks about a "mysterious priesthood of poverty". Such words make clear to us that Bernanos considered the essential fulfillment of Christian discipleship to be the reception of a sacrament and the performing of a priestly function, not of course only in the sense of a "common priesthood of all the faithful", but in the special sense of a spiritual (and therefore real) function.

These forms of the sacramental reality, however, remain existential reflections, as it were, of the actual sacraments of the Church: they are their exegesis through concrete living, so to speak. The horizons to which they point, and on the basis of which they become realities, are the sacraments as vessels of grace bestowed as gifts by the Lord on his Church. It is in this context that we are to consider Bernanos' attempt to develop his central concept of the death agony and of dying as such on the basis of the sacrament of last anointing,[86] also his understanding of priestly existence on the basis of the grace of priestly ordination, and above all his interpretation of all the laws governing the life of the "communion of saints" (including the mysterious vicarious "substitutions" at times called for by the individual's most

---

[83] *Robots*, 169–70.
[84] *Anglais*, 152. (The italics are von Balthasar's.—TRANS.)
[85] *Bul.* 6, 2.
[86] *Bul.* 9, 11.

intimate destiny) on the basis of the Sacrament of the Altar. All of this will be discussed at its own time.

For the moment, as a sort of check test, let us briefly look at a text from *An Evil Dream* that casts light on what for Bernanos was the absolutely decisive event of sacramental confession, which he considered to be the authentic form of all attempts by modern psychology to "redeem" man by having him express himself. The murderess Simone has lived "outside the law" ever since her youth, and she has always looked with curiosity on those who possess the "power of the keys". One of them "had almost succeeded in opening up her poor little soul, . . . which was both eager and distrustful", and as a result of that conversation she had nurtured throughout her life a "longing for confession":

> There was in her a fundamental lie the full reality of which had surely never dawned upon her consciousness. Each new year sealed this lie within her more deeply and tightly, to the point that she could not have gotten to it all alone. Most of the time, alas, revealing one's secret to another only adds a new lie to the existing ones; and what can we expect from a sincerity caught up in despair and poisoned by shame? *Only a certain kind of sacramental humility can keep from festering the wound inflicted to the heart when a secret is wrested from it.* But such humility cannot exist without total self-renunciation; otherwise it will be searched for in vain, and this vain search will almost surely confer on an already mediocre life a particular character of degradation.[87]

The novel's last sentence hints that Simone will confess her crime, and nothing else about her destiny interests the narrator any longer.

A novelist who takes as his subject the sacramental life of the Church can naturally not consider the sacraments with the abstraction normal to theologians. He cannot deal with them a priori as self-contained realities and divorced from their actual reception and the way they pass over into a person's living reality. Such a novelist can work with the sacraments only in their concrete reality as acts dispensed by men and received by men. He can only allow the sacraments to gain their concreteness from the perspective of these two specific existences: that of the priest, who "effects" the sacrament and who has put his whole

---

[87] *Rêve*, 227.

existence at the disposal of this event, and that of the believer, who receives the sacrament and who likewise becomes a person through and through determined by the sacrament because he has surrendered his existence to God by virtue of the *opus operatum*. The "experiences" lived by each in this process are of a wholly particular kind. On the one hand, they cannot be reduced to the categories of psychology, because the sacramental event at its center is not a psychic but a christological and ecclesial reality, and the psyche merely participates in it by association, although really and necessarily so. And, on the other hand, neither can they be reduced to the categories of mysticism in the narrow sense of the word, because it would be an abuse of the words involved if we were to equate the normal, *transpsychological*, sacramental experience of a living faith with mysticism: by so doing we would cancel out the possibility of delineating the new level of Christian life specific to the mystical experience properly so called.

Being the central Christian experiences, the experiences connected with the sacramental life are to be located within the continuum between the psychological and the mystical extremes. Since they are genuine *experiences*, they have a psychological side and are therefore accessible to the novelist. And, as genuinely *sacramental* experiences, their meaning and our understanding of it gravitate toward a reality that is greater than the soul, but also a reality toward which the soul gapes open and is intensely inclined. The soul makes itself available to the sacraments' higher sphere of meaning "instrumentally", as it were, so as to be marked by it even in its "psychology". This interior transcendence of the sacramental act can be more clearly grasped in its experiential quality through the greater expressive capacity of mysticism, and this is why Bernanos the novelist focuses with predilection on the mystical experience as a hermeneutic tool and not for its own sake. What engages him here is not so much the mystical experience as something exceptional but the truth of common Christian experience that becomes manifested through the mystical experience as through a magnifying glass.

Suddenly we can understand better why the reading of Bernanos' works elicits at the same time the impression both of an astoundingly penetrating psychology and of an unheard-of narrative technique (wholly foreign and unclassifiable for the unbeliever, especially in *Monsieur Ouine*). This technique was at times tentatively identified with that of psychoanalytical surrealism or existentialism, only to meet at once with Bernanos' outraged protests. The only point of comparison between Bernanos and these other literary movements is that, in the latter, the psyche is interpreted on the basis of a deeper level of being—mostly its own depth dimension—which it is not fully conscious of, because this level has been variously "concealed", "repressed", or "atrophied". Consequently, the psyche is seen to say and do things that are different, deeper, more mysterious, and more significant than it knows. *In Bernanos this depth dimension is not the soul itself but the Church, which is one and the same as Christ's redemptive mystery in the world, one and the same as the communion of saints*: it is the demands and the graces of this communion that flood the soul in its depths. And the Church's reality becomes a presence and an event every time a sacrament is dispensed and received.

In a polemical tirade against a stale literature of edification, bent only on moralizing, Bernanos writes: "The same priests who spend their time exhibiting, through inept little books, their contented ignorance of the anguished heart of men . . . would not think of doing both God and their own priesthood the honor of imagining that the sacrament of baptism, for one, is supposed to mark a person so profoundly that this mark would give his perversion—should there be such—a degree of malice proportionate to the grace he had received."[88] And a little farther down: "I live within a kind of spiritual universe, whose existence so many men do not even suspect. This being the case, you cannot possibly imagine that I think myself guilty of only the same faults as these unsuspecting fellows, arguing that the faults involved bear the same name in the dictionary!"[89] No: the reality that underlies the psychic acts of a baptized person is wholly other than outside the Church. It revalues the meaning and import of these acts, both for the good and for the bad. Nowhere can this be demonstrated more forcefully than in the sacramentally ordained priest, who has turned over his entire existence to the service of the sacraments and who experiences his own instrumentality on a daily basis. After her long struggle, the countess wants to entrust herself to the little country priest, "and to him alone". To which he replies: "It's as if you were putting a gold coin into a pierced hand."[90] But

---

[88] *Cimetières*, 238.
[89] Ibid., 240.
[90] *Curé*, 190.

a few sentences later it is he who stretches out his arm into the fire in order to rescue from the flames the medallion the countess had thrown into them. A moment earlier he had said to her: "This poker is only an instrument in your hands. If the good Lord had given it just enough awareness for it to choose to make itself available to you whenever you needed it, that would tell you approximately what I am for all of you, what I would like to be."[91] After the long struggle with this woman, who puts up a fierce resistance, the instrument knows exactly how very much the triumph comes from God: "It seemed to me that a mysterious hand had just opened up a breach in some invisible wall, and peace was entering on all sides, majestically assuming its proper level. It was a peace unknown on this earth."[92] To the little priest it appears that he is but an instrument that merely "attends" the event: "I would really have to be crazy to imagine that I played a role, a real role. It's already too much that God should have done me the grace of being present at this reconciliation between a soul and hope, to attend this soul's solemn nuptials."[93] And yet, the assisting "instrument" was present with his whole person and his utmost human participation. Once reconciled with God, the woman senses this when, just before her death, she calls him "her child" in the place of the other child God had taken from her: "The despairing memory of a little child held me far from everything, in a frightening solitude, and it seems to me that another child has delivered me from this solitude. . . . It is from you that I have received peace."[94] As he ponders the events in the presence of her corpse, the country priest for his part writes as follows: "Although I am nothing but a poor little priest, in the face of this woman, so superior to me only yesterday, . . . I have indeed understood what it means to be a father."[95]

But there is more. By participating in the process of this painful confession, the country priest experienced how the power to continue along his assigned way was given him precisely at the moment when he himself had used up his last drop of strength: "At the same time, sadness took hold of me, an indefinable sadness against which I was wholly powerless. This may have been the greatest temptation

---

[91] Ibid., 165–66.
[92] Ibid., 187.
[93] Ibid., 196.
[94] Ibid., 192–93.
[95] Ibid., 198–99.

in my life. And at that very moment God helped me: I suddenly felt a tear on my cheek. One single tear, the same you see on the face of dying people who have arrived at the outer limit of their misery."[96] That same sadness had been the price for this tear, and, according to what the Curé de Torcy had once said to him, this is how every truly priestly word must be paid for: "When the Lord haphazardly draws from me a word that is useful to souls, I know it by how it hurts."[97] Perhaps this is where the true, living "knowledge" proper to the sacramental ministry lies: "It's not at all a matter of coming to know your power, my dear Father. The whole question is how you use it, because it's precisely this that makes the man. What's the good of a power you never use, or which you only half-use? In both great and small matters, you yourself bring all of yours to bear, probably without even realizing it. This explains many things."[98]

When Chevance was called around midnight to come to Cénabre, he expected from him a confession of sins: "What misdeed could possibly have found him unbending? Or what slimy pit repulsed him? Already his hand was going up in benediction, and *the divine mercy that so filled him groaned in his palm, commingled with the outpouring of his own life.*"[99] These words say it all. But, when what the other confesses is that he has "lost his faith", there is for the moment nothing to absolve, and then Chevance has the astounding thought that he should instead ask his dismal brother for *his* blessing:

> In the awful trial in which I see you enmeshed, every other action of our ministry would surely be impossible to you. But which of us [priests], even at the devil's very feet, could not bless another in the name of the Father and of the Son and of the Holy Spirit? Ah, my friend: this is indeed true, this is a certainty! You are quite capable, without incurring sacrilege, to call down such a grace upon a brother who is scarcely less miserable than yourself—to call down a grace of which you are at present devoid. Just listen to me. At least make the sign of blessing, even with indifference, even with a perverted will! What does it matter whether, at this very moment, you have faith! . . . If you are incapable of begging for mercy for yourself—oh, at least, at the very least, make

[96] Ibid., 182.
[97] Ibid., 65.
[98] Ibid., 203.
[99] *Imposture*, 50.

the sign that bestows it on the sinner! Only wish, only wish for me to be happy![100]

This is Chevance's way of asking from the nearly dead man for some imperceptible sign of life,

> something like a consenting wink on the stony face of a death agony, a mere trifle, a slight breach in the wall upon which God's tremendous pity could then bear down with all its immense weight, for Chevance could hear the divine mercy roaring all about the poor reprobate who was still alive. This had just been revealed to him, in a flash of lightning, he could not have explained how. And he would forget it just as quickly. He was wholly caught up in his effort and was not gauging the extent of the blow he was inflicting. Well beyond his own reason, at a thousand leagues from his feeble body, which even now retained its posture of fearful humiliation, it was his charity and it alone that discerned, judged, and acted. Who could see through the eyes of an angel? The man he was trying to wrest from the darkness still stood there before him, with his broad shoulders, his pale forehead without a single wrinkle, his eyes downcast. But they were embracing in heaven.[101]

How could we doubt that what was then occurring in Cénabre at "an unheard-of depth" and "with all his superior faculties lying passive" was a check test, a kind of satanic *opus operatum*,[102] a power reaching into heaven itself?[103] In the character of Ouine we encounter an explicit antipriesthood. In some of the women characters we see a symbolic portrayal of the ultimate perversion of sacramental actions (especially in *A Crime* and *An Evil Dream*). But all of these are negative demonstrations, mirror-image inversions of the actual truth that in the very end necessarily exhibit their powerlessness.

The things that can be clearly seen in the priest and his ministerial function may also be detected in ordinary believers by a vision of faith that penetrates into hidden reality. In the course of everyday experience such a depth is wholly concealed; but there are exceptional circumstances that bring what is hidden into a kind of penumbra:

---

[100] Ibid., 54.
[101] Ibid., 55.
[102] Ibid., 55–56.
[103] Ibid., 63.

The host is something tiny. And there also exist here and there, lost in the enormous mass of people, persons who go by unnoticed by you—old shy priests, men, women, little children, well behaved or not, what does it matter! . . . What they have in their hearts is rarely expressed in their features, and, besides, they themselves don't know what they have in their heart. But God knows it. A mysterious exchange takes place between the white host and this humanity that is so little worthy of being observed and photographed. This is what counts, and I have the honor of pointing it out to you. However you may explain this fact, it thrusts itself on us and has always done so in the course of the ages. As soon as any threat begins to imperil, not the Church's treasures or her prestige, but the Church's faith, then these poor insignificant devils I speak of become martyrs, and you know this as well as I do. They calmly say *No!* to powerful figures whom only the day before they greeted with humility. . . . Then we begin to witness the slow fermentation of the crude dough whose leaven they have become. Religious bigots become long-suffering, and their pharisaical wives charitable. Misers begin to give lavishly, and casuists become simple as children. Calculating, cerebral types run into the arms of risk, and conniving political prelates lose all their guile. And the tyrants—masters of palaces and basilicas paved with gold—suddenly begin to listen with amazement, anxiety, and fear to the ancient, rejuvenated Church singing in the depths of the catacombs. . . . Only in times of trial does Christianity give the full measure of her strength. . . . *And I repeat: I am not speaking here of mystical realities, but of simple experience.*[104]

4. Transcendence and Mysticism

Any Christian experience deserving the name is rooted, not in psychology, but in the sacraments or, in other words, in faith. Bernanos' unspoken presupposition is the truth of faith and sacrament, which means the possibility for a person to live from the reality of participation in Christ's life, and he asks himself what results when a person lives rigorously *out of that center*. In this case, a person's life is not determined by the laws of his own psyche but by the laws of a vitality, proper to Christ and his Church, which do not belong to him by nature. The full effects of this life, moreover, may be successfully ascertained only in a person who has consciously and deci-

---

[104] *Anglais*, 156–58. (The italics are von Balthasar's.—TRANS.)

sively realized the leap out of his own self and into the life of Christ and the Church, a person, therefore, who is prepared no longer to live himself but to allow Christ to live in him. This, in other words, would mean living, not with faith as an ideal *toward* which one strove, but from faith as a center *out of* which one already derived one's life.

The writer who chooses the first of these ways—faith as an ideal to strive after—will naturally always appear to be the more understanding and humane, and he is sure to elicit his readers' sympathies. He specializes in portraying weak and failing men as they wrestle with a high ideal that is always beyond the reach of human nature. He compassionately accompanies his all-too-human characters' temptations, falls, and remorse, shedding much psychological light on all of it. Each of us recognizes himself in the unfortunate protagonist and feels understood. Such a "human" book can be such a consolation! The Christian ideal remains high above us like a ceiling we vainly stretch out to touch, much as the Jews vainly spent themselves trying to fulfill "Old Testament" law. We then come to view New Testament love as little more than a compassionate understanding for this inability on man's part. Thus, Christian love is reduced to the action whereby grace transfigures and makes up for man's incurable incompleteness, but in such a way that the interior understanding of others' guilt by a writer and his readers derives from their own experience of being just as guilty.

The vehemence with which Bernanos rejected the novels of François *Mauriac* can be understood only as his emphatic rejection of this whole way of looking at things. We here introduce Mauriac only as a point of comparison, as a representative of a current in Catholic literature diametrically opposed to Bernanos' own. And so Bernanos launches his tirade against Mauriac:

> One day, Monsieur François Mauriac . . . boasted of holding by the hand the little girl Hope of whom Péguy speaks. . . . I readily admit that he is full of good intentions. He overflows with good intentions, and he asks for nothing more than to be allowed to share everything he has. The misfortune is that the only thing he has is anxieties. . . . I reject Monsieur Mauriac's anxieties. I refuse to call by the name of "hope" this complacency in every manner of anxiety that he indulges, this sort of morbid delectation. I am not in the least fooled by all the reproaches I receive for allegedly pushing people to despair through my

inflexible attitude. I would like to pry them forcibly out of a state of
resignation in which, at bottom, they feel quite comfortable because it
dispenses them from having to choose. It is this lachrymose resignation, perpetually prostrate with grief, that is the authentic form of a
lethargic despair. . . . I have no reason to nurse a personal animosity
against Monsieur Mauriac. The good Lord, who can read the innermost
secret of our consciences, probably knows that the tortured author of
so many books in which carnal despair oozes through every page like
muddy water through the walls of a dark cellar has gained more merits
by being mistaken than I have by seeing things clearly. But not even
for love of him can I allow him to confuse optimism with [Christian]
hope.[105]

Bernanos indignantly refused to be counted among the "searching
souls", "in the manner of Mauriac and many others, who are motivated by a deep restlessness of heart and have found their mainstay in
a certain form—a rather abstract one, I fear—of obedience and discipline. . . . I, for my part, have never been a restless soul. Contrary to
what some pitiable priests think, with all the coarseness of my nature
I feel coarsely at home with obedience and discipline. In no way do
these bring me the elation (or the appeasement) of a difficulty that
has been overcome or a humiliation to which one has acquiesced."[106]
Two years later, in another letter to Amoroso Lima, Bernanos again
stressed the fact that he "has absolutely nothing in common with
Mauriac",[107] whom he elsewhere describes as "the bloodless Mauriac"[108] who revels in a "funereal eroticism".[109]

Why, at bottom, was Bernanos so trenchant in this manner of dis-
sociating himself from Mauriac and everything he represented? The
reason was that Bernanos was not interested in the sin of the flesh
as autonomous theme, and he devoted to it about as much energy as
did Christ and the apostles. Seen in the correct Christian light, carnal
sin amounts to pure and simple boredom: by no means could it be
considered an "abyss of evil". From the front, Bernanos writes as follows to his fiancée: "How quickly cowardice rises from the senses to
the heart! . . . Certain otherwise decent people (*honnêtes gens*) harbor

[105] *Liberté*, 130–32.
[106] *To Amoroso Lima*, January 1940; *Esprit*, 192.
[107] Ibid., January 16, 1942; *Esprit*, 208.
[108] *To Gallimard*, December 1947; *Croix*, ix.
[109] *Croix*, May 1941, 117.

an unavowed sympathy for human beings whose behavior has made them bestial despite their winning caresses. They forget that the good Lord's pity goes out to criminals about to be hanged rather than to these soft wills that helplessly yield to languid vices."[110] And eleven years later he writes to a friend: "You still seem to be mesmerized by the *enchantments of sin*. . . . Does your Satan really have the gift of tears?"[111]

Bernanos was quick to lavish his contempt on the boundless sexualization of modern French literature. Issuing a public protest against a famous script writer who wanted to handle his *Diary of a Country Priest* in the style of Claude Autant-Lara's *Le Diable au corps* [The Devil in My Body], Bernanos concludes: "Very soon the modern world will no longer have any spiritual reserves left to commit any real evil. Already one sector of modern literature, which considers itself the most advanced in the ways of damnation . . . , is proclaiming this failure . . . without knowing it. . . . At the far end of its desperate efforts to say everything, a certain kind of literature will indeed have *said* everything but *expressed* nothing. The crisis that threatens it is a crisis of infantilism."[112] This declaration on his part is in harmony with much older texts: "The [soul's] real drama begins at a much higher level [than that of the flesh]. It begins at the place where disobedience is loved for its own sake and remorse becomes the indispensable food of the soul or, indeed, the soul itself: yes, Remorse, that accursed son of divine charity, which, like God's love, prefers to have nothing if it cannot have everything."[113] "We should remember that all revolutions were made by eunuchs: Jean-Jacques Rousseau, Robespierre, and Cromwell all suffered from strangury."[114] Even when he described a criminal, Bernanos was never interested in sensual sin for its own sake but, at most, as a symptom for a spiritual illness lurking at a deeper level. What did interest Bernanos in criminals, however, was that "genius for evil" that is the antithesis of authentic faith and is located at the same level. Mauriac's heroes interested Bernanos only as symptomatic of a deep-set disease in society: "Come, now! You judge the bourgeois human beings in the novels of Monsieur François

---

[110] *To his Fiancée*, 1915; unpublished letter; *Erbarmen*, 24.
[111] *To Vallery-Radot*, January 17, 1926; *Bul*. 1, 3.
[112] Letter to the weekly *Samedi-Soir*, November 8, 1947, reproduced in *Bul*. 7–8, 4.
[113] *To Vallery-Radot*, January 17, 1926; *Bul*. 1, 3.
[114] *Joie*, 191.

Mauriac to be realistic, and yet you don't think that the smell of blood could some day go to these people's head?"[115]

But there is another element that is decisive here. The person who does not come to terms with his drives and whose religion risks becoming an endless struggle between "duty and inclination"—the threat of a Kantian Jansenism—is precisely the person who will most readily appeal to "casuistry". By contrast, the person who does not strive *toward* an (unattainable) Christian ideal but who lives already now *out of* the substance and reality of faith—the person after Bernanos' heart, that is—is the *saint* in the Pauline sense of the word, and for him the casuistry of the law has become absorbed by the simplicity of the truth. In Bernanos this simplicity goes by the name of "honor": it stands in stark contrast to a "duty" that is imposed and consists in a reaction of noble feeling and noble thinking coming from deep within the person. Against a bourgeois mentality and a despairing moralism, Bernanos proposed the ethos of chivalry, which for him was intimately related to the ethos of the saint, as is strikingly shown by the conclusion of the *Country Priest*.

A page of *We the French* sums up the reasons why Bernanos rejected every morality based on casuistry:

> Allow me simply to point out that, the more a sense of Christian honor becomes debilitated, the greater the abundance, indeed superabundance, of casuists. At the very least, the man of honor offers you the following advantage: he spares the casuist all his labor. A case of conscience does not pose itself to the average Christian; it is the average Christian who poses a case of conscience, in the hope that someone will find him a viable formula and solution. What business is it of mine if he uses such a right, if indeed it is a right? I am content with measuring the social value, for instance, of the characters Monsieur Mauriac presents to us under twenty different names: each time, his aching genius manages to create a new being from the same material. I find their value to be nil. A naturally

---

[115] *Cimetières*, 102. (To understand this statement correctly, we need to read it in context. Bernanos had been an observer of the Spanish Civil War, and in none of the camps did he find that sense of "honor" that was an "absolute" for him. He said he would never have had the "ridiculous idea" of going to look for such a sense of honor in Machiavelli, Lenin, or what he calls the "Casuists" [*Cimetières*, 98]. What most struck him in Spain was the extraordinary cruelty exhibited by the upright members of the Catholic middle class. Addressing the *bien-pensants*, he warns them that the taste for terror is easily acquired once a sense of "honor" has been lost.—Note of the French trans.)

chaste woman, one who is such by virtue of a tradition of honor and
dignity, may have less merits than some other woman, but her social
value incomparably surpasses her own merits. A man obsessed with lust
may obtain heaven at the price of a life truly crucified at the level of the
gutter, but, even if he never commits a grave sin, such a self-absorbed
creature surely possesses no social value. The moment a person feels the
need to consult the casuists in order to know the amount starting from
which stealing money may be considered a mortal sin (currency does,
after all, become devalued!), we may say that his social value is nil, even
if he abstains from stealing.[116]

The noblest offshoot of humanity is the saint, who grows out of the
ground of the Church's sacramental life. The sphere of sanctity cannot
be constructed through purely human efforts, and it can therefore be
understood on the basis of nothing but itself. It is a dimension that
has a foundation and a summit, a presupposition and a development
that it makes possible. The foundation is the act whereby a person
makes the truth of his own life identical with ecclesial, sacramental
truth. This enjoins total self-surrender to the God of grace, an all-
encompassing assent to him. This act is the simplest that can be expected of a person: by virtue of it, all the confusion (because untruth)
of sinfulness and distance from God becomes dissolved. Typical of it
is the simple and bare demand Chevance makes of Cénabre: "My reverend Canon, *all* you have to do is leave everything, hand everything
over."[117] And the country priest says to the countess: "My daughter,
you don't haggle with the good Lord. You must turn yourself over
to him without conditions. Give everything to him, and he will give
you even more in return."[118] This simplicity was also the reason for
Joan of Arc's victory over the theologians and the doctors, immured as
they were in their hermetically sealed and politicized systems.[119] Such
simplicity manifests great psychic health, while somehow there is always something neurotic about the complexity of sin. For Bernanos,
the basis of sanctity is the fact that the saint does not question the
rightness of normal ecclesial existence. None of the great priest fig-

---

[116] *Français*, 239.
[117] *Imposture*, 62. The emphasis is Bernanos'.
[118] *Curé*, 187.
[119] *Cimetières*, 272,

ures he created (including Cénabre) entertains doubts or difficulties in connection with the institutional Church. In *Under Satan's Sun* we see the foundational portrayal of a normally organized prayer life[120] according to ordinary and wholly traditional methods. We witness an ordinary confession to a quite ordinary priest, and the exercise of ordinary ecclesial obedience, which then changes levels smoothly, without any interruption, as the priest is led down his path by rather extraordinary situations.

Menou-Segrais is the ideal type of director Donissan needed. His repugnant experiences of ecclesiastical and clerical life have not so embittered him that he calls into question the very basis of this life: "I would have wanted to be adequately used. But it doesn't matter. It was all over already, and I was too weary. A certain baseness of outlook, and the distrust or hatred of greatness that these wretches termed 'prudence', had filled me with bitterness. I've seen the superior man hunted down like a prey, and I've seen great souls being torn apart. Nevertheless, I have a horror for confusion and disorder, and I possess a sense for authority and hierarchy."[121] The Abbé Demange describes him as having "a wildly independent spirit and a good sense that is so to speak irresistible, but the exercise of which cannot always take place without apparent cruelty".[122]

The Curé de Torcy is the same type of person. His often curt and exacting joviality is only the transparent veil for a wonderfully lively, wholesome, and vibrant heart: he belongs to the "race of those who stand erect".[123] At the beginning of her story, Chantal is being directed in a very exact and uneventful manner by the modest Chevance, who firmly conceals his rather extraordinary graces.[124] Accordingly, Chantal is initially filled by an interior joy, without a shadow of anguish or disquiet to trouble it.[125] Likewise, a perfect peace[126] and, indeed, a deep joy were the point of departure that led to Donissan's horrific experiences.[127] This foundation of wholesome normalcy merely

---

[120] *Soleil*, 148–49.
[121] Ibid., 94.
[122] Ibid., 87.
[123] *Curé*, 93.
[124] *Joie*, 38f.
[125] Ibid., 47 and passim.
[126] *Soleil*, 112.
[127] Ibid., 121, 139.

appears to be left behind by everything that rises above the ordinary. But it is in fact the continual ground and presupposition for every other Christian dimension, and it is never really left behind, much less transcended. And it is to this foundation that the ethos of honor belongs that, in its natural and supernatural unity and catholicity, was something exceedingly important to Bernanos.

In the *Country Priest*, this ethos of honor is portrayed in the figure of Olivier, who is juxtaposed to the sickly young priest by way of fraternal clarification. Only on this basis can the process of authentic transcendence begin: within the Church and rooted in the foundation of the Church, and only then rising into the free spaces where a Christian may be led and sent by God himself in a most personal and unforeseeable way. The vertiginous adventure of sanctity cannot, of course, be determined by any hard and fast rules; and yet it must take its point of departure from the one ecclesial foundation and always remain intimately related and bound to it. Consequently, despite all the contradictions inherent to the realm of experience, supernatural darkness cannot be understood as anything other than a particular mode of the Christian's joy in his faith, supernatural anguish as anything other than a higher form of tranquil certainty, and the sense of having lost both one's way and one's director as anything other than a particular further development of trustworthy direction by the Church. The decisive act whereby a person lets go of all worldly security and entrusts himself to God alone does not first occur during the ascent from the foundation to the solitary heights; clearly and emphatically, it occurs much before this, already at the level of the ecclesial foundation.

This does not keep the saints' adventure from possibly becoming a terribly burdensome trial for the "base"—the ordinary Church— and likewise a touchstone that causes the crumbling of many a "foundational man" or "pillar of the Church". But the manner in which these foundational men participate in their particular mode of sanctity is above all by *accompanying the saints through their direction of them.* For this, they must have the same open disposition of self-surrender as the saints themselves, hanging on all the whims of a Providence that can cut right across the most revered forms of tradition. Such is the case of Blanche de la Force in *Dialogues of the Carmelites*, with her vocation to live in fear, a shameful and humiliating fear that in the end can knock the most elementary feelings of honor out of a person's head. And yet, for Bernanos, the basis that makes everything about Blanche's fear understandable is the at once natural and supernatural honor of both the old French nobility (represented by the old prioress, Madame de Croissy) and the good common people (represented by the new prioress, Madame Lidoine). This sense of honor is something so profound that it can reach a familiar understanding even of so extraordinary a destiny as a person's intimate participation in the mystery of Gethsemani. Carmel as the scene of the action can here be viewed as the best possible symbol for the ecclesial sphere: being a part of the Church's institution and foundation, Carmel represents in an outstanding way the point of departure for the most unusual adventures by those God calls, and of this Teresa of Jesus and John of the Cross gave splendid examples. If anywhere, it is here that the rule is proven by the exception, and the women who are the guardians of the Rule are quite aware of both the basis and the summit of the structure, and they never lose from sight the inviolable relationship between the two. This becomes very clear in the important mediating figure of the subprioress, Marie de l'Incarnation, whose basic error it is to want to lay down the exception (martyrdom of blood) as a regular requirement of Christianity and to incorporate it into its foundation. By so doing, she upsets the whole ecclesial economy. At the same time, it is she who clings to "honor" in an immoderate manner[128] and who wants to turn an evident weakness into a higher form of "honor".[129] For this she must atone by being "dishonored",[130] namely, by being denied participation in what she had so longed for: her sisters' procession up the scaffold to the guillotine and their martyrdom in community. For Marie de l'Incarnation this privation is a real spiritual martyrdom and the actual form her atonement takes. But Sister Constance, too, with her continual easy laughter, is an indispensable check test for the fearfulness of her friend Blanche. To use the language of the art of the fugue, we may say that the two novices stand in a "counterpoint" relationship to one another: Constance demonstrates *in recto* what Blanche exhibits *in inverso*. Very far from heroic sanctity being a continual reproach hurled at the base earthly heaviness of the ecclesial foundation (as is the case with Mau-

---

[128] *Carmélites*, 60, 109, 119.
[129] Ibid., 131.
[130] Ibid., 228.

riac and all of psychologizing Catholic literature), for Bernanos the summit of sanctity is rather the permanent justification for the institutional basis. This is true even when Blanche flees Carmel and breaks with this form of ordered life. Indeed, with her flight she seems only to announce prophetically the coming collapse of the whole structure, when the monastery is abolished and the nuns executed. In this respect, too, Blanche's life ends in a confluence of her destiny with the current of community life in the Church, which, through the death of the first prioress and the prayer and assumed responsibility of the second, had vicariously borne for her in advance the burden of her fearful anxiety. It is her reintegration into the mainstream of ecclesial life that in the end makes it possible for Blanche to complete the song she had broken off at the scaffold.

These considerations now make it possible to understand more precisely the place that mysticism occupies in Bernanos' work. It refers to the extraordinary path of a particular vocation to sanctity; but this "path" is conceived only as the full-blown exposition and extrapolation of ecclesial normalcy itself, which means it is a function of the community. To be more precise still: mysticism involves a vicarious sacrifice offered up by the ecclesial community in a direction that can be none other than that defined by the *Via Dolorosa*, the way of the Passion of Jesus Christ. This way leads away from the world to a shut heaven, that is, into the darkness of godforsakenness, pathlessness, and descent into hell—and this for the sake of the sinner who is perishing in such a condition of loss and to grasp whose hand the saint comes. If we consider these three characteristics of mysticism together—a sacrificial offering by the Church, a way leading into the night of the Passion, and a communion with lost and condemned sinners— then we will understand both the strong role played by mysticism in Bernanos and his polemic against the whole direction mystical theology was taking in the Church. Bernanos had to inveigh polemically against a mysticism of flight from risk-taking into a superterrestrial sphere of security, against a mysticism of ever purer light in which the "nights of the soul" only connote temporary "purification", and against an individualistic mysticism whereby isolated persons undergo sublime adventures apart from the ecclesial community, and in particular apart from the "communion of sinners". The ruthlessly direct criticism made by the country priest, at the beginning of his diary, against the average form religious orders normally assume in the concrete at the same time extends to an ideology of mysticism that some of these orders have developed and sanctioned.

For the Curé d'Ambricourt, monasteries are sanctuaries for an artificially induced "favorable atmosphere" that makes it possible for certain spirits to soar sublimely. But, like certain homemade wines, reports of these spiritual flights in the cloister "do not travel well" and must be "consumed on the spot".[131] An example of this is the exclaustrated nun who now works for the Curé de Torcy and whose symbolic mania for cleaning cannot coexist with this world's dirt.[132] And the priest is not easier on choir monks: "They make music. . . . I have nothing against them: to each his occupation. All music apart, they're also florists. . . . In short, your contemplatives have all the tools to provide us with beautiful flowers, and they're real too. Unfortunately, sabotage does at times take place in monasteries like everywhere else, and too often what they palm off on us is paper flowers."[133]

> You'll perhaps say to me that I don't understand anything about mystics. . . . But allow me to burst out laughing right under the nose of people who sing in a choir before the good Lord has even raised his baton. . . . I have my own ideas on young David's harp. Of course he was a talented boy, but all his music-making did not preserve him from sin. I know that our conventional writers of pious books, who manufacture "Lives of Saints" for exportation, imagine that any good fellow can find shelter in mystical ecstasy: it's nice and warm there and as safe as in Abraham's bosom. As safe! . . . Ah, yes, of course: at times nothing is easier than to climb to those heights; God himself carries you there. The real question is knowing how to stay there and, if necessary, how to come back down. You'll note that the saints—the real saints —showed much embarrassment on their return. Once caught at their acrobatic labors, they began by begging people to keep their secret. . . . They were a little ashamed of the whole thing, don't you understand? Ashamed of being the Father's spoiled children, ashamed of having tasted the cup of blessedness ahead of everyone else! And for what reason? For no reason at all, out of favoritism. Such graces! . . . The first movement

---

[131] *Curé*, 13.
[132] Ibid., 18.
[133] Ibid., 20–21.

of the soul is to flee from them. After all, we can understand in different ways the words of the Good Book: "It is a fearful thing to fall into the hands of the living God!"[134]

These are artificial paradises, while Christ's apostle is called to graze the stubborn, spiritless herd in this world's darkness and dirt. For this reason, until we arrive at the last book, we will find nothing but secular priests in Bernanos. These priests do not have the option of acting like an abbot who dismisses a black sheep in order to deal only with Christians of good will. Secular priests are sent specifically to the recalcitrant and the lost. Donissan's mysticism has meaning only when he looks her in the eye and experiences her self-damnation as his own.[135] We are here at the antipodes of that whole current of contemplative, individualistic mysticism of interior ascent that is more influenced by Neoplatonism than by the Gospel and that strongly colors both the Patristic and the Scholastic periods. Even in our day it occasionally is allowed too much weight in the Church's mystical theology. The mysticism Bernanos considers authentic "is not at all like what we read in books".[136] For him, mysticism means, pure and simple, being evicted out of all shelteredness, not only of the world but also of a supernaturally and ecclesially secure existence in faith, to be cast out into the abysses above and the abysses below, into nights within which, when you are in them, you can no longer distinguish what comes from above and what from below, for forsakenness by the Father means being abandoned to the abyss.

In his first novel Bernanos executed this insight, doubtless valid in itself, with such fierce intensity that in the end the manner of its expression was skewed for sheer obsessive coherence. In *Under Satan's Sun* the night of the soul was for him nothing but abandonment to the demon, and this condition was seen to constitute the all-pervasive, existential core of all mysticism with its various charisms. The mystic simply mediates the light that he himself does not feel and that he believes he has lost. Thus, it is out of the depths of abandonment by God that Donissan sets about working his miracle, and the attempt

---

[134] Ibid., 21–23.
[135] *Soleil*, 191.
[136] *Joie*, 230.

fails him right in the midst of his action. For, insofar as the priest, in his utter abandonment, is the prey of both God and Satan, the obedience exercised in such a situation remains intensely fraught with danger on account of its very ambiguity. The face of satanic *hybris* makes its appearance precisely in the most perfect act of interior denudation.[137] God's very purity is "equivocal, and the miracle itself is not pure".[138] At the very moment when Donissan is sure he has seen the dead child open his eyes, he is also "met by the ironic leer of the demon's defiance".[139]

The saint is the truly possessed person. He has been delivered over to Satan's power. His soul and his capacity to feel and to think are demonically inhabited. During the nocturnal hallucination out in the field, what is happening is that the demon is attempting to take possession of Donissan's innermost heart. In order to understand correctly the mystical events that take place in *Under Satan's Sun*, we would have to examine again many things that have not been heard in the Church since the days of the witch trials. From these records we would only have to omit all references to sexual matters, something we must always do with Bernanos. Satan becomes omnipresent, even in the "most sublime experiences"; and this is exactly what must occur if what is involved is a mysticism based on the saint's vicarious experience of hell and damnation for the sake of saving another. The history of mysticism unquestionably records cases of such an experience of passive abandonment to the demon and of phenomena of possession as an expression of authentic, God-willed mysticism. We have only to think of Christine von Stommeln, Marie des Vallées, and Père Surin. Nevertheless, it would be a false move simply to stamp this real possibility as *the* normative type of the mystical night. We cannot do this even when, following Bernanos' correct lead, we understand the mystical night, not primarily within a scheme of Neoplatonic "purification" (preliminary to "illumination" and "union"), but rather as a genuine imitation of Christ in his vicarious suffering for all mankind, starting at Gethsemani and going all the way to the Cross and to the descent into the underworld. For we must not forget, first, that the devil does appear in the episode of the Lord's temptations in the

---

[137] *Soleil*, 258.
[138] Ibid., 244.
[139] Ibid., 301–2.

desert but is nowhere to be seen throughout Jesus' Passion. In the end, the Passion is Jesus' taking upon himself the world's sin before the face of the just Judge—his Father—something more terrible than any battle with the devil. And, in the second place, neither must we forget that the experiences of the dark night of the soul by mystics —offering distant analogies to the scenes in Bernanos' novel—by no means always present demonic phenomena. The "hell" that must be gone through is just as often a hell in which no "devil" is encountered; it is, rather, an experiential confrontation with the interminable monstrousness of the world's guilt.

We must call the mysticism of *Under Satan's Sun* excessively one-sided in the sense that it raises one particular variety of the dark night of the soul and makes it the norm for all mystical experience. But we must also judge it right and proper when it sees the meaning of the mystical night to be ecclesial: it lies in a saint's being delivered over to the darkness in the place and for the sake of sinners. Can we doubt the fact that the mystic is exposed and imperiled in ways the nonmystic will never know? This is why so many mystical vocations end in error and disaster! But, in *Under Satan's Sun*, Bernanos did not yet sufficiently see the truth that, during the unfolding of the event of the night in the soul, and in the very midst of abandonment by God, God himself provides a protection that the mystic feels not at all or only seldom but that keeps the interior event from aborting. The genuine mystical night somehow participates in the Church's infallibility insofar as the doorway leading into it is total ecclesial obedience. If it is genuine, the dark night of the soul is a reserve belonging wholly to God. And if the demon should appear within it, he would be fettered and could move about only within the exact space permitted him by God.

In Bernanos' next few works, the forced element disappeared from his portrayal of mysticism. Already in *Joy* a certain balance was restored, but without weakening any of the radicalism of *Under Satan's Sun*. In *Joy* the Church's sacrificial gesture is more clearly delineated, even if the hands of the priests that raise the species are the invisible hands of one already dead. Here, too, we again encounter a certain distrust of the secure world of the cloister: against the general expectation and her father's insistence, Chantal does not enter monastic life: "Any other young woman in the place of this fearless girl would doubtless have been overwhelmed by her feeling of solitude and, in her bewilderment, would have thrown herself into a convent as a last refuge. But for too long she had been schooled to seek her rest only in God. She was incapable of fleeing or even of hiding before her hour. She was always ready to face what came."[140] To her father, Chantal says: "Neither you nor the dean of Idouville nor anyone else in the world—not even an angel—could convince me to enter religion one hour too early. . . . Monasteries are not places of refuge or infirmaries."[141] Like his model Jean-Marie Vianney, Donissan longs for the contemplative's cell out of humility and the hunted prey's need for rest, which devours him;[142] but such repose is not granted him. Chantal, too, knows she must renounce any such idea and fight her battles in the world without protection. Her mysticism as well will increasingly consist of her abandonment to the demons. Like Mouchette's spiritual director, she too will be led from a vision of her torturer to a physical confrontation with him.[143] All monastery doors have been locked in advance against the country priest; it is as if he were too humble even to consider a mystical refuge as a possibility for himself.

Finally, Blanche is both symbolically and actually driven out of Carmel by her fearfulness, in order to be in a position to live in her body, and exhibit for all to see, precisely the highest reality Carmel represents: extrapolation out of the Church so as to be more deeply within the Church. It is true that Blanche initially flees to the monastery. Her father said the following to her as a warning: "One doesn't leave the world out of disdain, like a freshman recruit who gets himself killed at his first heated incident only because he fears he'll lack the necessary courage. He thus uselessly deprives both king and country of his services."[144] Blanche, however, does not flee out of cowardice but out of the same supernatural fear that has dictated all her steps and has nothing to do with cowardice. And, indeed, she flees in vain since her fear accompanies her. The mystical dimension within her drives her in and out of fear as the wind drives a dry leaf. She will nowhere find the refuge she has unconsciously expected from

---

[140] *Joie*, 47.
[141] Ibid., 95–96.
[142] *Soleil*, 101–2, 255.
[143] *Joie*, 255.
[144] *Carmélites*, 28–29.

the cloister. At one point she says to the prioress: "It must be sweet, Mother, to feel so advanced along the way of interior detachment that one no longer knows how to trace back one's steps." And the prioress replies: "My poor child, sheer habit in the end detaches one from everything. But what would be the good of a religious who was detached from everything if she were not detached from herself, which is to say, from her own detachment?"[145]

In the *Dialogues of the Carmelites* Bernanos leads us for the first time into the world of the cloister, and he does it so perfectly that he appears never to have moved in any other world. All the reservations he had earlier expressed about monasteries are not indeed effaced—he does, after all, show us the nuns with full human and all-too-human realism—but they are surpassed by a deeper level of quiet affirmation. By making the extraordinary way of little Blanche's life branch out from the orderly way of monastic life, Bernanos casts a final, clarifying light on his earlier saint figures. All of these, even though living in the "world", belonged to the category of "the excluded", that is, of those wholly consecrated to God: these were persons obedient to the Church who, for the sake of their ecclesial mission, also had to be virginal and poor, persons who, even outside the institution of the religious orders, exhibited by their lives the essence of the evangelical counsels in all their fullness and purity.

No one can seriously raise against Bernanos the objection that he disregarded the values of marriage or the values of the Christian's freedom and his responsibility for the world. The whole of his political and cultural writings speak of nothing else, and they pillory a Christianity that would flee from such a hazardous enterprise. But when Bernanos set about portraying the mission of qualified saints to substitute themselves for sinners, he had enough Catholic instinct not to allow himself to be seduced by a foolish mania for consistency and, for instance, to declare that the age of monasteries, religious orders, and evangelical counsels had ended and that, in any event, all of this had to be gone beyond sooner or later. Bernanos' vision in this regard was also more soberly and transparently Catholic than Claudel's, whose dramatic cruxes almost always aimed at secularizing the principles of the religious state so as to transform them into principles of the lay Christian state in the world: this entailed a secular-

[145] Ibid., 32.

ization of specifically ecclesial sanctity and its transformation into a Romantic cult of the "absolute religious personality" in the world. The mystical night, however, is unyielding: it will not allow itself to be transmuted into the night of eroticism, which is the case in all Claudel's works, from *Break of Noon* to *The Satin Slipper*. Nor will it allow itself to be exploited on the stage, because neither the mystical state nor its effects are conveyable by ready-made social relationships or psychological insights but remain the property and secret of God alone. In this Bernanos was more consistent than Claudel; and it is satisfying to see the same author, who in *Under Satan's Sun* did not escape certain dangers in his dramatization of mysticism (both in the struggle with Satan and Mouchette and in Mouchette's concluding conversion), then correct these wisely in later works. It can occur, in exceptional cases, that God himself shows forth to the world some fruit of suffering. But it is impossible to turn this into a dramatic principle.

Bernanos is the sole Catholic writer of modern times who, with his characteristically lucid vision, demonstrated the inalienable connections existing between the mystical experience and the evangelical counsels. And he did this while at the same applying an at once sharp and salutary critique of everything that is mere human contrivance within the historical developments of the religious state in the Church. As he dismantled this complex structure, what he unearthed was precisely the unmovable foundation: the ecclesial, sacramental, and hierarchical figure defined by every authentic form of supernatural Christian experience.

Did the cause for this "ecclesialization" of mysticism lie in a particular *kairos*, that is, in a corresponding "mysticization" of the Church in our time? Could this process of transcendence of the Church within the Church, which failed Luther, possibly be a call to today's Church to actualize her mission to the world with an orientation toward experience, maturity, judgment, and the risk of decision implied therein, and to do this more thoroughly than at any other earlier period of Church history? One is inclined to see things in this way after becoming familiar with Bernanos' appeals to the Church in the modern world. Ever since the French Revolution—which was but the final, rumbling chord that concluded a long crescendo—the Church has been basically living in a continual state of self-transcendence. She

has been forcibly separated from her natural foundation, which is a
Christian social order, and she relates to the "world" more polemically than organically. Consequently, the Church seems to have to
do without the natural field in which to sow her seed, which is at
the same time the natural soil that nourishes her own transcendental
form. In a dangerous sense, she threatens to be *at a loss of the world*.
The danger would consist in the Church's becoming satisfied with her
own sacramental and hierarchical foundation and thereby engaging in
a flight from the times and, simultaneously, in a deceptive mimicry of
the times. This would deprive her of the energy necessary to undergo
the experience of Christian transcendence. As we have seen, the latter
consists in the Christian's—and the Christian Church's—denudation,
extrapolation, self-abandonment, and hazardous risk-taking.

   In his struggle to achieve a positive Christian interpretation of the
French Revolution, Péguy had already confronted the problem, as
did Claudel even more emphatically in his play *The Hostage*. Both of
them had seen that, since the Revolution, the Church had been cut
off from the two sources of her living tradition—namely, the nobility
and the people—and that democratic and socialist civilization constituted for her a real vacuum. Her transcendence, therefore, can only be
understood as the sacrificial gesture whereby the Church completes
the oblation of ancient "Christendom", a society at once temporal
and spiritual. Bernanos took up the problem precisely at this point,
most explicitly in the *Diary of a Country Priest* (in the character of
Olivier) and in the *Dialogues of the Carmelites*: like the old prioress,
Blanche comes from the nobility, as do Sister Constance and Sister
Marie de l'Incarnation, while all the other nuns represent the solid
Christian people bound to the soil. The type of person capable of
undergoing and enduring to the end the experience of transcendence
—which is to say, the type of the saint—is thus seen to presuppose
the type of Christians who are rooted in the base. Vallery-Radot is
right in pointing out in this connection that Péguy's concept of the
"carnal" overlaps Bernanos' concept of the "sacramental".[146] These
are the two words that describe ancient Christendom. In the best of
cases, the relationship between ancient "Christendom" (at once aristocratic and popular) and the modern "Church" (at once the prey of

---

[146] "For both [Bernanos] and Péguy, the word *carnal* took on a sacramental sense", Vallery-
Radot remarks. *Bernanos au Brésil*, 2; *Bul*. 6, 5.

the world and lacking all bonds to it) would be that between sacrificer and sacrifice, foundation and summit, state of repose and state of being hurled. This indeed reveals to the writer all the grandeur of the Church's contemporary situation but also its questionableness. For, what becomes of the summit when the foundation already belongs to the past?

III. THE WORLD OF
BAPTISM AND CONFIRMATION

1. Sanctity

"There is one archetype of the Christian man, and this model is consecrated by the Church herself. It is the saint."[1] This means that sanctity, as Bernanos understands it, is the privilege of the Christian and
that it has its origins in baptism as the foundational act of the Christian
life. Furthermore, it means that the Christian as such is defined by
sanctity and that he is all the more a Christian the more he embodies
the idea of sanctity. Hence, sanctity is the simple, not the complex.
Indeed, it is the point of *departure* of both Christian understanding
and Christian action, and not some distant and unattainable vanishing
point.

The saints are human beings in the full sense of the term.[2] Only
through the saints can the Church be what she is.[3] They are the "fo-
cal points" (in the literal sense of "fiery centers") that transform into
lived existence the grace lying fallow, as it were, within the institutional offices and sacraments. In the saints, God's grace becomes the
center of a whirlpool that draws all around it toward itself. Monsieur
Ouine senses this: "I only know—experience has taught me this—
that an innocent person is always the center and core of a certain
ferment. The earth ferments around the innocent, and that's a fact!"[4]
The nature of sanctity is not psychological: holiness is rooted in the
depths of the sacramental mystery. Precisely for this reason, sanctity
has a compact unity that shatters all attempts by sinful reason to analyze it. The things Bernanos says in this connection are among his
most astounding insights:

> Certain specific forms of renunciation escape all analysis because *sanctity*
> *draws at every moment out of itself what the artist must borrow from the world*

---

[1] *Anglais*, 245.
[2] *Enfants*, 199.
[3] *Anglais*, 157.
[4] *Ouine*, 137.

of forms. Sanctity is always becoming more and more interior, until it loses itself in the depths of Being. We can no longer grasp the relation between acts and motives, and, once this contact has been lost, it can never again be recovered. *As the observable facts enter more and more strictly into the logical order peculiar to them, they appear to us on the contrary to become detached from all order and dissolved in absurdity.* In order to retie the broken thread, we would have to jump by one sheer leap—something impossible!—all the way up to the sublime goal of which the hero had caught a glimpse already with the first step of his ascent. This goal his keen yet patient desire had thus been able to possess in advance, and the goal was nothing other than *the profound unity of his life.*[5]

Hidden and simple unity of life, striven after and yet already received as sheer gift ahead of all effort: this is sanctity. And this unity is fullness, the precise spot from which all ecclesial grace flows. It is a single, undivided mission that nevertheless contains within itself a whole world of possible new forms of sanctity, as we clearly see in the great *primary missions of the founders of religious orders.* With his prophetic insight, Bernanos understood the full theological and ecclesiological depth of these missions more profoundly than most professional theologians: "The great destinies [of these founders], more than any others, are beyond the grasp of all predetermined rules: they beam, they blaze with resplendent freedom." By contrast to the "genius", whose "personal presence in his work is minimal" and who generally achieves his work "by a kind of monstrous specialization that depletes all his soul's energies", we could say of the saint that his work "is his very life" and that "all of him is to be found in his life." Just as æsthetic judgment can find here no point of connection, so too for morality and psychology:

Our experience of men teaches us how to penetrate quite deeply into their intentions by merely comparing (this is already cruel enough!) the public and the private aspects of their lives. There is no attitude, no matter how well or how patiently kept up, that does not bear within itself its own contradiction, and there is no lie, no matter how tightly constructed, that does not have a crack somewhere or that at least could not be taken the other way around. Just as the surgeon learns about life from observing death, and the biologist analyzes organic waste products in an attempt to discover in them the secret of physical processes

---

[5] *Imposture,* 75. (The italics are von Balthasar's.—TRANS.)

and functions, in the same way the moralist knows he has before him a character made up of craftiness and deceit, a corpse in disguise that fools us as often as others. The charade will go on until, on the other side of death, that first glance from the Judge will make it all fly into smithereens. *But the Saint is, already before us, what he will be before the Judge.* With a look of astonishment in our eyes we know that, in the saints, we are coming into contact, not with a diminished life continually curtailed by mortification (as many would have us believe), but with life at the moment of its pristine outpouring, with life at the moment of its burgeoning splendor: with life itself—a wellspring we are only now discovering.[6]

And Bernanos continues in this vein: "Sanctity has no formulas, or, to put it more precisely, it has them all. It gathers up and magnifies all human energies. It brings about the horizontal concentration of man's highest faculties. Even to know something about sanctity we are required to make an effort and to participate to some extent in its rhythm and mighty impetus." Within this unity, the holy founder of an order is something like the sun of his community, scattered throughout time: "If it were within our power to look upon God's works with a uniquely penetrating and pure vision, we would see the Order of Preachers as the very charity of Saint Dominic realized within space and time—his visible prayer, as it were." It goes without saying that this unity is wholly beyond the reach of "the modern methods of historical criticism". Such criticism may be capable of describing a life that is passionate in an earthly sense, since passion is something universally human and, in the end, "nothing is more monotonous than passion." It

takes everything you give it and gives nothing in return. Charity, by contrast, gives everything, but even more is given it in return. What kind of superhuman bookkeeping could give an account of this wondrous exchange? If the historian insists on applying an exact rigor to his investigations, he will not be able to tell us much about a saint's existence. The old legends can tell us much more, because what they do is transcribe profound realities into symbols. They have a naïve quality about them that seems expressly intended to overturn our own logic and experience. And how could they not be naïve? Every life of a saint is like a new flowering, the miraculous naïveté of Eden itself showering

---

[6] *Dominique*, 8–9. (The italics are von Balthasar's.—TRANS.)

down on a world that the heritage of sin has made the slave of its own dead.[7]

This is Bernanos' portrayal of Saint Dominic. He only lightly touches on details of the external life, and the mystery of Dominic's interior riches evokes the reverence proper to a fullness that cannot be hastily exposed and interpreted: "This young cathedral canon . . . *is* the Order of Preachers, which was not formed by virtue of abstract calculations but by the unrestrained outpouring of its founder's life. Here everything is pure, everything new, everything strives toward the heights, like the cosmic rising of the dawn. . . . He doesn't appear to have any plan, and he never knows where his way is leading. But he has something better than any plan: radical detachment, interior freedom",[8] and this freedom allows itself to be flung at every moment into the crucible, there to be recast by the Spirit.

"*Every predestined person has, at least once in his life, thought he was sinking and hitting rock bottom. The illusion that everything has been taken from us at the same time, the feeling of total dispossession, is the divine sign that, on the contrary, everything is only now beginning.*"[9] In order for their new way of life to receive ecclesial form and recognition, "Saint Francis and Saint Dominic first had to offer themselves in sacrifice so as to prove that that new way was possible. For such is the lot God reserves for his saints."[10] And thus it was given them to become new wellsprings of Church life, at a depth beyond the reaches of the flux of time: "If sanctity exhibits the unfolding of a history, it would have to be something like a succession without repetitions in which every moment is unique. The point is not that the 'work' is ripe but that *charity* is ready and willing, that an individual has been quickened by the Spirit and has now attained his highest degree of excellence." The curve described by a saint's life is governed by its own mysterious law, which is a "free, docile, and pure" will having nothing in common with the so-called "destiny of great men".[11] The saint's destiny is determined by a very different rhythm: "The beginnings are slow, often wearisome. The conflicts come from the outside, and

[7] Ibid., 11–12.
[8] Ibid., 18–19.
[9] Ibid., 22. (The italics are von Balthasar's.—Trans.)
[10] Ibid., 23.
[11] Ibid., 26.

they also seem to come from within. Then, once the work has found its mysterious balance, it's as if it were wrenched from the earth and released to pure flight."[12]

The life of the saint, thus, possesses a center to which Bernanos tirelessly points and which defies all analysis: *this simple center is the love that consists of being perfectly pliable in God's hands and permanently available to his good pleasure.* Bernanos would later give this the name of spiritual childhood and *childlikeness.* Such love *turns toward the world and, without at all changing, reveals to the world the unassailability of the true simplicity and the bold vigor and maturity of perfection.* The canon of La Motte Beuvron says to the country priest: "What can I say, my child? These people do not hate your simplicity. They're protecting themselves from it, because it is a kind of fire that burns them. You walk through life with a poor humble smile on your face that begs for pity but also with a torch in your hand that you seem to take for a shepherd's staff."[13] To go to God means feeling "in the depths of your soul and in the very marrow of your bones a sacred self-surrender, which is the threshold and the gateway to all sanctity."[14] It means being a "soft and malleable thing in [God's] hands. The saints never stiffened against temptations, and they never revolted against themselves. Revolt is always a thing of the devil."[15] Thus, what the saint is always receiving more and more of from God is the renunciation of his own reserves and powers; in a word, poverty of spirit: "We must never count on anything except the sort of courage God bestows day by day, penny by penny, as it were."[16]

These last statements come from the final phase of Bernanos' life. Even though *Under Satan's Sun* already contains his essential intuitions, this first novel portrays sanctity with the exaggerated characteristics of a supernatural heroism: "What a thing, sanctity! In his sublime naïveté [Donissan] consented to being transported all at once from the lowest to the highest rank, by divine command. And he did not

---

[12] Ibid., 30.
[13] *Curé*, 204.
[14] *Joie*, 121.
[15] *Carmélites*, 63.
[16] Ibid., 155.

try to evade this. *You must rise to the place where God is calling you*, the other had said to him. He was being called. *Rise or be lost!* He was lost.''[17] When the unity of the word of command whereby the saint accepts his vocation takes on such a coloring, the rupture between the ideal and the real appears absolute,[18] and supernatural charity then yields not only to despair but to self-hatred.[19] Incapable of living in his own presence, such a saint bears within himself, like a divine fire, the brand of the judgment against him, and he is impelled to inflict excessive mortifications on himself. Bernanos did not describe these trials in order to impress the reader of his first novel but simply because at that time he considered them to be the true reality of a saint's life. In Donissan, these self-inflicted tribulations still constitute the very flames of divine love, burning in the depths of the mystical night. Without this fire losing anything of its radical exactions, its flames will later on become as gentle as the humility itself of the saints, who inflict mortifications on themselves only secondarily, as it were, without giving it any thought.[20] And this self-hatred, which posed an unfathomable problem to Bernanos and never ceased tormenting him, will in the end become nothing but a forgetting of self carried to the highest degree, or simply a humble love of self in Christ.[21]

Bernanos' first novel, *Under Satan's Sun*, has an uncanny resemblance to the first phases of the lives of the saints, full of a dark violence that to us seems to overstep all boundaries. Later on, having become wiser, they will look back from a higher level, but to arrive here it is necessary for them to have climbed these slopes strewn with fallen rocks. When he describes these trials, even though his intention is precisely to surpass the psychological plane, Bernanos is still talking like a psychologist: "In everything he acted as if the sum total of his energy were constant—and perhaps it actually was. At certain moments, when he is about to renounce everything, the only rest he can envision is descending within himself and examining himself with intensified rigor. For this extraordinary man, fatigue is but a bad

---

[17] *Soleil*, 122.
[18] Ibid., 122–23.
[19] Ibid., 132–33.
[20] *Dominique*, 39.
[21] *Curé*, 321.

thought."[22] Who knows if Bernanos is not right after all? Perhaps the
saints are capable of overcoming the laws of energy governing things
here on earth, not only because they receive special aids in the order
of miracles, but because they must themselves necessarily overstep the
boundaries of nature. The idea itself is defensible; only its expression
is forced. "Forced" is the very term Bernanos applies to Donissan:
"What does that matter to the crude peasant, who is forced even in
his highest hope?"[23] And the style is itself not less "forced" in the
lines that follow, which describe the "elemental feeling" that "keeps
the Curé de Lumbres on his feet", like a "superhuman wrath, . . . the
rage of a child or a demigod". We must reiterate, however, that in
Under Satan's Sun we should see a bastion erected against the present
era and its spiritual idols. If a destructive violence takes surprising
forms in it and Bernanos occasionally lapses into a declamatory tone,
we should not judge him too harshly. In order to make us understand that God always uses unusual and ever-new ways to deal with
his saints, Bernanos must himself use striking and uncommon means.
"The work God accomplishes within us is rarely what we expect. Almost always the Holy Spirit appears to us to be acting nonsensically,
to be wasting his time. If the piece of iron could have some inkling
of the file slowly wearing it down, what rage, what exasperation
would take hold of it! And yet, it is precisely thus that God wears us
away."[24]

However, as life little by little instills in Bernanos the virtue of humility, superhuman traits occupy less and less space in his work. In
1947 he writes: "The saints are not sublime. They have no need for
the sublime. It's rather the sublime that has a need for them. The saints
are not heroes, at least not in the manner of Plutarch's heroes."[25] In
1939, when he was writing *The Humiliated Children* and *The Scandal
of Truth*, he should doubtless have used very different language. But
he explains: "A hero gives us the illusion of surpassing humanity.
But the saint does not surpass it: he assumes humanity; he strives to
realize it as well as possible. Do you understand the difference? He
strives to come as close as possible to his model, Jesus Christ, which

---

[22] *Soleil*, 145.
[23] Ibid., 303.
[24] Ibid., 234.
[25] *Liberté*, 286.

is to say, the One who was perfect man, who was man with perfect simplicity, who was man to the point, precisely, of disconcerting all heroes."[26] Toward the end of his life, when he speaks of the saints, Bernanos prefers to use the categories of magnanimity, generosity, and commitment. He emphasizes the risk the saints accept running, the risk of making a total gift of their soul and of their life, to the very limits of exhaustion and self-depletion. It is on such paths that the saint nonetheless advances toward the Kingdom that belongs to him, that Kingdom of God where the continuity is reëstablished between the exceptional hero and the little soul, a continuity that could hardly be detected in the works of Bernanos' first period.

To the holy country priest there is juxtaposed, as brother, Olivier, the knightly soldier. "Refusal is the law of the world—but we don't refuse anything."[27] In *The Humiliated Children*, Bernanos the soldier calls himself and his comrades in the Great War "saints of lesser quality".[28] In his own cruder language, this seems to translate the message of Saint Thérèse of Lisieux. Elsewhere he muses:

> You would be wrong to think that here I am speaking only of the saints of the calendar! There are millions of saints in the world known only to God, who by no means deserve to be raised to the altars. I speak of a very inferior and very rustic sort of saints, saints of very low birth who have only one drop of sanctity in their veins and who resemble real saints much as an alley cat resembles a Persian or a Siamese that has won first prize in contests. Normally, nothing sets them apart from the mass of ordinary people. Nor, by the way, do they set themselves apart from others. They think they are just like the others, and the Church herself is careful not to disabuse them on this point.[29]

This is sanctity in the world, submerged in the world like leaven in the dough, and this is why such saints are so unselfconscious. These are precisely Bernanos' favorites:

> I don't exactly hold Péguy for a saint, but he's a man who, although dead, remains within speaking range, and even closer. He remains within

---

[26] Ibid., 282f.
[27] *Curé*, 264.
[28] *Enfants*, 11.
[29] *Anglais*, 246–47.

reach—within reach of each one of us, and he answers every time we call him. This at least proves there wasn't much of the liar about him, barely what was needed to survive and live this poor, dear dog's life of ours—and no more: there was no deceit about him. He answers when you call him, and he even answers in a low voice. I'm not saying that this last particular is a sign of sanctity, but at the very least it's a quite special mark of friendship with God and something God has not always granted his saints. There are saints who are wholly incapable of speaking to us from the other shore without raising their voice, and we mustn't listen to these right after hearing the Gospel, because we'd become deaf by contrast. I suppose that these saints must one day have alienated a part of themselves they didn't regard as very precious and which they probably judged to be too human. And they were never able to gain it back, even at the price of countless sacrifices. That neglected part of themselves was a certain simplicity, a certain freshness, given by grace wholly free of charge, which could never thereafter recover its original form, even at the cost of fasts and mortifications.[30]

The hard-boiled analyst La Pérouse is defeated less by Chantal's "charity" than by this miracle of her freshness: "Even today, at this very instant, I would search in vain in your face for some mark, some sign, some imperceptible blemish left by the past. But for you, O marvel, there is no past! When one has scrutinized so many visages that, from a distance, appear to be alive but are in fact only scowls frozen into fixity, for centuries perhaps, by some hereditary disease, what a surprise it is suddenly to discover one person—free, intact, the most humble of beings—who is in profound harmony with herself!"[31] This innocence, this perfectly fresh start without a past of sin, is the mystery of sanctity, but only because what is contained here is the mystery of Christian baptism as such. Baptism bestows on every Christian this miracle of a new beginning, of absolute genesis, the mystery of the *Quasi modo geniti infantes* ("Like newborn infants . . . ," 1 Pet 2:2) that the Church celebrates especially on the Octave Day of Easter. This mystery triumphs over both time and the deterioration it brings: it is the mystery of an eternal youth that blossoms amidst the graying of hair and the inevitable march to death's scaffold.

---

[30] *Enfants*, 95–96.
[31] *Joie*, 226.

2. Childhood and Hope

Judging from the way Bernanos defines the heart of sanctity—as spiritual childhood, as an existence continually springing up anew from the divine Source, as elemental hope—we could conclude that he is simply a disciple of Péguy. But what could be the meaning of discipleship once one has penetrated so profoundly into the hearth of divine truth? Surely not that the younger of the two is an epigone, but that they both drink in their vision at the very same Source and that they both possess the same literary and human force to give shape to that vision through imagery and dramatic situation. It is as if both Péguy and Bernanos were equally intimate initiates, standing at the heart of the message of spiritual childhood proclaimed by Saint Thérèse of Lisieux: they are both direct fruits of the Carmelite's fecundity, established in the world over against the sterility of a Christianity that has become bourgeois and decrepit. So strong is this sign that it is infinitely more than the nostalgic reaction of a civilization grown old and longing for its ancient unities: such had been the tenor of early Romanticism and the *Wandervogelbewegung*—the "Birds of Passage" movement of German youth. Lisieux means the solemn and earnest command whereby grace calls Christians back to the Source.

Even stronger than with Péguy, it was Bernanos' experience of his own childhood and youth that provided him with the dominant image for this conception of a Christian existence. There are central passages in his work where Bernanos speaks of the crucial role played by childhood in the development of his imagination. Two of these are the great programmatic introduction to the *Cemeteries*[32] and the corresponding passages in *The Humiliated Children*.[33] These pages strike one at once with their tremulous pathos bordering on tears. Here we see Bernanos wholly intent on rediscovering the lost paradise of the "child I was", a child whom he does not solely want to elevate as the ideal *norm* of his work (only that is valid which can sustain this child's gaze) but who is considered the real *source* of this work: "As soon as I take pen in hand, what at once begins emerging before me is my childhood, a very ordinary childhood like all the others; and yet, it is from it that I draw everything I write as from an inexhaustible foun-

---

[32] *Cimetières*, iv–v.
[33] *Enfants*, 195–96.

tain of dreams."[34] This is why, ten years later, he writes to another correspondent that "childhood is always magical."[35] And, in the album of a young Brazilian woman, he weaves a garland of inextricable images consisting of children, poets, and the poor:

> Girls extend their album to *grownups* in the same way that the poor extend their hand. And generally they are both disappointed, because the only truly disappointed people in the universe have always been those whom the Beatitudes regard as privileged, which is to say, the poor and children. . . . But you have also extended your hand to poets. And I think that the poets—O miracle!—have given you without stint, because poets are by nature generous and bountiful. Never again forget that what still keeps this hideous world from falling apart is the sweet conspiracy—always attacked yet always reborn—of poets and children. Be faithful to the poets, remain faithful to childhood! Never become a grownup![36]

Thus, Bernanos' first hero, Donissan, whose mission it is to enter into the night of sin, cannot be better characterized than by the simplest law of life: to live means to turn one's back on childhood, to put ever more distance between oneself and childhood's source and light:

> A thousand memories return from his childhood, so strangely united to God, and from his dreams, those very dreams whose dangerous gentleness—O fury!—he had so feared and which he had little by little buried in his harsh zeal. . . . This, then, was the unforgettable voice that is heard for only a brief span of days, before silence closes over it forever. Without knowing it, he had fled God's outstretched hand—the very sight of the face full of reproach—and then the last cry heard from the top of the hills, that final distant call weak as a sigh. Every step drove him farther into the land of his exile, but he remained forever branded with the sign that God's servant had a short while before discerned on his forehead.[37]

And, if these last words reflect his mystical vocation, the same thing is fully expressed in the statement Donissan later on makes to Menou-Segrais in one of their conversations: "As for me, I have ever since

[34] *To Madame de la Noue*, 1935; *Bul.* 1, 5.
[35] *To Assia Lassaigne*, November 3, 45; *Bul.* 5, 11.
[36] *Bul.* 12–13, 4.
[37] *Soleil*, 123.

childhood lived less hoping for the glory to come than regretting the glory we have lost."[38] But surely Donissan is an exception. He is a child of God raised to the second power, a child of God, that is, in whom we can no longer discern the first power: that of a supernatural childhood that is opposed to the natural law of life. He experiences joy only in the manner of lightning, as a consuming fire,[39] and if he tastes of it, it is only to be deprived of it the more efficaciously. Only the girl Chantal will offer us a picture of graced spiritual childhood, but even this comes at the moment when she can no longer perceive what she has received.

Before we turn to Chantal, however, it is important for us to see how deeply hope is rooted, for both Péguy and Bernanos, in the *nature* of our ephemeral existence. Péguy does not establish very sharp boundaries between natural and supernatural hope; he simply stands astonished before the inconceivable miracle that life, subject to constant disappointment as it is, nevertheless daily begins each morning with renewed hope. Bernanos distinguishes more sharply between *espoir* and *espérance*, both of which must be rendered as "hope" in English. Doctor Lavigne, an unbeliever, defines *espoir* as "a beast within man, a powerful, ferocious beast", while *espérance* means nothing to him: "No one", he says, "has ever observed this particular divinity from close up."[40] Bernanos himself had painful knowledge of all the possible perversions of hope, the chief of which is "optimism", which he hounded with sarcasm. Bernanos wanted to have nothing to do with that optimism the world routinely equates with hope.[41] But this did not keep true *espoir*, like a time of youth that is genuinely lived, from coming mysteriously close to sanctity and divine childhood in Bernanos' eyes: such hope enables one to enter into the unconditional character of sanctity and spiritual childhood. This is all the more so as the spark of hope is found in the poor man and the sinner in an envelopment of utter hiddenness, humiliation, insult, and misery. In the novella *A Night*, the dying mestizo hopes for the to him unknown sacrament of baptism and for the likewise unknown truth of faith; but he does not receive them, because the "Christian"

---

[38] Ibid., 238.
[39] Ibid., 121.
[40] *Curé*, 294.
[41] *Cimetières*, 260 and passim.

has forgotten them. But the reader senses that he has been saved as far as Bernanos is concerned, that his *espoir* has been raised by grace to become a living *espérance*.[42]

To be sure, as Christian realities, both youth and old age are to be regarded as something primarily supernatural;[43] but the power of being a child, which is conferred by baptism and holiness, leaves a profound mark on the whole man, down to his physical aspect. Why, for instance, do nuns who are happy in their cloister always retain such an incredibly youthful appearance throughout their lives? And it is no coincidence that the country priest, already mortally ill, recovers all the glorious vitality of his physical youth while riding a motor-cycle. He had, in fact, never been young, because his childhood had been too harsh for that: "I never was young, because no one ever wanted to be young with me."[44] Now, in his sudden friendship with the young soldier, he is overcome by the joy of pure love, and it re-juvenates him: "By what miracle did I at that moment feel young, so young—ah, indeed, so very young!—as young as on this triumphant morning? . . . I understood that youth is a blessed thing, that it is a risk that must be run, but that this very risk, too, is a blessed thing." He well knows that God is giving him this gift of happiness in order for him to renounce it, that his sacrifice might be perfect. But he first had to know the reality of this joy, "which is a kind of pride, of exultation, an absurd and purely carnal hope, the carnal form of hope".[45]

Nor is it a coincidence that the country priest so loves the early morning: "The deliverance brought by morning is always such a sweet thing for me. It's like a grace from God, a smile. Let all mornings be blessed!"[46] And it is likewise no surprise that, for Monsieur Ouine, morning is the unbearable time of day: "His morning anguish is the curious extension of his insomnia, something like its intolerable blossoming. This acid freshness, this cleanness, this murmuring of invisible streamlets, this wholesale renewal of all things isolates his sleeplessness more painfully than does the nocturnal silence or the

---

[42] *Nouvelles* (Plon ed., 1955), 94–99.
[43] See *Curé*, 157.
[44] Ibid., 256.
[45] Ibid., 255–57.
[46] Ibid., 252.

darkness, in which his nerves find a sort of repose, a funereal security. The morning appears to exclude him disdainfully from life and to cast him out with the dead. He hates it."[47] For precisely morning is the time of children and of hope, "of which by evening there remains not a single crumb but which mysteriously reinvents itself by morning".[48] This human and incarnate experience of the grace of youthfulness conferred by sanctity belongs to the sacramental mystery whereby the spiritual becomes carnal. This is why Bernanos so loved contemplating sanctity in literally young figures, such as Joan of Arc and Thérèse of Lisieux, who together provided the model for Chantal de Clergerie and whose spirit permeates all Bernanos' books.

The whole of *Joan, Heretic and Saint* is one uninterrupted hymn to youth. Over against her stand the old men, scholastics and politicians, the desiccated and the loveless—vampires feeding at the saint's young heart: "The Old Man felt alone. . . . 'Is the heart still beating?', he asked himself. But the heart of the world is always beating. The world's youth is this heart. If it weren't for this sweet scandal of childhood, avarice and guile would have drained the earth of substance in one or two centuries at most. . . . But the spirit of old age that patiently conquers the world always loses it again at just the right moment."[49] The tribunal that judges youth and burns it at the stake is made up of old men. For Bernanos, modern France since 1870 was a "kingdom of old men, which consecrated itself at birth to the demons of old age".[50] With the reign of Vichy they reached their apotheosis, and "the old foxes of finance, the Academy, and the Church" borrowed from Hitler's Germany "the only armored police force capable of protecting their privileges and their lucre from the rage of the people".[51]

---

[47] *Ouine*, 144 (corrected text).

[48] *Lettres brésiliennes*, 1942; *Bul.* 5, 8.

[49] *Jeanne*, 10–11.

[50] *Cimetières*, 283. (In another passage of this work, Bernanos criticizes the former fanatics of anti-Germanism who suddenly discovered the virtues of Hitler's Germany out of their fear of Communism. He writes: "The formidable East, which only yesterday still began at Saarbrücken, has now made itself at home in the very center of Paris, in rue Lafayette. What can I say? These old men have grown older still. They prefer having barbarism as close as possible to them, within easy reach of their wheelchairs" *Cimetières*, 328.—Note of the French trans.)

[51] *Croix*, July 1943, 361–62 (BBC broadcast).

This universal and ever-tighter conspiracy of old men against youth was at the same time a conspiracy against sanctity, for "the reign of the old men is precisely the opposite of the Kingdom of God." [52] But the height of their mischief was that they dared to profane what they actually hated by usurping it:

> They have all betrayed youth, but they exploit it. They exploit it as a sacred sign: they call themselves young and speak in the name of youth. Who now would dare to look into the face of German youth, that cruel dwarf? And what has Mussolini done to Italian youth? As for the youth of Spain, it has been lapping up fresh blood from a saucer for six years now. Its wet nurse was Torquemada. At birth it began sucking his black teats. Indeed, they have all betrayed youth. But we French, at least, have betrayed it publicly. France threw herself publicly into the Old Man's arms, delivered herself over to decrepitude, to the spirit of senility. [53]

In 1937, as Hitler's troops are invading Austria, Bernanos writes: "With the rolling of the cannons and tanks, all the youth of Europe has just died in Salzburg, along with Mozart the child." [54] A series of articles in *Le Figaro* (November 1931 to January 1932, with a diatribe against the "spirit of the old men") shows the extent to which, for Bernanos, the whole problem of contemporary culture must be seen under the sign of a senescent civilization that has lost its youth. In *Monsieur Ouine*, the woman mayor says to the doctor: "In my time, you see—I'm speaking of my youth, of course—the old men didn't possess half the vice of today's old men. In my opinion, that's where our malady is coming from. The world is in the process of rotting on account of its old men." [55] In *Monsieur Ouine*, and even more so in *An Evil Dream*, Bernanos portrays with a precise realism that could only come from supreme indignation the gruesome work that "the old men" perform on youth, the subtle craft whereby they hollow it out and suck its lifeblood. We recall here the portrait Bernanos paints of the two young men Philippe and Olivier. True representatives of contemporary youth, they lack the capacity for faith and even more so for hope. They have fallen victim to the dandyism of the existentialists and to every form of self-poisoning. They are at the same time

---

[52] Ibid., 361.
[53] *Anglais*, 48.
[54] *Cimetières*, 346.
[55] *Ouine*, 191 (corrected text).

fellow travelers of the Communists and suicidal. The reality Bernanos here evokes is cruel in its precision but far from unjust. With what passionate ardor and youthfulness does the fifty-year-old Bernanos distance himself from these masks as he says of himself: "I have lost my youth, and I can gain it back only through sanctity."[56] Turning his back on today's false youth, Bernanos sets about inventing genuine youthful saints. As models for his own creations, he exalts Thérèse of the Child Jesus, Joan of Arc, and last but not least the Blessed Virgin with her childlike countenance. And he yearns for eternity and "the most mysterious of all angels, the one who on the day of the resurrection will make us again into little children".[57]

Thérèse of Lisieux is ever present in Bernanos' work. Cénabre already writes an article about her, in order to prove "that her heavenly smile . . . will forever remain the most bleeding rose—and the most protected—of the gardens of paradise".[58] Chantal's figure is expressly modeled on her traits, and in *Joy* Bernanos is continually alluding to images and turns of phrase reminiscent of Thérèse. And so we have the happiness of being weak in God's hands,[59] the lightness of the person who "allows herself to float",[60] the "bird within the still point of the storm",[61] the grayness and banality of everyday existence,[62] the little girl,[63] the ball thrown in a corner,[64] the vocation to small and not great trials,[65] the divine eagle that swoops down upon the prey of a mortal heart,[66] and the "abundant smallness" that is guaranteed to dissolve all relationship with the devil.[67]

---

[56] *To Paulus Gordan, Bul.* 5, 6.

[57] May 27, 1934; *Bul.* 1–2, 18.

[58] *Imposture*, 69–70.

[59] *Joie*, 67.

[60] Ibid., 91.

[61] Ibid., 119.

[62] Ibid., 221–22.

[63] Ibid., 228, 244.

[64] "A little trifle of a light thing, made to be of service for only an instant, to provide delight for one single instant, and then thrown away without a thought" ibid., 241.

[65] Ibid., 243.

[66] Ibid., 249. (In Bernanos' context, the eagle is the death agony.—Note of the French trans.)

[67] "She had never been much concerned with the devil and his attacks. She was sure she would escape him on account of her abundant smallness" ibid., 65.

The country priest, too, is full of Thérèsian traits. He continually refers to his own insignificance, which at the same time explains all the failures and mystical experiences of the little pastor and also veils their true meaning from him, dulling their impact as it were. In the midst of all this, we witness the pathos of the formula "all or nothing"[68] and, at the novel's conclusion, the "small, trivial death, as little as possible"[69] and the fear of not being ready to face death.[70] Here, we have Thérèse's message applied at a deep level, no longer now, as in *Joy*, with a direct copying of her specific characteristics, but with supremely free variations on her fundamental concerns and a transposition of the earthly into the spiritual.

In *The Great Cemeteries under the Moon*, Bernanos begins by sharply stigmatizing the "fraud of Lisieux"—the touching up of the saint's pictures and writings in an attempt to render them inoffensive. But then again he justifies the procedure in a deeper sense. For, he says, he "attaches no importance whatsoever to this deceit": if Thérèse's "little innocent hands", if her "terrible little hands" were "experts in cutting paper flowers", it is because "this mysterious girl perhaps had it in mind to bestow with a smile on our poor world one moment of great respite during which it could catch its breath for a while in the shadow of its own familiar mediocrity." The essential thing is that Thérèse, with these same hands "all bitten by chlorine on washdays and by frost", should have "sown a seed that nothing can keep from sprouting".[71] After Thérèse, it is "the spirit of childhood that will judge the world". Twenty years before the First World War, Thérèse had promised a rain of roses; but doubtless she did not know that the roses raining down from heaven could come to assume the form of bombs.[72] And the transition from the paper flowers to the real blossoms, and from these to the bombs, is just as astonishing and natural as Thérèse's own transition from playing at being a saint to earnest sanctity: "We could say that she became a saint by playing saints with the Child Jesus, in the same way that a little boy, by playing endlessly

---

[68] *Curé*, 260.

[69] Ibid., 304.

[70] Bernanos had already made Madame Dargent, the murderess, utter the statement "I'll never finish dying" (*Nouvelles*, [1955 edition], 10), which echoes Saint Thérèse's own formula, "I'll never know how to die."

[71] *Cimetières*, 241–42.

[72] Ibid., 247.

with an electric train, can gradually become a railway engineer, or simply a station master, almost without giving it any thought. . . ."[73]

The unbeliever, however, whom Bernanos puts in the pulpit on the feast of Thérèse of Lisieux and who presents the saint to the congregation from his own standpoint vehemently demands of his listeners that Thérèse's spirit be translated into a language that contemporaries can understand. To be sure, the saints are marvelous human beings, at once heroes, geniuses, and children. But what can the world do with them? "What can our politicians and moralists do with a Thérèse of Lisieux? In their mouth, her message would lose all meaning, or at least every chance of being effective. It was written in your language, and only your language can express it. We lack the words necessary to translate it without betraying it. . . . It is clear that you alone can and must communicate the saints' message; but, alas, you are very far from having always discharged this duty to the best advantage for us [unbelievers]. I am sorry to have to tell you that we are paying dearly for your neglect."[74] The unbeliever then shows Christians the ways to accomplish such a "translation". He shows them what, at bottom, Bernanos was attempting to do throughout his whole work. There is a childlikeness, an impulse of youthfulness, which the world understands because the world naturally loves what is young and knows from experience what it was to be young; and this same childlike and youthful impulse can also be the expression of a most profound, supernatural childhood—the expression of sanctity itself. But this reality needs to be lived by Christians convincingly before the world. Instead of a senile, abstract faith, the world should be shown a vibrantly youthful and really *believing* faith: "Hurry up and become children again, that we in turn might do the same!"[75] Friends of Bernanos attest to the fact that Saint Thérèse's *Novissima Verba* was always found among his favorite books.

The figure of *Joan of Arc* has already been mentioned. For Bernanos she comes right after Thérèse, representing in action the same spirit that the Carmelite represents in contemplation: both of them are, through and through, children. With her absurd, utopian hope, Joan fulfills

---

[73] *Liberté*, 265.

[74] *Cimetières*, 267.

[75] Ibid., 272.

a most difficult task as in a dream, and she succeeds in "putting the professors of the University of Paris in her pocket".[76] In the small work he dedicates to her, Bernanos cannot see her as anything other than a child. Joan stands there like a bronze statue erected against all the corrosion of the faith effected by rationalism and bureaucratic craftiness. But her victory does not derive only, or primarily, from the words she hurls with childlike boldness at her judges, sempiternally and unmovably true to their corrupted natures: her victory is rooted in her defenselessness, in her weakness, in the night of her soul and body. It is the child in Joan that is condemned[77] and forsaken by all; it is the child in her that is tortured much more cruelly than the little children for whose sake Ivan Karamazov renounced his faith and refused an admission ticket to eternal beatitude. The Russian cry for justice against the God of love—this cry of modern man, who feels so superior to the Christian—has a comic effect in the face of little Joan. She was actually the last Christian soldier, the last knight of Christendom, and—according to Olivier in the *Country Priest*—it is precisely for this reason that the clerics burn her at the stake.[78] Joan signals the end of a Christianity that is at the same time spiritual and temporal: after her we witness the emergence of the clerical Church. She is the last to realize the synthesis we saw the atheist preacher demand from the Christian community on the feast of Saint Thérèse. This is why Bernanos cannot praise her highly enough, indeed not as a "prophetic saint", but as the living image of Christian action taking root in the world and transforming it from within. In his *Letter to the English*,[79] Bernanos does not conceal the fact that it is Joan's help he needs in his wartime articles against Vichy.[80] It was her he had already invoked against the Francoist "crusades",[81] and it is again she who reappears in the last lines of the *Great Cemeteries* "among those old foxes, the *professors of morality* and the casuists, in the dense air of the judicial chambers": here, Joan is like a "little paradoxical theologian who appeals to God, to his saints, and to the invisible Church, while every crafty question strikes her deftly in the breast and hurls her to

[76] Ibid.
[77] *Jeanne*, 41f.
[78] *Curé*, 266.
[79] *Anglais*, 38, 40, 43, 107, 161, 250–51.
[80] *Croix*, 9, 16, 86, 96.
[81] *Cimetières*, 96.

the ground, dripping with sacred blood".[82] Likewise, at the conclusion of his *Letter to the English*, Bernanos once again stands by her and her simple wisdom. While the politicians no longer knew where to turn to escape, Joan "demanded, against the very will of the churchmen, that the first thing to be done was to make an anointed king out of the young prince". With mysterious ambiguity, Bernanos the monarchist then concludes his *Letter to the English* with the sentence: "When man will have lost everything, then we will demand for him too—whether he likes it or not—the Anointing that divinizes him. We will open for him the way to his crowning as king."[83]

Thérèse and Joan are like the accessible outer bastions of an unapproachable fortress. Bernanos' love for *the Virgin Mary* is too deep and too delicate for him to set up her image on every street corner. Only once in his works does he expressly call upon her and conjure up her image, at a moment when he could no longer go on without her. Only once does he have Mary emerge out of her invisible omnipresence in his books. This occurs at the conclusion of the country priest's *Via Crucis*, at the moment when everything begins to collapse around him. His friend, the Curé de Torcy, introduces the subject, in precisely the same manner in which it will be developed later on:

> And the Blessed Virgin: Do you pray to the Blessed Virgin? . . . Do you pray to her as you ought? Do you pray well to her? She is our mother, we know that. She is the mother of the human race, the new Eve. But she is also its daughter. The old world, the wretched and suffering old world, the world before the advent of grace, long rocked her on its desolate heart—for centuries upon centuries—all during its dark period of waiting, without understanding, for a *virgo genitrix*. . . . For centuries upon centuries the world protected with its old, heavy, crime-stained hands the marvelous little girl whose name it didn't even know. A little girl, the Queen of the Angels![84]

To be sure, "the Holy Virgin knew neither triumph nor miracles. Her Son did not allow human glory so much as to graze her, not even with the finest tip of its great wild wing. No one has ever lived,

---

[82] Ibid., 361.
[83] *Anglais*, 251.
[84] *Curé*, 229.

suffered, or died with such simplicity and in so great an ignorance of her own dignity—a dignity that nevertheless places her above the Angels." And then we hear the following profound and astounding affirmation from the Curé de Torcy's mouth:

> For, after all, she had been born without sin. What amazing solitude! She was *so pure and so limpid a fountain, a fountain so limpid and so pure, that she could not even see her own image reflected in it*, since it had been made solely for the joy of the Father. O sacred solitude! . . . Do you realize what we are for her, we of the human race? Naturally, she does detest sin; but, in the end, she lacks all experience of sin—an experience that even the greatest saints did not lack, not even the saint of Assisi, seraphic as he is. *The Virgin's gaze is the only truly childlike gaze, the only gaze of a true child ever to dawn upon our shame and our misery.*

"She is the youngest-born of the human race."[85]

It is into these eyes that the country priest peers when, with all his forces exhausted, he collapses into his particular night: "It was the face of a child, or of a very young girl."[86] Péguy, too, had known all of this; but, instead of Mary, he chose to evoke the vicarious figure of our primeval mother Eve, the moving ancestor of Mary, her youngest daughter. For Eve had known the eternal youthfulness of paradise and had tasted the infinite loss of it. Bernanos, however, here focuses on the contrary aspect: that eschatological youthfulness that never abandoned paradise and that, in Mary, in union with Eve, became the Mother of all sorrows precisely because she moves so ineffably alone among all sinners. And this is why her face is "the very face of sadness", but "a sweet, unfathomable sadness, a sadness without revolt, like a wide and gentle unending night".[87] There is nothing tragic about this solitude, because from it is born all communion among the children of God. And yet, this solitude cannot be leapt over in order to arrive at once at the ready-made community; for Mary's holy solitude is very much a reality: *it is the nocturnal basis for all ecclesial existence*, for all the love found in the redeemed. This mystery is deeper and more nocturnal than all the nights of sin and hell. It is one with the night whose praises Péguy sang so memorably. This

---

[85] Ibid., 231–32. (The italics are von Balthasar's.—TRANS.)

[86] Ibid., 237.

[87] Ibid.

night has nothing gloomy about it but exudes pure, radiant humility. It is a great undulant veil of mercy, an ocean of virginal motherhood, and the primal fountain of ultimate childhood.

~

But the Christian child has to confront the world; the sheep must come face to face with the wolves; and it is the sacrament of *confirmation* that strengthens the Christian for this encounter. Confirmation does not bestow on the Christian a new and different external hardness to compensate for his internal softness; rather, it transforms the Christian's hope and love and self-surrendering faith into weapons of the spirit. If it is true that "the grace of God makes the most hardened man into a little child",[88] that "the spirit of youth and the spirit of charity can never be found one without the other",[89] and that childlikeness is the sole condition that creates joy, delight, and merriment,[90] then it is precisely this "spirit" that is incomprehensible for the "old foxes" and a source of terror to them since they cannot conquer it. The sheep does not become a wolf. Exteriorly, it remains quite vulnerable. As with Joan, it can be bound and burned on the sacrificial altar. But the spirit is unconquerable. Indeed, such a death is itself a privilege of youth: "When everything wilts, rots, and returns to its original muck, it is given to youth alone to die, to know death."[91] This is so true that old people, whose only prospect is perfect decay, must search in themselves for a scrap of untouched youth in order to be able to die at all. Simone Alfieri declares to Ganse that she does not believe anyone "has ever quite succeeded in uprooting totally the little child he once was. . . . In any case, if such a thing still exists within you, don't let go of it. It isn't very likely that there's enough of it to help you live, but it will surely be of use to you to help you die."[92]

---

[88] *Ouine*, 201.
[89] *Cimetières*, 298.
[90] See *Curé*, 29.
[91] *Ouine*, 25.
[92] *Rêve*, 80.

This power, proper to the child, which refuses to die and which desperately fights off the resignation and cynicism typical of adult life: this power is conferred by the sacrament of confirmation. Thus, Bernanos takes up the "despair" that has been so fashionable in the twentieth century and transforms it into a "desperation" that he then puts at the service of his "tiny hope". Such desperation can be the power of hope in this hopeless world. It is identical with Saint Paul's "hoping against all hope" (Rom 4:18): *"In order to meet hope we must first go to the other side of despair.* When you trudge on to the very end of the night, you meet another dawn. . . . Optimism is a false hope, made to console cowards and imbeciles. Hope is a virtue, *virtus*, a heroic resolution of the soul. The highest form of hope is despair that has been overcome. . . . An optimistic courage can tackle only middling difficulties. However, if you consider circumstances of capital importance, the expression that naturally comes to your lips is '*desperate* courage', '*desperate* energy'." [93] "Hope is a disinterested and heroic act of the soul of which cowards and imbeciles are not in the least capable. These possess illusion in the place of hope." [94] "People think it is easy to hope. But the only ones who can really hope are those who have first had the courage to despair of all the illusions and lies in which they had found security and which they falsely took to be hope." [95] "There you have it! I invite you to despair of your illusions, and in this way I am putting despair at the service of hope." [96] As in Péguy, hope is here the power that swims against the current: the current of time and ephemerality, of sin and decay unto hell. Hope must have at least as much dragging power as the despair against which it is taking a stand; and if it intends to stride upstream, it will need even more power. The saints, "those magnificent hopers, always fight like desperadoes". [97] A figure like Chantal knows nothing of either mournfulness or resignation. [98]

In Bernanos' diary for 1946, three lapidary aphorisms are emblematic of the final form that hope takes in the life of the writer himself:

---

[93] *Liberté*, 14-15; cf. *Bul.* 5, 4. (Bernanos himself underscores the word "desperate" in the last sentence. The other italics are von Balthasar's.—TRANS.)

[94] *Croix*, May 15, 1945, 494.

[95] *Liberté*, 132.

[96] Ibid., 249.

[97] *Dominique*, 26.

[98] *Joie*, 110.

—"An unyielding despair, which is perhaps nothing other than the unyielding refusal to despair."

—"A man who, on an evening of disaster when he has been trampled by cowards and is despairing of everything, shoots his last cartridge while weeping with fury: such a man, without knowing it, dies in the midst of an outpouring of hope. To hope means to confront."

—"What does it matter to me to know whether or not I have hope? It's enough for me to have the works of hope. Only the future will tell whether or not I have hope's works. The future will tell whether each of my books is not a particular despair that has been overcome."[99]

From this we see that hope is an "infused, supernatural virtue" and that it does not need to be verified experientially any more than faith or love. Bernanos would like to offer some help to the *New Mouchette* who throws herself in the water: "At such a moment, anger and shame could have taken the place of hope for her, for such passions are not without a dark desire of revenge."[100] Even the figure of Drumont sketched by Bernanos is wholly based on this substitution of conventional hope by a darker reality that here bears almost existentialist traits but that actually is but the expression of the violence necessary to "swim against the current":

The man [Drumont], who, planning only to confront his time and age, was able to muster such a tremendous effort, did not for a single instant believe in success: he conceded nothing to the possibility of an improbable victory. Truly naïve as was his genius, his hope was even more naïve and existed on a different level of greatness where he did not even look for it. To be precise, his hope offered no manner of prey to his powerful hands. His hope simply gave him the slip. *As in the case of most sacrificial beings—persons haunted by the idea of sacrifice—the image of death took for him the place of hope. This image provided his nature with the indispensable portion of confidence and security it needed.* . . . But this is not by far saying enough. In the first place, any man capable of hoping to triumph—or at least who undertakes a task in order to triumph— would never have had the patience of carrying to full term—until the age of maturity and to the very threshold of old age—this preparatory meditation that any fortuitous event, whether favorable or calamitous, could all at once have rendered as vain and as sterile as the most diligent

[99] *Journal de ce temps*, in: *La Plume*, 1946, 6, 4.
[100] *Mouchette*, 216.

daydreams of a maniac. . . . A man bent on success would have made his book lighter, while Drumont visibly overloaded his, as a man stuffs with explosives a ship from which he no longer expects anything.

An "unflinching despair" is what gives Drumont's lifework "an air of majesty".[101]

Now, Bernanos by no means intends to make a Christian hero out of this anti-Semitic journalist; but his portrait fits too well in the series of Bernanos' other figures (including his own self-portrait) for us not to mention it. Bernanos, in fact, portrayed Drumont in his own image and likeness.

If Bernanos makes use of such shrill colors, it is in order to render to his portrayal of hope the brilliance that bourgeois habits of thought have made opaque. Strictly speaking, hope is a mystery: "The spirit of youth is a reality that is as mysterious as, for example, virginity."[102] "A young human life, all ignorance and boldness, this truly perishable portion of the universe, sole promise that will never be kept, unique marvel! . . . True youthfulness is as rare as genius, or perhaps genius itself is a defiance of the order of the world and its laws: a blasphemy!"[103] Ouine's ecstasy in the face of youth is here but the echo of Péguy's and Bernanos' ecstasy before the mystery of hope. But supernatural hope is not simply the absurd contravening of the trends of the times—believable only on account of its absurdity. Supernatural hope is accessible: it can become the quintessence of a life and thereby demonstrate its own nature as the power of truth. From where else could we derive the mysterious kinship obtaining between youthfulness and the religious state?[104] And, even more so, the kinship between hope and poverty as a state of life?

Modern man shrugs his shoulders at the idea of such a chaste betrothal with the future. The world no longer has time to hope, to love, or to dream. In its place, it is the poor who hope, in just the same way as it is the saints who love and atone for the rest of us. The tradition of hope is in the hands of the poor, just as the old lacemakers of Bruges hold the secret of a certain lace-point that the machines will never be able to imitate. You object that the poor necessarily have nothing but hope

---

[101] *Peur*, 140.
[102] *Cimetières*, 286–87.
[103] *Ouine*, 25.
[104] *Enfants*, 39–40.

to live on and that their hoping has no more merit than their living. Granted! And you could even add that, the more difficult life becomes for them, the more they have to hope—as compensation! . . . But the day will come when . . . the word of God will perhaps be fulfilled, and the poor shall possess the earth, simply because they alone, in a world of men in despair, will not have lost the habit of hoping.[105]

How could we otherwise explain the deep kinship between hope and sanctity? No: for Bernanos, life, with its natural aging, is not simply a fatalistic process that is ever driving us farther away from the sources of life. He does indeed like to portray our rebirth as children in an eschatological manner:

> Like every other poor Christian, I am awaiting eternal life, I can even say that that is the only thing I am awaiting. I know that it will be as simple as this present life appears complicated. The devil is a great artist who has been doomed by his taste for the bizarre and the monstrous. When his reign will have come to an end, we'll again become children. The Angel of distortion, who delights in carving up like a horse-chestnut childhood's sincere and sacred face, the ferocious humorist to whom we owe the creation of those two caricatures of childhood—the "mature man" and the old man—will then be unable to inflict any further harm on us.[106]

In other texts, however, Bernanos admits the possibility of growing old while retaining the spirit of childhood:

> The rhythm of modern life is much too swift to allow for the late blossoming of the human animal, for the beautiful flowers of a declining autumn, those who bore the name of Joinville—marvels of prudence and faith, heroism and fidelity, noble hearts full of compassionate sadness, still open to all the fresh images of a childhood they never rejected. In the present state of the world, it is almost as difficult to become an old person as it is to become a saint. You think you enter old age simply by seniority, imbeciles that you are? You're not old persons: you're merely obsolete, retired from life![107]

And so, the whole question is whether the hope of Christians is still young and vital enough to hold its own against a superannuated civilization: "Are you capable of rejuvenating the world, yes or no?

---

[105] *Croix*, September 1942, 252–53.
[106] *Français*, 134–35.
[107] Ibid., 201–2.

The Gospel is always young; it's you who are old."[108] "The only position you still must take is the one to which Saint Thérèse invites you: you must yourselves again become children and rediscover the spirit of childhood."[109] Could what Bernanos utters prophetically be really true, namely, that "the Christian West has not lost its child's heart"? "Chartres cathedral, for example, is actually much younger— that is, much more fitted to young hearts and minds—than so many monuments that your millionaires, fifty years ago, considered the last word on modernism. Europe is not old; it's her institutions that were too old for her. The peoples of Europe are not old; it's the élite classes of Europe that need to renew themselves and that refuse to do so, all the while dumping their refuse on us. Beware of Europe, you of the Americas!"[110]

In such a Europe, France has the vocation, "not to give the world greatness and riches, but to keep hope alive within it".[111] Despite all the disappointments afforded him by his motherland, and despite all the humiliations of his own youth, Bernanos holds fast to Péguy's vision:

My youth was saddened by infallible augurs who reeked of incense and patchouli and glistened with self-satisfied vanity even more than all the lamentable cosmetics then in vogue. They lambasted me with their fore-sight and accused me of childishness. However, since then they have had the experience of another sort of childishness—a monstrous crisis of [French] youth humiliated, bullied, and trampled by their unctuous skepticism, their optimism in the style of the Academy, their gutless humanism, their sordid talent for avoiding the heroic responsibilities of life. Which of these clairvoyant puppets could have foreseen Hitler, Mussolini, Franco, and the vast musical charnel houses[112] created by the wars, from which songs resound with one accord for as long as the shape of a song can subsist in a rotting mouth? They did not believe in childhood: they thought they were stronger than childhood. Well, then: the children they had trampled arose again from under their feet. But

---

[108] *Cimetières*, 269.

[109] Ibid., 262.

[110] *Anglais*, 179.

[111] *Croix*, July 1943, 358.

[112] Bernanos here has a macabre pun, creating the expression *charniers chantants* (singing charnel houses) as an echo of the *cafés chantants* (music halls), with their happy-go-lucky frivolity, which were so popular in Europe just before the First World War.—TRANS.

these were no longer the children you placate with a little jam. The red jelly they heaved from full throats, and laughing, did not smell of ripe currants. And they went on marching in their own muck, and always laughing—these youths who had been monstrously disowned—strong as an animal and untamable with their bulls' hearts.[113]

3. Mediocrity and Scandal

You can tell the spiritual level of a Christian by how deeply he is capable of suffering on account of the scandal offered by the Church. The vehemence of Bernanos' suffering in this regard is treated by many, particularly priests, with a sort of well-intentioned indulgence, as if they were dealing with an illness that excused the patient's occasional fits of madness. One can come to take such an attitude toward Bernanos only after having practiced a thorough leveling of the concept of truth, that is, after looking at the Church as if everything factual in her, and everything that can be confirmed about her, stood on the same level and possessed the same divine sanction as truth and as if there did not exist certain "facts" at whose existence a Christian can primarily react only with the indignation of his whole being. Péguy was of the opinion that, at the affirmation of the truth that many of his fellow men within or outside the Church are forever damned, a Christian could only react with the revolt of every fiber in his being, or, what amounts to the same thing, with the staking of his greatest treasure—his own salvation—in order to cancel the validity of such an affirmation. This was the import of his first *Joan of Arc* and of the subsequent *Mystery of the Charity of Joan of Arc*. As we will later see, Bernanos surely shared the same opinion; but, for him, the thorn of the unbearable contradiction is already to be found in the Church herself, which should be a community of God's holy children but instead offers Christians and non-Christians alike a spectacle of the most hopeless mediocrity in the form of a lukewarmness that is worse than any chill. If it were not for this lukewarmness, how could Christians, unperturbed, accept as established, self-evident fact what is actually the worst of all rents in the fabric of truth, namely, the impending threat of their own brethren's damnation?

---

[113] *Enfants*, 92–93.

In his panegyric on the feast of Saint Thérèse, the unbeliever declares:

> You have no interest in unbelievers, but unbelievers are enormously interested in you. . . . It's ever so tempting to observe you close up, to try to plumb you. For it is said you believe in hell. Could the look you give us, as fellow humans, then, possibly reveal a hint of the pity you would certainly not refuse someone condemned to death? Don't misunderstand me: we don't at all expect any ridiculous show of compassion. But, after all, in the end—in the end that will end all ends—should not a man be changed by being able even to imagine that a certain number of his buddies and associates, the very ones with whom he has danced, skied, and played bridge, will perhaps spend all eternity grating their teeth and cursing God? In a word, we thought we found you interesting. And yet, alas, you're not interesting at all, and we are hurt by this disappointment. We are hurt particularly by the humiliation of having hoped in you, which is to say, of having doubted ourselves, doubted our own unbelief. . . . It is true, then, that you really believe in hell. But you fear it only for yourselves, the believers. For us, you actually expect it. It is extraordinary that, under such conditions, you should be so completely lacking in pathos![114]

The wrath of both Péguy and Bernanos, then, is aimed at the same object. Like Bloy and Péguy, Bernanos is a wrathful Christian—not as if his wrath had topmost importance for him (this position is occupied by love, hope, and faith), although it does follow at once in second place. And the question is how this wrath, which flows spontaneously and naturally from an indignant heart, can even in the third and last instant become one with what is of first importance, thus becoming through and through a *Christian* wrath.

In a friendly way, the atheist's sermon tells the congregation of bigots, both men and women, any number of stinging truths. That, like hell, so too grace has failed to make any lasting impression on them. That no trace of joy or redemption whatever can be detected in them. That they possess a rare hardness of heart, not to say obduracy. That the Church's hierarchical ministry, particularly in its representatives, exhibits clearly Judaic and pre-Christian traits. That the world expects so much from Christians and receives so little. That Christians should

---

[114] *Cimetières*, 251-52.

be the salt, and not the syrup, of the earth.[115] That they don't allow the holiness of the saints to beam out over the world. That they have shown they no longer have a living or incarnate faith.[116] In the end, the question arises whether the Church really has the right to assert that she is an irrefutable sign of God's presence among the peoples of the earth.

It is precisely such a claim that makes "the bad example that anyone can give" into a real "scandal": "It is we who disseminate throughout the world this poison, which we have refined in our distilleries."[117] And the more we fall into the grip of a stale and insipid mediocrity, the less we realize that *we* are the ones, that it is we who are the spreaders of the poison: "The worst sort of imprudence is to underestimate the mediocre. Mediocrity is a colorless and odorless gas that we peacefully allow to accumulate, and then it suddenly explodes with incredible violence."[118]

Speaking of his former classmate in the seminary, who has now taken up in Lille with a hospital aide to whom he is doubtless "sincerely attached", the country priest remembers him to have been "sentimental": "The mediocre priest, alas, is almost always sentimental. Could it be that vice itself is less dangerous for us [priests] than a certain inaneness? Some suffer from blandness of the brain. Blandness of the heart is worse."[119] The symptom of a person suffering from the latter condition is a certain harmless-seeming unawareness. He has lost all sensitivity for the signs of the times,[120] something intimately related to the salt's growing stale. And he is completely surprised when anyone calls his attention to the fact.

Now, since the Church's hierarchical representative is the first to lay claim to being the salt of the earth, the responsibility for mediocrity naturally falls first of all on him: "The debasement of souls consists of apathy in the proper sense of the word: that is, the loss of the ability to suffer, something a thousand times more terrible than the worst intoxication of the senses. And the party mainly responsible—perhaps solely responsible—for the debasement of souls is the

---

[115] See *Curé*, 20.
[116] See *Cimetières*, 249–75.
[117] Ibid., 241.
[118] *Anglais*, 152–53.
[119] *Curé*, 90.
[120] *Croix*, February 1942, 183.

mediocre priest.''[121] For Bernanos, the great scandal remains the mediocrity of the clergy. He strives to penetrate its secret by placing it
squarely before the apocalyptic decision between cold and warm. On
the one hand, he holds before the mediocre priest those who fulfill
the priestly mission most rigorously—the saints, from Donissan and
Chevance to the country priest. On the other hand, he holds up to
the mediocre priest the mirror of someone like the Abbé Cénabre,
who personifies the horrible possibility of committing a great ''imposture''[122] on souls and on the world: he first gives up prayer, and
this leads to loss of faith, which eventually makes him the easy prey
of Satan. To be sure, Cénabre is too great a lord in the kingdom of
evil for him to be mediocre himself; it is he, after all, who initially
tears off the mask of mediocrity from the face of Pernichon, who is a
miserable and hopeless puppet of Catholic Action: ''Your mediocrity
naturally tends toward nothingness, which is the state of being indifferent to both good and evil. The only thing that gives you some
illusion of life is the way you harbor a few pitiable vices. . . . The
world is full of people like you, and they smother the best of us under
their sheer number. What could you possibly have come to do in our
battle of ideas?''[123] And yet, the central scene of *The Imposture* gives
full rein to the *danse macabre* of the clerical representatives of a certain
Catholic Action, and the portrayal is bizarre indeed: a vain, effemi-
nate, jovial bishop full of unction; a writer; a former collaborator of
Combes; an idiotic count; a couple of avaricious, calculating laymen;
do-good ladies with literary pretensions. All of them are gathered in a
fashionable salon that intends to preserve the heritage, by now phantasmal, of both the Enlightenment and nineteenth-century Traditionalism. Throughout the tatteredness of the scene sneers a wild grotes-
querie. This cloistered world of the deceivers and the deceived moves
under the shadow of the great ''impostor'', Cénabre. It is meant to
represent a carnival in hell and is unmasked as such. Pernichon is
present as victim only in order to make evident the cold and cruel
power struggle being played out behind the veil of religious conventions. As in some princely portrait by Goya, ''Catholic society''

---

[121] *Peur*, 185.

[122] *The Imposture* (*L'Imposture*) is the title of the novel that has Cénabre as protagonist.—
TRANS.

[123] *Imposture*, 16–17.

is here exposed and subjected to a cool and seemingly disinterested analysis:

> Nothing can any longer perturb these cruel hearts: their weightlessness makes them airtight against all the bad surprises of their incoherent life. The one condition is that a certain indispensable agreement, a certain rhythm, must be maintained at all cost. . . . Their little artificial society lives and prospers in a closed jar, and the passions that thrive there, violent as you may suppose them to be, are expressed only by conventional signs and made subject to a severe control and a formal discipline that quickly modify both their character and their symptoms. In the long run, nothing has less the appearance of an open and daring vice than this same vice transformed by necessary dissembling and cultivated in the depths. This phenomenon may be observed everywhere, but never more profitably than among these peculiar people who live at equal distance from the world of religion and the world of politics. They are then free to insinuate themselves, patiently and diligently, between one and the other, protected naturally by the very shadows of their eternally secret maneuvers. They are officious go-betweens who are continually being disowned, slaves by birth of all circumstances and junctures, shameful demagogues suspect in their orthodoxy. They have nothing that really comes from themselves—not their doctrine, which they naïvely borrow from every triumphant party, and not even their language, which bizarrely mimics the style of clerical reports and encyclicals. . . . What an undertaking, all to uproot souls! How could we not feel pity for these wretches whom professional hypocrisy—at times almost unconsciously—has made so sensitive to the open air![124]

Driven from the drawing room, the despairing Pernichon takes refuge in the bishop. But, behind the prelate's friendly words, the poor man meets with nothing but procrastinating evasion—at bottom, the icy egotism of a person who will not commit himself to anything and simply lets events take their course. And so, with one last glimmer of hope, Pernichon returns to the writer, an old debauchee invaded by the rot of every stage of perversion and his fond meditation on the process. This is what he then hears from the writer, a character very likely modeled on Gide: "His Excellency, the bishop of Paumiers, my old classmate? What an imbecile! Young man, this is doubtless a law of my nature: mediocre priests hold for me a kind of fascination. It

---

[124] Ibid., 138–139.

awakens an appetite in me. . . . I speak of mediocre priests, because, once they've given us the slip and are enjoying their freedom, then —just between us—all they become is very tiresome old boys. Case in point: that Loisy I was so fond of and who's now become a raving pedant who bores me to death.''[125] But he advises Pernichon to commit suicide,[126] while his own home turns out to be a real "hell".[127]

Bernanos, however, considered that the horizons of such a world had been drawn too narrowly, and he had to proceed to explore the phenomenon more broadly and also in a more concrete historical fashion. Thus, three years later he produced the tremendous canvas entitled *The Great Fear of the Right-Thinking*, in which for the first time he exposed the full range of his thoughts on this subject. Historically speaking, the mediocrity of Christianity is on the rise; this is occurring in proportion as the virtues proper to the priest within his own priestly sphere—above all his instrumental function and his ecclesial obedience—have been exalted and made into the fundamental virtues of the whole Christian people. As a result, a vague general compliancy and eagerness to oblige have been equated with, and substituted for, Christian obedience. Bernanos drew an alarming portrait of the evolution of a certain sector of Catholic France since 1870. We would be hard-pressed to assert that it is false as a whole. Events have only shown him to be all too much on target. It is the story of an ever more radical *émigration de l'intérieur*, a withdrawal into a hallowed inner-churchly sanctum, out of which fortress the increasingly self-cloistered inmates issue pathetic protests and make attempts at political sallies that are blessed by the Church but that they hardly believe in themselves. What concerns them almost exclusively is the preservation of traditional positions that guarantee the material possessions of the ruling classes. In contrast to what freethinkers like to imagine as defining pious hypocrisy in the style of Tartuffe, Bernanos paints the following sad picture:

> The world of the devout offers us few cases of actual Tartuffes, and maybe not any at all, because Tartuffe isn't any more native to the mediocrity

---

[125] Ibid., 173–74.
[126] Ibid., 178.
[127] Ibid., 183.

he exploits than the worm is native to the nut. . . . When the unbeliever comes close up for the first time to examine believers—a category of men he knows poorly—he is only too eager to find them ridiculous. His desire for God, if it exists at all, is still so confused and carnal that, without very much despair, he agrees in finding believers contemptible, quite in keeping with their portrayal by apostates. The actual disappointment is that believers are in fact neither holy nor contemptible but rather mediocre, and this in such a strangely complicated and even—despite the coarse exterior—refined way that their mediocrity calls to mind the hereditary defects of very ancient races: their unconscious perfidy, the cunning and jealous impotency of a class in decay. You need a lot of time, perseverance, and love to come to understand that the Church's greatest anguish is precisely this fleshless flock, kept together by habit or fear, for which the divine barely amounts any more to anything but an alibi for its laziness, for its horror of all manly struggle, for its sickly relish for undergoing, enduring, and experiencing the force of a master. But, who would take them in if not the Church? The only thing the Church is after is people's consciences, since the only kingdom she aspires to ruling is an interior realm to which God alone has access. Political parties, by contrast, ask for contributions first and foremost. . . . The Church is nothing less than a pantheon of great men. She is the refuge where, under the eternal raging of the wind and the rain, the most wretched of mortals come day after day, for better or worse, to receive their subsistence from God and his saints, until the dawning of universal forgiveness. Unfortunately, all that is needed is some insidious and covert persecution, such as Catholicism has been enduring in the world for a century or two, and certain bargains begin inevitably to be struck. These risk putting in the limelight—under the heading of "Catholic party" and by a disgusting equivocation—that aspect of Catholicism that is surely the least noble, the least healthy, and the most ready to engage in shady transactions, in the same way that the merest hint of bankruptcy is like a mating call to whole legions of maggoty profiteers.[128]

All the political writings that followed, beginning with the *Great Cemeteries*, would likewise have this one problem as their central concern. The explanation Bernanos believed he owed his unbelieving brothers burned in his soul: namely, that the entity they see before them and that bears the name of "Catholic Church" is indeed a source of scandal, but in a deeper and different sense from what external observers imagine.

---

[128] *Peur,* 105–6.

In *The Humiliated Children* there are reflections concerning the essence of "imposture" that hearken back to the novel of the same name and that question "whether Cénabre was really an impostor or not". For, "in order to deserve the name of impostor one would have to be wholly responsible for one's lies, one would have to have *begotten* one's own lies. And yet, all lies have only one Father, and this Father is not of this earth." Every extraneous lie finds in each of us "another lie that becomes its accomplice and is in mysterious and tacit agreement with it. An abject sort of fecundity thus becomes possible." [129] A veritable "kingdom of mendacity" stretches throughout the world, and it is difficult to say how guilty the person is who subscribes to it. It is precisely the mediocre who often are spared, and the plague descends parasitically on strong and healthy bodies. Very few men, "ashamed of their weakness and their vices", have not been tempted at a given moment in their lives "to slip out of themselves on cushioned wolf's paws". The way back to oneself can then never again be found, and one is condemned to living outside oneself as a true impostor. The modern state finds its choicest recruits precisely among such people who, being alienated from themselves, become its ideal subjects: "The sham judge, the sham soldier, the sham thinker . . . value their *function* above all, since they no longer value *themselves*. . . . The multiplication of impostors is far from endangering the State; on the contrary, it reënforces its power." [130] "The problem of imposture appears to me essential. Solve that, and you'll have the key to all the others." The impostor is not simply "a second-rate actor who occasionally goes to the dealer in old clothes to freshen up his wardrobe. Impostor and imposture are actually one. A real fatalism underlies imposture. . . . The impostor defends his imposture as he defends his life, because in fact it *is* his life." And the modern State relies on such deformed growth when it conscripts into its service people who have become alien to themselves. [131]

What occurs, moreover, when this impulse to flee from oneself takes place within the sphere of the Church—as a flight from the sinful world and into the refuge of the supernatural Church? Does not everything then become spurious and fallacious from top to bot-

---

[129] *Enfants*, 120. (The italics are the translator's.—TRANS.)
[130] Ibid., 121–23. (The italics are the translator's.—TRANS.)
[131] Ibid., 196–97.

tom? Such is "the illusion of all those wretches who, by ensconcing themselves in the deepest recesses of mediocrity, think they are
safeguarding themselves from the sins called "mortal", which are the
only ones that are officially defined and therefore feared". And "the
deepest recesses of mediocrity" in fact constitute an infectious focus
of sin that is all the more deadly as it is less apparent.[132] Indeed, one
comes to see that a real conspiracy exists among these three: *modern
Man*, with his tendency to flee from himself; a *Church* that more and
more is becoming filled with such men and that, as an organization
made up of men, behaves in all too human a manner; and, finally, the
State, which knows how to profit from this peculiar form of human
being and which in fact, being totalitarian, requires nothing better.
Once the reality of this conspiracy has been seen in its full extent,
the theme of mediocrity becomes an obsession, and Bernanos, the political and religious pamphleteer, found inexhaustible material here.

Bernanos' letters are full of evidence that points to an existence
pushed to the very edge of death by the stress of mediocrity: "At
times we are beset by incomprehension, injustice, and a particularly
troubling and haunting—although inferior and larval—form of imposture called *equivocation*: a form of mediocrity so concrete that it
appears to have its own weight, shape, and smell. What this provokes
in us is less revolt than nausea, repulsion, a repulsion of the soul, and
as a result there is then nothing we can ingest without at once vomiting it."[133] The whole of today's world seems to be permeated by
mediocrity, as is each of Bernanos' contemporaries as well: "There is
something like a principle of mediocrity in each of us, in each person
belonging to our miserable generation, and it can be detected even
among the greatest, in Claudel, for instance, and Valéry. If we are not
exactly a 'failed' generation, then at the very least we are 'lacking'
something, but what?[134] What loss did we suffer that we have never
known how to make up?"[135]

If man continues to become more and more average, what will
then happen with the Christian as he is trained in Christian schools
to become a true representative of the mediocrity of this age?

---

[132] *Peur*, 85.
[133] June 2, 1946, *C. du R.*, 55.
[134] Bernanos is here punning on the two senses of the verb *manquer*.—TRANS.
[135] *Liberté*, 67–68.

You have no need to produce average young Christians. The modern world has fallen so low that *average Christian* no longer has the meaning of "ordinary, decent person". There's no point in trying to form average Christians, since they will naturally grow up into such. Surely, only God can plumb men's hearts. But if we're talking mediocrity, and considering only the results, any responsible leader can tell you that an average Christian has all the defects common to the species, and in addition a good dose of pride and hypocrisy, not to mention a regrettable aptitude for solving all cases of conscience in his own favor.[136]

And what is true of education in Christian high schools (which is here the context) applies equally to the training of priests in seminaries, according to the opinion of Canon La Motte-Beuvron: "I'm well acquainted with the way a seminary education levels characters, to the point, alas, of homogenizing them all into a common mediocrity."[137]

This fact jumps up so evidently that no one can fail to see it, except for the affected parties themselves, and the real scandal consists in the fact that the Church at all costs wants to hide the truth of what is common knowledge. But, for Bernanos, the only therapy for mediocrity would precisely be the admission of one's own insufficiency, the bringing of the truth out into the light. If in earlier ages a loyal "ecclesial prudence" could still be expressed in an apologetics that veiled and disguised certain aspects of the life of the Church and individual Christians, this is no longer possible in an age in which the press and the other media ruthlessly turn their spotlights on every detail of human affairs. The scandal can be erased, if at all, only through humility.[138]

Just in time, however, Bernanos remembered that he himself, a sinner, was a member of the Church and that he had no right to summon her as defendant before his own tribunal, since those "who are most qualified to take scandal at the Church's defects—namely, the saints—are the very ones who never complain about them".[139] It was at this point that he perceived a deeper level of vision, one he had

---

[136] *Cimetières*, 229–30.
[137] *Curé*, 203.
[138] See above, 112f., the text from *Cimetières*, 114–15, in which Bernanos invites the Church to confess her faults.
[139] *Liberté*, 285.

never really ignored but that had been partly concealed by his burning indignation: *the level at which the particular mediocrity of Christianity becomes harbored within the particular mystery of the sacramental Church as Mystical Body of Christ.* The problem here is not only an "exterior inaccessibility" ("The mediocre priest is of all men the most impenetrable"),[140] but also "the incurable mediocrity of the clerical party, . . . the causes of which are deep and probably escape the judgment of both the moralist and the historian: they require a supernatural explanation."[141] But this last remark, dating from 1930, was insufficient; Bernanos gained greater fullness of insight only at the time of the *Country Priest* (1936), when suffering had gone a long way in purifying him: "The mediocre person is a trap set by the devil. Mediocrity is too complicated for us: it's God's own business. In the meantime, the mediocre person should be able to find shelter 'under the shadow of our wings'. Some shelter, some warmth—and do they ever need warmth, those poor devils!" This image itself, in turn, revealed to Bernanos an even higher truth:

> And what if Jesus Christ were waiting for you precisely under the appearance of one of these imbeciles you so despise? Don't you know that he takes up and sanctifies all our miseries, with the exception of sin? This coward is only a poor wretch crushed under the immensity of the social machine like a rat pinned under a beam. That miser is only an anguished creature overwhelmed by his own impotency and devoured by the fear of *being found lacking.* A person who seems to be pitiless could be suffering from a real phobia of the poor—there have been cases of this—and such terror is as inexplicable as the fear evoked in high-strung people by spiders and mice. Do you look for our Lord among such people?[142]

From this the thought follows that, in actual reality, mediocrity must belong to the manner of God's concealment in the Incarnation. The same Bernanos who tells pious hypocrites to their face, "You were an intolerable scandal to the child I was, a scandal I could only escape by striving to understand you", can also say to them in the same breath, "But it is necessary for this scandal to exist. Within it, Christ wants

---

[140] *Soleil,* 335.

[141] *Peur,* 177.

[142] *Curé,* 134.

to hide from our reason. . . . You are the sacramental species of the Sacrament of God's Permanent Humiliation!"[143]

Herein lies the test: whether or not one is done in by this insight concerning the scandal given by Christians. Doctor Delbende, a character beaming with nobility of stature and greatness of soul, nonetheless took his own life in the face of such scandal. The letters written during the last months of Bernanos' life speak continually about this mystery: "Our disappointment will, after all, never be worse than that of the Jews who underwent the ridicule of seeing their Messiah under the form of a poor man suspended by nails by the side of the highway, amidst an indifferent or jeering crowd going up to Jerusalem."[144]

> If the reality of the Church coincided with your dreams, she would have already turned this world into an immense Brotherhood, the very miracle of that, within History, would be a proof of the divinity of Christianity, as clear as two and two are four. We are disappointed by the Church *such as she appears to us*, just as the Jews were back then by the Messiah. . . . The curse hurled at the rich consists precisely in the fact that the rich will always exist. Otherwise, God would have cursed the poor, and there would no longer be any poor. Poverty has been sanctified and divinized, not abolished. Here lies the scandal. . . . Humanly speaking, the Gospel is nothing but contradiction and scandal. God wants us to search for him as he hides within doubt and anguish—up to the last second. "Father! Father! Why have you abandoned me?" That was the very moment we were saved.[145]

Two things result from this. One is theoretical and has to do with a way of going beyond the protests of the sixteenth-century Reformers and of coming to terms with Luther. The other is practical and is concerned with how the mediocre are to be saved.

Luther always interested Bernanos as intensely as Hitler did. In the *Country Priest*, the Curé de Torcy, who himself bears the Christian name of "Martin", assures us that he daily prays for Luther. And he confides: "At this moment [of difficulty] I understood Luther. He

---

[143] *Anglais*, 152.
[144] *To a Priest*, June 2, 1946; *C. du R.*, 55.
[145] *Reply to a Questionnaire* (draft), 46; *Bul.* 4, 8.

[too] had a strong temper. For, in his monks' dungeon at Erfurt, it was surely his hunger and thirst for justice that were devouring him. But the good Lord is not pleased when someone starts tinkering with his justice, and his wrath is a little too potent for us poor devils. It inebriates us and makes us worse than wild animals. . . ." This is what happened to "old Luther", who "ended up taking his hay to the feeding troughs of the German princes" and finished his life as a "paunchy old boy". "Although fundamentally a just man, his anger poisoned him little by little and turned into useless lard— that's all."[146] Bernanos truly followed the Reformer to the very border of revolt. It is doubtful whether he suffered less than Luther interiorly at the scandals offered by the Church. But, at this border-crossing, he took leave of Luther by way of the very substantial draft of an essay entitled *Brother Martin*, which he began in Brazil, read out to Gordan, "moved to tears",[147] and then lost, until Carneiro found it again in 1951 among the papers Bernanos had left behind in Barbacena. Albert Béguin then published it in *Esprit*.[148] In this essay Bernanos writes:

> I don't intend to force anyone to follow me in this, but I have always believed that the great heresiarchs who wasted the Church could just as easily have become her glory. They had been chosen, set apart, and marked for some extraordinary design, some marvelous adventure. Logically, I am then compelled to believe as well that they had received priceless graces, which they then proceeded to squander, casting to the wind and losing through vain disputes immense, incalculable spiritual riches, which would perhaps have been sufficient to sate for centuries the hunger of an innocent Christendom. . . . When you read certain pages of Luther's correspondence—but what Catholic has ever read Luther's letters?— you clearly see that he was fully aware of the fatal dilemma that ruled his life and that more than once—at least when he was young, alas!— he tried to obey the soft voice speaking to his heart and lovingly urging him to remain humble.[149]

Now, what this "soft voice" said must have been something like this:

---

[146] *Curé*, 71–72.
[147] *Bul.* 6, 4.
[148] *Esprit*, October 1951.
[149] *Frère Martin*, in: *Esprit*, October 1951, 442–43.

My son Martin, it is I who have put this bitterness within you. Beware! *It is with me, through me, and in me that you are suffering on account of my Church's wretched state. So don't come parading this suffering before me!* Others, who love me a thousand times more than you are yet capable of loving me, do not feel such suffering to the same degree as you, or barely at all. What throws your conscience into revolt appears to them merely a dream, a bad dream they turn away from whenever they want because they live in another world. As for you: I have decidedly made a place for you in *this* world. The material I used to create you was solid and heavy, and so I made you into a carnal man. I shall hurl you against other men who are as carnal as yourself, made from the same material: I want them to feel the force of your blows, for, if you remain faithful to me, it is through you that I intend to break their pride and avenge my people, whose souls they have put up for auction. But make no mistake, Brother Martin. This task is neither the greatest nor the most sublime of all. It is simply made to your measure, and that's all. I have given you health, strength, and a popular eloquence and genius for controversy almost equal to those of my son Augustine. Be well aware, however, that these are not my saints' favorite weapons. They will be useful to you only for clearing the terrain, for tearing out and eradicating the rotten rootstock.[150]

Saint Paul, too, was a man who "kicked against the goad" and did not know how to suffer in peace; but he did not for all that take to flight!

From the beginning my Church has been what she still is and what she will be until the last day: a scandal for strong spirits, a disappointment for weak spirits, and a test and a consolation for interior souls who seek only me. Indeed, Brother Martin, whoever looks for me there finds me, but that is where I must be found. And in the Church I am more hidden than people think, or than some of my priests want to make you believe —harder to find even than in the little stable at Bethlehem, for those, that is, who do not approach me humbly, in the tracks of the Magi and the Shepherds. For it's true that they've built me palaces, with endless galleries and peristyles, magnificently lit by night and by day and thronging with guards and sentinels. But, to find me there—the same as on that ancient road of Judæa buried under snow—the cleverest among you still has only to ask me for the one thing necessary: and this is a star and a pure heart. In the days of Saint Paul, Brother Martin, no more and no

---

[150] *Esprit*, October 1951, 443. (The italics are von Balthasar's.—TRANS.)

less than nowadays, you would have seen in my young Church things
to make you lower your thick skull and make your shoulders quiver,
like a bull tormented by flies. Just think of it! After fifteen centuries,
you still see people everywhere who boast of being better than others,
simply because they belong to me. You'd think I'd chosen them for
their beautiful faces and their lovely souls! Poor children! . . . If such
people are so proud of occupying a choice place in church, it's not hard
to imagine the pride of some of the baptized Jews who had seen me
with their eyes—or who thought they had seen me—on my Galilean
treks and who could say they belonged to my people and to my very
kin. Do you think that these welcomed Saint Paul very kindly when he
began to preach that a baptized Gentile, a *goy*—even if he had never
set foot in Jerusalem, even if he had never left his idolatrous country—
belonged to me no more and no less strictly than a circumcised Jewish
Christian?[151]

What attitude, then, are we to take before the scandal offered by the
Church? Bernanos boasts of being well acquainted with such scandal,
but he then goes on: "I distrust my own indignation and revolt. Indignation has never redeemed anyone, never purchased anyone's freedom. But it has probably doomed many souls, and all the simoniac
bacchanals of Renaissance Rome would not have profited the devil
much if they had not succeeded with the master stroke of hurling
Luther into despair."[152] But Luther could no longer understand the
mystery of the Church:

> The Church has a mystery about her. No one, without ridiculous self-
> contradiction, could set out to demand from an unbeliever that he be-
> lieve in the mystery of the Church. But, if we should see him lurking
> about her, we have the right to say to him that he is totally wasting his
> time if he stops short at all the frivolities, that is, if in the Church he is
> looking for anything other than Christ. . . . Yes: let him look for Christ
> in the Church or else abandon the undertaking altogether. For, if in the
> Church he is not looking for Christ and Christ alone, he will infallibly,
> and in spite of himself, be duped by—and become an accomplice of—
> that very mediocrity that so scandalized him from the outset. He will
> himself become a part of this mediocrity and be inevitably condemned

---

[151] Ibid., 444–45.
[152] Ibid., 438.

along with it. . . . No, it isn't the certificate that makes the priest, it's the sacrament, and it's in the name of the sacrament that he climbs the pulpit. . . . If it is true that Christ continues to reveal himself to the world, at every moment of our days and nights, naturally we cannot suppose that this massive infiltration by the Divine could take place using the same methods as those in vogue at the Rockefeller Institute, thanks to which a rigorously selected personnel initiates the natives of the tropics to the mysteries of hygiene. What I mean is that God's great enterprise could not be subverted to any significant extent by the mediocrity of its instruments. *It is not enough to say that this mediocrity is corrected and compensated for. By being used by God, it is somehow absorbed into God's designs like inert matter: once introduced into the living body, it becomes blood and lymphatic fluid. The mediocrity itself is quickened into a living reality.* Within the Church, mediocrity probably destroys only those who are themselves mediocre, by a process of self-digestion—like a stomach seared by an ulcer. *We know that the gastric juices, which can be lethal for those suffering from ulcers, are nevertheless an essential part of the normal man's digestion.* . . .

The particular kind of mediocrity I am speaking of would be difficult for a stranger to our faith to distinguish from other sorts of mediocrity; but I insist that it constitutes a variety all its own. To what extent, then, could we say that this specifically Catholic and ecclesial mediocrity is mysteriously related to Sanctity, if only by the challenge it poses? I have already quoted many times the statement, unforgettable for me, uttered by Père Clérissac, a young Dominican killed at Verdun: *Cela n'est rien de souffrir pour l'Église, il faut avoir souffert par Elle:* "It is nothing to suffer *for* the Church. We must learn how to suffer *at her hands.*"[153]

"There is surely a particular kind of virulence about ecclesiastical pharisaism, which tests the patience of the saints very cruelly, while, with poor Christians like myself, it most often succeeds only in embittering us and making us revolt."[154] As the country priest notes, God handed himself over to man; "he delivered himself into our hands —Body and Soul—God's Body, God's Soul, God's honor into our priestly hands."[155] And it's very possible for a priest to be a Judas: "I am not speaking of the bad priest. Or, rather: the bad priest is the mediocre priest. The other is a monster, a monsters escape all human measures. Who can know God's designs on a monster? What is he

---

[153] Ibid., 436–37. (The italics are von Balthsar's.—TRANS.)
[154] Ibid., 438.
[155] *Curé*, 270.

good for? What is the supernatural meaning of such an astonishing fall from grace? Do what I might, I cannot for example believe that Judas belongs to the world—to that world for which Jesus mysteriously refused to pray. . . . Judas does not belong to that world."[156] No, like a terrible and dismal shade, he belongs to a much more intimate order, one much closer to the Heart of God. This is why Cénabre, who also is a monster, was in the end struck by the lightning stroke of grace. This, too, is why Bernanos expects the same manner of salvation for Luther: "*Who can, in fact, know where God's sweet mercy will hide those it has stolen from hell, by an irresistible maneuver that will forever confound both the just and the wise?*"[157] In his *Saint Dominic* we find a similar thought: "The blossoming of heresy is always . . . a very mysterious phenomenon. When a certain vice in the Church reaches the peak of its ripeness, as it were, then heresy sprouts all by itself and at once begins to send out its monstrous branches. Heresy has its roots deep in the Mystical Body. It is a deviation and a perversion of this Body's most intimate life."[158]

This is why, in some sense, heresy is the mirror in which the Church sees her own reflection. Heresy can thus be the Church's humiliation because it shares in something of her truth: it belongs in this way to the mystery of the Church's vitality as she strives to follow after her Lord. This results in the practical consequence that Bernanos formulated unsurpassably in a late letter to a religious (1947):

> We all resemble one another, alas, in the fact that we suffer from other people's mediocrity within our own mediocrity, which is so different from theirs. And how much it's cost me to learn this! But now I know it. *In a word, other people's mediocrity opens in us a wound that should not cease to suppurate and make us suffer. Otherwise, if it closed up, it would infect the entire organism.* It's very pleasant to have preached to us that we should resign ourselves to the mediocrity of others, since this normally, perhaps infallibly, also brings with it the acceptance of our own mediocrity! Once the spectacle of mediocrity is no longer a torture to us, it means that we ourselves have become mediocre from head to foot—unless God's sweet mercy, which can be mischievous on occasion, has first made saints of us without our knowing it.[159]

---

[156] Ibid., 89.

[157] *Esprit*, October 1951, 439. (The italics are von Balthasar's.—TRANS.)

[158] *Dominique*, 27.

[159] August 1947, *C. du R.*, 58–59. (The italics are von Balthasar's.—TRANS.)

So it is that, in his *Luther*, Bernanos could apply in conclusion one last brushstroke to his portrait of mediocrity in the Church, which he could understand only in function of her sanctity: this, incidentally, is also the reason why we had to deal with mediocrity in this chapter on the Church's sanctity. This last stroke reveals Bernanos to be the arch-Catholic who in the end lay his own impatience, scandal, and fury at the feet of the mystery of the God who suffers in this world:

> Whoever pretends to reform the Church with . . . the same means used to reform temporal society: not only will he fail in his undertaking, but he will infallibly end by finding himself outside the Church. I say that he finds himself outside the Church before anyone has gone to the trouble of excluding him from her. I say that it is he himself who excludes himself from her by a kind of tragic fatalism. . . . The only way of reforming the Church is to suffer for her. The only way of reforming the visible Church is to suffer for the invisible Church. The only way of reforming the vices of the Church is to lavish on her the example of one's own most heroic virtues. It's quite possible that Saint Francis of Assisi was not any less thrown into revolt than Luther by the debauchery and simony of prelates. We can even be sure that his suffering on this account was fiercer, because his nature was very different from that of the monk of Wittenberg.[160] But Francis did not challenge iniquity; he was not tempted to confront it; instead, he threw himself into poverty, immersing himself in it as deeply as possible along with his followers. He found in poverty the very source and wellspring of all absolution and all purity. Instead of attempting to snatch from the Church all her ill-gotten goods, he overwhelmed her with invisible treasures, and under the hand of this beggar the heaps of gold and lust began blossoming like an April hedge. Ah, yes: I'm well aware that in these matters comparisons aren't worth much, especially when seasoned with a little humor. Would you still allow me to say, however, in order to be better understood by some readers, that what the Church needs is not critics but artists? . . . When poetry is in full crisis, the important thing is not to point the finger at bad poets but oneself to write beautiful poems, thus unstopping the sacred springs.[161]

---

[160] By an obvious mental lapse, Bernanos here writes "Weimar", which von Balthasar corrects with "Wittenberg".—TRANS.

[161] *Esprit*, October 1951, 439–40.

4. The "Imbecile"

Despite the suffering involved, it is possible to overcome the scandal offered by the Church provided the person witnessing such scandal is also a believer who strives to be humble. But what is the man to do who confronts scandal without being equipped with such weapons? This is the man whom Bernanos in his personal shorthand calls the "imbecile". He means this word to convey first of all the nuances contained in the Latin *imbecillus*: one who is mentally weak and untalented. From there we go to the more average meaning of "imbecile" as a colloquial term of contempt: the "blockhead", the "idiot", the "hopelessly unteachable dunce" who sees everything backward and who simply cannot come to see things as they are. Finally, the word assumes for Bernanos a deeply compassionate Christian connotation signifying the presence in a person of a poverty and neediness of spirit that naturally is not aware of itself and is unwilling to recognize its own pitiful reality—something that makes it even more abysmally poor. Starting with Bernanos, "imbecile" is as fundamental a concept in Christian sociology as the "individual" of Kierkegaard and the "humiliated and offended" of Dostoyevsky.

To be sure, there have always been dumb people. But their dumbness was somehow sheltered and neutralized by being contained within a very broad sociological framework erected by the not-dumb, which imperceptibly communicated even to the existence of the dumb a certain rightness and reasonableness. But what if the imbeciles should gain the upper hand and become the ones who erect the framework for all? And what if this state of affairs—which is in fact the modern development—should have subterranean and yet demonstrable connections with the scandal of the Church? This is the direction of Bernanos' thought, above all in his three most important works that elaborate a theology of culture: *The Great Fear of the Right-Thinking*, *The Great Cemeteries under the Moon*, and *The Humiliated Children*. The first of these is especially concerned with the history of the emergence of the modern imbecile and its relationship to the political history of the Church. *Cemeteries* then examines the devastating consequences of this development in our present age. Finally, *The Humiliated Children* attempts to expose the metaphysical and theological background of such a phenomenon. The chief result has been a massive fatalism deriving from men's guilt

—particularly Christian men's guilt—and assuming superhuman proportions:

> It was imprudent folly to have uprooted the imbeciles, and Maurice Barrès was the first to see this truth. A given colony of imbeciles, solidly attached to its native soil like a school of mussels to a rock, can subsist harmlessly enough and even furnish the State and industry with precious material. Imbeciles are above all determined by habit and rank prejudice. Wrenched from his habitat, he retains between his tightly closed shells some of the water of the lake that nourished him. But modern life does not only transport imbeciles from one place to another: it knocks them about and whips them into a fury.[162]

Such agitation is communicated to their interior—although their shells remain tightly shut—and becomes the "imbeciles' wrath that today fills the world".[163] The infantile ideologies that have been substituted for an adult conception of the world, with all their "right" and "left" and other idiotic classifications, constitute the imbeciles' normal *ersatz* for thought, and it is the imbeciles who become empowered by making these ideologies their own and who in their name begin to wage world wars: "There is one effort of which they are seriously incapable: thinking. They prefer killing to thinking, and that's the calamity!"[164]

> The world is filled with the wrath of the imbeciles. What rattles them in their wrath is the idea of redemption, for this is at bottom the origin of all human hope. The same instinct made Europe pounce on Asia at the time of the Crusades. But at that time Europe was Christian, and the imbeciles belonged to Christianity. Now a Christian can be this or that —a brute, an idiot, or a fool—but he cannot be an imbecile through and through. I mean born Christians, Christians from the Christian people, from Christianity, who grew up free and who fulfilled their existences' whole cycle of seasons whether by sun or by rain. God preserve me from comparing them with those sapless morons that clerics cultivate in little pots, protected from every wind. For a Christian raised in Christendom, the Gospel is more than an anthology a selection from which is read out each Sunday: it is a reality that permeates everything—laws, customs, efforts, and even pleasures.[165]

---

[162] *Cimetières*, 4.
[163] Ibid., 5.
[164] Ibid., 11.
[165] Ibid., 15.

But, once the Gospel ceases to be the salt of the earth, then, sociologically speaking, we witness the rise of the "supernaturalist" or the "Pharisee" and, in his wake, likewise the emergence of another scientifically verifiable phenomenon—the imbecile:

The cretin, the fool, the idiot all belong to the good Lord, and we should believe that he willed them to be as they are and that these unfortunates give him glory in their own way. But the imbecile is your work, a creation of society, or at least such a perfect deformation of man that it amounts to a new creation. In order to understand the situation of the imbecile within the society that both exploits and protects him, . . . we have to think of the situation of the bigot among Christians. . . . The Church has an all-too-human aspect to her and, therefore, a good share of the scandalous, and this scandal must be overcome. God demands this of us. Like the imbecile, the bigot prefers stultification to scandal. Before calling them cowards, we should ascertain whether the test they underwent was proportional to their strength. Neither open injustice nor cynical criminality would appear to account adequately for the existence or the multiplication of imbeciles. This sort of scandal provokes either indignation or disgust and creates either rebels or victims who are conscious of their plight. What poisons everything, however, is imposture. On a given day we have all known its piercing bite—the dull, interior pain it causes, the aching tremor of a human being's deepest root, the sharp spasm in the soul. It is not only possible but probable that our Lord also experienced it. The curses he hurled at the Pharisees convey a unique tone of wrath and anguish and express a kind of unbearable amazement. We can easily understand the attitude imbeciles take before certain truly excruciating forms of hypocrisy. These wretches then prefer to accept everything in a lump, which is one way of rejecting everything. Like one of Léon Bloy's heroes, these are people who just don't want to know. Naturally we could say they've taken refuge in the letter. But listen well to what I'm going to say: If they've done this, it's because you first drove them from the Spirit. . . .

I ask myself . . . by force of what disappointments and what countless humiliations—gulped down in helpless silence—there gradually came into being, in the course of centuries, the laughable arrogance and absurd dignity of a race worn down by scandal and slowly established in its function of sacrificial victim—a victim not only resigned but also unaware of what was happening, because the Pharisee has a sensitive heart and hates to see anyone weep. The imbecile makes atonement for the Pharisee, just as the poor do for the rich. . . . I do not here mean modern freethinkers—brilliant, literary, skeptical. The Pharisee has nothing to fear from these *poseurs*, because they know his secret. But the mass of imbeciles do not know it, or, if they ever knew it, they have voluntarily forgotten it and buried it in the depths of the collective memory along with their recollection of the horrors and agonies once endured by their ancestors when, poor wretches, they still clung grimly to the two ends of the chain, torn between yes and no, thesis and hypothesis, practice and principle, relative and absolute. Imbeciles will fight tooth and nail to the bitter end for a conception of the world, society, and life that dispenses them from having to judge and choose. And what then? I'll gladly tell you: The imbeciles' fury will fill the world, and pharisaical civilization, monstrous daughter of an aborted Christianity, will have fulfilled its destiny.[166]

At such an advanced hour in the world's history it appears essential to Bernanos not to abandon the imbeciles to their hopeless situation. In the *Great Fear* he had sought to show them how they had been created by the Church's scandal, had sought to heal them too by scandalizing them with a new scandal, as it were, thus renewing them spiritually: of this, naturally, they did not have the faintest idea. In the meantime Bernanos had learned that it is a part of Christian atonement to abide in the company of the imbeciles just as they are: "I can no longer quite tell the difference between myself and the rest of the flock, and, if you want to know the truth, I like myself better this way. At first I would go out to the imbeciles somewhat as society ladies go out to the common people. But that's over now: I no longer look at myself going out."[167] Earlier on he had set out to scandalize the imbeciles, but now he sees that

either the statement has no meaning or what it means is: I shall never tire of being scandalized, of sharing the imbeciles' scandal. For this is really the scandal I share, the scandal I'm best fitted for. . . . The idea of justice I have is that of the humblest peasant who has taken seriously the words of sermons preached at High Mass. I share the imbeciles' scandal and am torn apart by the same contradictions. . . . Imbeciles, for instance, do not pay any less attention than I do to certain manifestations of pious opportunism. They're quite aware of the fact that the churchmen who approved the conquest of Abyssinia, tolerated the Holy Week coup in

---

[166] *Enfants*, 174–79.
[167] Ibid., 179.

Tirana, and blessed the bombings of Barcelona and Guernica are scarcely qualified to condemn the invasion of Finland—which, in any event, had been snatched from the Russians by the treaty of 1917. The imbeciles, too, know it is ridiculous to heap flowers on persecuted German Jews in the name of the same principles once used to justify their extermination by Catholic kings. They know that the personal vow of poverty taken by saintly religious is in distressing contrast to the wealth and avarice of a significant number of religious congregations. The imbeciles sense all of this and many other things besides. . . . Caught between the splendor of the institution and the natural mediocrity of men as between the jaws of a pair of tongs, the Christian has only the choice between becoming a saint and escaping into sanctity or protecting himself against being crushed by despair. The imbecile has found another way: he hoodwinks the scandal offered by a pitiful religiosity by himself becoming a bigot, and the scandal of clericalism by himself becoming clerical. From such conformism the imbecile expects precisely the same benefits as the skeptic expects from his systematic doubt: both of them profess they cannot be surprised by anything so as to spare themselves the trouble of having to grow indignant over anything.[168]

In order to understand what Bernanos means here, we have only to look at characters like Pernichon or Jérôme in his novels. And we finally understand what in his concluding analysis he calls "the imbeciles' sense of shame"—something he has detected in his own reactions: a very physical anguish, a feeling of suffocation induced by

certain cynical manifestations the world normally looks upon with indulgence. Is this not, in fact, an imbecile's reaction, a way of shrinking back into oneself, a veiled refusal to understand? But the genuine imbecile can be told by the fact that such repeated trials strengthen and harden him, increasing the thickness of his hide. He receives in silence the blows dealt him; in this, he uses the little bit of judgment he has as sparingly as a boxer uses his breath. He isn't even sure he's been hit: his nose strikes the punches as if these were a wall. He feels no indignation at all against those who hit him, because the blows aren't personally intended for him. He staggers among lies and hypocrisies like a peasant shoved about by passers-by as he's trying to learn how to walk in Paris. The imbecile hates to talk about what scandalizes him: this is a reserved matter, the secret of a progressive initiation the trials required by which are best left unmentioned so as not to provide jokesters with reasons to laugh. In

___
[168] Ibid., 213–15.

short, if you've been born credulous or even a sucker, you'd better not discuss certain disappointments any more than your sexual experiences.

Precisely this "strange sense of shame" has imperceptibly taken the place of an "ecclesial sense" and become the secularized form of the *sentire cum Ecclesia*: "We have here a permanent conspiracy created by shameless exploiters in league with those cowards who, falling short of approving their behavior, nevertheless attend the performance with proud and earnest decorum, as if witnessing a game the rules of which they do not know."[169]

The people who have grown silent, and who no longer dare make any judgments because they have seen too much, are not by far harmless people:

> The respect imbeciles have for the established powers is not as favorable a sign as the *bien-pensants* would like to think. . . . Principles no longer protect the masters of the world—ever since, that is, the masters of the world have been seeking to take refuge behind principles without nevertheless believing in them. . . . The masters of the world have too much abused the extraordinary tolerance inherent in principles. By a slow but irresistible movement—which, if you would, I'll compare to the contractions of the uterus during childbirth—the principles are softly but surely pushing the masters outside.[170]

The imbecile, then, is "something like a creature that has been handed over for sacrifice", and his basic characteristic is a "reflex of self-defense". "From generation to generation, the imbeciles have developed the habit of understanding things amiss or not at all." "The imbeciles' legendary sense of security comes . . . from the fact that they are made for only two dimensions. They know the third dimension as we know the fourth—by hearsay."[171] "For the imbecile does not have at his disposal any mental instrument allowing him to enter within himself. All he can do is explore the surface of his own being."[172] This, too, is why no real dialogue can take place with an imbecile: there is no possibility of convincing him of his actual condition: "I have always been of the opinion that the *Enfant Terrible* and

---

[169] Ibid., 218–20.
[170] Ibid., 222–23.
[171] *Liberté*, 277.
[172] *Cimetières*, 16.

the Imbecile are one and the same being, whose real and sacred name will be revealed to us only later on. Only God has spoken to the *enfant terrible*, and in his own language. Only the logic of the Beatitudes in the Gospel is capable of shattering like glass the logic of the imbecile, of making him exit his shell still alive."[173] Bernanos, therefore, does not argue with them. The only thing he does is place them just as they are alongside true Christians or alongside the mystery of the Church. For instance, he juxtaposes the defrocked priest Dufréty, now become a traveling salesman, and the country priest—Dufréty being Bernanos' most successful example of the species "imbecile", with his ideology of progress, his half-baked drawing-room culture, and his fad for personality development. Or he places alongside Donissan all the different types of the species: the cultured priest, the unbelieving doctor, and, at the center, the caricature of the aged Anatole France. We see all three of them, like blind men on an open stage, groping their way with ridiculous gestures toward the Curé de Lumbres.

They are one and all half-cultured individuals, at least at the level that is decisive for Bernanos: "Experience has long since shown me that imbeciles are never simple and only rarely ignorant. Should the intellectual, then, by definition be suspect? For sure! When I say 'intellectual', I mean the person who gives himself this title by virtue of his accumulated knowledge and degrees. I am obviously not speaking of the scientist, the artist, or the writer, whose vocation it is to create and for whom intelligence is not a profession but a vocation. . . . The intellectual is so frequently an imbecile that we should always take him to be such until he has proved to us the contrary." He is particularly at home in the modern world of technology and numbers. In such a world he can climb to very high positions without giving away his half-culture.[174] "To be informed about everything and hence condemned to understand nothing: such is the fate of the imbeciles."[175]

The terrible thing is that this is a new form of poverty—a poverty of spirit—but a form of it whose radical sterility opposes it to the ideals of the Gospel. This is why the revolt of such people lacks a

---

[173] *Enfants*, 175.
[174] *Robots*, 181–82.
[175] Ibid., 205.

goal: they do not know what they want.[176] They firmly believe in progress;[177] this is their way of coming to terms with the problem of poverty and worldwide misery, so urgent in our day.[178] Here the imbecile has attained the peak of his development: "He will stop evolving at this point, in my opinion. We are now in possession of a certain kind of imbecile capable of resisting all catastrophes, until the moment this unhappy planet is burst to smithereens."[179] And world events "take the course prescribed by the imbeciles' logic: that's the truth of it". As for this logic, Bernanos adds,

> I'm far from ignoring its ruthless rigor. For, taken individually, each imbecile is nothing but an imbecile; but the accumulated experience of all imbeciles weighs down upon the world as a tremendous burden. The prudence of imbeciles consists in treating everything cautiously and with respect because, like certain primitive marine organisms, they can subsist only in calm waters. The least disturbance destroys them. By an extraordinary abuse of language that would have stupefied the ancient Greeks, it is this prudence of the imbeciles that Modern Society in our day has come to term "a spirit of moderation."[180]

Throughout his life Bernanos listened to the voice of the imbecile. Vallery-Radot tells us the following: "He would knock at my door at about nine in the morning, his pockets stuffed with newspapers. He always had a passion for newspapers. And he often chided me for not paying them as much attention as he did. Newspapers were his connection with the hundred-mouthed voice of Stupidity, which the creators of the great Press can call 'public opinion' with a straight face."[181] But Bernanos also knew that, with the imbecile, he found himself at one of the central hubs of the world, perhaps even at one of the deepest of mysteries, which, if it can be solved at all, then only from a Christian perspective. He saw here a necessary and, within certain limits, useful evil: "We should not waste our time cursing imbeciles. Imbeciles are parasites, and, if nature has willed that parasites exist, it must be because they are not useless. But our observation of

---

[176] Ibid., 201–3.
[177] *Cimetières*, 24.
[178] Ibid., 27–28.
[179] *Robots*, 157–58.
[180] *Anglais*, 79.
[181] *Souvenirs, Bul.* 2–3, 29.

the animal kingdom has unfortunately proven to us that, when parasites are tolerated for too long, they end up by imposing their own
laws on the superior species at the expense of which they subsist."[182]

For some inscrutable reason on the part of Providence, imbeciles
are indispensable: "As an old peasant woman once told me who was
unmercifully beaten by her drunk and lazy husband: 'What else do
you expect, sir? It takes all kinds to make the world.' It does indeed
take all kinds: even imbeciles and sluggards, even prodigal sons."[183]
A letter of 1946 draws the conclusion for us: "The good Lord sets
up imbeciles as a counterforce, not in order that Christianity might
annihilate them, but as a dike to raise its water level. I think of this
every day, and more and more often with each passing day. In our
distraught world it is difficult for simple people not to swell the ranks
of the imbeciles. I think the phenomenon is somewhat analogous to
the proletarization of the middle class",[184] "for the middle class is
almost alone in producing true imbeciles".[185]

The Church of the saints—which is to say, the Church of the baptized
and the confirmed—is always also the Church of scandal. Otherwise
she would not be the Church of God's Incarnation: "As long as the
parish holds together, sinners and the rest form but one great body
in which God's mercy and grace circulate like sap in a tree. . . . But,
alas, even the smallest group of human beings is not without a great
deal of filth. What should then be said of towns and big cities? But
once night has come, the city awakens and begins to inhale by all its
pores the filth of the day that has just ended. The city mashes its filth
into cesspools and sewers until it is reduced to an ooze that little by
little flows out to the sea in immense underground rivers."[186] The
meaning of this image is still far from clear; our next chapter will
throw some light on it. But it also points us toward the mystery we
are now considering. This is the mystery of the Church, which, as
greatest of all cities, also has the greatest accumulation of filth. And
yet the Church processes her refuse, comes to terms with it, excretes

---

[182] *Anglais*, 79.
[183] *Français*, 15.
[184] *To Benoît*, October 25, 1946; *C. du R.*, 57.
[185] *Cimetières*, 3.
[186] *Ouine*, 163.

it, and changes it back into the original chaos, which is to say, into hell. Filth is part and parcel of running a household in this world: "A parish is necessarily something dirty. And all of Christendom is something dirtier still. Just wait for the great Day of Judgment and you'll see what the angels will have to clear out of the holiest monasteries, by the shovelful: what a feat of cleaning! So, my boy, this proves that the Church has to be a tough housekeeper, tough and practical."[187]

The Reformation, on the contrary, dreamed of a "pasteurized, germ-free world".[188] It is not possible for the Church to get rid of her black sheep, and this is the best proof for the fact that the Church is no cloister.[189] On the other hand, this is what makes her a true *people* in whose midst things happen in a very human way, which is precisely the basis for their also happening in a Christian way.[190] This is so true that it is the Church that has given the concept of a "people" and a "homeland" the ultimate, definitive meaning and content for us of the Western World:[191] "After all, the Church is not an ideal still to be realized. She already exists and [this whole people] is already within her."[192] The dean of Blangermont knows what he is doing when he confronts the idealistic little priest with the solid ground that is the basis of the Church and her hierarchy (something conceived by Christ with the mediocrity of men particularly in mind) and makes him aware, too, of the Church's understanding of the hustle and bustle of earthly life: "On the battlefield, a soldier does not think of himself as a murderer. Likewise, the businessman who collects interests from loans does not consider himself a thief. After all, he could never conceive of taking a penny from anyone's pocket. What can I say, dear boy? Men will be men! If any of these business people were suddenly to decide to follow rigorously what theology prescribes concerning legitimate profits, they would surely be ruined."[193]

Paulus Gordan is right when he says that Bernanos "loves the Church with a deep, unshakable love".[194] He knows that all that God

---

[187] *Curé*, 19.
[188] Ibid., 129.
[189] Ibid., 26.
[190] Ibid., 28–29.
[191] Ibid., 269.
[192] Ibid., 42.
[193] Ibid., 82.
[194] *Bernanos au Brésil*, in: *Bul.* 5, 5.

suffered on account of the world's sins lies stored up in the Church's treasuries—all the suffering of that incarnate God of whom we could say much more emphatically than of any Christian that he suffered, not only *for* the Church, but *at the hands of* the Church.

IV. THE WORLD OF
HOLY ORDERS AND CONFESSION

1. The Kingdom of Evil

Already in Part One we saw that the problem of communication with evil[1] is a central concern of Bernanos' theory of knowledge. If all things can be known only from within, and if admission to evil is denied, how then is evil to be known? And the nature of evil must come to be known if we are to understand the redemption and if the struggle against evil is not to be blind. Despite its intrinsic powerlessness, evil possesses a definite ascendancy over man: it has the power to "seduce" and to lure man into the bottomless abyss, so that the man who would set out to "fathom the depths of Satan" (Rev 2:24) would necessarily be lost in them. The question may be solved only by reference to Church and sacrament: this is where a man can be outfitted with the required "armament" as with a diver's suit, and the armament is not drawn from the arsenal of human psychology but from the supernatural storehouse of the sacraments. Thus equipped, he can penetrate into the house of the Evil One dispassionately, as one fulfilling his mission, to emerge from it unscathed after having robbed the devil of his goods (Mt 12:29).

It is peculiar to Bernanos to conceive of this battle as above all a battle of the spirit and, hence, of vision, understanding, and judgment,

---

[1] In German there is an ambiguity in the genitive and dative cases of the adjective *böse* (evil) when used as a substantive. This makes it uncertain whether what is meant in a given case is the more abstract neuter noun *das Böse* (evil) or the personal masculine noun *der Böse* (the evil one), referring of course to Satan. Nor does context always solve the ambiguity. This same ambiguity occurs in Greek and Latin in the last petition of the Lord's Prayer. The title of the present chapter could therefore also be "The Kingdom of the Evil One", and the present sentence could equally read: "the problem of communication with the Evil One. . . ." I here opt for the neuter noun because of the occurrence of *das Böse* later in the paragraph. The grammatical point is important, as it points to the fact that in Judæo-Christian theology the concept of "evil" is inseparable from its source: the initiative and the person of "the Evil One". It is also relevant to the æsthetic-theological methods of Bernanos the novelist, for whom "evil" always exists in concrete forms that may be experienced by man. This makes it a fit subject for literary dramatization.—TRANS.

all of which are for him inseparable from prayer. This is why the sacrament of orders, which equips man in a special way for battling with the Evil One, is conceived by Bernanos primarily as the conferral of a supernatural grace of office that bestows vision, insight into the essence of guilt, which is something required before one ventures the judgment whereby the priest can truly become a vicarious cojudge along with Christ and can really exercise the power of binding and loosing. This battle with the Evil One, furthermore, often specifies itself in the sacrament of confession, which is par excellence the "sacrament of struggle". The sacrament of confession is, consequently, the only sacrament that receives explicit portrayal in Bernanos' fictional works: it is preëminently the sacrament in which the Christian is engaged as existential actor or agent, and the theologians describe his "acts" as penitent as constituting the *materia sacramenti*. In this sacrament, the psychological states and actions that are accessible to the narrator attain as such to a directly sacramental and therefore transpsychological significance, and this no less in the father confessor than in his penitent. In this way the event of confession becomes a decisive victory over what in our unbelieving modern world constitutes a dangerous and demonic substitute for confession, namely, depth psychology. With the latter Bernanos fought a bitter struggle in order to snatch back from it what originally did not belong to it and what it had vainly usurped: for Satan cannot be driven out by means of Satan (Mt 12:26). La Pérouse, Ouine, and Cénabre are characters consumed by curiosity: "The curiosity of the Abbé Cénabre is not of the kind that can be sated even by anguish—and it survives all else."[2] Bernanos himself, by contrast, and his priest characters are not curious beings. They are even less curious than Dostoyevsky himself, and perhaps even than Bloy. Rather, they are servants of the truth, and in creating them Bernanos borrows for himself a little of the priestly grace of office in order to accompany his figures, in the spirit of confession, down into hell and back again.

Bernanos' first concern was to break through the shallow moralism of his time and awaken anew an awareness, first, of the very existence, then of the depth, and finally of the "suction-power" of the

---

[2] *Joie*, 282.

satanic abyss. To do this, he had to turn his back resolutely on a certain Romantic tradition of "compassion with Satan" (from Milton to Hugo and Quinet) and of a morbid interest in his mysteries (from de Sade's sexual fantasies and Baudelaire's *Flowers of Evil* to Flaubert's *Temptation of Saint Anthony*, Rimbaud's *A Season in Hell*, all the way to Lautréamont's *Songs of Maldoror* and Jouhandeau's creations). For Bernanos, all of this represented, not an aid, but an obstacle to the Christian understanding of evil. The latter can be attained, not through an exploration of the weaknesses and yearnings of the modern subject, but rather through an objectivity possessed only by saints and priests. So it was that Bernanos was compelled to turn to the figure of the Curé d'Ars, not as a historical, but as a mythic and symbolic figure from which the writer could draw the decisive traits useful for his literary purposes. How does Jean-Marie Vianney view hell? What shape does its powerless might assume before his eyes and heart?

There was perhaps a touch of impatience in the way Bernanos descended on this material, wanting to bring the abyss to a standstill and extract from it a clarification of its nature. By making hell emerge into the world of men in so naked and disincarnate a fashion (with the exception of his portrayal of the possessed Mouchette), Bernanos unconsciously remained dependent on the Romantic tradition mentioned. In the famous demonic scene involving Ivan Karamazov, Dostoyevsky showed himself to be more experienced in the matter, since to the end he leaves open the question of whether the gaping of hell's jaws was a reality or a hallucination. In other words, he does not rule whether the demon is an independently subsistent person in himself or whether he acquires such personhood only within Ivan's evil spirit. By deciding to confer on the demon a definite personality in the human sense, which then entails a definite demonic psychology, Bernanos remains within the tradition of a mythic portrayal of the demonic. Together with Donissan we hear the devil's famous laughter with reference to the Cross,[3] and the saint once again hears it in the laughter of the half-crazed mother at the time of the failed miracle.[4] But we also experience Satan's urgent need to cuddle up in a human heart, there to warm himself, in order finally to pull his host down

---

[3] *Soleil*, 284.
[4] Ibid., 305, 309.

into his abyss.[5] Satan longs to kiss the soul in a carnal embrace: "I, in turn, have filled you with myself, dear fool—you who pride yourself in being the tabernacle of Jesus Christ! . . . I deposit my kiss on all of you, both sleeping and awake, both the dead and the living. That's the truth of it. It is my delight to be with you, little god-men that you are, such very peculiar creatures! If you really want to know, I don't often leave you. You bear me within your dark flesh. . . . None of you escapes me. Just by sniffing you I would recognize every single beasty in my little flock."[6] But Satan also suffers from contact with his anointed partner: "Your hands have hurt me greatly . . . as well as your forehead, your eyes, and your mouth. . . . I will never warm them again. They have literally turned my marrow to ice and frozen my bones. It's no doubt the fault of your anointings, your smearings with sacred oils—pure witchcraft."[7]

When Donissan peers for the first time into Satan's eyes, he sees there the vertigo of the abyss:

> A man tied by both hands to the peak of the mast and suddenly losing the balance of gravity would see the rending and swelling beneath him no longer now of the sea but of the cosmic abyss of the stars—and, seething trillions of leagues away, he would see the foam of nebulas in gestation through the gaping void that nothing can measure and that his everlasting fall is about to traverse. Such a man would not feel in the hollow of his chest a more absolute vertigo [than Donissan now felt]. . . . The daring man, in some sense bending forward and sucked from the earth by the immense call of nothingness, saw himself this time irretrievably lost. And yet, at this very instant, his final thought was still a confused act of defiance.[8]

As the priest then immobilizes the demon and chases him away with a firm "Get thee hence!", "the frightful creature takes a leap, turns on itself several times with fantastic agility, and then is violently hurled a few paces away as if by an irresistible trigger. He was then seen with both arms outstretched, like a man trying in vain to regain his balance."[9] It is then that Donissan becomes aware of his

---

[5] Ibid., 162f.
[6] Ibid., 166.
[7] Ibid., 169.
[8] Ibid., 170–71.
[9] Ibid., 172.

own power, and the devil, who undertakes to tempt him with it, accomplishes nothing since it is the power of the sacrament and not of
the person. Donissan can now deal his decisive blow, which is none
other than that of his vision: " 'It is given me to see you', the saint
of Lumbres said slowly. 'As far as this is possible for human sight, I
see you. I see you crushed by your sorrow, to the very limit of anni-
hilation—something that shall not be granted you, O of all creatures
the most tortured!' At this last word, the monster rolled from the
top to the bottom of the embankment by the road, and it twisted in
the mud contorted by horrible spasms. Then it became still, its loins
furiously arched, and it leaned on head and heels, like one afflicted
with tetanus."[10]

The spiritual result introduced by this scene is extraordinary indeed: it is the gift of reading people's hearts, which Bernanos very
expressly derives from this encounter with the abyss. Nevertheless,
the scene remains mythic in a manner that is not acceptable even for
a novel. We fully realize this when we compare it to the conversation
between the country priest and the countess that Bernanos wrote ten
years later. Only here does he attain to the true dialectic of damnation. The countess is a despairing mother who is in revolt against the
divine order, and she says she hates God because he has robbed her of
her son. In that case, the priest replies, even her son would not be able
to love her, because in hell there is neither love nor communication
and, hence, nothing that corresponds to our concept of personality:

> We judge hell by this world's criteria, but hell is not of this world.
> It is not of this world, and even less of the Christian world. . . . The
> most wretched of living men, even if he believes he can no longer
> love, nonetheless retains the power of loving. Even our hatred is re-
> splendent. . . . Hell, Madame, is not to love any longer. "Not to love
> any longer" sounds in your ears like a familiar expression. For a living
> person, "not to love any longer" means to love less or to love something
> else. *But what if this faculty, which seems to us to be inseparable from our being
> —indeed, which seems to be our very being, since to understand is still a way
> of loving: what if this faculty of loving were to disappear altogether?* Not to
> love any longer, not to understand any longer, and yet to remain alive
> —O terrible wonder! The error common to all of us is still to attribute
> something of ourselves to these forsaken creatures [in hell], something

---

[10] Ibid., 173.

of our perpetual mobility, while in reality they are outside time, outside movement, confined in an eternal fixity. . . . Surely, if a living person, one like ourselves—even if he were the lowest of all, viler than vile— were to be cast just as he is into this burning chasm, I would want to share his fate and would go to wrench him back from his tormentor. "Share his fate" indeed! . . . The misfortune, the inconceivable misfortune of these glowing stones which once were humans is that they no longer have anything to share.[11]

The mythic element in all this consists in the fact that Donissan speaks and has to do with a demon who laughs, weeps, and writhes as if they were the same kind of being. Indeed, the devil harangues him and tells him *the truth!* "We are allowed to test you, from this day to the hour of your death." "What did you want with me?", Donissan then asks, and he adds: "Don't try to lie. I have ways of making you talk." And Satan replies: "*I don't lie.* I'll answer you. But soften your demand a bit. What would be the good of my obeying? He has sent me to you to test you. Do you want me to tell you what the test consists of? I'll tell you. Who could resist you, O my master?"[12] One can have a human relationship with a devil who tells the truth, even if the relationship is a hostile one. And so Bernanos is here attributing to his spiritual hero a quality he will later on identify as the characteristic of all deceptive conversations with the abyss. This is "a boundless *curiosity*", which is not, to be sure, "a vain appetite for knowing" but rather the need to "snatch some of his secrets from the killer of souls".[13] But from yielding to such a desire there is only one step to the "inexplicable tremor of *compassion*" for the doomed creature felt by the saint of Lumbres. When "the monster" cries out: "Enough! Enough! You anointed dog! You torturer!", Donissan listens "with fear to this *lament* uttered with words and yet coming from outside the world".[14] What Bernanos here wanted to portray was an ineffable acquaintance with the abyss. In *Under Satan's Sun* this portrayal still had an unmistakably Romantic-mythic coloring that threatened to spoil the project. But Bernanos began to correct this anomaly already in his next novel, and then ever more decidedly with each new

[11] *Curé*, 180–81. (The italics are von Balthasar's.—TRANS.)

[12] *Soleil*, 174. (The italics are von Balthasar's.—TRANS.)

[13] Ibid., 169. (The italics are von Balthasar's.—TRANS.)

[14] Ibid., 172–73. (The italics are von Balthasar's.—TRANS.)

one. Had he not, he would infallibly have landed in that theologically untenable sentimentalism that Papini was soon to revive and that can never be a viable Christian alternative.

The kingdom of evil is henceforth portrayed by Bernanos as an absolute impotency opposed to God that becomes the dominant potency[15] in the person who surrenders to it. The intensity of his vision has by no means been diminished; by moving closer to man, it has only become all the more uncanny. The plunge into the abyss even becomes much more vertiginous. In *The Imposture*, by way of exception, it is not a woman who is possessed and damned but a representative of the ecclesial ministry. The Abbé Cénabre's confinement to the satanic depths is described step by step, with all its stages and states of mind, with hauntingly clinical precision and objectivity. Beginning with his lightning-like insight into his pride ("he saw himself naked"),[16] we follow the priest through his experience of loss of faith,[17] the slipping away of his own interior reality, his anxiety and fear, the revelation of his intrinsic lying and playacting, the void at his center, "the silent dissipation of his being",[18] his hatred for himself, and the "impossibility of his remaining any longer at home in himself".[19] And the conversation Cénabre has with the Abbé Chevance, whom he has summoned in the middle of the night, only exhibits the extent to which he, Cénabre, is walled in within himself: "Whether pleas, threats, lies, or cries of rage or despair—it seemed that nothing could cross the magic circle [around him]."[20]

A few pages later Bernanos describes this diabolical dispossession of self with perfect precision:

> Little by little, consciousness returned to the Abbé Cénabre. . . . What was taking shape in him was quite beyond the reach of the intellect. It was wholly unlike anything he had known and remained distinct from his life, even though his life was shaken by it at an astounding depth. It

---

[15] Von Balthasar here plays on the two words *Ohnmacht* (impotence, powerlessness) and *Übermacht* (dominant power, superforce).—TRANS.

[16] *Imposture*, 31.

[17] Ibid., 35.

[18] Ibid., 37.

[19] Ibid., 38.

[20] Ibid., 53.

was like the exultation of another being—its own mysterious *realization*. He wholly ignored both the meaning and the goal of this process; but this passivity of all his higher faculties, at the epicenter of such massive agitation, was, to tell the truth, a delectation that made his body quiver to the very roots. He admitted and welcomed the mysterious force into his own nature, enduring it with a terrible joy. . . . Its hold upon him was all the stronger as it had sunk its claws unforeseen. All resistance had been broken by a single blow.[21]

Chevance finally leaves, as he can do nothing more, but not before learning Cénabre's secret, and this will be enough to liberate the latter in the end from his prison within himself. When Cénabre remains alone he begins to reflect on his condition,[22] and three distinct times he hears his own laughter, something that frightens him to the core. In *Under Satan's Sun*, Donissan had heard the laughter of the mythical Satan; here, Cénabre hears himself but cannot recognize his own sound. It is the echo of a bottomless malice in himself that is revealed to him as by a stroke of lightning. What he discovers in this instantaneous light is "the taste of lying, its ardor and frenzy, the delight of its continual exercise, leading to a truly monstrous splitting of one's being".[23] The "key to his life" is henceforth a "nearly absolute hypocrisy". And when he again hears the laughter of this voice from his own depths, he accepts it and makes it his own: "His immediate reward was an immense relief, an immense allayment. Nothing could give a better idea of this unexpected deliverance than the bursting of an abscess", a real "release".[24]

Cénabre feels hell, but he cannot see it: "The idea of [demonic] possession didn't even graze him."[25] He feels free but does not know from what. He has shaken off his past, but the future before him is just as hollow and empty—a new lie that he must assume, an equally great state of boredom.[26] As for sensuality, he has long since seen through this small coin of hell's realm: he feels "a miser's disdain for this sort of squandering". Thus, all temporal duration has been taken from him, and he no longer has any locus in which to live or any

[21] Ibid., 55–56.
[22] Ibid., 68f.
[23] Ibid., 76.
[24] Ibid., 83.
[25] Ibid., 85.
[26] Ibid., 86.

dimension of hope.[27] Even the gun he reaches for to put an end to things refuses to shoot; his attempt at suicide is at base superseded by the condition in which he exists: he is incapable of any action and can only endure and observe.[28] Now his self-hatred turns into a sense of disgrace and humiliation, which has contradictory effects of hardening and softening him:[29] this amounts to an attack on the innermost core of his person and leads to total self-contempt. He clings to this self-contempt "as if it were the only fixed point in the midst of this universal shipwreck. Pride—whose tenebrous strategy is at once the subtlest and the strongest—felt threatened for a moment and, in order to survive, seemed to sacrifice something of itself. In reality, what it was offering to the wretched soul in its death throes was but a sacrilegious facsimile of divine humility."[30] Like a last offer on the part of heaven, he is given the gift of tears; but, as these run down his face, "all his fatigue flowed out of him along with them, and he felt an immense power quaking within himself." According to Bernanos, it was then that "his fate was sealed", for "no one is hurled into the abyss without first having detached his own heart from the terrible and gentle hand whose clasp he feels and rejects. No one is abandoned without first having committed the essential sacrilege: to have denied God, not in his justice, but in his love."[31]

Now this portrayal of damnation, hewn from Cyclopean blocks, dispenses with myth and follows a psychological approach rather closely. The books that follow *The Imposture*, especially *Joy* and *Monsieur Ouine*, will go even farther in their description of interior states. However, it would be a fundamental mistake to think that the object Bernanos is exploring—the kingdom of evil—can be adequately confronted with "psychology" in the usual sense of the term. Let us hear what he himself says in this connection: "*The simplest feelings are born and grow in a night that can never be penetrated. They merge or clash there in keeping with secret affinities, like electrical clouds, and on the surface of the darkness all we can perceive are sudden flashes of the inaccessible storm. This is why the best psychological hypotheses may be able to reconstruct the past, but they can by no means predict the future. And, like many other hypothe-*

---

[27] Ibid., 87–89.
[28] Ibid., 92.
[29] Ibid., 94.
[30] Ibid., 95.
[31] Ibid., 102.

ses, all they do is veil from our eyes a mystery the very idea of which over-whelms our mind."[32] This "leap", whereby evil always runs ahead out of the reach of all psychological analysis, makes sin an unfathomable reality.

Under Satan's Sun already endeavors to catch a glimmer of deeper layers of reality through the crack of what is allegedly "experienced" at the surface: "How many lovers thus take in their arms a total stranger, the perfect and supple enemy!"[33] Swamp creatures emerge for a moment from the depths, only to plunge down again.[34] Under the cover of what we experience exists a bond of solidarity among all sins, which makes them practically interchangeable with one another: "All sins have a family resemblance. Only one sin really exists."[35] "What is terrifying is this solidarity in evil! Regardless of how atrocious crimes may be, they do not communicate the true nature of evil any more than the most exalted works of the saints communicate the splendor of God. . . . The world of evil, in a word, totally escapes the grasp of our minds! And, in any event, I cannot always succeed in imagining it as a world, a universe. It is and will forever remain but a rough draft—the mere sketch of a hideous, stillborn creation at the extreme boundaries of being."[36]

The inventiveness of people who are bent on blaspheming God appears to the country priest to be inferior indeed in comparison with the real mystery involved: namely, that in the kingdom of evil what is truly central in the end is not at all the evil individual but rather his dissolution in the anonymity of flames and slime:

What does the Monster care about one criminal more or less? On the spot he devours his crime, incorporates it into his own frightful substance, and digests it without for a moment leaving his terrible, eternal immobility. But the historian, the moralist, and even the philosopher want to see only the criminal: they remake evil in the image and likeness of man. They have absolutely no idea of evil itself, which is an immense inhalation by the void, by nothingness. Be sure of it: if our species is to perish, it will perish of repulsion, of *ennui*. The human person will have

[32] *Soleil*, 37–38. (The italics are von Balthasar's.—TRANS.)
[33] Ibid., 33.
[34] Ibid., 75.
[35] *Curé*, 156.
[36] Ibid., 161–62.

been slowly gnawed from within, like a beam invaded by an invisible fungus that, in just a few weeks, turns a sturdy oak plank into matter so spongy that one finger can crush it without effort.[37]

The person thus becomes a function of this supra- or infra-personal chaos, and not the other way around. Time and again the same image we have so often encountered again emerges: that of an apocalyptic morass of fire in which the specific contours of sins—as elements distinguishing person from person as particular constitutive elements —are dissolved. Concerning Monsieur Ouine, for instance, we read: "He saw and could almost touch these mountains of excrement, these lakes of slime."[38] And, in the *Country Priest*: "There exists a communion of saints, but also a communion of sinners. In the hatred and disdain they bear one another, sinners unite, embrace, collect, commingle: one day, in the eyes of the Eternal One, they shall be nothing but this lake of ever-oozing slime through which the immense tide of divine love is perpetually passing and repassing—always in vain —the same oceanic tide of living, roaring flames that fructified the primeval chaos."[39] This is also the image of hell that the country priest describes to the countess: "The inconceivable misfortune of these glowing stones that once were humans is that they no longer have anything to share."[40] The "mysticism of sin" that Bernanos develops in certain characters who appear to have been "chosen for evil"—as counterparts to those who are "mystics of grace"—is for him only an occasion to mirror upward, into the dimension of what can be experienced, an area of reality that normally seethes unexperienced beneath all conceivable sin: "How often, alas, in the midst of our soul's struggles, there bursts out in our interior this heinous joy! But we do not hear it. And certain rare and singular circumstances are doubtless required for evil thus to violate the borders of its solemn empire and betray itself to our senses just as it is, in a glance or the sound of a voice."[41]

---

[37] Ibid., 162.
[38] *Ouine*, 164.
[39] *Curé*, 156.
[40] Ibid., 181.
[41] *Imposture*, 84.

Much more emphatically than *The Imposture*, *Monsieur Ouine* is the attempt to portray the transpersonal character of evil as such. This is the actual subject of the novel, and this is why the person of Ouine is portrayed precisely in its decomposition and dissolution into anonymity, while "the dead parish" as a whole, in its collectivity, is set up as the counterpole and symptom of the presence of this shapeless disorder. Both titles of the novel, then—"Monsieur Ouine" and "The Dead Parish"—are equally justified and refer to one another.[42] The area that is to be "mirrored up" lies underneath all individual sinful acts, within a general condition of sin; consequently, every specific sinful action is only referential and symptomatic; the relative insignificance of the question of who actually committed the murder points to the importance of universal guilt. The manner in which such an unusual subject is portrayed in *Monsieur Ouine* is quite adequate to the subject, as may be inferred from the novel's only seemingly surrealistic diction, which in the end we come to see as being actually "transpsychological" and theologically based. The murder does not come to light because no one is concerned with justice,[43] and Bernanos is not about to nourish the general curiosity of the characters. This is also why the question of the origins of the Devandomme family remains open.[44] The whole thing is a "morass. There are marshes that are calm and as if sleeping. But the ooze of this particular one has appeared to be damned active for some time now. You'd think you could almost hear it boiling and hissing—although don't forget, my friend, that this is barely an image. Some day we will learn the laws—still mysterious to us now—that govern fermentation of this kind, whether by accelerating it or slowing it down."[45] A casual crime suffices to throw the demoralization of a village into a state of crisis.[46] It now resembles "a huge top gone crazy, which turns and rumbles and would knock down the walls".[47] "Now there is a corpse in every house."[48] "Only one grain of leaven too many is required for the whole dough to rise. The evil was already in you, but now it's started to come out of the

---

[42] See footnote 80 in Part 1, Chapter 4.
[43] Ouine, 129, 154, 225.
[44] Ibid., 37f.
[45] Ibid., 138 (corrected text).
[46] Ibid., 140.
[47] Ibid., 222.
[48] Ibid., 139.

very ground and walls, as it were."[49] "Curiosity itself, the most powerful instrument of disintegration, . . . cannot overcome the resistance
and pliant elasticity of this magma."[50] The process is irreversible; for
this dead parish it is simply "too late".[51] The mayor of the village is
quite aware of it: "Why talk of absolution? Such as I am, such I will
remain."[52]

The character of Monsieur Ouine symbolizes this condition of the
village, and the most meaningful text in this connection is a passage
from the end of the novel containing the metaphor of the "empty
bottle".[53] " 'I too am empty,' said Monsieur Ouine, 'and now I can
see to the very bottom of myself. There isn't any obstacle now—
nothing to block my view. And there is nothing there. Don't forget
this word: Nothing."[54] Emptiness—the void—is the final word of
everything in this novel. In the words of Ouine's protégé, Philippe:

> In the depths of his [Ouine's] eyes you can see something I can't quite
> name that makes you understand why people are so ridiculous. Once
> you remove this ridiculousness, they are no longer of interest: they are
> empty. Life too is empty—a big empty house into which each of us
> comes in turn. Through the walls you can hear the trampling of those
> who are about to come in and those who are on their way out. But they
> never meet. Your steps resound in the hallways, and when you speak,
> you think you can hear the answer. It's the echo of your own words,
> nothing else. And when you suddenly find yourself face to face with
> someone, you've only to look a bit closer: you'll recognize your own
> reflection in the depths of one of those worn, greenish mirrors, under
> a layer of dust.[55]

The description of Ouine's death is evidently meant to convey his
descent into hell; but it is portrayed as the irruption of the absolute
nothingness that was always present in radical evil yet only now reveals itself as the façade of the person is demolished: "If nothing existed, then I myself would be something—whether good or bad. But

---

[49] Ibid., 165.

[50] Ibid., 146.

[51] Ibid., 166.

[52] Ibid., 202.

[53] Bernanos lost this portion of the manuscript before it got to the printer's, and it was
Albert Béguin who published it in 1951 in *Bul.* 9.

[54] *Bul.* 9, 16, and edition of the Club des Libraires de France (1955), 271.

[55] *Ouine*, 218 (corrected text).

it is I who am nothing."[56] What is here involved, however, is not the nothingness of the philosophers, what the Platonists once identified with evil. We here have a nothingness of quite different vehemence: the hunger that can no longer be sated with anything, the sucking that is incapable of any more gulping. "Nothing can fill me any more. . . . In vain have I opened myself up to things and dilated my being: I have been one huge orifice, nothing but inhalation, ingestion—body and soul. With my whole self I have gaped open. . . . Instead of sating my hunger, I have done nothing but desire. I have lived bloated with desire. I have taken nothing substantial into myself, neither good nor bad: my soul is nothing but a wineskin full of wind. And now, young man, it is sucking me up whole into itself. I feel myself melting and disappearing into this famished gullet. Even my bones have turned watery."[57] Now there can be no question of repentance, for the soul has become one with its cravings and drowned in its appetites: " 'I don't even have a morsel of repentance to throw at it. . . . The very word has lost all meaning. . . . I can no longer even imagine such a division within myself, such a disavowal of myself, such a weird fragmentation. I would need nothing less than a whole lifetime in order to produce one single act of repentance. . . . A new childhood, an entire childhood', Monsieur Ouine whispered in a low voice, with the inflections of unbounded lust."[58]

Ouine had already compared himself with a jellyfish: "Like those medusas living at the bottom of the sea, I too float and ingest"; but precisely such movement betrays the fact that he contains nothing within himself, not even "some poor secret".[59] This statement, spoken early in the novel, will be repeated by Ouine on his deathbed: "I have no secrets. . . . Even in the event that I once had any, I now have no more secrets. That's the trick God is playing on me, young man."[60] Nevertheless, Ouine continues:

> I need a secret. I have the most urgent need for one single secret, even the most frivolous you can imagine, or more repulsive and hideous than all the devils in hell. . . . Do you know what I mean by "a secret", my child? I mean something hidden worth the trouble of confessing: an

[56] Ibid., 240.
[57] Ibid., 235.
[58] Ibid., 236.
[59] Ibid., 25.
[60] Ibid., 237.

admission, an exchange, which would allow me to unburden myself to another. . . . I can no longer give anything to anybody, that I know, and most probably I can't any longer receive anything either. But what of it? Something could still *fall* from me like fruit from a tree, or at least— since there can no longer be any question of flower or fruit—like rocks from a boulder. The slightest shove would do it, the merest flick,

and down would come "the tiniest pebble". But even this is no longer possible, because "the door yawns open, the phials are empty, the poisons have become diffused in the air, completely diluted and rendered harmless. . . . Pure water—no, not pure, but tasteless, colorless water, without any freshness or warmth, water that no cold could deaden and that could extinguish no fire: Who would want to drink of this water with me? Steel is less hard, lead less heavy, and no metal could make a dent in it. Such water is not pure—in the exact meaning of the word—but rather untouched, unchangeable, polished like a diamond mirror. And my thirst is like it. My thirst and this water are but one."[61] As he lies dying, only his quiet, gurgling laughter still flows out of Ouine, "like the sobbing of water in the clayey bed of a stream, the burbling of the rain over pebbles. . . . [His laughter] flowed in the shadows like a slender thread of clayey water—elusive, inexhaustible, without beginning or end."[62]

This portrayal is masterly, even if the writer is compelled to work with nothing but contradictory images. What would be the use of concepts when the subject to be portrayed is the quintessential contradiction: the "second death", a state of being simultaneously alive and dead? Before we go any farther, however, we must now consider a most unusual and extreme intuition of Bernanos, a sort of "outer limit" to his thought. Until now Bernanos has been concerned with the specific ontological quality of evil as such, and this he could portray only as dissolution, decomposition, and disintegration. Now, however, the question imposes itself concerning the direction in which this whole process is moving. Granted, an immanent finality could never be ascribed to such a procedure of "denaturalization". Nevertheless, as with decomposition in the natural economy of things, some comprehensive purpose or precise locus in cosmic life should perhaps be sought for the process whereby a person is

---

[61] Ibid., 238–39 (corrected text).
[62] Ibid., 244.

irreversibly and totally corrupted by evil. Is there any such thing as a conclusive result to sin's process of putrefaction, for instance, its successful dissolution into separate components and neutral elements? Occasionally Bernanos' thought appears to move in this direction, as when he writes concerning those secrets "that finish rotting in our conscience, there consuming themselves ever so slowly",[63] or when he has Donissan say to Mouchette as she is struggling with Satan: "Stir up your slime a bit, and you'll see that the vice you so flaunt has long since rotted away there."[64] As early as 1919, in fact, he was already writing to Maître: "At the bottom of ourselves there is the refuse of thirty years, in full rot."[65] In the end, then, what occurs could be something like a depreciation of the depths of evil, precisely by virtue of its nothingness. After hearing confessions for a whole day, the country priest writes in his diary: "What do we know of sin? Geologists tell us that the ground that appears to us to be so firm, so stable, is in reality but a thin film above an ocean of liquid fire, a membrane that is always quivering like the skin that forms on milk that is ready to boil. . . . What is the thickness of sin? How deeply would we have to dig before we rediscovered the abyss of azure light?"[66]

But we should not interpret this thought as meaning that sin now becomes a part of the nature. The chaotic waters into which Ouine is dissolved, characterized by diamond-like impenetrability, are mysterious in a way very different from any element of the natural world. What Bernanos means is something quite different: namely, that the sinner should not cling to his sin in a kind of infantilism that, out of a false curiosity and delectation or even out of a false contrition, refuses to admit that sin obeys an inherent process that makes it transitory and, eventually, a thing of the past. Such infantilism simply refuses to let go of sin, and, at the same time, it seeks to confer on the kingdom of evil a consistency that by its very nature it cannot possess since it is a pure principle of dissolution that consequently must destroy itself.

---

[63] *Joie*, 100.
[64] *Soleil*, 207.
[65] *To Maître*, August 26, 1919; *Erbarmen*, 36–37.
[66] *Curé*, 90.

Bernanos' continual focus, then, is the experience of the abyss as this manifests itself on the surface of sin. Individual sins are by no means neglected or underestimated, but they are regarded as symptoms. And, since sin is always a lie, it can be that the apparent, perceivable forms sin assumes at the surface level, if they are to be understood, may have to be interpreted as the precise opposites of the realities they indicate: "The sensation of an invisible presence that is surely not God's",[67] the gliding of the interior glance "over the surface of another consciousness, of another mirror, quite unknown to me until now":[68] these are the things that unsettle the country priest. What lurks underneath and behind such perceptions? The experience also makes one more objective, as with a physician in the face of an illness: "Naturally, you don't want to look farther than the fault committed. And yet, the fault is after all nothing but a symptom. And the symptoms that are most impressive to the layman aren't always the gravest and most disturbing."[69] Indeed, it could be that the very essence of the sinner as sinner is his refusal to engage the full depth of his being and make it something vital: at base, the sinner is someone who lives at the surface of himself: "If that's the way they are, what can they say about sin? What do they know about it? The cancer gnawing at them is like many tumors in that it is painless."[70] Following this scent left by the contradictoriness between what appears at the surface and what actually lurks in the depths beneath it—obviously part of the demon's tack to lead astray willfully—Bernanos then goes about unearthing images that will show the correspondence between the essence of appearance and reality, images that will thus make perceivable the spirit of lies.

Lying, according to Bernanos' intent, must be experienced in the novels as the all-enveloping atmosphere and living milieu that forces those living within it "to devour one another; for such is the power of lies".[71] Lying is experienced as self-abolishing contradiction (Ouine is at once *oui* and *non*), as being deceived (Donissan is led around in a

---

[67] Ibid., 33.
[68] Ibid., 16.
[69] Ibid., 123.
[70] Ibid., 124.
[71] *Joie*, 18.

metaphorical circle by Satan),[72] as the power and the measureless joy
of lying to the very end and of giving birth to an infinite number of
lies (as with Mouchette).[73] Lying, as the self-disintegration of being,
is already hell itself: "Lying is the cruelest thing man has invented
to torture himself with."[74] Lying makes evident what the already-
mentioned difference is between petrification of the person (which
is hell) and decomposition of the person (which has an end and can
therefore have a redemption): "Only lying escapes putrefaction: it
dries out without rotting and little by little assumes the polish and
hardness of stone. Lying is a mineral substance. I can ask for nothing
better than the possibility of rotting. I am fully aware of the fact that
what my books contain by way of merely human truth will be the
first thing to be eaten by the worms, along with myself."[75]

But standing right next to *Mensonge* (lying), as masculine satanic figure, Bernanos sees his feminine counterpart, *Injustice*, which he understands as the rejection of all the elementary laws and requirements
of human existence, in both the private and the social realms. Lying
and injustice are but one: the expression of the very same kingdom of
evil, on the consistency of which Bernanos is ever intent on speaking:

> Somewhere in creation, Injustice has its will, its consciousness, its mon-
> strous memory. . . . Who would dare deny the fact that evil enjoys or-
> ganization, that—with its sinister landscapes, its wan sky, its cold sun,
> and its cruel stars—it has produced a universe that is more real than
> the one perceived by our senses? Evil possesses a kingdom that is at
> the same time spiritual and carnal, with prodigious density and almost
> infinite weight. Compared with it, the kingdoms of this earth are like
> mere figures and symbols. It is a kingdom that is really opposed only by
> the mysterious Kingdom of God, the name of which slides from our lips
> even though, alas, we do not know it and cannot even conceive of it, and
> yet we await its coming. Thus, Injustice belongs to our familiar world,
> but not all of her[76] belongs to it. Her pale face is indeed among us—

---

[72] *Soleil*, 151f.

[73] Ibid., 45–46.

[74] *Enfants*, 196.

[75] Ibid., 201.

[76] The context requires the feminine personification of "Injustice", by contrast to masculine "Lying". In the French original, of course, this corresponds to the grammatical genders
of the nouns involved.—TRANS.

rictal grin resembling that of lust and rigid with the hideous rumination of unthinkable cravings; but the monster's heart is throbbing with slow and solemn rhythm somewhere outside our world, and it will never be granted any man to fathom its designs.[77]

"If God were to open up our senses to the invisible world, which of us would not fall down dead—yes, *dead*—at the sight, at the mere sight, of all the hideous and abominable creatures evil has spawned?"[78]

The Curé de Torcy warns his colleague, the younger country priest, from becoming obsessed with this kingdom of injustice. He is not to stare it down like a lion tamer, because it does not yield to any man's glance: "Do not look at it a second longer than you have to, and never look at it without praying";[79] "to bear with injustice is the very condition of mortal man."[80] This kingdom of nontruth and nonjustice has its own spiritual form of (un-)truth or (non-)logic, and these are all the stricter as the logic of divine love is yielding and supple and sovereignly beyond all rigid laws: "The logic of evil is as strict as hell. The devil is the greatest of logicians, or perhaps, who knows, he may be logic itself."[81] "The devil is the greatest logician. No logic is comparable to the logic of hell."[82] "The poor souls of the damned in hell are eternally arguing with themselves—with the greatest of logicians, whose name is the devil."[83] Against the eternal Word—who is the Way, the Truth, and the Life—the devil is forever opposing his own eternal Anti-Word: "I am the door that is forever shut, the way without a goal, mendacity and perdition."[84] But this inexorable logic is in fact the sum total of all nonlogic and the perversion of all authentic thinking: "Satan is always seeking to grab hold of God's thought. But not only does he hate it without understanding it; he actually understands it in reverse. Unawares, he's bent on swimming backward up the stream of life instead of floating down it, and he spends himself in absurd and frightful attempts

---

[77] *Cimetières*, 81–82.

[78] *Ouine*, 164.

[79] *Curé*, 73.

[80] Ibid., 95.

[81] *Robots*, 156–57.

[82] *Anglais*, 155.

[83] *Letter*, August 1946 (?); *Bul.* 4, 5.

[84] *Curé*, 30.

at remaking, in the opposite direction, the immense effort of the creation."[85]

The person who surrenders to lying does it out of pleasure in deceit, in a kind of game that both knows and does not want to know the lying involved, since both things contribute to the enjoyment. The "reversal" in question (or the "perversion" in the literal sense of the word), as deliberate and conscious deed and whatever the form it take, constitutes the specific element of pleasure in evil. This pleasure may primarily reside, as initially with Mouchette, in a sensation of liberation and bold daring,[86] in the "trembling feeling of being free".[87] The "first revolt" can be "like a second birth", like a "beautiful flower full of poison that blossoms for a single day."[88] With time, however, what comes more and more into the foreground is the enjoyment of the perverse as such; in other words, delectation in the shameful: "Just between us—ever since the first day, have we looked for anything else? Something that both attracts and repels you. Something you fear and yet flee from without haste. Something you encounter again every time with the same shriveling of the heart. Something that becomes the air itself you suck in. Our very element: *shame!*"[89] Understood here is *remorse*, that form of relationship to oneself that consists in a "biting" of conscience and appears to be like the perverted sting of passionate love: "When disobedience is loved for its own sake, then remorse becomes the indispensable nourishment of the soul—indeed, becomes the soul itself. It is a cursed offspring of divine love, and it resembles its parent in that it has nothing until it has it all."[90]

It is here that *the* great metaphor for sin as ontological lie becomes relevant—the reality that, in all its ramifications and modalities, becomes the plastic language for the expression of evil without itself nevertheless being in the least evil: we speak of *sexuality*. If we can make such a claim for sexuality, it is simply because in this fugue-

---

[85] Ibid., 86.
[86] *Soleil*, 26–27.
[87] Ibid., 40.
[88] Ibid., 46.
[89] Ibid., 59, and see *Joie*, 198–99; *Ouine*, 156.
[90] *To Vallery-Radot*, January 17, 1926; *Bul.* 1, 3.

like faculty of human nature—in which the corporeal both can and should become the locus for the manifestation of spiritual love— every possibility is made available for concealment rather than mani- festation, for perversion rather than straightforward self-surrender and for the abuse of love itself and, hence, for the disintegration of the core of the person. Bernanos is wholly free of every suspicion of both Manichaeism and Jansenism;[91] no one has spoken about sexual mat- ters in a more wholesome, naïve, and objective way than Bernanos. Precisely his Christian freedom from concupiscence has allowed this particular writer to expose the false mystery play that sin choreographs around sex.

To anticipate one aspect of Bernanos' treatment of sex: Part of his sovereign freedom from all collusion with sin consists in his utterly illusionless manner of speaking about the whole gamut of sexual sin, including its first glimmers in early childhood. In so doing, he knows exactly the extent to which the cancer of sin eats its way into the heart of the person (as with the children in the country priest's cate- chism class, especially poor Séraphita, who lost her innocence so early on)[92] and how radically a loving communication can be broken off ("the demon of lust is a mute demon").[93] And he also knows how, in the midst of this devastation, one part of the person can remain untouched[94] and a sense of shame can lead to repentance.[95] Bernanos is not much interested in sexual matters for their own sake; he does not exhibit one spark of curiosity in this connection, considering it a sign of infantilism to be still feeding such concerns in one's ma- turity. For Bernanos, marriage is a part of the toil of a Christian life, sanctified by the blessing of the sacrament but not a particularly rich source of light. Marriage is the only sacrament that does not, in Bernanos' literary work, receive full development into a dimension of existence; consequently, we can present these dimensions only under the emblem of six rather than seven sacraments. Bernanos nowhere impugns marriage; but he would not be the spiritual brother of Péguy and Claudel, the admirer of Dostoyevsky, and a descendant of Pascal

---

[91] *Bul.* 2, 17.
[92] *Curé*, 37, 112f.
[93] Ibid., 87.
[94] Ibid., 241.
[95] Ibid., 248f.

and Kierkegaard—and beyond all this, he would not be one of those laymen who renounce the ministerial priesthood for the sake of a particular Christian mission—if marriage fundamentally represented anything more in his work than the earthly house through whose windows we sought a vision of eternal things. . . .

Thus, in the first instance, the sexual act becomes an occasion for Bernanos to portray the contradictions of sin and spiritual egotism. A nearly invariable feature of Bernanos' novels is the manner in which individuals who have already despaired in their revolt pounce on one another so as to experience a desire that has already been outdistanced and turned to boredom in the very act of craving. The first Mouchette strikes the typical note: "The violence of the impact numbed her. The big man was carrying her off like a prey. She felt herself thrown roughly on the leather sofa. A minute later she could see only two eyes that at first were ferocious. Then, little by little, she could see anguish rise within them. And, finally, shame."[96] "After her crime, Gallet's love was for Germaine another secret, another silent challenge. She had first thrown herself in the arms of the soulless cad, and now she clung to this other wreck. But the insubordinate child, with her unerring cunning, had quickly lanced this heart like an abscess. She did this, to be sure, both to take delight in evil and to enjoy a dangerous game: thus, she had turned a ridiculous puppet into a poisonous animal—known only to her, hatched only by her, like those chimæras that haunt adolescent vice. And in the end she came to cherish this creature as the very image and symbol of her own abasement. However, she was already becoming weary of this game."[97] Thus, the last act portrayed is but the expression of a hellish cruelty.[98]

In *Joy*, everything leads up to the rape of the virginal Chantal by the demonic Russian: the sexual crime, followed by the criminal's suicide, is a symbol of the most extreme manner in which the power of evil can violate the holy.[99] In *Ouine* we witness a series of sporadic assaults—barely more than resounding slaps—as the expression of hatred and triumphant power.[100] In the *New Mouchette*, the girl's rape by

---

[96] *Soleil*, 48.
[97] Ibid., 55.
[98] Ibid., 61.
[99] *Joie*, 309f.
[100] *Ouine*, 116.

the drunken bum is only a metaphor for her humiliation and hurt, for the elimination in her of every possible basis for love.[101] In *An Evil Dream*, we move emphatically into a deeper dimension of evil, in which all symbolic possibilities appear to have been left behind: here, the act of coition between Ganse and Simone is nothing but a grotesque and brutal boxing match.[102] The pleasure here indulged in can be heightened by the knowledge that the adultery stands in imminent danger of being discovered by the legitimate spouse,[103] and this in turn is a metaphor for the way evil affords joy by providing a dare. But the bed of love can also become a deathbed when a woman, while embracing her man and nestling him on her heart, "bewitches his rebellious look with her own and thus conquers all resistance" as, with the other hand, she prepares the gun.[104]

Fornication involves an intrinsic contradiction: that between sexual acts as a sign of love, on the one hand, and, on the other, sexual acts as the very opposite of the love they are supposed to express. This contradiction brings the country priest to his profound meditation on the connection, and perhaps even the identity, between fornication and *insanity*. Although the words of Saint Paul in 1 Corinthians 6:18–19 are not expressly quoted, they nevertheless provide the basis for this interpretation: "Shun fornication. Every other sin that a man can commit is outside the body; but the fornicator sins against his own body. Do you not know that your body is a shrine of the indwelling Holy Spirit, and the Spirit is God's gift to you? You do not belong to yourselves."[105] The young priest has a dark intuition that he has not lost his faith *because* the spirit of bodily impurity has not been able to subject him. Already as a child he had become familiar with the face of impurity, and the sight instilled anguish and terror in him, for he understood "that the mask of pleasure, once stripped of all hypocrisy, is nothing but the mask of anguish".[106] He is not prudish: as a child he had had to see too much. He is disposed to consider most sexual

---

[101] *Mouchette*, 86f.

[102] *Rêve*, 95.

[103] *Soleil*, 62.

[104] *Ouine*, 154–55.

[105] *New English Bible*.

[106] *Curé*, 140.

indulgence as trivial decadence; "but, just because there are harmless maniacs in the world, are we to deny the existence of dangerous madmen? . . . We do not understand lust any better than we understand insanity, and, without admitting it, society protects itself against both these things with the same sly fear, the same secret shame, and almost the same means. . . . What if insanity and lust were one and the same?"[107] Bernanos seeks proof for this in the secondary figure of the mayor of Fenouille, always lurking in the background. This man is a sexual psychopath who at the same time exhibits a furious yearning for purity, purification, and absolution. But such spiritual hunger is diseased because nothing can free it from itself, and, in the end, it leads to open madness. In a concluding scene we see the mayor running in pajamas through the streets of the town, fleeing the impurity that possesses his entire being and that has become intolerable.[108]

It cannot surprise if, behind the metaphor of the sexual act, another metaphor now emerges in Bernanos: that of *homosexuality*. Throughout his entire work this theme is only a symbol, but an intrinsic and necessary one, since, for Bernanos, homosexuality is a kind of sacramental sign of evil. Here we see the reason for Bernanos' unceasing interior dialogue with Gide, who served as model or point of departure for Ouine. While he always speaks of Cocteau only with the greatest disdain,[109] Bernanos does not portray Gide as being the paragon of vice but rather recognizes his particular excellence when he calls him "a great writer, one of the greatest in [French] literature".[110] Nevertheless, he joins Claudel in sensing the demonic element in Gide: "In order to turn the Sermon on the Mount into a burning hymn to savagery,[111] all one has to do is interchange its terms by virtue of that diabolical inversion the secret of which the old Gide seems to run after, crawling on all fours from book to book as he sniffs the ground with his carnivorous snout."[112] Once again,

---

[107] Ibid., 141.
[108] *Ouine*, 108f., 183f., 199, 207.
[109] *Peur*, 43; To Amoroso Lima, April 1939, in: *Bul.* 15–16, 15.
[110] *Croix*, February 1, 1945, 479.
[111] Bernanos here has the more generic *sauvagerie*, which von Balthasar renders more specifically as *Raubtierdasein*, "the existence of a beast of prey".—TRANS.
[112] *Peur*, 194.

Bernanos is not at all interested in homosexual acts as such, so little interested, in fact, that he usually leaves open the question whether and how they have occurred. But there is no end to his fascination with the phenomenon of a perversion of love turned to one's own sex, which is to say, turned to one's own faculty of loving (if, indeed, the word "love" still has any meaning here). The center of concern is a relationship to self that reaches its ultimate consequences in the figure of Ouine.

In the boy Philippe, Ouine sees his own youth, and it is this he craves with all his soul. At one point he says: "I have just seen myself again like a dead man looks at his past. . . . I have seen the little boy I once was—I could have touched him, heard him."[113] Ouine's inversion is at bottom metaphysical: "To go back into oneself is not a game, my boy. It wouldn't have cost me more to go back into the womb that made me. I've literally turned myself inside out. I've made my inside to be my outside. I've turned myself inside out like a glove."[114] What Ouine is here bent on is self-encounter in the other as in a mirror.[115] Thus, it is difficult to understand from a psychological standpoint, but quite normal from a metaphysical, when so complex a being as Philippe looks back at him from that mirror as someone sexually cruel, cold to the marrow of his bones, and nevertheless capable of a "shapeless compassion as voracious as hatred and ready to burst into tears".[116]

The relationship between the two young men in *An Evil Dream* goes beyond the dimension of normal love. As each recognizes the other in his solitude, we see that their relationship is of the same sort as that between Ouine and Philippe: "He softly slipped his arm under his companion's, and for a moment they remained pressing each other close in the window's pale light."[117]

But homosexuality as a metaphor for metaphysical perversity may best be evidenced in Bernanos in his portrayal of women. The full *gestalt* of inversion is developed in the relationship between Michelle and Daisy in *Ouine* and especially in that between Evangeline and her friend in *A Crime*. From the total concealment of this origin de-

---

[113] *Ouine*, 87.
[114] Ibid., 244.
[115] Ibid., 218.
[116] Ibid., 26.
[117] *Rêve*, 33.

rives the equally concealed crime, the eventual discovery of which points back to this source. The similarity of traits points the groping judge on his way to the truth: with rigorous logic, he is continually grazing the secret of the perversion, but he cannot quite unmask it. This similarity of traits in the end points to a similarity of sins: "You won't refuse to admit that, between individuals who are more or less bonded by the same secret and the same lies, there can exist a certain resemblance—what plain folk call 'a family likeness'."[118] In his fever-induced delirium, the judge sees moiling before him a confusion of faces, which "resemble one another by their vaguely unfinished and ambiguous appearance. The women's faces are too tense, too harsh, almost virile. That of the priest from Mégère[119] bears the traces of melancholy, a sort of pathetic sadness the reflection of which he had seen again—not without a certain uneasiness—on the passionate and feminine face of the altar boy."[120] This whole plot, quite incredible from the standpoint of the novel, is for Bernanos nothing but the portrayal, perceivable by the senses, of the "incredible perversity"[121] of the essence and condition of sin.

We can here also note in passing the significance of *morphine* as a metaphor in Bernanos' works. The taking of morphine is the quasi-sacramental act whereby man's divine hope for grace is rejected and substituted for with a self-reliant act of violence that wants to take by storm an Eden that nonetheless remains inaccessible. It is symbolic of the fact that the sinner has given up the quest for the reality lying beyond the present life's dreamlike existence, replacing it with the addiction to a willful dream of pleasure. Involved here is the flight from the ghastly boredom of Godlessness into an "artificial paradise".[122] Concerning Madame Alfieri, Bernanos assures us that, "long before drugs, lying had been for her a marvelous form of escape, a sort of relaxation that always did the trick: repose, oblivion. . . . She was one of those

---

[118] *Crime*, 197.

[119] This is actually the sham "priest", who is the murderous Lesbian in disguise.—Note of the French trans.

[120] *Crime*, 148.

[121] Ibid., 147.

[122] In the last two sentences, von Balthasar has a play on words involving *Suche* (quest, search), *Sucht* (mania, addiction), and *Flucht* (flight, escape), verbal transmutations that correspond to the metaphysical process described.—TRANS.

people—more numerous than we think—who love lying for its own sake and employ it with profound subtlety and lucidness. Such people really value lying only when it succeeds in commingling true and false in so thorough a fashion that they become as one, having a life of their own and creating another life within the given life."[123] Hope is a heroic act; in its place sinners put illusion, "which is just as much a poison as heroine and morphine, and for the same reasons".[124]

Bernanos himself always refused to have morphine or any other strong pain-killer administered to him, both in the period after his accident, when he underwent such excruciating pain,[125] and on his deathbed.[126] He had to be given injections while he slept. In *Joy*, Fiodor and La Pérouse are morphine addicts.[127] In the *Country Priest*, it is again the doctor, Lavigne, who uses the poison as a substitute for faith and prayer.[128] Madame Dargent has recourse to it,[129] as do Evangeline's murderous friend in *A Crime*[130] and Madame Louise in the same novel.[131] Madame Alfieri, in *An Evil Dream*, is herself an addict,[132] and at one point, without saying a word, she hands the young Mainville "the mock golden tinderbox, . . . filled with a white powder".[133] Her plan to pervert him succeeds so well that later on it is she who will say to him: "It's not right for you to overdo drugs in this way, poor little sweetheart!"[134] Likewise in *An Evil Dream*, Doctor Lipotte sees in the drug a means of fighting off the chill of a new "Glacial Age". He indulges in it because he "is afraid of death".[135] The needle that breaks in Simone's hands as she is injecting herself so as to find the courage to commit her crime[136] is a metaphor for the uselessness of this lifelong lie and for the ineradicable contradiction inherent in perversity.

It is an inescapable fact that the kingdom of lies receives most consistent symbolic portrayal in Bernanos through the figure and actions of *women*. To be sure, we do find in him the most dazzling portrayals

---

[123] *Rêve*, 193.
[124] *Croix*, May 15, 1945, 494.
[125] *To Vallery-Radot*, November 1933; *Bul*. 9, 2.
[126] Pézeril, *C. du R.*, 354.
[127] *Joie*, 17, 197.
[128] *Curé*, 288, 291.
[129] *Nouvelles* (Plon ed.), 8.

[130] *Crime*, 94.
[131] Ibid., 174.
[132] *Rêve*, 200.
[133] Ibid., 48.
[134] Ibid., 142.
[135] Ibid., 116–17.
[136] Ibid., 237.

of feminine sanctity (Joan of Arc, Chantal) and the most penetrating representations of masculine infamy (Cénabre, Ouine). Nevertheless, the first great symbol Bernanos creates stands there permanently with a kind of finality: this is Mouchette, the "bride of hell", who so dramatically contrasts with the sanctity of the priest Donissan. Cénabre is chosen for this because he is a priest, and moreover Bernanos always stressed the feminine side of priests. Ouine is chosen because he is a pederast and hence is playing a feminine role, something underscored by his total passivity. The respective heroines of *A Crime* and *An Evil Dream*—to whom we must add so strong a figure as Jambe-de-Laine—attain to such fantastic density of evil only because they are women. And the second Mouchette—despite all other differences— by no means lags behind the first in her capacity to be attracted by the suctioning power of the abyss. The old woman keeping wake for the dead in this same story is in reality a vampire. Michelle, in *Monsieur Ouine*, despite all her "sweetness", is the very embodiment of pure egotism, even with regard to her own son.[137] As C.-E. Magny has rightly pointed out, she is at bottom the one who keeps the absent father (an image of God) far from their son's life. In the *Country Priest*, all the demonic elements the priest encounters are found exclusively in women: in the young girl Séraphita; in the taciturn Mademoiselle Louise, who triggers the tragedy at the end; in the countess who is in revolt against God; and, finally, in her daughter Chantal, equally in revolt and always brushing against the demonic. The defrocked priest Dufréty is more pitiful than evil.

The initial symbolic pairing of Mouchette and Donissan remains normative: Simone had been a priest's mistress,[138] and her story concludes with her encounter in the street with an unknown priest to whom she will presumably make her confession. The very center of *The Diary of a Country Priest* is the scene between the priest and the countess, and this scene provides something like a spinal column to a book that would otherwise consist of loose anecdotes. In the early novella *A Night*, there is a character who rounds off this panorama: the mulatto sorceress Bisbillita, who is placed between the two men as these produce a parody of the grace of baptism. She too is a murderess.

---

[137] *Ouine*, 9.
[138] *Rêve*, 228.

Must we then conclude that Bernanos is at base a misogynist? Such a conclusion would be unthinkable. The only other possibility for his representation of women is the symbolic character of his language. The ministerial priesthood has been reserved for the man, and, hence, it is he who is the representative of the Church and of the Kingdom of Heaven. He must therefore exhibit before the world the face of a humility that serves but also of a manly conviction always ready for battle. Only exceptionally, deep in the background, do we now and then see the shimmer of the Church's feminine, Marian countenance. The nether abyss with which this Church stands in dialogue —or rather, struggles—is feminine. This abyss is man's undoing: it sucks him in, never again to release him. It is a promise that "cannot be kept".[139] It is a hope for love that is actually a mirage and a *maya* of love, perhaps even the quintessence of arrogance, as the protagonist of *Conversation among Shadows* says of herself: Françoise defies all the rules of love and refuses to get married, but she begs the man she loves to take her as a mistress. Primal pride occupies in her a place deeper than loving self-surrender. Self-surrender is the act of an individual person, while pride is impersonal and generic, and Françoise has it in her blood from her father and a whole line of forebears. Her pride is something stronger than she: "How could I have hoped to liquidate a pride whose roots are not in me?"[140] The sexual gesture that clamps a person frightfully as in a vise, pulling him into itself, receives in Bernanos the names of "embrace" and "espousal": Mouchette is the demon's "beloved",[141] and "their nuptials were enacted in silence."[142] But, in his coarse humility, it never occurred to Bernanos to symbolize the soul's union with God using such bridal imagery, not in the context of Chantal's very intimate mystical experiences in *Joy*, which naturally lent itself to this, nor in the quasi-official mystical language of the Carmelites, characterized by a cool liturgical restraint that addresses God as "His Majesty".[143]

---

[139] *Dialogue d'ombres* (Plon ed.), 108.
[140] Ibid., 138.
[141] *Soleil*, 59, 201, 217ff.
[142] Ibid., 221.
[143] *Carmélites*, 220.

Sin is the pretense of love where there is no love, the evocation of rapture (as through morphine) where there is no rapture, and simple perversion (as in homosexuality). Through all these modalities and metaphors, sin is a relationship that turns backward on itself, "self-love" in the sense of a refusal of genuine love, and therefore a *self-consuming hunger*. This is so much the case that, in Bernanos, the most "advanced" sinners are the ones who have already left love, sensuality, and sex behind in order to withdraw completely into the mysteries of the self, which in this instance are mysteries and pleasures of contempt, shame, and especially repulsion and tedium. Thus, Simone can confess the following to Olivier after Philippe's suicide:

> We are wretches, you and I. We are outside this world. I don't ask you to love me. But what binds me to you is something much stronger than love. . . . Before meeting you I felt I was no longer alive. To feel no longer alive is the thing that crushes me! . . . I have never loved anyone with real love. Neither my heart nor my senses—no power on earth shall ever tear me from myself and make me the thing of another, all happy and fulfilled. How many women are like me, women who will never yield to anyone! . . . My solitude does not frighten me; it puts me to shame. It puts me to shame because I never wanted it, and I often seem to myself to be merely enduring it. . . . *If I could only prove to myself—prove to myself once again, one final time*—that the heart can grow silent and the senses can fail, *that I can bring about in my soul's very silence and with nothing but my will what others (who are called "lost women" and who were only poor creatures in love) accomplished through frenzied mania and sheer madness!*

To which Olivier replies: "In other words, you want to love as Philippe killed himself, in the same manner and for the same reason. . . . At bottom this is what in another age would have been called 'sins of the spirit'. There is no remission for such sins, my dear. These are dazzling sins, the sins of angels. . . . All I am in your life is an occasion, a pretext."[144]

We here again encounter the concept that what is interior is greater than its expression, that the thought is greater than the deed it produces.[145] What this implies is that sin becomes weakened by its sense-

---

[144] *Rêve*, 154–55. (The italics are von Balthasar's.—TRANS.)
[145] Ibid., 89, 90, 183, 187, 189.

perceptible expression, in comparison with the "deliriums of pride"[146] raging in a soul alone with itself. As Simone says, what is involved is by no means a mere "crime in thought only", but rather "a true crime —well constructed, keenly alive, with all its proper parts". When Ganse asks her if the "baby-crime" is kicking yet, the future murderess replies: "If you put your hand on the right spot, you'll feel its heartbeat."[147]

Mention must be made here of one last metaphor. It is only an image, but an indispensable one. We speak, not of onanism, which could easily have been expected in this context if Bernanos did not harbor such disdain and lack of interest for this infantile vice: rather, we speak of *suicide*. Suicide is not significant for Bernanos as the despairing deed of a person who has been overwhelmed by a destiny extrinsic to himself and who can therefore not find a way out of this dead end. The importance of suicide, rather, lies in the way it incarnates the magnetic power of the abyss, that "suction by the void"[148] and long-premeditated attack upon Being that constitute so mysterious a process that Bernanos speaks of a particular "predestination" to suicide and even of its own unique "charism". "Not just anyone can commit suicide", he observes;[149] "not everyone who feels like it can kill himself."[150] "The penchant for suicide is a talent, something like a sixth sense: you're born with it."[151] By no means is this taste for suicide a sign that the person does not fear death; on the contrary, "the void fascinates those who do not dare to look it in the face. They hurl themselves into it for fear of simply falling."[152] The act of suicide owes its fascination precisely to the fact that it lacks all reason and foundation. In *An Evil Dream*, Philippe commits suicide for no other reason than its being *the* senseless act par excellence,[153] and his friend Olivier wants to imitate him.[154]

What suicide represents for Bernanos is a universal phenomenon:

Mankind is afraid of itself, afraid of its own shadow, afraid of its hands on the table, afraid of the half-opened drawer where the pistol's well-oiled barrel shines softly. When voluntarily—and, as it would seem, inevitably

---

[146] Ibid., 157.
[147] Ibid., 89–90.
[148] *Joie*, 158.
[149] *Cimetières*, 240.
[150] *Curé*, 185.

[151] Ibid., 292.
[152] Ibid., 174.
[153] *Rêve*, 38, 112f.
[154] Ibid., 157.

—mankind gradually begins to restrict its own inherited liberty, it may claim that what it is doing is sacrificing freedom for the sake of future happiness; but don't for one moment believe it! In this case, mankind is sacrificing its liberty to the fear it has of itself. It is like someone obsessed with the idea of suicide who, when he must remain alone in his room at night, first has himself tied to his bed so as not to be tempted to turn on the gas.[155]

According to La Pérouse, the psychiatrist in *Joy*, "suicide is, of all obsessions, the easiest one to detect",[156] and his hunch proves right in connection with Fiodor. But this assault on the self is secretly present as the basis of every sin. We already see this with Mouchette: "One night, by an irremediable stroke, she had killed not only the harmless marquis but her own deceitful image as well."[157] The murder Madame Alfieri commits may even be said to be a calculated suicide as well: "A murder that is premeditated, long in the hatching, carried out in cold blood, and undertaken without remorse achieves, in the most precise possible manner, a total and definitive rupture with human society and its detested order. It is a form of suicide."[158] There can be other causes of suicide, even honorable ones, as in the case of Doctor Delbende, who could not accept the God-established order of the world but who belonged to the race of the "upright" who "hate the mediocre".[159]

Nor is the second Mouchette, either, the very picture of sin; rather, as she is drawn by the bottomless pit and disappears into it in the end, she embodies an inescapable misery. She, too, belongs to the elect of the abyss, although differently from Delbende: "The gesture of suicide really terrifies only those who are not tempted—and doubtless will never be tempted—to undertake it, because the black abyss welcomes only the predestined. A person who already possesses a murderous will still ignores this fact and will become aware of it only at the last minute."[160] The truly suicidal are those who are plotting an attack on Being itself. One of these is the mayor of Fenouille, whose flight into insanity is an attack on himself: "In my opinion,

---

[155] *Liberté*, 215–16. See also his reflections on the suicide of Stefan Zweig, in: *Croix*, February 1942, 195.

[156] *Joie*, 197.

[157] *Soleil*, 53.

[158] *Rêve*, 245.

[159] *Curé*, 134.

[160] *Mouchette*, 220.

a madman is a person who exits his house, locks the door behind him, and throws the key away into the cistern, . . . a person who has cursed himself, denied himself, and even spit on himself!" To which the priest of the "dead parish" adds: "Of all hatreds, hatred of self is probably the one for which no forgiveness is possible."[161]

It is to this center that all of those suicidal states of mind point —concentrically, as it were—that Bernanos exposes and forces the reader to see. In the first place we have *ennui*, the "acedia" of the ancients that may also be described as weariness of life, terminal boredom, absence of every healthy strain.[162] Secretly bound up with such tedium are the *greed* that lurks behind all sensuality,[163] *contempt* for others,[164] the *disgust* so often mentioned by Bernanos and about which the mayor of Fenouille says that it "resembles death", or, more precisely, the feelings a corpse might have while it rots "in its coffin, while up above life goes on as usual".[165] Finally, there is the *indifference* that is the quintessence of Ouine and impresses us as an anticipation of Sartre. Extreme, borderline experiences always have something "supernatural" about them, and this is why hell's adepts can frequently be taken to be religious, priestly, and mystical personalities.[166] Indeed, in his portrayal of Cénabre and Simone, Bernanos even sees clear connections between the extraordinary vocation to sanctity and the failure of the same, which inevitably leads into the satanic realm. Hence, the suspicion begins to dawn that the whole attack upon Being that constitutes evil bears such sacral traits only because it is the (useless) attack upon an all-encompassing supernatural mystery of purity and grace. As the Curé de Fenouille says to the local doctor: it is possible that one day warped analytical methods will have triumphed over all Christian common sense, and the faith instinct itself will have been destroyed, and mankind will flatter itself for having abolished the "fundamental contradiction" in human na-

---

[161] *Ouine*, 203.
[162] *Soleil*, 54f., 208f.; *Joie*, 163; *Curé*, 9f.; *Ouine*, 118, 192 (to which must be added the significant text that appears only in *Bul.* 11, 13: "It all began with boredom. Boredom descended upon them, melted over them"); *Rêve*, 63, 65, 132, 166; and passim.
[163] *Crime*, 117.
[164] *Joie*, 230.
[165] *Ouine*, 199.
[166] Simone Alfieri, for instance, is "a peculiar sort of saint", "a sad saint", and "she is taken for a mystic" (*Rêve*, 24, 64, and 117, respectively).

ture. When all of this will have come to pass, there will still survive something in the deepest and most unconscious core of nature and its memory that will perhaps be felt only as a dull, poisonous goad: "The love of purity: this is the real mystery! The love of it in those who are most noble and, in the others, sadness, regret, an indefinable and piercing bitterness that is dearer to the dissolute than their very uncleanness."[167] Is grace thus in the end to extract a new meaning and value from the revolt of sin? Is the will to evil and contradiction in this way to become a prisoner of God's even greater will and verdict? Are perdition and damnation thus to become a function of redemption?

2. Physicians of Souls

Evil is a great No! uttered against God. But, at the same time, the No! is a denial of this God. The question, therefore, is whether the abolition of evil requires the restoration of God or not. The therapy of evil itself confronts the frightful decision for or against God. We must choose between one of two radically opposed courses of action: Will we seek to fortify the patient fully in his No! to God (since he is right, after all: there *is* no God) and thus help him come to full harmony with himself? Or will we seek to wrest his No! from him and lead him back to God? Two different therapists, therefore, offer their services to the sinner: the physician as analyst and the priest as confessor. The first of these attempts to transcend the sphere of guilt by "dissolving" it (the literal meaning of "analysis" in Greek): he transforms so-called "guilt" into a transparency for a deeper and more valid psychic reality and thus makes it vanish. The second of these, moreover, also transcends the sphere of guilt, but by making his own person, by virtue of the sacrament of holy orders, into an instrument for the divine judgment over the guilt. This occurs within that other sacramental event, confession, in which the sinner encounters the judgment of mercy with full ecclesial and existential concreteness.

Bernanos' decision, of course, goes for the second of these alternatives; but to the end he must still wrestle with the figure of the analyst. For the spiritual world in which his characters move is the world of modern unbelief, and this world for the most part has no

---

[167] *Ouine*, 208.

direct access to sacrament. The analyst has installed himself within the modern world as the precise form of help it requires—he who in fact is nothing but the faithful mirror of its spirit. The gallery of doctors we encounter in Bernanos' work testifies to his earnest desire to be just: La Pérouse (in *Joy*), Malépine (in *Ouine*), Delbende and Lavigne (in the *Country Priest*), Lipotte (in *An Evil Dream*), and the physicians in *A Crime* and *Dialogues of the Carmelites*. These are all courageous men, precisely because they are willing to become prisoners of the same "damnation" as their patients, in order to understand them better from within. Nevertheless, despite their courage, they are also men in despair. Delbende is a soulmate of the Curé de Torcy and of the little country priest: "Torcy," the doctor once exclaims, "you and I belong to the same race of men. . . , the race of those who die standing."[168] He is someone who "faces what he must" and who tells Torcy to his face: "Come on, now! Admit that you would hold out whether paradise existed or not!"[169] Nevertheless, in the end Delbende commits suicide.[170] Lavigne is someone destined for death.[171] Instead of praying, something that he as an atheist cannot do, he injects himself with morphine in order "to kill in little installments" his "rage to learn", that "curiosity", or *libido sciendi*, that afflicts all of Bernanos' unbelieving heroes.[172] Lavigne possesses the "taste for suicide, which is a talent, a sixth sense". But he is a decent and honest man despite all his cynicism, and he tells the country priest the truth of his condition.

La Pérouse and Lipotte are the theoreticians of cynicism. The first of these develops a full-blown theory of analysis[173] in which health

---

[168] *Curé*, 93.

[169] Ibid., 94. (An important textual nuance, evident only in the French, here reënforces the spiritual kinship and intimacy growing between priest and doctor. Even though on the previous page Delbende was still addressing Torcy with the formal *vous* ["Torcy, vous et moi, nous sommes de la même race"], now he suddenly switches to the familiar *tu* ["Conviens donc que tu tiendrais le coup, avec ou sans paradis"]—TRANS.)

[170] Ibid., 128f.

[171] Ibid., 293.

[172] Ibid., 292.

[173] *Joie*, 171, 192. The original text of this chapter was twice as long as what Bernanos finally gave the printer. The parts edited out were subsequently published by Albert Béguin in *Esprit* (December 1952, 949–63). Here we find a number of explications and applications of the theory of inhibition; an explicit identification of the "flight into illness" with the "flight into God" (949–50); a cynical analysis of the case of Clergerie, who transferred to

becomes a "hypothesis" and indeed a "chimæra", and life as a whole becomes an "abject secretion" and a "disease of nothingness".[174] The "little violence" at the center of his treatment aims at leading the patient in the end to a total disillusionment with the existence of any value whatever. Chantal, the young woman filled with God, can only be a scandal to him: she must be subjected to treatment.[175] But Bernanos unmasks this pseudoscientific apparatus. Despite "its costly and deceptive bibliographical arsenal, its tables, its schemas and statistics", the whole construction is doubtless the product of "the ruminations of a timid and fantastic adolescent imagination, incapable of overcoming the terrors, desires, and loathings of puberty".[176] This insight humbles La Pérouse, and in the end he must face the truth that there exists a genuine, Christian form of analysis such as Chantal attempts with her old grandmother.[177] For, despite all his cynicism, La Pérouse is a seeker: "I have spent my life", he avers, "searching for pure wellsprings, and it seems to me that I can scent their presence through the world, through people. . . . What have we to learn from our patients, I ask you? Almost nothing. All our results are vitiated. Nine times out of ten the pretense is evident, and even the most incisive interrogation succeeds in isolating the lie."[178]

Lipotte is in a situation similar to that of La Pérouse; but, while the latter is attempting to beset a genuine mystic, Lipotte has to deal with a case of genuine demonic possession, a woman who evades his competence in the opposite direction.[179] While the subject La Pérouse has to analyze is a mere weakling, Lipotte confronts Ganse, someone superior to himself. Nevertheless both Ganse, the future member of the Academy, and Clergerie, the old novelist, are at the end of their rope, something their sudden burst of tears makes clear enough. Both of them are driven to their end by their immediate environment but

---

his daughter Chantal his love for his dead wife, all the while being jealous of Chantal on account of her superiority; finally, certain remarks on the relationship between poetry and sexuality (955). In 1954 the "Club du Meilleur Livre" published a complete critical edition restoring all the texts to their original place in the chapter.

[174] *Joie*, 181–82.
[175] Ibid., 186.
[176] Ibid., 173.
[177] Ibid., 214f.
[178] Ibid., 185–86.
[179] *Rêve*, 47.

also by an invisible wound deep in their interior. While pointing out to Clergerie the benefits of psychoanalysis (it "cleans out not only the conscious but also the unconscious"), La Pérouse must also admit "the benefits of confession in the form that the Catholic Church proposes to her faithful".[180] By contrast, Lipotte can only jest concerning the traditional examination of conscience, a practice that a "miserable canon" has recommended to Ganse "as a remedy for all [his] ills". How could he possibly recognize under all its improbable masks "a bad childhood dream that has been long forgotten"?[181] Only the analyst can "put his hand on the precise spot, at the very root of the ill"[182] that the patient "doggedly protects, almost without realizing it, as if it were dearer than life".[183] And yet, Lipotte himself is a morphine addict and the prey of "an abject fear of death",[184] and he openly admits that man's worst enemy is *la honte*, "shame": "Cynicism is only a deviation, a deformation of the feeling of shame, in the same way that a certain form of impiety is a caricature of true devotion."[185] A certain "residue of shame" is the poisonous dregs of a Christianity in the process of dissolution, and it is such a residue that has determined the quality of the spiritual life of the generation to which he too belongs.[186] He has played the part of a scurrilous priest who goes about gathering up and taking in the psychopaths who, in former times, used to find their shelter with confessor priests, under the Church's protection.[187]

Finally, we have Malépine, who, together with the Curé de Fenouille, faces the most difficult of all analyses: that of the "dead parish", in which all events, even the most frightening, are but symptoms of a hidden disease. His "frightful solicitude weaves its magical threads around the mayor".[188] He sees that a crime has been commit-

---

[180] *Joie*, 179.

[181] *Rêve*, 108.

[182] "Ill" here translates the French noun *le mal*, which can refer both to the theological concept of "evil" and to a medical "illness" or "disease". In the present context, it is noteworthy that the translator must select the medical, rather than the theological, nuance to refer to an affliction of the soul as diagnosed by the positivist Doctor Lipotte.—TRANS.

[183] *Rêve*, 110.

[184] Ibid., 105.

[185] Ibid., 110.

[186] Ibid., 115.

[187] Ibid., 119.

[188] *Ouine*, 57.

ted. He also sees that the mayor's illness, which is a manifestation of the general guilt of the community, "is the priest's concern as much as the doctor's".[189] However, he must also listen as the priest tells him the harshest truths: for instance, that he and his science "have sealed up the name of God in the hearts of the poor", and that all of the spirit's subterranean ills—"the poisoning of reason, the inversion of the instincts"—must be traced back to this banishment of God and of the longing for God in present-day humanity. The priest's idea that "the three theological virtues" can pass over "from the invisible world into the visible world, transformed into malignant tumors" Malépine finds to be both comical and insane;[190] but the priest, unshaken, presses his point as the doctor accuses him of being a dangerous fanatic, and he challenges Malépine with the words: "We have left the miserable man in your hands long enough!"[191]

The next conversation between doctor and priest concerning their patient clarifies the theme of the debate even more: What is the meaning of insanity?[192] "Today's priests", notes the doctor, gloating, "quite gladly turn over to us for observation people with certain mental conditions that formerly would willy-nilly have been taken to be instances of mystical states."[193] The priest does not deny this; but he is convinced "that a certain impoverishment of the religious sense could become manifested in pathological phenomena that could go as far as effecting a profound transformation of the species".[194] As far as Malépine is concerned, the mayor suffers from nothing but a banal sexual obsession. But what the priest discovers in the mayor instead are the final causes of a process that, even though it could be dressed up in medical categories, nevertheless in reality is nothing less than a self-consuming longing for purity, the nostalgia for "what we call, by its true name, the primeval paradise on earth, the yearning for lost joy",[195] for God. The doctor is right in a superficial sort of way—in the foreground, as it were; but, because he cannot see the background, which is the all-decisive factor, he is in reality totally wrong.

---

[189] Ibid., 185.
[190] Ibid., 189.
[191] Ibid., 190.
[192] Ibid., 204–10.
[193] Ibid., 205.
[194] Ibid., 207.
[195] Ibid., 209.

And the mayor himself discovers the sources of his madness: it is that *he* can no longer abide being with himself, with his sin, and that *he* everywhere smells the disintegration and putrefaction of his own being, using for this a nose abnormally enlarged by herpes. The only door left open to him is insanity.[196]

In another context—the first, unsuccessful project to film the *Country Priest*—Bernanos provided the most precise commentary on this entire process: "For modern man, who suffers from such nervous exhaustion, evil is not a revolt but an escape, a way for man to rest by 'distracting' himself (from *distrahere*: 'to disperse' or 'squander'), a way for him to get out of himself and into the open, a method, alas, for man to strip himself of his person, just as a snake sheds its skin."[197] In the old grandmother in *Joy*, Bernanos had already described this voluntary flight into the kingdom of insanity.[198] Chantal sees through the fictitious character of her grandmother's madness. She comes to understand the connection between the illness and the woman's feelings of guilt, and this finally leads to her insight into the diseased nature of all sin and sinners.[199] Because she knows this, Chantal can undertake truly effective "analysis", just as the country priest can extract the truth through "analysis" out of his parishioners' souls in revolt by virtue of his naïve, unreflected, but very accurate knowledge of human nature. Despite the mockery of the doctors, the sentence from *The Imposture* retains its full truth for Bernanos:

> Examination of conscience is a profitable exercise, even for those who profess amorality. It defines our remorses, names them by their true name, and in this way holds them in the soul as in a closed jar, under the light of the spirit. If you do nothing but repress them, you should fear giving them real consistency and fleshly weight. We prefer to suffer in the darkness of ignorance rather than having to blush for shame. You have introduced sin into the dullness and density of your flesh, and the monster . . . will grow splendidly fat on your blood. He will feed on you like a cancer—clinging to you with unabating diligence, allowing you to live as you please, going and coming, seemingly healthy as ever, only somewhat uneasy. You'll go on in this way, growing secretly in your

---

[196] Ibid., 203.

[197] Interview in *Samedi-Soir*, November 8, 1947; *Bul.* 7–8, 4.

[198] Unfortunately, the most significant page in this connection was cut by the author; but it may be found in *Bul.* 12–13, 2–3.

[199] *Joie*, 209–10.

separation from others and from yourself, your soul and body split by
an essential divorce, existing in a state of lethargy that will be suddenly
routed by the thunderclap of an anguish that is the hideous bodily form
of remorse. You'll awaken in the midst of a despair that no repentance
can redeem because, at that very instant, your soul will have expired.[200]

Bernanos by no means underestimated the importance of doctors. He
himself sought treatment for his states of anxiety. He made a gift of
the manuscript of *Joy* to Doctor Lafitte, a friend in the medical profession. In Brazil he met Jorge de Lima, whom he admired both as
a doctor and as a writer and whose medical help he requested in his
frequent bouts of anxiety. On the one hand, Bernanos sees the partial
competence enjoyed by the doctor, especially when he is a Christian
who recognizes the deeper competence of the priest and the sacrament
of confession. On the other hand, he sees how the doctor has become
the priest of the unbelieving soul. "He's the parish priest of the re-
publicans", he writes.[201] And at one point Gallet says to Mouchette:
"You're speaking to a friend, to a father confessor."[202] Doctors' offices are the modern confessionals.[203] But this is where Bernanos'
distrust begins to set in: "The best psychological hypotheses"[204] do
not penetrate to the depths that alone matter. "You approach man
with your techniques, your statistics, your tests, and every possible
instrument for psychological measurement, just as other technicians
approach a poem by Baudelaire." But all these "vivisectors" with
their "reddened hands" are incapable of helping anyone understand
the wonder of one single soul.[205]

Seen from the outside, confession appears to be a somewhat anti-
quated but reliable form for the analysis of the soul. The old writer in
Under Satan's Sun who is a caricature of Anatole France asks himself,
while in the little church of Lumbres, why he should not himself try
out this "method of psychotherapy". For, after all is said and done, "is
a professor in his clinic doing anything different from what a simple

---

[200] *Imposture*, 28–29.
[201] *Soleil*, 21. (In a French context, the political term "republican" must be understood as
the opposite of "monarchist".—TRANS.)
[202] Ibid., 78.
[203] *Rêve*, 119.
[204] *Soleil*, 38.
[205] *Liberté*, 152–53.

priest does in the confessional: provoke self-revelations, elicit confi-
dences, so as then to influence at leisure by suggestion a patient who
has been soothed and released from tension?"[206] In *Joy*, too, Bernanos
claims that Sigmund Freud discovered nothing new, since this whole
world of illusions—precisely in the region where soul and body meet
—was thoroughly familiar to the old mystics of the Middle Ages.[207]
Certain laws do, of course, govern the relationships among members
of the same family, and Bernanos did not shy away from applying such
laws, for instance, in the *Country Priest* (Chantal and her father)[208] and
in *Monsieur Ouine* (Michelle and her son). But he insists that Freud's
"Taylorized medicine"[209] can at base understand nothing of what it
denies. Gallet has no inkling about the depths of Germaine's demonic
immersion,[210] any more than La Pérouse understands the sublimity
of Chantal's mystical experiences. Bernanos does not hesitate to use
certain narrow concepts from Freud's referential universe; as he does
so, however, he endows them with their true proportion and import.
For him, "a true novelist" is one "who has truly dreamed his book,
or who has drawn most of its situations and characters from the storehouse of his subconscious experiences: here are kept those precious,
irreplaceable, and incommunicable experiences of childhood that the
crisis of adolescence almost always plunges again into the night."[211]
This world of childhood, however, like the world of the death agony,
is sheer existence in grace before God and, hence, superior to every
form of psychology; and it is from the standpoint of childhood and
the death agony—these two extremes of life—that a human life is to
be interpreted, so that no psychology whatever can understand man
correctly and no doctor can substitute for the priest and father confessor.

Mouchette is released from a medical clinic "fully cured",[212] and
yet she is still in full possession of her demon: only Donissan the
priest will be able to free her from it in a violent struggle with the
fiend. Similarly, Chevance fell out of favor with his bishop for having

---

[206] *Soleil*, 356.
[207] *Joie*, 65.
[208] *Curé*, 171.
[209] *To Fernandez*, 1936; *Bul.* 1, 6.
[210] *Soleil*, 59.
[211] Interview in *Samedi-Soir*, November 8, 1947; *Bul.* 7–8, 2.
[212] *Soleil*, 82.

very naïvely exorcised a possessed woman who had three times spent long periods in insane asylums and had come out of them only more frantic. The doctor had diagnosed her imminent death, but the exorcism cured her.[213] The fact that in our time it is the psychiatrists who have an exclusive hold on the interior life of so many people[214] becomes the suspicious caricature of sacramental confession. The definitive judgment that psychology pretends to pass on genuine mysticism, the very feasibility of approaching the mystical dimension with the categories of analysis: these things are part and parcel of the form of the crucified servant assumed by the experience of God in Christianity.[215] And La Pérouse does not hesitate almost to equate the ideal analyst with that most delicate and hidden of mysteries—the true priest: "What composure is required! What purity of intention! What pureness! Yes, what pureness! One would need the simultaneous genius of both sexes—the power of the one, the modesty and delicacy of the other, a kind of androgyny: my dream!"[216] Here we have something like a caricature of what places the priest above all sexual distinction, or, if one prefers, a caricature of the priest's "femininity", which we call such, not on account of celibacy, but because he represents the Church, which is always feminine.[217]

The state of a soul that has been "sealed shut" by the "fundamental lie" can be broken open only by confession, which is what Simone's dilapidated soul yearns after whether she knows it or not.[218] Even in the context of psychoanalysis and its revelations, "only a certain form of sacramental humility" can come to terms with the ever-new perversions of which pride is capable. Arsène, in *Monsieur Ouine*, is the other example of this. When he indulges in a pathological confession of sins at the grave of the murdered child, before the whole community—a reminiscence of Caux[219]—the scene evokes the true image of confession, but as in a distorting mirror.[220] But Bernanos

---

[213] *Imposture*, 39–40.

[214] *Robots*, 209–10.

[215] *Soleil*, 246f., 283, 305.

[216] *Joie*, 188–89.

[217] *Soleil*, 224; *Curé*, 89; *Crime*, 94.

[218] *Rêve*, 227.

[219] Von Balthasar here alludes to certain methods of public confession practiced by the Moral Rearmament Movement, adopted in turn from the Oxford Movement.—Note of the French trans.

[220] *Ouine*, 173–74.

prefers this confession, vainly shouted into the wind, to dressing up the dilemma "scientifically" through psychoanalysis. In this grotesque form, the shout of guilt can be more easily understood and taken up by the divine mercy, just as the disconsolate cry of the half-breed in *A Night* for a baptism he will never receive[221] is more significant for Bernanos than the sterile and inconsequential baptism of so many nominal Christians. Indeed, Arsène refuses a possible absolution by the parish priest because it arrives too late, when everything is already frozen into an eternal doom; and yet this is preferable for Bernanos to a mechanical bourgeois confession, since he is certain that that authentic cry from the depths of damnation must ascend to reach the ears of God.

It was not curiosity that made Bernanos wrestle so intensely with *the figure of the priest* in his novels but the necessity to understand this figure correctly: it is here, after all, that, according to God's will, the supernatural power of evil is brought to a halt and overcome by virtue of the power of absolution the priest receives from God. If the moralists were right with the image of man they have constructed, then the psychologists' methods would suffice, and vice versa. But the dimensions of evil as found by Bernanos in Christianity are beyond the reach of both moralists and psychologists. Let us listen to what Bernanos wrote in an unpublished document that was supposed to serve the publisher of *Joy* as an advertisement for the book:

> If the moralists accounted for all of man, such a book as this would make no sense. But, within their clever calculations, it is sin, and not guilt, that remains the irreducible element. "I am convinced", says Barbey d'Aurevilly, "that for certain souls happiness lies in hypocrisy and deceit." And Léon Bloy speaks magnificently of the "abominable glory of having left all human deceit behind in order to plunge into the hypocrisy of the Angels."—Neither the outpouring of love of neighbor nor the intuition of a fraternal heart can discover in each one of us the secret, reserved part where evil grows and feeds its root. On this point our reciprocal ignorance is profound. We can doubtless walk along for a long time in a merry company, but in the end each of us holds between his arms only his own lie, the one that fits him perfectly. One sins alone, just as one dies alone.—The fanfares of vice are for numskulls, but its

secret lament is heard only by very few people. Who could doubt that the worldview of the Curé d'Ars was more pathetic than any other? He was quite aware of the fact that evil is loved for its own sake, that hell too has its cloisters. To be sure, the dark Angel is rarely caught in action: he strikes and vanishes. . . . But there is another kind of slower and more careful work that clearly reveals his presence. The first symptom is remorse, his masterpiece, the cursed child of divine Love, no less full of desires than its parent, and also anguish, the hideous bodily form remorse assumes.[222]

Only the mystery of holy orders is capable of staring down this mystery of evil. The devil himself recognizes this when he comes up against Donissan, whom he demeans as an "anointed brute"[223] whose priestly unction has "chilled him to the bone".[224] The Curé de Luzarnes, who had shared in Donissan's horrible battle with the devil, exclaims at one point: "For the first time I seemed to peer through to the true goal of my life and the majesty of the priesthood."[225] For unbelievers, the priest remains an object of continual fascination,[226] and for all alike, including believers, he remains an object of distrust and hatred on account of the challenge his very existence poses, and both these things are intensified in proportion as a given priest fully lives his mission. When the count turns his back on the country priest, it is with the words: "Both your character and your habits appear to me to be a danger for the parish."[227] And this hatred has been increased to nearly demonic proportions by the fact that a priest is necessarily in disharmony with the unbelieving society in which he finds himself in our day. In *Monsieur Ouine* Bernanos attempts to elucidate this phenomenon:

Hatred of priests is one of the deepest sentiments in man, and also one of the least known. No one doubts the fact that this rancor is as old as the human race, but our present age has raised it to an almost prodigious degree of refinement and excellence. This is because, despite the priest's being in appearance so closely involved in social life, the decay or disappearance of other sources of power and authority have turned

[222] Published in *Bernanos*, 160–61.
[223] *Soleil*, 173, 179.
[224] Ibid., 169.
[225] Ibid., 291.
[226] *Rêve*, 225f.
[227] *Curé*, 214.

him into a very peculiar being, less classifiable than any of those magical old men whom the ancient world kept locked up like sacred animals in the innermost precincts of temples, where they enjoyed familiarity only with the gods. The modern priest is all the more peculiar precisely as he doesn't recognize this fact: he is almost always fooled by the crude appearances—the irony of some and the servile deference of others. But opposition to priests—an opposition that is less religious than political and that has long fed their pride—little by little becomes a sort of hostile indifference in the end. As this occurs, their growing sense of solitude throws them unarmed into the very heart of social conflicts that they pride themselves naïvely in being able to resolve by means of texts. No matter! The hour is coming when the new order will be born on the ruins of what still remains of the old Christian order: this will truly be the order of the world, the order of the Prince of this world, of the Prince whose kingdom is of this world. Then, under the harsh law of necessity, which is stronger than all illusions, the pride of the churchman—for so long sustained by simple conventions that had survived real beliefs—will have lost its very object. And the steps of beggars will once again make the earth tremble.[228]

This magnificent text has as a companion piece the other text in which the Curé de Fenouille explains to the doctor the greatest danger to the cleric, which is something much deeper than the naïve vanity in which he usually indulges. That deeper danger is pride:

A pride all our own. . . . [For] we stand alone. Like greed, pride is a solitary vice. It quietly slipped into us without our realizing it in the course of those years of humble struggle that seemed short to us because a tight discipline . . . governed every hour, every minute. We were to be made into apostles, people whose kingdom is not of this world. But we clung to this world, we clung to it by secret fibers. Ah no, it's not a small thing to uproot greed from the hearts of little peasants! After all this, it could be that our inner spring is shattered, but often it's only overwound. They think we've been humbled, reciprocating indifference with disdain. Our experience of men and their misery is at once so naïve and so profound! But we couldn't give you any proof of this because we don't speak the same language. While you laugh at our naïveté, alas, we have already weighed you in a very exact scale: we have judged *you*![229]

---

228 *Ouine*, 171–72 (corrected text).
229 Ibid., 186–87 (corrected and completed text).

Such is the peril lurking in the background. What we see in the foreground is precisely the naïveté alluded to, which confuses itself unconsciously with the principle of the ministerial office that the priest represents: "Who could hope to hold the Curé de Luzarnes between the arms of the tongs? He has never seriously doubted any of the truths he teaches, simply because he has never doubted himself, his own infallible judgment."[230] From this derives the need for self-defense, or, what amounts to the same thing, the need for "saving the face" of the Church, a subject that elicited so many bitter pages from Bernanos.[231] This is also the reason for his struggle to clarify the true image of the priest, the particular form of sanctity appropriate for one destined for a ministerial existence. Fundamental in the saints is the way they combine a childlike unselfconsciousness where they themselves are concerned with a superior clairvoyance in matters involving the world and men. Such clairvoyance may be more a charismatic gift, as in the cases of Donissan, Chevance, and the country priest, or more something acquired through study, experience, and suffering, as we see in Menou-Segrais and the Curés de Torcy and de Fenouille.

In this innermost locus of his person, the priest is brother to the Christian writer, for both must come to know the world of evil. This knowledge comes through contact with sinners, while the personal purity of both priest and writer must be preserved. It comes through the experience conferred, not by acquired guilt, but by the face of the brother who is recognized with love, and this face is only really seen when one's own face is forgotten.[232] This is why Jean-Marie Vianney's life and destiny never ceased to fascinate Bernanos. He studied his life[233] and took him as model for Donissan.[234] But the softer, more human traits of Vianney—precisely those that do not play much of a role in *Under Satan's Sun*—again become manifested in the *Country Priest* and in the Curé de Fenouille in *Monsieur Ouine*. There were in this connection many features that initially appeared forced, as we

---

[230] *Soleil*, 341.

[231] *Vérité*, 56f.; *Cimetières*, passim.

[232] *Joie*, 48.

[233] Vallery-Radot, *Souvenirs*, in: *Bul.* 2, 25.

[234] *Soleil*, 248: "a new Curé d'Ars"; 270: "like a second Curé d'Ars"; 253, 277, 313f.: evocation of the confessional at Ars and the throngs of people flocking there; 342: the Curé's fasting; and passim: the battle with the demons, the suspiciousness aroused in superiors, the attempts to flee to a monastery, etc.

have seen: the overtaxing of the ministerial office as one ceaseless experience of human despair, the Christian life as consisting at bottom in a continual and awesome transport beyond the point of death, all of this portrayed inflexibly and abstractly as in Karl Barth's dialectical theology, contemporary with *Under Satan's Sun*. Such uncompromising harshness and exaggeration later on became malleable, to make possible the admission of a mystery of grace that had truly become humanized. In the country priest, the most splendid of all Bernanos' priest figures, the central characteristic is a naïveté so pure that it can be continually humiliated without the priest's realizing what is occurring. This is how Bernanos describes his hero-in-the-making in a letter to his friend Vallery-Radot: "I've decided to write the journal of a young priest, at the moment he arrives in a new parish. He is going to create the most unlikely situations, do the work of four men, start fantastic projects that will of course fail, more or less allow himself to be taken in by imbeciles, vicious gossips, and real bastards, and, when he thinks all is lost, he will have served the good Lord to the very extent to which he believes he has served him badly. In the end, his naïveté will triumph over all else, and he will die quietly of cancer."[235] A few days later Bernanos sent the first fifty pages of the novel to the same correspondent, adding: "You guess right that my friend is going to be hemmed in by a village in revolt. But this revolt will be inarticulate, and he himself will never become aware of it." He will have the advantage of having become like his flock in all things "save sin", although he is naturally a sinner like everyone else. Only grace raises him above the rest, and yet he is not elevated above the others externally and for his own sake: "All of us are wretches. But, from among the mediocre, God selects certain friends to raise them up to himself. To these he gives everything: wealth, endowments, titles, courtly offices, and their very name. Everyone loves them because he loves them. They are prayed to and venerated for the same reason. And so I find it useless to rail at the others because, alas, we are those others!"[236]

The life of the little priest is made up very humdrum events; even the extraordinary manifests itself in the ordinary; and his interior el-

---

[235] *To Vallery-Radot*, January 6, 1935; in: *Bernanos*, 173.
[236] Ibid., January 10, 1935; in: *Bernanos*, 174.

evation wears the humble mask of banality. He is awkward,[237] shy,[238] and impractical.[239] His troubles are "absolutely ordinary".[240] He has a sense of his "own mediocrity".[241] Whereas he should be "the leader" in his parish, instead he goes from door to door "like a miserable beggar", and he doesn't "even dare to knock".[242] He has no talent whatever for administration and is incapable of giving an order, and he perceives both these things as a real defect precisely because this "son of poor peasants" has a keen sense of rank and nobility, and yet this does not keep him from seeing through the façade of the count and the whole household up in the château.[243] His origins in the lowermost classes of society[244] make him perceive as quite normal most of the disagreeable things that come his way; however, he is the opposite of what Nietzsche calls a "Chandala". He suffers from hereditary alcoholism,[245] and he drinks a nasty warm wine partly because he can eat nothing else and partly in unconscious solidarity with his forebears. But it never occurs to him to set himself, the atoner, apart from them, the sinners.[246] On the contrary, this law of heredity and the psychology it entails become for Bernanos the improbable but most adequate metaphor for God's Incarnation and for genuine solidarity without sin. Like the Lord on the Cross, the little priest can affirm with interior conviction at the end of a life that has overflowed with indignities and humiliations that he has never been a "victim of injustice",[247] and he can thus return his spirit to God fully reconciled with life, indeed loving life from the bottom of his soul.

Even his sorrows and sufferings appear to him to have something laughable about them ("a man with nausea is always so ridiculous", he notes);[248] and yet, this does not make him into a bitter person, any

---

[237] *Curé*, 47, 304.

[238] Ibid., 247, 297.

[239] Ibid., 106.

[240] Ibid., 283.

[241] Ibid., 302.

[242] Ibid., 159.

[243] Ibid., 55f., 85.

[244] Ibid., 43f.

[245] Ibid., 92, 227, 247.

[246] There is a play of words here involving *ein Sühnender* (one doing atonement) and *die Sünder* (the sinners).—TRANS.

[247] *Curé*, 316.

[248] Ibid., 117. (However, the French expression for being nauseous [*avoir mal au cœur*] could

more than does the uselessness of his preaching[249] and all his other efforts[250] or the tatteredness of his entire existence.[251] Whether he is submerged in an interior night[252] or prayer is withdrawn from him, whether his most beautiful priestly experience is turned into the bitterest, and he skirts the temptation to suicide[253] and the sin against hope:[254] not for a single instant does he exalt any of this into any sort of "heroism". Rather, he does not even feel the extraordinary nature of his fate, and he even sees the passive experience of being stripped of all things as part of the ordinariness of life, indeed, as an aspect of his own gaucheness and inability to give of himself: "My God, I give you everything, and with a glad heart. Only, I don't know how to give. I give in the same way that other people have things taken from them. The best thing is to stay quiet. For, if I don't know how to give, You certainly know how to take. . . . And yet, I wish that, for once, for one time at least, I could have been more lavishly openhanded toward You!"[255]

Right behind the "children" saints, in the second row, Bernanos places the elders, the adults who sustain and vouch for the first group: these are Menou-Segrais, Torcy, and the other men of education and culture who possess a great interior serenity,[256] priests who know how to oppose everything half-baked, trashy, and hypocritical in both the Church and the priesthood without nevertheless losing their peace of mind. But they also know how to commiserate with all the suffering their spiritual "children" undergo, how to share their anguish and enter into their interior nights, although this solidarity in no way weakens their solid guidance. Still behind these Bernanos sees the priests who simply hold a ministerial office and whose heart has gathered something of a layer of dust. Nevertheless, Bernanos appraises them

---

be translated literally to mean "to be ill at heart", "to suffer heartache", or even, most literally, "to have evil in one's heart". Thus, the physiological turn of phrase, as uttered by the country priest, carries an important moral and metaphysical resonance.—TRANS.)

[249] Ibid., 39–40.
[250] Ibid., 51.
[251] Ibid., 99.
[252] Ibid., 121.
[253] Ibid., 219.
[254] Ibid., 125.
[255] Ibid., 303.
[256] Ibid., 30, 131.

positively: such are the dean and the canon in the *Country Priest* and, in a sort of twilight, figures like the Curé de Luzarnes.

These have all been made to be "shepherds and not hunters".[257] Like the Curé de Fenouille, they have all been sent out into the hazardous mystery of an anguishing pastoral task:[258] "We don't have any place of our own, and we belong to no one. We have left our families, our homes, our villages, and, once we've finished with our notebooks, our books, our Greek, and our Latin, we're sent out among you. Our only instructions are, as the saying goes, to *manage the best we can*, to do as much good as possible. And that's just as it should be: What other order could be given us?"[259] They are to go out and win souls. But souls do not want to be won. Their mind is on something else, and they don't want to have anything to do with the man in black: "It's possible the parish no longer exists. . . . It is dead."[260] The village of Fenouille stands like a solid mass over against its shepherd, like a surface off which every arrow rebounds. The *Country Priest*, begun one year after *Monsieur Ouine*, opens with the same contemplation of the village and the community: the little priest looks down on it yearning to discover its countenance, the face of his bride,[261] and he is eager and ready to offer her the ineffable riches the Church makes available in the ordained priest. Everyone will let him know that he should keep his distance: "A priest is like a notary public", he hears. "He's there in case of need. You shouldn't go pestering anybody."[262] The internal logic of this novel, however, demands that a few souls, resist as they might, will nevertheless open themselves up to the light of the sacrament as a result of their formidable duel with the young priest. In *Monsieur Ouine*, by contrast, what we see is the ruthless portrayal of an eerie, apocalyptic absence of events that surpasses all the spiritual combats of the *Country Priest*: the Church existing in

---

[257] *Croix*, October 1944, 453.

[258] Von Balthasar here separates the technical word *Seelsorge* (care of souls, pastoral work) into its two elements, writing instead "*Seel-Sorge*" (either "grief of soul" or "sorrow caused by souls"). The pun, reinforced by quotation marks, is no doubt intended to evoke the real suffering inevitably occasioned in devoted priests by a ministry that can often appear to be a mechanical and impersonal "job".—TRANS.

[259] *Ouine*, 161.

[260] Ibid., 162.

[261] *Curé*, 9, 38.

[262] Ibid., 215.

an utterly ruinous condition. Are we to say that this second vision belongs to a later stage in the history of spiritual decay?

> His eyes cast a glance—a heavy glance—up at his church. Fear, or at least an indefinable distrust, seemed to pull him backward. Fear of what? Of what danger? . . . Here, he had ever only been like one passing through, and the old church pushed him away without anger, just as this village —whose roofs he could see—rejected him, since church and village were but one. As long as the ancient citadel sent up her[263] tower in this place, as long as the belfry hurled its summoning cry out into space, this church would take sides with the community, would stand on the side of the people over against him. They could profane her or knock her down, but she would belong to them to the very end. Down to the last stone, she would never deny them. Yes: even prone on the grass, she would still offer her beautiful disemboweled flanks to both traitors and perjurers. Their little ones would come to play among her ruins. . . . As step by step he goes up the rocky path, he once more casts a stolen glance of jealousy behind him. . . . When his courage fails him, the only image capable of giving him peace and quieting his nerves is that of a beggar on a road, a real beggar with his satchel on his back and being chased by dogs.[264]

3. Two Sorts of "Seer"

The priest is a man who, by God's omnipotence and grace, has been ordained to the ministry of serving the truth. To him God's Word has been entrusted, and he is to bring it to men as what it is: the absolute, fruitful, burning, and all-consuming truth. "God's Word is a red-hot iron", and the priest is to "take hold of it, not with tongs, but with wide-open hands", and "feel the wound it inflicts on him". It is by the "pain he senses" that the Curé de Torcy knows when a word useful to souls has been "extracted" from him.[265] " 'Give me back my Word', the Judge will say on the last day."[266] If the priest proclaims the Word as he should, "the hard truth . . . will have wounded him

---

[263] The context requires the feminine personification of the church building.—TRANS.

[264] *Ouine,* 195–96.

[265] *Curé,* 65.

[266] Ibid., 73.

before it does you. You can really feel that he has wrenched it from his heart."[267]

The priest, therefore, is also a man who can transfer the sinner into this sphere of the Word's truth. He does this, not only because he is himself a sinner who can point his sinful brother in the direction of God's truth, but especially because, in the sacraments, he coöperates with Christ in judging sin and, by judging it, also in redeeming it. In order to do this, however, the priest must know and "see" sin. Seeing and judging, passive a posteriori verification and active finding of the truth, are the two sides of reason. Bernanos greatly stresses *judgment* as active engagement, creative daring, and personal responsibility. But he could not do this unless he equally promoted *vision* as counterbalance—the simple act of spiritual seeing that looks into innermost reality and reads (*intel-lectus*) what is there. Everything this writer is about, every aspect of his pathos, could be traced back to these two functions, which belong inseparably together.

Already the philosopher can justifiably ask the question concerning the origin of the light of absolute truth, which must fall on the relative objects of this world if a more than relative judgment about them is to be possible: Does it come directly from the light of the active intellect, which itself derives from God? Or, does it come from an illumination by the divine light as it falls on both the object and the reason contemplating it? These questions of the philosopher take on a double urgency when asked in the sphere of the supernatural. For in this realm the burning concern is the vision and judgment of souls, their turning away from and back to God, in the light of God's grace in Christ, a grace that chooses and redeems. By virtue of his office, the priest receives a particular share in this light; moreover, it belongs to Bernanos' prerogatives as a writer to make this sacramental participation graspable and visible through the expressiveness of his charismatic vision. And it would not be erroneous for us to take this interpretation of the ordained ministry by the writer's charism to be more than mere poetic license; rather, we should see it as an exegesis on the basis of interior kinship with it. For what should occur through such "charismatic interpretation" by a Christian imaginative writer is that what is contained within the ordained office as an objective possibility now becomes more clearly raised into consciousness

---

[267] *Soleil*, 117.

as the subjective sanctity to which the holiness of the office obliges the one entrusted with it.

We cannot fail to see the fact, however, that this highest grace, which consists of looking into others' souls with the eyes of God, permanently exists in a state of impending crisis. For, how could such a grace not be the object of the Evil One's most intense greed? "Your eyes will be opened", hissed the serpent to Adam and Eve, "and you will be like God, knowing both good and evil" (Gen 3:5).[268] The vision of souls from within, the consuming enjoyment of this vision: for Bernanos and his somber heroes, such is the strongest lure of the abyss. It is in this regard that Monsieur Ouine becomes a veritable antipriest, the Pontiff of Hell. The same act of seeing that in Bernanos' holy priests presupposes the greatest purity and humility and evinces the greatest intimacy with the divine Seer, who plumbs the depths of the heart, becomes in Ouine the exponent of every kind of spiritually impure and perverse pleasure: it becomes a vampiric act that sucks out the very marrow of souls, the embodiment of the "voraciousness"[269] of the abyss. These two sorts of "seer" thus stand diametrically opposed to one another: they are the *clairvoyant* and the *voyeur*.

But it was not on his first attempt that Bernanos grasped this mutually exclusive opposition; rather, at the outset he was so fascinated with the mere phenomenon of being able to see into souls that he confused the two forms of vision to the point of equating them—the gaze from heaven and the peering out of the abyss, God's vision and Satan's vision. It is here that we can appreciate the deepest ambiguity contained in *Under Satan's Sun*. Should we say that this book evinces a desire to portray the mystic's absolute abandonment by God himself to the darkest abyss as meaning that the divine light, on the basis of the humiliation of the Cross, has taken on this modality of a satanic light? Or, rather, should we say that the book bespeaks Bernanos' lingering fascination with Charles Maurras, whose demonic identification of God and Satan held Bernanos under its spell for a while with its indolent equivocation? Later on, in 1939, in the second appendix of *We, the French*, Bernanos translated Maurras' Latin dedication of his *Enquête sur la monarchie* (Inquiry on the monarchy) and offered it almost without commentary for his reader's consideration:

---

[268] *New English Bible.*
[269] *Soleil,* 325.

> To him who is even worse (or better)
> Than the Best (or the Worst),
> Whether God or Demon,
> Both of whose names are ineffable,
> This is dedicated.[270]

It is taken for granted that "the sun of Satan" must be shining in order for the priest to be able to look into the spectacle of Satan's kingdom opening before him. And, since this glance into the world of evil is a prerequisite for the sacramental judgment of sin in the light of God, the light of the abyss becomes commingled with the light from on high. We must now look again at the same central texts we have already studied in our search for the basic criteria of Bernanos' poetics; but this time we will probe them for their sacramental content.

In the decisive scene between Donissan and the demon, we detect the following train of thought, which is governed by an inexorable and incisive logic: Donissan looks tensely, indeed, "with a boundless curiosity", at the face of his opponent, "the killer of souls from whom he must wrest certain of his secrets".[271] And now the eyes of the abysmal pit fasten upon him; he feels their monstrous suctioning power; "the dauntless man" feels "wrenched from the earth by the fierce beckoning of nothingness".[272] "I have been given to see you . . .", he says to the fiend; "I see you to the extent possible for human vision."[273] Satan himself asserts, however, that he is only "obeying someone more powerful than himself" and that his role is to "test" Donissan "from this day forward, till the very hour of [his] death". At this moment his features blur, and he disappears like

> the spokes of a wheel turning at full speed. . . . Then the features of his form reassemble once more. And the curate of Campagne suddenly sees before him his double. The resemblance is so perfect and so subtle that it would have to be compared less with the reflected image formed in a mirror than with the singular, unique, and unfathomable idea each of us entertains about himself. . . . And yet his conscience, trained as it was in

---

[270] *Français*, 287f.
[271] *Soleil*, 169.
[272] Ibid., 171.
[273] Ibid., 173.

self-examination, could never have arrived all by itself at such a fantastic duplication. Even our most penetrating observation, when turned to the universe within us, can focus on only one aspect at a time. But what the future saint of Lumbres was discovering at this moment was both the whole and the detail, his thoughts with all their roots and ramifications, the infinite network binding them among themselves, the least stirrings of his desires—much as a flayed corpse would show the throbbing of life in the design of its arteries and veins. This vision, at once one and manifold, . . . was so perfect that the poor priest saw himself, not only in the present, but also in the past and in the future. He could see his whole life before him. . . . What's this, my Lord? Are we then so transparent to the enemy lying in ambush for us? Are we then released wholly unarmed to his calculating hatred?[274]

This is not, however, the vision Donissan is after: "This is not what I need. What is this sort of self-knowledge to me? The particular examen, without further lights, is enough for a poor sinner."[275] And yet "the vertigo of a supernatural curiosity, which would forever remain ineffectual", impels him to go forward. He cries out to Satan: "I must wrest your secret from you!" To which Satan replies: "Today you've been granted a grace. You have paid dearly for it. And you'll pay for it more dearly still." At this point Donissan should surely not have posed any questions, but an instinctive curiosity pushes him to ask: "What grace?" At this, his adversary feels "a shiver of joy" and replies: "In the same way you saw yourself a moment ago (for the first and last time), so too will you see . . . will you see . . . ha! ha! . . . Just as you've seen yourself, I tell you, so will you see certain others."[276] When Donissan regains consciousness, Boulainville the stonemason is alongside him in the night, and he gives the priest a drink from his flask. Immediately Donissan realizes he is looking at the world with new eyes. He walks through the darkness behind his companion, "looking down at the ground, his eyelids almost shut". And yet "he could have sworn that at the same time he was moving through a soft and friendly light, a cloud of golden dust." He felt summoned to an immense joy, aware that the power leading him is "imperious but beneficial" and that he would not be able to resist

---

[274] Ibid., 174–75.
[275] Ibid., 176.
[276] Ibid., 177–78.

it. He is certain that the stonemason is "surely a friend", and that doubtless they have all along been bound by "a heavenly friendship, a friendship of heavenly clarity. . . . Tears came to his eyes. Thus it was that, on a bright morning, two of the chosen met in the gardens of paradise, born one for the other."[277]

Donissan's senses, however, do not accept this new mode of vision without a struggle. The battle with the demon had been its price: "Now he sees with quiet trust—without a will to see through the light, but with the certainty of being transfused by the light. . . . He could see; with his fleshly eyes, he could see what remains hidden from the most penetrating vision . . . : a human conscience." Such vision was clearly distinct from the natural knowledge of self that comes through introspection, because the self-observer "must *descend* into himself, and the deeper he descends, the more the darkness thickens, until the lowermost tuff is reached—the bottom of the self where the shades of ancestors whirl about and where instinct bellows like subterranean water." Donissan was experiencing nothing of the kind: "Here was this wretched little priest finding himself suddenly transported to the most intimate part of another being, doubtless to the very spot on which the eyes of the Judge fall. . . . Without being able to express it (for he never could express it), he felt *that this knowledge was in keeping with his nature* and that the intellect and the other faculties men take pride in were here playing a very slender role. He felt that this knowledge was simply and exclusively the effervescence, the expansion, *the prolongation of charity"*, of love for God and neighbor. And it almost seemed to him that it was his fault if he had received this knowledge so late: "Once he has taken hold of the new sense just given him, a man born blind is not less astonished [than Donissan was] to be able to touch with his sight the distant horizon that until now he could reach only with so much effort, trudging through bogs and briars."[278]

These new eyes, moreover, were not given to the saint of Campagne in order for him to be able to discover in the stonemason "an unknown just man"; rather, they were given him for the sake of the next encounter this same night still holds for him, to enable him to penetrate the heart of Mouchette, "the final and supreme actor of this

---

[277] Ibid., 184–85.
[278] Ibid., 186–87. (Except for the word *descend*, the italics are von Balthasar's.—TRANS.)

unforgettable night".[279] The light that in the meantime had gone out in him is now rekindled, and this time he feels how he is opening out to it: "Radiating from a secret glow, flowing through him from a fountain of inexhaustible brightness, a hitherto unknown sensation invaded him, infinitely subtle and pure, absolutely unalloyed, and little by little this flood reached the very principle of life, transforming him in his very flesh. Just as a man dying of thirst opens up wholly to the keen freshness of water, he did not know whether what had pierced him from side to side was pleasure or pain." Bernanos cannot insist enough that this new mode of knowledge is a supernatural intuition "that precedes all hypotheses and imposes itself on its own initiative", and that, in its simplicity and sovereign power, it is like the a priori of all knowing, which is unattainable for man and yet always intended and, indeed, a presupposed requirement.[280] To be sure, such intuition is bestowed on the priest, not to make him capable of pure contemplation, but for the sake of the bitter and earnest battle of confession he must now fight to the end with Mouchette. Supernatural intuition is the final weapon he uses against her revolt, and it unmistakably manifests his superiority over her: "When the spirit of revolt still raged within you, I saw the Name of God written in your heart." The girl is "pierced through" by his voice and his gaze, and these are so "fatherly" because Donissan himself had "tasted the poison and savored its long bitterness" and thus, too, because the gift of *cardiognosis*—reading in people's hearts—in the end comes to him, whole and entire, from Satan.

Let us now look again at the very dense page in which Bernanos strives to attain a decisive insight into the nature of this light: He writes,

Human language cannot be sufficiently coerced to express in abstract terms *the certainty of a real presence, because all our certainties are deductions, and experience, when night falls on a long life, will be seen to be but the end of a long voyage around their own nothingness. The only evidence springing forth from reason is logical evidence, and the only universe offered reason is that consisting of species and genera. The only fire that can compel the ice of concepts to melt is the fire of God.* And yet, what at this moment is being revealed to the eyes of the Abbé Donissan is not a sign or a figure: it's a living soul, a

[279] Ibid., 191.
[280] Ibid., 193.

heart sealed off to everyone else! No more than at the moment of their extraordinary encounter is he now capable of justifying through words *the exterior vision* whose splendor remains the same *and which blends with the interior light that pervades him. Similarly, the initial glance a child casts on the world is so full and so pure that he cannot at first distinguish the universe he has just gotten hold of from the shuddering of his own joy. The colors and forms of all things simultaneously blossom in his triumphant laughter.*[281]

Two fundamental things are said in this decisive text. In the first place, Bernanos here affirms the superior character of an intuition into the real presence of the being of another (and, hence, of *Being as such*), an intuition that as such transcends all evidence coming from this world. By contrast, the sum total of what men call "experience" has as its center not so much Being as Nothingness—what Bernanos has termed "dream" in the pejorative sense. And, in the second place, the text stresses the form of *identity*, in such supernatural and absolute knowledge, whereby interior and exterior light, knowledge and object, come to coincide with one another. But all of Bernanos is here revealed in the fact that he approximates this superabundant modality of the intellect to the primal beginnings of existence by closely associating it with the first glance of the child, which, as we know, is one and the same as the final glance of the dying person: the insight that comes with the death agony. All the tribulations and all the vanities of poor earthly knowledge fall within the confines of this closed circle.

In the second (and older) part of *Under Satan's Sun*, the uncanny demonic ambiguity of this mode of vision is insisted on from the outset. Knowledge *is* temptation; therefore, supreme knowledge can only be supreme temptation—not a carnal temptation, of course, but rather "the other kind of concupiscence awakens in this naïve and stubborn heart, that rage for knowledge which undid the mother of all the living as she stood, erect and reflective, on the threshold of good and evil. *To know only in order to destroy, and, by means of this destruction, to renew one's knowledge and desire: O sun of Satan!* You are the yearning for nothingness, sought for its own sake, you are the most abominable offspring of the heart!"[282] Thus it is at least a kind of atonement and compensation when Donissan must in the future pay with express mortal anguish for the gift of reading into the hearts

---

[281] Ibid., 199–200. (The italics are von Balthasar's.—TRANS.)
[282] Ibid., 257. (The italics are von Balthasar's.—TRANS.)

of sinners in the confessional: "He replies as in a dream, but with extreme lucidity. Never had his brain been freer, and his judgment more prompt and clear, whereas his flesh was conscious only of its growing pain. . . . This pain has penetrated so deep that it seems to have reached the division of body and soul and to cleave the one man into two parts. . . . In his agony, the saint of Lumbres now has dealings only with souls."[283] It is out of this agony that the extraordinary concluding prayer is uttered, a prayer that, through the Church, bears before the presence of God the word of those suffering souls who cannot justify themselves. It is a word that itself consists of suffering and that can therefore be seen, grasped, and assumed from within by the saint in death's throes. But to the end Bernanos imposes a radical ambiguity on the mystical experience: the "abandonment of the saints" here exhibits the "deceptive image" of Satan's "despair". And we hear Donissan exclaim to the fiend: "You were suffering and praying with me—O hideous thought!"[284]

Donissan makes a double sign of the cross on the breast of a raging Mouchette;[285] in this way, he applies the knowledge derived from love in a manner consonant with this love: "Like charity, reason too is a form of our knowledge."[286] This is precisely the reason why, in his later books, Bernanos had to eliminate the original ambiguity of spiritual knowledge and remove every intrinsic demonic element from the divine light. "God is light, and in him there is no darkness at all" (1 Jn 1:5).[287] Chevance possesses the same gift for "seeing through" Cénabre and his work "with superhuman clairvoyance".[288] But, "of your unhappiness, I have only a vision that cannot be communicated. God help me! I see you in so terrible a way, and I have nothing left! How does he intend for me to make myself understood by you? . . . I swear to you that it's the Spirit inspiring me! I swear that you are as open to me as the eyes of a child are to its mother!"[289] And the country priest has received the gift of *cardiognosis* even more emphat-

---

[283] Ibid., 315.
[284] Ibid., 362.
[285] Ibid., 199, 361.
[286] Ibid., 200–201.
[287] *New English Bible.*
[288] *Imposture*, 63.
[289] Ibid., 66–67.

ically, although, like all other supernatural elements in this novel, this gift has taken on in his case a veiled form dissolved in the quotidian. At first it appears to be a keen sense of observation, a heightened knowledge of men.[290] Then, in his encounter with a Chantal consumed by her revolt, it appears he can read in her "by a kind of vision", and the priest asks himself "whether the ability isn't bound up with [his] prayer or perhaps is this prayer itself".[291] By virtue of this vision, he can say and do things he could never have accomplished naturally.[292]

But, to the same extent that the vision of the saints becomes purified of its demonic elements in Bernanos' later works, the demonic origin of the knowledge enjoyed by the "antipriests" comes into relief as the specific characteristic of the "voyeurs"—Cénabre and above all Ouine; for, in Donissan, an undifferentiated identity still obtained between the divine image and its hellish counterpart. Donissan's temptation, formulated as we have seen, could be the motto writ large over the destiny of both these characters: "To know in order to destroy, and, by means of this destruction, to renew one's knowledge and desire: O sun of Satan! You are the yearning for nothingness!"[293] Cénabre, who analyzes the saints without loving them,[294] must nevertheless "see [himself] naked"[295] in their light. "The sacrilege of a curiosity without love" leads him in the end to a "rabid self-contempt", and to use his shame like a dark fire that serves as perverse organ for the acquisition of knowledge.[296] Chevance attempts in vain to introduce the situation of the miserable man into the sphere of confession so as to begin to make some sense of it. Chevance's supernatural light is eager, but Cénabre shuts himself off from it—the same Cénabre who, at the beginning of the novel, in his capacity of father confessor, had profaned this sacramental light by his cold and disdainful analysis of poor Pernichon.

---

[290] *Curé*, 136.
[291] Ibid., 151.
[292] Ibid., 153, 163, 167, 174.
[293] *Soleil*, 257.
[294] *Imposture*, 30.
[295] Ibid., 31.
[296] Ibid., 36–37.

But only Ouine presents the picture of the perfect voyeur. Ouine wants to do evil in thought, because it is here that evil has its root and primal force; and so he has transferred into the dimension of knowledge all of the sensual lust that normally characterizes the sins of man. Ouine thus becomes a spiritual devourer of men, a vampire who sucks, not their bodily blood, but the lymph of their being and existence. In order to savor this kind of pleasure through knowledge, he does not even require particular secrets; the most "modest confidence" suffices to afford him the enjoyment of the "God-like pastime".[297] He takes pride in being an entomologist who observes souls without having to touch them: *"Their Creator has not known them better than I. No possession by means of love can be compared to this infallible grasp I enjoy*, which does not hurt the patient. It leaves him intact and yet completely at our mercy."[298] What does it matter, Bernanos muses, whether Ouine has in fact murdered the little shepherd or abused Philippe, when these deeds would at most be a weak echo of his infinitely deeper and more perilous peering into the souls of others? His clairvoyance, moreover, presents a form similar to that of the saints. Just as the Curé d'Ambricourt demands of Chantal that she give him the letter she is concealing, so too Ouine presses the Curé de Fenouille for the anonymous letters he has.[299] He sees through Philippe, Jambe-de-Laine, and Anthelme, and by this spiritual penetration, made possible by a perverted sacramental light, he subjects them to himself. Without expressing his intuition in theoretical terms, Bernanos has here entered the innermost sphere of his epistemological and ontological convictions. A subject's penetration through knowledge into the openness of another's spiritual being can be defined as an act of truth, in the strict sense, only by being grounded in love—the love of God, which God makes available to his creatures. In the absence of such love, the medium of knowledge can only be love's opposite: the concupiscence of hell. Here there can be no neutral middle ground. The knowledge of another's spirit must either be creative through love or destructive through greed: for the other's spirit, as spirit, necessarily stands before God and is therefore inaccessible without God.

---

[297] *Ouine*, 241.
[298] Ibid., 242.
[299] Ibid., 140.

4. The Battle of Confession

Supernatural vision is the prerequisite for supernatural judgment. "Judgment" connotes the action of a judge. If this action is in fact the priest's sacramental cojudgment with the God who redeems by judging, then its meaning is the actualization of *the* decisive event par excellence: the process and drama wherein a soul that has shut itself off from the light is now brought to open itself up to the light by the very light that strikes it, struggles with it, and defeats it.

"Come and see", Philip says to Nathanael. But, when the latter does come, the judgment is revealed to him: "I saw you under the fig tree before Philip spoke to you." The light has all along been enveloping him, overtaking him, locating him within a truth unknown to him, and he now capitulates before this truth: " 'Rabbi,' said Nathanael, 'you are the Son of God; you are king of Israel' " (Jn 1:46f.).[300] But, in order to be so intensely sharp and effective and to fight so victoriously, Christ the Light of God has made himself a "two-edged sword, penetrating even between soul and spirit, joints and marrow, and judging the reflections and thoughts of the heart" (Heb 4:12).[301] This Christ has done through his temptation and Passion. Out of the Word's helplessness on the Cross and in hell emerges his might, which, possessing the "keys of death and hell" (Rev 1:18), also possesses the keys to every soul that has been mortally and infernally locked. And he can bestow these keys on others. In these, the impotency of the Word has a possibility of repeating itself in order for the sacrament to be efficacious in the present. Thus, the Word "is strong only in weakness" (2 Cor 12:9–10; 13:4, 9).

In *Under Satan's Sun*, besides the profoundly dramatic character proper to it, confession still retains certain features of an ambiguous, mythic battle with Satan. The way in which a priest is exposed to evil in this sacrament is portrayed as a heroic enterprise in dragon killing, a picture that is impressive but distorted.

The figure of Donissan is distorted to the extent that in him, the

---

[300] *New English Bible.*

[301] *New American Bible, Revised New Testament.* But, with von Balthasar, we translate "judging" where the NAB has "able to discern". This more literal rendering of the Greek κριτικός is necessary for the point he is making regarding the effective *judgment* involved in confession. —TRANS.

clairvoyant priest, lurks something of Ouine the *voyeur*. This is all the more fatal as it involves a sacrament, and the most delicate of them all. The penitent who goes to confession must confront God and by no means a superman. The priestly office in this sacrament demands an almost impossible transparency in the confessor. His own person must assume such lightness that, as mediator, he must exhibit a thoroughgoing transparency even where he must actively intervene with very strong and exacting words and judgments. In the absence of total human humility and sober modesty in the priest, the truth of a ministerial judgment that represents the Church, and is in fact a co-judgment with God's judging action in heaven, becomes something hybrid and intolerable. Precisely because they are but instruments in the hand of the Most High, both the Church and the sacrament must bow in humility under this hand.

This is what Bernanos did not quite understand at first. Donissan explains to his colleague Sabiroux that he has not been gifted with "visions, apparitions, or unusual temptations" but that the only supernatural thing he has been given to see is the souls of sinners:

> You see, no one knows what a sinner is. What is the meaning of a voice in the darkness of the confessional, mumbling and hurrying through, slowing down only for the first syllables of the *mea culpa*? This is all right for children, poor dears! What one must really see is the faces, the faces and the looks that say everything graphically. Human eyes, Sabiroux! There's no end to what could be said about them. I've assisted many people at the moment of dying, and that's nothing. They no longer frighten you. God covers them with his mantle. But the wretches I've seen before me —arguing, smiling, fighting back, and lying, lying, lying, until one final anguish casts them at our feet like empty sacks! Their sort still cuts a smart figure in the world, don't you know? They prance before the girls and swear with style. . . . For a long time, alas, I didn't understand it. All I saw was strays that God gathered up in passing. But something stands between God and man, someone who is not a secondary character. . . . There is . . . there stands this dark being who is incomparably subtle and relentless, this entity whose only analogue would be monstrous irony or cruel laughter. God delivered himself into his hands for a while. It's in us that he's grabbed and devoured. It's from us that he's torn. Since time immemorial the race of humans has been put in the winepress. Our blood has been squeezed out in streams, to the end that even the tiniest bit of the divine flesh should offer delectation and laughter to the loathsome little hangman. . . . Ah, how profound is our ignorance! What

is the devil to a learned, courteous, and civil priest, pray tell? . . . They have read too many books and heard too few confessions. . . . We're in the first rank of a battle to the death, and our successors are right behind us. They are priests, but they still can't hear the cry of universal misery! The only confessions they hear is their sacristans'! Could it be that they've never been face to face with a human countenance in the throes of anguish? Have they never felt pierced by one of these unforgettable glances, already full of hatred for God, belonging to people to whom one has nothing left to give—nothing? The miser gnawed through by his cancer, the lecher looking like a corpse, the ambitious entrepreneur consumed by his one dream, the ever-watchful coveter. . . . What am I saying? What priest has never wept with helplessness before the mystery of human suffering, the mystery of a God reviled in man, his refuge? . . . But they don't want to see! They don't want to see![302]

Donissan, however, has been chosen precisely to "see". Ever since "the young taciturn priest first offered himself, in the darkness and silence, to sinful man—his master who would never let go of him while alive",[303] he was initiated into "his secret". Later on he did battle with Mouchette, who had expressly invoked the devil to help her.[304] Donissan points her to the God dwelling within her: "But, you see, God supports us even in our madness, and when man rises up to curse him, it's he alone who upholds man's feeble hand!" He also tells us that Christ descended much more deeply than she into the abyss of evil. He even extricates her from guilt over the murder she has committed: he says to her that she has been "a simple toy in Satan's hands, like a child's ball".[305] As he speaks thus, a transformation begins to take place in her. His gaze and his words gradually bind up into one all her sins, and she both senses and understands what is happening. The same fundamental passages that had served to summarize Bernanos' poetics must now be recalled again as basic to his heroine's experience:

> What she was hearing was not a judge's verdict or anything that surpassed her understanding . . . , [but rather] her own story, the story of Mouchette, not at all dramatized by some theatrical director and enriched with strange and peculiar touches, but *quite the contrary: her own story in*

---

[302] *Soleil*, 286–88.
[303] Ibid., 119–20.
[304] Ibid., 201f.
[305] Ibid., 202–3.

summary, reduced to nothing, seen from the inside. That particular sin that is eating us up: how little substance it leaves our life with! *What she saw being consumed in the fire of his words was . . . herself, and she could conceal nothing from the pointed and sharp flame that penetrated into the last nook, into the last fiber of her flesh.* In rhythm with the rising and falling of that formidable voice that resounded in the bowels of her being, she felt the heat of her own life increase and decrease. *The voice was at first distinct*, using everyday words, and her terror welcomed it like a friendly face in a frightening dream. Then the voice became *more and more commingled with the interior testimony—the wrenching whisper of a conscience polluted at its own deep source*—to such an extent that the two voices blended to form but a single lament, like a solitary gushing of crimson blood.[306]

In her shock she asks whether she has said anything, told a confidence, and she answers herself in the affirmative. In fact, it is he who has confessed in her stead by drawing out of her soul the hidden and deeply concealed word and assuming it in the light of truth into the divine Word. Again her hackles begin to rise, but "the spirit of revolt in her has lapsed into a heavy slumber."[307] Eventually Donissan's vision "recedes"; and yet he knows that, for the length of one moment that could never be undone, eternal truth has bent low over the abyss of time, and during this moment—"a minute, an eternity! —he too had been raised above his own nature by an almost divine effort."[308] From the perspective of this elevation, he can point out the nothingness and the self-destructive quality of the sin behind which Mouchette wanted to entrench herself against God: "You've brought to bear nothing but false crimes, just as you've given birth only to a lifeless fetus. Search farther! Stir up your slime a bit, and you'll see that the vice you so flaunt has long since rotted away there. . . . Out of yourself you've drawn nothing but vain dreams, ever-disappointed dreams."[309]

This is not yet enough, however. The penetrating gaze becomes ever keener and must dig down to a greater depth. The sinful destiny of little Mouchette cannot be considered in isolation. It finds both its reality and its unreality only in connection with the sins of all others, especially the ancestors, both known and unknown, who dissolve

---

[306] Ibid., 203–4. (The italics are von Balthasar's.—TRANS.)

[307] Ibid., 205.

[308] Ibid., 206.

[309] Ibid., 207.

into the night of the past: "Each of your acts is the sign of an act by those from whom you descend—cowards, misers, lechers, liars. I can see them. God allows me to see them. It's true that I've seen you in them, and them in you."[310] And now the priest's soft voice begins "with great simplicity" to draw them up, up from the depths of the generational conscience that is more deeply within Mouchette's conscience than the light of her consciousness can reach—a buried sphere into which we can nevertheless gain access only through the shaft of our individual consciousness as sinners. What is thus brought up is the truth of humanity's sin in all its social amalgamation and unity, just as it is seen by the eyes of the Judge and just as the cojudging priest must see it in the sacrament, implicitly most of the time and explicitly when a charismatic light is bestowed. This is "history seen from within, the most hidden and most zealously guarded aspects of history, not considered in the melding of effects and causes, acts and intentions, but history reduced to a few fundamental facts, to the primal sins that generate all others."[311]

As she listens, Mouchette finds in herself the confirmation of everything the priest is saying: in her flesh, in a race unified by inherited sin, in a memory emerging from much farther away than her own limited life. However, the self-disintegrating and dissolving chaos of collective guilt, with its spectral procession of the conjured dead, is exorcised by the light, by the word, "by the irresistible dominant emerging through a storm of sounds, by the active and dazzling will that pours the chaos into a stable mold".[312] And there now occurs for collective guilt the same thing that had occurred for individual guilt:

> The swarming multitude, in which a moment earlier she had recognized all her relations, gradually began to contract. Faces blended with faces, until they all formed but one face—the very face of vice. Vague gestures began to unify into one single attitude, which was the quintessential gesture of crime. Even more: at times evil left in its wake a prey that was nothing but an amorphous heap in full process of dissolution, swollen and digested by evil's poison. The misers formed a mass of living gold, the lustful a pile of entrails. All around sin was bursting its wrapper and let show the mystery of its begetting: dozens of men and women

[310] Ibid., 208.
[311] Ibid., 209.
[312] Ibid., 210.

bound together by the fibers of the same cancer, and the hideous bonds shrinking back like the amputated arms of an octopus, back to reach the very core of the monster—the initial sin that none had seen in the heart of a child. . . . And suddenly Mouchette saw herself as she never had before. . . . She had recognized herself in her kin and, at the climax of her delirium, she could no longer tell herself apart from the flock. Was it possible? Could she not find one single action in her entire life that did not have a double in someone else's? Not one thought all her own, not one gesture that hadn't long since been rehearsed? Her actions, thoughts, and gestures were not even similar: they were the very same! She wasn't repeating them: they were but one! . . . She sensed the enormous trick underlying her wretched little life, the gargantuan laughter of the Trickster.[313]

Later on we will deal with the mystery of collective guilt. What concerns us at present is the might of the words spoken in confession. These do more than simply descend into the unconscious with analytical tools and bring to light as in a mirror the realities of personal history and inheritance found there. By virtue of the power of divine judgment, the confessor's words confer on that enormous and yet "unreal" reality the only truth it can have in the sight of eternity. Just as Donissan's words at the decisive moment become identical with Mouchette's conscience, so too here: they now become identical with the elusive collective conscience, which in the end can attain any consistency only through the priest's words. The world of sin is subject to an ineluctable process of reduction whereby the apparent individuality of one person's guilt becomes dissolved in a deeper identity of species and kind. True uniqueness may be claimed only by the divine and the good; the satanic enjoys only the appearance of uniqueness. Thus, just as the guilty individual must experience the dread of seeing himself dissolve into the generic as he is stripped of all uniqueness, so too, in turn, the generic must see itself convicted of its naught before God. It is of no avail for Mouchette to flee from this revelation by hurling herself into one last encounter with Satan as his bride[314] and, finally, into suicide.[315] She is hemmed in on every side, and God's Word watches every route of escape. She kills herself precisely because she realizes the despairing nature of her situation.

---

[313] Ibid., 211–13.
[314] Ibid., 220.
[315] Ibid., 221.

As she dies, she requests to be taken to the church. Donissan accedes and carries her bleeding body there, and the scandal of the scene seals his fate: five years of banishment to a Trappist monastery.[316]

He then returns to his "poor confessional at Lumbres, which smells of gloom and mold",[317] in order to complete his task on earth: "Kneeling before him, his penitent children could hear only a sovereign voice coming from beyond eloquence, a voice that crushed even the most hardened hearts, a voice imperious as it pleaded and inflexible in its very sweetness. Out of the sacred gloom where the unseen lips moved, the word of peace went out, expanding like a ripple, more and more, until it reached the heavens, drawing the sinner out of himself until it left him bondless and free."[318] But, in the very measure in which he acts, he also suffers; he remains devoid of what he gives to others ("he distributed with full hands the peace he was bereft of"),[319] and the victory he so strenuously achieves has the form of a deeper defeat. The monotonous murmur of sin floods over and buries him: "Until the moment you die, raise your hand, forgive, absolve—you, O man of the Cross: always beaten in advance!"[320]

In *The Imposture* and *Joy* (which together constitute one novel in two volumes), the theme is how a soul can be broken open that has surrendered to the forces of hell and that, like hell itself, is shut off to all else. Like Donissan, Chevance is a timid and childlike priest who possesses a "divine simplicity" but is not gifted with eloquence.[321] His superiors have sent him from place to place and, thanks to Cénabre, he finally receives an appointment to a parish in Paris, where, according to a local wit, he busies himself as "confessor to maids".[322] Cénabre is perfectly aware of the special grace as confessor that his former student in the minor seminary of Nancy has received—a grace Chevance himself ignores—and on the night of his spiritual collapse, when Cénabre discovers with horror that he has "lost his faith", it is Chevance and no other that he summons. When Cénabre reveals his crisis to him, Chevance automatically assumes the attitude of a

---

[316] Ibid., 247.
[317] Ibid., 265.
[318] Ibid., 266.
[319] Ibid.

[320] Ibid., 315.
[321] *Imposture*, 40f.
[322] Ibid., 42.

confessor, but this throws the renegade into a rage. The "poor priest's humble gaze" gives forth "a sacred assurance", as he says to Cénabre: "I have nothing else to give you. . . . On my own I am nothing. Allow me to yield my place to God. I won't commit the madness of trusting my own lights. No, I will not incur such folly!"[323] "His eyes pleaded so humbly that Cénabre involuntarily yielded to him. 'I have lost my faith', he said." Later on the avowal of suicidal thoughts comes about just as involuntarily. But when revolt again rears its head in Cénabre, Chevance rises and says to him "with extraordinary dignity": "From this moment on I can hear what you have to say only in the sacrament of penance."[324]

But the wrestling match continues. Chevance realizes the extent to which the other priest has become entangled, and, when Cénabre asks to be heard in confession, Chevance refuses to collude in what would only be a "sacrilegious illusion". The resounding No! he hurls at Cénabre goes out of him, likewise involuntarily, "like a bullet", and he is the first to be frightened by it.[325] Because he is so completely given to God, this priest will always be saying things that transcend his own intellect and will. The confession does not take place, and absolution is impossible. But Cénabre has nevertheless revealed the state of his soul, and he has no idea of the consequences for him of having in the future a confidant ready to hear his confession, someone who has seen his hellish refusal in the light of absolution. Cénabre now forever has "this obscure judge, the intimate of one hour who had again disappeared into the crowd but who was a thousand times more dangerous because of his very obscurity: someone henceforth beyond his control."[326] Even in hell he can no longer be alone. From this hour on, however, Chevance will be in a position to die a vicarious and horrible death that practices a permanent breach in the prison wall of the miserable Cénabre.[327]

After having "bared himself to Chevance", Cénabre realizes he has also "disclosed himself to himself": "Just for once, just one time, he has heard the deep ring of his nature, the lament going up from his bowels that even the prodigious skill of his lying had not suc-

[323] Ibid., 49.
[324] Ibid., 52.
[325] Ibid., 59.
[326] Ibid., 60.
[327] *Joie*, 261, 308.

ceeded in smothering."[328] He questions Chantal "eagerly about the last moments of the Abbé Chevance on earth".[329] He gets a sense of the true context.[330] The "unstable balance" of Cénabre's imposture has not been "broken":[331] he has said too much; he has revealed too much about himself, even to Chantal, who has now somehow taken the place of the dead priest[332] and who, thanks to her own gift of vision, has now become just as much of a confidant.[333] His secret has been stolen from him; the only thing left for him to do is to hand it over voluntarily.[334] *Indeed, Chantal's light has penetrated inside him and is bursting him open from within:* "A stream of light had made its way within him."[335] The violence done him, moreover, is so strong that his mind is ready to explode. The blow that strikes him and henceforth plunges him into madness to his dying day is nothing other than the expression of this powerful explosion. He advances toward his deliverance "with a dagger in his heart".[336] He is "drained of all strength and has stopped fighting back, like a dying man who has already felt the first shiver of agony in the hollow of his chest, close to his heart" and who at long last "abandons himself".[337] This new experience of self-abandonment, in its certitude, can only coincide with the total anguish that is the organ through which he perceives it: he is now "broken open, incapable of containing any lie, delivered over beyond self-defense to what his whole life long he had feared more than any other danger, namely, exposure to the curiosity of others and to the cruelty of human judgment."[338] And so he escapes into the night, but in vain: he is really escaping toward his own destiny; for it is now that he receives the news of Chantal's sacrificial death. Before she dies, and before he himself descends into madness, she forces him to utter the words "Our Father"—the words that finish him off as he pronounces them "with a superhuman voice".[339]

In *The Diary of a Country Priest*, all of this again emerges in a more humanized and serene form, but also rendered a bit too inoffensive. It is the country priest's vocation to crack shut souls open with the

[328] Ibid., 298.
[329] Ibid., 169.
[330] Ibid., 260.
[331] Ibid., 275.
[332] Ibid., 282.
[333] Ibid., 272.
[334] Ibid., 283.
[335] Ibid., 304.
[336] Ibid., 305.
[337] Ibid., 306.
[338] Ibid., 308.
[339] Ibid., 317.

pincers of grace. Like Donissan, he could have chosen the way of easy sanctity[340] instead of becoming a fighter against Satan. Like Chevance, he is a weakling who lacks the gift of words but who on the spur of the moment says more than he is aware of or intends.[341] He too triumphs in the end in his decisive battles, but he must leave the field of battle as one thoroughly beaten in the human dimension: the daughter and the husband take their revenge on him for the conversion of the countess by attributing to his words the emotional shock that caused her death. They also resent his silence concerning the countess' last words, which he considers a secret of the confessional.[342] It will be left to him, too, to strike the decisive blows against the power of hell, for he will have to disclose the revolt out of despair afflicting the soul of the offended mother and wife and to trace this revolt to its origin in the jaws of the abyss.[343] At the same time, however, he is able to show her that the deepest revolt can be overcome by an even deeper love and that man's eternal revolt has been transformed mysteriously by the greater present (and presence) of the Passion into a thing of the past: "You could wave your fist at him, spit in his face, beat him with rods, and finally nail him to a cross. . . . What would it matter? *All of it has already been done to him*, my daughter."[344]

All of the other duels gyrate around this centralmost battle: for instance, the confession of the live-in tutor, Mademoiselle Louise, who is also the count's mistress. Her spiritual insufficiency makes evident the fact that the battle of confession demands a certain interior grandeur, a certain quality of soul, also in the penitent. "Be proud!" the priest advises her. At that, she looks at him in amazement, surprised "to hear these words from [his] mouth", and makes some reference to humility. In reply the country priest utters one of the principles of Bernanos' creed: "The finest thing is to rise above pride, but to do this one must first have reached at least that level."[345] And to himself he muses: "Never have I better understood my own powerlessness in the face of certain misfortunes into which I simply cannot enter, do what I might."[346] He prefers dealing with Chantal, the daughter of the count and countess, who is indulging in a vast

---

[340] *Soleil*, 129.

[341] Ibid., 197, 269; *Curé*, 166–67.

[342] *Curé*, 191f.

[343] Ibid., 180f.

[344] Ibid., 189.

[345] Ibid., 244.

[346] Ibid., 245.

revolt and who hates him. She would like to hate God too and thus hurl herself into hell; but the priest says to her face that he "vouches for her" and that her revolt is already a form of approaching God. "I'll avenge myself," she mutters, "I'll do evil for the sake of evil!" To which the priest rejoins: "At that very moment, I tell you, you'll find God. . . . You run away by giving your back to the world, because the world is not revolt but above all acceptance, and in the first place the acceptance of lies. Hurl yourself forward to your heart's content, then. Some day the wall will have to give, and all breaches open out to heaven."[347]

In the background there are the ordinary confessions, those of the children especially, so questionable in their validity,[348] and those of the adults with all their crustiness and deceit:

> I cannot for the life of me . . . understand what frightful transformation makes people unable to give anything more than this kind of skeletal and indecipherable image of their interior lives. . . . It's so easy not to go to confession at all! But there's something worse than this: the slow crystallization, around the core of conscience, of all sorts of petty lies, sly maneuvers, and equivocations. The simple matter is that the visible crust vaguely retains the shape of what it conceals. By sheer force of habit, and with the passing of time, the less subtle among them end up creating a full-blown language all their own, which remains incredibly abstract. It isn't that they're concealing much to speak of, but their cunning frankness reminds me of drinking glasses made opaque by long use that only admit a diffused light: the eye can't make out what's in them.[349]

We must finally mention another aspect of confession that constitutes something like its "upper limit": a certain impossibility to confess when God has deprived a soul of the ability to look at itself, at its own humility, and assent to his will, when, in a word, the soul has in some sense been dispossessed, as in the case of Chantal and Donissan. Chantal is repulsed by "the apparent mediocrity of her confessions", by "their insignificance. . . . She chided herself inwardly for mani-

---

[347] Ibid., 277.
[348] Ibid., 90.
[349] Ibid., 102.

festing her soul so badly to the dean of Idouville. . . . But what was she to tell him?"[350] The elderly priest of Larieux hears Donissan's confession every Thursday, and he finds "nothing extraordinary in the utterances of his penitent". Donissan had chosen him "without fuss" simply because he was "the oldest priest around", and every week he would "listen to the little speech" the old man gave him—this priest whom Menou-Segrais considered an "imbecile". And he listened "with so much love that the good man, surprised and flattered, in the end began to find some meaning in his own jumbled mumbling".[351]

This "upper limit" never exists for the penitent himself; it can be detected from the fact that he has been drawn more deeply into the sacramental mystery of the Church contained in all the sacraments—the mystery that consists in suffering along with her Bridegroom for the sins of all. Here, so strong, personal, and demanding a relationship is established to every sin committed that the distinction between one's own sins and those of others is beside the point. In this way the mystery of confession transcends itself and becomes one with the mystery of communion, so much so that the former can no longer be understood in isolation from the latter. Every sacramental confession necessarily contains such a limit, since it is an avowal made to the representative, not only of God, but also of the communion of saints. And, since anyone who sins against God also sins against the communion of saints (and every human being), his sin by its very nature has a social significance and, all the more so, his repentance.

Perhaps more than any other Catholic in modern times, Bernanos was crucial in reviving the ecclesial meaning of the public confession of guilt. The truth must be brought to light, even if this truth consists of the sins of Christians and of the Church's representatives. Only the confession of the truth can heal and absolve in every sense of the word, never the concealment and sly renaming of the truth. The whole polemical side of Bernanos' literary work should be seen exclusively within a sacramental context: above all, *The Scandal of Truth*, *The Great Fear of the Right-Thinking*, *The Great Cemeteries under the Moon*, and the famous "Letter to Amoroso Lima" of January 1940, which Bernanos himself considered to be a kind of definitive

[350] *Joie*, 46.
[351] *Soleil*, 142–43.

programmatic document.[352] Within the communion of saints there can, strictly speaking, be no purely private guilt and therefore no purely private absolution either. And, just as the individual sinner has an obligation to confess his sin (and this obligation cannot be substituted for by anything else, not even interior repentance), so too something analogous exists within the realm of history. To be sure, we speak here of something that is *only* an analogy, something that must still be verified by theology since Bernanos presents it more as an exploratory intuition than a clearly conceived idea. The substance of Bernanos' insight, however, remains inseparable from confession, since it refers to the exact point of connection between the two sacraments of confession and the Eucharist in their relationship within the total organism of all the Church's sacraments.

5. Damnation and Redemption

Never has there been so much talk about hell and damnation in literature as we see in our time. The rediscovery of the demon and his somber abode has led further to modern man's making himself at home in those realms of experience that ancient Christian dogma had described as characteristic of hell; most of the "existentials" of the philosophy in vogue today[353] belong to this locus of the spirit: here we would have to mention Sartre, Thomas Mann, Kafka, and their lesser satellites. If we followed a strict logic of thought, we would see that the theme of hell should be the common denominator of today's spiritual and intellectual battles. Bernanos participates in these with all the Christian earnestness he can muster. Nowhere else does he show himself so intent on thinking and speaking on the basis of and in obedience to revelation. Nor should we expect any less from someone who was familiar like few others with modern man's abysmal rejection of God.

Leaving aside the Romantic influences we have noted in his first novel, *Under Satan's Sun*, which vanish later on as we have seen, we can identify three distinct sources of influence that contributed in a

---

[352] All the letters to Amoroso Lima—from September 26, 1938, to December 1942—published in *Esprit*, August 1950, 187–209, are of great interest.

[353] The original edition of the present work is dated 1954.—TRANS.

general way to Bernanos' position on this problem. Although all three of these influences are expressions of a particular spiritual situation in history, Bernanos submits them to the judgment of Christian revelation: to it alone are they to bear witness. In the first place, Bernanos is concerned with making eternal damnation palpable to an existential faith and to do this by means of the possible experiences of damnation and perdition to be found within the temporal world. Here Bernanos is doing in the Christian camp the same thing as Sartre, Camus, and Kafka (to name but three) are doing on the non-Christian side. He then undertakes to test the social problematic of damnation critically and appropriate it, an endeavor in which he follows Péguy above all, but also Dostoyevsky and the Russians. Finally, Bernanos seeks to consider hell in the light of Christ's Cross, his descent into the netherworld, and his Resurrection; in other words, he puts the problem of hell within a soteriological context, which is where it must be approached like all other mysteries of revelation without exception. It is obvious that all of this cannot be more than an essay and an approximation, for no one can speak "systematically" about hell. We can only deal with aspects of it, as indeed revelation itself does.

Unlike so many Christians, Bernanos does not "reason" about damnation: rather, he leads to a vision of it *by way of experience*. "When it reaches its term, sin gives birth to death" (James 1:15). Spiritual death lies hidden in sin like a ripening fruit, growing and finally complete in all its members, a fruit that falls fully ripe from the tree only at bodily death. Writer and priest never appear so tightly intertwined as in the face of this subject: it is the task of each of them to expose this concealed fruit in his own way. They do this by instilling the consequences of faith into conscious experience, or, what amounts to the same thing, by drawing the consequences of faith from the depths of the contradictions people live out. While attempting this, Bernanos is fully aware that only approximations are involved, since "no one ever penetrates to the depths of his own solitude."[354]

Under Satan's Sun was meant to awaken the world by all means possible to the actuality and presence of hell: in the sinner who, like Mouchette, throws herself open to it and in the priest who, like Donissan, becomes its vicarious victim. One day Mouchette abruptly

---

[354] *Curé*, 243.

asks her lover: "Do you believe in hell, sweetheart?" When he answers no, she finds him insipid for being afraid of his wife but not
of Satan.[355] The ridiculously "enlightened" figures whom Bernanos
gathers in the rectory at Lumbres on the last evening of the saint's
life are intended to show, with all the clarity of the absurd, that the
age of not believing in hell is now past. *The Imposture* goes farther
down the same road; but hell, in objectivized form, here becomes
the innermost core of objective sin. The demonic libertine Guérou
declares: "The good thing about vice is that it teaches you to hate
man. Everything is just fine until the day you begin hating yourself.
I ask you, my boy: hating your own kind in yourself—isn't this hell
itself? Do you believe in hell, Pernichon? . . . *I* believe in it. . . . See
here, not to go any farther: my own home is a hell."[356]

Cénabre's progressive descent through all the circles of hell, until
he reaches its Luciferian center, still retains something of the heroic
Romantic element and no doubt reveals too great an interest on
Bernanos' part in such peregrinations. He does not succeed in de-
priving his hero of a certain spiritual grandeur and dark radiance, not
even when he has him strolling at night through Paris in the company of a tramp: "Cénabre's life is . . . one of the very few examples, perhaps the only one, of absolute refusal. To have some idea
of so desolate and sterilized a soul we would have to think of hell,
where despair itself is stagnant, where the shoreless ocean has neither
ebb nor flow."[357] He has repelled not only every form of faith and,
naturally, of love but expressly every form of hope as well, and he
lives in the proximity of nothingness[358] and in a hopeless contemplation of death from which he cannot henceforth be separated by
any event of whatever magnitude.[359] The only thing he has left is his
enormous curiosity, which for Bernanos is always the infallible sign
of an evil disposition: Cénabre is forever expecting "a new and imminent revelation, but coming from himself".[360] Thus, he can "enjoy
what tortured pride is always eagerly seeking: the brief and precari-
ous refreshment of shame. For humility is not, as dolts would have it,

[355] *Soleil*, 72–73.
[356] *Imposture*, 183.
[357] Ibid., 194.
[358] Ibid., 195.
[359] Ibid., 198.
[360] Ibid., 200–201.

an exclusive prerogative of heaven, made only for the godly minded. Even fallen nature, all the while hating it, cannot altogether dry up the wellsprings of humility within itself. . . . It suddenly wells up, unexpected and unrecognizable. . . . Full consciousness of evil does not belong to this world. Perfect, absolute remorse would make hell shoot up within a man and consume him on the spot."[361]

But what cannot occur all at once must inevitably occur gradually in "one indefinable process of gliding":[362] Cénabre must finally lose the God whom he has not quite been able to shake loose. He has sworn to himself that he would never be like those "renegades . . . who seem to drag their despised god along with themselves like a chain-gang companion, all the while insulting him". He himself, Cénabre, would "remain impenetrable until the end, until his very death".[363] And he really does succeed in changing by degrading and disintegrating himself. He becomes sloppy and dirty, not out of neglect, but in order to snuff out the image of himself always before his eyes. His internal dissolution manifests itself in acoustic phenomena: "He moved to and fro through a kind of muddled din, which not even sleep could altogether silence" and which brought about "sudden outbursts of violence". These attacks dispelled "the tireless rumbling, but only for a moment, and it then started up again ever so softly and carefully".[364]

Bernanos gives us one last image of this voyage to hell, perhaps the most significant of all and one that retains for him a strange ambivalence:

> *At bottom [Cénabre] was not changing. It seemed rather that he was regressing into the past, retracing his steps to his origin. He was not discovering a new man but again encountering the old. He was finding himself again little by little.* Such was the unexpected, the unforeseeable and supernatural result of having embraced lying—wholeheartedly, irreversibly! The strong image of himself he had formed, the artificial and fraudulent character that ev-

---

[361] Ibid., 212–13.

[362] Ibid., 215. (Nothing can approximate the stunning onomatopoeia of the original here: *un glissement indéfinissable*, consisting of sibilants, liquids, and the obsessive repetition of the vowel "i". Not enough attention has been paid to the specifically poetic techniques in which Bernanos' prose excels. He often approaches Dante himself in his use of linguistic devices that render evil palpable.—TRANS.)

[363] Ibid., 217.

[364] Ibid., 220.

eryone (beginning with himself) took to be the true man of flesh and
bone, was now falling apart little by little, was now breaking away from
him in tatters. . . . Just as in a night of rioting you can see emerging
on every side forgotten men, suddenly disgorged upon the town by the
dungeons and prisons, and, dazzled by the light, they grope stealthily
with hasty, silent steps toward the uproar and the conflagration: so, too,
the Abbé Cénabre could have recognized and named one by one the
thousand faces of his childhood. . . . All the dark corners swarmed with
fierce, embryonic life: thoughts, desires, lusts that were barely developed,
reduced to the essential—their germ, slumbering but alive.[365]

This very potent picture remains ambiguous because, for Bernanos,
the movement toward childhood always connotes the recovery of lost
sources. We have already seen that in Bernanos the most extreme evil
has the tendency to pass from self-disintegration to a return, through
self-dissolution, to its constitutive elements, and we will soon have
to examine the truth of such a conception. Even after the great efforts expended in the writing of *The Imposture*, Bernanos still felt he
had not reached the bottom of the abyss he could only half perceive.
He came to see more and more that this could not be done through
the portrayal of the extraordinary ("this soul, predestined above all
others", he had said of Cénabre) but by manifesting the presence of
damnation at the root of every actual sin. The ray of supernatural
light that priest and writer project on such damnation could result in
a revelation of hell. In the notes for the *Life of Jesus* he began in Brazil,
we read the following decisive phrase: "The hell of this world is hell
itself. It is its portal and threshold."[366] A few years earlier, speaking of
Maurras, he had written in *The Scandal of Truth*: "[Maurras] is cruelly
divided against himself. He has a passion for certain truths, and he
relentlessly strives to bend his thought to the discipline they impose;
but his very being rejects those truths, rejects their eternal substance
and profound reality. The temporal destiny of this man, therefore,
impresses me as one of the most cruel forms of damnation possible
in this world."[367] The country priest, for his part, writes the following words in his journal on the eve of his departure for Lille: "Doubt

[365] Ibid., 221–22.
[366] *Bul.* 6, 2.
[367] *Vérité*, 28–29.

concerning oneself is not humility. I even think that at times it could be the grandest, almost delirious form of pride: a kind of ravenous jealousy that makes a wretch turn against himself and devour himself. The secret of hell must lie here."[368]

Such affirmations are only intended to point to the presence of hell in this world. In order to isolate the essence of hell more plainly, Bernanos sets about excluding the passion and fire of revolt, since these are too intimately bound up with the wholesome and necessary vitality of our temporal existence: "Elemental woe is calm, solemn, like a king on his throne, mute as a shroud", says Fiodor in *Joy*. "As for despair: it confers on us an empire equal to God's."[369] And, speaking of the child he once was, Bernanos himself says: "I'd rather see him in revolt than jaded by disappointment, because most frequently revolt is but a form of transition, while disappointment of this sort no longer belongs to this world: it is brimming and dense as hell itself."[370] In the countess the country priest comes up against "all the harshness of hell".[371] What Bernanos puts in highest relief, however, is the coldness of hell, no doubt echoing Dante unconsciously: "I am cold itself. The essence of my light is unbearable cold", Satan declares to Donissan.[372] "His masterpiece is a peace that is mute, aloof, frozen, comparable to the thrill of nothingness."[373] Chevance says to Cénabre: "Alas, Sir, in blasphemy some love of God may still be found. But the hell you inhabit is the coldest of all."[374] And Chantal says to her father: "The world for which our Lord did not pray, the world you think I know nothing about—pshaw! It's not so hard to find it: it's the world that prefers cold to hot."[375] In his one and only sermon—at the grave of the murdered shepherd—the Curé de Fenouille says to his "dead parish": "All of you feel chilled to the bone, frozen cold. People always speak of the fires of hell, but no one has ever seen them, my friends. Pure cold is hell!"[376]

The nature of fire is different. In the words of the mayor of Fenouille, fire "triumphs over everything. There's no filth and no smell that can resist fire. The purest water is not as pure as fire: fire would

---

[368] *Curé*, 271.
[369] *Joie*, 150.
[370] *Enfants*, 195.
[371] *Curé*, 185.
[372] *Soleil*, 168.

[373] Ibid., 221.
[374] *Imposture*, 68.
[375] *Joie*, 103.
[376] *Ouine*, 166.

find something to consume even in pure water, don't you agree? . . . Water can do nothing for our miseries, but nothing is above fire. Fire is God, I do declare."[377]

Fiodor, the Russian in *Joy*, views the matter differently: "The secret of this house is not evil—no: it is grace. Our cursed souls drink it like water and find it tasteless, insipid, even though it is the fire that will consume us all eternally."[378] These elements, however, are but images; we must consider the thing itself they signify. The country priest knows that "hell is no longer to love",[379] but what this means exactly no one knows. It is the breaking off of all solidarity, something that for us is strictly unimaginable. It is a "sacred solitude" based on "a total and definitive rupture with the society of men",[380] or, what amounts to the same thing, it is the state of a person who has never really engaged his soul: "Could not damnation be to discover too late, after one's death, that one has never used one's soul?"[381] This had been the country priest's view: "I believe—in fact, I am sure —that many men never engage their being, their deep sincerity. . . . Once stripped by death of all the artificial limbs society furnishes to people of their kind, they will find themselves just as they are and just as they have been without realizing it: hideous undeveloped monsters, mere human stumps."[382] Thus we can understand the statement that "we always end by hating the truth we have deliberately disregarded. This is one of life's great secrets and also the secret of everlasting hell."[383]

These reflections bring us to the second question. Bernanos cannot ignore the objection raised by Péguy: it is the ancient Christian objection taken up by the nineteenth-century Russians and made out of a sense of human solidarity. In his first *Joan of Arc*, the socialist Péguy formulated the question as follows: Must I not fear eternal damnation just as much for any of my brethren as I do for myself? Can I be happy as long as a single one of them is excluded from the eternal light? Must I not therefore offer and lay down my soul in order to

---

[377] Ibid., 203–4.
[378] *Joie*, 154.
[379] *Curé*, 181.
[380] *Rêve*, 245.

[381] *Liberté*, 282.
[382] *Curé*, 123–24.
[383] *Enfants*, 47.

share the lot of those who are far from God, regardless of the just reasons and real guilt that led to their condemnation?[384] Bernanos must here agree with Péguy, having as he does the tendency to view the existence of evil as a monstrous "calamity" and a horrendous "destiny" that has befallen man. He feels that the most anguishing of questions—that concerning the salvation of one's brethren—should leave no man, and especially no Christian, indifferent. The frightening proclamation of judgment made by the Gospel is not intended to set our minds at rest but rather to jolt us ever anew to a mortal dread beyond systematization. Hell is not one of those facts to which one can "become resigned"; God himself, according to Péguy's Joan, will never "become resigned" to it.[385] In his sermon for the feast of Saint Thérèse, the atheist takes up the same theme in an ironical and provoking manner.[386]

Péguy mockingly reproached Dante, the visitor to hell, as a tourist who left the place just as he had entered it. His Joan vows herself to damnation if only she can share the lot of her brethren. And Péguy understood this lot of no-exit damnation in the first place in an earthly manner: as sheer misery, as the very condition that underpins a life of strictest, inexorable hopelessness.[387] He transposes the essential qualities of damnation to the earthly scene, to what is despairing in an earthly sense, while he compares the ordinary poor man with the inhabitants in Christian purgatory who enjoy a hope for heaven and the communion of all those who love. By contrast, "the horizon of the damned is barred off with an infinite barrier; hell is encircled." Likewise, "since all hope is forbidden the miserable, his misery has no limit. It is literally infinite. There is no need for its cause or its object to be infinite in order for it to be infinite. A cause or an object

<hr />

[384] "Et s'il faut, pour sauver de l'Absence éternelle / Les âmes des damnés s'affolant de l'Absence, / Abandonner mon âme à l'Absence éternelle, / Que mon âme s'en aille en l'Absence éternelle" [If, in order to save from the eternal Absence the souls of the damned ranting at this Absence, I must abandon my soul to the eternal Absence, then let my soul go to the eternal Absence]: Charles Péguy, *Jeanne d'Arc*, in: *Œuvres poétiques complètes* (Paris: Éditions Gallimard, Bibliothèque de la Pléiade, 1957), 959.

[385] "Jésus, votre Saint, ne s'y habitue pas. Vous ne vous y résignez pas" [Jesus, your Holy One, does not get used to it. Don't you become resigned to it either]: *Pages retranchées du Mystère de la charité de Jeanne d'Arc* (Pléiade), 1347.

[386] *Cimetières*, 251–52.

[387] *De Jean Coste*, miniature edition, 18f.

that is not infinite for an external science like physics may nevertheless occasion in a soul an infinite feeling if this feeling fills the whole
soul."[388] And Péguy adds with pathos: "Many an old man would have
returned to Catholicism if it were not for this single article of faith:
he descended into hell, and the interpretation the Church gives of it.
A very great number of serious young people have renounced their
Catholic faith primarily and even exclusively because they could not
accept the existence or the preservation of hell."[389]

We cannot here enter fully into Péguy's solutions to this problem;
we can only show the direction they pursue. In the first *Joan of Arc* we
witness Joan's blind solidarity with her damned brethren, to the point
of being thrown out of the Church and being burned at the stake.[390]
Joan's last utterance is still an anguished appeal for the eternal salvation
of all men.[391] In the second *Joan* what we have is a declaration of solidarity with God's innermost Heart, made by saints revolting against
hell, and their strengthening in this by the "sign"[392] and indeed the
inner certitude of the progressive redemption of all.[393] And yet, significantly, this part was not published. Rather, its place was taken by
the second "mystery", *Le Porche du mystère de la deuxième vertu*, which
has hope as its theme. The ever-greater confidence of which Péguy's
"little hope" is capable banishes un-Christian "certainties" in a very
Johannine and Thérèsian manner. Simultaneously—and for the first
time in Péguy—the meditation pierces through to the depths of the
mystery of eternal doom and attempts to approach it experientially
in the terrible mystery of the "dead wood": the process of stiffening

---

[388] Ibid., 26.

[389] Ibid., 30.

[390] "Et je serai damnée à l'exil éternel, / Et je fuirai honteuse et douloureuse et gauche, /
En l'exil infernal à jamais exilée. . . . Et moi je serais là / Sans avoir un espoir d'espérance à
jamais / D'apaiser la douleur d'un seul des douloureux, / D'en consoler un seul du mal fou
de l'absence" [And I shall be damned to the eternal exile, / And I shall flee ashamed and
pained and awkward, forever exiled to infernal exile. . . . / And I shall be there, never again
to have any glimmer of the hope / of soothing the sorrow of a single one of the sorrowful,
/ of consoling a single one of them from the savage malady of absence]: *Jeanne* (Pléiade),
1191, 1192.

[391] "Pourtant, mon Dieu, tâchez donc de nous sauver tous, mon Dieu, Jésus, sauvez-nous
tous à la vie éternelle" [Still, my God, do try to save us all, my God. Jesus, save us all for
eternal life]: ibid., 1205.

[392] Ibid., 1348f.

[393] Ibid., 1370-71.

and hardening that turns a living soul into a woodlike object, until it skirts the borders of everlasting death.[394]

In what concerns the problem of solidarity and that of earthly misery, Bernanos fully follows the lead of his predecessor Péguy. In Brazil he sketched an outline for the "Life of Jesus" he intended to write, and this outline shows us the extent to which the double mystery of solidarity and misery lies for Bernanos at the very heart of Christianity and of the redemptive event enacted by Jesus Christ:

> I would like to write this book for the most miserable of men. I would also like to write it in their language, but this is not allowed me. One cannot imitate either misery or the language of misery. One would have to be miserable oneself in order to participate without blasphemy in the sacrament of misery.
>
> Christ came into this world, and he came for all, not just for the miserable. Around his manger could be seen the Shepherds and the Magi, but neither Shepherds nor Magi were in misery. It's possible that the Good Thief was one of the miserable, but we can't be sure of it. Contrary to what the moralists generally believe, true misery does not lead to crime; it does not result in either good or evil; true misery does not lead to anything at all. The true misery of the miserable leads only to God.
>
> Misery leads only to God, but it doesn't want to lead anywhere. It shuts in within itself. It is walled in, like hell. And yet Christianity must go down into it. As long as we tolerate a hell in this world we shall be forced to await the Kingdom of God in the privacy of our homes. The hell of this world is hell itself. It is its portal and threshold. Satan is the dispenser of riches, but Mammon's treasury is empty. Satan has barricaded himself in the inaccessible depths of misery, to the confusion and consternation of the rich themselves. Gold is only a likeness, a counterfeit, a trap of him who calls himself the idol of the world. While humanity watches the buzzing of the flies, it does not see how the circle of the horizon is shrinking: it descends slowly into misery; it is inhaled by misery. You cannot judge the power of misery by the number of the miserable, which is to say, by the number of people who lack absolutely everything necessary. It's possible that modern society will put an end to poverty, if only by eliminating in each generation those who are born poor, the misfits and the unadaptable, thanks to a program

---

[394] *Note conjointe.*

for the regulation of births and a strict selection process. I do not for a moment believe that you can reduce the number of the miserable by reducing the number of the poor. On the contrary, I believe that the merciful priesthood of poverty was established in this world precisely in order to redeem it from misery, from the savage contagious despair of the miserable. If we could dispose of some means to detect hope as the spring-finder discovers underground water, it's by drawing close to the poor that we would see the hazelwood rod bend down between our fingers.

The poor man is not a person who lacks life's necessities on account of his condition. He's a man who lives poorly, according to the immemorial tradition of poverty, who lives one day at a time from the work of his hands and who "eats out of God's hand", as the old popular expression has it. He lives not only from the labor of his hands but also from his brotherhood with the other poor, from poverty's thousand little resources, from the foreseeable and the unforeseeable. The poor have the secret of hope.[395]

Here we find the same distinction Péguy made between misery (as hell) and poverty (with its saving hope), the same demand that poverty should voluntarily descend into the world of misery—that "the saints go down into hell"—the same identification of eternal with temporal doom. But this trend of thought is radicalized beyond Péguy: Bernanos seems to say that misery, being the locus of most extreme exposure, already in and of itself has something to do with redemption. Satan, who inhabits misery, can only be a trickster dispensing emptiness with "full hands", and it is the rich who will be put to shame and not the miserable. These are walled in below all hope in a no-exit situation; but they do have one escape—that "leading to God". And so the single objective would be this: to turn the mystery of hope *hidden* within the hell of hopelessness into a *manifest* mystery of hope, by means of the voluntary presence of the true poor in this hell. No absolute wall of separation need exist between the misery of the modern world and the poverty of Christians.

The texts that are pertinent in this regard are not so much those describing Donissan's descent into the interior realm of the first Mouchette: for our present theme no longer concerns the battle against revolt but something deeper, something that can no longer

---

[395] *Bul.* 6, 1–2.

be dealt with by means of force but only through an accompanying presence. More relevant, therefore, are the texts describing the descent *into the world of the New Mouchette*, which, properly speaking, is the world of misery. Bernanos has never portrayed misery more thoroughly than here. This is a walled-in universe with no exits, and this condition intensifies more and more until its shut-in despair becomes perfected in suicide. But such intensification only manifests what this world had concealed within itself from the outset. For the man buried in misery, all things work together unto doom. Every new encounter with another human being—the teacher, the tramp, her mother, the woman waking the dead—leads inescapably to an even deeper plunge into the abyss of misery and the inexorable solitude misery entails. Mouchette has only one companion, but he cannot tell her he understands; he may not emerge from the darkness and intervene: for this sole companion is the novelist himself. His literary deed becomes for him an act of hidden coredemption. The latter, however, must remain hidden, since misery's sole escape is in God. Bernanos' manner of accompanying Mouchette here is an incomparably more Christian act than his accompaniment of Cénabre, for instance, because the former companionship is utterly free of any kind of curiosity concerning the world of evil. It is a deed of humility and poverty. The only thing that remains significant about Cénabre is his descent into the world of the vagabond and his searching in this way for an escape through human contact, also the fact that in this episode the misery of the one who denies God proves to be infinitely more hopeless than the beggar's. The scene that brings these two characters together is something like the onset of a final, fundamental separation of interior states.[396]

Increasingly, what we find in Bernanos is the same development as in the late Péguy: a relentless distinction and divergent evolution between the two kinds of hell—the hell of misery, which does not *know* love, and the hell of those who do not *want* to love. The latter is the condition of the woodlike, the petrified, those who have died the second death. These two hells clearly diverge from one another as the pre-Christian Hades, with its drab hopelessness, and the hell of the Christian dispensation, which is a consuming fire for absolute negators. Both Péguy and Bernanos might perhaps have preferred to see the two conditions as one, but they simply could not do that.

---

[396] *Imposture*, 205–46.

And, what Péguy learned with the years, Bernanos proclaimed with clarity: namely, that a descent into Hades in the invisible footsteps of the Redeemer is something conceivable but that communication with actual hell is inconceivable since here only the deadest wood burns, and this is an inert matter that it is no longer possible to "accompany". When a person can in all earnest no longer love, when he has no spark of love left, then his intellect, his reason, and the core of his personality have also been destroyed. In a most horrifying way he has become a "thing": "Alas! Were God to take us by the hand to one of these aching things, even if it had been our dearest friend, what language would we speak to it? No doubt about it: if a living man (one like us, the lowest of all, vile among the vile) should be thrown just as he is into those burning chasms, I would want to share his lot. I would go and try to wrench him from his torturer's claws. Yes, share his lot! . . . But the calamity, the inconceivable calamity of these burning stones is that they no longer have anything to share."[397] Even the image of "dead wood" is, according to Péguy, but a memory of a life that once was.

We must now consider our third theme. The distinction we have attained between pre- and post-Christian hell is in the end a distinction made by the humble obedience of faith, which does not seek to rob the Judge of the living and the dead of his freedom and mystery. It is a part of the Church's treasury of faith that Christ conquered Hades and the *pœna damni temporalis*, that through his descent into the world of the dead he has shattered its iron gates, and that Christians may follow his footsteps and partake in this mystery of discipleship too. It is equally clear that this same Christ is also the Master of all who revolt against him and that no one has the competence or the possibility to know in advance what the final verdict of the Crucified over his executioners will be, that is, to affirm how far the grace of redemption will extend. Christ is as much the Lord of hell as he had been the Lord of Hades; he is this not only by virtue of his divinity but equally by virtue of his humanity—of his vicarious suffering for all and his descent into godforsakenness, which, being a case of God forsaking God, far surpasses all possible forms of godforsakenness in

---

[397] *Curé*, 181.

sinners. The Christian sets his hope on this fact: that the Cross surpasses all possible hells; the hope of the Christian, therefore, is by its very nature unlimited. It is of this hope that Bernanos speaks when, following the path of the mystics, he too undertakes a descent into the hell of those who do not want to love. In this sphere man has even lost the right to distinguish between different kinds of hell: for here what is involved is the victory of Christ over—and his thoroughgoing elimination of—all that is lost in creation.

Bernanos says the essential in a 1927 conference entitled "Satan and Us":

> This little Mouchette emerged (from what nook in my conscience?), and immediately she gestured to me with her eager and anxious look. . . . I saw the mysterious young girl between her beer-brewing father and her mother. Little by little I spun her story. I walked right behind her, letting her go where she would. I felt she had a daring heart. . . . She was free. But with what sort of freedom? You see, I couldn't help it: one by one, all familial and social bonds were shattering behind her— those that make each of us some kind of disciplined animal even at the penultimate degree of abasement. And I felt that, as this was happening, my pitiable heroine was plunging more and more deeply into a lie that was a thousand times fiercer and stricter than any discipline whatever. Around the wretched child in revolt no avenue was open, no possible escape could be found. The crazed impetus that drove her toward an illusory liberation could lead nowhere but to death or to nothingness.
>
> Let us be clear. The Catholic dogma of original sin and redemption came up here [in the novel], not out of a text, but as a result of the concrete facts, circumstances, and junctures. Once the problem was stated, no other solution but this was possible. *At the extremity of certain kinds of humiliation and certain ways of squandering the human soul sacrilegiously, the idea of redemption suggests itself to the mind: I say the idea, not of reform or of turning back, but of redemption.* Thus, the Abbé Donissan did not suddenly appear on the scene haphazardly: he was called there by Mouchette's savage cry of despair, which made him indispensable. This is what Paul Claudel expressed in one of his magnificent formulations: "Your book sets everything in motion", he wrote to me, "just to come to the aid of this little crushed soul."
>
> Mouchette's character is so offensive to the need fools have of security that a great number of pious critics have asked me to get rid of her. However, not only is she necessary to the interior balance of the novel; she *is* this very balance! I don't give a hoot whether or not she

has "verisimilitude"; but she must be *true*, otherwise the work loses all meaning, and the terrible atonement carried out by the Curé de Lumbres is reduced to an atrocious and insane episode. Once the passions reach their climax . . . , do they or do they not attain a sort of lucid madness, the willful and deliberate search of evil—evil loved for its own sake— and finally total, absolute revolt, for which no maneuver of our reason could give a satisfying definition? Such revolt, however, is far from being unknown to human experience, since all men have for millennia had a clear consciousness, or at least a presentiment, of hell—of its traps, its mirages—in a word, of the Sun of Satan![398]

It is therefore hell that generates the idea of mankind's "buying back" or redemption. It is also hell that kindles, in God, the idea of the need for a redeemer and, in the writer's head, the idea of an atoner who makes manifest the here-and-now of redemption: the sacramental and mystical, but also the poetic, re-presentation (literally, "the making present") of the event of redemption, the redemption *in fieri* (that is, even as it is happening), and this redemption cannot be comprehensible without the reality of hell. The divine thought of creating a new way for man is kindled on the flint of the hopeless no-exit inherent in the way of sin. Mouchette becomes more and more the exponent of utterly doomed mankind, and Donissan a transparency of Christ. The young girl's revolt is fundamentally overtaken and hemmed in on all sides by the presence and sheer givenness of another, greater deed; and it is precisely the awareness of this fact that drives Mouchette to her final act of despair and mutiny—her surrender to Satan and her subsequent suicide.[399] But even this suicide comes too late, since it has already been reckoned with in Donissan's atonement. The express portrayal of Mouchette's salvation as she is dying[400] is a concession by the writer that later on, in the story of the second Mouchette, he will prudently omit. The girl's salvation was finally to accompany the narrative only as unspoken, implicit leitmotif. *Abyssus abyssum invocat:* "abyss calls out to abyss", an emblem that the incisive language of *An Evil Dream* elucidates as follows: "Precisely because [Simone's] instinct had already convinced her that she had been born outside the law, outside all laws, did she darkly desire to abide in this

[398] *Satan et nous*, in: *Bul.* 12–13, 26. (The italics are von Balthasar's.—TRANS.)
[399] *Soleil*, 217–18.
[400] Ibid., 247.

mysterious world where the only rule is God's fancy, his mysterious preferences, the adorable iniquity of an omnipotence that turns itself into mercy, forgiveness, poverty."[401]

This meeting of the two abysses occurs beyond the middle ground of morality and "catechism theology",[402] and it makes us glimpse something like a negative predestination, an idea in Bernanos that does not allow systematization but that strikes a very distinctive note. "Not everyone who feels like it can kill himself";[403] not everyone can go into hell who would want to.[404] For all the inventiveness sinners are capable of has been overtaken in advance by the Cross;[405] indeed, all the extravagances of the modern age in this connection are beginning to show signs of the bankruptcy of the exertion and fantasy whereby it has attempted to set up a new order based on perversity: "The modern world will shortly no longer possess sufficient spiritual reserves to commit genuine evil. Already . . . we can witness a lethal slackening of men's conscience that is attacking, not only their moral life, but also their very heart and mind, altering and decomposing even their imagination. . . . The menacing crisis is one of infantilism."[406] As an attack upon Being, sin is so traumatic that the wound it inflicts always squanders something of the power of negation, which thus dries up progressively. The very force of sin always destroys a part of its own fortifications: "He had just lost a part of his life, of consequence no matter how petty we may consider it. A part of himself had been dealt the death blow and had been abolished even as he continued to live. Through what mysterious wound and what *open breach* of the soul had it thus slid off into nothingness?"[407] Together with this we must recall the famous statement of the country priest: "Hurl yourself forward to your heart's content. Some day the wall will have to give, and *all breaches open out to heaven.*"[408]

---

[401] *Rêve*, 226.
[402] Ibid.
[403] *Curé*, 185.
[404] Ibid., 277.
[405] Ibid., 188f.
[406] Interview with *Samedi-Soir*, November 8, 1947; in: *Bul.* 7–8, 4.
[407] *Ouine*, 121. (The italics are von Balthasar's.—TRANS.)
[408] *Curé*, 277. (The italics are von Balthasar's.—TRANS.)

Paul Claudel's play *Le repos du septième jour* [The repose of the seventh day] was written in 1896. In it, the emperor of the Middle Kingdom sees his realm threatened by the blind disorder of the Kingdom of the Dead. And so, in Act II he descends into the Kingdom of the Dead, where he encounters his dead mother as a sorrowing, wandering shade. He then meets the demon, who informs him about hell. Finally, the angel of the Kingdom instructs the emperor on how the threat of the Dark Kingdom is to be overcome in the future. Despite certain Chinese and Greek influences, this journey to hell is conceived in a basically Christian manner: third in line with Péguy and Bernanos, Claudel here makes this great attempt at connecting with Dante. None of the three poets is dependent on the others, but all of them converge in constructing common solutions. In all three instances, the descent is atoning and vicarious and, like Christ's, efficacious. In all of them, the descent forges onward until it reaches the experience of interior darkness and doom, and this experience of eternal darkness exhibits a point both of entrance and of exit for the one descending. The essential aspect of Claudel's view is the identification of the fire with heaven, with the place of purification, and with hell: in the final analysis, the fire is God himself, Light of the spirit, who becomes a consuming fire for those in revolt.[409] Ordinary sinners go blind in the everlasting night, but the elect of the Dark Kingdom, who have sinned against the divine Spirit, receive "the Antiwisdom", "the black Splendor", "the inverse Knowledge", all of which constitute "the hermetic Mystery".[410] Thus it is that they come to be nearest to Satan. For:

> Satan's eye penetrates into the depths of the divine energies,
> And it sees light, wisdom, love and justice, meekness, generosity,
> All of which had created him in the beginning and which now
>   make him subsist.
> And just as the godless, the mad, and the wicked
> Use the world as if it had been created for them, so too Satan,
>   knowing God,
> Subordinates Him to himself like a cause to its end.
> And such is the supreme Incest and the Mystery of Quietude.[411]

---

[409] *Le repos du septième jour* (Paris, Éditions Gallimard, Bibliothèque de la Pléiade, n.d.), 757.
[410] Ibid., 762–63.
[411] "L'œil de Satan pénètre dans la profondeur des énergies divines, / Et il voit la lumière,

The emperor, who has greeted and touched the "bottom of the world",[412] will return to his kingdom aboveground with a leprosy that will make him into his empire's priest and sacrificial victim. Thus he will say:

> I have touched the bottom of everything, and my hand has
> left its trace there.[413]

And he becomes the express type of Christ:

> O ye thieves! You had stolen from your Creator his work, and his
> very precious good—your will:
> And he, repaying you in kind,
> Robs you (behold!) of your crime, and, snatching up your nature,
> he brings about its restoration.[414]

However, Christ's descent into hell suffers from severe defects in Claudel, especially in his equation of Hades and hell. Strictly speaking, the Kingdom of the Dead that the emperor visits is *sheol*; but the doctrine concerning it that the demon expounds is taken *quæstio* by *quæstio* from a treatise of Thomistic theology on hell. Claudel again took up this problem and expanded it in his *Conversations dans le Loir-et-Cher*. Here again, Flaminius begins by developing in lapidary fashion certain traditional propositions, this time borrowed from Báñez:

> As for me, I say that even at this price—even at the price of such an eter-
> nity of torture—it is better to have been a Christian than an unbeliever
> or a pagan. Being is always preferable to Nonbeing. If we don't bear
> witness through light, we at least bear witness through fire, and if we
> don't participate in mercy, we at least participate in justice. A believer,
> even if he is damned, affirms more about this God he has known [than
> an unbeliever who is not damned]. Fire is always fire. How beautiful a

---

la sagesse, l'amour et la justice, la mansuétude, la générosité, / Par lesquelles il fut créé au commencement, et par lesquelles maintenant il subsiste. / Et comme l'impie, le fou et le méchant / Use du monde comme s'il était créé pour lui, c'est ainsi que Satan, connaissant Dieu, / Comme la cause à la fin, se le subordonne à lui-même. / Et tel est le suprême Inceste et le Mystère de Quiétude": ibid., 768.

[412] Ibid., 747.

[413] "J'ai touché le fond de tout et ma main y laisse son vestige": ibid., 768.

[414] "O larrons! Vous aviez volé à votre Créateur son œuvre, et son bien très précieux, votre volonté: / Et lui-même, vous rendant la pareille, / Voici qu'il vous dérobe votre crime, et, s'emparant de votre nature, il opère la restitution": ibid., 770.

thing fire is, even *that fire that never dies*. It's a beautiful thing to nourish it with our most immortal parts. . . . The damned person serves a purpose: . . . he shines eternally with the very light he rejects.[415]

But Flaminius goes even farther:

> "For his works follow after him." If his evil works follow the damned man, so too his good works! He has not done only evil. And, in the definitive world, both these kinds of works yield their definitive fruits. By this I don't mean only a lightening of his sentence, but something positive, some part of the damned man himself that is incorporated into his being, a portion of his earnings as condemned prisoner. And even his bad actions: Have they not possibly been the source of many good and wholesome things? . . . His dim association with all the saints whose halo he has enhanced shall not come to an end. Hell is not something that lacks all solidarity with paradise, even though the two are separated by a profound disorder.[416]

The whole of this "winged" conversation revolves more and more around the subject of communion and community, finally culminating in the glorious "Canticle" where Palmyre announces that every single creature is necessary to her own beatitude: "Not one of our brethren, even if he should wish it, is capable of becoming a missing person from our circle. In the coldest of misers, in the heart of the prostitute and the filthiest drunkard there is an immortal soul, busy with the holy act of breathing. Banished from the daylight, it practices nocturnal adoration. . . . Very many souls exist, but there isn't a single one of them with whom I am not in communion through the sacred point in it that says *Our Father!*"[417]

By a train of thought very different from Bernanos', Claudel is here seeking to integrate the damned into the communion and community of all (redeemed) creation. When the country priest spoke of the process in hell whereby those "burning stones" that had been men turned into "things", however, and when he stressed the absolute break in communication between them and the living, could he not have been setting up a logical deduction as conceptual ultima-

---

[415] *Conversations*, 70–72.
[416] Ibid., 72–73.
[417] Ibid., 119.

tum, intended to break open the encysted feelings of the mother in her revolt against God? Even if Bernanos and Claudel do contradict each other in their literal text, must they therefore also contradict each other in the realities they actually intend? Bernanos does not allow himself Claudel's grandiloquent syntheses; instead, he leans with the cooler eye of a physician over the hidden and secretive wounds of evil. Nevertheless, as a man of his time, he cannot help joining Péguy's Joan and Claudel's Palmyre at the heart of their concerns. Where the other two poets round off the great arc of their thought to a satisfying conclusion, Bernanos prefers to tear open chasms: through their rending cry, however, these gulfs speak the same language as that of the more harmonious singers, perhaps even with more affecting penetration. For, also for Bernanos, the world of confession is but the entrance into the world of communion and of the most mysterious of the sacraments—anointing, which takes hold of man at his most intense moment of weakness in order to open up to him the great gate.

V. THE WORLD OF
ANOINTING AND COMMUNION

1. Death Agony as Boundary

Confession and the battle it involves make present in the life of the confessing penitent the *agon Christi*, Christ's own struggle on the Cross and in hell against the concerted might of Satan. This being so, then the penitent's conversion and return to God is, as the central-most act of his life, rooted in the ultimate act of Christ's life, which is to say, his death. Thus, confession and anointing, confession and death agony,[1] belong together. Now, the bursting open of the sinner's solitude and his insertion into the community of love has its sacramental seal in Communion; but Communion is the consuming of the Lord's flesh and blood, offered up through his death as a sign of a "love that perseveres to the end" (Jn 13:1). Thus, the "communion of saints", which is to say, the Church, stands under the same sign of a death agony. And when the two boundaries of existence—birth and death—become identical as transitions from eternity into time and from time into eternity, then the osmosis between baptism and anointing becomes evident. Finally, when in this way it becomes clear that entering into the life of faith means entering into the mysteries of

---

[1] The reader should note that, as used here by von Balthasar, the meaning of the word "agony" remains close to its Greek root ἀγών. The first meaning of ἀγών is an "assembly", especially one "brought together" (literal meaning of the verb ἄγω) to see competitive games. By extension, it refers to any struggle, contest, or battle, or even an action at law or a trial. Thus, Christ's ἀγών is one fought by the divine and human Hero in the presence of heaven and earth, to regain the divine image in man that had been lost through sin and Satan's trickery. The form this contest takes in Christ's life is his Passion, Cross, death, and Resurrection, and hence it is the specifically Christian context that henceforth associates "agony" with suffering and death, in union with Christ's paschal mystery. Ἀγωνία, even more specifically, refers to gymnastic feats, particularly wrestling, and connotes a *struggle for victory*. The theological importance of this full range of images and meanings should be evident, above all by its objectivity and public, communal nature. The anguished *psychological* state of mind normally evoked in us by the English word "agony" is present in the Greek only very tenuously and as a byproduct of the efforts in endurance required by the struggle. —Trans.

Christ's death, then confirmation, which strengthens us in our faith, becomes our fortification for a life in death and out of death, becomes a certainty and a joy out of anguish, a power out of impotency. These connections lead us into the very heart of our writer's worldview. They must be unfolded carefully, step by step.

At the source of it all in Bernanos' life lies a sacramental happening: it was at his First Communion that the boy first had an experience of death. This is how the seventeen year old describes things to a former teacher: "At the moment of my First Communion the light began to shine on me. And I said to myself that it was not so much one's life we had to strive to make happy and beautiful but one's death, the conclusion of everything."[2] This was also the time when anguished fear entered into the life of the child, an experience about which the letters of his youth provide such an eloquent testimony and which will remain the mysterious underlying tone and *basso continuo* of all the melodies of his life: "I fear death and, unfortunately (although perhaps my guardian angel would say fortunately), I'm always thinking about it. The slightest indisposition appears to be the prelude to this ultimate illness I so fear." Then and there, he decided to live wholly for God and to die for him, "thus I'll no longer need to be afraid of this hideous death."[3] But only two months later we again hear: "I'm so afraid of death and of the inevitable decomposition it entails, which almost makes the hair on my head stand on end."[4] Hence, Bernanos' first act of self-surrender to God appears to have been motivated by the will to overcome this panic and to attain a sort of Stoic superiority over the hideousness extending its shadow over all of life: "I think very often about this death I so fear, which can arrive at any moment like a thief. Compared with death, even the most brilliant lives are so sad and so empty!" He adds that he has found a good confessor and that he has read the "good and beautiful books" of Ernest Hello, which have helped him understand "that self-sacrifice and total self-forgetting are the only way of becoming somewhat valuable for God and his cause and *that the best means of attaining contempt for death is to offer up one's life and death in sacrifice*."[5]

---

[2] *To Lagrange*, March 1905; *C. du R.*, 19.

[3] Ibid., 18–19.

[4] Ibid., May 31, 1905; *C. du R.*, 22.

[5] Ibid., 21. (The italics are von Balthasar's.—TRANS.)

From here it was only a step to the heroic and aristocratic attitude of alleged superiority to death proffered to the young Bernanos by the ideology of the Action Française. This he was only too eager to embrace and try to graft onto his own lived experiences. We sense this attitude in his letters from this time, and we see it clearly dramatized in Drumont, the hero of *The Great Fear of the Right-Thinking*, whose portrait by Bernanos owes its decisive features to the influence of Maurras, which by that time he had almost overcome: "As in the case of most sacrificial beings—persons haunted by the idea of sacrifice—the image of death took for [Drumont] the place of hope. This image provided his nature with the indispensable portion of confidence and security it needed" and put his work "under the sign . . . of "an unflinching despair".[6] "A human life reckons its own value numerically as long as it has not made a free gift of itself; but sacrifice confers on it another and mysterious value. *Whoever lords it over his own death can gamble away his life, no matter how high the stakes.*"[7] "He is not afraid to question his heart, his nerves, his muscles, and, in the face of greatest peril and death itself, to hear his whole being reply: 'I'm ready!'—What inebriation!"[8] The fundamental thought underlying this astonishing book is thus that a life should be constructed that the power of death steels for anything and everything. Such death must obviously have no part of fear; it must be exalted to the sphere of the pure, the sublime, the childlike:

> We have seen people die. We know what dying is. It's not a difficult thing. The survivors of the last war, on the contrary, know that it's a very simple thing, a very simple and a very pure thing. To sum it all up we could say that, *if fear did not at times alter its sacred sincerity, dying would be a childhood affair*, something accepted with a child's heart. On the other hand, we are not at all displeased that an idea that has matured in our brain should one day go to pay its tribute to peril and return to us humanized and ennobled—dripping with nuptial blood—after having consummated its espousals with death.[9]

---

[6] *Peur*, 140.
[7] Ibid., 126. (The italics are von Balthasar's.—TRANS.)
[8] Ibid., 168.
[9] Ibid., 63. (The italics are von Balthasar's.—TRANS.)

However, intermingled with such formulations, which proclaim a sort of right-wing existentialism, we already perceive at the same time other ideas that reject all entrenchment in heroic gestures: "[Drumont] expected a great deal. He expected too much from the act of a man who loyally, honestly, unreservedly, and unconditionally puts his entire life as a man at the disposal of the truth whose eyes he feels upon himself. And, without his knowing it, what the truth looking at him expected from him was, precisely, his silent and powerless agony."[10] Thus it happens that the statement by Drumont that Bernanos quotes with approval has, in the very quoting, already been surpassed by Bernanos' appropriation: "Every man who is ready to die can influence events. Behind all events there stands a man who is ready to die."[11]

The temptation of a heroic cult of death is strong, and it will take Bernanos a long time to overcome it completely. It is the temptation to render the abyss of death *useful* and extract from it a more abysmal knowledge concerning life and experience, or, in other words, the temptation to reflect back over limited temporal consciousness that knowledge and vision which open up precisely in stepping beyond the limits of his own life. The earlier Bernanos believed that a person would come to know everything if, at the moment he *relinquishes* consciousness and loses his concentration on his own narrow little world, he could only set up a mirror next to himself in order to learn what he is doing in such a surrender. This is why Bernanos was fascinated with the French colloquial expression *se voir mourir* (to see oneself die), that is, to experience one's own death consciously: it contains an essential part of the theory of knowledge he long sought after.

Already in 1917 he writes to a schoolmate: "We mustn't *watch* ourselves live, but simply live. We must only watch ourselves die, when the time comes. Just think that we shall keep for all eternity the face we make for ourselves at that moment."[12] His first story, dating from 1922, begins with the sentence: "She doesn't realize it: she *shall not see* herself die",[13] but this statement is wholly reversed by the narrative

---

[10] Ibid., 134.
[11] Ibid., 136.
[12] *To Maître*, March 1917; *C. du R.*, 32. (The italics are the translator's.—TRANS.)
[13] *Madame Dargent* (Plon ed.), 5. (The expression *se voir mourir* should normally be trans-

itself, since Madame Dargent's death becomes a moment of supreme self-recognition, of insight into the nature of things, and an expression of her whole life:

> "I'm trying to fool myself, to imagine I'm falling asleep, lapsing into oblivion, gliding steadily away. . . . What's the good? My thought's never been clearer or my memory more precise and marvelously active, bathed in a harsh, blinding, implacable light. . . . I can no longer see you. There's a great expanse of water that must be a lake. I can't go any farther today. Wait. . . . Wait, I need to lean over it. . . . Hold me tight!" . . . She fastened an indecipherable look upon him, a look that was wonderfully alert and transparent but also one in which the great shadows of interior collapse glided to and fro. "I've seen myself in the water", she said. . . . "Stay a while! Stay forever! . . . Did you think I was already dead? I was only reflecting. . . .[14] Can this really be called reflecting? There's a frightful void in my head: my whole life is reassembling here", she whispered as she struck her forehead, "feature by feature. Every second a new memory—the oldest and most secret of all, the one most thoroughly dissolved by the past—floats up like a bubble and bursts on the surface. . . . Could it be that I'm dead? Little by little, as my familiar self is destroyed, another self is taking shape higher up, and I've just seen its true face: it's as if I would now be seeing it forevermore!"[15]

The dying woman's entire confession of her life was made possible by its becoming reflected in the mirror of death.

A significant indication of the evolution of Bernanos' thought is the fact that he refuses Monsieur Ouine the vision of his own death: "Well-intentioned people like to say of a person who dies quietly that the poor man 'didn't see himself die'. For me these words hold a hidden sense. Is it possible that I myself am no longer capable of 'seeing myself die'? At least no longer capable of that interior glance from which I've derived too much delight and which now is gyrating on itself like a delicate little machine gone berserk at the approach of the only thing that deserves being seen and that I now cannot see. If only I could see it through your eyes!"[16] Ouine's insatiable curiosity has

---

lated "to realize one is dying", but here we translate literally to keep to Bernanos' episte-mological nuance.—TRANS.)

[14] The reader should note the two senses of the word *reflecting* in this context. Bernanos surely intends both.—TRANS.

[15] *Madame Dargent*, 9.

[16] *Ouine*, unpublished chapter: *Bul.* 9, 11; "Club" ed., 268.

exhausted his seeing capacity. What he would like to have is the mental enjoyment of his own death: "Could I perhaps have two souls like some animals have two stomachs? Or perhaps two consciousnesses? Which of them will be snuffed out first? It would be interesting to watch the process."[17] But Ouine cannot "watch" his own death, and this precisely is the punishment with which his creator afflicts him.

Bernanos, for his part, hoped that "he would see himself die", although in a humorous letter he says he does not want to live in himself but in the ideal image of him that his loving friends have created: "An eternal divorce from the frightful old gentleman . . . I sometimes encounter in the mirror; nothing any longer in common with him, nothing but an eternal divorce from him! I am what all of you in your friendship want me to be. I will not meet up with the other me until the end of ends, and not for long even then, only the split second needed 'for the last croak', as Rimbaud says."[18]

The final step was taken, however, only when Bernanos' whole trend of thought regarding death moved out of the danger zone of a higher self-mirroring and transcendental reflection and became immersed in the mystery of Christ's death and agony. Henceforth, the thought of human death remained unfathomable outside the reality of Christ's own dying. It is the death agony of God's Son that provides a meaningful anchor both for the inward turning to self and for the fear of exiting from self. The false heroism of the Drumont portrait is in this way definitively overcome, as it yields to a glorification of powerless agony that even then was inchoate. This agony, however, is no longer that of man abandoned to his own helplessness but that of participation in the darkness of the Cross—a participation that is most real, albeit unconscious, for the one undergoing death in the night of impotency. In the end, each person dies another's death because Christ has died the death of each of us for us. This is the meaning of the first prioress' death agony in the *Dialogues of the Carmelites*:

MÈRE MARIE: I thought, Mother, that all your anguish had been appeased last night. . . .

---

[17] Ibid., unpublished chapter: *Bul.* 9, 10; "Club" ed., 267.
[18] *To Vallery-Radot,* June 12, 1933; *Bernanos,* 116.

THE PRIORESS: It was only a slumber of the soul. But God be thanked for it! I could no longer see myself dying. Well-intentioned people like the expression "to see oneself die". . . . Indeed, Mother, it's true I can see myself dying. Nothing distracts me from this vision. Of course I feel your concern and I'd like to respond in kind. But nothing can help me anymore. For me the rest of you are only shadows, barely distinguishable from the images and memories of my past. I am alone, my good Mother, absolutely alone, without any consolation. My mind remains quite capable of forming reassuring ideas, but these too are only phantoms. They cannot comfort me any more than the shadow on the wall of a leg of mutton can satisfy one's hunger. . . . I've meditated on death every hour of my life, yet now that's no good to me at all.[19]

Here, both things have become one: namely, absolute, open *vision* (such as already Madame Dargent with her lucidity possessed) and an absolute *helplessness* that is so great that it can only be understood as unconscious participation in Christ's anguish in the face of death. And so, what initially had been the spirit's encounter with itself, or the merging of its conscious with its unconscious will, can finally lead to the merging of our human willing ability with its apparent opposite, namely, the will of Christ. We may regard the following entry, already quoted, that Bernanos made in his "Agenda" shortly before his death in 1948, as the capstone of all his thought:

We really and truly want what He wants. Without knowing it, we really want our sorrows, our sufferings, our solitude, and we only imagine that what we want is our pleasures. We imagine that we fear our death and want to flee from it, whereas we really desire this death as He desired His. Just as He sacrifices Himself on every altar where Mass is celebrated, so too does He undertake to die again in every man entering his death agony. We want everything He wants, *but we don't know that we want it. We don't know ourselves; sin makes us live at the surface of ourselves. We will again go back into ourselves only to die, and it's there He awaits us.*[20]

Death and its agony, therefore, can be rightly understood only from Christ's perspective, and so Bernanos' focus turns more and more to him. Christ's death is what the Gospel "has most carefully unfolded. Nothing has been left out, while his triumph is a kind of children's

---

[19] *Carmélites*, 56–57.
[20] *Agenda*, January 24, 1948; *Bernanos*, 147.

parade, . . . a benign parody."[21] For Christ's death is the redemption of all, the locus where the destinies of all sinners can really and in earnest be gathered up and recapitulated in Christ as Head: "Fear of death is a universal feeling that necessarily comes in all sorts of forms. Some of these are surely beyond the reach of human language. There is only one man who has known them all, and this is Christ in his agony."[22] "From the Garden of Olives to Calvary, our Lord has in advance experienced and expressed all agonies—even the most humble, even the most desolate. . . . Many theologians believe that, in Jesus Christ at the moment of his Passion, human nature was abandoned to the experience of every feeling a man is capable of."[23] Thus, even new and unknown forms of anguish we have yet to discover may be seen as already anticipated by the Lord's Passion:[24] "The Nazis loved to contrast the Most Sacred Agony of Christ in the Garden of Olives with the joyous death of so many young Hitlerian heroes. Christ does indeed want to blaze for martyrs the glorious highway of a death without fear, but he also wants to precede each one of us through the darkness of mortal anguish."[25] And the following snatch of conversation between two Carmelites is very relevant here:

SISTER MARTHA: In the Garden of Olives Christ was no longer master of anything. Human anguish had never risen to that pitch of intensity, nor will it ever reach that level again. Anguish had submerged everything in him, except for the uppermost tip of the soul where his divine acceptance was realized. . . .

SISTER CLAIRE: The martyrs were upheld by Christ, but Christ himself was aided by no one because all help and all mercy come from him. No living being ever went into death more alone and more unarmed than he.[26]

Sin is for all sinners a kind of armor, a thick crust that hardens them and renders them incapable of the highest suffering. Only the Sinless

---

[21] *Curé*, 230.
[22] *Cimetières*, 85.
[23] *To Maître*, August 26, 1919: *Bul.* 1, 3; *C. du R.*, 37.
[24] *Cimetières*, 85.
[25] *Liberté*, 286.
[26] *Carmélites*, 158-59.

One has the sensitivity to feel the subtlest suffering.[27] And, by feeling and enduring everything possible and yet uttering no complaint, he shuts the mouth of hell: "Even on the Cross, as he brought his Sacred Humanity to perfection through his anguish, our Lord did not declare himself a victim of injustice. *Non sciunt quod faciunt*—'they know not what they do': these are words that even the smallest children can understand, words we would almost call childlike; and yet the demons have been repeating them to themselves ever since they were uttered, but without understanding them, much to their growing terror. Whereas they were expecting thunder, what came instead was an innocent hand that gently closed the pit of the abyss over them."[28]

The novel *Under Satan's Sun* did not fail to dramatize to an unbearable degree this situation of the Lord agonizing in the face of hell. What is unbearable about it, however, is not the Lord's suffering in itself but, once again, the ambiguity that commingles Satan's vision of the Cross with that of the human gazer:

> At certain moments just seeing is in itself so harsh a trial that one wishes for God to shatter the mirror. . . . It is hard to remain standing at the foot of the Cross but even harder to look at it unswervingly. . . . What a spectacle, my friend, is offered when innocence undergoes agony! But, after all, this death is nothing. . . . One could perhaps finish it off, accomplish it, with one fell blow; one could fill this indescribable mouth with earth so as to smother its cry. . . .[29] But no: the hand gripping him is wiser and stronger; the glance feasting on him does not come from human eyes. Everything is given, everything handed over to the terrible hatred that gloats over the just man as he dies. The divine flesh is not only torn apart; it is coerced and profaned by an absolute sacrilege reaching into the very majesty of the death agony.[30]

A wild dialectic leaps across the distance between Christ and ourselves; Bernanos is so bent on actualizing the Cross that he forces an identification:

---

[27] *Agenda*, January 24, 1948: in *Bernanos*, 147; see *Carmélites*, 159.

[28] *Carmélites*, 316–17.

[29] This is precisely what the murderess in *A Crime* does (63–65) in order the more quickly to reduce to silence the priest agonizing by the roadside.—Note of the French trans.

[30] *Soleil*, 283–84.

The "drama of Calvary," you say. . . . But it's so vivid it could almost pluck out your eyes: nothing else exists! Listen to me, Sabiroux: I who am speaking to you, I have heard, yes, I have heard, even in the cathedral pulpit, things . . . I cannot repeat. . . . People talk about the "death of God" as if it were some old fable. . . . They embellish the tale, they add to it. Where do they get it all from? The "drama of Calvary"! Watch out, Sabiroux. . . . God casts us between Satan and himself as his last rampart. It's through us that for centuries now the same hatred has been trying to reach him. The unspeakable murder [of God] is perpetrated in the poor flesh of man.[31]

Already in his next novel Bernanos is careful to respect the distance between Christ and ourselves. We could not for a single instant speak of identity between Chantal and Christ, although the whole destiny of the girl as well as that of her confessor make sense solely in the light of Christ. A kind of identity obtains (and is demonstrated) only between Cénabre and Judas, and we will speak of this later on.[32] Even though the theme of the saint's death in darkness may be traced consistently from Bernanos' first to his last novel, nevertheless a marked evolution in its meaning and emphases is clear. Donissan's is a "bitter death" that comes after a life that was "one uninterrupted furious struggle".[33] His trial will last "to the very hour of [his] death".[34] Indeed, the freethinker waiting outside his confessional "suddenly discovers him with a frightful face, as if struck by lightning".[35] But Donissan's story has a tragic aftertaste: "The human race expresses itself through its cry of pain, through the wail wrenched from its sides by a supreme effort. . . . Even the vilest of men takes his secret with him—the secret of a suffering that is efficacious, purifying. . . . Because your pain, Satan, is sterile!"[36]

Dying appears here as man's highest art, and in fact the concern with an *ars moriendi* long haunted Bernanos' mind. But early on he must already have been familiar with the cry of pain of Thérèse of Lisieux, who brackets such an art with an anguished question mark: "Oh, Mother! Is this the end? How am I going to manage to die? I'm never going to know how to die! . . . If this is the death agony, what will death itself be like? . . . I can't breathe, I can't die. . . . Isn't it

---

[31] Ibid., 285–86.
[32] *Joie*, 253f.
[33] *Soleil*, 129.

[34] Ibid., 174.
[35] Ibid., 360.
[36] Ibid., 362.

over yet, then? Am I not to die?"[37] Bernanos several times referred to these words, for instance in his *Letter to the English*[38] and in a letter to Prouvot.[39] Already Madame Dargent echoes the sentiments of Saint Thérèse: "I can't die. . . . Oh, Charles, it's much more awful than I thought! I hope this is going to end. . . . I'll never finish dying!"[40] The country priest, too, has similar feelings in the face of death: "More than once I've felt the dread of not knowing how to die once the moment arrives." But he then takes hold of himself: "I can see how a man who is sure of himself and of his courage would want to make his death agony something perfect and complete. But I'll have to make do. My death will have to be what it can manage, and nothing else."[41] This is already the destiny of the Abbé Chevance, only writ large: "As with a sacred gesture a child flings his arms open to death, [Chevance] abandoned himself from the first moment, incapable of imagining any defense for himself. Not only was he resigned to suffer but, in the extraordinary simplicity of his heart, to suffer in a low and paltry way, to suffer as a coward, and, thus, to scandalize his neighbor."[42] Every action of the Abbé Chevance is qualified as "humble", so too his death agony[43] and, more generally, "the humble disaster that was his life".[44] The alien burden he carries into his death robs it of all majesty and even humanity, and the death rattle issuing from his throat is nothing more than the "hollow sighing of a hounded animal".[45] To the shocked and frightened Chantal he cries out: "I don't want to. . . . I don't want to. . . . I don't want to die. . . . You cannot save me from this situation, neither you nor the others. It's hard to die, my daughter. . . . It's not good for you to watch me die. It's a worthless sight, a worthless sight I tell you. Go away!"[46] But, in the end, "the mysterious humiliation of such a death" is embraced by Chantal, made her own, "espoused" for all eternity.[47]

Saint Dominic, too, is seen by Bernanos as dying without understanding his situation,[48] and the same holds even more true for Joan

---

[37] *Novissima Verba*, 188, 191, 195.

[38] *Anglais*, 34.

[39] *To Prouvot*, February 21, 1941 (unpublished); *Geduld*, 78.

[40] *Madame Dargent*, 9–10.

[41] *Curé*, 318.

[42] *Imposture*, 265.

[43] Ibid., 295.

[44] Ibid., 310.

[45] Ibid., 312.

[46] Ibid., 313–15.

[47] Ibid., 318.

[48] *Dominique*, 42.

of Arc. Chantal herself will die in a condition of public shame that she cannot understand, this as the true disciple of Chevance, who had died "in a very paltry and insignificant manner, just as one would wish to live".[49] It was the cook of the Clergerie family who uttered her best possible funeral oration: "I tell you, sir, she renounced everything, even her own death."[50] And the country priest follows suit: "The kind of heroism that suits me best is precisely not having one, and, since I'm lacking in strength, what I wish for now is a very small death, a death of no account at all. I wish for a death just like all the other events of my life."[51] In *The Great Fear of the Right-Thinking* Bernanos spoke of the "classic illusion of the dying man": as long as he has a little consciousness left, he "does not want to believe that he'll have to take that final step without fanfares and that the death agony is just like any of the disgusting things he's already familiar with. Thus, he slips full of shame into death's slumber."[52] Even those who are already reconciled with God receive in Bernanos, at the moment of death, a different countenance, one that is alien and inaccessible. Such was the case of the countess in the *Country Priest*: "I so much wished for her to smile, with that impenetrable smile of the dead that goes so well with their silence! . . . She did not smile. Her mouth, drawn slightly to the right, had an air of indifference about it, an air of haughtiness, of scorn almost."[53] And the young priest will experience this himself when he learns the deadly nature of his illness: "By what frightful wonder was I able to forget the very Name of God? I was alone, unutterably alone in the face of my death."[54] According to Dufréty's account, after his death his face "seemed to express a great anguish".[55] Finally, the death of the prioress in the *Dialogues of the Carmelites* intensifies and summarizes all of this, endowing it with a kind of statuesque eternity: fearful anguish experienced as shame, as the incapacity to accomplish well precisely the thing for which one has prepared oneself through a whole lifetime, her death as a scandal for the whole community; but her death also as something with such immense presence that it fills everything in the house and whose majesty makes every living thing inwardly tremble with humility.[56]

[49] *Joie*, 283.
[50] Ibid., 316.
[51] *Curé*, 304.
[52] *Peur*, 149.
[53] *Curé*, 194-95.
[54] Ibid., 298.
[55] Ibid., 323.
[56] *Carmélites*, 63-72.

"God wants us to search for him in doubt and anguish—until the very last second."[57]

Things can also be approached more externally, simply by considering the great number of death scenes and persons destined for death in Bernanos' stories. Already his very first creative attempt, *La Muette* (The mute woman),[58] is a death scene. The novellas *A Night* and *Madame Dargent* are drawn-out portrayals, as with a slow-motion camera, of two death agonies. *Conversation among Shadows* ultimately takes place in the presence of death, since the partners in conversation are really shadows themselves. Deaths abound particularly in the later novels; all the protagonists are conceived in terms of their death, and everything in the narrative leads to it. Thus we have Chevance and Chantal, the new Mouchette, Simone Alfieri, and Philippe. In the *Country Priest* all the main figures are destined for death: the priest himself of course, but also Torcy, the countess, Doctor Delbende, Doctor Lavigne, the priest's tubercular friend Dufréty, and the "consort" he has contaminated. In *Monsieur Ouine* everything is constructed in terms of the "hero's" death scene, and all around him characters drop like flies: Anthelme, Fanny, old Devandomme and his grandfather, as well as Eugène and his wife. Nowhere in Bernanos does death enjoy greater ascendancy than in this book that portrays a world without hope. Concerning Steeny's grandfather, Michelle asserts: "He finally died . . . after an interminable agony, which dragged on for months in the grip of his own powerlessness and of his relatives' sarcasm. His death was as slow as his life."[59] Ouine made himself a veritable teacher of death. Philippe had barely met Ouine when he says to him: "Death has never frightened me less than this evening." To which Ouine replies: "I will teach you how to love her.[60] She is so rich! The reasonable man receives from her what fear or shame keep us from seeking elsewhere—even the initiation to pleasure. Don't forget this, Philippe: you'll come to love her. A day will even come, I fear, when you'll love her and only her."[61] It is the superior power of the dead—above all the war dead—that rules the whole land of the

---

[57] "Reply to a Survey" (draft), 46; *Bul.* 4, 9.

[58] In *L'Avant-Garde de Normandie*, December 7, 1913; *Bul.* 2–3, 9–11.

[59] *Ouine*, 5.

[60] The context's erotic nuances call for the feminine personification of death, *la mort.*—TRANS.

[61] *Ouine*, 20.

living,[62] deciding destiny and determining the course of the world.[63] Little Guillaume has much to say about these dead: They did not die out of weakness but were surprised by death; and yet, being warriors, they awaited death with every fiber of their consciousness and were wholly bent on it. In the end, they took their life, barely begun, along with them to the other side of death. Whoever has ears to hear can hear these dead, just as, far inland, you can hear the tossing of the waves on the coast if you set your ear to the ground.[64]

Finally, we have the extraordinary experience of Fanny, who feels death growing within herself and obliterating all else when she hits Steeny with her car:

> I thought I too was dead, just imagine. It's like an immense cry, a very great cry I could hear, but not with my ears. Can you understand? One single great cry coming . . . from where? Perhaps from the soul? . . . Surely death, real, actual death, is this same cry, rising, rising, rising, until the last, tiniest bit of silence is wiped out—whoosh! How about it, Philippe? My idea is that there won't be any silence in the other world. My God! I've never felt my body to be so fragile, nothing but a membrane, a mere membrane of skin you can see through, a skin membrane that a little prick with a pin would burst—poof! And then the cry was entering me from all sides, roaring, and I was sinking straight to the bottom in this noise like a scuttled ship.[65]

As portrayed in *Monsieur Ouine*, death is far indeed from anything resembling a Christian death. But even such death, exerting so much power over a world without faith, is real and grips Bernanos profoundly. By this time he is very far from any kind of heroic triumph over the death agony, or from trying to exploit death so as to achieve a more intense feeling for life. In his youth Bernanos had already mocked the Stoic approach,[66] and, in *The Scandal of Truth*, he satirized the Stoic attitude toward death, saying that "this sort of courage" is "but a form of refusal".[67] The country priest, too, turns his back on such an approach: "Since nothing is more foreign to me than Stoic indifference, why would I wish for the death sought by

---

[62] Ibid., 97.

[63] Ibid., 48.

[64] Ibid., 48

[65] Ibid., 79.

[66] *To Dom Besse*, September 3, 1918; *Bul.* 11, 5.

[67] *Vérité*, 7–8.

the imperturbable? What Plutarch's heroes inspire me with, at the same time, is fear and boredom. If I were to enter paradise in such a disguise I think I'd make even my guardian angel smile."[68] No; the "hero" in Bernanos, who, in the face of the child's fear of death, for a while lashed out at himself in secret, despairing self-defense, had in the meantime capitulated before "the tender majesty of the death agony".[69] Now, the mature Bernanos overcomes death in a Christian sense, which is to say, in the place where rigidity dissolves into the softness of assent to weakness, shame, decline, and decay, the place where our writer comes to understand that the death agony is an act of love.[70] In a totally new way, a character's death now becomes for Bernanos the writer the touchstone of his life. Whoever has exercised love, whoever has made a habit of throwing open his arms—this person will know how to die. But whoever has striven to bring the world's injustice to its knees—this person will die in despair.[71] And many a person who has consecrated his life to God will have a more laborious death than could have been foreseen.[72]

For Bernanos personally, and in direct echo of his own words, death became more and more the cherished and yearned-for moment when he would cross the boundary from a life destined for death over into the manifestly seen truth of eternal life. Not for a second did he ever doubt the fact that he would personally see God and come into paradise: "Fortunately, every day a little more of my own sad *self* passes over quietly into my books. When there isn't any left, you'll look for me in vain, and you won't be able to find me. Except in paradise! Except in paradise!"[73] "Five minutes of paradise will make everything well."[74] "I am sure that's the way you'll appear to me in paradise, when you arrive there and your familiar voice will say at the threshold, in a tone I know so well: 'Where is Monsieur Bernanos?' Listen carefully: My word of honor that, with God's grace, I'll be there!"[75] And he inscribes a book to his nephew as follows: "In paradise you'll

---

[68] *Curé*, 319.
[69] *Rêve*, 53.
[70] *Curé*, 318.
[71] *Cimetières*, 83.
[72] *Curé*, 318.
[73] *Letter* of 1935; in *Bernanos*, 122–23.
[74] *To a woman friend*, November 24, 1934; *Bul*. 2–3, 22.
[75] Ibid., June 17, 1936; *Bul*. 2–3, 22.

meet up again with . . . an old uncle and an old aunt who'll still be a little singed by the fires of purgatory, and a little tired from having had to walk for so long, but they'll be very happy at having arrived."[76] There are many other such passages in his letters, as when he expresses the desire for his friends to gather around his deathbed: "May you be present there, to pluck something of my first glance . . . only just barely opening on what I have so much yearned for!"[77]

When at the end of his life Bernanos then stood in earnest face to face with death, the most wonderful combination took place of everything that had gone into the making of the man Bernanos, and the result was a gripping unity of childlike spirit and manliness, Christian humility of spirit and joy in the resounding word, self-surrender and bravado, earnest anguish and humor, all of it blended together by naked, self-abandoning love. Here, nothing was the product of human art. But, according to Bernanos, does not art only fully become itself once it enters the realm of grace? Everything beautiful and strenuous that his life had created became in his death a malleable material ready to be molded by grace.

2. Death Agony as Center

When the agony that closes a life so emphatically becomes that life's measure and judgment, we may say that it has moved from the periphery and established itself as the center. That agony will then be seen as what imparts the innermost substance to the act of living. If death is "the great adventure"[78] that raises every life from anonymity and seals it with uniqueness, then all of earthly life is in this way ennobled, and it becomes an eternal adventure. In Bernanos, the inevitable *basso continuo* can very easily harmonize with the melody of joy in life and affirmation of life that is composed over the bass line. He chides the Germans for having a contempt for death, "something that appears to us [French] even crasser than a contempt for life": it seems to be the privilege of his race to love both at once.[79] Man does, after all, come into existence under a sign that is mysteriously

[76] *Dedication to His Nephew*, December 24, 1939; *Bul.* 5, 7.

[77] Inscription to a friend on a copy of *La joie*, 1933; *Bul.* 2–3, 15.

[78] "Satan", in: *Bul.* 12–13, 24.

[79] *Anglais*, 35.

related to the sign of his end. In Ouine's death this elemental truth becomes evident. Bernanos writes that Ouine's voice "did not appear at all suited for expressing a feeling as simple and naïve as that of surprise, *a surprise, so to speak, in its pure state, culled at its very source without any admixture of curiosity or irony. . . . As for both surprise and fear: most people know only their shimmering, glistening surface, which is similar to that of the watery abyss. The double secret remains buried in the memories of earliest childhood . . .* , that childhood without words and almost without eyes that remains unknown and inviolable—for the crib is not less deep than the grave."[80] This is why Bernanos stations a midwife by Ouine's deathbed, someone who treats him as unsentimentally as she would a newborn baby: "There he now lies, just the same as he was when first coming out of his mother's womb. Poor Monsieur Philippe! What could you do for a baby who's just been born? Keep him clean and warm and not expect to be thanked."[81] But that first movement of astonishment and surprise that overwhelms us at birth and from which our very existence takes its departure, that impulse that emerges again only when we are in the grips of the fear of death: it is this feeling that makes an individual life something unrepeatable, that makes it exactly what it is before God: "The confused heap of childhood impressions, the first part of life swarming with movement, and also the last to enter into death's immobility: this it is that doubtless confers on every human death agony its own incommunicable character and makes each one of them a particular and unique drama."[82] This is the reason why "*sweet childhood is the first thing to emerge out of the depths of every death agony*",[83] and our childhood—inexhaustible and untouchable at the foundation of ephemeral time—is also what helps us and makes it possible for us to endure our death struggle. Simone says it to Ganse: The little of his childhood that remains unspoiled is surely the only thing that will help him die.[84] Consequently, "the last obedient steps" of the man condemned to death are one and the same as "those first steps he took toward life", consisting of the "same terror, the same haste, the same trust,

---

[80] *Ouine*, 233 (corrected version). (The italics are von Balthasar's.—TRANS.)
[81] Ibid., 228.
[82] Ibid., 145.
[83] Ibid., 94. (The italics are von Balthasar's.—TRANS.)
[84] *Rêve*, 80.

the same dazzled surprise, the same sacred awkwardness".[85] Hence, the one who had most thoroughly died during his lifetime—the boy Bernanos—will be the one with fullest life in the midst of death and "the first one to enter the Father's House".[86]

Thus, both of life's boundaries—birth and death—are connected by a subterranean stream, and under the surface of life they meet, touch, and interpenetrate one another. And from both of them comes that most elemental of all feelings that imparts to existence its fundamental coloring: the unity of *wonderment* and *anguish*, which is to say, of childlike self-entrusting to another and deepest shuddering in the act of surrender. We may note that these two poles constitute the two basic attitudes and cognitive means for both ancient and modern philosophy. The specifically Christian unity of wonderment and anguish, moreover, rests on the suffering that God's eternal Child underwent on the Mount of Olives. In the language of the Gospel's teaching, this is the unity of poverty of spirit (the condition of being stripped of all personal power and self-defense) and the bliss that comes from having permanently outstretched arms.

For Bernanos, this is so much the crux of the matter that he very closely relates *faith* and *anguish*, as in this passage: "Who was the first to teach me that faith is a gift of God? I don't know. My mother, most probably. It could then be withdrawn from me? . . . From this moment on I came to know the anguish of death, because after so many years I still cannot separate one anguish from the other. This double fright slipped through the same breach into my child's heart."[87] The Bernanos who says this is the same one who elsewhere affirms with total confidence that he has never had the slightest doubt in connection with faith and that he does not want to be mentioned in the same breath with those who are called "restless souls".[88] When he speaks of this "breach" in his "child's heart", moreover, he means something far deeper than at first meets the eye, as is shown by the rest of the passage: "Faith has never appeared to me to be a constraint. The idea has never occurred to me to take up the defense of faith

---

[85] *Joie*, 239.
[86] *Cimetières*, iv–v.
[87] Ibid., 239.
[88] *To Amoroso Lima*, January 1940; *Esprit*, 192.

against myself. It's faith itself that sees to my defense: it represents that portion of my freedom that I could never give up without dying. In order for me to be able to confront my faith some day as if we were strangers, the same kind of mysterious and incomprehensible psychic split would need to take place as precedes the act of suicide and alone can explain it."[89] What Bernanos is speaking of, therefore, is not a doubt of faith but a most inward shudder at that seam in the fabric of existence where nature and supernature blend together, that juncture where what is grace and, conjointly, innermost freedom could be lost. Let us compare this passage of *The Great Cemeteries* with a statement by Bernanos at seventeen: "I have this fear that my *conversion* may be only half-sincere, that it will last only a little while, and that I'll soon relapse into the baseness and platitudes of life and God as conceived by the Philistines. It must be so hard to live without ideals, without faith, and hence without hope! You must pray intently that this never happens to me."[90] Almost forty years later, when Bernanos was living as a recluse on his Brazilian farm, he could declare even more clearly: "As if faith were an inexhaustible source of consolations that makes us immune to the misfortunes of this life, and even to its simple annoyances, whereas faith really is a crown of thorns that makes us participants—most often, alas, despite ourselves!—in the Most Holy Agony [of Christ]!"[91]

This vision is confirmed by the wartime letters. The young man's faith took on during this terrible time the mode of inward shuddering: "Of all his gifts, God has left us only with the profound feeling of his absence, which is a mark of his predestination." He feels how God's justice is gathering up in the world like a storm, to explode in the midst of time when the right tension has been reached. What he means here is not a bare justice but the superior power of love, which will spend itself elementally over sinners:

> My anguish is full and continual. Some days are horrendous. We would be branded with ignominy for all eternity if we still pretended to pit our feeble forces against the pitiless thunder of grace, which multiplies its blows as if the time for this were exactly apportioned to it. And so it is. In these decisive days that precede the Judgment, impatient mercy is

---

[89] *Cimetières*, 239–40.
[90] *To Lagrange*, May 31, 1905; *C. du R.*, 22.
[91] *Croix*, October 1944, 447.

no longer out to lure souls: rather, it ravishes them, snatching them to itself with armed hand. It is with mighty blows that the pitiful flock is driven home to the foot of the Cross. . . . Nevertheless, there is a day on the rise, a frightening brightness. Will it be given to me to see this day?''[92]

In his important letter on anguish, dating from 1919—the very year of the birth of Expressionism!—Bernanos describes the fragility and exposure of Christian life in the face of eternity, particularly of the life of those entrusted with the highest Christian missions. Perhaps his exalted pathos now and then sounds an artificial note here; but Bernanos is the first to sense the theatrical element behind his words, and he himself deplores it. But we cannot doubt the truth of the profound experience hiding behind words that cut the air like whizzing swords:

Alas, alas! Until daybreak, until the rising of the frightful sun, sheltered under hope's highest peak, circled with darkness, what is it that we can then still hold out over the abyss in our torn hands? From down below, the dismal multitude is calling out to us with its neighing. At the bottom of ourselves there is the refuse of thirty years, in full rot. . . . The divine glance has settled upon us, so firm and yet so tender . . . : we must either break our bonds or die. My dear boy: I write this with the anguish of hope, shaken with sobs at the foot of the Cross. The only thing we have left by way of strength—and this one thing we have in abundance, lavished, squandered, thrown up with full hands—goes by the name of agony. Do you get the picture? I am the weakest of all, the most unstable, the most cowardly—*a slave*—and, if anyone, it's *me* who shall have to crawl along the long, the very long road, with my sensitivity flayed alive, until I reach Him!''

He then quotes two psalm verses that contain a raw appeal to God out of the depths of abandonment, and he comments: "This cry, this sublime challenge, is the whole substance of our heritage. We live *within* this extraordinary word. . . . As in a bronze casting, everything has here been seized at its most vital and been set for all centuries to come."[93]

---

[92] *To Maître*, September 17, 1918; *C. du R.*, 33–34.
[93] Ibid., August 26, 1919; *C. du R.*, 36–37. (The italics are von Balthasar's.—TRANS.)

Faith itself is here "agonic", "agony" in the most literal sense of the word, as we have seen: struggle, contest, wrestling with the angel through the night, above all an immense hunger and thirst, an emptiness crying out for the fullness of God. The proud man wants to be his own self-sufficient fullness and sets out to construct himself a personality using his own materials and often undergoing great privations. But, Bernanos exclaims, "what can I do with such scraps? I now see that what must be done here is, not build, but create, and Another possesses the secret of the word that creates. . . . Only, he doesn't speak. . . . The ideas I was fondest of, the richest of my feelings, are now emptied of all substance."[94] Here faith is considered, not as the Creed of the Church—since this is unassailable—but as an existential attitude and stance: a nakedness before God, a will to be taken by Another precisely where one has nothing left to give, an appeal to God for him to tear away the last protective layers: "No one gives himself totally. And yet this is what must be done. One must open oneself up to the truth from top to bottom."[95]

This shuddering of the denuded man becomes in Bernanos a precise cognitive organ, *his* own particular "eyes of faith": shivering, he perceives changes in weather conditions that others, being clothed, cannot feel.[96] Of Mouchette we read: "It was this very dread that lived and thought in her stead. For, *at the boundaries of the invisible world, anguish is a sixth sense, and pain and perception come to be but one.*"[97]

As we have already seen in the biographical portion of this book, no one will probably ever be able to ascertain the precise nature of the states of fear and anxiety that haunted Bernanos throughout his life. It is enough for us to know that a condition that surely had a psychological and perhaps even pathological substratum was put at the service of a greater network of meanings and, thus, was sublimated and transvaluated into a function of his authentic mission as Christian writer. This fact is not contradicted by what Dom Paulus Gordan describes as Bernanos' tendency to observe himself during his phobic crises and "to record and analyze all his sensations with a

---

[94] *To Dom Besse*, September 3, 1918; *Bul.* 11, 5.
[95] Ibid., Ascension 1919; *Bul.* 11, 11.
[96] *Enfants*, 225.
[97] *Soleil*, 209. (The italics are von Balthasar's.—TRANS.)

lucidness that only increased his suffering".[98] But the condition here
must be that these anxiety attacks, which surely were not imagined,
must not be turned into actual "mystical" states: they must be left
in the intermediary realm of a psychological makeup that has been
markedly transformed by supernatural grace. In this location we may
see such states as constituting a necessity and even an indispensable
prerequisite for his activity both as creative writer and as critic of his
civilization. Bernanos would have been the first to protest against a
systematic identification of faith and anguish. Nevertheless, something
of the situation of faith in *today's* world (and thus of faith as such) is
indeed manifested in an exemplary and perhaps even vicariously atoning manner by the destiny of Bernanos' bare and seismographically
sensitive heart. Bernanos is the trenchant Christian (and not merely
existentialist) answer to the philosophical method of Heidegger and
Sartre, who exalted anguish and alienation as privileged means and
medium for ontological experience. Anguish had nothing interesting
to offer Bernanos in a literary sense: for him, it was a horrible, elemental experience. In Bernanos we can discern what may be true and
valid about the positions of Heidegger and Sartre, but much more besides: namely, what precise Christian meaning the whole experience
of anguish may contain and how all of Being becomes denuded before
God and, once utterly exposed, then becomes immersed in the all-
encompassing and graciously enveloping Passion of the Son of God.

What Bernanos' chief characters experience in their suffering, therefore, may all along be said to exist in a movement *underway* from their
own anguish toward the anguish of Christ, which is to say, from
philosophical-anthropological anguish toward theological anguish. It
is obvious that these two kinds of anguish cannot be distinguished in
the experience itself. For, who would venture to pinpoint the place
where personal human suffering passes over into universal human suffering conditioned by original sin, where the latter then passes over
into the universally vicarious suffering of the Cross, and finally where
this all-encompassing suffering of Christ is communicated to the individual "member" of Christ as personally experienced anguish, to
the precise degree pleasing to grace?

This movement of individual suffering going out to meet Christ's
suffering is most beautifully portrayed in the country priest's medita-

---

[98] *Bernanos au Brésil*, in *Bul. 6, 3*.

tions. He asks himself "through what breach in being" this anguished sadness could have penetrated into the depths of his soul, since "no power of reasoning in the world could provoke" it. But, to tell the truth,

> it did not "enter": it was already in us. More and more I have come to believe that what we call sadness, anguish, despair—as if to convince ourselves that we're dealing with certain movements of the soul—is actually the soul itself. Ever since the fall, man's condition is such that *he is incapable any longer of perceiving anything within or outside himself except in the form of anguish.* Even the person most indifferent to the supernatural nonetheless retains, even in his pleasures, the dark awareness of the frightening miracle that is the burgeoning of a single joy *in a being capable of conceiving his own annihilation. . . . It seems to me that, but for God's ever-watchful mercy, man would crumble again into dust the very first instant he became aware of himself.*[99]

Human self-awareness is thus conceived as anguish, but enveloped, shielded, and essentially made possible by the sweet mercy of God. This is why a few pages later, if he had had the courage, the little priest could have revealed to this friend from Torcy the spiritual locus of his election, vocation, and mission, and hence of his foundation as both man and Christian. The Curé de Torcy himself comes close to the truth when he states: "Much before our birth—forgive me for speaking human language—our Lord met us somewhere, maybe in Bethlehem, in Nazareth, or on the roads of Galilee. On that day of days, his eyes transfixed us, and our vocation received its particular character according to the place, the hour, and the circumstances." At this point, the Curé d'Ambricourt burst into tears: his friend had touched the deepest place in his heart. Later that night he writes in his diary:

> The truth is that I've always been in the Garden of Olives. And at the moment—yes, it's strange—at the very moment when he puts his hand on Peter's shoulder and asks the question—the very useless and almost naïve but oh so courteous and tender question—*Are you sleeping? . . .* I opened my mouth and was going to answer, but I couldn't. Too bad! Is it not enough that today, through the mouth of my old friend and counselor, our Lord has done me the grace of revealing to me that noth-

---

[99] *Curé*, 217–18. (The italics are von Balthasar's.—Trans.)

ing would ever me snatch me from the place chosen for me from all eternity, my position as *prisoner of the Holy Agony?*[100]

While other of Bernanos' figures participate at times in aspects of Christ's agony, the whole existence of the country priest as such is submerged in it, offering in its totality a mute and humble testimony to this mystery. He admits at once that he has a fear of death,[101] and he wants to feel no shame in the face of a fear that reappears every time he spits up blood.[102] This is an anguish that, as he correctly observes, "is something very different from mere fear. It lasts but a moment. I'm at a loss as to what to compare this lightninglike impression with. Perhaps with the cutting lash of a whip across my heart. O Holy Agony!"[103] He wants to await his own agony humbly,[104] without bravado, his soul at peace.[105]

Here we see the great extent to which Bernanos was working exclusively out of his own deepest inspiration when he was asked to write the movie script for Gertrud von le Fort's *Die Letzte am Schafott* (Song at the Scaffold). We can in no way speak of a literary dependency on the German poetess, since the theme of anguished fear had always permeated even his earliest novels and novellas. Not even Thérèse of Lisieux, who saw herself positioned at the same point in the Passion as Bernanos, could be said in this connection to have been any more for him than a confirmation of what had all along been the heart of his life and experience.[106]

Already in *Under Satan's Sun* existence and temporality themselves are an anguish and an agony. On the first page of the first part (which afterward became the second), we see the saint of Lumbres standing at night before an open window: " 'My God! My God!', he repeated, unable to weep or to pray. . . . As at a dying man's bedside, minute after minute trickled into this darkness, irretrievable."[107] Before Donissan's encounter with Mouchette, Bernanos manages, evidently with the greatest effort, to compress into words of astounding

---

[100] Ibid., 222.
[101] Ibid., 174.
[102] Ibid., 319.
[103] Ibid., 253.
[104] Ibid., 316.
[105] Ibid., 273.
[106] *Anglais*, 34–35.
[107] *Soleil*, 252.

plasticity the priest's total metaphysical and theological experience of anguish:

> Ah! What agony is endured by a man who feels his will, his concentration, and finally his very consciousness running out as through a sieve, while his somber interior is suddenly exposed exteriorly, like the leather of a glove turned inside out. He suffers *a most bitter agony for the length of an instant that no pendulum can measure.* But this poor priest, when he doubts, has doubts not only about himself but about his one and only hope. If he loses himself, he's losing a more precious, indeed a divine good: God himself. *By the last lightning of his reason he measures the night* in which his great love will now lose itself.[108]

Anguish is again the central point of *Joy*. Chevance sums up his director's legacy to his spiritual daughter Chantal by reference to anguish: "When you think you are lost, it'll mean that the little task entrusted to you will be very close to its end. At that moment, don't try to understand. Don't torture yourself. Do nothing but remain very quiet. Even prayer can at times be an innocent ruse, a means like any other to flee, to escape, or at least to gain some time. On the Cross, our Lord prayed, and he also cried out, wept, gasped for air, and gnashed his teeth like any other dying man. But there's something even more precious: that minute, that long minute of silence after which all had been consummated." The old priest "had often talked about this with a kind of mysterious stubbornness, as if he were speaking, not of a probable danger, but of a juncture that must certainly come, and as if he feared nothing for his beloved spiritual daughter except for one supreme movement of self-defense on her part, something almost involuntary, a final startle. Was this not, in addition, the lesson taught by his death, the hidden meaning of an agony as humble and as forlorn as his?" Another of his statements had struck Chantal: " 'I've had too great a disdain for fear', he confessed one day. 'I was young. My blood was too hot.' At which she exclaimed: 'What? Could it be you saying this? You? Are you now going to bring fear into paradise?' And Chevance answered: 'Not so fast! Not so fast! In a certain sense, *fear is already God's daughter, redeemed on the night of Good Friday.* True, she's not pretty to look at, not at all! Now she's mocked, now she's cursed, and she's repudiated by

---

[108] Ibid., 190. (The italics are von Balthasar's.—TRANS.)

all. . . . And yet, make no mistake: *she is at the bedside of every agony, interceding for the person.' "*[109]

With Chantal, too, it is less a matter of sudden crises of anguish than the slow unfolding of an interior state that has been there all along. And her "condition" remains wide open toward eternity; in this world it has no possible expression or explanation: "*The thought did not occur to her that she was perhaps suffering for no reason or object, that the question, asked in this way, had no possible answer, that her anguish existed only in order to become lost, along with so many others, within universal serenity, in the same way that a cry does not go beyond a certain circumference in space: outside that circle, it becomes nothing.*"[110] This "beyond" is the moment after the "It is consummated"; this, and not the Mount of Olives as in the case of the country priest, is Chantal's proper spiritual locus. This is why, "sure of being struck unawares", Chantal has the same "Stoic docility" as a man condemned to death, who thinks only of "using up one by one every minute of grace he has left". But, "in his effort gradually to destroy and confine to nothingness by this *great impulse toward the void* the final seconds that uselessly prolong his agony, the man enters into the night he is summoning *and is no longer one of the living.*"[111] By taking this step into emptiness, Chantal can no longer understand her own fear;[112] "the only thing she now awaits is the night, the void, the fall, the swift and quiet gliding." And now the sentence that builds a bridge between Saint Thérèse and Heidegger: "At this moment, full significance was attained by the certainty of having been—in each and every circumstance—nothing but a light and useless little thing, made for only an instant's utility, for the joy of a single instant, a thing of no account that is then cast off without a thought. She had indeed been thrown away (*jetée*)."[113]

This is what explains why, as she goes to her final confrontation with Cénabre, Chantal feels "weary, weary, weary unto death",[114] why "an immense fatigue"[115] may be read in her eyes, why she has the

---

[109] *Joie*, 236–37. (The italics are von Balthasar's.—TRANS.)
[110] Ibid., 109–10. (The italics are von Balthasar's.—TRANS.)
[111] Ibid., 239. (The italics are von Balthasar's.—TRANS.)
[112] Ibid., 240.
[113] Ibid., 241.
[114] Ibid., 234.
[115] Ibid., 277.

feeling of being "reduced to utter powerlessness",[116] why the phrase "*too late*—those two disconsolate words that contain all the wretchedness of our race—" should come "to the lips of Mademoiselle Chantal with a smothered moan", why it seems to her that "the little universe" she has not "succeeded in saving" has been "lost in oblivion", and why finally the idea of an "eternal solitude without appeal" should in the end break her resistance.[117] Moreover, all of this occurs beyond the limits of vital human activity, beyond the pull of the force of gravity, as it were, at the place where God himself takes over the active role and the full responsibility: "She already knew her struggle was hopeless. She knew that, either willing or coerced, she had gone too far, to the precise point where unknown laws carry the day",[118] laws which it is absolutely futile to try to forecast or avert. "In the certainty that the blow would strike her precisely from the direction she least expected, and that she therefore could in no way stave it off, she pondered no self-defense whatever."[119]

Chantal thus undergoes the experience of crossing over into death and nothingness beyond the limits of life itself, and this crossing-over itself is the substance of her anguished fear. As a result, she comes to know something deeper: namely, that her own passivity is her assumption into and repossession by a more universally valid agony— God's. Here Bernanos is speaking with theological precision: Chantal had, he writes,

> the superhuman certainty of so thorough an annihilation that she could not any more live than die, so much so that, if God were pleased to destroy a wretched little creature as perfectly dispossessed as she, he would have to share his own agony with her. . . . Just as a child repeats, without understanding them but with sacred docility, the words he receives one by one from his mother's lips, so too would she go forward step by step into the darkness of an Agony whose threshold no angel had yet crossed. Groping in the dark, she would collect every crumb of this terrible bread. . . . That very moment, the silence she was summoning rolled over her and covered her.[120]

---

[116] Ibid., 244.
[117] Ibid., 245–46.
[118] Ibid., 238.
[119] Ibid., 239.
[120] Ibid., 248–49.

At the very end, however, she hesitates. Would Chevance have approved of her taking this path? And Bernanos very keenly observes: "It was not the impulse of her ecstasy that made her take the final step but, on the contrary, the barely conscious effort she made to draw back and get a hold of herself. What does it matter, though? She had now gone too far into the Presence that nothing limits. She could only let herself collapse like a runner at the end of his race; and, while she thought she had again rejected the sublime gift of which she felt unworthy, the divine Agony had in fact alighted upon her mortal heart and was carrying it away in its claws."[121] Now she was "with the solitary God who had taken refuge in the night like a humiliated father in the arms of the last daughter left him, slowly filling the measure of his human anguish by the shedding of blood and tears, under the black olive trees."[122] Chantal, too, was led into this garden of agony because it was in this place, and no other, that she had to await the betrayer.

We will have to speak more of this later on. But the point here is the unique form of anguish that has overcome the watershed between the anguish of man as sinner and the anguish of God on the Cross, so that as a result Chantal now sees and experiences her own anguish from the standpoint of God's. Bernanos' words in this connection are bold indeed; compared with the real experience of the mystics, they may even be a bit too rectilinear: "Whereas ordinary anguish cannot be separated from a certain secret shame that loosens our last forces and completes our degradation, this anguish [of Chantal's] tortured the soul *without in any way troubling it*. Its dazzling pain was so transparent and pure that it made it blaze *well beyond the world of flesh*. And yet the extraordinary young woman recognized her faithful companion, the humble and sincere friend of a lifetime—her own suffering —in this sort of prodigious and unbearable brilliance that was the very suffering of God."[123]

Bernanos is here obviously making an extreme effort to construct the inaccessible experience of the elect with the small fragments of his own experience of anguish coupled with the contemplation of his faith. In so doing, however, he falls victim to his own drive for sub-

---

[121] Ibid., 249.
[122] Ibid., 250.
[123] Ibid., 252–53. (The italics are von Balthasar's.—TRANS.)

limity and heroism. Later on, in the *Country Priest*, he will be better advised to abide near a suffering that is both more hidden and more carnal; in so doing, he will remain closer to the mystery of the Cross, while in these passages from *Joy* (especially the phrase describing a pain so pure that it "blazes well beyond the world of flesh") he is striking Gnostic resonances that remind us of Giraudoux. His intentions become clear once we compare them to a passage in a letter written at almost the same time (January 1927): "We hate pain because we have become incapable of producing it in its full purity, in its state of pristine birth. We hate it, but doubtless we do this under a name that is not its own. Besides, ever since the earthly paradise, we no longer know the name of anything."[124] What he could not attain in himself —the pure, cloudless horizon of cosmic suffering, what Rilke called "the constellations of pain"—that Bernanos wanted to touch at least through his heroes. Nevertheless, he never again forgets (as he had in *Under Satan's Sun*) to emphasize the childlike and simple beauty of self-surrender, which triumphs even in the midst of terrors,[125] nor does he forget to temper his somewhat overwrought "sublimity" into a soberly authentic pilgrimage through a pathless desert: "Everything is giving way under me. I seem to be walking in slime. If I go forward I'll surely sink, and if I don't move I'll sink just the same."[126]

In the cases of Donissan, Chevance, Chantal, and the country priest, Bernanos is intent on showing clearly the meaning and criterion for authentic Christian anguish: it is its character as vicarious, atoning *representation*. If a Christian is robbed of light, it is only that he might radiate light all the more abundantly. In an unpublished page concerning *The Imposture*, Bernanos refers to Chevance as "a saint who hands out to everyone the joy he is deprived of". And he applies the same formula to Donissan: "He gave out with full hands the peace he was deprived of."[127] Later on we read this concerning the Curé de Torcy: "The supernatural force emanating from him was in no way affected. Visibly devoured by anguish . . . , he remained a maker

---

[124] *To Raymonde Laborde*, January 29, 1927 (unpublished); *Geduld*, 59.
[125] *Joie.*, 253, 271.
[126] Ibid., 270–71.
[127] *Soleil*, 266.

of calm, certitude, and peace."[128] This same priest says the following to the younger country priest, after the latter's dramatic scene with the countess: "It's possible the good Lord is making you abide in sadness. But I've always noticed that, regardless of how much they may trouble us, these sorts of trials never cloud our judgment when the good of souls requires it."[129]

Such visible radiance, however, is proper to those entrusted with the care of souls, and for the present purposes we may number Chantal among them because of her role toward Cénabre. It is no longer characteristic of the world of pure contemplation and the suffering proper to it; only exceptionally do the two coincide. This concealment of what man would most like to see occurs most radically in Bernanos' last work, the *Dialogues of the Carmelites*. Here, the visible effects both of the prioress' death and of Blanche's anguished fear are only accidental, intended more for the audience of either film or play than for the *dramatis personæ* themselves. In this work, anguish has really become as anonymous as sin in *Monsieur Ouine*. Here, too, anguish has lost the heroic sublimity with which Bernanos had hitherto characterized his heroes, including the country priest. It has finally become one with *shame*, that other characteristic of Christ's suffering on the Mount of Olives and on the Cross, which is what makes it wholly human and wholly representative of all mankind. In this way, the rift is also bridged between Bernanos' own experience of anguish and that of his heroes; for Bernanos' personal anguish is based on his sense of lowliness, which wholly excludes any possibility of heroism for himself. We can see this clearly in a capital passage from *Journal de ce temps*, his 1946 diary: "The shame and the remorse occasioned by this fatigue weigh more heavily upon me than the fatigue itself. . . . My fatigue is the agony that comes from participating in the universal shame of a universe that has failed, from participating in man's betrayal of the universe. It's as if Being had lost its color because of the poisons added. . . . Have mercy on us! Forgive us our fatigues! Cleanse us of them! Wash us from this filth! We don't want to roll before your Face dead with fatigue!"[130] Already in 1925 Bernanos expressed his feeling of universal pollution in a letter to Vallery-Radot:

---

[128] *Curé*, 128.

[129] Ibid., 223.

[130] *La Plume*, 1946; *Erbarmen*, 123.

"The air we breathe from the moment of birth is not pure. No, it is not pure."[131]

Dialogues of the Carmelites marks Bernanos' definitive farewell to a pathos of honor and greatness of soul that had been sustained by anguish and for the sake of anguish. Chevance's ideal of dying in a small, insignificant way here becomes the highly un-ideal ideal of life itself. Whose nerves would not be irritated by Blanche de la Force and her continual panic, by her avoidance of all situations that call for steadfastness—an attitude that cannot be interpreted other than as cowardice? In this connection we can ask whether, with such qualities, she can at all be considered the "heroine" of a play or even of a film and whether this instance does not demonstrate that the Cross simply surpasses the sphere of anything that may be portrayed by human beings. (A "passion play", for example, can do no more than represent the exterior scenes through a kind of naïve liturgy. Who would dare even to crack open the interior scenario of the Lord's suffering?) Blanche's anguished fear, like Bernanos' own, first emerges in the dimension of psychological pathology; but it is already taken up in advance into Christ's mortal fear, which is what makes it possible and grounds it, and, in union with Christ's, Blanche's fear can itself become atoning. Between these two poles there clearly intervenes the world of "honor", of the old nobility and its worldview: Blanche herself comes from the nobility, and she feels bound to Sister Constance, herself a noblewoman, in the same way as the country priest feels bound to Olivier, the gentleman soldier. Blanche's father, her brother, the prioress Madame de Croissy, and above all the subprioress, who is puffed up with the pride of the nobility: the whole world of all these characters becomes bracketed by a situation that, while not denying the value and meaning of honor, nevertheless transforms its uses into something higher and apparently contradictory. The prioress, who dies a frightfully anguished death for the sake of Blanche, comes from a world of spiritual nobility that knows nothing of fear as a psychological and pathological affliction. Her anguish is imposed on her from a purely supernatural direction. But this living liturgy belongs to the form and ceremonial of Carmel, in which the hereditary ideals of honor and nobility have already been transposed to a spiritual and ecclesial dimension: it is only within *this* scenario, as objective

---

[131] *To Vallery-Radot*, 1925; *Geduld*, 29.

framework, that Blanche's fearfulness can be taken up effectively into the agony of the one great Passion.

Blanche is described by her brother as "a being marked by destiny. . . . Life was for her like a stream overflowing with a delicious nectar that turned to bitterness the moment she touched it with her lips."[132] For she bore within herself "a fear that had been stuffed into the deepest part of her being . . . , like frost in the heart of a tree".[133] "Fear is perhaps a sickness", she herself affirms,[134] and she feels she is totally unprotected against its outbreaks.[135] Indeed, all her frantic escapes into shelters of different sorts result time and again in her being exposed in the utterly unsheltered. She has a vocation to the cloister, but her manner of following it can only be an escape, in the sense, not of contempt for the world,[136] but of the simple inability to live in the world. The prioress warns her: "Believe me, one enters our Rule badly by throwing oneself into it in a reckless manner, like some poor man pursued by thieves." Blanche replies: "It's true I have no other refuge." But the prioress insists: "Our Rule is not a refuge. It's not the Rule that keeps us, my daughter, but we who keep the Rule."[137] But Blanche nevertheless clings to such a shelter. To her brother, who has come to beg her to follow him into exile, she says: "It's true I no longer fear anything. Where I am nothing can harm me."[138] However, the very brother to whom she says this knows she is no longer safe in the company of her sisters ("You are no longer safe here"),[139] and that the only thing keeping her in the monastery is "the fear of fear". And so he entices her away from the cloister by appealing to her duty to her father and, at a deeper level, by challenging her to face her fear: "We must learn how to risk fear as we risk death. True courage is to be found in this risk."[140]

And now Blanche must witness the horrible crumbling of the prioress, Madame de Croissy, the pillar to which she clung for her life: for the prioress had chosen her precisely, the weakest of all, to be present during her death agony and its excruciating anguish.[141] Then too the convent's chaplain must flee, and, without knowing it, he

132 *Carmélites*, 110.
133 Ibid., 16.
134 Ibid., 116.
135 Ibid., 54, 72, 116.
136 Ibid., 29.
137 Ibid., 40–41.
138 Ibid., 107.
139 Ibid., 103.
140 Ibid., 104.
141 Ibid., 71.

gives her a sign when he announces he will have to put on a dis-guise.[142] Circumstances keep her from making her vows; indeed, the new prioress must refuse her this "necessary consolation and its for-tifying effects" because she does not dare "sacrifice to Mademoiselle de la Force the safety of all [her] daughters".[143] All the events now unfolding in Carmel seem to conspire in thrusting her back into the world. Literally speaking, it is she who is first "sacrificed" for the good of Carmel, then dismissed and forsaken.[144] In actual fact, she had never been accepted into the community; she had always remained a stranger among the nuns. But precisely for this reason she never belonged anywhere else but in Carmel, in its solitude[145] and its par-ticipation in the Lord's Passion.[146] When she finally does flee with mortal fear—first as far as the drying room[147] and then out of the en-closure altogether after the ceremony of the heroic vow[148]—Blanche has become nothing but "the plaything of circumstances",[149] a leaf in the storm whose place is naturally much less on the outside than within the cloister. In her own father's house she now becomes "a wretched maid" whom all mistreat;[150] but the heart of her experi-ence now is drinking her fear to the dregs, imbibing her shame in full drafts: "I was born in fear, I have lived and still live in fear. And, since everyone has a contempt for fear, it is only just that I also live in contempt."[151] Some months earlier she had already said to the prioress: "I no longer hope to overcome my nature . . . or come to terms with my shameful wounds."[152] The last we see of her before the final scene of her death on the scaffold reminds us of the passage in Mark's account of the Passion where we witness the fleeing of the naked young man who leaves his tunic behind (Mk 14:52). Both the subprioress and the chaplain have gone searching for her, but now she perceives all Christian love only as claws ready to seize her: "Completely beside herself, Blanche looks at the priest with a distracted expression, escapes from him brusquely, and disap-pears."[153] The fact that, in the end, she is able to climb the scaffold

---

[142] Ibid., 124.
[143] Ibid., 130.
[144] Ibid., 143–44.
[145] Ibid., 37.
[146] Ibid., 158–59.
[147] Ibid., 177.

[148] Ibid., 188.
[149] Ibid., 182.
[150] Ibid., 205.
[151] Ibid., 204.
[152] Ibid., 144.
[153] Ibid., 213.

wholly free of fear[154] is a miracle whose explanation must be sought in another context: that of vicarious representation and substitution.

It is by such paths that Blanche enters the imitation and discipleship of Christ.[155] She does it, not on her own strength—which wholly fails "Blanche of the Weakness"[156]—but by her being dragged along against her will and being constantly threatened from within. There is no way to understand Blanche's destiny other than from the perspective of the Cross. Her shameful fear, which makes her drop and shatter the statue of the "Little King of Glory" on Christmas Eve[157] and thus properly distances her from the Cross, is the weapon God engages as being most efficacious against evil: "I have always feared", says Madame Lidoine, the new prioress, to her daughters, "that you may be deceived when your generosity inspires you to oppose zeal for evil with zeal for good, as with two potent voices that strive to drown one another out. It's precisely when evil is making the most noise that we should make all the less. . . . Indeed, it's just when the power of evil—which is nothing but appearance and illusion— manifests itself most dazzlingly that God again becomes a little child in the crib, as if to escape his own justice, the demands of his own justice, and, so to speak, to delude it."[158] The misery of sin cannot be abolished by means of good works—not even martyrdom—but only through the humbling of everything that, within the realm of grace,

---

[154] Ibid., 230.

[155] Ibid., 158–59.

[156] Ibid., 162. (An important symbolism of names comes into play here. "Blanche of the Weakness" [in French, "Blanche de la Faiblesse"] is, of course, an ironic inversion of the protagonist's actual name, "Blanche de la Force". There is a second irony here as well, based on the Carmelite practice, upon taking a new name in religion, of adding a "title" signifying the nun's particular devotion to a saint or a mystery of the faith ["Thérèse of the Child Jesus and of the Holy Face," "Elizabeth of the Trinity"]. Blanche's "title" comes to her wholly unofficially, by "nature" as it were, since she never really became a nun or took vows. Ironically, it refers to her chief *difficulty* in serving God, precisely because her weakness and fearfulness, drunk to the dregs, become the particular occasion for her to receive the grace of supernatural courage. The actual Carmelite name Blanche herself had chosen ["Blanche of the Agony of Christ", see below] would in some sense be supplanted by this name given her by grace, because she could not suffer Christ's agony other than through her own natural weakness, which she continually attempted to escape. Finally, a third echo here reminds us of the German poetess who created the character, Gertrud *von le Fort*.—TRANS.)

[157] Ibid., 141.

[158] Ibid., 187–88.

could still have the appearance of earthly power:[159] "The Lord always lived and still lives among us as a poor man. . . . He wished to live among the poor. He also wished to die with them. For he did not stride forward to his death like a baron at the head of his men. . . . He did it among poor people who, far from dreaming of defying anyone, rather made themselves very small in order to pass unperceived for as long as possible. . . . Truly, according to the expression of Sacred Scripture, he was 'the lamb led to the slaughter'."[160] This is so much the case that all weakness henceforth belongs to him: "Every night a person enters is the night of the Most Holy Agony."[161] Thus, when the prioress asks Blanche if she has not already, "for some extraordinary reason", chosen her name as Carmelite, in the event she should be admitted to probation, Blanche answers without hesitation: "Yes, indeed, Mother. I would like to be called Sister Blanche of the Agony of Christ."[162]

Carmel's life form, like that prescribed by monastic rules as such, is wonderfully elucidated from this perspective: "Our vocation is not at all to oppose injustice but simply to atone for it, to pay the ransom for it. And, since we possess nothing other than our wretched persons, we ourselves are this ransom."[163] The heart of the monastic life is not self-elected heroic sufferings, as the subprioress is inclined to believe (it is she who pushes through the community vow of martyrdom), but first and foremost sober prayer,[164] whereby interior poverty becomes reflected in the form of "simplicity of soul"[165] and especially of "modesty",[166] that is, humble submission to the duties of state. The *nobility* inherent in Carmel's life form has not been borrowed from worldly culture, any more than Benedictine *mâsze* (measure, moderation); it is an intrinsic necessity that corresponds to the hiddenness of Christ, of his love and his sacrifice.[167] Madame Lidoine begs "Divine Providence only for those modest virtues that the rich and powerful readily hold in disdain: good will, patience, the spirit of reconciliation. More than any other, these virtues are suitable for poor handmaids such as we."[168] In the end, the prioress rises to the

---

[159] Ibid., 134–35.
[160] Ibid., 146.
[161] Ibid., 23.
[162] Ibid., 41.
[163] Ibid., 134.
[164] Ibid., 38–39, 82.
[165] Ibid., 40.
[166] Ibid., 135.
[167] Ibid., 99.
[168] Ibid., 81.

insight that Christian courage itself inwardly possesses the form of poverty:

> Come what may, we must never count on anything except the sort of courage God bestows day by day, penny by penny, as it were. This is the courage suitable for us, the one that best harmonizes with the humility of our state. And maybe it's too much presumption to ask him even for that. Better to beg him humbly that fear may not test us beyond our strength, that we may feel only its humiliation without its pushing us to any blameworthy action. When you weigh fear and courage from within that Garden of Gethsemani, where all human anguish became divinized in the Lord's adorable Heart, then the distinction between them appears to me close to superfluous. Both fear and courage appear to us to be mere baubles.[169]

The subprioress herself will voice this doctrine in the end: "Courage could very well be one of the devil's phantasms. . . . Only one thing matters: that, whether brave or cowardly, we should always be exactly where God wants us, entrusting ourselves to him for all the rest. Yes, there is only one remedy for fear: to cast oneself recklessly into the will of God, just as a deer, pursued by dogs, plunges into the cool, black water."[170]

On the whole, *Dialogues of the Carmelites* is an agonic piece. The existence of all the women in it unfolds with the Mount of Olives as real locus. This is made ever more conscious to them by the impending threat of martyrdom, with the same blinding clarity that characterized the agony of Madame Dargent; but the martyrdom is only the occasion and not the substance of their interior vocation. The latter is constituted by the agony of the Redeemer himself, which is so spacious a land that there is room within it both for fear and for courage, for the highest nobility of attitude and for the greatest invasion of anguish, for the merry and childlike laughter of Sister Constance, who finds everything amusing (even the Lord's Passion, seen from the perspective of the angels), and for the gray daily routine of all the others, with all its little frictions and very pedestrian viewpoints. If there is anything Bernanos succeeds in doing it is the demonstration of his thesis that the space within which the plot of the *Dialogues* develops is the divine agony itself. Because this is so, the whole drama represents, not a torture, but an ineffable liberation.

---

[169] Ibid., 135–36.
[170] Ibid., 149.

It purifies like a sacrament (which is never the case with Claudel), and it has something of the rigors and exactions of the flames of purgatory, which are to be nothing other than the flames of God's suffering love. Here, Bernanos' personal anguish has been wholly put at the service of the Church and of art. The colors in his palette have been provided by his anguished fear; what he has produced, however, is not his own anguish but a much higher one in which his own is forgotten and assuaged.

Once the locus and meaning of ultimate anguish are determined, then the thousand forms of anguished fearfulness and its thousand uses can move freely within and around that space in the most contrary directions without their ever becoming contradictory. Bernanos' statements in this connection are almost unlimited, covering the whole field of psychology. They portray anguish itself, shine a keen light into its foundations, and show all its variations.

The Great Cemeteries under the Moon portrays "true anguished fear" as a "raving delirium. . . . It is the cruelest folly of which we are capable. Nothing equals its impetus, and nothing can withstand its impact. Similar to it is anger, but this is only a passing state, a sudden dissipation of the soul's forces. But fear is as durable as hatred."[171] It is different from mere apprehension[172] because of its incomparable penetration and depth.[173] It is as manifold as the gamut of human individuals: every instance of anguish in the face of death is unique, if only because the childhood recurring in it is unique.[174] Fear can intensify to such plenitude that it forces one to fight "against an apparently indefinite number of fears—a fear for every fiber of one's being, a multitude of fears". The country priest has the impression

---

[171] *Cimetières*, 83–84.

[172] Both the French and the German here make semantic distinctions that are more difficult to make in English with any consistency. In the original, French *peur* and German *Angst* (fear, in the stronger sense of "dread", "terror", and "anguish" as permanent states of soul) are being contrasted to *crainte* and *Furcht* (fear, in the lighter sense of an apprehension about specific things). The linguistic situation is complicated by the fact that the other two words *angoisse* (anguish, mental suffering, in German *Angst*) and *agonie* (agony) are freely used throughout this chapter as virtual synonyms for *peur* and *Angst*. I have frequently rendered these in English as "anguish" or "anguished fear" to emphasize the complex character of the phenomenon that, as analyzed by Bernanos and von Balthasar, is not only psychological but, properly speaking, metaphysical and religious.—TRANS.

[173] *Curé*, 253.

[174] *Ouine*, 145.

of hearing "the whispering of an immense, invisible crowd cowering at the bottom of [his] anguish as if in the deepest of nights".[175] In this most extreme form, fear turns against existence itself:

> When nervous frenzy passes a certain point and dread (*épouvante*) it-self seems to have found its balance in a frightful immobility, then the strongest instinct of which a living being is capable—self-defense—appears in effect to have been abolished. For the poor wretch caught in the throes of this condition, it is then a question no longer of escaping from his pain and anguish but of exhausting it. At its climax, every form of madness succeeds in baring the bottommost foundation of man's soul —that secret self-hatred that is the deepest part of his life, and probably of every life.[176]

It is therefore not difficult to see through the mask of fear, above all to see that "the mask of pleasure, stripped of all hypocrisy",[177] reveals nothing but fear behind it. The expectation of enduring pleasures, and hence desire (which the world often confuses with hope), are thus functions of fear.[178] In the *New Mouchette*, fear as the foundation of pleasure is ruthlessly probed and exposed.[179] But Bernanos specializes in exhibiting the phenomena of modern culture in the light of fear. Fear is what he sees as underlying the democracies,[180] fear too as the foundation of the different forms of totalitarianism:[181] what rules on both sides is fear.[182] And the basis for the civilization of the future could well be a new and unheard-of combination of hatred and fear:[183] "Mankind is afraid of itself. . . . It is sacrificing its liberty to the fear it has of itself. It is like someone obsessed with the idea of suicide who, when he must remain alone in his room at night, first has himself tied to his bed so as not to be tempted to turn on the gas."[184] The atom bomb was invented purely by fear: "Modern man is man in anguish. Anguish has taken the place of faith. They all call themselves realists, pragmatists, materialists, raging to conquer the goods of this world. We are very far from suspecting the true nature of the disease gnawing at their insides. All we see is their frenzied activity,

---

[175] *Curé*, 280.
[176] *Rêve*, 237–38.
[177] *Curé*, 140.
[178] *Enfants*, 250–51; *Soleil*, 326.
[179] *Mouchette*, 86, 100.

[180] *Enfants*, 234.
[181] *Cimetières*, 113; *Français*, 17.
[182] *Cimetières*, 116, 126.
[183] Ibid., 84.
[184] *Liberté*, 215–16.

but we don't realize this is the degraded and debased form assumed by their metaphysical anguish."[185] Fear is also the residue left by the two world wars.[186] But it had already been the motor force of the history of France between 1870 and 1914 at all levels—culture, politics, and even official religion. The title Bernanos gives to his biography of Drumont says it all: *The Great Fear of the Right-Thinking*. Much fear, too, lurks behind the political strategies of the Church. And fear is the fundamental emotion underlying the French Revolution: "Are the French cowards?", asks Sister Constance. And Sister Mathilde replies: "They are afraid. Everybody is afraid. They contract fear from one another like the plague or cholera in times of epidemics."[187] Could it be that bravery is nothing but the fear of fear?[188] Finally, "a sordid fear of death"[189] is what Bernanos discovers behind the skepticism and irony of much of modern literature, whose representative par excellence is Anatole France.

It goes without saying that the common ground for this fear intrinsic to mankind is sin. If fear before the eternal Judge were not the basis of sin, then Christ's trepidation on the Mount of Olives would have been pointless. Mouchette's first experience of fear is sin-induced;[190] fear makes her jovial and talkative.[191] Gallet, too, "howls with fear" when he sees himself implicated in his mistress' guilt.[192] In *A Crime*, the murderess endures for hours on end "all the humiliations and tortures of a gigantic pride in the throes of agony".[193] Cénabre languishes out of a pure fear that is identical with his rejection of faith,[194] and Chevance explains to him that his fear has come too late and must remain unfruitful: "Nothing can now be done with the anguish you speak of. . . . Do not accuse God, reverend Canon! God had tendered this anguish to you, so to speak, as one persuades a little child to drink his medicine sip by sip. But you wouldn't as much as taste it. Now you must swallow it all down in one gulp. Drink up quickly!"[195] Bernanos, however, takes great care to distinguish the agonies of sinners from those of saints. Ouine's anguish in the face

---

185 Ibid., 176.
186 *Enfants*, 54.
187 *Carmélites*, 148.
188 *Curé*, 263.
189 *Soleil*, 325.
190 Ibid., 68.

191 Ibid., 75.
192 Ibid., 77.
193 *Crime*, 234.
194 *Imposture*, 36.
195 Ibid., 62–63.

of death is a "false agony",[196] a totally insignificant agony.[197] "Our death agonies bear the sign of remorse: they testify against our past; they break all sorts of bonds, and, anticipating the unspeakable judgment to come, they enact a full denunciation of our shame. . . . But a saint's sublime life concludes by plunging into the death agony like a cataract into a gulf of light and tenderness."[198] Hence the loving intensity with which Bernanos handles the agony of Joan of Arc:[199] "We must consider this agony face to face, or better still, we must enter into it. How deep and dark it is! All the fire of the stake cannot melt its chill."[200] From this standpoint we can understand Bernanos' statement as he lay dying: "I am now taken up into the Holy Agony."[201]

Bernanos doubtless belonged to that class of men who, according to his own formula, are made for agony. We can apply to him what he says about Léon Daudet: "More than any of us . . . he was made for the sweat of anguish, for that other kind of purifying tears—intimate and profound like none other—which were seen to flow on that night of nights by the prophetic olive trees. There are men whom nothing can appease: these find their refreshment, not in the living water promised to the Samaritan woman, but in the bile and vinegar of the total Agony."[202] For these, the plain human face is not expressive enough; they need a *mask* that settles down snugly upon every facial feature and contour. This is Bernanos' favorite image for describing the death agony: "Anguish", says the prioress, "clings to my skin like a wax mask";[203] Cénabre has "the petrified face of agony;"[204] Donissan wears "the mask of one in the throes of the death agony",[205] and this in the midst of life's activities, long before the member of the Academy finds him dead in his confessional, with an "awesome face, lit up by God's lightning".[206] During his struggle with the countess' daughter, the country priest suddenly sees before him "a bizarre face, contorted not by fear but by a deeper and more inward panic. I know from experience how a similar alteration of the features can take place. But until now I had only observed this on the faces of

---

[196] *Ouine*, unpublished chapter, in: *Bul.* 9, 7.

[197] *Ouine*, 228.

[198] *Dominique*, 36–37.

[199] *Jeanne*, 45f.

[200] Ibid., 60.

[201] Daniel Pézeril, in: *C. du R.*, 355.

[202] *Cimetières*, 339.

[203] *Carmélites*, 67.

[204] *Imposture*, 55.

[205] *Soleil*, 278.

[206] Ibid., 360.

the dying, and I naturally attributed it to some banal, physical cause. Doctors speak of the *mask of agony* as a matter of course. But doctors are often mistaken."[207] Most characteristic perhaps is the interminably drawn out death agony of the murdered priest in *A Crime*. He can no longer utter a word because his mouth has been filled with soil and rocks. He has become all mask. And yet he knows everything. Before such a witness, at once mute and all-knowing, the shrewd brain of the murderess consumes itself feverishly but in vain to find new strategies. The wisdom that comes with the death agony sits in judgment on all the partial wisdom of life; but the mask of death becomes a "confessional secret" belonging to the afterlife, something that could never be betrayed.[208]

~

This realization of the way the terrible mask of agony settles upon our living face should not make us forget that all human anguish remains comprehended within God's redeeming anguish. And, like everything else God shares with us, this gift too is conveyed within an ecclesial and sacramental vessel. Bernanos did not explicitly deal to any great extent with the sacrament of *holy anointing*, but everything he says about the death agony is implicitly uttered within its sphere. Mankind, however, has nowadays become so interiorly impoverished that it no longer realizes the treasure bestowed on it in this sacrament. In the same way as the young Frenchman in the virgin forest forgets the words of baptism, so too Mouchette has become so pitifully distraught by the time she descends into the water that she does not have the slightest idea of the wonderful balm available to salve her wounds. Together with the Church, this sacrament enters a stage of invisibility, which does not mean it loses its efficacy. It is as if the individual sacraments were becoming concealed within the total sacrament of the Church, to operate from that concealment. When one of them can still manifest itself in its uniqueness, it sheds a special light: "Our death agonies . . . are a wholesale denunciation of our shame. Oh,

---

[207] *Curé*, 150.
[208] *Crime*, 91, 125.

if only the sheet could cover for an instant the humbled and empty body, where only the anointed spots gleam!"[209] The anointing makes smooth the way leading to the threshold of eternity, which anguish and fear have muddled to the point of disappearance.

One time only did Bernanos attempt to portray the effects of anointing, namely, on the occasion of Ouine's death. During his lifetime, Ouine had so thoroughly abused his gift for reading into souls that, as he lies dying, he himself confesses that "it is possible that I myself am no longer capable of 'seeing myself die'—at least not with that interior glance from which I've derived too much delight and which now is gyrating on itself like a delicate little machine gone berserk at the approach of the only thing that deserves being seen and which I now cannot see." Such is the textual passage from the "forgotten chapter" of *Monsieur Ouine* that Albert Béguin published subsequently. But, in a footnote, Béguin gives the variants as they stand in Bernanos' successive drafts of the text, and these variants are very relevant to our present purposes. We here give them verbatim:

> It is possible that I myself am no longer capable of "seeing myself die" —at least not with that interior glance from which I've derived so much delight [and which no anointing with holy oils can] that now it is probably no more than an opaque orb [gyrating vainly on itself *and which an anointing with Holy Chrism drives berserk at the approach of the moment of decision*] [pivoting] [gyrating berserk] [gyrating vainly on itself and which no anointing with holy] [which no anointing with Holy Chrism] [turning vainly] [pivoting vainly on itself at the approach of the only unknown thing that deserves being seen] gyrating wildly on itself [and which no anointing with Holy Chrism could] at the approach of the only thing that deserves being seen and which it will not see.[210]

Ouine's sickness of soul should be interpreted within the horizon of the sacrament of anointing. The holy oil becomes a standard, a thermometer, a judge of his perverse form of vision. It does not open these tarnished eyes but rather blinds them definitively: so misused an organ cannot experience healing. The only way Ouine could have

---

[209] *Dominique,* 36–37.

[210] *Bul.* 9, 11. (The italics are von Balthasar's. All the phrases within square brackets, and hence the allusions to the Holy Chrism, were crossed out by Bernanos. He here seems to have backed away from attempting to express the ineffable.—Note of the French trans.)

crossed the threshold of eternity would have been for him to be *carried* across it after abstaining to make any contribution of his own.

In the end, it is precisely the King of Creation, who squandered all his goods on the prodigal son, who is anointed, like that poor *dauphin*, Prince Charles, "whom the wise little girl from Lorraine had consecrated and anointed king by the churchmen against their will". For, "when man will have lost everything, then we will demand for him too—whether he likes it or not—the anointing that divinizes him. We will open for him the way to his crowning as king."[211]

3. Death Agony as Communion

Everything we have said thus far concerning anguished fear and death acquires its Christian meaning only when understood within the mystery of Christ: for this is where most extreme solitude (and all fear is aloneness) becomes the wellspring of deepest communion. From the wine press of Gethsemani's anguish, the Blood was made that foams up in the chalice of the Church. For Bernanos, all possible aspects of human existence have their point of reference in this mystery. He understands this so radically that he cannot conceive of what we call spirit, person, and unique individual being without their being rooted in the soil of such communion. For Bernanos, a wholly "autonomous" person would be a contradiction in terms, ultimately because of the *imago Trinitatis* in man. For our writer, moreover, the communion he intends is never neutral, as if all it implied were a common rootedness in the one nature of Adam. In his view, communion always means an osmosis of concrete destinies, which are either grace-filled or godless. Thus, there exist from the outset a communion of saints with one another and a communion of sinners with one another;[212] but, just as primevally, there also exist a communion of saints with sinners and, consequently, a communion of sinners with saints. The saints' participation in the fate of sinners partakes in Christ's partic-

---

[211] *Anglais*, 251.

[212] The German word *Gemeinschaft* may be translated as either "communion" or "community", depending on whether the interior event or its social result is meant. But German also has the two more specific words *Gemeinde* and *Kommunion*, referring respectively to the more visible social community and the more spiritual communication in grace. All of these words are used in the present section.—TRANS.

ipation in the perdition of all. This vital involvement by Christ and his saints has burst open a great breach in the condition of loss sinners are submerged in: it is the master "stroke" that "pounds [Cénabre] from behind" and finishes him off as sinner;[213] and it is simultaneously the "loss of substance" that afflicts him[214] and the "flood of light" that streams in through the wound in his soul.[215] Because this is so, we are entitled to call the total community of saints and sinners *communio sanctorum*, the "communion of saints", on the basis of the event that creates it in the first place. Its deepest foundation is to be found in the divine *circumincessio*—the reciprocal indwelling of the three Persons in one another—and in the *communicatio idiomatum* —their reciprocal exchange of love and their participation in each other's properties. We could say that, for Bernanos, this is where the whole meaning of revelation lies: the Incarnation now makes possible as well a *communicatio idiomatum* between God and man, an *admirabile commercium*, that is, an awesome transaction and exchange between grace and sin. The Church is the locus where all of this takes place. The sacraments are the continuation and the making present of this event, and Christian life is its perfection and full realization. But this whole edifice is grounded in suffering.

Time and again Bernanos calls our attention to the literal meaning of the word *sym-pathy*: "participation-by-suffering-together-with": "All true sympathies are painful, as already the etymology suffices to show."[216] Speaking of himself, he writes nobly: "With all my soul I am fully a part of that suffering flock—the human race. I would like to love them enough to be able to suffer with them in their sorrows rather than using these, even for edifying ends."[217] And Ouine exclaims in his cynical mode: "Oh yes, of course: sympathy, compassion, *sym-pathein*, 'to suffer with'. What we should really say is 'to rot along with'!"[218] But Guillaume, the young invalid, penetrates more deeply, because for him suffering, involving concrete contact, has become a cognitive organ. He describes to his friend Philippe how his uninterrupted suffering is always whispering something to him:

[213] *Joie*, 302–3.
[214] Ibid., 299.
[215] Ibid., 304.
[216] *Erbarmen*, 115; *Croix*, May 30, 1945, 500.
[217] *To Jorge de Lima*, February 25, 1940; *Lettres inédites*, 20–21.
[218] *Ouine*, 137 (corrected text).

I know more about it than you now, more than any of them, because I've suffered a lot. You see, suffering is something you learn. At first it's like a little whisper deep inside you, day and night. . . . Weeks and weeks pass by and then, all of a sudden, wham! You begin to understand. Yes, I know, there's understanding and there's understanding. Of course, I don't mean ready-made words and phrases you can repeat. But a conversation has been struck, and now you're not alone any more. You'll never be alone again. Even when you feel completely hollow, completely empty, *suffering asks the question and gives the answer: it thinks for you.* All you have to do is let it work. When I just think of what I was last year, Philippe, I feel ashamed! So blundering, so rude! I wouldn't have been any good to you at all. . . . *Now I'm not eager to understand you any more. I don't need to. It's as if all your hurts were passing through me.*[219]

Philippe is made furious by this last statement, but now he has received from Guillaume the same wound that Chantal had inflicted on Cénabre—a wound that can be made only by a person who becomes responsible before God for a soul on its way to damnation. Guillaume has already seen Philippe in hell: "O Steeny! My dear Steeny! I saw you the other night in a dream, nailed through the middle of your chest onto an arid boulder—a kind of flaming wall made of salt—and, before I could even utter one word, you screamed out to me: 'No, no, stay there! Don't move! Leave me alone!'—exactly as if you were already damned."[220] In a similar way, the country priest has to struggle to defeat the countess' will to damn herself. The countess says to him with arrogant despair: "Do you think you can dispose of my destiny against my will? I *will* damn myself if I so please." To which the country priest instinctively replies: "I'll vouch for you soul for soul."[221]

This is, strictly speaking, a Christian mystery; the "unbeliever" reminds the congregation of the fact in his famous sermon in *The Great Cemeteries*:

> You'd think that this great dogma of the communion of saints, whose majesty astounds us, only added one more privilege to all your others. Is not its complement that other dogma of the reversibility of merits? We [unbelievers] are answerable only for our own acts and their material consequences. The solidarity binding you to all other men belongs to a

---

[219] Ibid., 43–44 (corrected text). (The italics are von Balthasar's.—TRANS.)
[220] Ibid., 39.
[221] *Curé*, 277.

much higher order. It seems to me that this gift of faith you've received, far from freeing you from men, rather binds you to them by bonds that are tighter than those of blood and race. You are the salt of the earth. When the world grows stale, to whom do you want me to turn? It's useless for you to boast of the merits of your saints, because you're nothing but the stewards of those goods. We often hear the best among you announce with pride that they don't *owe anything to anybody*. Such words make absolutely no sense in your mouths, because you literally owe everything to everybody, to each of us, including myself.[222]

The fact that Christians have forgotten this is the origin of all the miseries of the modern world:

I say that the solidarity of all of Christendom has not been kept in the face of major, intolerable scandals. Christians have reacted each for himself. If in a defeated army the soldiers scream out "Each man for himself!", what we hear Christians scream, scattered as they have been by the thundering offensive of the forces of evil, is "Each man must save himself all alone!" Each man for himself indeed! Redeemed humanity has been made a partaker of divinity, as the liturgy of the Mass teaches us, and now it hangs from the Cross by nails: But what do the Pharisees care, since they have paid their tithes and observed the Sabbath?[223]

Bernanos sums up the vocation of the writer in the following terms: "A true writer is only the steward and distributor of goods that do not belong to him, goods he has received from certain responsible consciences in order to pass them on to others. If he fails in this duty, he is less than a dog. In my opinion, this is only one aspect of that universal collaboration among souls that Catholic theology calls the communion of saints."[224] Likewise, the justification for monasteries is that people do not enter them seeking only their own personal salvation, but, as the prioress Madame de Croissy explains, monasteries are "houses of prayer", of "universal" prayer, because God has permitted "us to pray in the place of others. Thus, every prayer—even that of a little shepherd keeping his flock—is the prayer of the whole human race."[225] And the country priest adds: "I picture the silence of certain souls as being like vast places of refuge. Finding themselves

---

[222] *Cimetières*, 257.
[223] *Croix*, March 1941, 98–99.
[224] *Lettres brésiliennes*, 1942; *Bul.* 5, 8.
[225] *Carmélites*, 39.

at the end of their rope, wretched sinners enter there gropingly, with their last drop of strength. They can sleep in peace and then leave refreshed and consoled, with no memory of the great invisible temple in which, for a short while, they have laid down their burdens."[226]

In a letter of 1940 Bernanos writes: "From where do you get the idea . . . that solitude distances you from other people and keeps you from understanding them? From a Christian and even a human perspective, I would have thought the contrary. It's in silence and solitude that one rediscovers oneself, rediscovers the truth about oneself, and it's through this truth that one gains access to that of others."[227] According to Bernanos, whatever can be said of prayer and silence can also be said to a supreme degree of Christian suffering. The extraordinary sufferings of all Bernanos' saints may be understood only as a "sympathetic" suffering with others, as the form in which they share in the wretchedness of their brethren—those who perhaps are utterly lost and abandoned to damnation. Donissan may be understood only through Mouchette: "The Abbé Donissan did not appear out of nowhere. Mouchette's wild cry of despair summoned him and made him indispensable."[228] Chevance and Chantal may be understood only through Cénabre and the whole hellish world around him: "Where are we both going?", Chantal asks her grandmother.[229] And, as she is carrying the old woman home on her shoulders after her collapse, Chantal whispers, catching her breath: "Mama, I seem to be carrying you, but it's you who are carrying me. . . . Don't ever let go of me!"[230] And, meditating on the fate of the countess, the country priest writes in his diary: "Perhaps God wanted to transfer to my shoulders the burden from which he had just delivered his exhausted creature."[231] The poor priest must pay with specific sufferings, either before or after the event, for every supernaturally successful deed of his. Finally, a person's death—that most valuable of all acts in a Christian life—becomes one of the choicest coins with which Christians pay for, and indeed commune with, one another. Of this we shall speak later on.

---

[226] *Curé,* 282.

[227] *To Amoroso Lima,* March 1, 1940; *Esprit,* 198; *Erbarmen,* 90.

[228] *Satan,* in: *Bul.* 12–13, 26.

[229] *Joie,* 132.

[230] Ibid., 137.

[231] *Curé,* 218.

Thus, all personal salvation depends on a person's investing his soul, on his putting it in circulation, so to speak, on his engaging it in the exchanges and negotiations that alone matter: "Whoever makes use of his soul, no matter how ineptly, begins by the same token to participate in universal Life and attunes himself to its vast rhythms: he enters body and soul into the communion of saints that belongs to all men of good will."[232] Staking one's soul for one's brethren in imitation of the Lord (1 Jn 3:16) is not a "heroic act of love" that soars high above ordinary Christian life. Staking one's soul for one's brethren, rather, is the alpha and the omega of ordinary Christian life. This investing and staking of one's soul for others is the solution to the theoretically unsolvable question of how a guiltless Christian can partake in the communion of the guilty, indeed, of how he can bear their guilt without himself incurring guilt. Ouine doubts whether "anyone has ever been able to share the ennui of man and at the same time safeguard his own soul".[233] And his interlocutor, the Curé de Fenouille, knows that all effective pastoral work rests on an absolute distinction: "Already at the age when children are all games, laughs, and songs, I had felt that you can't compromise with evil, that justice and injustice are two separate universes." And yet, he goes on, "I don't rise up in revolt against evil, because God himself did not rise in revolt against it: rather, he assumed it. I don't even curse the devil."[234] Or, must we believe what Clergerie affirms of his daughter, namely, that she had to have "a certain experience" or "at least a foreboding" of evil in order to escape its snares?[235] Is not precisely the Immaculate Conception— she who can look on evil only with uncomprehending and astonished eyes—the most solitary and excluded of all?[236] In an existential sense, this is one of the darkest, most impenetrable of questions.

In order to begin prying it open, we must ask whether and in what sense there exists a *"communion of the wicked"*. The country priest expressly endorses the concept, in the sense that all sins at bottom constitute one single sin and that the very sinners who hate and murder

---

[232] *Liberté*, 283.
[233] *Ouine*, 138.
[234] Ibid., 142.
[235] *Joie*, 98.
[236] *Curé*, 231.

one another are made companions for all eternity precisely by their common acts and attitudes.[237] Indeed, he is of the opinion that, "if God were to give us a clear idea of the solidarity binding us one to another, both in good and in evil, we would scarcely be able to go on living."[238] Mouchette and Gallet understand this: "We are both at the bottom of the same hole",[239] partaking of the same anguish; the doctor sees himself "bound forever to his hideous friend".[240] Ouine enjoys a sort of vampiric communication on the basis of his desire and curiosity,[241] and, in *The New Mouchette*, the woman sacristan is a true vampire who grows fat by sucking the life of others.[242] In *An Evil Dream*, the problem always lurking in the background is that of a "complicity in the darkness".[243] Over against all this, however, we have the statement of the Curé de Fenouille to his "dead congregation": "*The devil, who can do so many things, will never succeed in founding his own church, a church that would bring into a common pool all the merits of hell, that would bring together all of sin.* From now until the end of the world, the sinner will have to sin alone, always alone. We shall sin alone just as we die alone."[244] The concept of a communion is not something neutral that may be subdivided into a communion of the good and a communion of the wicked. These two forms move in exactly opposed directions. The communion of the wicked is something so negative and dissolute that it can be constituted only by the refusal that all the alone hurl at goodness. This is best symbolized by the manner in which the "dead congregation", at the end of the sermon, breaks out into a common laughter that welds it together into a hellish community,[245] a community of the spiritually dead who are already, indeed, in a state of putrefaction: their contact with one another is based on a process that dissolves all contour and limit among creatures. It leads to that chaos and primal slime that makes up the infernal sludge,[246] the "layer of pus no surgeon can now eliminate".[247]

The dead state in which these persons find themselves leads to that dismal derealization and world of the "evil dream" that has no ex-

---

[237] Ibid., 156.
[238] Ibid., 184.
[239] *Soleil*, 74.
[240] Ibid., 77.
[241] *Ouine*, 241.
[242] *Mouchette*, 196–97.

[243] *Rêve*, 174; see also 208, 248, et passim.
[244] *Ouine*, 166.
[245] Ibid., 172–73.
[246] Ibid., 164.
[247] *Cimetières*, 137.

its, because the crime whereby one attempts to break through the
dream and redeem oneself only immerses one in it the more profoundly.[248] At this stage, however, the wicked who are communing
in their shared decomposition encounter a new mystery, different yet
related to the previous one: that of *sexual communion* in one flesh,
which since Adam has been a sinful flesh. How can we avoid seeing
the dimension in which persons are dying the "second death" through
self-dissolution as being one and the same as—or at least as leading
to—the dimension of the union of the sexes, from which new persons are always emerging through procreation? Bernanos' tumultuous
portrayal, in *Under Satan's Sun*, of universal guilt as rooted in hereditary, sexual guilt points in this direction.[249] The extraordinary passage
deserves being compared to the third of Rilke's *Duino Elegies*. The
concept of inherited guilt, and of community of guilt on the basis of
communion between the sexes, is the form in which Bernanos most
fatally experiences the *communio peccatorum*. This can already be seen in
Conversations among Shadows, in which Françoise vainly seeks to tear
her abysmal arrogance out of her soul by throwing herself into an
all-consuming love. But the truth is that the sin is older than herself:
Françoise is actually bearing the sin of her whole family, above all her
father's sin. "How did I ever hope to eradicate a pride whose roots
are not in me?"[250] The first Mouchette likewise bears the burden of
a father who keeps her at a distance from all religion; and the second
Mouchette must carry a hereditary burden in the proper sense: it is
significant that, when her drunken father beats her, she feels "in dark
solidarity with his ferocity, as if she shared in his hatred".[251] Beyond
this, she remains paralyzed by the dull torpor of the flesh. She can
feel and know (or better, *not* know) only through the flesh and must
therefore remain as mute as the flesh.[252]

The lesbian's wrongdoing in *A Crime* is seen as deriving almost
totally from the sin of her mother.[253] But Chantal, too, feels weighed
down by her heredity,[254] and, even though the doctor declares her
free of such influences,[255] she is in fact the precise recapitulation of
her whole ancestry: she can recognize herself in all their traits and

---

[248] *Rêve*, 244.
[249] *Soleil*, 208f.
[250] *Nouvelles*, 138.
[251] Ibid., 250.

[252] *Mouchette*, 112.
[253] *Crime*, 242–43.
[254] *Joie*, 175.
[255] Ibid., 226.

deeds.[256] What with Chantal remained largely a part of her imagination becomes literal reality with the country priest. He is the child of alcoholics, and the first cause of his continual thirst is physical: "You suffer from a thirst that is not yours."[257] He is aware of his situation, and he also knows the good things he owes his lineage, for instance, his mother's "endurance" and "wild clinging to life".[258] The metaphor of heredity here becomes a transparency of the reality of redemption, that is, of the experience and the suffering of the guilt of others in oneself, in one's own flesh and spirit. The wretched black wine he cooks up with dry bread is the only thing the country priest, suffering from stomach cancer, can still digest. Without discarding its external form, his alcoholic addiction becomes an interior work of reparation, in the same way as, on the Mount of Olives, the addiction to sin may only be drunk to the dregs by Christ in the form of its punishment, as a work of atonement. For him who has eyes to see, sin's brand of disgrace is perfectly visible on the country priest, just as the agony, disgrace, and repugnance of Gethsemani openly proclaim that here Someone has "become sin" for our sake.

Chantal can therefore say to Doctor La Pérousse: "There was a time when I feared evil, I don't mean as we should fear it, I mean I was horrified by it. Now I know we shouldn't be horrified by anything. . . . Sin, for instance: all of us are immersed in it, some of us to enjoy it, and some of us to suffer because of it; but, when all's said and done, it's the same bread we're all breaking by the fountain's edge, mouth watering—the same repugnance."[259] The only question is, however, whether the line can be drawn so strictly between pleasure in sin and atonement for sin. Bernanos does not have to enter fully into the mystery of the Lord's Passion and into the other mystery whereby Christ chooses certain persons (such as Chevance, Chantal, and the country priest) to share in his work of atonement: Bernanos already knows how much every pleasure brings with it its own thorn, its own repugnance and tedium. A point may be reached where the collective element—the weaknesses and burdens of a whole family of ancestors—gains the upper hand over personal guilt in a given gen-

---

[256] Ibid., 137.
[257] *Curé*, 227; see also 92, 247.
[258] Ibid., 283.
[259] *Joie*, 230.

eration, which then sees its whole existence as such as a punishment: this is the case of the generation of the young in *An Evil Dream* and of Philippe's generation in *Monsieur Ouine*. And the point may also be reached where a will to solidarity may become expressed as a will to be present in the world of sin, not so much out of bravado as out of a spirit of camaraderie. The foreign legionnaires Olivier describes are just such a strange troop of "monks in the world" who have their distant forebears in the wandering minstrels of the Middle Ages, in Rabelais, and in the musketeers: "In the spirit of these good fellows, blasphemy is a way of burning one's bridges behind one: you get used to it. I find it idiotic, but not dirty. Having become outlaws in this world, they make themselves outlaws in the other. . . . One more blasphemy for good measure, so as to run the same risks as one's comrades and avoid acquittal as a favored minority and then . . . croak! and it's over."[260] This is the same caliber of people Olivier finds in his own family: "They are eager and hard, never satisfied with anything, with an intractable center to them that must be the devil's part in us —something that makes us our own terrible enemies, to the point that our virtues look like our vices. The good Lord himself will have a hard time telling the bad boys from the saints in the family, if, that is, by any chance there are any!"[261]

There exists a wholly unwitting kind of solidarity. It shares others' joys and sorrows so unselfconsciously that it does not realize what it is doing. One instance of this is the dying mother of the second Mouchette: "Without at all realizing it, the old woman is taking on herself the whole family's weight of misery. . . . On the sad galley where they were rowing together, the mother was the figurehead on the prow, facing the wind and spouting foam with every new attack of the sea."[262] This is a humble form of sanctity that remains wholly hidden from itself. And surely the ethos guiding Bernanos in all his portrayals of the communal entanglement of human destinies rests on the deepest sort of compassion, the kind that leaves to God's judgment the impossible task of separating the good from the wicked and that walks in the shoes of each and every person both mournfully and resolutely: "The great misfortune is that the justice of men always

---

[260] *Curé*, 262.
[261] Ibid., 260.
[262] *Mouchette*, 133.

comes too late. It represses or stigmatizes certain acts, without ever tracing these either higher or farther back than the person who has committed them. But our hidden faults poison the air others breathe, and what results in a specific crime was first a germ carried about by some unsuspecting wretch: without this principle of corruption, the full fruit of the crime would never have ripened."[263]

The darker the dusk of solidarity in guilt, the brighter the dawn descending from the much more unfathomable abyss of *vicarious atonement*. The *Dialogues of the Carmelites* plays such an artfully interwoven fugue on this theme that its intricacies escape the analysis of even the cleverest contrapuntalist. In this way, the work succeeds admirably by pointing us to the ever more perspectivistic hall of mirrors that is Christian solidarity in redemption. Every instance in this work when a person's self-substitution for another is seen to bear a concrete effect is intended only as a metaphor, brought out into the light for the sake of the audience: for within the tapestry of salvation itself the threads are interwoven a thousandfold, so much so that no one thread can be pulled out and shown forth in isolation from all the rest.

Plagued by her anguish, Blanche is the one character who is constantly in peril. Three others want to make themselves answerable for her: the old prioress Madame de Croissy, the subprioress Marie de l'Incarnation, and her young friend Sister Constance.

Constance takes responsibility for Blanche at just the decisive moment: the vow of martyrdom must be unanimous by the whole community, and Blanche is the only one to vote against it; but Constance speaks her agreement in her stead. They both kneel down side by side, and Blanche utters the vow, "using up her last reserve of strength" and having to rely beyond that on Constance's forces. The moment she has "offered up her life to God for the salvation of Carmel and of France", Blanche flees definitively into the world.[264] Constance personally lacks all notion of fear, but she possesses a keen sense she cannot explain to herself for what is agitating her dear sister. Ever since their very first conversation, everything has developed "as if [Constance] were beginning to understand, but she didn't exactly know

[263] *Curé*, 183.
[264] *Carmélites*, 184–86.

what".[265] Her intuition tells her with certainty that Blanche "would return".[266] She even understands the mystery of the "exchange of deaths".[267]

The *prioress* dies the death of the young Blanche for her; Constance already knows that the little novice would go to her death "easily", astounded "to feel so comfortable within it", for "we don't die each for herself, but one for another, or even one in the place of another."[268] The prioress offers her "very poor death" for "the dearest and most endangered" of her daughters,[269] and, when God hears her plea, it seems to her she is receiving a false death, one too small for her. But Blanche must be present and thus participate interiorly in this work accomplished for her sake. She must undergo the trial of this death; she must "gather" it like a precious fruit by reading the words and the will of the dying nun on "her incessantly moving lips".[270]

But *Marie*, too, presses the community to take the vow of martyrdom on the basis of the mystery of vicarious substitution that lies at the heart of the Carmelite vocation. Her problem is that she *provokes* martyrdom; to the commissioner who threatens to destroy the monastery, that "lair of superstition", Marie replies: "And don't fail to destroy us too, down to the last one."[271] Madame Lidoine, the new prioress, completely disavows such an attitude.[272] In fact, she refuses to recognize a vow taken in her absence.[273] But when the sisters are in prison awaiting the moment of climbing the scaffold, Madame Lidoine ratifies the vow made by her daughters. At first she does so only for herself, hoping to the very end that her own sacrifice would suffice and that "the youngest ones" at least would "go unharmed". For, she reflects, "if those people aren't complete monsters, or if they know something about our Holy Rule, whom else would they attack but me?"[274] The prioress, in other words, willingly takes the place of Marie and of the whole community; but these do not want to leave her alone. At the last moment she will only be one Carmelite among others, and yet she will have taken the place of Mère Marie, who instigated the vow but is now kept by obedience from coming to the

[265] Ibid., 36.
[266] Ibid., 222.
[267] Ibid., 78.
[268] Ibid., 79.
[269] Ibid., 61–62.
[270] Ibid., 70–72.
[271] Ibid., 122.
[272] Ibid., 135, 188.
[273] Ibid., 198–99.
[274] Ibid., 223–24.

prison and, hence, from dying with her sisters.[275] "My daughters,"
says the prioress, "the hour has come for you to remember the vow
you made. Up to this moment it has been my desire to be solely
answerable for it. But now I can only assume the part allotted to me,
and even so I can claim it only with humility in the name of our admirable Mère Marie de l'Incarnation. It's her part that's now allotted
to me, unworthy though I am."[276] Then takes place the astounding
reversal of which Madame Lidoine had already had a presentiment.
When Marie had wanted to die heroically for "the weakest and perhaps most miserable one", the new prioress had replied: "It's you, my
daughter, who will be sacrificed to this weakness and perhaps delivered over to this disdain." And Marie had said at once: "I will gladly
consent."[277]

Marie is a very positive figure in Bernanos. She represents the ideal
of honor.[278] She understood her novice's weakness but wanted to turn
it into something honorable for the whole community through an act
of heroism.[279] She knows how to obey;[280] she is full of insight in what
concerns Blanche, discerning from the outset that she "lacks character", and she wants to "help her by particular acts of penance".[281]
Marie knows that the crux of the matter is not fear or courage but
"casting oneself body and soul into the will of God".[282] She is always
"extraordinarily simple and natural",[283] and this enables her in the
end to bear her terribly bitter humiliation, which she perceives as a
"dishonor":[284] she is the only one excluded from fulfilling the vow
of martyrdom she herself had instigated. But she realizes that she has
brought this too on herself by her extravagant attitude. Offering to
go into Paris to look for Blanche, Marie says to her prioress: "Reverend Mother, I ask you to forgive the fault I have committed. May
God grant me to atone for it so intensely that no one but me will be
hurt by it."[285] It is this trip into Paris that separates Marie from her
community and deprives her of the martyrdom she has so ardently
desired. But precisely this circumstance is the occasion for Marie to
suffer the all-important *spiritual* martyrdom that calls her, in her soli-

[275] Ibid., 214.
[276] Ibid., 226.
[277] Ibid., 131–32.
[278] Ibid., 60, 109, 119, 131.
[279] Ibid., 131.
[280] Ibid., 82.
[281] Ibid., 84–86.
[282] Ibid., 149.
[283] Ibid., 180.
[284] Ibid., 228.
[285] Ibid., 89.

tude, to offer herself in the place of all her sisters and so establish an even deeper communion with them. When she declares herself to be someone "dishonored" by destiny, the priest replies: "That's exactly the word I was expecting! And, mind you, I don't reproach you for uttering it! On your lips, it is the howl of nature in its death throes. This is the blood, yes, this is the blood God is asking of you and which you must pour out!"[286]

So it is that Blanche is carried over the threshold by the willingness of these three nuns to take her place. (If we counted Madame Lidoine, there would be four, and many more if we included the other sisters.) In the end Blanche goes to her death fearless and singing with a clear voice.[287] However, none of this should make us forget that all these works of willing, vicarious substitution have their foundation in Blanche's weakness and that they derive their efficacy and power precisely from the way Blanche herself represents the essential weakness of all men before the ultimate challenge: Blanche drinks the cup of fear to the dregs both for herself and in substitution for all others. Bernanos has no intention of disentangling this admirable web; it is enough for him if we come to see that neither in love nor in sin does a person live merely his own destiny. Rather, parts of others' destinies are allotted to him, and he also finds his own destiny lived out in others'. Bernanos wants us to see, too, that, in an infinitely more intimate manner than even Christians suspect, life and death are interchangeable within the one Body that must truly be called mystical.

4. Communion as Night

"Communion of saints" happens when every member of the Body surrenders his whole being and opens it to becoming but a part of the whole, when he allows his integrity to suffer wounds that make possible the passage through him of the Blood circulating throughout the whole. Such a wound, moreover, has its archetype in the death agony Christ suffered in Gethsemani, where his very Being ran out as anguish. The utter freedom with which love is given assumes the

---

[286] Ibid., 228.
[287] Ibid., 230.

suffering form of futility: "I have the impression", writes the country priest early in his diary, "that my life and all the energies of my
life are running out of me and becoming lost in the sand."[288] And
at the end, when he is about to face death, he says: "I cried with
wide-open eyes, I cried as I've seen the dying cry. And still it was
my life flowing out of me."[289] Thus, too, from the beginning, Chantal bore "a mysterious wound . . . from which a more than human
charity flowed, a carnal charity that could discover God in man".[290]
And at the end of her story we read: "Her own suffering no longer
belonged to her. She would not have been able to keep it for herself.
It was as if the precious blood of another heart were being poured
out of her torn, her devastated flesh."[291] And concerning Saint Dominic: "Around the dying father who has now emptied himself almost totally of his mystical blood, of his truly divine charity, the Order [of Preachers] is buzzing like a beehive in an outpouring of austere
tears."[292]

The need for love to assume such passional form derives from
sin. Sin is the "mysterious wound . . . , the open breach" through
which the soul "slides off into nothingness", "the black, putrefying
wound".[293] The "form of sin" exacts from love the horrific experiences Donissan must undergo, all of them summed up in the frightful certainty of already being defeated in advance, before the battle is even engaged.[294] To Satan's scornful jibe: "Man of the Cross,
conquered in advance!", Donissan can only reply: "The man of the
Cross is not on it in order to conquer but in order to bear witness to
the point of death."[295] He will have "the unbearable feeling of having

---

[288] *Curé*, 40.
[289] Ibid., 299.
[290] *Joie*, 49.
[291] Ibid., 248.
[292] *Dominique*, 38. (Here we have another good example of what amounts to a veritable prose poem of great pathos and lyric intensity. The reader deserves a look at the sounds and rhythms of a magnificent original whose compression, cadenced word order, and oxymorons make every attempt at translation awkward: *Autour du moribond qui achève de se vider de son sang mystique, de sa toute divine charité, dans une effusion de larmes austères, l'ordre bourdonne comme une ruche.*—TRANS.)
[293] *Ouine*, 121.
[294] *Soleil*, 295.
[295] Ibid., 315.

been caught in a trap",[296] until all hope is eclipsed in his heart[297] and his one need will be "to die, just as you long to pour out tears", a yearning for eternal night, for "something more secret than solitude: the vertigo of an everlasting fall into all-engulfing darkness".[298] "A strange childhood, a naïve eagerness similar to the first wound of the senses, heats up the old blood and throbs in his scrawny chest. . . . Gropingly he seeks death, caresses death through so many veils with a weak, trembling hand."[299] And the *forma peccati* advances until it overlaps perfectly with the person, until the difference between the two can no longer be told: " 'To *die*,' he says in a low voice, 'to *die*. . . .' He spells out the word so as to become imbued with it and digest it in his heart. . . . And now he feels it in the deepest part of himself, in his veins—this word, a subtle poison. . . . He persists, he doubles his efforts with a mounting fever. He'd like to drain it in one gulp and so hasten his end. His impatience has about it something of the sinner's need to plunge into his offense, always deeper, there to hide from his judge. . . . Indeed, nothing separates the humble wonder worker from his rest except a final movement of his sovereign will."[300] In Donissan the form of sin assumes that extreme severity that God's Providence allows only very exceptionally: namely, vicarious demonic possession: "That thing he can't name, crouching in his heart, so voluminous and heavy", is at the same time "his anguish" and "Satan" himself: "He drags this burden around within him, and he doesn't dare cast if off. Where would he be casting it? Into another heart."[301] The Curé de Luzarnes would say of him: "I thought I saw him in the burning lake."[302] Evil is so close to him that it blocks off all light; only plunged in his own infernal disconsolateness can he console the souls of others,[303] for "everything in him and about him bears the sign of wrath."[304] This is why evil appears to him to be invincible,[305] as he exclaims: "What priest has never wept out of helplessness before the mystery of human suffering?"[306]

Thus, when Donissan offers God his own eternal salvation as ran-

---

[296] Ibid., 125.
[297] Ibid., 242.
[298] Ibid., 256.
[299] Ibid., 257.
[300] Ibid., 257–58.
[301] Ibid., 260.

[302] Ibid., 268.
[303] Ibid., 265–66.
[304] Ibid., 150.
[305] Ibid., 254.
[306] Ibid., 287–88.

som for the salvation of souls and chooses hell as his lot, he is at
bottom doing nothing but ratifying the condition he is already in. At
first it seemed as though his love were accomplishing its self-sacrifice
consciously: " 'If I could do it without hating You, I would surrender my salvation to You. I would damn myself for the sake of these
people You, as a kind of joke, have entrusted to me—wretch that I
am!' In this way did [Donissan] defy the abyss, summoning it up with
a solemn vow, with a pure heart."[307] But in reality he had ever been
predestined to arrive at such a pass,[308] at this "pact with the nether
darkness", at this "kind of moral suicide whose reasoned, subtle, and
secret cruelty make one shiver".[309] "He compared himself to some
old defiled wall on which passers-by inscribe obscene words, a wall
crumbling little by little and full of laughable secrets."[310]

All of this constitutes the experiential aspect of "being used" by
souls,[311] the most radical possible application of the Christian recipe
that requires one to "use up" one's soul and "put it in circulation".[312]
For, how could one make use of one's soul, precisely, without using
it up and without feeling the "futility" of it all, the wasteful squandering of one's "efforts"?[313] Bernanos' other saints stand under the
same sign: Chevance, whose sacrifice takes the form of powerlessness, of the inability to give anything;[314] Chantal;[315] and, above all,
the country priest, who is plunged into the same night as Donissan,
only more humbly and humanly: "The saints all experienced such in-
firmities and failures. . . . But surely not this numb revolt, this surly
and almost spiteful silence of the soul. . . . The same solitude, the
same silence. And this time no hope of overcoming the obstacle, of
getting around it. In fact, there's no obstacle there at all, nothing.
God! I breathe the night, I inhale it. The night comes pouring into
me by I don't know what inconceivable, unimaginable breach in my
soul. I myself am night. . . . My solitude is perfect, and I hate it. I
have no pity on myself. What if I'm losing the ability to love?"[316]
"The spirit of prayer has left me of itself, without making the slightest tear, like a fruit that falls from the tree. Dread arrived only later.

---

[307] Ibid., 139.
[308] Ibid., 238f.
[309] Ibid., 146.
[310] Ibid., 255.
[311] Ibid., 205.

[312] *Liberté*, 283.
[313] *Soleil*, 205.
[314] *Imposture*, 66–67.
[315] *Joie*, 245.
[316] *Curé*, 121.

I understood the vessel had broken when I saw my hands empty."[317]
"God has withdrawn from me. Of this, at least, I am sure."[318]
   The degree of mystical vehemence attained by such passages is
rooted in a very sober and penetrating experience on the part of
Bernanos himself: he had discovered the truth that loving, commu-
nicating oneself, distributing oneself like bread, all make the loving
person into a solitary: "Once you have not only said what you think
but said everything you think, then you come to know a very bitter
form of interior solitude. Those who know how to keep jealously,
for themselves, a part of the truth available to them can at least nourish themselves secretly with it. The others, having given away everything, feel very empty."[319] People "only really began to distrust me on
the day I resolved to understand and love them. The more I advance
in this kind of life, the deeper my descent into solitude."[320] Thus,
Cénabre can say to Chantal: "Whatever may be the gift you have
received—whatever its importance or character—you will eventually
have to share it with others, and that first act of sharing may well be
for you worse than death, a type of death much more difficult than
physical death because it leads to a more frightful solitude."[321] The
whole mystery of Carmel is founded on this truth: "Our business is
to pray, just as the business of a lamp is to shed light. It wouldn't
occur to anyone to light a lamp in order to shed light on another.
'Each man for himself!,' such is the law of the world. And our law is
a little like it: 'Each man for God!' My poor dear! You've dreamed of
this house like a child full of fears, whom the servants have just put
to bed: in your dark room you dream of the living room with its light
and warmth. You know nothing of the solitude in which a true religious becomes vulnerably exposed both to life and to death."[322] This
mystery is connected with that of the solitude of the innocent within
the world of the communion of sinners. Ouine mumbles something
about it: "Innocence can resist everything; it is harder than life itself.
Alas! I who am speaking to you have known a few of these unfortunates. . . . Society defends itself against such monsters. It pushes

---

[317] Ibid., 143.
[318] Ibid., 158.
[319] *To Amoroso Lima*, March 5, 1939; *Esprit*, 190.
[320] *To Jorge de Lima*, April 7, 1940; *Lettres inédites*, 26.
[321] *Joie*, 276.
[322] *Carmélites*, 36–37.

them little by little out of its midst and isolates them."[323] The Curé
de Fenouille, for his part, admits to Ouine: "Solitude had already depleted me much before the time I was old enough to endure it."[324]
And "in one split second" Chantal recognizes "her frightening, her
elemental solitude, the solitude of the children of God",[325] while the
Curé de Torcy speaks of the "astonishing solitude" and the "virginal
sadness" of her who "was Innocence itself", the Mother of God,
"born without sin".[326]

We need only let this tender bud blossom in order to discover the
truth lying within it: the pure Flesh and Blood of the Son of God,
given to sinners, delivered over into the hands and hearts of sinners.
To be sure, the Church orders that the sinner should examine himself
before he approaches the Eucharist.[327] But what could the result of
such a self-examination ever be except "Lord, I am not worthy"? And
from where could purification come if not, always, from precisely this
Flesh and Blood, handed over on the Cross and reviled by sinners,
whose sacramental distribution (since the Last Supper precedes the
Crucifixion) leads only subsequently to the paschal institution of the
sacrament of confession? The Church's order of the sacraments remains in full force; but Bernanos goes back to the archetypal event
behind it. By a radical "stripping of the altars" as on that fateful night
from Holy Thursday to Good Friday, Bernanos returns to the primal
Cross, to that initial and elemental surrender of the pure Flesh to the
impure sinner, until he is squarely before the communion of Judas,
concerning which John speaks so unambiguously. In fact, this act of
eucharistic communion is the only one John mentions,[328] as if this
most critical of cases included all other less extreme instances of sinful

---

[323] *Ouine*, 136.

[324] Ibid., 142.

[325] *Joie*, 120.

[326] *Curé*, 231, 237.

[327] "A man must test himself before eating his share of the bread and drinking from the
cup. For he who eats and drinks eats and drinks judgment on himself if he does not discern
the Body" (1 Cor 11:28-29, *New English Bible*).

[328] " 'In truth, in very truth I tell you, one of you is going to betray me. . . . It is the man
to whom I give this piece of bread when I have dipped it in the dish.' Then, after dipping it
in the dish, he took it out and gave it to Judas, son of Simon Iscariot. As soon as Judas had
received it, Satan entered him" (Jn 13:21, 26-27, *New English Bible*).

betrayal, and as if this one case were the proof for a "love that goes to the end" (Jn 13:1). Behind every "use" of the holy Flesh lurks the massive *abuse* of the holy—and also of the saints—at the hands of sinners.[329] Behind every honor rendered lurks an elemental dishonor and profanation. God ran this risk with his Incarnation, which necessarily led to the Cross: "The divine flesh was not only torn; it was violated and profaned by an absolute sacrilege, until it reached the majesty of agony."[330] In *Under Satan's Sun*, Bernanos' first novel, the whole drama unfolds between God and Satan, and man appears only as a "last rampart" cast between them.[331] In the double novel *The Imposture* and *Joy*, however, Satan enters man, and this makes possible for the first time the concrete portrayal of the *figure of Judas*. Here, the eucharistic Flesh is represented symbolically in the body of the pure girl who is sacrificed.

As Chantal, without knowing it, is awaiting Cénabre's arrival for the decisive battle, in spirit she is actually in the upper room of the Last Supper, where

> He, blessing the firstfruits of his impending agony as he had this very day blessed the vine and the wheat, consecrated his work, his sacred BODY, for those who were his own, for the sorrowing human race, and so offered himself to all men. . . . He lifted his Body up once, once and for all, while still in the full splendor and strength of his youth, before surrendering it to fear, before leaving it face to face with hideous fear during this interminable night. . . . Doubtless he was offering his Body to all men, but *he was thinking of only one, of the one man to whom this Body truly and humanly belonged as that of a slave belongs to his master: He thought of the one who had gotten it by ruse, by disposing of it as his own legitimate possession by virtue of a perfectly valid sales contract drawn up in correct form. This was thus the only man who could defy mercy and enter body and soul into despair, who could make of despair his dwelling, cover himself with despair in the same way that the first murderer covered himself with night. This was the one man among men who really possessed anything, who was fully provided for, and who would henceforth look for nothing from anyone, for all eternity.*[332]

---

[329] *Soleil*, 242.
[330] Ibid., 284.
[331] Ibid., 285.
[332] *Joie*, 251–52. (The italics are von Balthasar's.—TRANS.)

Bernanos is not so naïve as to believe, or have others believe, that a sacrilegious communion absolved Judas. He is the first to know that "the blood that flows from the Cross can kill us."[333] Nevertheless, he insists on this conception of "rights" that strikes us as a dramatic intensification of Anselm's "juridical" theology of the redemption; indeed, Bernanos underscores his point repeatedly by having Cénabre defend his "rights" to Chantal and Chevance. As someone who has already surrendered to hell, Cénabre has no love available to him; and so he can express his claims only with all the coldness of juridical form. *These "rights" of his rest on the fact that the destiny of both Chevance and Chantal may be explained only in terms of Cénabre, the Judas figure: their condition as sufferers is a function of him as sinner,* just as the Crucified Jesus deigned, not only to suffer at the hands of all Judases, but to reproduce their destiny and their godforsakenness in himself: "What an extraordinary thing, this First Communion of the human race amidst a carnival of soldiers, Jewish priests, and dolled-up girlies!"[334] Just as the mouthful swallowed by Judas was what precipitated him out into the night, so too it was the decisive confession that Donissan coerced out of Mouchette that precipitated her into her infernal nuptials and her subsequent suicide and, likewise, the climactic conversation between the countess' daughter and the country priest that propelled her into the lethal hatred of her revolt. And thus it is that Chantal, too, sees Judas, "that strange, incomprehensible creature who renounced hope, who sold the hope of man for thirty denarii in cash, and then hanged himself". She sees him, not in the act of betrayal, but "at the hour when he had already accomplished his destiny, when he had already been set up forever as the black fruit of a black tree at the entrance of the shameful kingdom of shadows—the strict, unbribable sentinel whom mercy accosts in vain and who will let no forgiveness pass through, to insure that hell consummates its horrendous peace with all tranquillity." Chantal listens to this "unspeakable lament" and takes it "into her soul just as a diver fills his chest with air", and, "very simply, just as she had offered herself up many times for sinners, with the same gesture she went toward this sinner of sinners with open arms. . . . As soon as she had taken the first step, this gibbet that had expanded so furiously began to shrink

---

[333] *Imposture*, 62.
[334] *Joie*, 231.

in size, and suddenly it was there before her, within reach of her little hand—nothing but a black and twisted olive tree. . . . The Abbé Cénabre stood before her."³³⁵ After the long discussion with him, Chantal kisses his hand,³³⁶ just before delivering unawares the blow that shatters his armor. Cénabre had communicated his "secret" to her—the secret of hell—but in sealed form: "What are you going to do with it . . . ?", he inquires of her. "What will it become in your hands? Whatever you touch immediately turns into something that resembles you, something with the marvelous ability to torture you."³³⁷ But Chantal explains to him how sorely God is lacking from her life: "And now I would doubtless be poorer, much poorer, than you if you had not miraculously given me this . . . this thing for safekeeping."³³⁸ Bernanos then releases Cénabre to insanity after he has spoken the words "Our Father". This was a dénouement that meant a great deal to Bernanos: "I entreat you", he wrote to his editor: "for God's sake don't change anything more! I must absolutely *reinsert* the note at the end. Otherwise it will seem that Cénabre is dead. It is better for God to strike his reason after the lightning bolt of grace."³³⁹

As a matter of fact, hell is no longer the same after the Passion as it had been before it. Bernanos concludes his life of Saint Dominic with an ancient formula encapsulating "the wondrous delirium" of the saint's "universal charity": "*ad in infernos damnatos extendebat caritatem suam* [his love extended even to those damned in hell]."³⁴⁰ What can be more quintessential of hell than its abandonment by God? And who could be more abandoned by the Father than the Son, who knows like no other who the Father is?

5. I and Thou

The vehemence with which Bernanos tears open the wound of Being, that the substance of life may flow out of it in the agony of love, points back to a most profound suffering occasioned by the self. His

³³⁵ Ibid., 253–55.
³³⁶ Ibid., 285.
³³⁷ Ibid., 283.
³³⁸ Ibid., 284.
³³⁹ *Letter*, December 1928, in: *Bernanos*, 162.
³⁴⁰ *Dominique*, 41.

outbursts against modern society, modern Christianity, and the "imbeciles" forced Bernanos to retreat ever more into the heart of an ideal of unusual and unique sacrifice as his final citadel, which he decked out with as much tragic glory as Reinhold Schneider expended on his kings and saints. In the end, however, we are no longer dealing with living human beings but with sacrificial victims who have been consumed by the raging multitudes. They possess their tremendous status as persons only in the condition of agony. It is much too little to say that suffering has a power to build up, to purify, to ennoble. The crux of Bernanos' view is that agony is what makes for the ultimate development of the person: among all the other states of soul portrayed by Bernanos, it is agony, the death agony, alone that breaks through dream's layer of fog and presents us with full reality. Thus, in the early novels we detect the danger of a Christian Stoicism, albeit of a very particular character: the greatest selves become unassailable precisely when they are wholly devoured as Orpheus was by the Mænads. This image is hardly misplaced, since Donissan, Chantal, Cénabre, and Ouine all have mythic, semidivine characteristics. It was the incessant humiliations inflicted by life that shattered Bernanos' ideal image both of himself and of his heroes; it took the figure of the country priest for us to have the first character in his novels who was almost wholly a man among men, although this in no way banalized the authentic Christian mysteries of suffering and solitude that the country priest likewise embodies.

Now, if I can be myself fully only at the moment of my death agony, then I am forced to declare all human love to be highly questionable. Does not love, like most other things, belong in the realm of shadows? Is not every intimate exchange that takes place between lovers always a "conversation between shades"? Is not their life a dream and their self-surrender a secret "poison, a drug to narcotize [their] ennui, to flee from the frightening reality of [their] truth"?[341] This flight is all the more probable as Bernanos always tended to construe the self's relationship to itself—the reflection that constitutes the person as person—as something hellish and unbearable that drives the spirit that consciously experiences it out of itself with a force akin to violence. The letters often speak of the abysmal repulsion that gripped Bernanos when confronted with his own person, an irrepressible urge to "hit"

---

[341] Vallery-Radot, *Souvenirs*, in: *Bul.* I, 10.

and "slap" himself, to "disappear no matter where, the farthest away possible". It is, therefore, easy for him to discover an uncannily self-destructive tendency to *self-hatred* as the foundation of the self, especially in those creatures he calls the "wretched" and the "miserable": those for whom life is not worth it, who have not gotten even as far as the threshold of human dignity. The second Mouchette destroys herself out of a self-hatred Bernanos means to be elemental rather than ethical, since at bottom it is not responsible for itself. The mayor of Fenouille capitulates to madness only in order to escape from himself, to "negate himself and spit on himself". But the village priest observes to him: "Of all hatreds, hatred of self is probably the one for which no forgiveness is possible."[342]

This is the reason why drug addicts are so important in the world of Bernanos: "What is truly abnormal in the addict is not the fact that he consumes a toxic substance; it's his having felt the need to use it, to practice this perverse form of escape, to flee from his own personality as a thief bolts from the apartment he has just burglarized. No attempted cure by detoxification could ever heal the unfortunate addict from his lie and reconcile him with himself."[343] The generation of the damned in *An Evil Dream* has lost all love for itself. Concerning Simone, who has gone the farthest in this direction, we read: "The only hatred she thoroughly knew, reveled in, and drank to the dregs was hatred of self. . . . She had hated herself ever since her childhood, at first unawares, then with a sly and hypocritical ambition, the kind of dire fawning with which a poisoner surrounds the victim she intends to decimate some day."[344] *An Evil Dream* lays bare "the bottommost foundation of man's soul—the secret self-hatred that is probably the deepest part . . . of every life".[345] Observing his peasant parishioners, the country priest writes: "A peasant rarely loves himself, and, if he displays such cruel indifference toward those who love him, it isn't that he doubts the affection shown him; rather, he scorns it." Therefore, peasants never improve their lot, because they view themselves as incorrigible. Their sole goal is "to feed themselves at the least expense like useless and costly animals". Speaking of certain "old rakes whose greed is nothing but a bitter rage" on old age, the

---

[342] *Ouine*, 203.
[343] *Liberté*, 155.
[344] *Rêve*, 243.
[345] Ibid., 238.

Diary adds: "In the very threshold of the death agony, anguish can still wrench certain words from the dying person that bear witness to the presence of a self-hatred for which perhaps no forgiveness exists."[346]

The chasms of self-hatred into which Bernanos descends in the company of Cénabre are for him not an æsthetic construct or a curious journey of discovery: they are the record of hard experience. It is all the more moving, therefore, to follow him to his victory over this darkest sort of danger. It was not natural ethics that persuaded him that man must love himself. Bernanos was a true child of an age for which interrelationships in the order of nature were only half-intact: they lay all about like the ruins of a bombed-out city. Consequently, he granted little weight to the natural law. For him, salvation from self-hatred lay in faith as "a supernatural knowledge of oneself in God" whose core is the target of sin's attacks: "You have lost all desire to know yourselves", the country priest says to unbelievers. "That deep truth that you yourselves are no longer interests you."[347] Only in God can the limitless self-hater become reconciled with himself. The following statement reveals how laborious and humiliating a task this was for Bernanos: "The hard thing is not loving your neighbor as yourself. It's loving yourself enough so that the literal observance of the precept will not do harm to your neighbor."[348] But in 1936, by the time he was writing the *Country Priest*, Bernanos was in a more conciliatory frame of mind toward himself: "Growing old, too, is a beautiful thing. It's a gripping experience to look in the mirror at a face that's become a stranger, to be tempted to hate it and yet to forgive it."[349] Ten years earlier he had placed Chantal before the mirror, to "smile at her pale reflection", and he had commented: "Her tragic face, made taut by distress, inspired her less with pity than with disgust."[350] And by 1939 he was writing to a friend: "The point is . . . to become simple enough to love oneself in one's work, just as God loves himself in his creation."[351]

The final, full-blown victory is recorded in the last few sentences

[346] *Curé*, 32.
[347] Ibid., 142–43.
[348] *Enfants*, 114.
[349] *Letter to a Woman Friend*, June 17, 1936, *Bul.* 2–3, 22.
[350] *Joie*, 66.
[351] *To Michaelis*, June 5, 1939; *C. du R.*, 49.

the country priest enters into his diary. Its strategic placement in the novel suggests to us that Bernanos here wanted to stress a wholly new breakthrough, something like the ultimate product of the young priest's suffering and vulnerability. It is a key passage, a signal set like a flag on the highest peak to measure the tremendous distance this climber has traveled and to mark the spot where he finally collapsed: *"Hating ourselves is easier than we think. The real grace is to forget ourselves. But, if all pride were dead in us, the grace of graces would consist in loving ourselves humbly like any other of the suffering members of Jesus Christ."*[352]

This is the reason it took Bernanos so long until he dared to free himself to love a *thou* beyond all suspicions. Such love is not possible until a person ceases attacking his own existence through self-hatred. For a long time he was led astray down all the problematic dead ends of looking at all relationships as mirror reflections of the self: his *Conversation among Shadows* is an eloquent example of this. It is already significant enough that Donissan can read in the souls of others only through the detour of his own self-awareness. The evil fruit of this seed becomes fully ripe in *Monsieur Ouine*, who cannot and will not encounter anything in the *thou* but himself: "A big empty house. . . . Your steps resound in the hallways, and, when you speak, you think you're hearing the answer. It's the echo of your own words, nothing else. When you find yourself in front of someone, you have only to look a little closer and you'll recognize your own image. . . ."[353] More serious still is the confession of the doctor in *Joy*: "To tell the truth, I have never loved anything. . . . Whom would I have loved? I've spent my life looking at myself in the face of my lunatics as in a mirror. . . . I know the specific and unchangeable meaning of each of my frowns. I can no longer make myself either laugh or cry."[354] And an even graver note is struck in the confession scene at the beginning of *The Imposture*, in which two sinners can see through one another because each of them recognizes his own sin in the other. The icy disdain with which Cénabre looks upon his penitent is returned in kind by the latter.[355] Hence the advice we find in *The Humiliated Children*: "If

[352] *Curé*, 321. (The italics are von Balthasar's.—TRANS.)
[353] *Ouine*, 218.
[354] *Joie*, 224.
[355] *Imposture*, 68.

you want to suffer all alone, keep quiet. Otherwise don't go, under the pretext of sympathy (*sym-pathein*), looking for your own suffering with sugar tongs in the heart of others and wrinkling your nose, like poor Monsieur de Montherlant."[356] What one would in the end find in the other is one's own sin, and sympathy would be reduced to "brotherly complicity",[357] that is, not at all a personal relationship but a oneness precisely in the factor effecting the person's dissolution. Such an illusion can in the end lead to a dazzling and frightful insight, as in the case of Simone when she finally sees her relationship with Olivier in a true light: "When the lie of her wretched love began to scatter gradually, she understood that what she had cherished in this love . . . was a kind of weak fellowship in guilt. And a pity she had never felt before was bursting her heart, flooding her chest with so burning a rush that she pressed both hands against it with a cry of pain."[358] But, regardless of how apparently cordial the arrangement may be, such complicity in evil can only lead to hatred of the other *because* it can only lead to hatred of self: "For it is natural for man to hate his own suffering in the suffering of the other."[359] "The author of *The Paschal Candle* . . . instinctively hates what resembles him, *and savors, without admitting it, the bitter inebriation of despising himself in others.*"[360]

The situation changes totally, however, when it is a question, not of sinner encountering sinner, but of sinner standing before saint as a mirror in which the latter can recognize himself. Indeed, where could Donissan find a clue to his apparently meaningless destiny if not in Mouchette? And it is Cénabre who holds the key to what happens to Chantal and Chevance: "None other than myself", he says, "is capable of helping you see clearly within yourselves."[361] This act of mirroring is genuine, ontological; it rests upon the wondrous possibilities of the "communion of saints", which, when really lived, make illusory the attempt to view oneself in isolation and outside of love. If

[356] *Enfants*, 35.
[357] *Mouchette*, 65–66.
[358] *Rêve*, 248.
[359] *Soleil*, 32.
[360] Ibid., 332. (The italics are von Balthasar's.—TRANS.)
[361] *Joie*, 277.

it is true that "to understand is already to love" and that "what separates two beings from one another and makes them enemies probably has no reality to speak of",[362] then it must be possible to offer the other more than just an illusory image of oneself and to encounter in the other more than just his own self-delusion. In this case, it is right and good to live in the image of us that a person who really loves us has created, as Bernanos writes to a friend: "Whatever reality remained to me (which wasn't much) has just turned into smoke. I am becoming a ghost, a dream, a picture—a beautiful picture, because it resembles you. . . . I am what all of you in your friendship want me to be."[363] And it is also right "to allow those who love me to carry the weight of my own life".[364] With this, the spectacle of the sin and mediocrity of others acquires a new face: it becomes a true, salutary mirror for our own blindness concerning ourselves: "When a person deliberately closes his eyes to his neighbor under the pretext of charity, he is most frequently breaking the mirror so that he will not have to see himself in it. The weakness of our nature is such that we search first of all in others for our own miserable defects."[365] "The mediocrity of others keeps open a wound in ourselves that ought never to stop hurting and suppurating. If it were to close, it would risk the danger of poisoning the entire organism."[366]

Despite all the ambiguities involved in the relationships among persons, and all the real or imagined isolation we must endure, the even greater miracle does nevertheless take place that sustains and explains everything: the grace of giving and receiving. When Bernanos gives thanks for the love that is offered him, he does so with "the vague feeling of not being the right recipient", that "a mistake has been made in the address." But to him it is a matter of indifference whether he is worthy of love or not, for "it's quite enough if others find in me what the good Lord inspires them to look for in me, what he himself puts there if only for an instant."[367] At this point a final certitude takes hold of Bernanos: true and real giving and taking is a grace; it is God in us, for God is an interchange among Persons. This is a grace,

[362] *Cimetières*, 78.
[363] *To a friend*, June 12, 1933; *Bul.* 2–3, 16.
[364] Ibid., October 14, 1933; *Bul.* 2–3, 16.
[365] *Carmélites*, 38.
[366] *Erbarmen*, 120.
[367] *To Amoroso Lima*, end of 1938; *Esprit*, 189; *Erbarmen*, 79.

however, that does not simply take effect over our heads, as it were: it makes us active participants as real givers and takers: "Life has taught me that no one is consoled in this world who has not first consoled and that we receive nothing we have not first given. Among us we can speak only of an *exchange*. God alone *gives*, only he."[368] "Between one man's hand and another's there intervenes, I firmly believe, more than just the density of this world. It may well be that, from so far away, all we are capable of is the *gesture* of giving. It is God who actually gives."[369] The great skill of the Christian, consequently, is that he can give infinitely more than what he has: "O marvel, that we should be able to make a gift of what we do not ourselves possess. O sweet miracle of our empty hands! The hope that was dying in my heart blossomed again in hers. The spirit of prayer I had thought irretrievably lost in myself was given back to her by God—who knows? perhaps even in my name."[370] "God sends us . . . to one another's houses bearing messages we cannot read and gifts whose value we absolutely ignore."[371] "Since I am coming to you with empty hands, it may well be that he will put there what you desire to find in them. It may also well be that I will find in yours what I am not looking for in them and what you have not put there."[372] "You have many things to say to me, many things you have never said to yourself and which nevertheless beam forth from you."[373] "The thing you want to give begins at once to burn your hand and passes right through it."[374] "Whoever cannot give more than he receives begins to decompose."[375] "*The law ruling a poor Christian is precisely to give what he does not have. Otherwise, where would charity be? Where would be the sweet miracle of charity?*"[376] "We are always unworthy of what we receive, my child, because we never receive anything except from God."[377]

---

[368] *Enfants*, 36. (Italics are the translator's.—TRANS.)

[369] *To Michaelis*, June 5, 1939, in: *C. du R.*, 49; *Erbarmen*, 103. (Italics are the translator's. —TRANS.)

[370] *Curé*, 198.

[371] *To Gordan*, in: *Bul.* 5, 6.

[372] *To Amoroso Lima*, February 2, 1940, in: *Esprit*, 197; *Erbarmen*, 89.

[373] Ibid., March 1, 1940, in: *Esprit*, 199; *Erbarmen*, 91.

[374] *To Michaelis*, June 5, 1939, in: *C. du R.*, 50; *Erbarmen*, 104.

[375] *Cimetières*, 271.

[376] *To Charreyre*, April 1946, in: *Bul.* 4, 5; *Erbarmen*, 108. (The italics are von Balthasar's. —TRANS.)

[377] *Carmélites*, 126.

However, precisely this is the proof of the fact that, poor though we are, we too can nevertheless give something to God: "What others expect from us—it's really God expecting it from us. . . . I truly believe that only this matters. All the rest is but pious literature."[378]

---

[378] *To Amoroso Lima*, January 1940, in: *Esprit*, 191; *Erbarmen*, 82.

PART THREE

CONTEMPORARY MAN

I. THE CHRISTIAN WITHIN TIME

1. The Face of the Present

The middle part of this book has dealt with the interior mystery of the Church. But the Church exists for the sake of the world. We have shown the manner in which the Church fulfills this function in her innermost center, that aspect of her mystery turned toward eternity: she does it by suffering, by standing in others' stead, by atoning. The Church's task, however, is not limited to this eschatological function; she fully lives up to the mandate she has received only when she intervenes within the sphere of temporality. The ineffable mystery of Passion within her heart is the secret source that nourishes her action. From the tenderness of her interior openness and self-surrender she derives the blinding severity and lordliness of her exterior. It was in this furnace that Joan of Arc's sword was forged, as well as the "dagger" of young Chantal, with which she put theologians and doctors of the Church to shame, to say nothing of the hidden "weapon" of the young, proletarian country priest, with which he fearlessly confronted his learned confrères and the nobility of the château and brought them to their knees.

Bernanos was the Christian in the world par excellence. Whatever might have been happening around him, our writer took a passionate interest in it: the resolutions of his own French people, those of the other peoples of Europe and the world, whether these were hidden determinations reached at the deepest level and bearing unforeseeable and most concrete consequences or more ordinary day-to-day decisions. Where others saw only superficial politics, Bernanos saw man's eternal destiny and, indeed, the destiny of God's Kingdom at stake. Just as an individual sins, plunges into the abyss, undergoes conversion, and confesses his wrongdoing, so too a country in a given epoch of its history. Bernanos trembled for his dear France, and, like Péguy, he feared lest it fall into the state of mortal sin; but this danger is just as great for all other countries that have entered into a dimension where they risk the enormous danger of modernity: the peril of losing the sense of man. The second half of Bernanos' life was ever more dedicated to this most urgent of Christian tasks. It appeared to him to be so imperative and, hence, so obviously a priority that the writing of novels (including the burning problems of dream and unreality) silently receded into the background. The novelist then reëmerged as genial journalist, the Bernanos who for decades followed the day's events, x-rayed and analyzed them, saw through them, and judged them. The same "prophetic reason" continued fulfilling the same task; and it was no less demanding to respond, with the total keenness and tautness of a Christian conscience, to the questions posed by every new day in the world's history than to answer the questions arising from the relatively more stable situation of the human spirit in a given age as dramatized within the framework of a novel.

We must renounce the feasibility of doing even fair justice to this other side of Bernanos' work: the endeavor would require another whole book of the same proportions as the present one and would call for an accomplished expert in the field of contemporary history. Still, it is impossible to speak about Bernanos without at least hinting at his judgment of the modern world. Since our inevitably more sketchy treatment will not be able to go into the concreteness of the situations Bernanos confronted, it will necessarily appear a bit thin-blooded and perhaps even inconsequential. To counteract such an impression, the reader will have to look up for himself the texts referred to and allow them to have their effect on him, for example, a collection of essays such as *The Way of the Cross-of-Souls*. Through such an effort, the reader would continually come to see what "situation ethics" can be when engaged in its best and least suspicious form: in the concrete, this involves standing within the "exterior" realm of history and answering its questions directly out of the depths of the "interior" realm of the spirit, without giving the impression that those "principles" that have their roots and validity primarily within the "interior" realm are simply being "transposed" as a secondary application to the realm of history. Bernanos did not respond to the great epochal questions with ready-made "solutions": this would have constituted the casuistry he so assailed. Nor did he emerge for a few moments at a time out of the mystic's interior depths and self-involvement in order to utter some oracle within the superficial world of politics. For Bernanos, depth and surface, life in God and life in the everyday world, response to eternity and response to today's immediacy, were all one and the same. In this he was a Christian layman through and through, seeking to fulfill his assigned task fully conscious of his responsibility.

If one were to ask the basis of the integrated vision out of which Bernanos spoke, we would have to refer him to the first chapter of Part Two: Bernanos' vision of man. Bernanos viewed man as a being who by his very existence is already imperiled, overtaxed, often defeated, a weak, poor creature lacking in understanding: in other words, man as Jesus saw him when his eyes rested upon him as he spoke the Beatitudes. Thus envisioned, man already has a hard enough time asserting on this earth his humble dignity and the little bit of freedom and humanity left him; but, as he enters the modern world, he undergoes the additional danger of landing in a desolation that robs him of every possibility of developing in a manner befitting his worth. The throbbing earnestness, full of barely restrained foreboding, which overwhelms us as we hear Bernanos speak shows that he was not engaging in or defending "cultural politics" or any other similar abstraction; rather, he was standing up as an advocate for the "humiliated and offended" of this earth, and he did so with the irrefutable knowledge of someone who has himself experienced their spiritual plight. The terms themselves in which Bernanos expressed this plight may be familiar to us from other contexts: threats to freedom, totalitarian transformation, slavery to the machine, self-concealment in anonymity, the impersonal mega-event that seems to occur all "on its own", and so forth. But the tone with which Bernanos demonstrated all of this on the example of the day's concrete events permits us no evasion into vague generalities but rather demands of us that we take an immediate personal stance as individuals against all that is wrong and unjust.

Such a trend of thought is familiar to us from Péguy; but the "modern world" Péguy accused and pilloried consisted primarily of the world of an intellectualism cut off from nature, for instance, the world of the "Sorbonne" and of socialist party ideology. For Bernanos, by contrast, the "modern world" was the total phenomenon of modern culture threatening man as such. Likewise, we have heard similar things from Karl Kraus, but without the simple nobility of the Christian: unlike Kraus, Bernanos did not wrangle and raise an outcry, insisting on pet dogmas with pigheaded stubbornness, and he took no joy in unmasking hypocrisy or in churning out pamphlets for the fun of it like his Jewish counterpart. Bernanos' ethos was comparable in many respects to that of Reinhold Schneider's historical analyses, particularly of the contemporary world: in both of them we find the same inexorable courage, demanding that their own age should make a confession of its guilt; indeed, both of them saw it as the writer's task to utter such a confession in anticipation of a more public and communal admission of sin.

By combining the literary task of the writer with the prophetic interpretation of the contemporary world, Bernanos, together with Péguy and Schneider, showed that he belonged within an illustrious tradition. The Greeks—Æschylus, Pindar, and Sophocles—did not hold out their characters into an atemporal void but proposed them to their contemporaries as images of solid action. The same may be said for Dante, Shakespeare, the Gœthe of *The Natural Daughter*, and the Eichendorff of *Presentiment and the Present*. In all of these, literary creation is political in the highest sense given this term by Plato. For this reason, the writer's word of challenge to his time is inseparable from the literary gift he makes to all time.

The most recent writers of the West, who may also well be its *final* writers, can do nothing other than create ultimate, believable forms and images drawing on the greatest values of the tradition. This they can do only with the most extreme sort of effort, because "writers of the West" are by definition an endangered and wholly isolated species. Their task is then to hold up their faithful creations within an age in the process of dissolution, an age in which it is unsure—not only factually, but essentially—whether anything like literary creation, in the traditional sense, can continue to exist.

The characters created by writers consciously within the Western tradition are shaped from material from the past; but they are thoroughly imbued with spirit in the process of their creation: Chantal is a Joan of Arc in spirit; Péguy's Christian is a Joinville in spirit; Reinhold Schneider's Christian is pure nobility, a king in spirit. The transposition of these characters from a historical past to a burning spiritual present and presence, unshackled by the limitations of historical specificity, results in a kind of prophetic ideal that looms over the writers' contemporaries. No one, not even the writer who creates it, can anticipate the particular human form this ideal will take. The prophetic warners are quite aware of the fact that only an imperceptible seduction, a small betrayal, would suffice to make life easier for themselves and to secure the applause of all. For writers and

proclaimers are very much sought after. *Les petits curés progressistes*—
the "petty progressive priests" on whom Bernanos could not heap
enough scorn—have made their own the slogan about "marching in
step with the times", and they engage in social politics with every
ounce of their being. Bernanos had nothing against "social concerns",
only he would have liked to pursue them in all their depth. He therefore bristled with questions and marginal comments when the *petits
curés* seemed to have forgotten certain pages of the Gospel all too
thoroughly.

Bernanos strove to view the horizon before him in all its depth
and width; he had to seek and point out the ultimate consequences
of certain developments about whose superficial advantages it was not
difficult to grow enraptured. He spoke to those who did not close
their eyes to the fact that half the world was Communist and that the
whole world had escaped by the skin of its teeth from being transformed into a Hitlerian concentration camp in the style of Auschwitz.
Bernanos' witness was proclaimed in the face of all the unfree technicians and capitalists who are shackled in their journey and convinced
of the metaphysical impossibility of changing the direction of socio-
historical evolution: they childishly rely on some phantasmal "world
reason" to guide and correct the course of their own unreason. By
contrast to these, Bernanos took his stance outside such unfreedom
as the man who is genuinely free because he is poor; from such a
location he could then radically question the determinism ruling the
lives of the majority and turn its dogmas upside down at least for his
own free person. Bernanos was convinced that the social and cultural
scales had been totally thrown out of balance by the ascendancy of
massive philistinism, and that the equilibrium could be restored only
by the free person. This being so, the counterweight he threw into
the scales was not so much a social and cultural doctrine as, precisely
—his own person. This is the coin with which he paid for everything. What we will now examine schematically, therefore, will not
have the significance or intention of theoretical theses concerning the
times but rather the import of ethical motivations directly addressed
to the reader. Such direct address can no more be reduced to theoretical propositions than the prophetic and eschatological manner of
speaking of the evangelists and apostles in Scripture can be reduced
to an abstract system.

Bernanos' diagnosis of our sick age is grave. Man, turned into a collective mass and handed over to the power of machines, is in the process, not only of losing his most inalienable goods, but of abandoning
them voluntarily. What was once freedom will soon be something unknown[1] and, indeed, undesirable. Man is becoming a trained animal.[2]
His own dignity is being radically debased by the machines;[3] he is
"at once degenerating and hardening";[4] and "the systems flaunted at
us are systems of decomposition."[5] He has become totalitarian in his
own intimate self.[6] Totalitarian man,[7] whose freedom is in the process
of decomposing, is logically followed by the totalitarian State: the latter is more "a symptom than a cause".[8] Here, it is man himself who
is being gambled away,[9] for, without freedom, man can by no means
continue to be rational, to be a "holy person": henceforth he can
only be a higher animal,[10] and, in his race with the machine, he can
only come out a loser.[11] Mankind has suffered so intrinsic a loss that
Bernanos compared this time and again to the chronic loss of vitamins
in an organism[12]—a radical feebleness that has long since abandoned
all faith in "health", that is, in freedom of the spirit.[13] The condition
is one of thorough depersonalization.[14] The ascendancy of technology
leads automatically to police terror;[15] the capitulation of freedom of
itself leads to the hypertrophy of the State; and both things together
lead to the substitution of truth by propaganda,[16] because the truth
becomes something indifferent or indeed repulsive to the personless

[1] *Cimetières*, 358.
[2] *Liberté*, 152, 218.
[3] Ibid., 31, 109, 125.
[4] Ibid., 198.
[5] Ibid., 208.
[6] Ibid., 19, 104.
[7] Ibid., 226.
[8] Ibid., 106, 197.
[9] Ibid., 57, 136–37.
[10] Ibid., 39.
[11] Ibid., 60.
[12] *Croix*, May 1940, 11; *Liberté*, 84, 119 (the diabetic syndrome compared to democracies that are decomposing into bureaucracies), 225 (avitaminosis and European de-Christianization).
[13] *Liberté*, 97.
[14] Ibid., 113, 142, 175.
[15] *Robots*, 26; *Liberté*, 141.
[16] *Croix*, March 1941, 99; *Liberté*, 92, 145, 255.

individual,[17] and because such an entity as "the personless individual" is too depleted to be able to judge responsibly, to choose, and to become committed to the end to a truth that has been acknowledged. But as the power of the State grows, its real worth declines because no one takes responsibility for it:[18] the State thereby becomes the intrinsic enemy of the free man, of the hero, and of the saint.[19] The "soft monster"[20] is ready for every atrocity,[21] indeed, for every impulse to destroy. The atom bomb is the symbol of the fact that might has triumphed over reason.[22] The possibility offered by technology to commit murder on a gigantic scale without any personal danger to the murderer, moreover, signals the end of any personal ethos of war: "The dismemberment, the flaying, and the tearing apart of several millions of innocent human beings has become a job that a gentleman can finish off without as much as soiling his cuffs or even his imagination."[23] And we can ask ourselves whether the big-time capitalist, too, does not "partake in this privilege of the demons: to be able to kill without even knowing what he is killing".[24] Mechanical civilization attacks man inwardly in the manner of a vampire: "It will stop producing its wares only at the moment it has succeeded in devouring all men. It will have devoured them in the wars in enormous masses, by the heapful; but it will also have devoured them one by one. It will have sucked them empty one by one of their marrow, of their soul, of the spiritual substance that made them men."[25] Thus it is that an image imposes itself here that Bernanos developed in great detail: that of the corpse undergoing decomposition according to schedule—the "order of putrefaction".[26] "As long as the corpse is nourishing the worm, it is the latter's mistake to take dissolution for history."[27] The massive abrasion suffered by the energies of the tradition will soon demonstrate that what we like to call our "dynamism" is in truth nothing but the liquefaction of everything that had been held together organically.[28] We have here a spiritual entropy of all foundational values that brings about the disease and death, not

[17] *Liberté*, 142, 217.
[18] Ibid., 117.
[19] *Peur*, 305.
[20] *Cimetières*, 26; *Robots*, 31.
[21] *Cimetières*, 185.
[22] *Liberté*, 34-35.
[23] *Robots*, 161.
[24] *Curé*, 85-86.
[25] *Liberté*, 250.
[26] Ibid., 192.
[27] Ibid., 193.
[28] *Enfants*, 253.

only of truth, but also of its opposite, mendacity.[29] An unconscious
panic then grips humanity, which launches a frantic flight out of the
burning bazaar.[30] But this breakout soon degenerates into a "suicidal
craze": the anxious expectation of the inevitable atomic war.[31] The
modern State has enough power to declare military service compul-
sory (something Bernanos considered an abomination)[32] and to drive
the docile herd of men to their slaughter on the fields of battle, to
the musical accompaniment of propaganda. In such a slaughterhouse,
millions are torn to shreds for an ideology of the right or of the left,
all in the name "of the sacred totality, the thrice-holy name borne by
totalitarian civilization".[33]

In the meantime, Bernanos made sure not to impute the guilt for all
this to the machine. Not the machine itself, but the use man makes of
it, is what brings on the deterioration of civilization.[34] The root of the
evil is a perverted ideal of man,[35] the decay of freedom, and its betrayal
by man himself.[36] "The aim is not at all to destroy the machines",
as was done by traditional weavers when the first weaving machines
appeared, "and to weave our own garments as did Gandhi".[37] Such
protests, however, do serve their purpose: they cast responsibility for
social devastation back upon man, instead of unburdening him of it
through a false determinism. The machine, too, is only a symptom.[38]
Indeed, Bernanos' whole purpose was to show that there is no intrinsic necessity in the development of the machine age.[39] As an advocate of freedom, he had to demonstrate that it is primarily man who
has abdicated, that the machine has gained power over him only for
this reason, and that even now man still possesses enough freedom to
hold the machine as his slave instead of his leading a slave's existence
subject to the machine. But we are not left with the impression that
this more positive train of thought really wins out in the end, that the
hope Bernanos normally infused into the last sentences of an essay
(actually an eschatological, not to say rhetorical, hope) is capable of
providing the counterweight to the reasons for despair he had brought

---

[29] Ibid., 127–29.
[30] *Croix*, June 1943, 343–44.
[31] *Cimetières*, 272–73; *Liberté*, 173,
215–16.
[32] *Liberté*, 43; *Robots*, 58, 102.
[33] *Liberté*, 245.

[34] *Croix*, January 13, 1945, 474.
[35] *Liberté*, 122, 137, 154–55.
[36] Ibid., 197.
[37] Ibid., 114.
[38] *Robots*, 139.
[39] *Liberté*, 84; *Robots*, 187–89.

forth. Our writer detected a despair and an anguish at the very base of the contemporary world[40] that disguise themselves in vain behind a threadbare optimism.[41] And, even though he always objected to being considered a pessimist,[42] his concluding judgments are clearly negative: "The thing we still call 'civilization' has outstripped every form of barbarism in accomplishing works of destruction. It now threatens to destroy, not only the works of man, but man himself. It is capable of modifying man's nature profoundly, not by enhancing it, of course, but by mutilating it."[43] In such a world, the Christian begins to run out of air to breathe and space to move around in. We may even say that this is the goal of a deliberate development: "The main thing is to make the experiment irreversible as quickly as possible by destroying all traces of Christian man. The world of tomorrow must be made as uninhabitable for the Christian as the world of the Ice Age was for the mammoth."[44]

Modern nonculture bears the mark of the Antichrist deeply engraved, not because it openly persecutes Christians, but because it is bent on realizing the movement precisely opposed to the Incarnation: "Man has made the machine, and the machine has made itself man, by a sort of demonic inversion of the mystery of the Incarnation."[45] "The misery and odium of the modern world, which so comically declares itself to be materialistic, is that it disincarnates everything it touches by accomplishing in reverse the mystery of the Incarnation."[46] "The debasement of man is signaled by the moment when ideas are no longer for him anything more than abstract and conventional formulas, a sort of algebra, as if the Word no longer became flesh and as if humanity were entering upon the road of the Incarnation, only undoing it in reverse."[47] And there is more: "The peoples have made a god out of their despair, and they adore it. We have lived long enough to witness despair assuming flesh—*et incarnatus est.* Perhaps we'll even see it die and rise on the third day, because the devil can ape God with great skill. We will see it return to judge the world."[48] "The devil's whole occupation being the aping of God, I am inclined

---

[40] *Français*, 174; *Liberté*, 92.

[41] *Liberté*, 94, 168, 176.

[42] Ibid., 13–14, 91.

[43] Ibid., 156.

[44] Ibid., 241.

[45] Ibid., 239–40.

[46] *Français*, 114.

[47] *Robots*, 167.

[48] *Français*, 173.

to believe that the birth of the Antichrist will not make much more noise in the world than the birth of our Lord Jesus Christ."[49]

This world-in-the-making will be a "spiritual wilderness", and in it men will die of thirst; if only for this reason, wars shall never cease, because the world will have to drink its own blood.[50] A hard and heartless age will dawn:[51] "Man was driven out of the earthly paradise as man, but he gets around the difficulty by forcing his way back in as an animal."[52]

So it is that, like Péguy before him, Bernanos took a stance against "the whole system" and all its basic postulates.[53] And he finally came around to demanding that the vague and anonymous machinery of order that calls itself "the modern State" provide proof of its legitimacy:

> The politics of Rome was cynical, but the people of Rome were religious. . . . The ancient world deified its masters. Knightly Christianity invented the legitimate lord, the suzerain, the anointed king of Saint Joan of Arc. What has the modern State preserved of all this? When it wants to bind consciences, what authoritative titles can it display before its citizens? It produces a twofold title: a certificate attesting to the fact that it controls the public services, the finances, and the army (in short, a certificate of existence—a birth or baptismal certificate is, of course, never requested) and the opinion of the first theologian to come along (using terms that are as general as possible, so as to remain flexible for whatever the future may bring) attesting to the fact that all established power comes from God since God has allowed it to establish itself. Nothing else.[54]

This already shows that the *cultural* diagnosis is intrinsically bound up with the *political*. Here, too, our concern is not so much the doctrines themselves as the mentality behind them and the human beings who create it. Bernanos, the disillusioned *camelot du roi* from his days in the Action Française, turned above all against the "realism" of the people on the right, not, however, because such realism is a doctrine of the right (to the end of his life, Bernanos would remain a monar-

---

[49] *Enfants*, 166.
[50] *Liberté*, 206.
[51] Ibid., 30.
[52] *To Charreyre*, August 1946 (?), in: *Bul.* 4, 6; *Erbarmen*, 110.
[53] *Liberté*, 149; *Robots*, 23; *To Charreyre*, August 1946 (?), in: *Bul.* 4, 6; *Erbarmen*, 110.
[54] *Français*, 274–75.

chist), but because political "realism" is the very significant cover term for the loss of all idealism: in its unconscious self-contempt we can see evidence for the withering of a genuinely political worldview and its decay into inauthenticity and, indeed, the cynicism of a mere ideology.

Bernanos' central thesis holds that, as ideologies, the "Right" and the "Left" are equally worthless and false,[55] that their opposition is idiotic,[56] and that the first task therefore is to break down such a false polarity at all costs. In March 1941, Bernanos wrote: "We have left two Frances facing each other as enemies: the France of the right and the France of the left; but our mission was to reconcile them."[57] But the problem is bigger than France. It is a matter of indifference to Bernanos whether mass-man is liberal or totalitarian, or whether he is trained on the American or the Russian model;[58] on a moment's notice one can be reduced to the other.[59] There was nothing fundamentally new about Hitler.[60] A democracy designed for mass-men of itself leads to dictatorship, as Plato had already observed,[61] and "democracies" are already "economic dictatorships".[62] Hegel may be found at the root of both Marx and Hitler.[63] The basis for the Soviet Russian system is a Western ideology imported from Germany.[64] How naïve, then, to construe Hitler's invasion of the U.S.S.R. as a Western "crusade of the right" against the East![65] At the same time, we should not overlook the Slavic assaults into East Prussia, which have left behind such a "savage and cruel" history:[66] "The totalitarian phenomenon, at least in what concerns its origins, is not properly speaking a European phenomenon."[67]

---

[55] *Liberté*, 42; *Cimetières*, 49; *Robots*, 211; *Croix*, January 1944, 399.

[56] *Cimetières*, 5–6.

[57] Ibid., 336; *Croix*, March 1941, 103.

[58] *Liberté*, 47, 59, 63, 104.

[59] Ibid., 55f.

[60] Ibid., 118, 235.

[61] Ibid., 145, 150.

[62] Ibid., 55.

[63] Ibid., 80.

[64] Ibid., 81.

[65] *Croix*, June 1941, 131.

[66] *Liberté*, 223–24.

[67] Ibid., 244. (Bernanos here seems, curiously, to exclude the Slavic world from the true

Bernanos never missed an opportunity to underscore the Anglo-Saxon and Calvinistic origins of capitalistic industrialism. German ideology imported from this source a ready-made fact. It was in England that the modern oppression of the worker began and that machines were first allowed to turn human beings into herds[68]—the very accomplishments that form the basis today for the rivalry between the United States and Russia.[69] When reflecting on all these statements, however, let us take great care not to read them as a directly political taking of sides. They are meant as warnings against tendencies and dangers lurking in the background, as an examination of conscience that is all the more rigorous the closer the patient stands morally to the examining physician, and all the more indulgent the farther away he stands. Only this explains Bernanos' relatively lenient tone when speaking about Hitler:[70] his reflections in this connection only serve as a background for his biting satires against the French right and the ignominious behavior of the collaborators. French distrust of England by no means kept Bernanos from praising the attitude of the English during the war as the most convincing of all, and in his *Letter to the English* he actually entrusts the destiny of France to Anglo-Saxon hands. Bernanos cannot be accused of any Communist leanings;[71] nothing could be more perverse to draw such a conclusion on the basis of his contemptuous rejection of contemporary democracies.[72] Communism appeared to him to be something so evidently depraved that there was no need for a special war against it. By contrast, how urgent a need there was in the years when Bernanos was at the peak of his powers for a steady and relentless unmasking of the totalitarianisms of the right, which moreover were the specialty of Catholic countries: Hitler, too, came from a Catholic background, and the "capital of

---

European tradition. We shall see in the last chapter of this book, however, that he professed a great admiration for Gorky. It is likewise curious that he nowhere deals with the official Catholicism of a Poland sympathetic to Fascism.—Note of the French trans.)

[68] *Français*, 281f.; *Robots*, 134, 140f.; *Liberté*, 60, 98, 158.

[69] *Croix*, November 1944, 459f.; May 30, 1945, 502.

[70] *Cimetières*, 126, 164, 338f.; *Enfants*, 159–71; *Français*, 49f., 127, 182, 258; *Croix*, 26f., 206.

[71] See, on the contrary, his trenchant judgments, especially in his *Letter to Jorge de Lima* of April 1939 (*Lettres inédites*, 15); also *Liberté*, 135, and passim. He reserved particularly devastating judgments for Catholic sympathizers with Communism (*Peur*, 314).

[72] *Cimetières*, 50, 53, 155, 225; *Anglais*, 86, 198; *Croix*, 193; *Liberté*, 95, 305.

the movement" was a Catholic city.[73] These totalitarian regimes of the right often set up an abominable caricature of Catholic obedience only a hair's breadth away from it, and for this reason some kind of "understanding" with these regimes time and again appeared a thing full of promise to Catholics. The ideology of Communism already appeared to Bernanos to be entering its dotage,[74] but that "collective greed called nationalism",[75] which perverts the Christian notion of "fatherland" into the idol of a "people's state", seemed to him still in 1947 to be thriving as strong as ever. As well, Bernanos was no great friend of the Jews, a habit of mind that was a residue of his Maurrasian beginnings—witness his admiration for Drumont and his permanent adherence to the latter's main theses. But, when the question concerned racism, then Bernanos became an eloquent advocate for the rights of the Jews, and he demanded of them, too, that they overcome race as the chief criterion for social grouping; instead, he favored a human community that would be a "human work", "a creation by man consisting of as many different elements as a poem or a symphony".[76]

Bernanos' polemics became violent and offensive only when he had been disillusioned in some deep love. Initially, he had ardently believed in the ideals of the rightist movement, in particular Charles Maurras, just as Péguy had lost his political heart to the socialists Lucien Herr and Jean Jaurès. Consequently, imperial Rome appeared to Bernanos later as the quintessence of the political "realism" he so hated, and he looked on its heirs—the Italians of both the Renaissance and of the Fascist present—with deep aversion. It was likewise a case of disillusioned love when he often spoke so bitterly about the clergy. Disillusioned love, as well, estranged him from the Claudel he had once so intensely revered. And only disillusioned love explains the steady stream of indignation against Spain that began pouring inexhaustibly, starting with *The Great Cemeteries under the Moon*, out of a Bernanos who had originally been so enthusiastic about Spain and who supposedly was himself of Spanish descent, much to his pride. Before his very eyes he saw how Spanish Catholics could murder in

[73] *Croix*, May 1941, 126.
[74] *Liberté*, 135.
[75] *To Gallimard*, December 1947, in: *Croix*, x.
[76] *Croix*, May 1944, 423. Concerning the Jews, see *Croix*, 416–24; *Français*, 224; *Enfants*, 226; *Cimetières*, 205.

the name of Christianity, how they sought the Church's blessing for their murderous weapons, how they abused the sacraments and made an art out of that fundamental confusion the unmasking of which was for Bernanos the most important, indeed, the only important concern of his cultural criticism: the blurring of the realms of ecclesial and political obedience.[77] Bernanos, the resolute and almost instinctual opponent of everything Calvinistic and Anglo-Saxon, especially in its American form, should have found in Spain and Latin America his natural spiritual allies. In Brazil he actually did find a sort of second home, despite all the sorrows of exile. His wrath over Francoist Spain, therefore, derived exclusively from Christian reasons and antecedents. Initially he could not help but sympathize with the Falange, in which his eldest son served time. Subsequently, however, his Catholic conscience wrenched an elemental cry of indignation from him. Here he could touch palpably the proof for the abominable suspicion that had been ripening within him like a nightmare. And, once he held the proof in his hand, he could in the future use it like a model for pedagogic demonstration. But this demonstration aimed above all at the democracies: their leveling of the different estates and classes within society,[78] their flattening out of spirit and persons tended toward the same result, whether they wanted it or not.

Only the person and his integrity interested Bernanos, and by no means a political system of any kind pursued for its own sake. If there was a system that saw it as its duty and mission to secure freedom, if there was a system that had grown out of the free responsibility of its citizens and not out of a secret interior abdication and spiritual defeatism, then Bernanos was not very interested in the specifics of that system's constitution. He also saw very clearly that every social order must be "realistic"; the only question, however, concerned the spiritual roots and the degree of such "realism": "No, I am not so naïve as to believe that human societies could ever be disinterested undertakings. But there are different kinds of egotism, and the sort that constitutes the very marrow and nerves of the capitalist world belongs to the basest species."[79] Bernanos knew that the era of mys-

---

[77] See especially *Cimetières*, 72f., 86f., 108f., 128f., 147f.; also *Vérité*, 66–68; *Anglais*, 53; *Croix*, 287, and passim.

[78] *Cimetières*, 230.

[79] *Croix*, December 25, 1943, 392.

tical politics was over and that in the age of the press and the radio the heads of state, too, had to "explain, excuse, and justify" their acts before the public.[80] He did not fight for the monarchy but rather for a type of man who would be free enough to want a monarchy: such a man would not perceive monarchy as oppression—as our democrats do—but as the liberating space within which something like human greatness could once again thrive.

2. An Ethos of Honor

Bernanos could not give the ideal image of man always before him in his struggle a better and simpler name than that of *honor*. This concept was not for him one important value chosen from among other possible ones; rather, honor was something like the absolute ethical foundation that imparts personal dignity, moral splendor, sublimity, and divine likeness to all the commandments and the fulfillment of the commandments. Honor was for Bernanos a shibboleth and a watchword: "Few words can resist the sleazy distortions that the politician, the ideologue, the banker, and the casuist successively practice on language. . . . Honor is one of those words."[81] Bernanos did not intend for honor to displace and substitute for charity, which is the supreme value of Christian life. Rather, honor has its particular and irreplaceable position in that locus where the values of Christian life become engaged in what Péguy called *the temporal*. Within this dimension, honor has a position similar to that of charity insofar as, without honor, the exercise of every sort of temporal duty and task becomes just as useless and vain as the Christian theological and moral virtues are useless without love. While the theological virtues of faith, hope, and charity, however, are pure gifts of grace from above, it is essential to honor that it be put into action and sustained simultaneously from above and from below—by God and by man, by the Church and by society, by both spiritual and worldly realities. Honor does not exist outside the point of intersection of both the realms that make it possible to begin with. Honor may even be said to be the

---

[80] *Anglais*, 90.

[81] *To the Students of the Action Française*, December 11, 1928, in: *L'Etudiant français*, December 25, 1928; reprinted in *Bul.* 14, 11.

proof that such a point of intersection exists—or, better, that such a point at one time existed and could, therefore, exist again. It is so important a capstone because it is so complex in its conditions. If it is lacking, the whole bridge collapses: not only does natural, personal, and social ethics decay into mere "moralism" and "casuistry" (which for Bernanos was the expression of such decadence), but the other pillar—the spiritual—also collapses, since it cannot stand on its own, being intrinsically secured within the buttress of the temporal. The retreat of the spiritual into self-sufficiency and self-satisfaction is a phenomenon that necessarily corresponds to the secularization of society. One consequence of such a retreat is that the spiritual itself becomes more and more worldly within its own realm: it is as if the spirit itself were becoming materialized out of the inability to perform its task of being the form of the matter of the world. The end result is that the alleged domain of the "spiritual" itself becomes politicized, and a whole "casuistry" must be elaborated to justify this transformation.

The layman finds his privileged post at the crossroads of the spiritual and the worldly, and the ethos of honor is above all the ethos of the laity. Priests and religious have renounced the world in order to consecrate themselves exclusively to spiritual realities, the same realities that claim the "soul" of the layman. But the layman must go forth from the realm of the spiritual in order to exercise his commission of stewardship over the realm of the worldly in obedience to the primacy of the spiritual. The renunciation of the worldly necessarily bears the appearance of a certain "infidelity" to the world, and the purely spiritual part of the Church will always risk giving this appearance. This is not in itself a danger, provided, that is, that the Church does not *as a whole* stand under the sign of this apparent "infidelity". Such would be the case if the Church required the layman to forsake the specific fidelity he owes the earthly, worldly realm on the basis of its God-created nature—if the Church required the layman, that is, to forswear the selflessness, conscientiousness, and steadfastness of commitment that the world rightly claims from him. All that would then be left is an artificial, merely "diplomatic" attitude on the part of the Christian layman toward the world, instead of the real pledge and risk of self alone worthy of a fully human act of stewardship. It is the peculiarity of Bernanos' thought in this respect that he did not consider the Church's vital center to be the realm of her functions and structures (even the most sacred and grace-bearing) or the different forms of life within the Church derived from these: for him, rather, the vital center of the Church is the point where these functions and structures, which in themselves are but means, attain to their goal —namely, *a Christian existence in the world but not of the world.* Only such an existence was considered by Bernanos to be the fullness of sanctity. This is the reason why he so treasured Joan of Arc and why he could write these telling lines at the end of his little book about her:

Let others govern the Kingdom of God in peace! . . . Let others tend the domain of the spiritual through their argumentation and legislation! As for us, we shall cling to the temporal with both hands, we shall cling with both hands to God's temporal Kingdom. We hold the heritage of the saints in our keeping. For, ever since God's blessing descended upon us and also on the vine and the wheat, on the stone of our thresholds, on the roof under which the doves make their nest, on our poor beds full of dreams and oblivion, on the road where our wagon wheels grate, on our boys with their crude laughter and our girls who weep by the fountain's edge—ever since God himself visited us: Is there anything in this world our saints have not had to assume? and is there anything they cannot give?[82]

Here is where Bernanos located the hub of honor, and we must allow him to unfold his views himself in a detailed manner. The first thing we should hear in his words is a certain bitterness of expression instilled in him by his agitation over the events of the times.

There is such a thing as Christian honor. But you'd be mistaken to expect the definition of this honor, for instance, from the Austrian epis-copate.[83] And, besides, there can be no definition. . . . It is at once hu-man and divine, and, just so as not to disappoint you, we'll define it anyway. *It is the mysterious fusion of human honor and the charity of Christ.* To be sure, the Church has no need of it in order to perdure. And yet, honor is not any less indispensable to her for all that. Experience must long since have taught you, dear Monsieur Hitler, that, in the face of any and all usurpers, the conclusions arrived at by the theologian aren't very different from those of the realist, at least in appearance. For the one

[82] *Jeanne,* 67–68.
[83] Bernanos is here alluding to certain attitudes of Archbishop Innitzer in the face of an advancing Hitlerism.—Note of the French trans.

as for the other, the true Master is the victor. Do I mean in the case
of the blacks in Ethiopia? No! I mean in the case of Vienna, too. The
churchmen have practically annulled the principle of legitimacy, probably thinking that they can confiscate it for their own benefit. . . . So be
it, then! This means we find ourselves freer than ever to claim an honor
our entitlement to which no one is disputing.[84]

*I by no means wish for the Church to bind her fate to that of legitimacy, because
she must stand in readiness to survive whatever may come.* Even less do I contest the principle of her "sacred opportunism". I find it right and good
for the Church to deal with the de facto regimes before her, because she
cannot stop her march anywhere. She is being borne toward the Eternal
on an unbending trajectory, much like a stone flung from a slingshot.
Our forebears knew this as much as we, but that did not unbind their
consciences. *The Church's sublime infidelity to everything that was not herself had as temporal counterweight the temporal fidelity of Christians.* It was
on this temporal fidelity that they based their honor; and, by extending
their fidelity from the princes of the visible realm to those of the invisible realm—the poor, the weak, the widow, the orphan, the forsaken
—our forebears by the same stroke established the reality of Christian
honor.[85]

"Our forebears did not believe in legitimacy. What they believed in
was their old legitimate Monarchy, period. 'Legitimate' here means
that it became legitimate, that it was raised to the dignity of being
legitimate by time, by the services it rendered, and by our forebears'
own fidelity to these services."[86]
An article of 1941 repeats the same principles for the purpose of
stigmatizing the politics of France's collaborationist bishops.[87] The real
problem is that the institutional Church must rely on power but cannot run "the risks of honor".[88] Thus, alongside his "saints" Bernanos
placed his "heroes" as in the second focus of the ellipse: "*Christian
honor . . . remains the indelible temporal sign of the baptism of Clovis and
of the Mystery of Royal Consecration.*"[89] Occasionally it happens that, in

[84] *Cimetières*, 356–57. (The italics are von Balthasar's.—TRANS.)
[85] *Français*, 138. (The italics are von Balthasar's.—TRANS.)
[86] Ibid., 176.
[87] *Croix*, January 1941, 85f.
[88] *Cimetières*, 94.
[89] *To the Students of the Action Française*, in: *Bul.* 14, 11.

imitation of Joan of Arc, the laity must forcibly take the defense of this honor into their own hands:

> To hold one's own against the doctors of theology, to give insolent answers to the Inquisitor of the Faith, *to appeal to God rather than to the churchmen*, to keep one's sacred word, to make oneself the judge of the legitimacy of princes when even the Holy See refrains from taking sides: what sacrilegious presumption! Yet, this presumption is ours. It isn't to the churchmen that the honor of the French has been entrusted. If we had ever thought of making French honor into one of the theological virtues, the churchmen would be holding a good hand against us, and not without reason. But French honor and French soil have not been entrusted to the keeping of the churchmen; our honor and our soil are but one. This temporal reality is ours, and we cling to it with both hands![90]

> There exists a Christian order. . . . This order is the order of Christ, and the Catholic tradition has preserved its essential principles. But the temporal realization of this order does not belong to the theologians, the casuists, or the doctors, but to us Christians. And it seems that the majority of Christians are forgetting this elementary truth. They believe that the Kingdom of God will happen all by itself, provided they obey the moral rules (which, in any event, are common to all decent people), abstain from working on Sunday (if, that is, their business doesn't suffer too much for it), attend a Low Mass on this same day, and above all have great respect for clerics. . . . This would be tantamount to saying that, in times of war, an army would quite fulfill the nation's expectations if its men were squeaky clean, if they marched in step behind the band, and saluted their officers correctly.[91]

If it is understandable for the churchmen to safeguard the prestige of the Church, nevertheless the adoption of this principle by the laity would, according to Bernanos, lead directly to a "Christianity of privilege", which is to say, to the petty-bourgeois Catholicism of the nineteenth century: The *bien-pensants* (the right-thinking) imagine "that we expect of them virtues unattainable by the majority of men. The truth is that we expect only one thing: for them to admit publicly what they are—mediocrities like everyone else, or distinguishable from every-

---

[90] *Français*, 25–26.
[91] Ibid., 35–36.

one else only by the absurd and sacrilegious pretension of belonging to
the chosen and privileged portion of our species, whereas the Gospel
on every page proclaims the futility of faith without works and the
universal justification of men of good will. It is this pretension that
the world hates in us."[92]

But the influence also moves in the other direction: "If the Church
must rely on force, it is up to us to see to it that the sense of fidelity
and honor be so strong in our country that it will far outweigh the
advantage of having temporary control of the army, the police, and
the coffers of the Banque de France. Then the churchmen will naturally rally as in former days around fidelity and honor, because even
the most realistic of realists could not possibly refuse to take into account what Bismarck called the 'imponderables.' "[93] "The disciplines
of the Church, for instance, are not enough to form the Christian
knight. . . . The Church is not a teacher of honor; she is a teacher
of charity."[94] "I don't think the churchmen have ever pretended to
form the citizen single-handedly, any more than the soldier or the
scholar. . . . It's all very nice . . . to draw up social programs on paper. The important thing is to know *what kind of men you're going to fill
them with.*"[95] "In order to become a holy man, don't you think, you
must first of all be a man."[96] "Is it too much to ask that one's word
of honor be an inseparable part of virility and that one would risk
losing one's honor only by being castrated? A eunuch can be saved
like everyone else, and yet you [bishops] refuse to ordain him. What
else does this mean but that a believing male does not always meet
the conditions necessary to be a Christian *man?*"[97]

> Honor is only a human virtue, granted. But it allows you to classify
> people. I'm not asking for it to be raised to the dignity of a theological
> virtue; I'd only like for us to make good use of it. The Church does
> not disdain human means, so why would she reject this one? Can it be?
> You cannot do without a certain amount of worldly pomp, claiming
> it adds to the Church's prestige, and you go to great expense for the

---

[92] Ibid., 39.
[93] Ibid., 177.
[94] Ibid., 237–38.
[95] Ibid., 241. (The italics are von Balthasar's.—TRANS.)
[96] *Croix*, July 1943, 355.
[97] *Français*, 249.

upkeep of palaces and museums full of anachronistic soldiers decked out
by Michelangelo, and at the same time you would dim the flame of
honor in the world practically to nonexistence? . . . We're quite aware
of the fact that the Church should run no risks, or at least that she is the
sole judge of the risks she can run. By no means do we expect her to
run ours. Wheel and deal, negotiate to your hearts' content. But allow
Christians to run the risk of fidelity and honor![98]

We must, indeed, take with Bernanos the final logical step demanded by his thought and say that the "sublime infidelity" of the
churchmen, bound up as it is with their necessary nonengagement
within the temporal, brings them into relation with the phenomenon
of power insofar as power can become detached from the organic
whole of the human order as this order is rooted within the temporal: "You love power," Bernanos once exclaimed somewhat crudely,
"but you don't run any of its risks."[99] In the *Country Priest*, Olivier
expressly interprets the symbolism of the burning of Joan of Arc at
the stake as the liquidation of the ideal of the knight and its substitution by the modern soldier as mere instrument of power, precisely at
the moment in history when "doctors of theology and casuists" were
gaining the upper hand in the Church. Nowhere else does Bernanos
follow Péguy's train of thought more closely than in this connection: "There is no more Christendom now, and there shall never be
again", Olivier observes with pathos to his friend the country priest,
"because there are no more soldiers. With no more soldiers, there
is no more Christendom. I know: you'll say that the Church has
survived Christendom and that that's the main thing. I agree. Only,
there will never again be a temporal kingdom of Christ—that's over
with. . . . The last true soldier died on May 30, 1431, and it's you, you
[priests], who killed her! Worse than killed: you condemned her, cast
her out, burned her." And, when the country priest asks somewhat
"stupidly": "What exactly do you rebuke the churchmen for, then?",
the young officer replies: "Me? Oh, not much! That they laicized us.
The first true laicization was that of the soldier. And it didn't happen yesterday. When you [priests] start whimpering nowadays about
the excesses of nationalism, you should remember how back then you

[98] Ibid., 147.
[99] *Cimetières*, 94.

emitted a pleasant little laugh and made eyes at the Renaissance jurists as they were busy tucking Christian law and honor away in their
pockets and—under your very noses and beards—slowly reassembling
the pagan State, which knows no law except its own welfare and sur-
vival. . . ."[100] "You [priests] have turned us over to the State. The
State, which arms, dresses, and feeds us, also assumes responsibility
for our conscience. It forbids us to judge, and often even to understand. . . . We're dispensed from being faithful. . . . In the near future, the best killers will kill without risk or responsibility. . . . Draw
up as many concordats as you like! Outside of Christendom there is
not in the West any place for either fatherland or soldier, and your
cowardly complacency will soon have permitted both of these to be
thoroughly dishonored!"[101]

Such straightforward soldier's talk conceals the worst wound possible to a Christian heart, as well as an abysmal fear over the disappearance of Christian *man*, for without a true human incarnation of
the latter, all hierarchies, infallibilities, and sacraments remain hanging in midair. Bernanos is quite aware of the fact that he is dreaming an "impossible romantic dream" when he mourns for past ages
of knightly Christendom. He knows that "modern life is always busy
making of honor a kind of snobbery and anachronistic affectation. . . .
There used to be such a thing as the honor of one's craft, but crafts
no longer exist. There used to be such a thing as the honor of a task
well done, but the machine has gobbled it up in one mouthful. There
used to be such a thing as family honor, but economic conditions, if
they don't yet condemn the poor man to celibacy, still deprive him of
the material means necessary to exercise the prerogatives of family life
with dignity." Moreover, "obedience" and "resignation" are no real
solutions, because "you need to be a saint to be able to work out your
salvation in dishonor. And you [priests] certainly do preach enough
about the exceptional character of heroic vocations! The trouble is,
my country is not populated by exceptions but by citizens."[102]

---

[100] *Curé*, 266–67. (It is evident that Olivier is oversimplifying history a bit, since it would
be difficult to consider jurists such as William of Nogaret and Marsilio of Padua as belonging
to the Renaissance.—Note of the French trans.)

[101] *Curé*, 268–70.

[102] *Français*, 242–44.

In the end, Bernanos could only be left awaiting the arrival of "a new order of knighthood",[103] which he proclaimed in prophetic tones. He well knew that the ancient and earnest manner of fighting wars was forever gone;[104] and so he appealed to the spiritual values of a person who still remembers his intrinsic dignity and wants to remain conscious of them as he engages his full existence. This appeal was made by means of a new word that conveys a kind of magical power: *fierté*—"pride." As Bernanos used it, it connotes, not the arrogance of *orgueil*, but rather interior mettle, noble-mindedness, and undaunted boldness of spirit: "Be proud!", says the country priest to Mademoiselle Louise, the governess, after she has been dismissed from the château. When she expresses her astonishment at such a suggestion by replying, "I never would have thought that pride is one of the theological virtues", the priest explains his meaning further: "The finest thing is to rise above pride, but to do this one must first have reached at least that level."[105] "Stand up proud!", Marie de l'Incarnation also says to Blanche;[106] and Bernanos himself exclaims to a young man: "Be proud! Under its arrogant airs the world is choking with humility, but a humility that is perverted, debased, one that is nothing but one of the forms assumed by cowardice of mind and heart. We are base but not humble. We must once again produce pride just as an exhausted body must again begin producing red blood cells and vitamins. Our charity must descend from very high if we want it to be efficacious. What a cringing Christianity, ours!"[107] Even martyrdom presupposes a certain *joie de vivre*, "that violent and jealous gusto for life that is just the stuff out of which martyrs are made".[108] It was to illustrate this that Bernanos invented Sister Constance, the Carmelite who found everything amusing and even knew how to cheer up her sisters in their dungeon on the eve of climbing up to the guillotine. Nothing could make Bernanos so indignant as confusing humility with defeatism—the laying of a pious mantle of "Christian humility" over the shoulders of political and moral defeatism. He was put beside himself by the appeals made by Vichy and Pétain to the na-

---

[103] *Cimetières*, 359.

[104] *Robots*, 169–71; *Français*, 39.

[105] *Curé*, 244.

[106] *Carmélites*, 109.

[107] *To Benoît*, 1948; *Bul.* 4, 10.

[108] *Peur*, 277.

tion for "repentance", "recollection", and recognition of faults committed.[109] He refused to receive these "sacraments of dishonor". Precisely from this plenitude of disgrace Bernanos expected an elemental outbreak of whatever feeling of honor might still be left Christians. Was it any different at certain points in the Middle Ages? Around the year 1000, for instance, after the

> double collapse of empires—that of the Cæsars and that of Charlemagne
> —. . . the world must have seemed to everyone even more decrepit
> than it does nowadays. Well, Monsieur Roosevelt, it was in just such
> a world—so old and so wasted that it drove wise men to despair and
> which the monks declared to be bound for the devil—it was in such a
> world that knighthood was invented. Chivalry was not born in an attack
> of optimism. It flourished out of the world's selfishness, savagery, and
> despair. . . . The flower of humanity simply met in one place: it's as if
> the flower of humanity had made a mysterious appointment to come
> together where no one expected it. . . . Knightly honor—which is to
> say, the overturning of the world's values, the disdain of money, the
> exaltation of poverty, power deriving its dignity exclusively from ser-
> vices rendered the weak, power become servant—such knightly honor
> became consecrated once and for all.[110]

None of this is going to be achieved by congresses and organizations, for honor is not a theory: "Christian honor is not a doctrine, a system, a philosophy, or even a mystical stance. A 'mystique of honor' no longer has anything to do with real honor. You have to reinvent *Christian Man*, and I'm afraid all you have left is 'the faithful'."[111] But no more than man can that mysterious point of life be produced synthetically that is above all morality and casuistry, and yet, without this superior vivifying point, both morality and casuistry are but members of a corpse, a mere residue of life.[112] In order to safeguard honor,

---

[109] *Croix*, June 1941, 129; July 1941, 133f.; September 1941, 145 ("Under the name of atonement, shame has thus become the legitimate spouse of the old sovereign, the first lady of the kingdom, the queen of France. . . . Shame will yet spill more blood than was spilt by honor"); January 1942, 177; October 1942, 260; September 1944, 445 (an article devoted to the "ridicule" constituted by Vichy, that "ballet featuring members of the Academy, society ladies, admirals, and archbishops, in the background a décor of bright blood—a ballet in a graveyard").

[110] *Anglais*, 203–6.
[111] *Français*, 234.
[112] Ibid., 238–39.

Bernanos secures it in the most unassailable of locations: "*Honor also belongs to childhood.* So, if honor escapes the analysis of the moralists, it's by virtue of this principle of childhood. For moralists can work only on the 'mature man', that fabulous beast invented by themselves to make their own deductions more facile. There's no such thing as the 'mature man'. There's no intervening stage between the two extreme ages: *whoever cannot give more than he receives begins at once to fall into decay.*"[113]

It is significant that Monsieur Ouine also poses as a professor of morality.[114] No expression was more suspect to Bernanos than *se faire une conscience*, that is, to say that one has "created a conscience for oneself" with regard to some matter.[115] The expression is redolent of machinations that already point to the lack of all honor:

> You have let the hour pass when it was still possible to instill a sense of shame in these weak souls. You allowed them the time to devise a morality for themselves, and now they're entrenched behind it. You'll never succeed in dislodging them. We already have an armistice morality, a collaboration morality, and soon we'll have a morality of the economic and military alliance. Like all the others, this one too will obtain the benevolent endorsement of the religious authorities. All those people are in perfect harmony with their conscience. . . . They don't have any honor, but they have a conscience. This state of affairs is much less rare than we think.[116]

Precisely such a passage should prevent us from establishing any link between Bernanos' views and those of certain like-sounding literary projects by Catholic German writers who, during the Nazi period, sought to transpose the official *Herrenmoral* (master-race morality) onto a spiritual Christian dimension, thereby saving the "kernel of truth" it contained and at the same time securing a position for themselves within the system. We must state this all the more clearly as we do, in fact, see that Bernanos was at one time heavily influenced by the ideology of Maurras and that certain formulas of his youth were imbued with a strong dose of *hybris*. Consider the following sentence, for in-

---

[113] *Cimetières*, 270–71. (The italics are von Balthasar's.—TRANS.)
[114] *Ouine*, 168.
[115] *Anglais*, 117; Croix, August 1942, 235.
[116] *Anglais*, 100–101.

stance: "Once the right moment comes, only honor (or, if you like, a high opinion of one's task and of oneself) can inspire the dauntless decisions that onlookers qualify at first as foolhardy but that posterity regards as solely manifesting the power, intuition, and superhuman foresight characteristic of genius."[117] As late as 1940 we find Bernanos writing as follows:

> The error of racism is not to affirm the inequality of the races, something that is as obvious as the inequality among individuals. Its error is to give such inequality an absolute character, to subordinate morality itself to the inequality in question, to the point of staging a confrontation between master morality and slave morality. *If there does indeed exist a master morality*, the only thing that distinguishes it from the other is the extent and severity of its requirements; but the public spirit has fallen so low, even among Christians, that the word "master" automatically evokes the idea of subjection and not of protection. *There are no privileges, there are only services:* such was at one time the fundamental principle of the ancient French monarchical legislation. But it can be understood only by a nation deriving from an age-old race, a lordly race, a nation for whom the most evident mark of base origin is to feel naturally tempted to serve oneself to the detriment of the weak rather than to serve the weak. When people speak of my country's "liberal" or "democratic" tradition, they forget that it expresses, often unconsciously, *an aristocratic conception of life*.[118]

If we add to this Bernanos' genuine and constant concern for the unprotected working classes (a concern that, for him, was inseparable from his aristocratic conception of life), then his kinship could appear even greater to the contemporary German panorama, which he nevertheless hated. By using Maurras as a bridge, it would be easy to make Bernanos into a kind of unselfconscious advance crusader for values that, in the end, he so ardently combated after having perhaps initially indulged a weakness for their theatrical fascistic form. Is not the very vehemence of this battle once again simply the sign that half of his bleeding heart had remained in the other camp?

---

[117] *Peur*, 80.
[118] *Croix*, June 1940, 13. (The italics are von Balthasar's.—TRANS.)

Not at all. Such a way of construing Bernanos' position would be wholly unfounded. Indeed, any noble heart would have to bleed at the sight of Fascism demeaning sacred values, and the mystery of value itself, in order to set up a screen to conceal the naked lust for power. But the crux of the matter here is not a superficial similarity of words and concepts but the spirit that contains these and the manner in which it discerns reality. The more the history of the world advances, the easier it becomes to speak an ideological language, and the more pressing it is for Christians to learn the art of the discernment of spirits. Bernanos would not have objected in the least to searching, with Reinhold Schneider, for the most genuine and purest source of the Prussian spirit, which is to say, the spirit of the Knights of Marienburg: precisely this *unity of soldier and monk* was for him the crux of his concept of honor and what his young hero Olivier praises as the salutary indicator of the right way. It was from this unity that the West emerged, and this unity can again be a source of healing for it.[119] "What those degenerate heirs of Christian knighthood" (he means the Fascists) "are most lacking is honor". And if today's youth "wishes to become a second order of chivalry, it must begin by saving the notion and reality of honor."[120] He did, of course, appeal to whatever residue of nobility, noble tradition, noble feeling for life, or noble lifestyle might still be in the people.[121] But he never envisioned any other foundation for a "rebirth of knighthood" than the most noble attitude of the heart: namely, service out of love.

Here again, it is the country priest who makes the decisive observation about modern traditionalists: "I have no objections against the order they propose. Except for one thing: it is without love."[122] Not for nothing did Thomas Aquinas construct his Christian ethics on a very broad natural foundation and show so much esteem for the values of the cardinal virtues and all their potential aspects, such as gratitude, generosity, boldness, magnanimity, magnificence (in the sense of performing great deeds), mercifulness, and reverence, to name but a few—all of them forms of greatness of soul with which the ancient world was already familiar[123] and which medieval man under-

[119] *Curé*, 264, 267.
[120] *Vérité*, 78.
[121] *Croix*, August 1941, 135–38.
[122] *Curé*, 263.
[123] See R. Gauthier, *Magnanimité* (Paris: Vrin, 1951).

stood in a deeper Christian sense. Péguy's whole ethics, nourished on Corneille's classical and Christian ideal, centered around this concept. His enthusiastic love for *Polyeucte* was based on the contest between the pagan and the Christian form of spiritual honor he there saw dramatized: the Christian hero does not defeat his judge on the field of supernatural virtues—something unknown to him—but on his own field of honor, which the Christian transfigures in the light of grace but in no way diminishes. Already Bernanos' first book of politico-cultural criticism, *We, the French* (which originally was to bear the bitter title *Démission de la France*, "France Abdicates"), had as sole object to expose the devastation brought about by an ethos of retreat into the shelter of the "supernatural" as parade ground for all the resentments stigmatized by Nietzsche, all of which had one thing in common: being a mode of dishonor. The dimension of the natural may not be skipped over with impunity: "The Lord came for the criminal, too, as well as for the coward. But, in order for the coward still to be able to hope . . . , the balance of justice must first be reëstablished. Human society must first show the coward in all his dishonor. For, if you honor the coward, you turn him into a monster. But the coward, in his frank dishonor, can enter naked into the kingdom of Christ's charity, poor among the poor."[124] Sacrifice, even of the ritual sort, always presupposes the integrity of what is to be sacrificed. A living person who offers his life to God must first sense the magnificence of being young, of high achievement, of earthly happiness: "What is happiness? A kind of pride, of gladness, an absurd and purely carnal hope, the carnal form hope takes."[125] Indeed, we are to "conquer nature: conquer it, but not violate it—and the distinction is full of consequences".[126] And "true humility begins with a certain decency, a certain balance."[127]

The type of man who both can and should make history in our day cannot be educated only by priests and monks,[128] because the supernatural virtues in which these specialize do not suffice for such a

---

[124] *Français*, 236.
[125] *Curé*, 257.
[126] *Carmélites*, 33.
[127] Ibid., 109.
[128] *Français*, 237.

task: "It's not up to the churchmen to form whole men. Father and mother should be enough for that and, along with them, all one's ancestors."[129] At this point we should say a word about the profound and very radical distrust Bernanos entertained of all boarding-school education, a distrust he extended to the whole Jesuit order as such— the only order to be thus continually stigmatized by him with bitter sarcasm. His fundamental objection has already been given: this order's endeavor to "produce" Christian laymen within a supernatural "closed jar", instead of an education undertaken by both priests and laymen at the open point where world and Church intersect. No amount of Baroque-style humanism could reconcile a fuming Bernanos with the fact that the truly free, chivalric Christian he envisioned had now become a well-behaved little soldier and that, indeed, a whole Christian culture had been designed on the blueprint of the ideal Jesuit preparatory boarding school—the Paraguay experiment being nothing but one expanded school of this type.[130] "It's as if you'd put the peoples of the world into one of your high schools!", was his roaring objection to the culture produced by the Counter-Reformation. There, people are "crushed" by their "experience" of the good fathers—their "wisdom", their "disciplines", and even their "measured, benevolent, and implacable justice".[131] "Ever since the seventeenth century, the Church has been distrustful of the young. . . . It's all very fine to protect little men from the dangers of adolescence; but wouldn't you say that the well-behaved young men whom you bring out during public competitions are a little lacking in character?"[132] The end of the episode is not far: "Yes, you've put the peoples of the world into one of your high schools. But your schools are emptying out, as at vacation time, and, unless Providence disposes otherwise, all that will soon be left is the faculty, along with the small number

---

[129] Ibid., 235.

[130] *Cimetières*, 215.

[131] *Français*, 153.

[132] *Cimetières*, 227. See also *Croix*, August 1942, 242–43. (Here, speaking with surprising lyricism, Bernanos praises "the composure, the boldness, and the infallible mastery of the artist or the gambler" that characterize the Brazilian landowners of vast properties on the Rio Grande do Sul. He then adds: "It's precisely such people who created the world of our forebears. Ever since they were replaced with peons, Europe offers the spectacle of a badly run high school. In the momentous affairs of the day, nothing can take the place of what we would be tempted to call . . . 'innate experience', something impossible to capture in formulas and incapable of being transmitted."—Note of the French trans.)

of those poor unfortunates who never go on vacation because they
have neither family nor means: all they can do is wander in their
melancholy about the deserted courtyards."[133] Bernanos' animosity
against the Jesuits may be encountered with great frequency.[134] His
central point of criticism was the "humanist priest", that "ape of the
Renaissance swarming with Latin verses like maggots on a corpse".
Those "raceless and countryless maniacs made our forebears cringe
with shame at the sight of their barbaric cathedrals, and they even
rejected our ancestral language as unworthy of eloquence." They replaced "the Celtic or Germanic Virgin" with the Roman Vestal[135] and
became the spiritual fathers of the Enlightenment.[136] For Bernanos, in
fact, it was the Jesuits who were responsible for the evolution from
the more "tempered humanism of the Baroque period" to the full-
blown Enlightenment of the seventeenth and eighteenth centuries.[137]
Beyond this, what appeared unpardonable to Bernanos was the manner in which the Jesuits extended their own ideal of obedience to the
whole Church in general and to the individual Christian in particular. He likewise found Jesuit missionary methods up to the recent
past unpardonable: these banked on the Church's splendor as a "grand
establishment" and played on the "terror of the Revolution" in order to enroll bourgeois Catholics in the ranks of the "innumerable
associations" controlled by the Society. These maneuvers amounted
to "a terrible injustice committed against the French proletariat".[138]
With regard to Saint Ignatius himself, Bernanos was ambivalent. He
was occasionally capable of harsh and spiteful words against him when
juxtaposed to Joan of Arc,[139] and then again he could praise him when

---

[133] *Français*, 166–67.

[134] For a mere sampling, see: *Peur*, 294; *Cimetières*, 94, 166, 225; *Français*, 76, 165, 196f.,
198, 217f., 222, 229; *Enfants*, 12f., 39f.; *Robots*, 75; and passim.

[135] *Français*, 165–66.

[136] *Cimetières*, 227: "It is no petty undertaking to reconcile—in the name of humanism—
the morality of the Gospel with that of La Fontaine. . . . The finest flower of the atheistic
encyclopædists issued from your schools."

[137] Ibid., 228f.; *Français*, 165; *Croix*, 104.

[138] *Anglais*, 124–25. (On the following page Bernanos underscores the "hypocrisy" and
"imposture" of an anti-Malthusian campaign that only began in earnest when the workers—
imitating practices traditional among the bourgeois—grew weary "of making children destined for the hospital and the graveyard and thus began putting cheap manpower at risk."—
Note of the French trans.)

[139] *Français*, 25: "Unless we're kept from it by God's grace, it's only too easy to imagine

holding him up, together with Joan of Arc, as the last representative of the chivalric soldier.[140] But Bernanos never knew how close his deepest convictions stood to those of this vigorous saint who prized above all others the virtue of magnanimity.

Bernanos sought an Archimedean point for our times: "We can argue endlessly about legality, rights, and justice itself, because, alas, it isn't always easy to draw the distinction between the letter and the spirit. But honor is hard evidence. It binds both the old man and the child, both the poor man and the rich, both the scholar and the ignorant, and it even seems that the noblest animals aren't entirely devoid of it. Honor is the salt of the earth."[141] "The world needs honor. What the world lacks is honor. The world has everything it needs, but it doesn't enjoy anything because it lacks honor. The world has lost its self-esteem. . . . Honor is an absolute."[142] Although the return of honor is not exactly imminent,[143] hopefully it is already clear that only it can save the world: "There is no solution for a crisis of shame other than an explosion of grandeur."[144] "A Christian knight of the twelfth century appears infinitely less outmoded today than a bourgeois intellectual."[145] Ideologies are tearing the world apart, "but, when everything conspires to separate us, honor can still be what we have in common."[146]

Our last word on this subject, however, should be that Bernanos did not overestimate honor. He quite readily admitted and defined its limitations: "I am well aware", he writes, "of the fragility and profound ambiguity of the concept of honor."[147] "I do not make a god out of honor, nor do I pretend that this god is French. Honor is an age-old

---

the kind of reception the Castilian nobleman would have given Joan of Arc if the poor shepherdess had been born late enough for her to reveal her ambitious projects to him, who was dry as a vine branch, yellow as bile, and haunted by death and hell."

[140] *Croix*, February 1941, 96: By waging war, Joan of Arc "not only remained in the state of grace but sanctified herself. And Saint Ignatius of Loyola himself may have left the military profession, but he by no means abjured it. With great piety he hung his sword at the altar of the Virgin."

[141] Ibid., May 1940, 10.

[142] *Cimetières*, 98.

[143] *Anglais*, 10.

[144] *Croix*, October 1944, 455.

[145] *Français*, 174.

[146] *To Gallimard*, December 1947; *Croix*, viii.

[147] *Français*, 232.

companion of man, . . . and, like us, he[148] too became a sinner. But, if he did become a sinner, then he too can be redeemed. . . . Our honor has been baptized. . . . There is more humility in him than in many an opulent parishioner who likes to take the first place in the church. What do you mean?, you say. Who has ever heard of such a thing as a 'humble honor'? Well, it *is* humble."[149] But there is more: at least after *Monsieur Ouine*, Bernanos began glimpsing something like a "sacrifice of honor". "At the far end of its stripping-down", little Guillaume's dream of honor is exchanged for a much more mysterious grace,[150] and the same holds true for his aged grandfather.[151] Such a transmutation is accomplished above all in the *Dialogues of the Carmelites*, in the "dishonor"[152] that the "admirable Mère Marie de l'Incarnation"[153] has to endure. She had indeed understood Blanche's weakness but had always wanted to extract some kind of "honor" from it,[154] whereas the dying prioress had already said to her: "The poor daughters of Carmel look upon the rule of worldly honor in the same way the Lord Jesus Christ and his apostles looked upon the ancient law. We are not here to abolish it but, on the contrary, to fulfill it by going beyond it."[155] Confronting the commissioner of the Republic, Mère Marie takes on an almost arrogant tone: "You ought to know, Sir, that even in the poorest daughter of Carmel, honor speaks louder than fear."[156] But the old prioress had been right; in the end, honor too has to be let go of like everything else, surrendered to God's designs: "To sum everything up with a word that is never found on our lips any more, even though our hearts have not disowned it: in whatever circumstance you find yourselves, think that your *honor* is in God's safekeeping. God has assumed responsibility for your *honor*, and it is more secure in his hands than in yours."[157]

---

[148] *L'honneur* is here personified in the masculine.—TRANS.
[149] *Anglais*, 37.
[150] *Ouine*, 133.
[151] Ibid., 157f.
[152] *Carmélites*, 228.
[153] Ibid., 226.
[154] Ibid., 131.
[155] Ibid., 60.
[156] Ibid., 119.
[157] Ibid., 63. (The italics are the translator's.—TRANS.)

3. Between Revolutions

When Bernanos spoke of honor, he had his own French people in mind—the people who had to understand what he meant by this word since the best things about this people may only be conceived from the standpoint of honor. These are also the people who, as Bernanos knew, are today "gambling their souls" like no other people of Europe. Thus far, we have excluded from the theme of honor the specific theme of France, because we had first to hear Bernanos develop his vision of honor in all its purity, applicable to us all. But, even though the other peoples of Europe may not be much inclined to listen to Bernanos' dialogue with his own nation, the case of France cannot be indefinitely excluded from such a discussion, because in Europe all peoples are in solidarity with one another and necessarily feel one another's "loss of soul" as their own destiny.

Bernanos loved his people with such a simple, deeply human, tender, and wholly nonfanatical love that there are few similar examples we could compare to him: "Being French is an occasion, not for pride, but rather for much ache and toil and great exertion."[158] His love sprang directly from the heart, without any ulterior motives of glory, power, or privilege in the world. This love was itself part and parcel of being French, wholesome and unspoiled by any deliberate reflection. But it is profoundly significant that this love, too, which came so naturally to Bernanos, should also be deeply Christian. What he loved in his people, as in man, was the creature loved and chosen by God, the creature inseparable from its Christian vocation. A France that would no longer be Christian could not continue to be the object of his love. But, in reality, such a thing is an impossibility, the only thing approximating it being a France that renounced (and had forgotten) its true mission: "There's no pride in being French," he writes. "We are still a Christendom on pilgrimage, a Christendom in the midst of toil. Pride is the vice of those who think they have arrived."[159] France is the country whose most secret mission is its Christian responsibility for more-than-France, that is, for the whole world. This is why Christian honor is something so essential to France. It is a nation that should live nowhere but at this cross-

---

[158] *Français*, 9.
[159] Ibid., 10.

roads between heaven and earth. The temptation of a *gloire* of the
imperial-Roman type would be one of France's two great aberrations,
an option Bernanos dispatched by rejecting "the Corsican of Genoese
extraction who was more a politician than a soldier and who scarcely
gave the word *gloire* the same meaning as his grenadiers".[160] France's
other aberrant temptation would be a piety alien to both the world
and common folk: "It's easy for moralists and bigots to preach detachment from all *gloire*. What could those imbeciles have in common
with what we mean by 'glory'?"[161]

> When we speak of "glory", what is conjured up by the upstart foreigner,
> the crowned yahoo, and the slave armed to the teeth is: Power, Riches,
> Domination. And the pious at once exhort us to despise such vanities.
> What can we reply? We know well that the glory we envision is neither
> a vanity nor a lie. We know this, but unfortunately this conviction is not
> one of those an ordinary Frenchman can justify in the face of theolo-
> gians, moralists, politicians, and philosophers. As soon as he pronounces
> this sacred word, the Frenchman finds himself in the holy of holies of
> his race. . . . But then he becomes a little bored. Fiddling with his cap
> between his fingers, he's ashamed of showing these old stones to the
> foreigners who can build such modern and comfortable structures. . . .
> Indeed, no! There's no pride in being French![162]

"And allow me to say it once and for all, in the same sense: There
isn't any honor either in being a Christian. It wasn't us who made
the choice."[163] In its most decisive hours and in connection with
its weightiest tasks, France's destiny appeared to Bernanos to be one
with the destiny of Christendom itself, inseparably spiritual and world-
bound. This becomes evident when we consider the French Revolution, which at the same time signaled a revolution in Christianity.

For both Bernanos and Péguy, France's path from the monarchy
through the Revolution and on to modern times was the subject of
continual contemplation and reflection concerning the most fundamental issues of human existence and attitudes. By observing this
evolution we can study the essence of both honor and dishonor and
learn to read the water level of both hope and resignation. The Rev-

---

[160] Ibid., 21.
[161] Ibid., 25. The very next sentence shows that Bernanos here means Ignatius of Loyola.
[162] Ibid., 22–23.
[163] Ibid., 26.

olution is the hinge on which the door of French history turns. Very much depends on evaluating it correctly. For Bernanos, the value and rightness of ancient monarchical and Christian honor remained unassailable: this honor, for him, was after all what maintained the tense unity in the duality of Christian and temporal realities, and it mirrored the heavenly Kingdom within an inchoative *Civitas Dei* on earth. All of this being so, what then was the Revolution? And what have its historical fruits been down to our time?

One of two paths could be taken in interpreting the French Revolution. The first was to adhere to the temporal products of the old Christian spirit, to the forms this spirit had generated and which had become a spacious dwelling place for the nation. By maintaining or restoring these forms, one could hope for the revival of a spirit worthy of the forms, even though the spirit would no longer be Christian. This was the path of Maurras. The other path opted, on the contrary, for letting go of all the temporal products of Christian culture swept away by the Revolution in order to adhere solely to the Christian spirit without the forms it generated. One could even go so far as seeing in the Revolution an anonymous and amorphous emergence of the Christian spirit and declare the Revolution, insofar as it was Christian, to have been the very heart of the Ancien Régime. This was the path of Péguy.

Initially Bernanos took the first of these paths, at least in an external sense, but from the outset he was intent on connecting with those aspects of the popular French tradition that still contained intact portions of the Christian heritage. He always strove to live the Action Française movement as an explicitly Christian undertaking. There is a letter of 1916, written in the usual pretentious and domineering tone of the movement, that holds forth as expected on the subjects of good taste, race, and style. However, it ends with the following remark, characteristic only of Bernanos: "From this [Christian] world, whose matter has been destroyed, we can at least save the spirit."[164] Very early on he clearly discerned the hopeless desiccation and institutionalization of Maurras' movement.[165] As well, Bernanos was

---

[164] *To His Fiancée*, May 30, 1916, in: *Erbarmen*, 25.

[165] "We see [the Action Française] becoming a State that, in order to survive, will legitimately substitute the leaders of its small army with a hierarchy of functionaries. And I lack both the taste for and the methods of the functionary" (*To Dom Besse*, 1919, in: *Bul.* 11, 9).

much too impatient and too "pneumatic" to be able to bear a life
dedicated to the cultivation of mere forms. He could tolerate forms
only as the products of a revolutionary and creative Christian power.
Thus, his swing in the direction of Péguy, once it was realized in a full
and conscious way, was actually the acknowledgment of something
that had long—in fact, always—been present in him. Together with
Péguy, Bernanos could henceforth understand the spirit of the Revolution as being crypto-Christian, or at least susceptible to Christian
interpretation and therefore redeemable. They could both, therefore,
appeal from a historical Revolution that could not carry its intentions
through and failed in its effects to a Christian Revolution of the future. The latter would have as its task the putting into practice of
the deepest Christian concerns: the defense of the rights and dignity
of the poor and the realization of a brotherhood among men that
would overshoot all boundaries and quarrels among nations (but not
in the sense of a totalitarian "equality"!), and this against all ostensibly Christian formalism and Jansenism, and also against the bourgeois
world of the nineteenth and twentieth centuries. This vision closes
the rift between the right and the left, without either direction having
to abandon its deepest soul.

At this point a thorough critique of *Maurras* becomes possible: a
"Christianity" without Christ, indeed without God, is an impossibility:[166] "Is it not an enormity to hear Monsieur Maurras speak in
the name of French tradition while willfully remaining a stranger
to the portion of our national heritage that to us is the most precious: the French Christian tradition? . . . As far as we're concerned,
the France of Maurras is as hollow and as empty as his Catholicism
without Christ."[167] Maurras, therefore, truly stands outside the living tradition.[168] His is an "aching and shut soul, with a wound that
has dried up since childhood and no longer seems capable of yielding a single drop of blood."[169] Maurras is system, petrification, "lucid and icy arrogance",[170] a hater[171] who is incapable of love (he

[166] *Cimetières*, 156.

[167] *Vérité*, 17.

[168] Ibid., 50.

[169] *Français*, 62.

[170] *Croix*, 265.

[171] *Français*, 78: "Lavish with his intelligence, Monsieur Maurras gives nothing of his soul
except his hatreds."

knows nothing of "the charity of Christ")[172] and who throughout his life produced other haters:[173] an absolutely tragic figure.[174] Bernanos never tired of juxtaposing Maurras to *Péguy*, his opposite in everything,[175] and he turned them into symbolic protagonists of: rationalism versus mystery,[176] State versus fatherland, spiritual Church versus world-engulfing Christendom.[177] Like Jaurès, Péguy's archenemy, Maurras belonged to the "party of the intellectuals".[178] Bernanos early on detected and exposed the spiritual threads leading from Maurras to Hitler, before history had made them evident.[179] The interesting thing is that he did this on the basis, not of their common rightist ideology, but of the most interior realities: their common death of soul, their skepticism, and their cynicism concerning the human community, which made them see it as a collective ripe for the advent of The Totalizer.

The love the young Bernanos entertained for *Léon Daudet* is something altogether different. It was not his ideology Bernanos loved but his "sensitivity, keen to the point of martyrdom", his "great-souled sincerity", his "psychological penetration, whose extreme bitterness is barely masked by an immense compassion", his struggle in a "Dantean hell" to conquer the prize of his "free will", with "redeeming faith" marching ahead of him and, behind him, "despair and nothingness".[180] All of this Bernanos felt within himself, and he strove to impress some shape upon it and thus tame it: for this reason did he pay such homage to Daudet.[181] *Drumont*, too, was hardly more than a mask and a double for Bernanos. He never admired "any of

---

[172] Ibid., 80f.

[173] *Vérité*, 39f.: "His misfortune . . . is that he really does not love his own thought. He bound himself to his thought by chains of iron. His strength is hating other people's thought with a watchful and discerning hatred, . . . with a carnal hatred that, by virtue of a moving contradiction, has the power and the impulse of love. This is what makes him capable of begetting thousands of imbeciles."

[174] *Français*, 89.

[175] *Cimetières*, 284f.; *Vérité*, 19f., 33; *Français*, 102.

[176] *Enfants*, 77f.

[177] Ibid., 83.

[178] *Vérité*, 37–38.

[179] See *Croix*, 272f.; *Cimetières*, 328; *Français*, 184, 101, 106 ("Those Frenchmen who follow Monsieur Maurras . . . are the ones who shout: 'Long live Mussolini!' 'Long live Franco!', if, that is, they actually still refrain from shouting: 'Long live Hitler!' "); *Vérité*, 44.

[180] *Léon Daudet romancier* (1909), in: *Bul.* 14, 9.

[181] See *Peur*, 267, 269; *Cimetières*, 281, 338–39; *Français*, 65; *Robots*, 125.

his doctrines"[182] but only his power to see clearly:[183] "He sees and teaches you how to see, nothing else."[184] Like Bernanos, Drumont too is "one called",[185] a broken-down solitary[186] with deep anxieties,[187] who is a snapshot of the coming cultural agony of modern times.[188] Clinging to the values of a bygone world,[189] he attempted to make a counterrevolution.[190] Finally, his old age and death[191] in deep poverty, disgrace, and misery[192] provided Bernanos with not unwelcome material for his novels.

For lack of the brighter light from the lamp of Péguy, whom Bernanos did not yet know, Bernanos' history of the wretched "abdication by France" was written under the somber influence of Drumont. Jewish ascendancy in culture and politics is not its central theme, only a symptom for the general decay of the French people.[193] The rising conspiracy between the State and money[194] and the ever-deeper entanglement of the ruling classes in the bonds of property, well-being, security, and self-protection at all costs intensified until all ideals, and indeed Christianity as such, secretly became a functional appendage of these property privileges, and the defense of Christianity became inseparable from an anxious power struggle for the conservation of class privileges. The bitter psychoanalysis Bernanos undertook of the Catholic bourgeoisie[195] reached its high point in his accusation of the privileged classes for their fear, cowardice, and egotism, of ecclesiastical politicians for short-sightedly closing ranks with these classes in decline and for expecting from them the defense of the Church's interests,[196] and of both the social élite and the churchmen for completely forsaking the workers in their plight.[197] The apparent conversion of the Voltairian bourgeoisie to the standpoint of the Catholic *bien-pensants* (while the workers were left to adopt the godless position of the Revolution) was retold by Bernanos with contemptuous sar-

[182] *Peur*, 96.
[183] Ibid., 149.
[184] Ibid., 313.
[185] Ibid., 125.
[186] Ibid., 134.
[187] Ibid., 137, 288.
[188] Ibid., 157.
[189] Ibid., 109

[190] Ibid., 75.
[191] Ibid., 257.
[192] Ibid., 295f.
[193] Ibid., 108f., and see 54, 127.
[194] Ibid., 148.
[195] Ibid., 68–70, 91f.
[196] Ibid., 86f., 120f.
[197] *Vérité*, 48, 55; *Français*, 98, 125f.

casm.[198] Nor was the battle over the schools under Combes exempt from his vitriol.[199] He saw it as a battle of the clerical rear guard of a defeated army that no longer believed in itself and was fighting for positions that had already been lost. The clergy's alliance with the rich classes,[200] the Church's pitifully late intervention in the battle for workers' rights,[201] the unjustified allowances made in the interest of capital,[202] the Church's alliance with the bourgeoisie against the new workers' front and against a materialism that "all too conveniently" made us forget the materialism wrought by a "liberal economy":[203] all these things appeared to Bernanos to be alarming symptoms of the emergence of a bourgeois Church and of the Church's detachment from her roots in the people, to which the modern worker belongs just as much as Christ the Worker himself belongs.[204]

Having thus become bourgeois through and through, France had to tread a path of fear and disgrace. The climax of this development was the catastrophe of Vichy, which for Bernanos was the point-by-point demonstration of all his earlier forebodings. These we can review at leisure in his long series of articles in *The Way of the Cross-of-Souls*, which he produced with a patience laced with rage. Despite all of this, however, France remained for Bernanos the land of hope. Against all hope, Bernanos clung tightly to his country's vocation,[205] which according to him consisted in its showing to all peoples of the world—and itself first treading—the way of the freedom of the person, of human dignity, and of the superiority of man over all slavery to money and technology.[206] This is why Bernanos looked rather positively on the lack of order and discipline of the French, on their stubborn individualism, and on their backwardness with regard to technological competitiveness.[207] France's isolation within the Ger-

---

[198] *Français*, 116, 123–24; *Anglais*, 68, 112; *Curé*, 83.

[199] *Peur*, 114; *Croix*, March 1941, 103.

[200] *Curé*, 97.

[201] *Français*, 135.

[202] Ibid., 164.

[203] *Anglais*, 123, 126; *Curé*, 67f., 83.

[204] *Français*, 11.

[205] *Croix*, May 1943, 330; *Liberté*, 41.

[206] *Cimetières*, 136, 351; *Français*, 21f.; *Anglais*, 184; *Croix*, 108; *Liberté*, 16, 21f., 41f., 86, 133, 163, etc.

[207] *Croix*, May 1943, 332 ("The undisciplined spirit that has been such a source of reproach against the French was an indispensable element in Christian order"), 341 ("Anarchy, which

mano-Anglo-Saxon coalition based on technological capitalism was
seen by Bernanos as analogous to the position of Athens with regard
to Rome:[208] "The Propylæa are absolutely defenseless before the machines",[209] since their effect comes only from their value. The only
thing France had to put in the scales to counterbalance the institution
was man.[210]

In its original meaning and during its "first phase", the *French Revolution* was the revelation of an idea of freedom that wanted to unite
all estates within society[211] and that was exceptional in that it conceived of such freedom not nationally but universally.[212] This project
was the result of an "overabundant trust"[213] that for a moment was
able to inspire the whole world with a like trust. Alas, this "Great
Movement of 1789", which was a kind of "prophetic illumination",
soon made way for a "realist and nationalist Revolution. Abandoning the idealism of Rousseau and of the Declaration of the Rights of
Man, this 'second Revolution' connected with the State absolutism
of Italian and Spanish jurists and their centralizing, unitarian tradition and quite logically resulted in the Napoleonic regime."[214] It was
later to be continued by the Marxist Revolution: "The Revolution of
'89 was the Revolution of Man, inspired by a religious faith in man,
whereas the German Revolution of Marxist type is a Revolution of
the masses, inspired, not by faith in man, but by faith in the inflexible
determinism of economic laws."[215] "The Revolution of '89 simply
came too late."[216] It should have been made much earlier by Christians.[217] As it was, it turned out to be a "failed revolution".[218] Despite
everything, "the France people love is always the France of 1789, the

---

is to say, the absence of order and a spontaneous disorder, is still more valuable than a perverted order"); *Liberté*, 133; see *Anglais*, 51.
[208] *Liberté*, 163.
[209] Ibid., 238.
[210] *Français*, 21.
[211] *Robots*, 37.
[212] Ibid., 41.
[213] Ibid., 130.
[214] Ibid., 73–74.
[215] Ibid., 77.
[216] Ibid., 84.
[217] Ibid., 83.
[218] Ibid., 126; *Peur*, 73.

France of new ideas",[219] and people also love the champions of that France.

In 1939 Bernanos wrote: "Charles Péguy was a man of 1789, and Charles Maurras is a man of 1793. The man of 1789 stands closer to us than that of 1900."[220] In 1944 his thought was further focused, but he basically remained faithful to the statement of the Count of Chambord: "Together, with you, whenever you want, we can take up again the great movement of '89." What the Revolution "could and should have done" was "to unite the French. And it did do it, but only for a short moment. . . . But no Frenchman has forgotten the memory of this heroic communion", because

> that magnificent experience was above all parties. . . . The great movement of '89 was at base neither monarchist nor antimonarchist, and the experiment could have very naturally been made within the framework of the monarchy's institutions, had these been reformed and renewed. The experience of '89 was neither clerical nor anticlerical (I don't say neither religious nor antireligious, because it derived from a deep religious inspiration), but it could have occurred within the framework of French Christianity. The experience of '89, in fact, grew out of our ancient Christian soil: it is wholly in line with our medieval tradition. . . . The experience of '93, on the other hand, grew out of a totally opposed tradition: that of the jurists of the fifteenth century[221] and the Renaissance, which was Roman in spirit. For those of my readers who know our history I will say that the experience of '89 connects with Saint Louis himself, that of '93 with Philip the Fair. . . . The men of '93 belonged to the tradition of absolute monarchy—that of Charles V, Philip II, and Louis XIV himself, who was so strongly influenced by the Spanish blood he had from his mother. The men of '89 left no real heirs: their task must be taken up anew. But the men of '93 . . . have sons they could not disown if they were still alive—I mean the heads of totalitarian States and their accomplices. To express my thought in an even more poignant way, I would have to say that 1789 means Péguy, while 1793 means Maurras and Lenin.[222]

---

[219] *Robots*, 125.

[220] *Vérité*, 26; see *Croix*, 407.

[221] Here we ought perhaps to read "fourteenth century", as suggested by the reference to Philip the Fair.—Note of the French trans.

[222] *Croix*, July 1944, 437–38.

All Bernanos could do was project 1789 into the future and begin
awaiting the true, Christian Revolution.[223] On December 25, 1943
Bernanos emitted a cry of the heart when he wrote: "In the West
and in the East, in both the North and the South, society is in a slow
process of petrification. The individual will soon find himself trapped
like a fossil in limestone, a fern twig in coal. Fellow Frenchmen, on
this Christmas Day let us make an oath to proclaim everywhere, as
early as tomorrow, the universal revolt of the human spirit against the
Revolution that was snatched from us and has become enslaved."[224]
Four years later, in 1947, Bernanos claimed to be seeing in the
world

> the first symptoms of a Revolution, the greatest revolution of all histori-
> cal time, or, even better, the sole Revolution of all the world's countries'
> histories—the one of which the others were but a pale image, generally
> unrecognizable. This Revolution is that of man created in the image and
> likeness of God, against brute matter, which, from century to century,
> is slyly gaining the upper hand over him even though he flatters himself
> with the illusion that he is subjecting it to himself. Friends of my coun-
> try, it's in France that this Revolution will have its head and its heart.
> And it's by virtue of it that France will again be—as never before—the
> head and the heart of a renewed humanity.[225]

Although weighed down with bitter sorrow, Bernanos welcomed
France's disgrace as it collapsed before Hitler's onslaught as a step in
the direction of truth, honor, and purification. Whether he really believed this or not is a moot point; but we are certain that this was
the substance of his hope. The thorough explanation for this collapse,
which he gave the whole world in his *Letter to the English*, was intended to accelerate the healing process in the manner of a vast clinical
history. In so doing, he was aware that what was at stake for France
was her soul, her eternal salvation.[226] His return home to France from
Brazil represented one final disillusionment that left him bereft of all
hope. To André Rousseaux he writes: "I get the impression that my
country has been dead for a long time, but I had never realized it.
I was its survivor without knowing it. Can I continue being a survivor

---

[223] Ibid., May 1943, 333f.
[224] Ibid., 393.
[225] Ibid., December 1947, xi.
[226] *To Amoroso Lima*, March 13, 1940, in: *Esprit*, 201; *Erbarmen*, 94.

now that I know it?"[227] And yet, six months before dying, he could still say: "Friends of my country! France is holding up." Both the Collaboration and the Resistance were "lies", and the "Liberation" was "the greatest one of them all". No, "you liars. You have not liberated France. It's France herself who, with the help of the undertaker, is liberating herself from you day by day."[228] At bottom Bernanos continued to do what he had done up to that moment: plunged into "France's long night" he endured suffering not only *for* his country but *at the hands of* his country",[229] convinced that, if "for two thousand years generation upon generation of Christians has had no other task but to live again one after the other the Lord's Passion, our own generation is entering upon the deepest secret of this agony: total solitude and total abandonment."[230] Precisely this statement shows that Bernanos' final exodus into the wilderness had nothing to do with desertion. To his last breath he remained at France's disposal. At the faintest authentic summons he would have run back with flying banners to participate in the genuine *Christian* French Revolution he envisioned. When Bernanos speaks about the conditions in France and the particular mission entrusted to her, he is uttering no doctrines belonging to a dimension above and outside of time but rather truths that apply to today and every day. Only truths that are thus spoken within time can have an effect on the time. Bernanos remains the watchman on the tower, perennially on the lookout for the truth that is coming.

---

[227] January 1946, *C. du R.*, 329.

[228] *To Gallimard*, December 1947; *Croix*, x.

[229] *To Rousseaux*, February 1, 1946, in: *C. du R.*, 329; *Geduld*, 100. (The italics are the translator's.—TRANS.)

[230] *To E. G. de Mata Machado*, June 16, 1942, in: *Geduld*, 95.

II. THE CHURCH WITHIN TIME

1. The Face of Christendom

The Christian is a man of his time. No one expects the Church's supernatural means of grace to shield him from the influences of his cultural environment, which always has both its bright and its dark sides. The central point of Bernanos' thought in this connection may be summed up very simply as follows: In the case of modern man, it is his personal freedom—the foundation of all genuine culture and religion—that is ever more imperiled. Machines and social conditions are increasingly narrowing man's horizons, to the point that he is more and more becoming a pack animal. At the same time, by contrast to other Christian churches, the distinguishing mark of Catholic faith is a strong ecclesial obedience. The logical conclusion, for Bernanos, is that nothing could be more devastating than a confusion, or even an approximation, of both phenomena: the drive to produce mass-man and the power of ecclesial obedience, as if the universal malleability and steerability of modern man nicely coincided with the Catholic principle of obedience, indeed, as if the weakening of human freedom and individual power of decision represented an advantage for the Church! The contrary, in fact, must be vigorously affirmed: Whatever weakens the interior powers of the ethical person by the same token deprives the Church of a portion of her efficacy in the world. If each and every Christian is a part and a representative of the Church in the world, then each and every Christian must, by the active engagement of his whole person, make the world realize something of the total freedom from and transcendence above the world that are the Church's.

On this point Bernanos could be alarmingly grave. He could not offer enough proofs to substantiate his anxiety in this connection or alert Christians loudly enough to the creeping, epidemic sickness secretly affecting freedom, since for him the soundness of Catholic obedience stood and fell, precisely, with the soundness of human freedom. By every means available he sought to persuade Christians that they too have somehow necessarily contracted the plague of the times and that they therefore have the duty to implement conscious countermeasures, for the healing of the world may be expected from no one else but Christians. Here we can really understand what Bernanos is all about only if we do not lose from sight the integrity of his loyalty to the Church. What he so sharply criticized in Christians—both those who command and those who obey in the Church—was whatever in them seemed to him to endanger authentic ecclesial obedience, which he did not for a moment question or turn into a problem.

"A good number of those who go to Mass on Sunday are not any less despiritualized than all the rest, appearances to the contrary notwithstanding. They ingest a food they are no longer capable of assimilating, like diabetics who seem to eat with good appetite but are in fact devouring their own substance."[1] The modern world, lacking all spirit and freedom, appears to Christians to be still far off, far outside their own ambit: "You tell me you'll have the time to see it coming. It has already come. It is within you, taking shape within you. How different you already are from all those who went before you in the course of the ages! With what ease you put up with things! How well you submit! But your children, alas, will be capable of putting up with even more things, of submitting even more."[2] Propaganda and the party are today what regulate individual conscience, "for instance, which injustices should make us indignant and which should leave us indifferent. Consciences nowadays revolt only on command against people subjecting women and children to abominable tortures. Unfortunately, this holds true as much for Christians as for everyone else." Now, since the watchwords put forth by propaganda are astoundingly short-lived and therefore full of inherent contradictions, those who are steered by propaganda become accustomed to a great malleability of conscience, and their conscience, exhausted by continually changing positions, becomes inclined to affirm a priori the truthfulness of propaganda. The consequences are palpable: "indifference to both the truth and lies", "spiritual anemia", "a faculty of judgment prostrate with fatigue and disgust".[3]

Someone will object, however, that the wheel of history cannot be turned back. Man is a historical being conditioned by situations

---

[1] *Liberté*, 122–23.

[2] Ibid., 141.

[3] Ibid., 142–44.

—or so we are unceasingly assured by existentialists of every variety, including the Christian. They do not even need to be Marxists and so reduce man's subjection to history to material and economic factors. Bernanos replied by saying that human society is less like a "locomotive hurled down a railroad track" than like a "work of art that the artist's imagination is fast at work shaping and reshaping interminably."[4] For Bernanos, *this very seductive thesis of man's subjection to history already contains within itself a denial of his freedom.*

Generally speaking, we imagine the devil as characterized by

> the spirit of revolt. This opinion is most pleasing to conservatives because it authorizes them to put all the malcontents into hell and all the policemen in paradise. I don't deny the fact that the devil staged a revolt all his own. But nothing proves his having planned to lead men astray in the same way he led the Angels astray. Experience rather shows that he deems it less easy to lead us to perdition by the spirit of revolt than to debase us by the spirit of servitude. Far from intending to raise us to the satanic dignity of the rebellious Angels, his clairvoyant hatred rather ponders how to make us descend to the condition of irrational beasts.[5]

"There is a ruination of consciences that is more deplorable than the ruination of bodies, more widespread and far-reaching than any heresy of past centuries."[6]

> This sclerotic hardening and stiffening of consciences, this drying-up of the soul's deepest wellsprings, is a universal phenomenon. But for thirteen long months I have been observing it in my own country, among my own people, with an inward, almost religious anguish and a sacred dread. God is going away, God is withdrawing from us, and how empty and heavy at once he is leaving us! . . . We have lost that interior freedom that was our inherited privilege, . . . and it's God we have lost along with it. In order to find it again, it will not be enough to desire it anew or to moan for its loss or to look in the pharisaism of social justice for some sort of alibi that doesn't fool God.[7]

---

[4] Ibid., 168–69.
[5] *Anglais*, 238–39.
[6] *To Jorge de Lima*, January 1941, in: *Lettres inédites*, 38.
[7] *Liberté*, 186–87. (Excerpt from a talk given in September 1946, at the Rencontres Internationales de Genève.)

Whatever anyone may say, freedom "can in fact come to die in the heart of men".[8] Even after the defeat of totalitarian systems, "everywhere in the world there remain focuses of infection of the totalitarian spirit,[9] because "the disciplines imposed by technology have gradually, if not wholly ruined, then at least considerably weakened the individual's self-defense reflexes against the collectivity."[10] Everything lures him to entrust himself blindly to the Providence of the great whole that provides for him so magnificently through all the stages of childhood, school, professional advancement, and social security—from maternity clinic to crematorium!

If we question Bernanos concerning the counterforces he envisions, his whole attitude and answers will at first surprise us, not indeed because he warns us against a false resignation[11] and the passive attitude of the victim,[12] but because throughout his life Bernanos opposed all Catholic "collaboration" and "presence" in the preparations for the "new world". He resolutely opposed the contemporary Catholic policy of "catching the [current cultural] wind in one's sails". Soon after the end of World War I, he was already expressing disgust over the modern methods of Catholic apologetics.[13] Despite his friendship with many Dominicans, we likewise encounter severe misgivings concerning fashionable Neo-Thomism.[14] And he was full of scornful distrust on the occasion of Cardinal Suhard's famous pastoral letter of 1947: "For fifty years now I've been hearing these impostors denounce a world without God—no God in the schools, no God in the world—and here they now are, reproaching me for not having enough *trust* in the world!"[15] This is a paradoxical statement, precisely because Bernanos was no less vigorous in attacking the ghetto mentality within the Church, as is amply shown by *The Great Fear of the Right-Thinking* and *The Great Cemeteries under the Moon*. And what disdain (with an aftertaste of youthful resentment) he piled on the "closed jars" that were for him the seminaries and the teaching or-

---

[8] Ibid., 178.

[9] Ibid., 106.

[10] Ibid., 107.

[11] Ibid., 129–30, 246f.; *Cimetières*, 225.

[12] *Liberté*, 128f.

[13] *To Dom Besse*, Ascension 1919; *Bul.* 11, 11; *Geduld*, 21f.

[14] *Croix*, November 1940, 63.

[15] *To Estang*, May 31, 1947; *Bul.* 1, 7. (The italics are the translator's.—TRANS.)

ders! What bitterness elicited by the lifelessness and languor of Catholic programs, with their defeatist vocabulary of "besiegement", "conservation", "defense", in short, "everything in the world except the vocabulary of victors".[16] The "museum-like atmosphere" of much Catholic discourse smothered him, and the sweet prettiness of many chapels "nauseated" him.[17] This apparent contradiction in Bernanos' attitude vanishes if, with him, we view occasional "sorties" outside the ghetto of the closed Church more as an enterprise in clerical politics than as a simple fulfillment of the Christian mission and if we take into account Bernanos' deep-seated distrust of the genuineness, maturity, and rootedness of such actions. So deep-set a distrust could appear to be unhealthy, and, despite its salutary function as warning, it could have the effect of paralyzing more people than it fired with zeal.

In order to understand such animus on the part of Bernanos, we cannot lose from sight the fact that, for both Bernanos and Péguy, the shrinking of "Christendom" to "the Church" and the loss of Christianity's self-evident claim upon and possession of "temporal existence" represented a colossal and irretrievable loss whose effects permeated the whole of Christian life and thought. Relative to this, it is a matter of indifference whether the modern Church tends to turn away more from the world or toward the world. Consequently, the first of these options would be imputed to the Church by Bernanos as "fear", and the second as "political opportunism". Occasionally Bernanos dared to dream the dream of ancient Christendom to its logical conclusion: "We were in the process of founding an empire, my boy, compared to the likes of which that of the Cæsars would have looked like sheer muck under our feet: peace, the *Pax Romana*, but the real one this time. A Christian people—that's what we could have created all together."[18] It was a vision of power and joyfulness, as the Curé de Torcy assures us. For a "Christian at home in Christendom", the Gospel does not merely imply "Catholic action"; rather, it is something that leavens the whole dough: "the laws, the mores, the sorrows, and even the pleasures" of human life.[19] A people cannot be

---

[16] *Français*, 212.

[17] Ibid., 268.

[18] *Curé*, 27.

[19] *Cimetières*, 15.

created with the "élites" grown in clerical hothouses,[20] especially not
with those "selected products" protected against the dangers of life
by the windshields of religious boarding schools—"fine young men"
who are turned into "old men" before they are allowed to be children.[21] The Christian thrives only in the open air, hardened by the
dangerous world in which Christ has placed him and into which he
has expressly sent him: "The Church has strong nerves. Sin doesn't
frighten her—on the contrary. She looks at it face to face, with great
calm."[22] The face of this world will be transformed, not by a Catholic
"action" that in its own quiet way engages in political strategies and
makes clever moves on the chessboard, but by free and courageous
Christians willing to give the best of themselves and risk all possible
dangers. Strategy is always bent on power, and, since it must always
hold its cards close to its chest, it can count only on a distrustful
opponent. Still, if it is true that the Christendom of old is dead a
thousand times over, is it not in the end sufficient for the individual
Christian to make the spirit of ancient Christendom continue to live
in him, with no thought given to "strategy" but only by virtue of a
daring feat of self-commitment? Olivier, in the *Country Priest*, thinks
this does suffice, and Bernanos along with him.

"Christendom created Europe. Christendom is dead. Europe is going to cave in. Nothing could be simpler."[23] This would indeed be
simple if the *spirit* of Christendom had died along with its earthly form
and been replaced with the spirit of mere "church politics", which
no dictator and no totalitarian state of either the present or the future
need be afraid of: "The modern State has a good understanding of the
Catholic busy in different 'works', the Catholic belonging to 'associations' and 'Catholic Action', in short, the Catholic with a purely clerical formation. . . . The modern State doesn't have much to fear from
such a fine young man because it knows his kind: it has supervised his
birth and upbringing, it has the certainty that it can keep him under
control for as long as it pleases, which is to say, for as long as it cares
to negotiate with the young man's responsible superiors."[24] Bernanos

---

[20] Ibid., 55.
[21] Ibid., 227.
[22] *Curé*, 27.
[23] *Cimetières*, 155.
[24] *Enfants*, 152, 153.

is here referring not only to the moral innocuousness of the type of man that is thus created but also to *the absence of a Christian dimension in him*: the lack of a certain depth of mystery that is not so much a mystery shrouded in unintelligibility for secular man as an ineffable mystery resulting from the inexplicable power of Christian presence and self-assertion in the world. The world cannot, in any event, do away with the scandal the Church represents for it,[25] not even by allowing the Church an ever more limited space within the world[26] and by seeing to it that the Church's air supply is cut off. The authentic scandal the Church must offer, however, is the one she provokes in the world by living the fullness and totality of ecclesial truth, not by the pathetic spectacle of an existentially diminished half-truth![27] The world must learn that no worldly power can make the Church pliable for its own purposes[28] and that it is an "idiotic maneuver" for the world to try to "associate" the Church with its designs, because the Church cannot be fitted into a network of "realistic" schemes.[29] The true scandal the Church offers is something liberating because it creates freedom, but this can occur only when the ideal with which the Christian confronts that of modern society differs from it down to the roots. The Gospel's most important values and categories must be shown to cut right across the icons of desire of a humanity on the ascendancy:

> "You shall know the tree by its fruits"—that's what Scripture teaches you. A certain kind of justice is also known by its fruits, even when it embellishes itself with the name of *social*, as we saw in Mallorca at the time of the imposture of Spain's "Holy Crusade", when we unmasked a certain "order" that also called itself *social* and even *Christian*. . . . Justice that is not according to Christ, justice without love, soon becomes a rabid beast. It would be mad to think that justice, even when it has been "debaptized" and de-Christianized and voided of all spiritual content, could still be something vaguely resembling real justice and at all use-

---

[25] *Anglais*, 235f.

[26] *To Maitre*, March 1917, in: *Bernanos*, 32.

[27] *Vérité*, 56–57.

[28] *Anglais*, 166. (In this text of September 1941, Bernanos addresses himself to President Roosevelt, saying that the American bishops' call "for a Crusade in favor of Christian Democracy" is a "momentous" event, but no more so "than the call of the Spanish episcopate in favor of the Phalangist Crusade" [*Anglais*, 163].—Note of the French trans.)

[29] *Anglais*, 158.

ful. . . . It would be like saying that a dog with rabies could still be a good companion to be kept by one's side.[30]

Such are the words—and these passages are not unusual—of the same man who spoke out so vigorously for the rights of workers against the hypocrisies of the bourgeoisie and who insisted so strongly on actual social engagement as opposed to the merely theoretical development of clerical programs. In this case, he much preferred to be branded a Romantic reactionary than to be aligned in the camp of the *petits curés progressistes*. Christendom can be produced only from the fullness of the Gospel and not from the clever mixture of equal parts God's Word and the demands of the times. Bernanos could not countenance the project of first responding to the demands of "progress", and then, "once the planet has been thoroughly accoutered with these industrious animals according to the best prescriptions of technology, there will always be time to convert and baptize them, that is, to give them what they would still be lacking. Such is the train of thought of a species of imbecile peculiar to certain Catholic circles."[31] What should rather be done, from the outset and with the full depth of one's being, is to inveigh—in the name of the freedom of the person —against an ideal of progress that, when promoted for its own sake, must necessarily imperil and indeed destroy the free person.[32] This opposition to "progress" is indispensable regardless of how difficult and exhausting it may be.[33] But the Christian never loses that hope that "cannot be taught like grammar and that, like faith, is a grace of God. It's enough for us to be ready to receive it."[34]

2. Obedience and Responsibility

At the level of principles it is not difficult to apply what we have been saying to the relationship between the Christian and the Church's hierarchical ministry. The central concern is how to safeguard the authentic Christian virtue of obedience from all infiltrations by modern

---

[30] *Liberté*, 166–67.
[31] Ibid., 205.
[32] Ibid., 7, 38.
[33] Ibid., 102, 207.
[34] Ibid., 248f.

defeatism. In other words the genuine, Christian, that is, supernatural childlikeness of obedience must be safeguarded from confusion with an all-too-nonsupernatural infantilism that is all the more nefarious when it hides behind an ideal of "blind obedience". In his novels[35] Bernanos showed how far the mystery of spiritual direction by someone in the sacramental ministry can lead a chosen individual: indeed, into the very night of self-surrender. Such direction, moreover, always opened the subject more and more to the highest forms and ways of Christian freedom and responsibility. What we are concerned with at present is something wholly different: namely, the dangers posed to the Christian person and his free responsibility by a flight to obedience, or, more exactly, a flight to conformism, "the blissful servitude that dispenses one from both willing and acting, that doles out a little task to each one and that, in the near future, will have transformed man into the biggest and most ingenious of insects—a colossal ant."[36]

With trepidation Bernanos recalled a motto used by soldiers during World War I to encourage one another in the blind execution of orders that may have been incomprehensible and even senseless. The motto ran: *Faut pas chercher à comprendre*—"You mustn't try to understand."[37] This formula, uttered by the *poilus*[38] in a tone of defeatist humor, took on a very humorless form in the German trenches across the way, where a Kantian moral imperative prevailed without which the rise of Nazism would have been unthinkable. In 1944 we see Bernanos summing up the situation: "The horrors we have just witnessed, and the far worse ones we will soon see, are by no means a sign that the number of untamable rebels, mutineers, and insurgents is increasing in the world, but rather a sign that what is steadily on the rise—with bewildering speed—is the number of the obedient and the docile, of those who, according to the famous expression of the First War, *didn't try to understand.*"[39]

---

[35] See above, the section on "Obedience" in Part 2, Chapter 2.

[36] *Peur*, 277.

[37] *Curé*, 12; *Enfants*, 48f.; *Français*, 143; *Robots*, 114, 217; *Croix*, 388.

[38] *Poilus*: the "shaggy ones", a popular term referring to French infantrymen during World War I.—TRANS.

[39] *Robots*, 215–17.

With a curiosity laced with terror, I am seeing a steady growth in the number of those persons who, while no less active or capable or lively than others in the defense of their temporal goods, are trying to live in the world as if they didn't live in it. They are contentedly working out their salvation all alone, for themselves alone, and, with a kind of spiritual rapture, they delight in repeating this formula: *I do not understand. I obey without understanding. I no longer understand anything. What bliss!* So doing, they think they've reached the peak of the contemplative life, but they don't for all that fail to keep a watchful eye on their bank account.[40]

"Ordinary people no longer try to understand anything, and they've even developed a taste for such detachment. Little by little they're falling into the superstitious optimism of the incurable, which above all refrains from asking the doctor for explanations even were he inclined to give any."[41]

"The saints were obedient, not docile,"[42] but the bourgeoisie "gladly leaves its conscience on consignment. It invests its conscience as it invests its money, not being very concerned with drawing huge interest as long as the household enjoys full security."[43] "The reverend Jesuit Fathers may boast of having shaped Catholic opinion. The only question remaining is whether such docility is based on indifference or not."[44] "Docility can for a while take the place of enthusiasm and love, but in the long run it enfeebles these. Whoever knows only how to obey his leaders blindly risks falling under the dominance of bad masters."[45] "Whoever *obeys* everyone without distinction no longer knows what it means to *serve*."[46] "Those trained to obey blindly are the same ones who will suddenly disobey blindly. To obey without discussion is by no means the same thing as to obey without understanding, and total docility is not as far as we think from total revolt. Christian obedience has by nature a heroic character."[47] *"Total obedience seems to me to be contrary to honor because a person cannot serve two*

---

[40] Ibid., 142–43.
[41] *Croix*, December 1943, 388.
[42] *Enfants*, 86. (The italics are von Balthasar's.—TRANS.)
[43] Ibid., 86–87.
[44] Ibid., 227.
[45] *Français*, 170.
[46] *Croix*, October 1941, 149. (The italics are von Balthasar's.—TRANS.)
[47] Ibid., December 1944, 465.

absolutes."[48] Here Bernanos is pitting what he most highly values—
honor—against another value—obedience—which, according to him,
has unjustly usurped the highest priority by unjustifiably overextending beyond its own sphere something that is good and desirable in
its proper place. Totalitarianism and, more specifically, "total war use
methods that are close to being something like a *sacrilegious and ironical
transposition of the 'Spiritual Exercises' of Saint Ignatius* in order to form
the sort of man who, *perinde ac cadaver* [in the manner of a corpse],
will be capable of all manner of submission and violence, going indifferently from one to the other."[49]

For all its audacity, such a statement is nonetheless formulated with
nobility and prudence. In order to understand it we must keep three
things in mind.

In the first place, the Christian tradition has always turned its back
on Tertullian's motto, *"credo quia absurdum"* (I believe it because it is
absurd) and instead always favored and defended Augustine's *"credo
ut intelligam"* (I believe in order to understand) and Anselm's *"fides
quærens intellectum"* (faith seeking understanding) as most closely reflecting its spirit. This applies so emphatically to obedience in matters of faith that already Paul declared the effort to understand to be
the urgent duty of every Christian—the effort, that is, to penetrate
as deeply as possible, in the light of God's grace, into the meaning
of the mysteries that are first believed on the basis of God's authority. However, like every other Christian, Bernanos always admitted
unquestioningly that such "intelligence" of the mysteries of faith is
possible only on the basis of an antecedent faith.[50] Furthermore, the
Catholic doctrine of the *præambula fidei* requires a preliminary intuition or recognition on my part of the credibility of the person who
is exacting an act of faith from me: *"Scio cui credidi"*, writes Saint Paul
—"I know in whom I have believed" (2 Tim 1:12). What holds for
the obedience of faith even with respect to God himself obviously
holds as well (a fortiori, we may say!) for the ecclesial obedience
derived from that primal act of obedience in faith. For the act of ec-

---

[48] Ibid., February 6, 1945, 487.
[49] *Robots*, 116. (The italics are von Balthasar's.—TRANS.)
[50] *Croix*, December 25, 1943, 391–92: The skeptic, precisely, is "a man who reasons before
believing, admiring, or loving".

clesial obedience is made by responsible persons endowed with the cognitive faculty, even if they (as with every form of obedience) are doing the will of another, in this case an other who is an authority set over them by God.

In the second place, the ideal of obedience put forth by Ignatius of Loyola did not propose a single novelty heretofore unknown in the Christian tradition. What he did do was cast much light on and rejuvenate the dimensions of Christian obedience, above all its character as bold venture, with respect both to the person commanding and the person obeying. Ignatius spoke out most energetically against a purely passive obedience that executes an order mechanically, without the full engagement of the whole person in this process. In other words, he opposed a mere "obedience of the will" that is not also an "obedience of the understanding", which is to say, a comprehending obedience that has understanding on the very basis of the personal movement to obey, much as ecclesial faith must inwardly possess a movement toward the *intellectus fidei*. We could really expect no other doctrine from Ignatius, very much a man of the Renaissance, whom we see sending his sons out to undertake tasks requiring a highly developed sense of personal responsibility. The delimiting concept of "blind obedience" is here necessary as a reminder that obedience (like faith) continues to deserve its name only as long as the motive of action does not coincide with the obeying person's subjective insights and self-assurance. Furthermore, "blind obedience" can constitute something like the exuberant culmination of a "visionary" obedience wherein the transcending of natural in favor of supernatural certainty, rooted in God and in the Church, takes on the character of a wholesale surrender and sacrifice of one's one vision to the divine and ecclesial view of things. This extreme possibility has its rightful place only in the sphere of loving trust proper to Christian childlikeness, something so highly praised by Bernanos. This exceptional ideal of "blind obedience", therefore, cannot be legitimately transposed to the secular plane of the State, as a mere glance at the ancient world, especially as portrayed in Plutarch's *Lives of Illustrious Greeks and Romans*, will make amply clear. Bernanos, consequently, was quite right to insist that "supernatural obedience and the other sort should not be put practically on the same plane."[51] In any event,

---

[51] *Français*, 147.

one thing is certain: "blind" obedience should be looked upon as an extreme manifestation and not as the ordinary form of Christian obedience.

In the third place, a particular possibility of obedience within the Church is offered by the obedience of the religious orders, which involves a surrender of one's own will by making it available to legitimate superiors. This surrender of the will in obedience parallels the surrender of the procreative faculty in virginity and that of personal possessions in poverty. Such a sacrifice can be easily understood in the context of traditional monasticism, which is predominantly contemplative. The question of how it can be justified in the newer, more active orders brings up somewhat more difficult problems that are beyond our present scope. For we should know that, whenever he spoke of Christian obedience, Bernanos was always careful to respect the particular character of obedience in the religious orders, and he explicitly excluded the latter from the discussion. In one letter, for instance, he protests against certain "travesties of the renunciation required by the Gospel"; but he adds at once that what he is saying does not apply "once a person has surrendered his freedom into the hands of his regular superiors in the context of the monastic life."[52] "Outside the religious state, blind obedience is something risky."[53] It goes without saying that he would like to communicate something of his own concept of obedience even to contemplative monasteries, which is why he has one of the senior Carmelites from Compiègne say to her sisters after their first night in prison:

> My dear girls! I can well imagine that, at your age, obedience still seems to you to be a soft pillow, and all you have to do is lay your heads upon it. But we who have more experience—we know that obeying, which appears so different from commanding, is also a burden. Yes, indeed, my dear girls! It is just as hard to learn how to obey as how to command. To obey is not to let yourself be led along passively like a blind man following his dog. An old religious like me desires nothing more than to die in obedience, but an active and conscious obedience. We dispose of nothing in this world, that's for sure. But it isn't any less true that our death is our death, and no one can die in my place.[54]

---

[52] *To Amoroso Lima,* March 13, 1940; *Esprit,* 202.

[53] Ibid., June 1940; *Esprit,* 204.

[54] *Carmélites,* 218–19.

Bernanos would not be Bernanos if he did not have a deep sense of the power of religious obedience, of the wondrous scandal exhibited when someone "who possesses all the necessary experience to command . . . and an outstanding faculty of will should nevertheless choose to live in the world with all the simplicity, innocence, and spirit of submission of a small child."[55] Such admiration for the value of vowed obedience, however, did not prevent him from protesting against the unexamined extension of this particular form of obedience and its imposition upon the ecclesial obedience of the Christian who lives a life of commitment within the world. He even objected to monastic obedience being held up as sufficient ideal and model for "ordinary" ecclesial obedience. As far as Bernanos was concerned, such a model would be as inadequate as holding up the life of vowed virginity as a model for married people, or the life of vowed poverty as the model to be imitated by people who own property and are responsible for its administration. This would be a new form of the Church's monasticization, which would not only contradict the whole spirit of the Church but would run directly counter to the Church's present task. Such a "monastic" transformation would be particularly dire at this moment in the world's history, when totalitarianism is rampant, when the Church, consequently, is responsible for safeguarding the world's legitimate and specifically *secular* freedom as well as the integrity of the moral person.

The line must therefore be drawn in a double sense: on the one hand, Christian obedience over against State obedience (most especially if the State is totalitarian); on the other hand, within the Church, lay obedience over against vowed obedience in the religious orders. The moment responsibility in the world comes into play, obedience can no longer be the sole norm—even though this by no means questions or "restricts" it. Already in the very first pages of his *Journal*, the country priest writes: "I'm quite aware that the superiors are there. Only, who is it that keeps the superiors abreast of realities? We do. So, when the obedience and simplicity of the monks are held up to us, I'm not too touched by the arguments, try as I might. . . . We're all capable of peeling potatoes and watching the pigs as long as a novice master is there to tell us what to do. But a parish? Ah, it's not so

---

[55] *Joie*, 94.

easy to lavish acts of virtue on it as on a simple community!"[56] The regard given to responsibility or to "honor" is not a "restriction" or an emasculation of Christian obedience; it simply makes obedience take into consideration the whole of Christian life, of which it is but a part.

The responsibility of the person obeying is so primary a factor that it necessarily engages at once the absolute responsibility of the person commanding for this responsibility of the person obeying. And, when a subordinate burdened with responsibility makes his person available to a superior in obedience to God, this gesture of trust on his part engages the *person* of the superior. It is a total impossibility for a personal relationship of obedience to remain completely one-sided, that is, for a superior to respond to a subordinate's offer of obedience merely with the impersonal attitude of an official administrator. This holds not only for the natural ethos of obedience, nor only for the common ecclesial obedience binding on every Catholic; it also holds for the special obedience of the religious orders, as is most splendidly seen in the spiritual fatherhood of the Benedictine abbot. The openness and self-surrender of the obeying person is something so extraordinary that the resulting "nakedness"—most graphically illustrated by Saint Francis in the central square of Assisi—must at once be embraced and covered over by the superior's mantle of personal love. In other words, even the most hierarchical and official of relationships between obeyer and obeyed does not dispense from love. And this principle results in other consequences: the reality of love can never be replaced with a mere sacramental office (this holds for the superior), nor can love be "bought" with merely official obedience (this holds for the subordinate). No superior in the Church is entitled to exact love from a subordinate (and true obedience is always love!) merely on the basis of his hierarchical office *unless he himself intends* to reciprocate love with Christian and personal love in the measure of his own capabilities. But if a superior nevertheless exacts an obedient love without intending to reciprocate it, then he becomes guilty of a serious fault against the subordinate who is obeying him out of love.

---

[56] *Curé*, 12.

This is the point at which Bernanos' criticism begins in earnest. It targets the kind of reverence given the holder of a hierarchical office when such homage corresponds to nothing real in the actual person of the officeholder. Bernanos observes how merely formal respect can often degenerate into sheer flattery and fulsomeness, and so he objects to the fawning attitudes shown

> the most insignificant superior of a major seminary who only yesterday was a total nonentity to his little flock and yet, on the day of his installation, is quite prepared to accept without blinking panegyrics that would have embarrassed a Saint Athanasius or a Saint Augustine. . . . Yes, I know: it's the dignity of the office that is being extolled, and I'm sure the office is worthy of such praise. But when an unknown person can appear to make such easy claims on our love, aren't we running the risk of atrophying in us a creative will that, in order to thrive, requires opposition from others and a measure of self-doubt just as a seed sown in the wild requires the stimulus of showers and wind? What serious writer or artist would not want to flee from the sickening atmosphere of family admirers, even if such admiration is sincere?[57]

The extravagant honors, occasionally bordering on hysteria, shown at times to the highest dignitaries in the Church—against the express teaching of the Church![58]—are often generated and exploited by interested, calculating parties who in this way "profiteer for their own enterprises".[59] And not seldom a "blind parroting" of the (alleged) official ecclesiastical line is confused with a *sentire cum Ecclesia* (thinking with the mind of the Church) that is genuine, virile, and responsible. In his famous "Letter to Amoroso Lima" of 1940, which he considered programmatic, Bernanos speaks with considerable bitterness of a danger inherent in Catholic Action: he means the policy of viewing—as the "sole totally legitimate activity" of the militant Catholic—the habitual "apology for ecclesiastical authority and its methods, the delirious exaltation of its least successes and the concealment of its failures".[60] In this Bernanos sees the upsetting of the equilibrium that ought to obtain between obedience and responsibility: "You say

---

[57] *Français*, 208–9.

[58] *Croix*, November 1944, 461 (referring to the "fetishism that some devout people are in the habit of exhibiting in connection with the Holy Father").

[59] Ibid., November 1944, 462.

[60] *To Amoroso Lima*, January 1940, in: *Esprit*, 193; *Erbarmen*, 85.

that . . . , by obeying, you don't run any risks! This is lying by telling only a half-truth."[61] "The freedom the Church allows us is a positive good, a positive right, and we have the duty to use it for her glory instead of burying it like the talent in the Gospel. There is a risk, of course there is. . . . There's a risk in everything. We must accept that risk humbly. The virtue of fortitude was given us just for this."[62]

These principles naturally apply above all where the inner-worldly policies of the Vatican are concerned and the Church's infallibility is not at stake. Bernanos was wont to criticize specific acts of Vatican politics with considerable frequency.[63] In so doing, however, he for the most part exempted from his criticism the acts of the pope himself as chief shepherd, out of deference to the sensibilities and opinions of ordinary Catholics.[64] At the same time, however, Bernanos underscored the difference in the times, which now no longer had the same sense of "prestige" that formerly was automatically accorded the dignity of office. The sophisticated means of information now in current use make it senseless to have recourse to simple public denials or hush tactics that in a previous era could still be effective as means of averting scandal.[65] After the Liberation, Bernanos insisted that the Church should herself discipline those of her members guilty of collaboration with the Nazis and, indeed, remove them from office in the case of clergy as the State had done with collaborators: "It is deeply regrettable that the Church should have been compromised by a certain number of heartless and brainless men. But how could we conceal a fact known by all? We cannot at the same time safeguard both the truth and prestige." By attempting to do so, Catholics would bring more damage than benefit to the Church.[66] Likewise, Bernanos was convinced that frank "irreverence"—such as he exhibits in the *Great Cemeteries* with regard to the attitude of the Spanish hierarchy during the Civil War—"will in the end be more beneficial [to the

---

[61] Ibid., 194; *Erbarmen*, 86.

[62] Ibid., 204; *Erbarmen*, 97.

[63] *Vérité*, 59f.; on Italy and the Church: *Vérité*, 64; *Cimetières*, 23, 169, 295f; *Enfants*, 226f.; *Croix*, 267f.; on Spain, see *Cimetières*, passim; on collaboration with the Nazis, see *Croix*, 86, 152, 179, 198, 271f., 280f., 325.

[64] *Croix*, 70, 227; see 409f.

[65] *Enfants*, 142f.; *Cimetières*, 201; *Vérité*, 63; *Croix*, 64–67, 345, 451f.

[66] *Croix*, October 1944, 450–52.

Church] than the blind submissiveness of conformists" and an official strategy of concealment.[67]

Behind all the various injuries and dangers to the Church exposed by Bernanos, the common denominator is always the one temptation: to abuse the supernatural guarantees of efficacy inherent in the hierarchical office by "overextending" the principle of sacred ordination into spheres where it cannot apply. From another perspective the same abuse could be described as the excessive exoneration of the principle of the morally responsible person, *as if hierarchical office could somehow conceal and compensate for deficiencies in the personal realm.* This danger touches all Catholics in the same measure; for, whereas the lukewarm or mediocre cleric relies too much on the sacredness of his "office", the laity relies too much on the "automatic" efficacy of the Church's "means of grace". The responsible pastoral parties must unceasingly be made aware of the dangers and possible detriments to the Church that can come precisely from greater advantages and privileges.[68] And this is just what Bernanos did, often bluntly and without genuflections but always with a deep honesty and childlike attitude. To doubt this in order to weaken his arguments would be a shabby move indeed. A person like him, who, as the saying goes, always "bore his heart on his tongue", was utterly incapable of underhandedness. He was engaged in a fight for the moral values he most highly treasured: honor, truthfulness, childlike sincerity, and the manly courage of the Christian who steps forward and is at all times ready to enter combat for his beloved Church, provided no one constrains him to use lying and dishonor as weapons in this struggle. His chief arm for doing battle was the truth and not strategy, and by "truth" we should here understand the fullness of supernatural truth reaching down to the most hidden depths of the mystery of the Church, as our analysis of his novels has amply shown. This being so, Christians should not react like overdelicate sissies if now and then a justified or even (in God's name) unjustified blow from Bernanos' sword should graze them. A good field of wheat is always grateful for a cleansing thundershower. Even if a few stalks should break, most of them come out refreshed and breathing more freely.

---

[67] Ibid., September 1943, 373.

[68] On the question of "infallibility" as a "two-edged sword", see *Croix*, July 1942, 226f.

3. Blessed the Poor in Spirit!

One of Bernanos' chief concerns was thus a reform of the spirit of ecclesial obedience—truly of the *spirit* by contrast to the choking overgrowth of the *letter* of obedience. Similarly, in the end, what most greatly concerned him was a renewal of the spirit of poverty. He meant this in so central and elemental a sense that all Catholics must listen in astonishment. For, in the first place, Bernanos was not interested in the factually fictitious material poverty of most people living in religious orders today: what interested him was literal poverty, the real lack of material and spiritual means of numberless people only a minority of whom are Christians and almost never religious with vows. Nor, on the other hand, was Bernanos concerned with purely social and economic questions, with the practical ways in which this plight of the poor could be helped. Rather, he was concerned with the gospel, with poverty of spirit, which for him was closer than we think to poverty as an evangelical counsel.

In a moment we will enter into the specifics of this rather difficult network of questions. But first we should consider that, if to his emphasis on responsible obedience and poverty of spirit we add the virginal character of Bernanos' saintly heroes, it becomes clear that the geometrical locus, so to speak, of Bernanos' view of Christian existence is that defined by the intersection of Christ's three evangelical counsels with fullness of existence in the world. The most authentic Christian locus, according to Bernanos, is the place where the two contrary forms and ideals of Christian life—that of the cloister or the religious orders and that of the laity in the world—open up to one another. At the same time, ecclesiologically speaking, this is the locus of the Church's essential transcendence into the world, the locus where the Church's innermost mystery must necessarily remain open with respect to the world. This sphere has long remained unnoticed, and yet, in today's situation, it has begun to cast a bright glow and attract the attention of all those intent on God's Kingdom. The "secular institutes" have sought to install themselves within this sphere and locus in an ecclesial form. Bernanos and Péguy—and in his own way Reinhold Schneider, too[69]—were primarily concerned, not with

---

[69] See Hans Urs von Balthasar, *Reinhold Schneider* (Cologne: Verlag Hegner, 1953) 237f.

practical projects of this kind, but with clarifying and understanding
the ecclesial situation and testing the waters through a living and, if
need be, painful experience. Bernanos, in particular, reflected on this
whole question in a state of total openness, preferring to say too little
rather than too much and to speak in paradoxes and apparent contradictions rather than narrowing the horizon and laying down inflexible
principles prematurely.

Both Communist ideology and the liberal West have agreed on
one thing: the poor should and must disappear. With the increasing
progress of culture and the steady rise in living standards, the poor
are basically condemned to die out. The Church has nothing decisive
to oppose to this unanimous resolve. As long as there (still) are poor
people in the world, the Church will strive to look after them. And
yet, we will scarcely find any Christians who give serious consideration to the Christian necessity that there be poor people in this world.
But Bernanos, for one, did entertain such thoughts, like Péguy and
Bloy before him. Much as they part ways on other issues, on this
one question they constitute so resonant a three-note chord that its
stentorian rumble should be enough to shake our consciences. We
will hardly be able to silence their deafening boom by objecting that
it comes from three men who were so incapable of living a practical
life that they had to raise their personal ineptitude to the plane of theories and systems. On the contrary, we cannot go too far in looking
on their earthly destiny as the specific material their lives had to work
on so that, through suffering, they might learn familiarity with the
gospel's way of thinking. Those who are sheltered in the "organized"
poverty of the monastic life do not have such direct or "easy" access
to the heart of the gospel.

Bernanos traced a bold question mark on the margin of the "poverty" of the religious orders,[70] although he was well aware of the
original impulse that motivated their founders.[71] And naturally he
knew as well that the main thing in the religious state is a "spirit"
of poverty that becomes keenest when the religious allows himself to
be expropriated and stripped down inwardly. When Blanche declares:
"I'm not afraid of poverty", Madame de Croissy, the first prioress,

---

[70] See, for instance, the speech he puts in the mouth of the Spanish bishops (*Cimetières*, 202–3) and also *Enfants*, 248, 260.

[71] *Dominique*, 24, 40.

replies: "Ah, there are many different kinds of poverty, down to the most miserable, and this is the one you will be sated with."[72] And in *Joy* Chantal says: "I was happy that God went to the trouble of laying me bare himself, and he did it so carefully that he made it impossible for me to become any poorer. I thought of myself as some wretch who had only a few coins left in his pocket and who all of a sudden realized that they were worthless, being precisely the ones withdrawn from circulation."[73]

This extreme spiritual poverty, however, has meaning and value only because Christ became the poorest one among us: poor in spirit —denuded of all power and self-defense before both God and man— and, signifying this, poor in the flesh as well: in the crib, in his carpenter's smock, in his public life, on the Cross. Christ's total poverty is unsurpassable: "The Lord lived and still lives among us as a poor man, and the moment always comes when he decides to make us poor like himself. He does this that he might be welcomed and honored by poor people, in the manner of poor people, and thus find again what he experienced so many times on the roads of Galilee— the hospitality of the wretched, their simple acceptance."[74] *The condition of poverty becomes a worthy and honorable thing by reference to Christ.* In clear contrast to riches, poverty is the garment and insignia of him who, "being rich, became poor for our sake" (2 Cor 8:9). The great hope Christianity brought into the world of the poor "was certainly not that of a dictatorship of the proletariat but that of a society in which the poor would be honored because God himself had made himself poor and had thus hallowed—not only the 'moral disposition' of poverty of spirit, as certain simoniac theologians sometimes let it be known—but the very social condition of the poor."[75] "The question is not how we can make the poor rich, since all the gold of your mines would probably not suffice for this. In any event, you'd only succeed in multiplying the pseudorich. . . . No, the question is not how we can enrich the poor but how we can honor the poor, or, rather, how we can give them the honor that is their due. It's obvious that neither the strong nor the weak can live without honor, but the weak need honor more than anyone else."[76]

---

[72] *Carmélites*, 62.
[73] *Joie*, 75.
[74] *Carmélites*, 146.

[75] *Anglais*, 199.
[76] *Cimetières*, 31–32.

This is patently a spiritual task, on the same level as the defense of
the honor of the "weaker" sex and of the aged:

It is dangerous to countenance the debasement of the weak, because the
putrefaction of the weak poisons the strong. How low would women
have fallen—I speak of *your* women and wives—if by common agreement, in the course of the ages, you had not prudently decided to respect them even though you possessed the means of subjecting them
to yourselves body and soul? You respect women and children, and it
wouldn't occur to any of you to consider their weakness something like
a slightly shameful affliction better not spoken of. If your mores have
won out over violence in this connection, why could we not see the
ignoble prestige of money also yield in its turn? Yes, the honor enjoyed
by money would be paltry indeed if you were not a sly and willing accomplice. . . . There shall never be a legitimacy of money. . . . Money
always seems to be ashamed of itself.[77]

But precisely for this reason "money, with its millions of suction
pumps, has long been sucking up day after day every bit of honor
still left in the world. . . . In the face of the monster, almost reduced
to inertia by this glut, the totalitarian State distends its cavernous gullet in order to swallow up all at once both honor and money."[78]

The men of the Middle Ages were not virtuous enough to disdain money,
but they scorned the money-men. . . . Christendom did not eliminate
the rich or enrich the poor, because it never saw the abolition of original sin as its goal. Christendom would have indefinitely postponed the
world's enslavement to money by maintaining the hierarchy of human
values and maintaining honor. By virtue of the same mysterious law that
covers with protective fur those species of animals transplanted from
temperate to polar regions, the rich, in a climate so little favorable to
their species, in the end developed a prodigious resistance and vitality.
Along with economic conditions, they patiently had to transform from
within the laws, mores, and very morality of society.

Thus, they became intent on emptying of value all the inventions of
technology and the discoveries of science: "Under the raging blows
[of the rich], Christendom perished and the Church totters."[79] The

---

[77] Ibid., 32–33.

[78] *Liberté*, 242–43.

[79] *Cimetières*, 41–43.

worst thing is that the rich have dishonored the poor in a new way: they have absorbed the poor into their own ideology, persuading them that poverty is a disgrace and wealth an honor. By so doing they have inflicted the most thorough, even if perhaps most unnoticed, attack upon the honor of Jesus Christ, and the cleverest of all attacks too on his Church, who "is the trustee of the poor, . . . and who is alone, absolutely alone, in safeguarding the honor of poverty. Ah! Our enemies do have an easy time of it!"[80]

Indeed, this protectiveness of the Church over the poor has nothing to do with fighting social backwardness, and even less with shielding off a deplorable state of affairs that nothing can change. The real crux here is *the power of the spirit* over against the power of all the world's "realisms". This power, which Christianity brought into the world and which it alone defends, is—contrary to what Nietzsche thought—not the exaltation of inferior values, but the glorification of a mysterious meta-value that transcends all forms of physical and economic will-to-power. Bernanos has written a magnificent passage on this theme:

> The right of the strong is real. It's a solid and dense matter. I agree it would be mad to believe that there is no place, precisely in a materialist society, for such solid and dense matter. *The right of the weak is spirit. Without the spirit, the weak are nothing but trash, useful only for the tiny portion of debased power still left in them. The residual power of the weak is so denatured that it becomes perceivable only if they gather in great numbers. The treasure of the destitute is spiritual, and doubtless the reason why Christ praised the social condition of the poor as blessed is that everything that falls away from the Spirit also falls away from the poor. The poor follow the destiny of the Spirit. . . .* I am a Christian because common sense and history persuade me that there will always be defeated men and that Christianity is the party of the defeated. I do not love the defeated out of some kind of morbid predilection for whatever wails and cowers. I do not want the defeated to wail or to cower. To love what wails or cowers is not at all according to my nature. Examine the history of the world up and down to your heart's content, and you will clearly see that the wretched have never been loved for their own sake. The best of mankind suffer them and tolerate them only out of pity. Through pity they are excluded from love, because the law of love is reciprocity, and reciprocity is not

---

[80] *Curé*, 74.

possible where there is pity. . . . God keep me from once again making the defeated of this world a promise that has never been kept! I
would only like to say to them that, throughout so many centuries, the
Word of Christ is the only good left them. Once I've told them this,
they can laugh in my face if they want, and I won't get angry. "What
good is a word to us?", they might ask. "Can you eat it?" And I would
reply: "Whatever the case, if this one word should be smothered, you
would become nothing. . . . Around you there is a mystery, an ineffable
presence, a spirit. You are sacred as a child is sacred. (Pay no mind to
what I say.) Whether you know it or not, the Word of Christ envelops
you because you dwell within it—you dwell within it along with your
misery. . . . You cannot eat the Spirit, that much is true. But it keeps
you from being eaten. Thanks to the Spirit, thanks to this Nothing,
your flesh is still untouchable (no offense meant!) like pork for Jews
and Moslems."[81]

Christ's statement, "The poor you will always have with you"—
that "saddest of affirmations in the Gospel"—was addressed by Jesus
to Judas, the "banker among the Twelve", who was already interested
in social welfare for the poor like any philanthropic millionaire. The
Lord's word to him meant:

Do not let the hour of mercy strike in vain. You'd do better to spend
the money you've stolen from me immediately than to turn the head
of my apostles with your fantastic speculations on the perfume market
and your projects of social works. Besides, you think that in this way
you're flattering my well-known weakness for tramps, but you couldn't
be more mistaken. I don't love my poor in the way old English ladies
love lost cats or feel sorry for the animals at a bullfight. That's the way
the rich behave. I love poverty with a deep, deliberate, and lucid love, as
equal loves equal—like a fertile and faithful wife. I crowned her[82] with
my own hands. . . . Not just anyone is capable of breaking with her the
bread of bitterness. I have desired for her to be humble and proud, not
servile. . . . If the right of the poor derived strictly from necessity, your
egotism would have soon condemned them to the strictly necessary, and
even this they would have had to repay with eternal gratitude and ser-
vility. . . . There will always be poor people among you for the simple
reason that there will always be rich people, which is to say, greedy and
hard men who look not so much for possessions as for power. And such

---

[81] *Français*, 159–61. (The italics are von Balthasar's.—TRANS.)
[82] Echoing Saint Francis, Bernanos here personifies *la pauvreté* in the feminine.—TRANS.

men as these exist among both the poor and the rich. . . . *Whether you are rich or poor, you should try to look at yourselves in poverty as in a mirror, because she is the image of your fundamental disappointment. On this earth it is she who occupies the place of the Lost Paradise. She is the emptiness of your hearts and of your hands.* The one reason why I have elevated her so high, taken her as my spouse, and crowned her is that I know your malice all too well. If I had allowed you to look on her as your enemy, or even as a stranger, if I had left you any hope of banishing her some day from the world, I would by the same token have doomed the weak. Because the weak will always be an unbearable burden to you, a dead weight that your haughty civilizations hand down one to the other with anger and disgust. I have put my sign on their forehead.[83]

The beatitude of the poor in spirit thus becomes the Magna Charta of the person and his dignity over against all claims and pretensions of the mass:

Christianity . . . divinizes man. Nothing less is required in order to balance out in some measure the enormous advantage enjoyed by the collectivity over the individual. Whoever claims to belong only to the human order will sooner or later fall victim to the brazen law of the cyclopean State. Whoever awaits only the coming of the kingdom of man will see himself deprived of the Kingdom of God, which is to say, of justice, because the triumph of man in this world can be obtained only by means of a pitiless rigor. And we will enter the earthly paradise only by riding on the belly of the poor, of the infirm, of all those precisely whom the Gospel of the Beatitudes exalts.[84]

At no moment of its evolution can the state of the world surpass and leave behind the principles of the Gospel as if they were anachronistic. Now, what the Gospel teaches us "on almost every page" is "poverty of spirit. Blessed are the poor in spirit, that is, blessed are they who possess the spirit of poverty, who retain the spirit of poverty even in the midst of opulence, because, even if they possessed everything, they would still cling to nothing."[85] This ethos is by no means a spirit and a work of supererogation: it is the fundamental Christian spirit, which should be at the center of the most elementary Christian attitude toward ownership and possession: "According to Christian law,

[83] *Curé*, 74–77. (The italics are von Balthsar's.—TRANS.)
[84] *Anglais*, 248.
[85] *Croix*, September 1942, 248.

the owner is actually but the steward of what he owns. He administers the goods for his own profit, no doubt, but also for the welfare of the community to which he is accountable. Christian law has never recognized the *jus abutendi* that allows big or small speculators the right to destroy essential articles and provisions at will so as to fix their price at a high level."[86] Even though here the chief concern is the "spirit", nevertheless this spirit can at no moment in the world's history be disjoined from the material reality of poverty or weakness that contains it: *the existence of the poor and the weak is the efficacious sign and, hence, the "sacrament", of poverty of spirit.* The spirit of childhood is inseparable from the spirit of poverty: "The poor and children are those most privileged by the Beatitudes."[87] And the spirit of childhood will always be nourished and enkindled by the existence of real children. Likewise the spirit of hope, which is also inseparable from the spirit of poverty, will always become really incarnate in the materially poor: "Hope is too sweet a food for the ambitious. It could risk softening their heart. The modern world has no time for hoping, or for loving or dreaming. It is the poor who alone perform a work of hope in and for our world, exactly as it is the saints who love and atone in our stead. . . . The meek shall inherit the earth simply because only they will not have lost the habit of hoping in a world full of people in despair."[88]

This is why the hope of the world rests on the poor: "I say that the poor shall save the world, and they will save it without intending to. They will save it despite themselves. They'll ask for nothing in return for sheer lack of any knowledge of the price of the service they have rendered. They'll succeed in this terrific transaction and will of course receive not one farthing for it."[89]

Building is always a work of love. Thus, sooner or later you'll have to appeal to a humanity you know hardly at all and with which you even refuse to acquaint yourself because its existence would reduce your theses to naught. It is an "unrealistic" humanity, in the sense you give to this word. It is a different humanity, a different species of men that you think never demands anything, but only because it doesn't need the

[86] *Croix*, 151.
[87] *Bul.* 12, 4 (dedication in an album); see also *Curé*, 304.
[88] *Enfants*, 251–52.
[89] Ibid., 248–49; see also *Croix*, 251.

same things as you. . . . But you'll never exhaust its patience, its holy
patience. Whatever you knock down, it will come right behind you
raising it up again—one time, ten times, one hundred times. It will pick
up untiringly everything you let drop. It will put it back in your hand
smiling. . . . You will never triumph over the patience of the poor—
patientia pauperum non peribit in æternum (the patience of the poor shall
not perish for ever).[90]

If all of this is true, why is the Church ashamed of the poor? Why
does she enter into disgraceful secret alliances with the bourgeois middle class? Why are the poor not to her what they were to her divine
Founder?

> After twenty centuries of Christianity—blast it all!—it should no longer
> be a shameful thing to be poor. Or, if it is, it's because you've betrayed
> him, your Christ! On this I won't change my mind. For God's blessed
> sake! You [priests] have at your disposal everything you need to humble
> the rich, to make them fall into step. The rich have this thirst for being
> fawned over, and the richer they are, the more they thirst. If you had
> only had the courage to shove them down to the last row of pews, close
> by the holy-water fount, or even out into the porch—why not?—*that*
> would have given them food for thought. They would all have leered
> toward the pew where the poor were sitting—I know them. Everywhere
> else they come first; but that here, in our Lord's house, they should come
> last: Can't you see it now? . . . The fact remains, though, that a poor
> man, a genuine poor man, an honest poor man will go all by himself
> and cling to the last places in the Lord's house, which is also his own,
> and that no one has ever seen or will ever see an usher—looking like
> a first-class hearse in his plumes—come looking for this poor man in
> the back of the church to invite him up into the sanctuary, with all
> the deference owed a prince, a prince of royal Christian blood. Such an
> idea normally makes your clerical confrères chuckle. Futile imaginings
> indeed! But why the devil do they lavish precisely such honors on the
> powerful of the earth, who lap them right up? . . . What do I care if they
> take me for an imbecile? In this I know I've got the truth by the tail,
> and the pope himself couldn't make me let go. And what I'm proposing
> here, my boy, your saints have *done* it, so it couldn't be as stupid as
> all that! In what posture do we see your saints? On their *knees* before
> the poor, the infirm, the leprous—that's how. A strange army indeed, in

---

[90] *Enfants*, 253–54; see also *Croix*, 254.

which the corporals limit themselves to giving a friendly, patronizing little pat in passing on the shoulder of the royal guest at whose feet the field marshals are prostrate![91]

These are the words of Doctor Delbende. Perturbed by the harangue, the country priest nonetheless understands that the Church is not merely "a sort of sovereign State, with its own laws, functionaries, and armies", and competent to assign to each person the social position proper to him. He realizes that, justified as Delbende's accusations may be, there is a deeper mystery hiding here beneath it all: The Church

> marches through the ages like a troop of soldiers through unknown lands where all normal provisioning is impossible. She must live on successive regimes and societies as a soldierly troop lives from day to day on the local population. How could she hand over to the poor man, God's legitimate heir, a kingdom that is not of this world? The Church is always searching for the poor man; she calls out to him on all the ways and byways of the earth. And the poor man is always in the same place, on the highest tip of the dizzying peak where he is face to face with the Lord of the Abyss, who for twenty centuries has untiringly been repeating to him, with a mellifluous and portentous voice, the one phrase: "All of this is yours if, falling down, you adore me!"

Only at this point does Bernanos fully unveil the improbable miracle of poverty: "*Power is within reach of the poor man's hand, but the poor man ignores this, or pretends to ignore it. He keeps his eyes lowered to the ground, and the Seducer awaits from moment to moment the one word that would deliver our race over to him. But this word shall not issue forth from the princely mouth that God himself has sealed.*"[92] No one is as vulnerable as the poor man, and yet it is precisely he, the most defenseless of all, who is also the one most protected by his misery. He is the friend of God. As Bernanos likes to repeat often, he "eats out of God's hand". God lowers his mantle over his nakedness. What, along with Péguy, Bernanos calls *misery* by contrast to *poverty* is something as walled in as hell itself; and yet it is open only to God and for God.[93] In *An Evil Dream*, the Russian says the following concerning misery Russian-style: "It is majestic, imposing, regal. . . . Indeed, it has all

[91] *Curé*, 96–98.
[92] Ibid., 108–9. (The italics are von Balthasar's.—TRANS.)
[93] *Vie de Jésus*, in: *Bul.* 6, 2.

the majesty of hell";[94] "it is as majestic and cold as hell."[95] One of
the elements of this misery is being deprived of faith, as the prioress
of Compiègne says: "In our prayer those who persecute us cannot be
told apart from all the other poor, or, if they can, it's only by their
greater poverty—better yet, by the most extreme misery conceivable,
since they seem bereft of the grace of God to the point of thinking
themselves to be the enemies of His Majesty."[96] The essential thing
here, however, is not the hatred of God but that condition of being
bereft of light, spirit, and hope that makes an existence in misery appear immutable. This is the state of the new Mouchette and of every truly miserable person: "Among the poor as among the rich, an
anonymous person in misery is alone, as alone as a king's son. At least
in this country of ours, misery is not something to be shared. Every
miserable person is alone in his misery. His misery belongs only to
him, like his face and his bodily members." In the Russia of olden
times, misery was the lot of a whole people: "If the Church could
raise a whole people to her altars and had chosen the Russian people
for this, she would have made it the patron saint of misery, the special
intercessor of the miserable."[97] This is why Bernanos so loved Maxim
Gorky and his memoirs of childhood, which he used as a model for
the diary kept by the country priest. They are at once a "lament" and
a "hymn", not in the sense of expressly religious prayer, of course,
but of something cryptically related to it: "I think that such misery—
a misery that has even forgotten its own name, that has given up all
search, all reasoning, and that turns its haggard face toward chance:
such misery, I say, shall one day wake up on the shoulder of Jesus
Christ."[98] This is already an "innocent revolt, which in order to express itself can only use the language of acceptance".[99]

The sick boy and the old man, who are the poor in *Monsieur Ouine*,
are the living images of this unending "lament of existence", this
"moaning" and "solemn sighing":[100] "For all that, he had no courage.
Nor did he suffer. All he did was bear with his sorrow in his own

---

[94] *Rêve*, 130.
[95] Ibid., 281 (notes and variants of the critical edition).
[96] *Carmélites*, 134–35.
[97] *Curé*, 63.
[98] Ibid., 64.
[99] Ibid., 320.
[100] *Ouine*, 132.

way, with one interminable sigh. . . . From head to foot he was all muteness, obstinacy, dark patience."[101] Such are the poor, "starving and dying of thirst",[102] to whom the beatitude is addressed, those who stand in close proximity to the Lord, at that point of existence which has throughout been the crux of the matter for Bernanos: the point of birth and death, the point of a pure hope that is forgetful of itself and whose content cannot be determined. It is from such a point that Bernanos takes the measure of man. To Vallery-Radot he writes: "How can you speak of 'entering into' dear poverty? You are already wholly within it. You are body and soul within its grandeur. It will beam out from within you when God wills it."[103] Bernanos described how he had been taught from childhood to respect the poor,[104] and he felt only gratitude for the bitter poverty he had to endure in his adult years. At the beginning of World War II he writes:

> Lady Poverty has always showered me with benefits. For a long while I did not know the price that had to be paid for these, because I obviously don't flatter myself with having a heart as magnanimous as hers. But I love her for her charity, for her tender lucidness, for her exquisite solic-itude. . . . The trials poverty has imposed on me have been fewer than the follies she has spared me. And if the poor—I say the poor and not, alas, the miserable!—wanted to be sincere, they would admit like me that their poverty treats them in the same way, that she is the marvelous and gracious steward, not of their goods, but of their life.[105]

Bernanos freely acknowledged that, both in the army of holy poverty and in the literal army, he never went beyond the rank of modest foot soldier, or, if you prefer, that "in the most ancient aristocracy of the world—that which has Jesus Christ as chief and Francis of Assisi as field commander—" he himself was but a very low-ranking noble-man. But this sufficed for him to feel "in humble solidarity with the honor of poor people". While not daring to compare himself with the "Princes of the Blood [in the court] of Poverty", with the "great lords of misery", he was of those who strove "to keep the Holy Rule of [their] Order with all honesty",[106] and this in an age of which Péguy

---

[101] Ibid., 133.

[102] *To Dom Besse*, July 1928, in: *Bul.* 10, 8.

[103] *To Vallery-Radot*, November 2, 1927, in: *Geduld*, 35.

[104] *Cimetières*, 44–45.

[105] *Enfants*, 243–44.

[106] Ibid., 246–47.

said that "the great adventurers of the modern world" are the fathers of families.[107] The world of the Beatitudes, the air of the Beatitudes: whoever attacks these and would declare them spent, even under the pretext of creating a better world and a purer air, is by the same token attacking what is holiest in man: "For there is a portion of misery and injustice in the world to which we cannot do violence without risking at the same time the destruction of man's freedom."[108]

> I fear that it's precisely the meek and the peacemakers who set no store at all by your confounded world. What do you expect? These poor devils were born breathing the atmosphere of the Beatitudes, and they don't do very well in your air. They'll do what they can to adapt to your world because they feel their solitude and can barely explain it to themselves. Thus, they are always ready to think themselves in the wrong, to flee to yet another shelter for lack of anything better, to flee to the words you've stolen from them—magic words like justice, honor, fatherland—as the bulls at a bullfight run into the gloomy enclosure that is a mockery of their cool and shady stall and that will open only to release them onto the bloody arena.[109]

There will no longer be a place for the poor in the rational and totalitarian world to come. Everything and everybody (including many Christians!) seems to agree that the poor are a species that should be wiped out[110] because poverty is "a kind of shameful disease unworthy of civilized nations" and that these are going to be "delivered of this filth in the blinking of an eye. But which of us would dare speak in this way of the poverty of Jesus Christ?"[111] It would be ridiculous to conclude from this that Bernanos belongs in the ranks of those "right-thinking" Catholics who try to dissociate themselves with a few alms and "works of supererogation" from the terrible scandal of world poverty, particularly in our time. Bernanos was definitely not one of those who, shrugging their shoulders, declare the permanent differences in social classes to reflect the will of God, who decrees both "the privileges of the rich" and "the privations of the poor".[112] Bernanos did, however, see an intrinsic connection between this re-

[107] *Français*, 34.
[108] *To Charreyre*, April 1946, in: *Bul.* 4, 6; *Erbarmen*, 109.
[109] *Cimetières*, 170–71.
[110] *Curé*, 61.
[111] Ibid., 69.
[112] *Français*, 116–17.

pugnant bourgeois ideology and the demonic ideology of the builders of the future State: both dishonor the poor; both look down on the dishonored poor either pharisaically or in the name of a loveless "justice", seeing in them "malcontents" and socially dangerous elements to be reckoned among those "irregular formations" from which an orderly society must be freed.[113] What an unbearable sight it would be if representatives of the Church "appeared before tribunals and pointed with trembling finger at the chest of the malfeasant poor", thus releasing them as prey for warmongers and crusaders! Bernanos thunders as follows in the face of the Spanish bishops: "When your children go astray, why in the name of God would you refuse to share the anguish of natural fathers? Your sort of anguish has a name: we call it 'shame'. . . . If sons were incapable of dishonoring their fathers, how on earth could they *honor* them?"[114]

> "But what about our works?", you'll object. Oh, yes! I beg your pardon. However, has not care of the sick, of the infirm, of old people, of the unemployed, the schooling of children and their technical postacademic training—has not all of this been taken over by the modern State? It has enormous capital at its disposal and a gigantic administrative machinery, and if you're not careful the day will come when the charity of Christ will be more expensive—yes, *will be more expensive*—for the miserable than the opulence of totalitarian welfare. . . . Compared to the "charitable" works of the powerful official establishment, your own works will run the risk of being nothing but leftovers from the past, mere symbols that don't go much beyond the status of venerable rites such as the washing of feet on Holy Thursday.[115]

Still, Bernanos did not fundamentally believe in the emergence of such an earthly paradise. The intrinsic doubtfulness of the whole construct, the demonic nature of the instruments of power used, and man's indomitable yearning for authentic spiritual values all block the way for the realization of such a project. Indeed, even if the ideal earthly city should be built, "a keen repugnance would soon develop as reaction to an *aurea mediocritas* (or 'golden mediocrity') raised to the status of

[113] *Cimetières*, 202–3.
[114] Ibid., 212.
[115] *Français*, 204–5.

universal rule, and we would witness everywhere, like a new springtime, a flowering of various forms of voluntary poverty."[116] Christ's
promise to the poor, or, what amounts to the same thing, his curse
over the rich, will triumph in the end over all projects proposed by
sociologists: "The curse hurled at the rich consists precisely in the
fact that the rich will always exist. Otherwise, God would have cursed
the poor, and there would no longer be any poor. Poverty has been
sanctified and divinized, not abolished. Here lies the scandal."[117] We
can also be certain that a totalitarian civilization would so hollow man
out and rob him of his essence that, in a very real sense, he would
become utterly poor and, indeed, miserable. The effects of such a
civilization would inevitably be brought home to him in this or in
some other very painful way. This is exactly what Bernanos could
hear when once listening to a discourse by Hitler: "He is stealing
our words from our mouths. He is attempting to dishonor us by pretending he believes us to be accomplices of a kind of disorder that he
has himself created. When we have reached a point of such confusion,
the only thing we really still have to oppose him with is the faith of
children, the patience of the poor, all those things we lack but which
the good Lord will surely give us."[118]

It goes without saying that, throughout these critical reflections,
Bernanos nowhere proposed concrete suggestions for the solution of
social problems either to the State or to the Church. All he had to
offer was a spirit, the spirit that should be the forerunner of all solutions. He saw very clearly that the truth he heralded puts everyone,
including himself, squarely before an *"insoluble problem"*: *"How can we
restore the poor to the justice due them without ensconcing them in power?"*[119]
Whoever succeeds in doing this will have established God's paradise
on earth. But the more these two things—justice and power—are
today held out to the poor as being of equal value, the farther away
paradise vanishes. And if, once the reign of foolishness and of money
(it's all one) has finally defeated itself, the "reign of the poor" should
dawn,

[116] *Curé*, 109–10.
[117] *Reply to a Questionnaire* (draft), 46; *Bul.* 4, 8; *Erbarmen*, 114.
[118] *To Amoroso Lima*, December 13, 1940, in: *Esprit*, 206; *Erbarmen*, 100.
[119] *Curé*, 109.

I am sure it will be of short duration. For, much as I may love the poor, I know that the power to dominate and subject others has not been given them and that their order and their justice are not of this world. The role of the poor in human society, rather, is comparable to that of the woman in the family, or, even better, to that of those older aunts who remain unmarried. Not infrequently these are the ones responsible for the honor and prosperity of many households. It is their lot to atone for the faults of each family member, and in the end they go to their graves gnawed by the remorse of having been a burden to everyone.[120]

Within the world of the temporal, the poor remain the element of the timeless, the salt of the world's hope, mankind's patience and its dogged expectancy of eternal life.[121] They have struck a covenant with holiness, because without poverty there is no holiness possible. Once having heard the Beatitudes of the Sermon on the Mount, who could still entertain any doubts concerning the mysterious connection that binds the poor with the Kingdom of God? The poor man can never belong to this world totally, not even when all his bitter striving goes to fighting for a little corner of the world, a spot he is in perpetual danger of losing.

Once there was a little man who loved poverty so much that he married her. He called her his lady and heralded her arrival: "No one, except this saint, ever believed seriously in the advent of poverty. No one, except this man, who was like a seraph come to earth, ever hoped to do homage to poverty in the presence of all the nations. . . . Once he had died, everyone got so busy honoring him that poverty became lost in the tumult of the holiday crowds. She even forgot her crown, the crown reserved for the royal anointing: it was solemnly placed instead on the head of the saint while all the rich cheered—so astounded were they to have gotten off so easily."[122] "Sheltered in the arms of sweet, vigilant poverty, the tragic Saint of Assisi" came to know her highest form.[123] "For every poor man has his own particular poverty, made in his own image and likeness. This is his guardian angel, his angelic Minister of Poverty. You can easily imagine that I have no claim to having received the same poverty as Saint Francis of

---

[120] *Enfants*, 261.
[121] *Croix*, September 1942, 251f.
[122] *Cimetières*, 243–44.
[123] *Satan*, in: *Bul.* 12–13, 25.

Assisi. My poverty is naturally of a much more modest condition, but precisely because of this we stand—she and I—on the same footing, and in the end we generally understand one another."[124]

"My dear brothers! I'll repeat now what I've already said, because it's always the same thing: If you had *followed* this saint instead of cheering him, Europe would never have known the Reformation, or the Wars of Religion, or the terrible Spanish repression. For it's you this saint was calling. But death was not partial: it struck everyone equally. And today we're facing a similar danger. . . ."[125]

[124] *Enfants*, 244.
[125] *Cimetières*, 269.

INDEX OF NAMES